General Jurisprudence

... alisation for understanding law. ... perspective, it critically reviews mainstream Western tradition of academic law, legal theory and human rights ... most processes of so-called 'globalisation' ... and that a healthy cosmopolitan discipline of law ... social relations and legal ordering. It shows how ... Western canon of jurisprudence should be critically reviewed ... account of other legal traditions and cultures. Written by a leading scholar in the field, this important work presents an exciting alternative vision of jurisprudence. It challenges the traditional canon of legal theorists and guides the reader through a field undergoing seismic changes in the era of globalisation. This is essential reading for all students of jurisprudence, human rights, comparative law and socio-legal studies.

William Twining is Quain Professor of Jurisprudence Emeritus of University College London. He has worked extensively in Eastern Africa, the Commonwealth and the United States and is a leading proponent of broader approaches to the study of law. His recent books include *Globalisation and Legal Theory* (2000) and *The Great Juristic Bazaar* (2002) to both of which this is a successor.

General Jurisprudence

Understanding Law from a Global Perspective

WILLIAM TWINING

CAMBRIDGE
UNIVERSITY PRESS

CAMBRIDGE UNIVERSITY PRESS
Cambridge, New York, Melbourne, Madrid, Cape Town, Singapore, São Paulo, Delhi

Cambridge University Press
The Edinburgh Building, Cambridge CB2 8RU, UK

Published in the United States of America by Cambridge University Press, New York

www.cambridge.org
Information on this title: www.cambridge.org/9780521738095

First published 2009

Printed in the United Kingdom at the University Press, Cambridge

A catalogue record for this publication is available from the British Library

ISBN 978-0-521-50593-2 hardback
ISBN 978-0-521-73809-5 paperback

To my students.

Table of Contents

The following text can be found online at www.cambridge.org/twining

15   Some basic concepts

16   Elusive isms: Instrumentalism, pluralism, scientism, realism

17   Law teaching as a vocation

Appendices

Preface

The aim of this book is to present a coherent vision of the discipline of law and of jurisprudence as its theoretical part in response to the challenges of globalisation. Western traditions of academic law have a rich heritage, but from a global perspective they appear to be generally parochial, narrowly focused, and unempirical, tending towards ethnocentrism.[1] *General Jurisprudence* presents an alternative vision and agenda for legal theorising that includes creating reasonably comprehensive overviews of law in the world; constructing and refining cross-cultural analytic concepts; critical evaluation of our stock of theories about law, justice, human rights, diffusion, convergence of laws, and legal pluralism; and the construction of a workable normative basis for co-existence and co-operation in the context of a world characterised by pluralism of beliefs and dynamic multiculturalism.

The central thesis is that most processes of so-called 'globalisation' take place at sub-global levels and that a healthy cosmopolitan discipline of law[2] should encompass all levels of social relations and of normative and legal ordering of these relations. The mainstream Western canon of jurisprudence needs to be critically reviewed and extended to take more account of other legal traditions and cultures, and of problems of conceptualisation, comparison, generalisation and critique about legal phenomena in the world as a whole.

What is a healthy discipline? One answer is given by a report prepared for the British Academy in 2004 on the actual and potential 'contributions of arts, humanities, and social sciences to [a] nation's wealth'. The title '*That Full Complement of Riches*'[3] is borrowed from Adam Smith. It doffs its cap to the modern climate of accountability and free enterprise, while making the point

---

[1] On ethnocentrism, see Chapter 7 below.

[2] 'Cosmopolitan' is used here descriptively to mean covering the whole world. 'Cosmopolitanism' is sometimes used in a narrower sense to refer to an idealistic vision of a unified world community constituted by universal moral principles (e.g Held (1995), (2006)). My reasons for preferring this adjective to international, transnational, and global, are discussed below in Chapter 1 and Twining (2002a).

[3] The full title is *That Full Complement of Riches, the contributions of the arts humanities and social sciences to the nation's wealth*. The Committee was chaired by Professor Paul Langford and is referred to as the Langford Report (2004). The report unashamedly makes the case for an increase in public expenditure and support for humanities and social sciences relative to the physical

that 'wealth' in this context cannot sensibly be restricted to economic prosperity, but must include cultural and intellectual enrichment, individual well-being, and new knowledge and understanding.[4] The report conceives of a healthy discipline in terms of this broad concept of 'enrichment' together with an understanding of major challenges of the age, such as climate change and poverty; contributing to public policy and debate; and providing a rigorous, beneficial and fulfilling education. In this view a healthy discipline of law is one that adequately performs these functions. In order to do so it needs to be conceptually well-equipped, ethically aware, and empirically informed throughout its various fields and specialisms.

Law as an academic discipline occupies a modest position that uneasily straddles the humanities and social sciences. Many non-lawyers envisage law as a dry, technical, 'applied' subject; many academic lawyers aspire to be recognised as genuine scholars. Almost everywhere, law is perceived as a 'cheap subject' involving worse staff:student ratios and smaller demands on research funds than most other disciplines. Law schools are institutionalised in a variety of ways.[5] Throughout the history of academic law there have been recurrent tensions about ideology, objectives, perspectives, and methods. Some of these have been expressed in terms of dubious dichotomies: liberal versus vocational; black letter versus contextual; formal versus critical; knowledge-based versus skills-based; pure and applied research; hard versus soft disciplines. These tensions have played out in a variety of patterns in different countries and periods of history. Pessimists view these conflicts as debilitating;[6] optimists prefer to talk of 'creative tension'. I count myself as an optimist. I am an enthusiast for my discipline. I believe that law can pervade nearly all aspects of social life, that it is potentially a marvellous subject of study, and that a legal perspective can provide important lenses on social and political events and phenomena. Law *is* important – for better or for worse.[7]

sciences. It is, in my view, a brilliant example of advocacy that convincingly answers the question: why are these disciplines important? The core of the message is that the contribution of non-scientific disciplines to the public good is systematically underrated, but that their health depends on an appropriate balance between short-term and long-term benefits, between 'pure' and applied research, and between instrumental uses of research and the advancement of knowledge for its own sake.

[4] Compare the recent broadening of the concept of poverty in the context of development in the Human Development Index, discussed at Chapter 11.1 below.

[5] They include professional schools (as in the United States), primary schools providing the academic stage of multi-stage process of professional formation (as in England, at least until recently), multi-functional centres of learning, Islamic law colleges, (e.g. Malat (1993) Chapter 1), institutions of mass legal education (in some countries serving as cheap depositories for excess demand for higher education), and specialised institutions, such as judicial training colleges. Legal scholarship reflects this variety.

[6] This attitude is captured by the title of a well-known article: 'The Law Teacher: A Man Divided Against Himself' (Bergin (1968)).

[7] This is a summary of views developed at length elsewhere. On the variety of law schools around the world and different conceptions of legal scholarship, see Blackstone's *Tower* (*BT*) *passim*; on controversies in legal education, see *BT* and *Law in Context* (*LIC*). On different perceptions of the importance of law see Chapter 11.3 below.

In the present context, which is concerned mainly with legal theory and legal scholarship, the discipline of law can be treated as being on the edge of the social sciences, but less 'scientistic' than some, with close ties to the humanities, especially history, philosophy, and literature. It is also subject to demands from a powerful practical profession. In many countries the trend over the past fifty years has been for law to become integrated into the university, with legal scholars sharing the basic academic ethic of being concerned with the advancement and dissemination of learning.

In my view, jurisprudence is the theoretical part of law as a discipline. The mission of an institutionalised discipline is the advancement and dissemination of knowledge and critical understanding about the subject matters of the discipline. Legal scholarship is concerned with the advancement of knowledge and critical understanding of and about law. Legal education is concerned with dissemination of knowledge and critical understanding – including the know-what, know-how, and know-why of its subject matters and operations. *General Jurisprudence* is concerned in first instance with legal scholarship and legal theory – with what is involved in advancing the understanding of law from a global or transnational perspective and only secondarily with the implications of this for the teaching of law.[8]

This book can be interpreted as a plea for a less parochial jurisprudence. It might even be read as a polemic that suggests that in recent years Anglo-American jurisprudence has been narrow in its concerns, abysmally ignorant of other legal traditions, and ethnocentric in its biases. This is partly correct. However, when talking of 'parochialism' it is useful to distinguish between provenance, sources, audience, focus, perspectives, and significance.[9] My argument does indeed suggest that we should pay more attention to other legal traditions, that the agenda of issues for jurisprudence needs to be reviewed and broadened, that the juristic canon should be revised and extended, and that there is much to be learned from adopting a global perspective. However, in some respects the perspective is also self-consciously quite parochial, reflecting my own biases and limited knowledge and the fact that I am addressing a very largely Western audience about the discipline of law as it is institutionalised in the West, especially in common law countries.

It may help to say something about where I am coming from. I was born in Uganda in 1934. I sometimes say that I had a colonial childhood, an

---

[8] At this stage in history, most forms of international and transnational legal practice are quite specialised. On the one hand, few law students and legal scholars can focus exclusively on a single jurisdiction; on the other hand, we are some way from a situation in which primary legal education can sensibly be geared to the production of global lawyers or Euro-lawyers, or even specialists in international law. A cosmopolitan discipline does not imply neglect of local knowledge. But law students can generally benefit from being presented with broad perspectives and from being made aware of different levels of legal ordering and their interactions. (Twining 2001, 2002a). They also need to be aware of the religious and customary doctrines and practices of ethnic minorities in their own country as they bear on different branches of law.

[9] *Globalisation and Legal Theory*, (*GLT*) 127–9.

anti-colonial adolescence, a neo-colonial start to my career, and a post-colonial middle age and beyond. Such a claim is open to several interpretations, as is the claim that we are living in a post-colonial era. I am based in Oxford and Florida, but I have travelled widely and have worked in several countries, mainly in Eastern Africa, the United States, the Commonwealth, and latterly the Netherlands. My background, experience, and outlook are quite cosmopolitan, but my biases and culture are British, my training is in the common law, and my main language is English. My perspective on jurisprudence straddles the analytical and socio-legal traditions: I was taught by Herbert Hart in Oxford and Karl Llewellyn in Chicago; at University College London I have been in regular conversation with Jeremy Bentham and his editors; my African experience stimulated an interest in legal anthropology and law and development, and a concern for radical poverty.[10]

In this book, my standpoint is that of an English jurist, who is concerned about the health of the institutionalised discipline of law, especially in common law countries, during the next fifteen to twenty years in the face of 'globalisation'. The aim is to develop and illustrate a vision of general jurisprudence for Western jurists in the early years of this Millennium. A jurist from a different tradition, or with a different personal background, would almost inevitably present a significantly different picture. Few of us can break away very far from our intellectual roots.

A cosmopolitan discipline of law must be concerned with all legal phenomena considered to be significant in the whole world throughout history. This is a collective enterprise. Given constraints of expertise, language, and time, any single scholar has to be selective even in presenting an overview. This book does not present a masterly synthesis or a Grand Theory. It suggests and illustrates some ways of studying legal phenomena and presents a particular vision of our discipline, but there are many other ways and visions. It emphasises theorising as an enquiring activity, more concerned with exploring questions than producing neatly packaged 'theories'.[11] If there is one single message it is a message of complexity.

About this book

General Jurisprudence is a sequel to *Globalisation and Legal Theory* (2000), which considered the significance of globalisation for Anglo-American Jurisprudence from an historical and analytical perspective. It also builds on Part A of *The Great Juristic Bazaar* (2002), a collection of more detailed studies of some leading jurists in the Anglo-American tradition, especially Jeremy Bentham, Oliver Wendell Holmes, Herbert Hart, and Karl Llewellyn together with some less obvious figures, including R.G. Collingwood, Boaventura Santos, Italo Calvino, and Susan Haack. Extensive cross-references are made

---

[10] See further *LIC*, Chapter 1.   [11] See further *LIC*, Chapter 6, especially pp. 110–13, 129–30.

to these two books, which provide a more detailed background to some of the themes developed here.[12]

The book is divided into three parts. Part A (Chapters 1–8) presents a critical overview of jurisprudence from a global perspective. The chapters suggest that classic Western jurists, including Kant, Bentham, Rawls, Llewellyn, and Hart, need to be reappraised in the context of globalisation and that the juristic canon should be revised, reinterpreted and extended to include a new generation of Western jurists, including Patrick Glenn, Boaventura Santos, Brian Tamanaha, Thomas Pogge, and John Tasioulas, as well as thinkers who throw light on non-Western ideas and interests. Part B (Chapters 9–14) develops and illustrates earlier themes by exploring in detail the implications of adopting a global perspective for a number of specific topics including diffusion of law, surface law, the roles of law in 'development' (with special reference to poverty reduction strategies), and extending the juristic canon to non-Western jurists. The website attached to this book makes available a series of self-standing essays (Chapters 15–17) and appendices that further concretise the general themes.

The chapters in outline

Chapter 1 presents an overview of Western traditions of academic law, a specific conception of legal theory as a heritage and an activity, and a cautionary view of 'globalisation' as a complex amalgam of processes that are making the world more interdependent. These processes present a series of challenges to our discipline and to jurisprudence as its theoretical part at different levels of human relations. The chapter sets out reasons for preferring the term 'general' to 'global' or 'universal' in relation to jurisprudence, and it introduces a particular positivist perspective.

Chapter 2 considers analytical jurisprudence, especially conceptual analysis, in light of these challenges and suggests that there are important tasks awaiting analytical jurists to develop a richer framework of analytic concepts that can be used to describe, analyse, compare and generalise about legal phenomena across different legal traditions and cultures.

Chapter 3 addresses the difficulties of constructing broad overviews of law that are not too simplistic. It examines past attempts to 'map' law in the world in terms of legal families, traditions, cultures, and state legal systems. Chapter 4, building on the work of Hart, Tamanaha, and Llewellyn, but going beyond them, constructs a flexible conception of law as an organising concept for

---

[12] In particular *GLT* deals more extensively with 'globalisation', legal and normative pluralism, post-modernism, comparative law, and problems of generalisation about legal phenomena. Part A of the present book consists of a complete reworking and updating of lectures given in Tilburg and Warwick in 2000–1 as a sequel to *GLT*. Parts B and C bring together in revised form a sequence of self-standing but linked essays, several of which have been previously published in widely scattered places.

viewing law in the world as a whole and for developing a framework of related analytical concepts.

Chapter 5 approaches normative jurisprudence through a detailed exploration of the implications of adopting a global perspective for classical utilitarianism and Rawls' theory of justice and considers the attempts of Singer and Pogge to move liberal theories onto a world stage.

Chapter 6 deals with human rights as moral, political, and legal rights. Here globalisation has stimulated a revival of debates about universalism and relativism and concerns about ethnocentrism.

Chapter 7 considers the main contemporary challenges to human rights theory in relation to three recent attempts (by Griffin, Tasioulas, and Sen) to provide a universalist justification for belief in human rights as moral rights.

Chapter 8 considers the challenges of globalisation to social-theoretical perspectives on law and justice with particular reference to empirical legal studies and comparative law.

The next four chapters (Part B) develop particular themes in more detail. From a global perspective diffusion of law – the spread of legal ideas and laws around the world is especially significant. Chapter 9 considers critically some assumptions underlying the literature on 'reception' and 'transplantation' of law and presents a new framework for the study of diffusion.

Chapter 10, 'Surface Law', critically explores alleged 'gaps' between the law in books and the law in action, aspiration and reality, appearance and reality, and theory and practice in a number of legal contexts and examines what it means to say that Alan Watson's 'transplants' thesis, convergence theories in comparative law, and attempts at unification and harmonisation of laws relate only to surface phenomena. Chapter 11 examines different perceptions of the role of law in 'development' with particular reference to the Millennium Development Goals and poverty reduction strategies, using Uganda as a case study.

Chapter 12 explores resistance to the idea of non-state law and shows that this is mostly based on fears that can easily be allayed. It illustrates how state-centric perspectives can lead to marginalising, ignoring, or even rendering 'invisible' normative and legal orders that are often as important to their subjects as official state law and that are particularly relevant in respect of diffusion, law reform, and confronting problems of multi-cultural societies.

Chapter 13, 'Human Rights: Southern Voices', considers the different perspectives and ideas of four 'Southern' jurists about contemporary political and legal approaches to human rights.

Chapter 14 draws together the main themes in Parts A and B.

Part C

The self-standing essays that are made available on the website linked to this book (www.cambridge.org/twining) also develop themes that are touched on in Chapters 1–14. The chapters are numbered sequentially from those in the text.

Chapter 15, 'Some basic concepts', is an exercise in applied analytical jurisprudence. It considers three sets of concepts: (a) relations, persons and subjects; (b) group, community, and society; and (c) the ideas of normative and legal orders, systems, and codes.

Chapter 16 considers four elusive 'isms' – realism, instrumentalism, pluralism, and scientism – as examples of the kind of conceptual elucidation that can be undertaken by a broadened and more relevant view of applied analytical jurisprudence.

Chapter 17, 'Law teaching as a vocation', revisits the International Legal Center's 1972 Report on *Legal Education in a Changing* World and presents a vision of the demands and expectations on scholar–teachers of law in today's world.

Audiences: how to read this book

This is a work of legal theory, but its perspective and approach are multidisciplinary and, it is hoped, it will be of interest to scholars in several other disciplines. It is addressed to three main legal audiences: legal theorists, academic lawyers concerned with the health of their discipline, and undergraduate and postgraduate students.

For jurists it presents an alternative view of the nature and tasks of legal theorising that diverges from predominant fashions in legal theory. This conception of legal theorising as an activity claims to be more coherent, more directly related to specialised scholarship, and more immediately relevant to current pressing issues such as human rights, poverty reduction, diffusion, harmonisation of laws, and corruption.

For academic lawyers generally, and for comparatists and human rights lawyers in particular, it provides a vision of what a genuinely cosmopolitan discipline of law might become and it sets a general context for more particular enquiries. Part A presents a general overview, Part B concretises this perspective at the level of middle order theory and Part C addresses a series of specific topics that will be of interest to different specialists.

General Jurisprudence is also designed for use in undergraduate and postgraduate courses in Jurisprudence or Globalisation and Law (by whatever name) or as general background reading. Part A attempts to give an overview of the implications of globalisation for analytical, normative, and social or empirical jurisprudence by considering both classic mainstream jurists from this perspective and by introducing the ideas of thinkers who have begun to develop different conceptions of general jurisprudence for the new Millennium. It also provides a basic introduction to the work of contemporary liberal philosophers who have tried to construct a philosophical justification for universal human rights as moral rights that avoids the pitfalls of ethnocentism (Griffin, Tasioulas, and Sen) and of contemporary 'Southern' jurists whose ideas deserve to be better known. The essays in Parts B and C are self-standing and can be read selectively in any convenient order. They deal more concretely with a range of specific topics and concepts that are of central concern to a global perspective on law.

The time is ripe for a radical rethink of taught jurisprudence. In addition to exploring the implications of 'globalisation' with a quite sceptical eye, *General Jurisprudence* presents an alternative conception of legal theory, extends the canon of thinkers worth studying, and establishes closer connections with contemporary issues and specialisms. The text sets out to be accessible, lively, and readable for students, with detailed references and more recondite points confined to the footnotes. It aims to contribute to the cause of making legal theory courses more directly relevant to understanding law in the twenty-first century.

Some general themes

The first ten chapters proceed on two axes. First, they examine critically the ideas of a number of 'canonical' jurists from a global perspective and introduce some other thinkers, who might be included in an expanded canon for general jurisprudence. The notes contain select references to a wide range of sources.[13] But this is not just 'a book about books'. While not advancing a 'grand theory', this book presents and defends a number of theses including the following:

- That most processes of so-called 'globalisation' take place at sub-global levels.
- That over-use and abuse of words such as 'global' and 'globalising' ('g-words') fosters a tendency to make generalisations that are exaggerated, false, meaningless, superficial, or ethnocentric. However, for some purposes adopting a global perspective is illuminating.
- That claims to 'universality' or 'generality' in respect of concepts, norms or empirical facts should be treated with caution if they are based on familiarity with only one legal tradition.
- That jurisprudence can usefully be viewed as the theoretical (more abstract) part of law as a discipline, and that a healthy cosmopolitan discipline of law needs to be underpinned by a conception of theorising as both a heritage and an activity that performs a number of intellectual functions.
- That the spheres of jurisprudence as activity can be conveniently divided into analytical, normative and empirical enquiries, but too much weight should not be placed on these distinctions, because most theoretical enquiries involve conceptual, normative and empirical dimensions.

---

[13] The notes and bibliography provide a starting-point for exploring a varied and rapidly developing literature. The bulk of the text was completed in July 2007. The notes contain references to a number of significant works published since then.

- That 'philosophy of law' is just one part of jurisprudence, which includes a variety of kinds of theorising at different levels of abstraction. Jurists should be concerned with 'jurisprudentially interesting questions', not just with 'philosophically interesting questions'.

- That the concept of 'general jurisprudence' should be interpreted broadly to include any general enquiries about law that transcend legal traditions and cultures. In this context, the idea of 'global' jurisprudence is too restricted.

- That the 'naturalistic turn' in jurisprudence, which emphasises the continuity of conceptual and empirical enquiries, is to be welcomed in its moderate forms, but not in extreme versions that suggest that there is no place for conceptual analysis.

- That one of the primary tasks of analytical jurisprudence is the elucidation and construction of concepts. In the past Anglo-American analytical jurisprudence has focused primarily on basic concepts of 'law talk' (legal doctrine and its presuppositions), usually within a single legal tradition. From a global perspective there is a need for the techniques of conceptual elucidation to be applied to a wider range of discourses (including empirical and normative 'talk about law'), especially analytical concepts that can be used to transcend legal traditions and cultures.

- Conceptions of law that are confined to state law leave out too many significant phenomena that deserve to be included in a total picture of law from a global perspective. General jurisprudence needs to work with a number of reasonably inclusive and flexible conceptions of law rather than attempt one master definition or concept. In particular, it is useful to conceive of law in terms of ideas (including rules) and of institutionalised social practices (involving actual behaviour and attitudes as well as ideas). A distinction between legal traditions and legal cultures usefully captures this dichotomy.

- Adopting a conception of law that includes 'non-state law' should not be interpreted as downplaying the importance of state law, nor should it be taken to imply that it is never legitimate to concentrate mainly on state law and to emphasise the distinctive characteristics of this form of law. Such a broad conception raises difficult issues about how to differentiate legal norms and practices from non-legal norms and practices ('the problem of the definitional stop'). My position is that where the line is most sensibly drawn should depend largely on context.

- In constructing a broad overview or map of legal phenomena in the world as a whole it is useful to differentiate different levels of relations and of ordering such relations. Such an overview can use law as a flexible organising concept, which provides a framework of analytical concepts that can be useful in interpreting, describing, comparing, and generalising about legal phenomena.

- Modern Western normative jurisprudence has been universalist and secular in tendency, as is illustrated by theories of natural law, utilitarianism, and human rights. This is challenged by pluralism of beliefs, recent religious revivals, and various forms of scepticism. Globalisation has stimulated fresh debates about universalism and relativism, about the compatibility of Western values with those of other traditions, and the prospects for cross-cultural dialogue and workable agreements on the conditions for co-existence and co-operation in the context of belief pluralism.

- There have been some valuable recent attempts to provide a philosophical justification for human rights as moral rights as part of liberal-democratic theory, but to date these have not paid serious attention to values rooted in other belief systems.
- That broader and more empirically oriented approaches to the study of law, exemplified by realism, law in context, and socio-legal perspectives have been absorbed into the mainstream of legal studies in a few countries. This is an important first step in the direction of increasing awareness of the empirical dimensions of law and justice, but we are a long way from making knowledge and understanding of law evidence-based, cumulative and explanatory, let alone 'scientific' in any strong sense.
- Feminism, human rights, critical theory, and other movements that cut across traditional classifications of legal theory and fields of law present further challenges to the development of our discipline in the context of globalisation.
- Diffusion, pluralism, multi-culturalism, and 'law and development' are among the general topics that become more salient when one adopts a global perspective.
- Comparison is a crucial first step on the road to generalisation and an empirically grounded comparative law will have a crucial role to play in the development of a healthy cosmopolitan discipline of law.[14]

Some of these themes are further concretised by the chapters in Part C (on the web). It is obvious that globalisation mandates the institutionalised discipline of law to broaden its geographical and intellectual horizons. My purpose here is to illustrate how this can be done within the common law tradition and beyond.

W L T

Coral Gables April 2008

---

[14] This theme is developed in *GLT*, Chapter 7 and at pp. 255–6.

Acknowledgements

This book has been in preparation for over fifteen years. During that time, as always, I have incurred many more debts than I can acknowledge. The early chapters and Chapter 9 grew out of work done in the wonderfully supportive atmosphere of the Center for Advanced Study in the Behavioral Sciences at Stanford in 2000–1. I am grateful to students in seminars in Boston, Miami, and London, where many of the ideas were first tried out. Individual chapters were discussed in seminars and conferences at many institutions, including Stanford, Columbia, Copenhagen, Granada, Stockholm, Oslo, University College London, the University of Miami Law School, Tilburg, and Warwick. John Tasioulas gave very helpful advice on Chapters 5–7. Chapter 8 owes much to comments by John Griffiths and Bronwen Morgan. The four 'subjects' of Chapter 13 – Abdullahi An Na'im, Francis Deng, Yash Ghai and Upendra Baxi – graciously agreed to be interviewed and to explain their work and its contexts and the Transitional Justice Institute, University of Ulster provided wonderful support and stimulation. The late Henrik Zahle stimulated the thoughts developed in Ch. 10. I owe a more general debt to Terry Anderson, Patrick Gudridge, John Griffiths, Oscar Guardiola Rivera, Susan Haack, Andrew Halpin, Neil MacCormick, Patrick McAuslan, Christopher McCrudden, Dennis Patterson, Robert Rosen, Alan Swan, and Brian Tamanaha. Among librarians, Sue Ann Campbell and Martin Reid have rendered regular assistance. So, in different ways, have Erna Stoddart, Gloria Lastres, and Ann Tucker. More than ever before, my wife, Penelope, went beyond support, encouragement, and tolerance to indispensable help by acting as a sounding-board, preparing the bibliography, and reading proofs.

The following have kindly given permission for republication of copyright material: Cambridge University Press, the *Law and Society Review*, the editors and publisher of *The Review of Constitutional Studies*, the Editors and publisher of the *Anales de la Catedra Fransisco Suareź*, the editors and publisher of the *Journal of Legal Pluralism and Unofficial Law*. Every attempt has been made to secure permission to reproduce copyright material in this title and grateful acknowledgement is made to the authors and publishers of reproduced material.

Abbreviations

ALI	American Law Institute
Bentham *CW*	*The Collected Works of Jeremy Bentham*, prepared under the supervision of the Bentham Committee, University College London
Bentham *Works*	*The Collected Works of Jeremy Bentham*, published under the superintendance of John Bowring (Edinburgh, 1838–43).
CEDAW	Convention on Elimination of Discrimination against Women
cls	critical legal studies
CPR	civil and political rights
EBRD	European Bank for Reconstruction and Development
EC	European Community
ECHR	European Convention for the Protection of Human Rights and Fundamental Freedoms
ECJ	European Court of Justice
ESCR	economic, social, and cultural rights
EU	European Union
FIFA	Fédération Internationale de Football Association
GATT	General Agreement on Tarriffs and Trade
HFH/HABITAT	Habitat for Humanity
IBRD	International Bank for Reconstruction and Development (World Bank)
ICANN	Internet Corporation for Assigned Names and Numbers
IESBS	International Encyclopedia of Social and Behavioral Sciences
IFI	international financial institution
IMF	International Monetary Fund
IOC	International Olympic Committee
LSA	Law and Society Association (USA)
MDGs	Millennium Development Goals
NAFTA	North American Free Trade Agreement
NBER	National Bureau of Economic Research
NGO	non-governmental organisation

OECD	Organization for Economic Co-operation and Development
OIC	Organisation of the Islamic Conference
PEAP	Poverty Eradication Action Plan
PRSP	Poverty Reduction Structure Plan
SLSA	Socio-legal Studies Association (UK)
UCC	Uniform Commercial Code
UCL	University College London
UDHR	Universal Declaration of Human Rights
UNDP	United Nations Development Program
UNESCO	United Nations Educational, Scientific and Cultural Organization
WHO	World Health Organization
WIPO	World Intellectual Property Organization
WTO	World Trade Organization

Further abbreviations

Some of the topics and thinkers introduced in this book are discussed at greater length in earlier works by the author; these are referred to by abbreviations as follows:

BT	*Blackstone's Tower: The English Law School* (London: Sweet and Maxwell, 1994)
GJB	*The Great Juristic Bazaar: Jurists' Texts and Lawyers' Stories* (Aldershot: Ashgate, 2002)
GLT	*Globalisation and Legal Theory* (London: Butterworth, 2000; reprint Evanston, Ill.: Northwestern University Press, 2001)
HRSV	'Human Rights: Southern Voices' 11 *Review of Constitutional Studies* 203 (2005)
HTDTWR	*How to Do Things with Rules* (with David Miers) (4th edn) (London: Butterworth, 1999)
JJM	'Karl Llewellyn's Unfinished Agenda: Law in Society and the Job of Juristic Method' 48 *University of Miami Law Review* 119 and *GJB* Chapter 6
KLRM	*Karl Llewellyn and the Realist Movement* (London: Weidenfeld and Nicolson, 1973; reprint Norman, Okla.: Oklahoma University Press, 1985)
LIC	*Law in Context: Enlarging a Discipline* (Oxford: Oxford University Press, 1997)
LTCL	*Legal Theory and Common Law* (Oxford: Blackwell, 1986)
RE	*Rethinking Evidence* (2nd edn) (Cambridge: Cambridge University Press, 2006)

Part A

Chapter 1

Jurisprudence, globalisation and the discipline of law: a new general jurisprudence*

1.1 Clean water

A few years ago a team of local and foreign consultants was asked to evaluate the health of the criminal justice system (including police and prisons) in an African country that was starting to rebuild after a terrible period of human and natural disasters. Under the general rubric of promoting 'democracy, human rights and good governance', their remit was to devise a strategy and set priorities for expenditure by Government and a consortium of foreign donors. Part of this involved setting priorities for prisons. Seventy per cent of the prison population was on remand, often illegally. Despite the best efforts of the prison service, prison conditions were appalling. Money was short, and many of the problems seemed intractable, if not insoluble.

It was difficult to know where to begin. The country had a newly minted Constitution (including a Bill of Rights). Legitimated and validated by an admirably democratic constitutive process, this Constitution was a source of both national pride and strong, but not universal, public support. One member of the team suggested that the first principle should be: 'Enforce the Constitution'. Brushing aside the argument that there were no sanctions against the Government for non-enforcement, the team adopted this as their starting point.

Article 24 stated: 'No one shall be subjected to any form of torture, cruel, inhuman, or degrading treatment or punishment.' Before considering complex problems of illegal detention, mixing women with men or children with adults,[1] extreme overcrowding, and forced labour, the team turned its attention to the seemingly simpler question of providing clean water and adequate food. Someone proposed that failure to provide these basic necessities was 'inhuman' and therefore unconstitutional. This proposal met with a sceptical response.

* Parts of this chapter were first published in Annales de la Cátédra Francisco Suarez No. 39 (Proceedings of the World Conference of Social and Legal Philosophy, Granada, 2005) (Twining 2005) and are reproduced here by kind permission of the publishers.

[1] Article 37(c) of the Convention on the Rights of the Child prescribes that 'every child deprived of liberty shall be separated from adults unless it is considered in the child's best interest not to do so'. I am grateful to Kerstin Mechlem for this point.

The first argument was that there had been no local precedents interpreting 'inhuman': it was a category of indeterminate or illusory reference. To which the reply was that the local provision was derived from many international and regional conventions and standards, including the non-binding Standard Minimum Rules for the Treatment of Prisoners. The Government was a signatory to many of these documents. There was accordingly a vast jurisprudence upon which to draw in interpreting Article 24, including persuasive precedents and commentaries within the same region.[2] The term 'inhuman' might be vague, but it was part of a universal principle of political morality upholding basic human needs for survival and reasonable health. From this one could infer that the Government had a duty to protect the life and health of all prisoners by providing clean water, even if the Government's international obligations were backed only by the moral sanctions in the tribunal of international opinion.

The next line of argument was about local conditions: 'About half of the rural population does not have clean water. Are you proposing that prisoners should be treated better than the ordinary people should? And will the test of cleanliness take into account the fact that many locals have developed some immunity to infections found in water? What about foreign prisoners, should they be treated equally?' After some debate, the team decided by a majority that the exact standard of 'clean' should be prescribed by regulation, taking into account local conditions (including costs), but not beyond a point that the water would be deleterious to health.[3] If that meant that prisoners were being treated better than some people, that was what the Constitution, backed by international and regional jurisprudence, prescribed.

The third line of scepticism came from within the team. The economist said: 'This is sheer legalism and mischievous nonsense. What precisely are you recommending in respect of water? (Running water, purification, or boiling?) What precisely is the test of 'clean'? Standards are not self-enforcing: Who will do the testing and who will pay? How much will this cost for all prisons in the country?' 'Does the provision of clean water have a higher priority than other claims of the prison service or the criminal justice system?' 'Are you sure that this Constitution is an institution that this country can afford?' The reply from the team was: 'The Constitution is the basic law. In interpreting terms like 'inhuman' there is leeway for taking into account local conditions and values, but it is absolute in regard to the principle that the Government has a duty to treat prisoners as human beings. We are not advocating Kelsenian purity.[4] We

---

[2] A good summary of the international jurisprudence is to be found in Rodley (1999). However, there does not appear to be much direct authority on standards for provision of food and water, and there are unsettled questions about omissions and intent in respect of 'inhuman and degrading treatment'. Some support for the team's interpretation may be found in the Standard Minimum Rules for the Treatment of Prisoners.

[3] The Committee on Economic, Social and Cultural Rights sets a higher standard: water has to be safe and not constitute a threat to a person's health. I am grateful to Kerstin Mechlem for this point.

[4] This is, of course, a misuse of Kelsen.

can tolerate some impurities so long as they do not seriously threaten health. But we reject arguments of the kind: 'Prisoners have no-right to food or clean water or freedom from torture, because we cannot afford such protections.' Article 24 is part of a worldwide consensus on non-negotiable minima.'[5]

The dilemmas in this situation are real; the issues are at the heart of legal theory. Indeed this text could be read as a *roman à clef*, incorporating phrases from several jurists. My object in starting with this tale is neither to defend nor to criticise the position taken by the majority of the team. The issues are contested. Rather, in talking about very broad, often abstract matters, I do not want to give the impression that I think that jurisprudence can be divorced from urgent, real life, historically specific problems. In talking about linking social science with the study of human values, Julius Stone wrote: 'Yet it still remains basic that this concern of jurisprudence seeks detailed empirical understanding and solution of *ad hoc* practical problems, and that concern with the larger more visionary enterprises ought never to obscure this truth.'[6]

1.2 Western traditions of academic law

Jurisprudence is the theoretical part of law as a discipline. How any discipline is institutionalised varies according to time and place and tradition. Law is no different. Because of this historical contingency, there is no settled core or essence of the subject matters of our discipline or of legal knowledge.[7] I shall argue for a broad (and pluralistic) interpretation of these subject matters, but not all of my readers will agree with me. The purposes, methods, and scope of the discipline are frequently contested.

If one adopts a global perspective and a long time scale, at the risk of over-simplification, one can discern some general tendencies and biases in Western academic legal culture that are in the process of coming under sustained challenge in the context of 'globalisation'. In a crude form, these can be expressed as a series of simplistic assumptions that are constituent propositions of an ideal type:

(a) that law consists of two principal kinds of ordering: municipal state law and public international law (classically conceived as ordering the relations between states) ('the Westphalian duo');[8]

(b) that nation-states, societies, and legal systems are very largely closed, self-contained entities that can be studied in isolation;[9]

---

[5] This is a fictitious story based on experience in several African countries.

[6] J. Stone, 'Trends in Jurisprudence in the Second Half Century' (at p. 30), printed in Hathaway (1980). This paper was written shortly after the publication of Stone (1966).

[7] On 'the core' of law as a discipline see *BT*, Chapter 7 (1994).

[8] The Peace of Westphalia (1648) refers to two treaties, which ended the Thirty Years' War and the Eighty Years' War. These events are often taken to signal the rise of the nation state and the start of the modern international system. This interpretation of history is contested, but it serves as a convenient reminder that the predominance of municipal state law is relatively recent.

[9] On Rawls, see Chapter 5.5 below and *GLT*, 7–8, 46–49, 72–5.

(c) that modern law and modern jurisprudence are secular, now largely independent of their historical-cultural roots in the Judaeo-Christian traditions;[10]

(d) that modern state law is primarily rational–bureaucratic and instrumental, performing certain functions and serving as a means for achieving particular social ends;[11]

(e) that law is best understood through 'top-down' perspectives of rulers, officials, legislators, and elites with the points of view of users, consumers, victims and other subjects being at best marginal;[12]

(f) that the main subject-matters of the discipline of law are ideas and norms rather than the empirical study of social facts;[13]

(g) that modern state law is almost exclusively a Northern (European/Anglo-American) creation, diffused through most of the world via colonialism, imperialism, trade, and latter-day post-colonial influences;[14]

(h) that the study of non-Western legal traditions is a marginal and unimportant part of Western academic law;[15] and

(i) that the fundamental values underlying modern law are universal, although the philosophical foundations are diverse.[16]

In short, during the twentieth century and before, Western academic legal culture has tended to be state-oriented, secular, positivist, 'top-down', Northo-centric, unempirical, and universalist in respect of morals. Of course, all of these generalisations are crude and subject to exceptions – indeed none has gone unchallenged within the Western legal tradition – and issues surrounding nearly all of them constitute a high proportion of the contested agenda of modern Western jurisprudence. However, at a general level this bald 'ideal type' highlights some crucial points at which such ideas and assumptions are being increasingly challenged. For example, it has been contended that:

(a) from a global perspective, a reasonably inclusive picture of law in the world would encompass various forms of non-state law, especially different kinds of religious and customary law that fall outside 'the Westphalian duo';[17]

---

[10] On secularism see pp. 404–5 below. There are books, including a *magnum opus* by Charles Taylor (2007), which talk of a secular age, or of human rights as a secular liberation theology. That is quite parochial. From a global perspective the demographers of religion, like Philip Jenkins, suggest that this is an era of religious revival, not only in respect of Islam, but of Christianity, Buddism, and the Yoruba religion; and not only in the 'Global South' – consider the challenges to Kemalism in Turkey and the rising importance of Islam in most Western countries. Misztal and Shupe (eds.) (1992). On Islam, see Rahman (2000); on Christianity, see Jenkins, (2007a) (2007b); on the Yoruba religion see Abimbola and Abimbola, (2007).

[11] On instrumentalism see Chapter 16.4 below.

[12] See *GLT*, 108–35, Tamanaha (2001) pp. 239–40.

[13] On the distinction between conceptions of law as ideas and as a kind of institutionalised social practice, see pp. 30–1 below.

[14] On diffusion see Chapter 9 below.   [15] On ethnocentrism see p. 129 below.

[16] For example, natural law, utilitarianism, and neo-Kantianism are all universalist in tendency. On different meanings of universalism see Chapter 5.3 below.

[17] See Chapters 4 and 12 below.

(b) sharp territorial boundaries and ideas of exclusive state sovereignty are under regular challenge;

(c) we may be living in 'a secular age' in the West, but much of the rest of the world is experiencing a religious revival;[18]

(d) while nearly all members of the United Nations and many international and transnational organisations are institutionalised in accordance with some model of bureaucracy, large parts of the world's population live in societies and communities that are differently organised;

(e) 'top-down' perspectives are being more persistently challenged by bottom-up perspectives that range from Holmes' Bad Man to user theory to various forms of post-colonial subaltern perspectives;[19]

(f) in order to understand law in the world today it is more than ever important to penetrate beneath the surface of official legal doctrine to reach the realities of all forms of law as social practices;[20]

(g) until the mid-twentieth century, imperialism and colonialism were probably the main, but not the only, engines of diffusion of law, but in the post-colonial era the processes of diffusion are more varied and there is a growing realisation that the diffusion of law does not necessarily lead to harmonisation or unification of laws;[21]

(h) the study of non-Western religious and other legal traditions is increasingly important,[22] and our juristic canon needs to be extended to include 'southern' jurists;[23] and

(i) the world today is characterised by a diversity of deep-rooted, perhaps incommensurable, belief systems; and that one of the main challenges facing the human race in a situation of increasing interdependence is how to construct institutions and processes that promote co-existence and co-operation between peoples with very different cosmologies and values. Insofar as belief pluralism is a fact, it is foolish to hope for achieving a consensus on basic values by imposition, persuasion or rational dialogue.[24]

The situation is rapidly changing and in many respects academic practice is ahead of legal theory. The object of this book is to interpret these changes, to give them some coherence, and to suggest some ways forward. As such it as much an exercise in trend-spotting as in trend-setting.[25]

---

[18] Misztal and Shupe (eds.) (1992). See n. 10 above.

[19] Nader (1984); Tamanaha, (2001) at pp. 239–40; *GLT*, Chapter 5; Baxi, (2002a) Preface; Rajagopal (2003).

[20] See Chapter 10 below.   [21] See Chapters 9 and 10 below.

[22] See, e.g. Glenn (2004).   [23] See Chapter 13 below.

[24] Hampshire (1989) and Chapter 7.4 below.

[25] In a friendly comment on my paper on 'General Jurisprudence' (Twining 2005/7), Brian Tamanaha (2007) suggested that my conception of general jurisprudence is impossible. This assumes that I was trying to launch a grand overarching theory. My response is that legal theorising as an *activity* is already responding to the challenges of 'globalisation'. My paper ended: 'si momentum requiris, circumspice' – in other words it is happening already.

1.3 Jurisprudence

Jurisprudence, as the theoretical part of law as a discipline, has a number of jobs or functions to perform to contribute to its health.[26] This requires some clarification. 'Jurisprudence', 'legal theory', and 'legal philosophy' do not have settled meanings in either the Anglo-American or the Continental European traditions. In order to be brief I shall stipulate how they are used here, rather than enter into controversies that are partly semantic, but also partly ideological. As we shall see, I treat jurisprudence and legal theory as synonyms and legal philosophy as one part – the most abstract part – of jurisprudence.[27]

Jurisprudence can be viewed as a heritage, as an ideology, and as the activity of theorising (i.e. posing, reposing, answering, and arguing about general questions relating to the subject matters of law as a discipline). The idea of heritage emphasises continuity. The idea of ideology, in a non-pejorative sense, links one's beliefs about law to one's more general beliefs about the world – whether or not they are systematic; and in the Marxian pejorative interpretation of the term, the notion of ideology is a healthy reminder of the close connections between belief, self-interest, prejudice and delusion.[28] All three perspectives on jurisprudence are adopted in this book.

(a) Jurisprudence as ideology

Ideology is important, because people's lives are ruled not only by law, but also by religion, political commitments, and other beliefs. In some contexts sharp distinctions are drawn between religion and positive law, for instance attempts to allocate separate spheres to state and religion. But in many places 'religious law' is important and is to a greater or lesser extent officially recognised. Important political activities, from social policy to terrorism, are publicly justified in the name of religion with varying degrees of sincerity. Values are imbricated into our understandings of law at all levels. At this stage in history humankind inhabits a world in which plurality of beliefs is a contingent but stubborn fact and, as we become more interdependent, issues about co-existence and co-operation are greatly sharpened. Differences in respect of cosmologies, values, political ideologies, cultures, and traditions are part of the essential background to understanding law.

[handwritten marginalia: basing decision because of religious belief – complicated]

---

[26] For more detailed discussions, see *LIC* (1997) Chapters 6 and 7.　　[27] See pp. 21–5 below.

[28] On ideology and law, see Halpin (2006a). The thesis that nearly all of our heritage of jurisprudence functions as an ideology to legitimate state coercion and violence, may have an element of truth, but is often overstated.

(b) Jurisprudence as activity

As an activity within our discipline theorising has several functions.[29] These include:

(a) Constructing whole views or total pictures (the synthesising function): this is one of the functions of both geographical and mental mapping.[30] In the present context it would include not only a total picture of law in the whole world (a notional atlas of world law), but also such constructs as a general theory of international law or comparative law or corruption or constitutionalism in the world as a whole or in some parts of it.

(b) Elucidating, constructing and refining individual concepts or, more significantly, conceptual frameworks or usable vocabularies that will travel well. This is the subject of Chapter 2. A classic example is Bentham's idea of a universal 'legislative dictionary'.[31]

(c) Developing normative theories, such as theories of justice or rights or human needs or values.[32]

(d) Constructing, developing, and testing middle order empirical hypotheses, such as Maine's famous generalisations, Alan Watson's 'transplants thesis', and Donald Black's boldest theses.[33]

(e) Developing working theories for participants (for example prescriptive theories of law making, adjudication, doctrinal exposition, advocacy or negotiation (including cross-cultural negotiation)). Much more of jurisprudence is taken up with this kind of enterprise than is generally acknowledged, especially in the Anglo-American tradition, no doubt because the culture of academic law is strongly participant oriented.[34] Some of the best known examples are particular to specific legal systems or cultures – such as Karl Llewellyn's theory of appellate judging and advocacy[35]– or else they are geographically indeterminate – such as Ronald Dworkin's theory of adjudication or standard works on negotiation such as *Getting to Yes*.[36] Participant working theories that claim to be of widespread application across jurisdictions and cultures need to be treated with caution.

(f) Finally, and probably most important, is the critical function, that is digging out, exposing to view, and evaluating important presuppositions and assumptions underlying legal discourse generally and particular phases of it.[37] Of course, this can operate in many contexts, using different methodologies; for my immediate purposes, critical examination of the assumptions and presupposition of mainstream sub-disciplines such as European Union Law, Public International Law and Comparative Law are

---

[29] See further, Twining (1974b).   [30] *GLT*, Chapter 6. See Chapter 3 below.
[31] Mack (1962) at pp. 151–8 ('the legislator as lexicographer').
[32] The problems of generalisation in this area are the subject of Chapters 5 to 7.
[33] See below Chapter 8.   [34] *LIC*, pp. 126–8, *GLT*, pp. 129ff.
[35] Llewellyn (1962).   [36] *GLT*, Chapter 2.
[37] *LIC*, pp. 130, 135–8. Chapter 9 below applies this approach to writings about diffusion.

a high priority.[38] This is one of the most important tasks for developing a cosmopolitan discipline of law.

(c) Jurisprudence as heritage

If one stands back and surveys the vast heritage of Western legal theorising about law, one is reminded of two tendencies that are in tension. First, our Western heritage is vast. However, viewed from a global perspective, that same heritage can be criticised for being insular, parochial, quite narrowly focused. Nearly all of it concentrates on the municipal law of sovereign states, mainly those in advanced industrial societies; it operates within and across only two of the world's legal traditions, common law and civil law, with other major traditions marginalised or completely ignored. Our 'Country and Western Tradition' of legal theorising and comparative law is vulnerable to charges of parochialism and ethnocentrism.[39]

Students coming to Jurisprudence for the first time are often bewildered and daunted by the disorderly profusion of our heritage of legal thought. Like a huge bazaar it presents a scene of loosely organised diversity.[40] One leading British student work discusses the ideas of over 100 thinkers, yet in the Preface to the seventh edition the author apologises for not finding room for many other significant figures.[41] On examination it becomes obvious that the work is focused almost entirely on modern Western, mainly Anglo-American, theorising about law. The index does not mention Hindu, Islamic, or Jewish jurisprudence and there are only passing references to Chinese, Japanese, Latin American and African traditions. So this presents only part of the total picture of the heritage of legal theory.

---

[38] On EC law see, for example, Weiler (1999), MacCormick (1997), Walker (2003), (2005) Ward (2003a), (2003b). On comparative law see *GLT*, Chapter 7, Edge (2000), Riles (ed.) (2001), Legrand and Munday (eds.) (2003), Menski (2006), Reimann and Zimmerman (2006); Örücü and Nelken (eds.) (2007). Since the mid-1990s there has been an outburst of theorising about Public International Law: notable works include Allott (1990) (2002), Franck (1995), Harding and Lim (1999), Hathoway and Koh (2005), Rajagopal (2003), David Kennedy (2004), Téson (1998), Koskenniemi (1999) (2005) to mention just a few. A useful overview is M. Evans (2006) Part I. 'New Approaches to International Law' (NAIL) are discussed by Riles (2004). On feminist perspectives, see Charlesworth (1991). An exploration of philosophical issues is to be found in Besson and Tasioulas (eds.) (2008). The ambivalent, sometimes cavalier, attitude towards international law of the administration of George Bush Jr, has provoked an extensive critical literature, see e.g. Sands (2005), Koh (2003), Lichtblau (2008).

[39] *GLT*, pp. 184–9.

[40] On the metaphor of jurisprudence as 'The Great Juristic Bazaar' see *GJB*, Chapter 11.

[41] Freeman (2001) Preface. Another recent student reader on Jurisprudence, Penner, Schiff, and Nobles (2002) tries heroically to give a broad conspectus by adopting a historical perspective, by regularly crossing disciplinary boundaries, by moving beyond Anglo-American authors and transnational classics such as Aquinas, Kant, Kelsen and Weber, to include modern Continental Europeans, such as Derrida, Foucault, Lacan, Habermas, and Luhmann. Although it extends over 1,000 pages, like Freeman, the focus is exclusively Western and the editors lament that they have been forced to make significant omissions for reasons of space.

Even if the focus is only on Anglo-American jurists, the picture is daunting. For example, the few students who study any of Jeremy Bentham's writings in the original usually focus on a few chapters of one early work, *An Introduction to the Principles of Morals and Legislation*. This represents less than one per cent of his *Collected Works*, which will in time extend to over seventy substantial volumes. Yet Bentham is only one of almost 100 English and American thinkers represented in Lloyd and Freeman's *Introduction to Jurisprudence*. No history of Anglo-American Jurisprudence can be sensibly restricted to thinkers who were English speaking lawyers. Even quite narrow conceptions of the agenda of jurisprudence recognise that at least some of the central issues are shared with other disciplines: For example, concerns about justice and rights are shared with ethics, political theory, literary theory, theology, psychology, economics, and sociology among others.

The extent and diversity of the heritage of Anglo-American jurisprudence poses problems of selection even within that tradition for particular purposes such as legal education and more generally for communities of scholars as well as for individuals. Texts and authors become 'canonised' partly on perceived merit, but as often as not quite arbitrarily. There are no agreed criteria of selection. Inertia, fashion, ideology, power, self-promotion, and serendipity often influence the choices that are made. However, surveys of jurisprudence courses and statistics of citation tend to converge in identifying a fairly consistent shortlist of individual authors who are widely read and studied at any given time.[42] There is a mainstream and something approaching a canonical core, but the core is constantly changing and there is a rather healthy pluralism surrounding it.

Fairly orthodox accounts of the Anglo-American tradition depict it as extending over several centuries, as multi-disciplinary, and by no means confined to anglophone authors. Plato and Aristotle, Kant and Kelsen, Marx and Weber, Foucault, Habermas, and post-modernists have been at least partly assimilated into the tradition. Yet if one adopts a global perspective, this heritage is vulnerable to criticism as being quite narrow and 'parochial' on three main grounds.

First, nearly all Anglo-American legal theorists, including those who claim to be doing general jurisprudence, work exclusively within the Western legal tradition. Their perspective is generally secular and they pay little or no attention to religions other than Christianity or to non-Western cultures and traditions.[43]

---

[42] See, for example, the series of surveys of taught Jurisprudence in the UK by Cotterrell and Woodliffe (1974), Barnett and Yach (1985) and Barnett (1995) (which also covers Australia and Canada). Ronald Dworkin remarks that: 'Contemporary jurisprudence courses differ wildly in content....There is no single subject, technique or canon.' Dworkin (2006a) at p. 96. This may be true of some jurisprudence courses, especially in the United States, but there is a mainstream and there is far less variety in books for such courses as is illustrated by the three surveys referred to above. See below Chapter 5, n. 1.

[43] 'We do not today... speak of Christian Law, though Christianity permeates both civil and common law. Neither Christianity nor Buddhism have sought to realise themselves through law (even widely defined), though they have had influence in various legal traditions.' (Glenn (2007) at p. 81.) Today the Natural Law tradition has both a secular and a religious strand.

Second, and related to this, almost all of Western jurisprudence has focused on state law, especially the domestic (municipal) law of sovereign, industrialised nation states. Herbert Hart's *The Concept of Law* (1961) dominated the foreground of Anglo-American Jurisprudence, with some justification, for forty or so years, until the advent of globalisation challenged the assumption that the law of sovereign states is for all intents and purposes the only proper focus of the discipline of law. Hart's picture of law as a system combining primary and secondary rules deriving their validity from a 'rule of recognition' is still useful in analysing the predominant legal orders of modern nation states, but it sits uneasily with various forms of regional law (e.g European Community Law); nor does it fit situations where custom or religious law or normative orderings emerging from self-regulation or commercial practice are important; nor does it capture the complexities of the interactions between national, transnational and supranational legal orders.[44]

Third, and most important from a global perspective, the *agenda* of mainstream Anglo-American jurisprudence seems quite limited. It has concentrated, sometimes obsessively, on a narrow range of issues most of which seem generally remote from the concerns of world leaders and 'Southern' peoples. From a global perspective, questions need to be asked about the actual and potential contribution of law and legal theory to the pressing problems of the age, such as the North–South divide, war, genocide, and environment, or those identified at the Millennium Summit including hunger, poverty, basic education, health, international and national security, colonialism, displaced persons, fair trade, or corruption.[45] From this point of view our heritage can look rather narrow and sterile, narrow in its concerns, ignorant of other traditions, and ethnocentric in its biases. In short, despite the richness and complexity of our heritage, from a global perspective, we are collectively open to charges of myopia, ignorance, parochialism, and irrelevance. The central argument of this book is that both the practices and discipline of law are in fact becoming more cosmopolitan and that jurisprudence as the theoretical part of law as a discipline needs to face these challenges. One of the tasks of *General Jurisprudence* is to evaluate, revise, and extend the inherited canon of juristic texts, both within our own tradition and beyond it.

(d) Domains of jurisprudence

In the Anglo-American tradition the heritage and the activity are sometimes classified into broadly defined, but overlapping, fields: Julius Stone categorised them as analytical jurisprudence, sociological (or functional) jurisprudence, and theories of human law and justice (censorial, critical, or ethical).[46] I prefer

---

[44] These issues are explored at length in Chapters 4 and 9 below.
[45] On possible agendas see Chapter 14 below.
[46] Stone (1946) Chapter 1 (discussed in Twining (2003a)).

to talk rather more broadly of analytical, normative, and empirical (or socio-legal) jurisprudence. Such classifications serve a modest purpose provided that two points are borne in mind: first, the boundaries between these activities are not precise; and, second, most practical questions about law involve a combination of analytical, empirical, and normative elements. So any classification of these broad fields or activities should not be expected to bear much weight.[47] Continuities between these domains of jurisprudence are a central theme of this book.

Anglo-American analytical jurisprudence has been primarily, but not exclusively, concerned with concepts and legal reasoning; the most stable relations have been with analytical philosophy. Normative jurisprudence deals with values and the closest relations have been with ethics and political theory. Other theoretical lines of enquiry concerned with interpreting, describing, and explaining actual legal phenomena in 'the real world' are sometimes assigned to Historical Jurisprudence and the Sociology of Law. Such labels can be misleading.[48] In the present context 'empirical jurisprudence' covers any general questions (that are not purely analytical or normative) about legal phenomena in 'the real world'. It thus includes 'Historical Jurisprudence', 'Sociological Jurisprudence', and much else besides. By using the word 'empirical' I do not intend to adopt an empiricist as opposed to a phenomenological, hermeneutic or other interpretive stance; nor do I wish to restrict this to a particular epistemology.[49] In this context 'empirical jurisprudence' is a rough category covering generalisation (including assumptions) about legal phenomena in the 'the real world'.[50]

1.4 The significance of 'globalisation'

Words like 'globalisation' and 'global' are used very loosely. Here, it is useful to distinguish between two primary uses. First, 'globalisation' is sometimes used to refer to certain recent tendencies in political economy – the domination of the world economy by a group of interrelated ideologies and practices, commonly referred to as 'The Washington Consensus'.[51] This is clearly illustrated by 'the anti-globalisation' movement, which has rather diffuse targets, including American hegemony, Western dominated international financial institutions, free market ideology, and capitalism in general. The issues are important, not

---

[47] Hart (1983) at pp. 88–9.

[48] On misleading uses of 'sociology' to cover all social sciences see Chapter 8.2 below.

[49] In so far as this is necessary, I am here prepared to take my stand on 'innocent realism' as set out in *GLT*, Chapter 8, based on Susan Haack (1998). On empiricism, see Chapter 8.2 below.

[50] I shall use the term 'legal generalisations' to refer to generalisations about legal doctrine – for example, interpretive or quasi-empirical claims that the basic concepts and principles of the law of contract are uniform throughout most of the world. See Chapter 10.2(c) below.

[51] See below p. 337.

least in respect of poverty and environmental matters, but this usage is too narrow in the present context. I shall use the term 'globalisation', following Anthony Giddens, in a much broader, less politically fraught sense, to refer to those processes that increase interaction and interdependence in respect not only of economy and trade, but also communications, science, technology, language, travel, migration, ecology, climate, disease, war and peace, security and so on.[52]

This second broader meaning can be quite useful, but it too is problematic. I teach a course called 'Globalisation and Law'. At our first meeting I usually ban all 'g-words' from the classroom – 'global', 'globalising', 'globalisation' etc.. There are two exceptions to this rule: first, for most of the course we adopt a global perspective; second, a student may use a 'g-word' provided its use can be justified in that particular context and that it is being used with clarity and precision.

There are two reasons for the rule. The first is obvious: 'g-words' are ambiguous and tend to be used very loosely. They are abused and over-used in many ways, often as part of generalisations that are false, exaggerated, misleading, meaningless, superficial, ethnocentric, or a combination of all these.[53] This can clearly be seen in much of the loose talk about global law, global governance, global law firms, global lawyers, and global jurisprudence.[54]

The second reason is especially important for lawyers: the literature on globalisation tends to move from the very local (or the national) straight to the global, leaving out all intermediate levels.[55] It is also tempting to assume that different levels of relations and of ordering are neatly nested in a hierarchy of concentric circles ranging from the very local, through sub-state, regional, continental, North–South, global, and beyond to outer space. But the picture is much more complicated than that: it includes empires, alliances, coalitions, diasporas, networks, trade routes, and movements; 'sub-worlds' such as the common law world, the Arab world, the Islamic world, and Christendom; special groupings of power such as the G7, the G8, NATO, the European

---

[52] Giddens, (1990) at p. 64. Cf. Giddens and Hutton (2000). See further *GLT*, Chapter 1, at pp. 4–10.

[53] Twining (2001) at pp. 24–6. Holiday Inns and CNN may circle the world and in that sense may be 'global'. But most global generalisations refer to surface phenomena, which may conceal more than they reveal. This theme is developed in Chapter 10 below.

[54] Not all such talk is inflated. For example, Harold Berman makes a sustained case for developing 'world law' underpinning global society along the lines of Wilfred Jenks's vision of a common law of mankind or a new *ius commune*. (Berman (1995), Jenks (1958)). While I place much greater stress on sub-global processes and institutions, the argument deserves to be taken seriously. Similarly, the New York University Law School's programme and concerns are sufficiently extensive that it may be pedantic to mock its claim to be 'a' or 'the' 'Global Law School'. However, a law firm with offices in less than ten metropolitan centres and many books, journals, and articles with 'global' in the title illustrate the general point.

[55] This is very common. See Westbrook (2006). Even Santos, who emphasises the complexities of 'globalisation', tends only to use four levels: global, regional, national, and local. See Santos (2002) at pp. 162–82 (placing the global and the local in counterpoint); See also p. 371 (showing a more flexible chart).

Union, the Commonwealth, multi-national corporations, crime syndicates, and other non-governmental organisations and networks. Talking in terms of vertical hierarchies obscures such complexities. It is especially important for lawyers to be sensitive to the significance of boundaries, borders, jurisdictions, treaty relations, and legal traditions.[56]

Even with these crude geographical categorisations, and even without reference to history, a ban on g-words sends a simple message of complexity. It also emphasises the point that in regard to the complex processes that are making human beings, groups, and peoples more interdependent, much of the transnationalisation of law and legal relations is taking place at sub-global levels. Furthermore there are also local and transnational relations and processes that to a greater or lesser extent bypass the state such as the Internet, networks of non-governmental organisations (NGOs), many of the internal and external relations of large corporations, and so on.

The purpose of this ban on 'g-words' is not to suggest that the processes that are loosely subsumed under 'globalisation' are unimportant; rather it emphasises that, if we adopt a global perspective in studying and theorising about law, our attention needs to be focused on all levels of relations and ordering, not just the obvious trilogy of global, regional, and nation state, important as these may be. There are, of course, genuinely global phenomena and issues (e.g global warming, the Internet, and nuclear proliferation).

Since World War II, a significant number of supra-national and transnational regimes and orders have developed and are a very important part of the legal landscape. It is reasonable to treat the World Bank, the International Monetary Fund, and the World Trade Organization as 'global' institutions, even if their geographical reach is uneven. The same applies to institutions and orderings such as UNESCO, the International Olympic Committee (IOC), FIFA, the Catholic Church, Amnesty International, or the law firm, Baker and Mackenzie.[57] However, at least as important are regional bodies and regimes, such as the European Union and the Council of Europe, the North American Free Trade Association (NAFTA), and the African Union. Most obligations under public international law are derived from multilateral and

---

[56] On levels of law see Chapter 3.3 below.

[57] Which of these various regimes, orders, and orderings counts as a 'legal order' depends on one's criteria of identification of law in a given context. See especially Chapters 3 and 4. Developing regimes for the Internet, corporate self-regulation, *lex mercatoria*, are all candidates for recognition as 'non-state' legal orders. Whether the system of internal governance of an institution such as Baker and Mackenzie, a law firm with over 3,000 lawyers and offices in over seventy cities (Bauman, 1999), counts as 'a legal order' depends on context. Similarly, given that in 2002 Baker and Mackenzie did not have offices in Africa, the Caribbean, the Indian sub-continent, and most of the Pacific (including New Zealand), and does set some geographical limits on the work it undertakes, raises the question of whether it is genuinely 'global'. This is a trivial question for most purposes, except perhaps to make the point that this is the law firm with the best claim to the label. Of course, some of these transnational fields have become highly specialised: for example, on WTO Law see Howse (2007), Palmeter (2003), Petersmann (2005) and Bermann and Mavroidis (2007).

bilateral treaties with very variable geographical application.[58] Hirst and Thompson point out that the bulk of the work of most multi-national companies is sub-global, often confined to two or three continents.[59] It can be useful to talk of 'the world economy', provided that one recognises that there are many sub-global economies, including unofficial and informal ones. Similar points apply to 'the world banking system'. How a recession in the United States or a decision to lower interest rates in the European Union affects other economies is an empirical question – one should not just assume changes at the global level. There are degrees of interdependence.[60]

Commonsense suggests that the extent of interdependence and interaction is likely to be greater where there is proximity in terms of space or such factors as historical association (ex-colonies, trade routes, traditional alliances) or language (English, Chinese, Kisawahili) or legal tradition (the common law, civil law, religious law) or patterns of migration (religious and other diasporas), or complex combinations of these. Legal patterns are closely related to other patterns of proximity. The important point here is that most institutions, regimes, orders, and orderings with which we are concerned operate largely at sub-global levels and in studying such phenomena it pays to have a reasonably realistic demographic picture of their scale and distribution across space and time.

This book is concerned with implications of 'globalisation' (broadly conceived) for legal theory. Here it is relevant to make two points relating to law as an academic discipline as it has been institutionalised in what is loosely called 'the West'. First, in the past 150 years or so the primary focus of academic law, legal scholarship, legal education, and legal theory has been on the municipal law of nation states. This is true not only of substantive and procedural law, but also of satellite subjects. Comparative law, at least until recently, has been almost entirely dominated by 'the Country and Western Tradition' which has been largely concerned with comparisons of private municipal law in 'parent' common law and civil law systems.[61] The more expansive 'Grandes Systèmes' tradition has often been dismissed as unscholarly or simplistic. In legal theory, only exceptionally have Western jurists looked beyond municipal law: in the Anglo-American tradition nearly all canonical jurists, positivists and non-positivists alike, from Bentham and Austin through to Dworkin, Raz, and Duncan Kennedy, have been almost entirely concerned with domestic

---

[58] On mild scepticism about the 'universality' of the international human rights regime see Chapter 6.3 and Chapter 10.2 below.

[59] Hirst and Thompson (1999).

[60] Some writers, accepting this point, use 'globalisation' to refer to any process that intensifies relations across national borders (e.g. the authors discussed in Woodman *et al.* (2004) at pp. 20–3). Similarly Goldman (2007 at p. 15) uses 'globalist' and 'universalist' to denote tendencies towards universality. Unfortunately, the magnetic pull of 'g-words' encourages tendencies to generalise and to over-simplify.

[61] Twining (2000a), *GLT*, Chapter 7.

state law. The few exceptions, such as Ehrlich, Maine, and Llewellyn,[62] are generally treated as marginal. In recent times, leading normative theorists, notably Rawls and Dworkin, have explicitly retreated into a peculiar kind of particularism. Dworkin states that 'interpretive theories are by their nature addressed to a particular legal culture, generally the culture to which their authors belong'.[63] Rawls makes a similar restriction to liberal or at least decent societies;[64] even empirical legal studies and sociology of law have, for most of their history, focused almost entirely on the municipal law of their own 'societies'.[65] The major exceptions to this tendency are public international law, human rights law and, recently, transnational commercial law.[66]

Similar patterns are discernible in Continental Europe. The phenomenon is familiar, well documented, unsurprising, and for the most part quite easily explained. One general reason is that, especially in the common law tradition, the culture of academic law is 'participant-oriented' and, at least until recently, professional legal training and practice (by judges, government lawyers, as well as private practitioners) have been almost entirely focused on local municipal law. In the present context, an important implication of this is that nearly all of our stock of concepts and theories has similarly been relatively local, or at least geared to a single legal tradition. Indeed, nearly all legal concepts, including many 'fundamental legal conceptions', that have been the focus of attention of analytical jurists are 'folk concepts'.[67] One of the main challenges to general analytical jurisprudence is the elucidation and construction of analytical concepts that 'travel well' across legal traditions and cultures.[68]

A second point is that adopting a global perspective may encourage reductionist tendencies – a search for universals, the construction of grand overarching theories, and a tendency to emphasise similarity rather than difference. Such tendencies are particularly visible in the movement to harmonise, standardise and unify laws.[69] In 1977 the World Congress on Philosophy of Law and Social Philosophy was launched under the grand rubric of 'A General Theory of Law for the Modern Age'. No such theory resulted. My contribution, entitled 'The Great Juristic Bazaar', was taken as satirising this title and emphasised the richness, pluralism, and complexity of the global heritage of theorising

---

[62] American commentators tend to focus on Llewellyn as a Legal Realist and commercial lawyer, but play down the significance of 'the law-jobs theory', which is treated by European jurists as perhaps his most significant contribution. See Drobnig and Rehbinder (eds.) (1994).

[63] E.g. Dworkin (1986) at p. 102. See Chapter 5, p. 162 below.

[64] 'The aims of political philosophy depend on the society it addresses' (Rawls (1999b) at p. 421, *ibid* at pp. 306–7).

[65] See Chapter 8.5 below.   [66] See generally, Braithwaite and Drahos (2000).

[67] On the shortness of the list of concepts dealt with by nineteenth-century analytical jurists as part of general jurisprudence see *GLT*, Chapter 2.

[68] This is the central argument of Chapter 2 below. On some of the methodological difficulties see Glenn (2004) at pp. 44–51.

[69] A powerful and eloquent critique of the tendency to privilege the similar over the different is presented by Pierre Legrand (2003).

about law.[70] I am not an extreme particuralist,[71] but problems of generalising about legal phenomena – conceptually, normatively, empirically, and legally – are a central concern of this book.

I make one general exception to the ban on 'g-words'. I encourage students to adopt a global perspective as a starting point for considering particular topics in the course. Thinking in terms of total pictures is mainly useful for setting a context for more particular studies. Grand synthesising theories, such as Glenn's account of legal traditions, or organising theories such as Tamanaha's, also have their uses.[72] They are examples of the synthesising function of legal theory. There may even be value in trying to construct a historical atlas of law in the world as a whole – although my own efforts in this direction have done little more than illustrate some of the obstacles in the way of such an enterprise: the multiplicity of levels of human relations and orde-ring, the problems of individuating normative and legal orders, the complex-ity and the variety of the phenomena that are the subject matters of our discipline, and the relatively undeveloped state of the stock of concepts and data that would be needed to produce such an overview.[73] Adopting a global perspective also helps to map the extent of our collective ignorance of other traditions. Despite progress towards a more cosmopolitan discipline, atten-tion will remain primarily focused on particular enquiries and local details. Jurists and legal scholars cannot live by abstractions alone.

To sum up: We may not be able entirely to expunge g-words from our vocabulary – indeed there are some genuinely global issues and phenomena, and a global perspective may be useful for setting a broad context and present-ing overviews. However, whenever we hear a g-word we should pause and ask: is it being used precisely, or in this context is it exaggerated, superficial, misleading, simplistic, ethnocentric, false or just plain meaningless?

1.5 'General jurisprudence'

Similar considerations apply to the term 'general jurisprudence' as to the over-use of 'global'. 'General' in this context has at least four different meanings: (a) abstract, as in '*théorie génèrale du droit*'; (b) universal, at all times in all places; (c) widespread, geographically or over time; (d) more than one, up to infinity.[74]

---

[70] Twining (1979) reprinted in *GJB*, Chapter 11.

[71] My caution relates to facile and misleading transnational comparisons and generalisations about law. This does not imply that there are no patterns, rather that they are not easily discerned and interpreted – see R. Hoffman (1998) on the theme of 'the same and not the same'.

[72] Discussed in Chapters 3 and 4 below.   [73] *GLT*, Chapter 6, and Chapter 3.3 below.

[74] Leslie Green's account of 'General Jurisprudence' (2005) is confined to contemporary analytical legal philosophy (general jurisprudence as the most abstract part of jurisprudence/legal theory) and does not quite fit any of these categories. The article contains some interesting insights, but ignores all broader discussions of the concept. On 'legal philosophy' as one part of jurisprudence, see Chapter 1.6 below.

The English distinction between general and particular jurisprudence is not quite the same as one common usage in Continental Europe. In his useful book *What is Legal Theory?*, Mark van Hoecke traces the history of civilian conceptions of 'general jurisprudence' (*théorie générale du droit, algemeine rechtslehre*) in terms of the ups and downs of a sub-discipline that has tried to establish itself between abstract legal philosophy and legal dogmatics.[75] This kind of legal theory reached its heyday before World War II in the *Revue Internationale de la théorie du droit* edited by Kelsen, Duguit and Weyr. In this interpretation 'legal philosophy' is abstract and metaphysical, removed from the details of actual legal systems. 'General jurisprudence' was empirical, concerned with analysing actual legal systems at a relatively high level of generality. 'General' in this context refers to level of abstraction rather than to geographical reach and 'general jurisprudence' is interpreted as a kind of middle order theory. In the English analytical tradition, on the other hand, 'general' referred to extension in point of space: Bentham, for example, distinguished between universal and local jurisprudence; Austin between the general theory of law common to maturer systems and the theory of law underlying a particular legal system.

Accordingly we need to distinguish between 'generality' in respect of levels of abstraction, in respect of geographical reach, and in respect of extent. Mobile phones or the Internet have a wide geographical reach without being very abstract; mobile phones are numerous; the Dutch concept of 'bileid', as I dimly understand it, is quite abstract but rather local.[76] Often, however, generalisation involves abstraction.

During the nineteenth century English jurists normally assumed that jurisprudence was general. The Natural Law Tradition was universalistic. Bentham developed a universal science of legislation. Austin, more cautiously, developed a general analytical jurisprudence for mature nations. Holland claimed that jurisprudence was a science and therefore must be general. Leaders of the Historical School, such as Maine, advanced sweeping Darwinian generalisations about law and social change.[77] However, during the early days of academic law in both England and the United States the focus became more particular. One reason for this was that the study of the fundamental legal conceptions of one's own legal system was seen to be more practical and

---

[75] Van Hoecke (1986).

[76] Blankenburg and Bruinsma (1994) at pp. 63–73. '"Bileid" is 'a very Dutch legal term', which has no English equivalent.' It is considered a key to understanding Dutch legal culture. 'It is generally used to describe the policies of a public body' in terms of intentions, guidelines, ethos, or standards by which its actions may be judged. It is used here as an example of an abstract term which has a limited geographical reach.

[77] For details see *GLT*, Chapter 2. '[Maine's] model was geology and he compared primitive ideas of law with the primary crusts of the earth, but his readers related his theory of legal evolution to the doctrine of biological evolution which became fashionable through Darwin's *Origin of the Species* (1859).' (Stein (1984) at p. 344).

relevant to the rest of the curriculum. Austin, Pollock, Gray, and others explicitly emphasised practicality.[78]

Nineteenth century proponents of general jurisprudence, influenced by scientific models of enquiry (e.g. Darwinism) and by universalism in ethics (e.g. both utilitarianism and natural law), tended to *assume* the universality of their theories. Today, however, claims to universality and generality need to be treated as problematic. A central issue of a revived general jurisprudence should be: how far is it meaningful, feasible, and desirable to generalise – conceptually, normatively, empirically, legally – across legal traditions and cultures? To what extent are legal phenomena context- and culture-specific? In treating general-isation as problematic, usage (d) from our list may be the most useful, because of its flexibility.

While Bentham and some nineteenth century jurists equated 'general' with 'universal' (b),[79] Austin and others explicitly limited their theories to 'mature' or 'advanced' societies (c). So by implication do Hart and his followers who treat modern state law as the paradigm case of law.[80] The geographical reach of much contemporary juristic discourse is strikingly indeterminate.[81] 'General' in senses (c), and (d) is a flexible, relative category in a way that 'global' and 'universal' are not.[82]

In the nineteenth century the term particular jurisprudence referred to the study of the concepts and presuppositions of a single legal system; general jurisprudence referred to the study of two or more legal systems and was quite often confined to advanced or 'civilised' systems. Universal jurisprudence was more like global jurisprudence, but was often restricted to the law of sovereign nation states. Generality and particularity are relative matters. Globalisation has implications for law and its study. It does not follow that what is needed is a global jurisprudence, if that means looking at law solely or mainly from a global perspective. That is too narrow. The old term 'General Jurisprudence' is broader and more flexible than 'global'. Here I shall use 'general jurisprudence' to refer to the theoretical study of two or more legal traditions, cultures, or

---

[78] Austin (1863); Pollock (1882) at pp. 1–41; Gray (1909) at pp. 128–44. There were also signs of a tacit legal relativism, exemplified by W. W. Buckland (1890) and (1945), discussed in *GLT*, pp. 24–35.

[79] Tamanaha's conception of 'general jurisprudence' is universalistic in tendency: 'The ability to gather information on *all* kinds of social arenas, on *all* state legal systems as well as on other kinds of law, is precisely what qualifies this proposal as general jurisprudence.' (Tamanaha, 2001, at p. 233).

[80] Galligan (2007) explicitly confines his focus to modern societies and argues strongly for treating state law as distinctive (*Ibid.* at pp. 21–2).

[81] *GLT*, Chapter 2. For example, it is sometimes difficult to be sure whether Dworkin's theory of adjudication is about American Federal Law, US law, Anglo-American law, 'the common law' generally, or extends to all liberal democracies or even beyond that.

[82] *GJB*, pp. 338–41.

orders (including ones within the same legal tradition or family)[83] from the micro-comparative to the universal.[84]

Why do I talk of 'reviving' general jurisprudence, when some prominent modern jurists, for example Hart and Raz, have claimed to have been doing 'general jurisprudence'?[85] A brief answer is that, while much of their work can be treated as *examples* of general jurisprudence, their *conception* of 'general jurisprudence' is quite narrow in being largely confined to state law viewed from what is a essentially a Western perspective. My conception is much broader than theirs and harks back to a time when jurists as different as Bentham, Austin, Maine, Holland, and followers of Natural Law were all conceived as pursuing different aspects of 'general jurisprudence'. The label itself is unimportant, although it has sometimes been misused. Furthermore, contemporary jurists who consistently do general jurisprudence are exceptional, for the great bulk of legal theorising in the Anglo-American tradition is confined to modern Western state legal systems, often very largely to the United States and the United Kingdom. Finally, my conception of general jurisprudence is intended to challenge tendencies (often latent) to project parochial preconceptions onto non-Western legal orders, cultures, and traditions.[86]

1.6 Jurisprudence, legal philosophy, and empirical legal studies

'Jurisprudence', 'legal theory', and 'legal philosophy' do not have settled meanings in either the Anglo-American or the Continental European traditions.[87] Here, I shall treat jurisprudence and legal theory as synonyms and legal philosophy as one part – the most abstract part – of jurisprudence. In this view, jurisprudence is the theoretical part of law as a discipline with a number of jobs or functions to perform to contribute to its health. A theoretical question is no more and no less than a question posed at a relatively high level of abstraction. Some topics, such as theories of justice, questions of metaphysics, epistemology, or meta-ethics, belong to legal philosophy in this restricted sense. Some questions, such as 'what constitutes a valid and cogent argument on a question of law in the context of adjudication?' are in part philosophical, as they are concerned with the nature of reasoning; but they also involve elements

---

[83] This chapter is mainly concerned with theorising across legal traditions and cultures. However, comparison and generalisation *within* a given legal tradition or culture can also be problematic and has tended be neglected by comparative lawyers. (On comparative common law see *GLT*, pp. 145–8).

[84] This conception has some affinity with nineteenth century usage, but differs from it in three important respects: (i) it treats generalising about legal phenomena as problematic; (ii) it deals with all levels of legal ordering, not just municipal and public international law; and (iii) it treats the phenomena of normative and legal pluralism as central to jurisprudence.

[85] See n. 74 above (Green 2005).

[86] On the concepts of order, culture, and tradition see Chapter 3 below.

[87] For a fuller treatment, see Twining (2005e).

about which philosophers have no special expertise – such as the distinction between questions of law and questions of fact, and the nature of adjudication.[88] One just cannot take for granted that courts and judges are institutionalised in the same ways in the Netherlands and England, let alone in the world as a whole.[89] One does not expect philosophers to contribute very much to clarifying such matters, yet theories of adjudication and legislation are an important part of the agenda of jurisprudence.

Herbert Hart wrote that 'no very firm boundaries divide the problems confronting [different branches of legal science] from the problems of the philosophy of law'.[90] He continued: 'Little, however, is to be gained from elaborating the traditional distinctions between the philosophy of law, jurisprudence (general and particular), and legal theory.'[91] I agree with the first statement, but dissent from the second for several reasons. First, there has been a tendency in recent times to treat legal philosophy and jurisprudence as co-extensive, but this is associated with a tendency to focus only on the most abstract questions and to neglect other important, but less abstract, issues. Similarly there has been a tendency to criticise all jurists at the level of philosophy.[92] However, by no means all questions in legal theory are solely or mainly philosophical questions and not all jurists are philosophers.

The idea of 'philosophically interesting' questions and concepts can build bridges between law and philosophy by pointing to shared concerns; but it can also divert attention from concepts and issues that are jurisprudentially significant.[93] Justice, rights, rules, causation, and reasons are familiar examples of concepts that are both important in jurisprudence and philosophically interesting; tradition, culture, institution, corruption, and torture, may be potentially philosophically interesting, but have not received the attention they deserve within jurisprudence. There are other concepts that could benefit from the methods of conceptual elucidation developed by analytical philosophers even if they do not raise issues of philosophical significance (e.g. lawyer, dispute, court,

---

[88] As we descend a ladder of abstraction, the need for local knowledge increases. For example: 'What constitutes a valid, cogent, and appropriate argument in common law/UK/English adjudication?' requires detailed knowledge of the institutional and cultural contexts, even more so if the question refers to a specific court (the House of Lords/ Crown Courts) or an individual judge or a particular case.

[89] Courts, adjudication, judges are all problematic as analytic concepts (*GLT*, p. 65). For a brave attempt to develop a general account of adjudication see Shapiro (1981). For an even bolder attempt to construct a general model of third-party intervention in conflicts of others see Black (1993) Chapter 6 (with M.P. Baumgartner).

[90] Hart (1967).

[91] *Ibid*. In the Postscript to *The Concept of Law* (1994), Hart revived the distinction between particular and general jurisprudence in order to differentiate his enterprise from that of Dworkin. In my view, he did not succeed (*GLT*, Chapter 2).

[92] See Leiter (1997) (review of Neil Duxbury *Patterns of American Jurisprudence* (1995)).

[93] *GJB*, pp. 81–3.

jurisdiction, unmet legal needs).[94] In the enterprise of understanding law, it is neither necessary nor sufficient for an issue to be philosophically interesting for it to be jurisprudentially interesting.[95]

The revival of close contacts between jurisprudence and analytical philosophy in the 1950s, for which Herbert Hart has been given much of the credit, has led to a range of work that has contributed much to the enterprise of understanding law. In addition to Hart's own work in both general and particular (or special) jurisprudence, his immediate successors included several substantial figures, of whom Dworkin, Finnis, MacCormick, and Raz are the best known. Although some of the debates about positivism seem to have verged on obsession and have recently descended into unseemly wrangling, Brian Leiter has reminded us of the contributions of the next generation of analytical philosophers to a wide range of topics.[96]

In the fifty years since Hart's seminal inaugural lecture there is much to celebrate, not only in terms of an extensive and sophisticated literature, but also because there is now a lively, loosely-knit inter-disciplinary community that includes philosophers interested in law, jurists interested in one or more areas of philosophy, scholars trained in both disciplines, and philosophers who have worked to acquire sufficient local legal knowledge to be accepted as honorary jurists. There is thus a large and quite varied pool of talent that is well-equipped to tackle a fresh range of issues.

Despite its many achievements, there has in recent years been a growing sense of dissatisfaction with the dominant mode of analytical legal philosophy both within and outside its somewhat closed circles. This is a complex matter because the criticisms come from different quarters, the reasons are varied, and

---

[94] For example, problems of constructing suitable analytic categories for comparing legal professions and legal education have bedevilled discussions of these subjects. At a more mundane level it seems likely that the underdevelopment of global and international statistics about legal phenomena is in part due to lack of stable concepts suitable for this purpose. See *GLT*, pp. 153–7. See further Chapter 2.3(b), and Chapter 8.7(a).

[95] For a recent example of the use of 'philosophically interesting' that is criticised here, see Dworkin (2006a). Compare a shift of tone in Dworkin (2006b) at p. 228: 'the [sociological] concept is not sufficiently precise to yield philosophically interesting "essential features". ...[T]he sociological concept, like the concepts of marriage, meritocracy, boxing, and other criterial concepts we use to describe social arrangements, has too much leeway for that: its boundaries are too malleable to support an essential feature philosophical investigation.' Arguing against Raz, Dworkin maintains that concepts relating to social institutions are not 'natural kind concepts' that have essential features.(*ibid.*, at p. 229) I agree with him on this, but differ on the judgement that enquiries about social institutions are neither important nor intellectually interesting. On 'essentialism' see Chapter 4 below.

[96] Leiter (2004). Leiter lists criminal law theory, the conceptual and moral foundations of private law, the elucidation of central concepts of abstract legal theory (such as authority, reasons, rules and conventions); the revival of natural law theory; and the exploration of the implications of philosophy of language, metaphysics, and epistemology for both traditional issues of legal philosophy and for fresh explorations of the foundations of various fields of substantive and adjective law (*ibid.*, pp. 166–70). One might add a wealth of literature on the borderland of legal and political theory, especially in theorising liberal democracy and justice, and some outstanding contributions to intellectual history, not least in relation to Bentham.

some of the more heated polemics have taken the form of personal attacks.[97] There are two main complaints: (i) that legal philosophy has become too detached from ordinary legal scholarship and legal practice; and (ii) that the agenda of issues addressed by mainstream analytical philosophers is too narrow. I believe that there is some merit in these criticisms, but there are encouraging signs that we are entering a new era.

The charge that analytical legal philosophy is out of touch with legal scholarship and legal practice relates mainly to the continuing debates about positivism – especially the Hart–Dworkin debate and discussions provoked by Hart's Postscript to *The Concept of Law*. For some years many law students have complained that there seems to be little or no connection between this kind of jurisprudence and other subjects in the curriculum. Similarly, many legal scholars feel that they find little illumination for their particular studies from such theorising. In this view, much legal philosophy has become too abstract, too esoteric, and perhaps too sophisticated to contribute much to the health of the discipline. In short, analytical legal philosophy has become a subject apart.[98]

Charges of narrowness against analytical jurisprudence are of long standing. They can refer to focus, or conception of law, or geographical reach. All three are relevant in the present context. The central thesis of this book is that as the discipline of law becomes more cosmopolitan, jurisprudence as its theoretical part needs to broaden its reach to take more account of non-Western legal traditions, a wider range of legal phenomena, and different levels of normative and legal relations and ordering.

For many years I have argued that Herbert Hart and his followers revolutionised the methods of analytical jurisprudence, but they tended to accept uncritically the agenda of questions they inherited, which in turn was based on a narrow conception of law that centred on legal doctrine and its presuppositions.[99] Although they treated law as a social phenomenon, their work proceeded 'in almost complete isolation from contemporary social theory and from work in socio-legal studies, with little overt concern for the law in action'.[100] As an example of this, Hart himself continued to focus almost entirely on concepts of legal doctrine or its presuppositions ('law talk') but paid almost no attention to concepts of 'talk about law', such as dispute, function, institution, and order,

---

[97] The recent round of public polemics involved Coleman (2001) criticising Dworkin, who in a long review responded with a fierce attack on recent debates about positivism, which he characterised as insular, ascetic, Ptolemaic, sterile and unworldly and analogous to Scholastic philosophy. (Dworkin, 2002). Leiter (2004) then dismissed Dworkin as wrong-headed, deeply implausible, and largely irrelevant to both legal practice and areas of legal philosophy ignored by Dworkin. In a thoughtful essay Halpin (2006b) argued that all the protagonists in these exchanges, and Joseph Raz, who stayed clear of the polemics, were out of touch with legal practice, as he interprets it. For a brief comment see Twining (2006d).

[98] See MacCormick and Twining (1986).   [99] Twining (1979) (reprinted in *GJB*, pp. 69–92).

[100] *Ibid.*, p. 561 (*GJB* at p. 73).

which were as susceptible to, and in need of, the same kind of conceptual elucidation.[101]

The effect of these recent sharp exchanges is more revealing than their intellectual content. They can be interpreted as symptomatic of a growing feeling that some enclaves of legal philosophy have got into a rut and there is a need to branch out in new directions. Part of my argument is that the challenges of globalisation present many opportunities to do just that. Rather than prolonging these polemics, I shall return at the end of this chapter to Dworkin's recent discussion of positivism in which he makes an important distinction that is quite close to the distinction between law as ideas and law as institutionalised social practice that is developed in Chapter 4.

1.7 Legal positivism

In academic law the terms 'positivist' and 'positivism' are sometimes used loosely, as terms of abuse, to refer to formalist or 'black-letter approaches', to someone who is uncritical or indifferent to questions of value, or to spurious claims to neutrality in enquiries that can be shown to be value laden.[102] Behind such charges lies the idea that 'positivism' involves a sharp distinction between fact and value (or between law as it is and law as it ought to be) and a claim that legal scholarship is or should be only concerned with the law as it is. Such attitudes are epitomised by a well-known professor who is reported to have thundered at beginning law students in University College London: 'This is *not* a Faculty of Justice; this is *not* a Faculty of Law; it is *the* Faculty of Laws.' I do not share that attitude.

In this book I adopt the standpoint of a legal positivist who has regularly been critical of 'black letter' approaches; who believes that questions of political morality and evaluation of legal institutions and rules are both central to the discipline of law, who frequently adopts a critical stance, and who, as a scholar, aspires to relative detachment without making any strong claims to neutrality or to being scientific.

'Positivism' in the present context involves no more and no less than two well-known propositions:

(1) that there is no necessary connection between law as it is and law as it ought to be (the separation thesis);[103] and

(2) that the existence of law is a matter of social fact (the social sources thesis).[104]

---

[101] *Ibid.*, at pp. 578–9 (*GJB*, pp. 90–1). See Chapter 2 below.

[102] 'The now pejorative term "Legal Positivism" like most terms that are used as missiles in intellectual battles, has come to stand for a baffling array of different sins.' (Hart (1983) pp. 50–1).

[103] Classic texts include Bentham (1776/1977) *A Fragment on Government* Preface (*CW*, 1977 Burns and Hart, pp. 397–8); Austin, *The Province of Jurisprudence Determined* (1832/1954) at pp. 184–5; Hart (1958) reprinted; Hart (1983) Chapter 2. Hart (1961) Chapter 9.

[104] Hart (1961) Chapter 9; Raz (1979) pp. 38–52.

This is not the place to justify a positivist position generally.[105] My reasons for adopting these positivist assumptions in this context are as follows:

First, for most of my professional life I have worked within the Anglo-American tradition of legal positivism, exemplified by Bentham, Hart and Llewellyn. When real issues have divided positivists and non-positivists, I have tended to side with Hart against Dworkin and Fuller, while considering that the significance of the issues that divide them is overblown.[106] In considering legal phenomena from a global perspective, I shall continue in this tradition by trying to build on, refine and go beyond some of the basic ideas of Hart, Llewellyn, and Tamanaha.

Second, the separation thesis is particularly important in looking at legal orders and phenomena from the outside (while taking into account the internal point of view of participants). Describing, and where appropriate evaluating, legal orders other than one's own, considering them as the product of 'other people's power', comparing legal phenomena from two or more legal orders, and mapping law in the world are activities that require relative detachment so far as is feasible. On the other hand, if one is participating in one's own legal system as citizen, lawyer, judge, reformer or critic, one's concern may indeed be to make the system 'the best it can be', to emphasise aspirations such as respect for rights or the Rule of Law or fidelity to law. There are some contexts in which the is/ought distinction breaks down, for example in presenting an argument or

---

[105] See *GLT*, Chapter 5, esp. pp. 119–21.

[106] My position on this point is close to Neil MacCormick: 'The best forms of positivism lead to conclusions similar in important ways to those derivable from the more credible modes of natural law thought, when we pursue rigorously the matters in hand. That is not to say no important matters are in dispute…Our conclusion ought to be, not that these important issues may safely be ignored by jurisprudence, but they ought to become the focal point of discussion in place of mock-battles over the question whether unjust laws can enjoy formal validity' (MacCormick (1981b) at p. 145). Recently MacCormick has moved from a gentle form of positivism to a position that: 'law is necessarily geared to some conception of justice, taking account of distributive, retributive, and corrective justice, to all of which respect for the rule of law is in the context of the state's capability for coercion, essential.' But he makes it clear that he is mainly talking about the point of law from the standpoint of participants in a particular state legal system: 'Hence you cannot sincerely participate in this enterprise without a serious orientation to these values, and you cannot intelligibly participate in it without at least pretending to have such an orientation' (MacCormick, (2007) at p. 264). MacCormick's arguments are subtle and persuasive, but they do not apply to the standpoint of a comparative lawyer or a member of Amnesty International considering the human rights record (its legal provisions as well as specific 'violations') of a foreign country or a jurist trying to construct an overview of legal phenomena from a global perspective. From such standpoints Hart's position is more persuasive: 'The contrary positivist stress on the elucidation of the concept of law, without reference to the moral values which it may be used to promote, seems to me to offer better guarantees of clear thought. But apart from this, the identification of law as morally legitimate, because oriented towards the common good, seems to me in view of the hideous record of the evil use of law for oppression to be an unbalanced perspective, and as great a distortion as the opposite Marxist identification of the central case of law with the pursuit of the interests of a dominant economic class.' (Hart (1983) at p. 12.) For a more detailed discussion see Twining (forthcoming Del Mar (2009)).

justifying a decision on a disputed point of law, but that is not the present context.[107]

Third, critics of positivism who argue that such a stance leads to an amoral, impoverished, even dangerous conception of law caricature the kind of positivism to which I subscribe. In this context, constructing overviews of legal phenomena in the world as a whole or substantial parts of it, it is useful to draw a clear distinction between describing, explaining and interpreting legal phenomena as they are and evaluating, criticising, recommending, and prescribing conditions for legitimating such phenomena.

Many of the concerns about the separation thesis relate to issues about legitimation, evaluation, constructive interpretation, and criticism of law – issues that in my view can be addressed as well within positivism as outside it.[108] A positivist of this kind is not amoral or indifferent to issues of morality and evaluation. Indeed Bentham, and to a lesser extent Hart, distinguished the 'is' and the 'ought' for the sake of the ought.

The closeness between this version of positivism and the position of Ronald Dworkin is illustrated by the distinction that is developed in Chapters 3 and 4 between law as ideas and law as a species of institutionalised social practice as part of the thesis that understanding law involves both conceptions. In his recent writings Dworkin[109] distinguishes between a sociological and a doctrinal concept of law:[110]

> We must take care to distinguish two questions both of which might be questions about the very nature of law. The first is sociological: what makes a particular structure of governance a legal system rather than some other form of social

---

[107] I am a weak positivist in that I consider that the is/ought distinction depends on context and standpoint. Hart was more emphatic about the distinction. (Twining (2006d)). Hart told me that he was a stronger positivist than MacCormick made out in MacCormick (1981a). (See now MacCormick (2008)). Recently the terms 'hard' (exclusive) and 'soft' (inclusive) positivism have acquired a technical meaning in a separate debate about the meaning of the 'rule of recognition'. (In this debate Raz and Leiter are clearly 'hard', but there is disagreement as to whether Hart was 'hard' or 'soft' (Leiter (2007) at pp. 121–2). The main concern of Hart's positivism was to set up a concept of law that involved no pre-judgement about its morality, social utility or other value. Description should be kept quite separate from prescription, evaluation and legitimation. For the jurist concerned with understanding law – including other people's law – it is important to attain relative detachment as far as is feasible, even if this involves disenchantment with the law. Dworkin (2006b) and MacCormick (2007) are right that for legal actors as participants in certain kinds of polity, law is and should be linked to justice and other aspirations.

[108] Raz (1979) at pp. 233–49.

[109] Dworkin (2006a). See a different formulation in Dworkin (2006b) at pp. 1–5.

[110] Dworkin also introduces a third concept, which is not in issue here. '[W]hat we might call an *aspirational* concept of law, which we often refer to as the ideal of legality or the rule of law. For us this aspirational concept is a contested concept: we agree that the rule of law is desirable, but disagree about what, at least precisely, is the best statement of the ideal.' (Dworkin (2006b) at p. 5) I agree with Dworkin that what is the best conception of the aspirational concept is a question of political and personal morality and that 'the central concepts of political morality – the concepts of justice, liberty, equality, democracy, right, wrong, cruel, and insensitivity – function for us as interpretive concepts as well' (*Ibid.*, p. 11). On formal and substantive conceptions of the rule of law, see Chapter 11.3(b).

control, such as morality, religion, force, or terror? The second is doctrinal: what makes a statement of what the law of some jurisdiction requires or permits or authorizes true? The sociological question has neither much practical nor much philosophical interest. The doctrinal question, on the contrary, is a question both of enormous practical and considerable philosophical significance.[111]

What is interesting here is that Dworkin acknowledges that there is such a thing as a sociological question about the nature of law, but he dismisses it as not philosophically interesting and of no practical importance for 'lawyers', presumably practising lawyers. As this book is mainly about what he calls 'the sociological question' and deals hardly at all with adjudication or 'the doctrinal question', it is relevant to respond to Dworkin's challenge.

First, Dworkin's conception of what is important in jurisprudence, and by implication in the discipline of law, is extraordinarily narrow. He is primarily interested in certain aspects of domestic state law. Within the parochial confines of a single legal system Dworkin is not even interested in argumentation about disputed questions of fact or sentencing, or issues that concern other actors besides judges and advocates. In short, he has a narrow and unrealistic view of adjudication. Forty or so years ago academic law in England was viewed as essentially 'a barrister's subject', concerned primarily with interpretation of legal doctrine in borderline cases. The Supreme Court still exercises an obsessive fascination for many, but not all, American academic lawyers. Dworkin's legal theory, his answer to 'the doctrinal question', is mainly presented as a working theory for superior court judges and superior barristers interpreting the law in hard cases in municipal common law systems in the doctrinal tradition of legal studies.[112] What he says about these is interesting and important, but my conception of jurisprudence and academic law (and, indeed, of adjudication) is much broader than that. We are interested in different questions.[113]

Dworkin's dismissal of questions in which he is not personally interested as 'not philosophically interesting' is doubly revealing. First, as was stated above, in the enterprise of understanding law our concern should be with jurisprudentially interesting questions, whether or not they are philosophically interesting. Second, under the cover of loosely using the pejorative word

[111] Dworkin (2006a) at pp. 97–8. The context of this statement is a debate with Schauer about whether Hart had a developed theory of adjudication. Schauer (2006) and others (including myself) (Twining 2006d) maintain that Hart had not focused much on adjudication in his descriptive theory of law. Dworkin argues that Hart's conception of validity commits him to such a theory and his position on this is 'more original and much more important' (*ibid*).

[112] Dworkin himself is cautious about making claims about the geographical reach of his ideas. But his work has been widely translated and has been considered in relation to civil law systems and European Union law. See further *GLT*, pp. 43–7.

[113] In the postscript to *The Concept of Law* Hart explained the main differences between himself and Dworkin in terms of their being interested in different questions. Dworkin challenges this by arguing that Hart's concept of validity links the sociological and doctrinal questions, so that Hart is providing a (flawed) answer to the latter. For present purposes it will suffice to accept Hart's distinction between identifying the existence of law anywhere and interpreting its content in the context of a particular legal system.

'sociological', by implication he dismisses as uninteresting the whole of legal history, comparative law, empirical studies, concerns about pluralism and diffusion, even those aspects of normative jurisprudence not concerned with 'the doctrinal question', and many other topics that are important for the enterprise of understanding law. All of these are of interest to jurists concerned with general jurisprudence as it is presented here.

Dworkin dismisses disagreements about 'the sociological question' as merely semantic and taxonomic. All that empirical researchers need to do is stipulate working definitions and get on with the job.[114] That is a caricature of the range of enquiries involved in understanding law other than enquiries about 'the doctrinal question'. Social scientists and socio-legal scholars will be surprised at the suggestion that there are no questions of philosophical interest relating to their disciplines when applied to law, that analysis of social science concepts is unproblematic, and that abstract moralising is more 'practical' than anything that empirical legal studies can offer.[115] There are, of course, questions of political morality (to which Dworkin himself has contributed) that are relevant to law beyond 'the doctrinal question'.

It is strange for a philosopher to feel the need to place so much emphasis on the practical value of his theory. In the pursuit of theoretical understanding, practical applications are incidental. However, I share with Dworkin a concern with maintaining connections between theory and practice in jurisprudence. How far his theory of adjudication and argumentation has been influential in practice is a matter of debate, but it is odd to dismiss all other lines of enquiry as having no practical value, especially as doctrinal questions centre on 'the law in books', whereas a central concern of empirical legal studies is with 'the law in action' – how law actually operates in practice, its technology, and its social and economic effects.[116] For example, one could point out that enthusiastic law reformers can benefit from understanding why importing foreign law often runs into difficulties, that many practising lawyers have to navigate across different legal cultures and cope with situations involving normative and legal pluralism, and that drafters of Bills of Rights might have something to learn from the rights-scepticism of Bentham and others.[117] My central concern is with the health of the institutionalised discipline of law; some of the ideas discussed here may have practical implications for teaching and research and

[114] Dworkin (2006a) at pp. 97–9. The tone in Dworkin (2006b) seems in some respects more moderate, but he still insists that the doctrinal question is more interesting and important than the others. Interestingly Dworkin refers to sociologists and other social scientists, but not to law-trained socio-legal scholars who are part of the legal academic community. On 'broadening the study of law from within' see Chapter 8.3(c) below.

[115] Contrast the Genn Report (2006) which treats socio-legal research as being more in touch with 'the real world' than 'textual scholarship'. (See Chapter 8.4(b) below).

[116] On difficulties associated with the distinction between 'law in books' and 'law in action' see Chapter 10 below.

[117] See Chapter 6.5 below.

beyond. However, the main point is theoretical: one cannot understand the subject matters of our discipline solely by answering 'the doctrinal question'.

Rather than engage in unnecessary polemics, it is worth emphasising that Dworkin and I share some significant areas of agreement.[118] Most important, in this book I shall use two conceptions of law that are approximately equivalent to Dworkin's twin 'doctrinal' and 'sociological' concepts. The empirical conception of law as a species of institutionalised social practice rooted in social facts is important as the basis for 'realistic' perspectives that capture the actual operations, roles, causes, and consequences of legal phenomena. Such perspectives include rules and doctrine and much else besides. Study of these matters involves many perspectives in addition to sociology. However, from a global perspective, it is also useful to think in terms of 'legal traditions', (i.e. following Glenn, the dissemination of ideas over time). This involves a distinction between law as ideas and law as practices. Accounts of legal traditions such as classical Roman Law, Jewish law, or Islamic law are typically histories of ideas that tell us little or nothing about how they were institutionalised and how, or even whether, they operated in practice. In that sense they are confined to 'doctrine' in the broad sense of ideas that are taught or handed down.[119]

To give a simple illustration: the term 'Islamic law' can refer solely to ideas, precepts and doctrines derived from the holy *Quran*, the *hadith*, and other sources. Or it can refer both to these ideas and how they have been institutionalised in fact through social practices involving people praying and fasting, disputing, imams, khadis, mosques, law schools, and other activities carried on in the name of Islam. In respect of a purely doctrinal conception, law and morality are largely indistinguishable in Islamic thought. This is one important context where the is/ought distinction breaks down and it is potentially fertile ground for Dworkinians to extend their range. On the other hand, when Islamic ideas are embodied in social practices they are often mixed in with customs, conventions and adaptations, some of which have no basis in doctrine.[120] In

---

[118] For example, we agree that agonising about borderline cases of 'law', such as whether commercial custom or Jewish Law or the internal governance of Baker and Mackenzie merit being classified as 'legal', is silly outside a given context (below pp. 72–3); we agree that adjudication is not so central to 'the sociological question', but that the sociological and doctrinal questions are linked. I also acknowledge that broad-brush overviews or an historical atlas of law in the world on their own may be of limited interest beyond establishing a general context for more particular studies; and we agree that law is not of a natural kind and has no essence. *Per contra*, Dworkin does not deny that social sciences can throw light on law. On the continuity of conceptual analysis and empirical enquiry see Chapter 2.4 below.

[119] In ordinary usage, 'doctrine' means different things to common lawyers, civilians, and theologians. I am interpreting Dworkin as referring to much more than explicit legal rules and principles. Whether his conception is broad enough to include all ideas involved in the Islamic legal tradition is an open question.

[120] E.g. Rosen (2000). On the one hand, controversial practices such as female genital mutilation can be shown to have no basis in Islamic doctrine; on the other hand, many, but not all, Muslims living in countries that prohibit polygamy accept monogamy as a social practice and adapt their behaviour in order to 'render unto Caesar the things that are Caesar's'. See, e.g. Ballard (1994), Bano (2007), but see also Menski (2006) cited at p. 368 below.

Chapters 3 and 4 I construct a framework of concepts that includes a notion of social practice that covers both normative doctrine and actual behaviour. In some contexts, for instance in discussing religious law, it will be important to keep the two ideas separate. But first we need to consider the implications of adopting a global perspective for analytical jurisprudence, especially conceptual analysis.

Chapter 2

Analytical jurisprudence in a global context

2.1 Introduction: conceptual questions

What is law?[1]

What should count as a 'legal system' or 'legal order' for the purpose of constructing a reasonably comprehensive historical atlas of law in the world?[2]

Does Hart's (or Kelsen's or Dworkin's) conception of law travel well?[3]

Does the European Union have a constitution? Should it have one?

We are told that legal pluralism occurs when two or more legal orders co-exist in the same time-space context. What counts as one 'legal order'?[4]

Do 'rights' have the same meaning in Islamic law and Western law?[5]

Can corporations have human rights? Can chimpanzees?[6]

Was Dinka traditional society genuinely democratic?[7]

To what extent does the interpretation of the precise scope of 'inhuman and degrading treatment' turn on universal moral principles or local culture and conditions?[8]

Is 'dignity' in the Universal Declaration of Human Rights so vague as to be meaningless?[9]

Transparency International, Western financial institutions (e.g. the World Bank) and aid agencies are promoting a worldwide campaign against corruption. Transparency International regularly publishes a Corruption Perceptions Index in the form of league tables. Is not what counts as 'corruption' culture specific?[10]

Is cronyism a form of corruption? When is a tip a bribe?[11]

What is meant by 'development'? How can it be measured?[12]

What is the essential nature of globalisation?[13]

---

[1] See Chapter 4 below.   [2] See Chapter 4 below.
[3] See Chapter 4 below.   [4] See Chapter 16.1.2 below.
[5] See, e.g. An-Na'im (1992) in Chapter 13.3 below.   [6] See Chapter 15.2 below.
[7] See Chapter 13.2 below.   [8] See Chapter 1.1 above.
[9] McCrudden (2008).   [10] See Leys (1965), Twining (2005b) at pp. 25–33.
[11] See Appendix III (on the web).   [12] See Chapter 11 below.   [13] See Chapter 1.5 above.

Mrs Thatcher said 'There is no such thing as society'; several social scientists have argued that 'society' is no longer a useful concept. Are they in agreement?[14]

Comparative lawyers talk about 'reception', 'transplantation', 'diffusion', and 'transposition' and 'importation' of laws and legal ideas. Are these all synonyms?[15]

Is it possible to draft uniform insolvency or copyright laws for countries with different legal cultures and traditions or different models of insolvency regimes?[16]

The European Development Bank has developed 'legal indicators' of the extensiveness and effectiveness of commercial law and financial regulation in countries in transition. How can these be meaningful?[17]

Are the U.S. Supreme Court, the European Court of Justice, the International Criminal Court, the gecaga *courts in Rwanda, khadi courts in Morocco, the Iran–United States Claims Tribunal, arbitration under the International Chamber of Commerce, and the courts of the Common Law Movement in the United States all 'courts' in the same sense? Are they sufficiently similar to be comparable?*[18]

We are told that country X has five times as many university law schools and law students per 100,000 of population as country Y. Are 'universities', 'law schools' and 'law students' comparable in this context?[19]

Is there a negative (or a positive) correlation between the number of lawyers in a given society and its economic health? Or is this a meaningless question?[20]

What are the problems involved in constructing standardised categories for global statistics on such matters as crime (e.g. murder, theft), levels of damages for personal injuries, delay in court, prisoners on remand, legal aid and representation, or the percentage of the national budget allocated to the legal sector or to judicial administration?[21]

Can there be an empirical science of law?[22]

---

[14] Discussed Thatcher (1993) at p. 626. Lady Thatcher's point was that 'society was not an abstraction, separate from the men and women who composed it, but a living structure of individuals, families, neighbours, and voluntary associations' (*ibid*). On quite different doubts about society as a useful analytic concept because of the weakening of national boundaries see below pp. 93, 228 and Tamanaha (2001) pp. 206–8.

[15] See Chapter 9 below.   [16] Westbrook (1999).   [17] Ramasatry (2002).

[18] On the 'gecaga' courts see Clark (2006), Newton (2007); on khadi courts see Rosen (1989); on the International Criminal Court see e.g. Cassese (2003); on the Iran–US Claims Tribunal and the International Chamber of Commerce see Dezalay and Garth (1996); on the Common Law Movement see below p. 73.

[19] See Chapter 2.3(b) below. Twining (2001) at pp. 28–31; see Twining (1997) Chapter 15.

[20] 'Do lawyers impair economic growth?' Symposium (1992) criticised in Galanter (1998) at pp. 743–7); see Galanter (1992) discussed in Chapter 2.3(b).

[21] This question refers to a fairly random selection of topics that I have encountered in discussions of 'globalisation' and law and development in recent years. Most of these are topics that might in principle be subject to quantification provided that standardised categories can be constructed and the phenomena can be treated as commensurable or otherwise comparable. For a preliminary discussion, see *GLT*, pp. 152–68. On commensuration see Espeland and Stevens (1998).

[22] See Chapter 8.9 below.

Questions like these arise throughout this book and in discussions of law and globalisation. They are of different kinds. Few, if any, of these questions are solely about words or concepts, but all of them have a conceptual dimension.[23] Concepts are important as thinking tools at all levels of practical legal activity as well as in academic law and legal philosophy. One of the implications of 'globalisation' is that it raises important issues about the adequacy of our inherited vocabulary and conceptual apparatus for describing, analysing, interpreting, comparing, and generalising about legal ideas and phenomena across legal jurisdictions, traditions and cultures. My thesis is that there is a lot of work to be done on usable concepts in cross-cultural and transnational legal discourse and that this is a task for analytical jurisprudence.

Semantic and conceptual questions are of many different kinds. Some can be resolved quite easily; some may require quite sophisticated techniques of analysis; and some raise profound philosophical questions. Anyone who has played *Scrabble* will be familiar with the question: Does this (e.g bik or hrrmph) count as a word? Such issues are typically resolved by appeal to a dictionary or other authoritative source. But, as lawyers should know, very few questions of interpreting words in a statute can be resolved by resorting to a dictionary.[24] Arguments are needed about the 'best' or 'correct' interpretation in a specific context. Before answering such questions, it is often useful to pause and ask: what puzzlement or other concern lies behind that question? If a foreigner asks me: 'What is law?' or 'What is corruption?', she may only be unfamiliar with the word and be asking for a translation. But if a jurist or law student puts the same question, even though they are familiar with the term, they are surely asking about something else. It may be that I have used an ambiguous word, and they are asking which of two fairly precise meanings is intended in this context. Or it may be that the word is vague and they want me to be more precise, perhaps by stipulating a definition. It may be that the question is a request for a correct or proper meaning of the word, in which case I can point out that they are making an elementary semantic error, by assuming that all words have correct or proper meanings.[25] Similarly if someone who asks 'What is justice?' means 'What kind of thing or entity does justice stand for?' I can point out that it is

---

[23] This chapter is concerned with analysis of *both* concepts and words. They are intimately related, for one uses words to label concepts, but it is important to keep them conceptually distinct. For example, a term may 'travel', but become attached to a different concept; the same word may refer to more than one concept; I may have a concept but be unable to express it in words; words may imperfectly capture a concept. I shall follow the convention of putting words in inverted commas (e.g. torture refers to the concept, 'torture' to the word). A variant on the use of inverted commas for words are scare quotes (e.g. 'globalisation' means 'so-called globalisation').

[24] On the tendency of commentators to underestimate the range and variety of 'conditions of doubt' in interpretation see *HTDTWR*, Chapter 6.

[25] On 'the proper meaning' fallacy see Hart (1953).

wrong to think that words like 'justice' stand for things or entities.[26] Or if the question means: 'What is the essential nature of law/justice/corruption?' I can suggest that it is wrong to assume that law/justice/corruption has an essential nature, but some serious thinkers will disagree.[27]

This kind of elementary ground clearing may resolve some questions, but genuine puzzlements may remain. Some concepts like justice, democracy, cause and, perhaps, law are said to be essentially contested concepts, that is they admit of different conceptions that are a battleground for profound substantive disagreements, often involving opposing theories.[28] Such puzzlements about law, justice, rights, causation, due process, and responsibility have been and continue to be at the centre of the agenda of traditional analytical jurisprudence. This is as it should be. My argument is that one of the implications of globalisation for the discipline of law is that, because the great bulk of scholarly and juristic attention has been focused on domestic law within a single legal tradition, we do not yet have so developed a vocabulary and conceptual apparatus for studying and generalising about law transnationally and cross-culturally.

2.2 Analytical jurisprudence

(a) The historical context

I was an undergraduate in Oxford in 1952 when Herbert Hart took up the Corpus Chair of Jurisprudence. Accordingly I experienced analytical jurisprudence both before and after his advent. At the time, the standard textbooks, such as Salmond and Paton,[29] devoted about half of their space to legal concepts such as sovereignty, rights, duties, acts, legal persons, *ratio decidendi*, possession, and ownership. The focus was on the meanings of these concepts in English law. In other words it was largely particular rather than general jurisprudence. A fairly standard essay would deal with one concept, drawing on cases and articles in addition to the textbook. For example,

---

[26] On hypostatisation or 'thingifying' see n. 112 below.

[27] On 'essentialism' see p. 66 below.

[28] Gallie (1956). There is a clear account in Dworkin (1977) at pp. 101–105.

[29] Salmond (10th edn, 1947), Paton (2nd edn, 1951). Dias and Hughes (1957) and Dias (1964), which appeared shortly afterwards, continued the tradition, but this kind of particular analytical jurisprudence has disappeared from most jurisprudence courses in common law countries, except India. Salmond's *Jurisprudence* continued to be used in India as a standard text long after it had been largely superseded in the United Kingdom. Sarkar (1973, 1981) speaks of it as having 'been with students, the Bench and Bar for the last seven decades'. (Preface). MacCormick (2007) Part 2 may mark a partial return to this style of analytical jurisprudence by devoting five chapters to analysis of the concepts of persons, wrongs, duties, rights and obligations, property, legal powers and validity, but without reference to a single legal system. Similarly, this book presents analyses of a number of analytic concepts, but goes beyond doctrinal concepts to include important socio-legal concepts, such as function, institution, group, and system.

in dealing with possession, one would read cases in larceny, bailment, sales, trespass to land and trespass to goods, and – despite looking at Savigny – one would conclude that the term had different meanings in different branches of English law. Our system had no general definition or theory of 'possession',[30] and in the best pragmatic tradition of the common law, it did not need one. Such exercises were valuable in getting students to think across different branches of law, but they would now be dismissed as 'atheoretical'. Certainly, the method of analysis was unsophisticated. Hart's inaugural lecture on 'Definition and Theory in Jurisprudence' seized on the methodological weakness. He argued that questions such as 'What is law?', 'What is a legal person?', 'What is a right?' were misposed, because they looked like requests for a dictionary definition (*'per genus et differentiam'*),[31] but this form of answer does not dissolve the puzzlements behind such questions. I remember feeling profound culture shock on reading 'Definition and Theory' and attending Hart's lectures that were the precursors of the *Concept of Law*. Words do not necessarily have a proper meaning; 'justice' does not stand for a thing; definitions are not true or false. My naïve semantics were shattered and I became an instant convert to 'linguistic analysis'.[32]

Within a short time of taking up the Corpus Chair in 1952, Hart revitalised English jurisprudence by re-establishing close links with analytical philosophy. His contributions to analytical jurisprudence included reviving the idea of general jurisprudence; adopting, refining, and applying Bentham's techniques of analysis of abstract concepts; and serving as a conduit of ideas developed by the remarkable group of Oxford philosophers that included Ryle, Paul, Waismann, and above all, J.L. Austin. Hart was a member of this close circle of colleagues who claimed to have brought about a 'revolution in philosophy' through careful and sophisticated analysis of language.[33] The central claim was that most philosophical problems could be 'solved' or 'dissolved' by careful analysis of ordinary usage of words.[34]

The term 'analytical jurisprudence' is sometimes treated as co-extensive with 'linguistic analysis', or with elucidation of abstract concepts. This is too

---

[30] Hart distinguished between definition and theory in his inaugural lecture. That was, for us at least, an innovation.

[31] A definition *per genus et differentiam* is a classificatory definition that takes the form 'M is a species of class N (*genus*) and is distinguished from other members of the class by characteristics o and p (*differentiae*)'. MacCormick (2007) rightly argues that an explanatory definition of law as a species of institutionalised normative order still has value.

[32] The basic ideas are explained clearly in Hart (1953). On its deleterious effects for a naïve enthusiast see Twining (1968) at pp. 5–7. On elementary semantic fallacies see Chapter 3, n. 1 below.

[33] The atmosphere of intellectual excitement of the time is evoked in Lacey (2004), Chapter 6. On the 'revolution in philosophy' see Ayer (1956).

[34] The claim that philosophical puzzlements could be dissolved by analysis is associated with Wittgenstein; the stronger claim that philosophical problems could be solved by such means is attributed to J.L. Austin.

narrow.[35] It is true that elucidation of abstract concepts was the main focus of attention of some analytical jurists in the Anglo-American tradition, including Austin, Holland, Hohfeld, Kocourek, and Salmond. However, it has not been their only concern. For example, Hart treated a number of other topics as part of analytical jurisprudence, including the study of the form and structure of legal systems, problems of legal reasoning, and problems of definition of law.[36] Hart also made it clear that he considered that critical analysis of assumptions and presuppositions of legal discourse was one of the main tasks of legal philosophy.[37] This broader view accommodates contemporary jurists such as Raz, MacCormick, and even Dworkin, who assimilated some of the techniques of conceptual analysis developed by analytical philosophers, including Hart, but moved on to deal with what they considered to be issues of substance.

From about 1960 there was a reaction against logical positivism and 'linguistic analysis' in philosophy.[38] Within jurisprudence Hart's own work soon came under attack from several different directions. In particular, English and American heirs of secular natural law, Devlin, Fuller, and later Dworkin, attacked Hart's positivist premises.[39] Second, empirically minded jurists, beginning with Bodenheimer, criticised the abstraction and lack of 'realism' of *a priori* analysis of legal concepts.[40] Third, rather later, critical legal scholars and post-modernists challenged the alleged neutrality of conceptual analysis and the assumptions about the relative determinacy of language exemplified by Hart's analysis of abstract terms in terms of core and penumbra. Morton Horwitz crystallised the main criticisms along the lines that analytical positivism as exemplified by Hart was unhistorical, unempirical, apolitical, uncritical, and based on a false hermeneutics.[41] Hart and his disciples robustly defended his position against such criticisms and managed to show that at least some of them were directed at caricatures of his own views. But over time he retreated on a number of fronts, most significantly in respect of the more extravagant claims about the value of linguistic analysis of ordinary linguistic usage.[42]

---

[35] The diversity of the lines of enquiry that tend to attract the label 'analytical jurisprudence' is illustrated by such recent books as Atria (2002), Coleman (2001), Dixon (2001), Frandberg and van Hoecke (1998), Halpin (1997), Herrestad (1996), Pintore and Jori (1997), Tamanaha (2001) and Unger (1996). This chapter is written within and in reaction to the mainstream Anglo-American tradition.

[36] Hart (1967/1983).   [37] Hart (1987) at pp. 35, 40.

[38] Gellner's *Words and Things* (1959) is sometimes treated as marking the start of the reaction. Leiter (2007) gives a useful account of subsequent developments through Quine to the 'naturalist turn' in philosophy, emphasising continuities between philosophical theorising and empirical enquiry. See further Chapter 2.4.

[39] Fuller (1957–8), Bodenheimer (1955–6), and Devlin (1959) first challenged Hart before the publication of *The Concept of Law* in 1961.

[40] Bodenheimer (1955–6); see Hart's reply (1957).

[41] Horwitz (1997). For a partial dissent, see *GLT*, p. 34.

[42] See especially, the Postscript to *The Concept of Law* (1994) and discussions of it. It is sad that in his reply to his critics, Hart concentrated on only one of them, Ronald Dworkin, and failed to re-assert the importance of the link between analytical jurisprudence and socio-legal studies. See Chapter 2.4(b).

Since the 1950s there have been significant developments in the philosophy of language, epistemology, and cognition. The most directly relevant to jurisprudence is 'the naturalist turn' stimulated by W.O. Quine, who in attacking any sharp distinction between 'analytic' and 'synthetic' statements raised profound questions about the nature of conceptual analysis and its relationship to empirical enquiry. This will be considered briefly below.[43]

I shall not enter these debates here. Suffice to say, my position is that Hart's contributions to jurisprudence, and to the discipline of law more generally, included bringing an increased awareness about the nature and limitations of language; some sharp and highly transferable techniques of conceptual analysis; some overblown expectations about what these techniques could achieve;[44] and a sense of intellectual ambition and excitement. Hart made an enormous impact by rejoining jurisprudence and philosophy in respect of method, but he barely changed the agenda he had inherited from his predecessors in the English positivist tradition.[45] I believe that Hart's techniques are still of real value, especially when applied to a wider range of concepts than he envisaged and within a broader conception of law and of its study. Herbert Hart himself often expressed the view that his kind of analysis was applicable to these broader inquiries, but in practice he very largely confined his attention to doctrinal concepts ('law talk').[46] He realised that his method had a potentially wide application, but his own agenda remained quite narrow.[47]

(b) Beyond doctrinal concepts

Almost all of the literature focuses on concepts used or presupposed in the discourse of legal doctrine ('law talk'). This book adopts a broad conception of the subject matters of law as a discipline and proceeds on the assumption that,

---

[43] See pp. 54–6 below. In my view some of these developments are indeed significant, but they do not invalidate or supersede Hart's main methods of conceptual elucidation. On the recent 'methodology debate' in jurisprudence, see Chapter 2.4 below.

[44] At its height the leaders of 'the revolution in philosophy' in Oxford, associated with J.L. Austin's circle, gave the impression that they believed that most philosophical problems could be solved by careful examination of language, especially ordinary usage. Despite denials that they made any such claim, there is little doubt that in the first flush of enthusiasm some analytical tools were overused. A good example was T.D. Weldon's *The Vocabulary of Politics* (1953), which had almost cult status when I was an undergraduate. Hart himself made a partial retraction (Hart, Postscript 1994) but in both England and the United States there was such a strong reaction that 'linguistic analysis' became a by-word for narrow, sterile, over-abstract logomachy (e.g. Gellner, (1959)).

[45] On Hart's assumptions about the scope of analytical jurisprudence see Hart (1983) Ch. 3, especially at pp. 88–9.

[46] See below p. 44.   [47] Twining (1979).

insofar as conceptual elucidation is important, it applies as much to discourse about law as to the more traditional 'law talk'. In particular, conceptual analysis has a lot to contribute to the normative and empirical study of law. It is part of my general thesis that conceptual analysis has an important part to play in reviving general jurisprudence, but that what is needed is a much broader conception of what is involved than those of Hart or Raz or even Stone. The central concern is with the development of adequate ways of expressing law and talking about law across legal orders, jurisdictions, levels, traditions, and cultures – ranging from comparison of two or more contexts to genuinely global generalisations. What travels well/badly, when, why, and how?

This conception of analytical jurisprudence builds on Anglo-American tradition in respects of methods, but differs in the following respects:

(i)   It is based on a wider conception of law that goes beyond municipal or state law and covers all levels of legal ordering including global, transnational, international, regional, municipal (including national and subnational), and local non-state.[48]

(ii) It focuses on a wider range of concepts than traditional analytical jurisprudence. It includes, but is not limited to, 'fundamental'[49] or 'essentially contested' or 'philosophically interesting'[50] or very abstract concepts.[51] More important, it is not confined to law talk, but extends to any general discourses about legal phenomena (i.e. talk about law).

(iii) It is concerned not just with individual concepts, but with *groups* of related concepts both in jurisprudence and in specialised discourses, such as the discourse of public international lawyers, or about prison conditions, or contract, or corruption.

Analytical method here includes not only logical, linguistic, and conceptual techniques developed by analytical philosophers, but also tools of analysis developed in neighbouring disciplines (such as ideal types, models, metaphors, and deconstruction). It would be as foolish to try to codify the

---

[48] See Chapter 4 below.

[49] On the idea of 'fundamental legal conceptions' in regard to Hohfeld and human rights, see Halpin (2003).

[50] On the type of intellectual snobbery that suggests that legal philosophers (aka jurists) should only concern themselves with issues and concepts that are 'philosophically interesting', see above pp. 223, 281. This is a different point from Dworkin's sharp attack on 'Pickwickian Positivism' in legal philosophy (Dworkin 2002). I have some sympathy with the view that much recent analytical jurisprudence has lost touch with legal practice, but I have a broader view of what constitutes 'legal practice' than Dworkin.

[51] For example, George Fletcher's excellent, but eclectic, book: *Basic Concepts of Legal Thought* (Fletcher 1996). Fletcher's selection is intriguing: I The Legal system: The Rule of Law; Law; Rules and Discretion; Discourse. II Ultimate Values: Justice, Desert, Consent; Equality. III Morality in the Law: Morality; Efficiency; Loyalty; Consistency.

techniques of conceptual elucidation as to attempt the same for translation or comparative literature. Sophisticated analysis of language may be based on an understanding of the properties, uses and limitations of language and on certain working principles, but it is nearer to art than science. It requires sensitivity, imagination, feel, patience, and detailed knowledge. Some issues of method are contested. Similar considerations apply to other relevant kinds of analysis.

However, there are some specific devices that are available and can be learned, such as:

  (i) Awareness of certain cardinal features of language that pose threats to understanding (e.g. vagueness, types of ambiguity).[52]

  (ii) Awareness of common false assumptions about language (e.g. the proper meaning fallacy, hypostatisation).[53]

  (iii) Techniques of division and classification.[54]

  (iv) Differentiating species of definitions; stipulative definitions;[55] explanatory definitions.[56]

  (v) Elucidation of concepts too abstract to be susceptible of definition *per genus et differentiam*.[57]

  (vi) Disambiguation.

  (vii) Elucidation of emotive and expressive terms (e.g. corruption, torture, terrorism) and the emotive use of language in law.[58]

(viii) Use of standard or paradigm cases and variants.[59]

  (ix) Use of ideal types as polar opposites, binary distinctions, or with variants.[60]

  (x) Use of analogies, models, and metaphors.[61]

  (xi) Wittgenstein's family resemblances ('game').[62]

---

[52] Hart (1958) at pp. 144–8, Empson (1947).

[53] Hart (1958). On 'hypostatisation' (the assumption that all nouns stand for entities or things) see below n. 112.

[54] Jolowicz (1970).   [55] Robinson (1950).   [56] MacCormick (2007) Chapter 16.

[57] Hart (1953) building on Bentham's techniques of paraphrasis and phraseoplerosis.

[58] This is a large subject for another occasion, see Twining and Twining (1973), Twining (2005b).

[59] See the analysis of 'bribery' and 'torture' below. See also the analysis of processes of diffusion in Chapter 9.

[60] See Appendix III (on the web) and Table 9.1 (models of diffusion) at p. 279 below. Ideal types employ concepts that themselves may need to be elucidated. For example, Mirjan Damaska has been rightly praised for his brilliant use of three ideal types in comparing procedural systems (managerial/reactive states; hierarchical/co-ordinate systems of authority; and inquest/contest systems of procedure) (Damaska 1986). His weakest point is the overuse of binary distinctions, especially in respect of states, and his contested distinction between inquest and contest in terms of purposes (see Markovits (1989) at p. 41; *RE*, pp. 180–2).

[61] M. Black (1962); Haack (1998) Chapter 4.

[62] Wittgenstein (1953) para. 66; (1969) 17; *HTDTWR* at pp. 194–6, 398–9. See further below p. 102.

(xii) Distinguishing between analytic (etic) and folk (emic) concepts and uses of concepts.[63]

(xiii) Deconstruction and immanent critique.[64]

(c) Legal and cultural relativism

'Cultural relativism' – the thesis that cultures are unique and are not subject to precise comparison and generalisation, nor to criticism from outside – has recently had a revival in connection with debates about whether human rights are 'universal'.[65] The fact that this chapter raises questions about our capacity to generalise across legal cultures and traditions, should not be taken as the assertion of a strong particularist or relativist position.[66] Legal anthropologists, such as Bohannan and Roberts, have emphasised the importance of 'folk concepts' in understanding the normative order of a different culture;[67] comparative lawyers have warned of the many pitfalls in attempting to compare conceptual schemes. For such reasons, functionalist approaches to comparative law have emphasised that convergence between legal systems is more often than not convergence of shared outcomes reached by different conceptual routes.[68] Implicit in such perspectives is a sub-text to the effect that ordinary legal discourse tends to be highly culture specific and lacks a vocabulary that is suitable for analytic purposes. Pushed to its limits this view suggests that lawyers are inescapably culture-bound: they cannot free themselves from

---

[63] This chapter is mainly concerned with 'analytic' as opposed to 'folk' concepts. The debate between Gluckman and Bohannan about 'folk' and 'analytic' concepts in legal anthropology (summarised in Nader (1969)) was part of a more general, rather convoluted, debate in social anthropology about 'emics' and 'etics' (especially Headland *et al.* (1990)). I have some reservations about these distinctions (Twining (2003b) at pp. 229–31), especially in relation to law, but in the present context we are mainly concerned with analytic concepts that can be used cross-culturally. For present purposes, the following working definitions by James Lett, a leading contributor to the anthropological debate are adequate: '*Emic constructs are accounts, descriptions and analyses expressed in terms of the conceptual schemes and categories regarded as meaningful and appropriate by native members whose beliefs and behaviors are being studied. ... Etic constructs are accounts, descriptions and analyses expressed in terms of the conceptual schemes regarded as meaningful and appropriate by the community of scientific observers.*' (Lett (1990) at pp. 130–1) (original italics). Emphasis on the importance of analytic concepts does not preclude 'thick description' (see Ziegert (2002) on Luhmann).

[64] e.g. Balkin (1987), Binder and Weisberg (2000) Chapter 5. Some, but not all, of the techniques listed are dealt with in books on logic or introductions to clear thinking (e.g. M. Black (1952) (1962); Walton (1989)). One might add to this illustrative list particular ideas such as the distinction between concept and conception, 'essentially contested concepts' (Gallie (1956)) and Dworkin's notion of 'interpretive concepts'. I shall not discuss here Dworkin's characterisation of Hart as a 'semantic theorist' and Hart's reply in his Postscript to *The Concept of Law* (1994), neither of which I find convincing.

[65] Discussed at Chapter 5.3 and Chapter 6.3 below.   [66] *GLT*, pp. 25–33, 42–7.

[67] Bohannan (1957), Roberts (1998). On the distinction between 'folk' and 'analytic' concepts see n. 63 above.

[68] e.g. Zweigert and Kötz, 1998 Chapter 2. For a balanced discussion of functionalist approaches in comparative law see Örücü in Örücü and Nelken (2007) pp. 47–53 and Twining (2000a) at p. 37. On functionalism generally see Chapter 4.3(d) below.

their cultural blinders and are hence incapable of doing valid comparative work across cultures. Simon Roberts comes close to adopting this position when he suggests that one needs to look to the social sciences rather than to law for an analytic framework for 'the comparative project'.[69]

Originating in different contexts (including analytical jurisprudence, legal anthropology, sociology, and comparative law), such particularist views seem to converge on a single thesis, which may be termed 'legal relativism'. A strong version of this thesis would be that law is inherently culture specific and legal discourse is largely confined to 'folk concepts'.[70] I personally share some of the concerns underlying this position because moderate versions offer some salutary warnings about the difficulties of comparison and generalisation in law. However, the strong version can be shown to be false. An obvious way to do this is to identify counter-examples – concepts and legal discourses that do 'travel well'. This is the subject of the exploratory studies reported later in this chapter.

The chief weakness of strong legal relativism is that it postulates a high degree of isolation of actual legal orders and legal discourses from other legal cultures and from other spheres of activity in the same culture. This seems implausible in most contexts.

First, one can hypothesise that terms of art, jargon, specifically legal concepts and other specialised legal language only form a very small part of 'law talk' in most legal orders. Legal language normally draws on and interacts with 'ordinary' and specialised 'non-legal' discourses. It is quite misleading to characterise law talk solely or mainly in terms of its uniquely legal meanings and features.

Second, legal orders rarely exist in isolation from other legal orders, systems, and cultures. For at least twenty years anthropologists have acknowledged the weaknesses and distortions of an earlier tradition that treated 'tribes' and 'societies' as isolated, self-contained, timeless units.[71] Alan Watson's 'transplants thesis', even in its weaker and more plausible versions,[72] draws attention to the near-ubiquity of diffusion and transplantation of laws, a fact which goes a long way to account for significant patterns in any realistic picture of law in the world.[73] Although I am personally quite sceptical about the value and

---

[69] Roberts (1998). This view is reminiscent of W. W. Buckland's scepticism about the feasibility of general analytical jurisprudence (Buckland (1945)) and the 'jurisprudential relativism' of Atiyah and Summers (1987) who argue that the primary subject-matter of jurisprudence should be 'the relevant phenomena of law in one or more particular societies' (at p. 418) and that Dworkin's model judge Hercules does not fit the English system of appointing judges 'who do not even want to emulate Hercules'. (*Ibid.*, p. 420, 264–6.). See *GLT*, pp. 25–53. See the position of 'difference theorists' in comparative law, such as Pierre Legrand (1999b) discussed below p. 305. See Hyland (1996).

[70] 'Legal relativism' as used here should be distinguished from Donald Black's only indirectly related theory of 'legal relativity'. This asserts that, while rules of law remain the same in their content, their consequences vary with the relational structure of each case (i.e. rules of law are only one of the variables affecting case outcomes). (Black (1995) (2007).

[71] Collier and Starr (1989).   [72] Ewald (1995b).

[73] *GLT*, Chapter 6. See further Chapter 9 below.

importance of large-scale efforts to unify or harmonise large bodies of law within the European Union and beyond, recent experience has shown that unification is sometimes quite feasible, at least at the level of 'law talk' and surface law.[74] Relativism and isolationism, in law as in other fields, are matters of degree. The extent to which they are plausible options today is best explored through detailed study of particular areas.

(d) 'Travelling well'[75]

My aim is to raise some questions about the adequacy of our stock of concepts for transnational, cross-cultural and cross-level legal discourse. This includes exploring what it is for a concept or group of concepts or models or frames to travel far and to travel well (i.e. so that they can be used with reasonable clarity and precision to express, describe, analyse, compare, generalise about, explain, or evaluate subject matters of our discipline across various kinds of boundary.)[76] My tests of travelling far and well are mainly empirical and pragmatic: Does it fit?[77] Does it work? Can the same concepts be used with roughly the same meaning in similar contexts in England and Italy, or in California, Tanzania and Japan?[78] For example, would this category or group of concepts be suitable for use in regional or global statistics, or in an international convention intended for local application in many countries, or in a genuinely comparative transnational study of some legal field or institution or set of problems, or in making some broad empirical generalisations about courts or lawyers?[79]

---

[74] Twining (2001: pp. 26–8). On surface law, see Chapter 10 below.

[75] There is a vast literature on transfer of knowledge and diffusion of ideas. See Chapter 9 below and Twining (2005d).

[76] In the present context 'travelling' should not be interpreted too literally to refer only to transfer across physical space. The concept of 'travelling well' in relation to concepts, ideas, and facts has been the subject of a major interdisciplinary programme at the London School of Economics 'How Well Do "Facts" Travel?' www.lse.ac.uk/collections/economicHistory/Research/facts/. See also Galison (1997).

[77] An example of bad fit would be applying 'chiefs' as an analytic concept to an acephalous society (i.e. a society without chiefs) or applying American constitutional concepts (e.g. separation of powers) to a polity with a radically different constitutional tradition.

[78] See the provocative claim by James Gordley (mainly in relation to contract doctrine): 'Both "common law" systems such as those of England and the United States and "civil law" systems such as those of France, Italy and Germany have a similar doctrinal structure based on *similar legal concepts*. They divide private law into certain large fields such as property, tort and contract, and analyze these fields in a similar way…*The organization of the law and its larger concepts are alike even if particular rules are not.*' Gordley (1991) at p. 1 (italics added). This passage is discussed further in Chapter 10 below in relation to surface law .

[79] Another context of 'travelling well' is the use of questionnaires in comparative law. A large proportion of ambitious comparative projects has been based on questionnaires, for example Rudolph Schlesinger's project on the common core of legal systems in relation to formation of contract (Schlesinger 1968) and, with more sophistication, the major comparative studies of precedent and interpretation of statutes led by Neil MacCormick and Robert Summers (1991) and (1997).

'Travelling well' is a metaphor associated with wine. Here it is used broadly to refer to the transferability of concepts and terms across different contexts. The contexts are many and the term is deliberately vague. The concern relates both to legal concepts, such as duty, person, contract, used in the formulation of laws (law talk) and analytic concepts used in describing, analysing, explaining and evaluating legal institutions and phenomena (talk about law).[80] 'Travel' can take place across legal cultures, languages, jurisdictions, levels, and fields of law.

I am sometimes asked whether I think that the idea of 'inhuman treatment' travels well in relation to the problem of provision of clean water in prisons in poor countries.[81] Clearly the term itself does not resolve the issues on its own. There is room for real disagreements about such questions as whether prisoners have a right to be given clean water when many people in the rural population do not have it; or how far economic considerations and priorities should affect the implementation of legally prescribed human rights. Is the phrase 'torture, inhuman or degrading treatment or punishment' restricted to intentional acts, or does it cover negligent or reckless acts or omissions?

I think that the concept of inhuman and degrading treatment does travel quite well in that context in that, first, it provides a framework for debating such issues; second, it provides a direct link to the idea of basic human needs; but, third, it allows some flexibility in respect of its interpretation and application in different social and economic contexts. The notion of degrading similarly invokes an abstract universal principle of respect for persons or human dignity, while allowing some latitude for different economic conditions and cultural attitudes to respect and shame.[82]

In order to develop and concretise the theme of concepts travelling well, I have sampled the literature on several topics, including discourse about legal rights, legal personality, corruption, comparative studies of legal professions and legal education, international standards for prison conditions, and the constellation of concepts associated with the concept of law itself. Some of these will be looked at in detail for other reasons in this and other chapters. Here it may be useful to briefly refer to three topics that illustrate the theme of concepts travelling well: on the one hand, transnational discourse about prison conditions is an example of a subject which, perhaps surprisingly, seems fairly amenable to generalisation; on the other hand, comparative study of lawyers and legal education is an example of an area that in the past has seemed

---

[80] Bentham, Austin and other pioneers of analytical jurisprudence emphasised the importance of 'basic', 'fundamental' or 'common concepts' in universal jurisprudence, but also cautioned that the number of such concepts is quite limited (Bentham (1970) pp. 6, 295; Austin (1863) 367–9, discussed in *GLT*, pp. 16–23). However, my argument applies more broadly to any important concepts employed in transnational or cross-cultural or cross-level legal discourse.

[81] See Chapter 1.1 above.

[82] Consider the practical problem of not mixing men, women and children in the same cell, especially in a poor country, in which most police stations in the country have only one cell. Is that 'degrading' treatment in the context?

bedevilled by terms and concepts that do not seem to travel at all well. More controversial is Professor Brian Tamanaha's attempt to construct a very broad conception of law without using any of the criteria of identification proposed by contemporary analytical jurists, such as Hart, Raz, or MacCormick. Next, we shall consider one set of concepts, Hohfeld's analysis of eight related concepts associated with legal rights, which are conventionally included on lists of 'fundamental legal conceptions' (i.e. analytic concepts that are generally thought to 'travel well'). In Chapter 4 we shall look in detail at a possible framework of analytic concepts that cluster round different conceptions of law, including function, rule, institution, order, ordering, social practices, acceptance by officials, sanctions and primary and secondary rules. We shall also touch on some meta-concepts of analytical jurisprudence, including criteria of identification, criteria of validity, and individuation. This list will be extended in later chapters to include, *inter alia*, conceptions of justice, human rights, legal pluralism, instrumentalism, person (subject), group, system, and emotive terms such as torture, terror and corruption.

2.3 Four case studies

(a) Prisons and airports

'Only the name of the airport changes' (Calvino)[83]
The first case study examined transnational terminology relating to state prison systems, as illustrated by the Standard Minimum Rules for the Treatment of Prisoners (SMR), Human Rights Watch's national and global reports on prisons, and Vivian Stern's *A Sin Against the Future: Imprisonment in the World*.[84] The concepts and terms used in these texts seemed to travel remarkably well, given the great variety in prison conditions, populations, ideologies, and policies worldwide. For example, the SMR has been widely used in assessing prison conditions and regimes in many countries and has had some influence on standard setting within some state prison systems.[85] The underlying philosophy (essentially based on rehabilitation) is no longer widely accepted, the application of these standards by foreigners is often resented, and few prison systems meet these minimum standards in fact; but there appear to be relatively few *conceptual* difficulties about applying these standards worldwide. One interesting feature is that the Standard Minimum Rules are expressed in non-technical English, which appears to travel better than the more technical terminology of prison laws.

In her powerful survey and polemic about imprisonment as a global phenomenon, Vivien Stern makes a number of sweeping factual generalisations

---

[83] Calvino (1974) at pp. 88–9.
[84] Stern (1998). For a longer account of this case study see Twining (2005b) at pp. 20–5.
[85] For example, it is used in several Human Rights Watch reports on prison conditions in over twenty countries. See Stern (1998).

about the state of prisons and shared problems in the world today. As descriptions of conditions these seem at least to represent testable descriptive (but not explanatory) hypotheses.[86]

The normative generalisations of SMR and Stern's empirical ones refer mainly to prison conditions and prison regimes. They apply less clearly to prison ideology and policies. The main reason for this seeming homogeneity is probably that 'the modern prison' developed as one of the first institutions of the modern bureaucratic state to be the subject of significant transnational networks of bureaucratising professionals. Prison ideology, rationales, and policies are more closely entwined with local politics, history and culture. They may be harder to compare or to subject to generalisation.

(b) Lawyers and law students

Concepts associated with legal education, legal professions, and lawyers on the whole do not travel well, even within the same 'legal family' or between contexts in a single jurisdiction.[87] For example, who counts as a 'law student' is problematic within the single jurisdiction of England. No definition seems to provide a sensible basis for comparison between the mass university systems in Italy, the multi-stage processes of professional formation, such as that in England and professional law school programmes in the United States. If 'law student' is defined as someone registered for a 'first degree in law', there are serious doubts whether this is a sensible unit of comparison.[88] If the definition is extended to include anyone involved in a professional training programme or in the process ending in initial certification, the problems of comparability are more complex. The difficulties increase if the concept of 'law student' is extended to include apprentices, postgraduates, specialist trainees, and students taking courses that include a legal element (e.g as part of police or accountancy training). Any comparative statistics about numbers of 'law students' under any of these definitions are almost meaningless, generally misleading, and often false. That is only the start of the difficulties.

---

[86] See Appendix II (on the web)

[87] For preliminary discussions of the semantic difficulties, see Twining (1996), (1998) (2001). For earlier attempts to construct analytical frameworks for considering issues of legal education policy transnationally see Twining (1997b) Chapters 13 (Access) and 15 (Law schools). On the Bologna Process directed to harmonising higher education in Europe see Terry (2007) and Lombay (2001) and (2004).

[88] I once identified approximately sixteen different usages of 'law student' in England alone. However, the problems of comparison relate not so much to the ambiguity of such terms, as that the institutional structures and traditions vary so much between countries. Do an English barrister, a French notaire, an American corporate lawyer, and a Muslim jurist belong to comparable 'professions'?

Similar considerations apply to 'legal education' and to terms like 'lawyer', 'legal profession', 'legal services' and 'legal work',[89] and to a lesser extent to 'judge', 'court', and 'trial'.[90]

The most notorious example of the elementary pitfalls surrounding terms like 'lawyer' is the senseless debate stimulated by Vice-President Dan Quayle when, in a speech to the American Bar Association, he asked rhetorically: 'Does America really need 70% of the world's lawyers?'[91] The speech was widely reported, repeated, and discussed thereafter. The term 'lawyer' was not defined and there was no basis in fact for this figure in respect of any of its possible meanings. In the ensuing debates Quayle's dictum was linked to the alleged 'litigation explosion' in the United States, regulation of admission to the legal profession, and the economic role of lawyers.[92] Several of the commentators agreed that the debate was 'debased', that the international data were weak, and that cultural and other differences made it virtually impossible to correlate lawyer populations with economic indicators transnationally.[93] For instance, Epp criticised Magee for purporting to compare figures about West German private practitioners with American figures that included government lawyers, corporate lawyers, judges and law teachers (all vague categories themselves).[94] Epp also mentioned similar silly mistakes in other contexts. Such mistakes are regularly repeated in reported statistics, law school league tables, and the like.[95]

'Law student', 'legal education', 'lawyer' and 'legal profession' may not be philosophically interesting, but these conceptual difficulties have been a serious obstacle to the development of comparative studies in this general area.

(c) Tamanaha's 'core concept' of law

An extraordinary proportion of the energy of analytical jurists has been taken up with trying to elucidate the concept of law. From a global perspective conceptions of law constructed around the modern nation state do not travel

---

[89] The comparative study of legal professions is one of the most developed fields of transnational legal sociology. The extent to which it is still hampered by basic conceptual problems is clearly illustrated in the pioneering studies of Abel and Lewis (1988–89) and more recently Barcello and Cramton (1999). However, I am persuaded that leading scholars in the field, such as Philip Lewis, Terry Halliday, and John Flood, have developed sophisticated conceptual tools for surmounting or by-passing some of the more elementary problems of comparison and generalisation. Moreover, legal practice is rapidly changing, not least in respect of corporate practice and 'global' law firms, whose partners may indeed travel well. See Chapter 8.7(a) below. Efforts of European integrationists to 'harmonise' legal education and increase professional mobility are creating new problems, as they purport to 'solve' them.

[90] See Chapter 1 at pp. 21–2.   [91] Quayle, (1991).

[92] For an excellent critique of this 'debased debate', see Galanter (1998) at pp. 743–7. See further Galanter (1992). Quayle's attack was taken up by economists (e.g. Symposium on 'Do Lawyers Impair Economic Growth?') (Symposium 1992).

[93] See, e.g. Cross, in Symposium (1992) at p. 654.   [94] Epp in Symposium (1992) at p. 597.

[95] See GLT, pp. 152–65. For an equally dubious use of comparative statistics about judges and lawyers see Posner (1996) pp. 21–2. I am grateful to Andrew Halpin for this reference.

well. Only recently have jurists tried systematically to construct general conceptions of law that encompass both modern state law and legal phenomena based on other legal traditions. The most important work to date is *A General Jurisprudence of Law and Society* (2001) by Brian Tamanaha. He sets out to construct a broad 'core concept of law' that fits both state law and important manifestations of 'non-state law', including international, transnational, religious, customary, and even natural law, while avoiding what he sees as the legal pluralist trap of being over-inclusive by failing to provide any criteria for differentiating law from other social institutions, such as schools, hospitals, and sports' leagues.[96] He accepts the main premises of Hart's legal positivism (the separation thesis and the social sources thesis), but in a brilliantly sustained piece of analysis he strips away all 'essentialist' and 'conventionalist' criteria of identification associated with models of law, such as Hart's, that treat state law as the paradigm case of law. For example, Hart's rule of recognition, acceptance by officials, the union of primary and secondary rules, efficacy, all functionalist assumptions, and even normativity, institution, system, and society are rejected as necessary features of a core concept of law. Tamanaha is left with the proposition that law is whatever those subject to it attach the label 'law' to.

We shall consider Tamanaha's approach and his methodology in detail in Chapter 4. Here the important point is that Tamanaha accepts that all the concepts that he rejects as candidates for *necessary* criteria of identification – such as union of primary and secondary rules, institutionalised law enforcement – are an *important* and *useful* part of the apparatus needed for describing, interpreting, and explaining legal phenomena. During the course of two books,[97] he illuminates a number of important concepts, including social order, custom, ideology and coercion, but because the focus is on the necessary criteria for identification of one concept, law, he does not deal with them systematically as a group.[98]

Legal rights and legal personality were two sets of 'fundamental legal conceptions' that I studied as part of the analytical jurisprudence as an undergraduate. In both instances, these were treated as 'doctrinal concepts' that were part of English law. They are still centrally important 'folk' concepts, but the question arises whether they can also serve as 'analytic' concepts that can apply to any, or at least a significant number of, legal orders belonging to different

---

[96] On the problem of 'the definitional stop' see Chapter 12.2(c) below.

[97] Tamanaha (1997) (2001).

[98] In a longer critique of this bold and illuminating effort, I have argued that Tamanaha's 'labeling test' does not work either as a 'core concept' (whatever that means) nor as an organising concept for a number of reasons, including that it involves using 'folk' (emic) concepts for cross-cultural 'analytic' (etic) purposes (Twining, 2003a). I concluded that 'I, for one, would have welcomed a more extensive analysis of many other concepts, including function, group, dispute, norms, normative orders, system, institutionalisation, and legal subjects. Analytical jurisprudence needs to move beyond focusing on individual concepts to concentrate on groups of concepts, conceptual frames, and specific discourses.' (Twining (2005e at p. 254). This book tries to fill some of these gaps.

legal cultures and traditions? In short, how well do they travel? Section (d) examines rights and related concepts in some detail; later we shall examine the concept of legal persons (or subjects).[99] I conclude that both can be interpreted in ways that make them highly transferable as analytic concepts, but that Bentham and Austin were right in suggesting that the number of such concepts is quite limited.[100]

(d) Hohfeld's fundamental legal conceptions

The most significant figure in American analytical jurisprudence, Wesley Newcomb Hohfeld, drew almost entirely on Anglo-American sources, focused on 'fundamental legal conceptions as applied in judicial reasoning' in the Anglo-American tradition, and explicitly addressed an American audience.[101] In short, his sources, audience and focus were quite particular, even parochial, but his contribution had a potentially broad significance.[102] I shall argue that his analysis of rights is broadly applicable to legal discourse in other cultures, at other times, and to at least some other contexts.[103] Hohfeld died young. In the United States his work was taken up by early Yale Realists, notably Corbin, Cook, and Llewellyn, first to criticise the over-use of abstract concepts in law talk (the narrower categories theme)[104] and later, usually quite quietly, to use it as a foundation for exposition in such projects as the Restatement on Contracts, the Revised Uniform Sales Act, and the Uniform Commercial Code.

Hohfeld's analytical scheme has been the subject of widespread misunder-standing, different interpretations, criticism, refinements and extensions. Questions have been raised about his choice of terms, about particular aspects of the scheme, the relationship between the two boxes (claim-right – power), its completeness, its limitations and its utility.[105] For present purposes, I shall assume that the basic scheme is valid, that it can be interpreted in a way that meets all the basic criticisms, and that it is useful in showing up confusions and ambiguities in many kinds of law talk, including judicial reasoning, legislative arguments, legislative rules, and expositions of doctrine. The question here is: how well does the basic scheme travel?

---

[99] See Chapter 15.2 below.   [100] See *GLT*, Chapter 2, especially pp. 22–5.   [101] Hohfeld (1913).

[102] On particularity and 'parochialism' in respect of audience, sources, focus and significance see *GLT*, Chapter 5.

[103] I shall not deal here with matters that might limit the applicability of Hohfeld's scheme, for example, whether it presupposes binary rules or whether it involves an ideological bias towards individualism.

[104] See Llewellyn's 'common points of departure of Legal Realism', No 7: 'The belief in the worthwhileness of grouping cases and legal situations together into narrower categories than has been the practice in the past. This is connected with the distrust of verbally simple rules – which so often cover dissimilar and non-simple fact-situations....' (Llewellyn (1962) pp. 27–8, 56–9, 413 discussed in *KLRM*, at pp. 137–8, 330–3).

[105] Halpin (1997).

The scheme decomposes all legal relations into their basic components, like atoms as they were conceived in Hohfeld's day.[106] It is commonly depicted in the form of two squares: A robust interpretation of the scheme can be summarised as follows:[107]

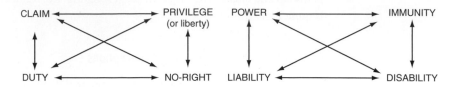

(1) The word 'right' is ambiguous. In legal usage it has four primary meanings: claim (another ought or must); privilege (I may); power (I can [alter the position of another]); immunity (another cannot).

(2) These four concepts denote relations between legal persons.[108] A statement of the kind 'A has a claim-right *vis à vis* B in respect of Z' denotes the relation between *two* persons (A and B) in respect of *one* subject (Z – activity, typically an act or omission) and *one* legal rule. Failure to recognise this is one of the most common sources of misunderstanding of the scheme.

(3) Each of the four terms has a correlative and an opposite, as follows:
- claim-right is the correlative of duty and the opposite of no-claim;
- privilege is the correlative of no-claim and the opposite of duty (i.e. no-duty [not]);
- power is the correlative of liability and the opposite of disability;
- immunity is the correlative of disability and the opposite of liability.[109]

(4) Because each of the terms in each box can be defined in relation to each other, only two of the terms are strictly necessary within the scheme:
A's claim *vis à vis* B = B's duty to A; and[110]
A's privilege *vis à vis* B = B's no-claim against A = A's no-duty (not) to B.
Thus in the first box, the three other terms can be expressed by duty or its absence. Similarly in the second box the four terms can be expressed by power/no-power. The extra terms are convenient to avoid circumlocution.

---

[106] Hohfeld had studied chemistry and Cook, his promoter, physics before moving into law. They both were given to using analogies from the physical sciences.

[107] This interpretation is quite close in respect of basics to the excellent article by John Finnis (1972).

[108] On relations between persons (subjects), see Chapter 15.2 on the web.

[109] As subsequent commentators have emphasised, Hohfeld's specific choice of terms is unimportant as the meaning of each term is stipulated in this context. For example, I have substituted 'claim' and 'no-claim' for Hohfeld's 'right' and 'no-right'.

[110] On whether some duties do not have correlative claim rights ('absolute duties') and whether there can be claim-rights without assigned correlative duties, see pp. 213–14 below.

I shall follow convention in treating duty and power as the main concepts, but this is for reasons external to Hohfeld's scheme.[111]

(5) The noun-form terms can be replaced by verbs without any change of meaning, for example:

- A has a claim-right against B=B ought
- A has a duty=A ought
- A has a privilege=A may (not ought)
- A has a power=A can
- A has a disability=A cannot
- A has an immunity=B (others) cannot

The substitution of verbs for nouns has the advantage of removing the danger of reifying noun-forms (hypostatisation)[112] and provides a useful link to the Bentham-Hart techniques of elucidation, for it is difficult to elucidate words like 'may' and 'ought' outside standard sentences of the kind 'I may', 'I can'.[113]

(6) 'The relevance of 'legal remedies' to the defining of terms in his scheme is left undetermined by Hohfeld.'[114]

(7) A natural language may or may not have a word or words with more or less equivalent meanings to Hohfeld's terms. Or it may have several approximate synonyms for one term. For example, Hohfeld's 'privilege' can be rendered by 'liberty' or 'licence', provided that it is defined in the same way. The English language distinguishes between 'ought', 'must', 'should', and 'shall'. When used to express norms these words usually suggest different degrees of emphasis or strength, but in Hohfeld's scheme they are all rendered by 'duty'. They are different kinds of 'ought'. Conversely, Hohfeld invented the term 'no-right' (= 'no-claim') and used 'power', 'disability', and 'immunity' differently from ordinary usage.[115] Thus, if one identifies a culture that has no words for expressing any of Hohfeld's terms, this does not mean that Hohfeld's scheme cannot be applied to that culture, any more than the fact that the Tiv may not have had terms or

---

[111] For example, if one accepts a distinction between absolute (e.g. a duty not to be cruel to animals) and relative duties, then some duties have no correlative claim-rights, but – in Hohfeld's interpretation – all claim rights are relative.

[112] A question phrased in the form 'What is ..... ?' invites an answer with a noun as the subject (e.g. a right is, law is etc). This sometimes leads people to hypostatise (thingify) (i.e. to assume that all nouns stand for entities or things). Clearly abstract words, such as justice and rights, do not stand for physical entities, but the idea of non-physical entities is an obfuscation. The fault lies in conflating grammatical form (here a noun) with meaning. A simple way out is to change the grammatical form without changing the meaning, for example: (X has a duty=X ought).

[113] Hart (1953). Words like 'require', 'permit', 'authorise' can be used to express the Hohfeldian scheme.

[114] Finnis (1972) at pp. 380–1.

[115] I do not discuss here some of the difficulties related to the second box over and above the choice of terms, nor criticisms of Hohfeld's use of 'opposites'. For a critical re-examination of Hohfeld's scheme, see Halpin (1997). In a recent article Halpin has argued that Hohfeld's 'square of opposition' should be replaced by 'a triangle of possibilities' (Halpin 2003).

concepts equivalent to latent function or phoneme or bilharzia does not mean that such analytical concepts cannot be applied to them. However, if there is a difficulty in rendering 'ought', 'may' or 'can' in a local language, this should set some lights flashing, suggesting that how the culture copes without them may be significant.[116]

On this interpretation, Hohfeld's scheme is best interpreted as an analytic scheme designed for scholarly use. It is a set of tools for decomposing 'law talk' into its basic elements. Some confusion has arisen as to whether or not it would be a good idea to use the scheme as part of the 'folk' concepts of English and American law (i.e. as concepts for expressing the content of legal rules). This point was discussed in relation to some of the early Restatements and the Uniform Commercial Code. The prevailing view was that Hohfeldian analysis should be used *sub silentio*; the draftsmen should check that their texts were consistent with the basic conceptual scheme, but the more awkward or less familiar terms should be avoided. Karl Llewellyn was also keen wherever possible to use verb forms rather than abstract nouns in drafting the Uniform Commercial Code.[117]

Assuming that this interpretation is broadly correct and that the scheme, so interpreted, is valid, how well does it travel? There is some evidence to support the thesis that it travels rather well across fields of law, geographical space, time, and even some other disciplines. For example, Hohfeld's own analysis showed quite convincingly that it transcended different fields of substantive Anglo-American law. Others have extended this to other common law countries,[118] to civil law systems,[119] to the European Union,[120] and to English legal history.[121] Hohfeld himself was cautious about its extension to non-legal contexts, but others have applied it to moral and political discourse. John Finnis has claimed that 'clear-headed familiarity with Hohfeld's scheme

---

[116] One example might be attempts by Western scholars to rationally reconstruct or 'restate' the norms of a group that is inarticulate or reticent about its rules or seems not to think in such terms (e.g. Hoebel's attempt to reconstruct the basic postulates of Cheyenne culture (Hoebel (1954) at pp. 142–3)) or the controversy surrounding the Restatement of African Law project (A. Allott (2000), Twining (1963); (1964) at pp. 32–53). A reluctance to articulate general rules does not preclude the use of 'ought', 'may' and 'can' in respect of particular situations.

[117] For example, Corbin reports that when Williston was made Reporter on Contracts for the American Law Institute he told Corbin that he accepted Hohfeld's analysis, but not his terminology, and he asked Williston and Oliphant to check that the drafts were consistent with Hohfeld's concepts. (Corbin to the author 1965 quoted in *KLRM*, p. 397) Corbin reported that Bigelow adopted Hohfeld's analysis in his preliminary work on the Restatement of the Law of Property. On the UCC see *KLRM* pp. 97–8, 137, 416. Compare the European Communities Act 1972, s. 2(1), which begins: 'All such rights, powers, liabilities, obligations and restrictions from time to time created or arising by or under the treaties, and all such remedies and procedures from time to time provided for by or under the Treaties are without further enactment to be given legal effect…'.

[118] For example, it is a favourite of older Indian and Australian textbooks on Jurisprudence (e.g. G. Paton (1951), M.M. Nair (1986)).

[119] Belvedere (1997); Van Hoecke (2002).   [120] Hilson and Downes, (1999).

[121] Paton (1951); Hallis (1930).

can bring with it awareness of the questions regularly begged when "claims of right" are raised in law, politics and moral debate.'[122] More controversially, Hoebel used it in his *The Law of Primitive Man*.[123] Some anthropologists have reported that they found it helpful, but it would require further investigation to test out its applicability to 'radically different cultures'.[124]

One way into probing its general applicability is to ask does it fit all normative systems? To put this in simple terms: can all normative systems be reconstructed in the language of 'ought', 'may', and 'can'? On my interpretation of Hohfeld, I believe that the answer could be in the affirmative; at least it has a very wide application. This is a complex issue, which depends in part on how the term 'normative system' is used, for the question may be tautologous. I shall not pursue it at length here, but it may be useful to give a simple example. You and I are playing chess. Towards the end of the game, you only have your king left. I see that if I move my knight to QB4 in accordance with the rules you will be in check. I *may* move my knight, I *can* by doing so put you in check (i.e. change your situation). As a result of this move you *must* move the king. I *may not* move my pawn backwards. I *cannot* mate you in one. And so on. My students sometimes object that it is odd to talk of a duty to move your king and of my claim-right that you move it. I reply that one does regularly use 'must', 'may', and 'can' in relation to chess moves and more important, one can reconstruct chess moves into this language. To be sure, it is an extension of ordinary usage to use 'duty' here, but analytically it is correct. Law, morals, politics and chess may have different kinds of 'oughts', but if 'I ought'='I have a duty' then a chess 'ought'=a chess 'duty'.[125] Thus relations under several normative systems can be decomposed into basic Hohfeldian units.

This argument is not dispositive. For we might identify a normative system that does not fit Hohfeld's scheme.[126] A different counter-example would be a culture or social system whose ways of social ordering do not depend on a normative system. This is ethnographically interesting in relation to debates about the extent to which 'customary law' can be appropriately articulated in terms of substantive rules without some distortion.[127]

A common objection to Hohfeld's scheme is that it is 'reductionist': he reduces all legal (perhaps all normative) relations to eight (or even two – see above) basic concepts. This is true, but some would take that as a compliment. It would be a criticism, if it can be shown that some legal relations are not reducible in this way. If the point is that Hohfeld's account of 'rights' is not comprehensive, this is correct and suggests a limitation. His analysis is only the

---

[122] Finnis (1972) at p. 377.   [123] Hoebel (1954).

[124] The phrase is borrowed from J. Barton *et al.* (1983).

[125] This formulation is intended to be neutral about the relationships between law, morals and politics.

[126] A borderline case would be a system of prudential rules of thumb (*HTDTWR*, pp. 14–15, 124–5, 136–8; Schauer (1991) at pp. 104–11).

[127] See above n. 116.

beginning of wisdom on rights. As Hart and others have shown, quite apart from any faults in the scheme itself, Hohfeld did not address such questions as: is there a common thread running through the four different meanings of 'right'? Are there significantly different kinds of duty, power, liability and so on? What is the relation between rights and other related concepts such as interests, benefits, entitlements, and needs?[128]

These are complex issues that require sustained investigation, interpretation, and analysis – just the kind of issues that should be addressed by general analytical jurisprudence. For my immediate purpose, it is sufficient to make a weaker claim that, if one accepts one or other version of it as valid, the Hohfeldian scheme is a powerful analytical tool that travels some distance across space, time, cultures, and disciplines.

2.4 Continuities between conceptual analysis and empirical enquiries

(a) 'The naturalist turn'

Since *The Concept of Law* was first published 'ordinary language philosophy' has been out of favour, although some of its methods have been assimilated. There have been significant developments in epistemology, logic, the philosophy of language and other areas of philosophy that bear on analytical jurisprudence. A particularly significant development has been 'the naturalist turn' in philosophy,[129] stimulated by Willard van Orman Quine, variously interpreted in philosophy, with one version diffused within jurisprudence by Brian Leiter. In some early papers, Quine attacked the distinction between analytic and synthetic statements that were the basis for the logical positivists' distinction between truth in virtue of meaning (*a priori*) and empirical (*a posteriori*) truth. Leiter explains Quine's thesis as follows:

> Without a domain of analytic truths – truths that are *a priori* and hold in virtue of meaning – it becomes unclear what special domain of expertise for philosophical reflection remains. If all claims are, in principle, revisable in light of empirical evidence, then should not all questions fall to empirical science? Philosophy

---

[128] Sen (1981); Hart (1982); (1983); Martin (1993). The reductionist argument is reminiscent of the exchange in Calvino's *Invisible Cities* between Kublai Khan (a prototypical reductionist) and Marco Polo (a post-modernist (?), opposed to closure). The Great Khan sees a game of chess, like his conquests, being reduced to nothingness: '...black square or a white one. By disembodying his conquests to reduce them to the essential, Kublai had arrived at the extreme operation...it was reduced to a square of planed wood. Polo on the other hand sees the same square as the start for an endless inquiry starting with the history of the tree from which it was cut.' (Calvino (1974) at p. 131).

[129] The starting-point of 'the Naturalistic Turn' was Quine's essay 'Two Dogmas of Empiricism' (1951). His position was later developed in essays collected in Quine (1953) and (1969). Goldman (1986), Haack (1993), Jackson (1998) and Leiter (2007) represent a wide spectrum of views in the ongoing debate within philosophy. On the so-called 'methodology debate' in jurisprudence, see Leiter (2007) at pp. 175–81.

would be out of business, except perhaps as the abstract, reflective branch of empirical science. And if analytic statements are gone, then too is conceptual analysis: since any claim of conceptual analysis is vulnerable to the demand of *a posteriori* (i.e. empirical) theory construction, philosophy must proceed in tandem with empirical science, not as an arbiter of its claims, but as a reflective attempt at synoptic clarity about the state of empirical knowledge.[130]

Quine's thesis has been differently interpreted by both supporters and critics.[131] As a result there have developed several species and sub-species of naturalism that are too complex to unravel here.[132] In the present context it is, however, helpful to distinguish between reformist and revolutionary naturalism. The latter holds that 'the traditional problems of epistemology are illegitimate or misconceived, and should be abandoned, to be *replaced* by natural-scientific questions of cognition'.[133] Reformists adopt various less radical positions on the question whether the traditional questions of epistemology can be resolved by the natural sciences of cognition or, more moderately, that the findings of such sciences are relevant to some or to all of the traditional problems.

Few philosophers have accepted the revolutionary or replacement version of naturalism.[134] The revolutionary (replacement) version of naturalism might spell the end of analytical jurisprudence interpreted as being primarily concerned with elucidation of concepts. The other, in my view, more plausible, versions concur in rejecting *a priori* conceptual analysis and in maintaining that findings in the natural sciences are at least relevant to conceptual concerns. For example, there are points at which cognitive psychology can help conceptual elucidation. The message for analytical jurisprudence is reasonably clear: *a priori*, intuitive analysis of concepts divorced from empirical knowledge of actual legal institutions, processes, rules etc. will not add much to our

---

[130] Leiter (2007) at p. 176. As Haack makes clear, there are some epistemological and conceptual questions that cannot be resolved by empirical science, for example, the problem of induction and the epistemic status of science. Within jurisprudence it is difficult to conceive how concepts like authority, rights, and responsibility could be settled by empirical scientific methods.

[131] Susan Haack (1993) has argued that Quine's own position is fundamentally ambiguous.

[132] Haack and Leiter both agree that there is important work for conceptual analysis and that philosophy cannot be exclusively an *a priori* discipline, but differ in their interpretations of Quine and which modest versions of naturalism to support (e.g. Haack (1993) Chapter 6, especially pp. 130–5, 152–7; Leiter (2007) at p. 34, n. 90). Brian Leiter uses his version of 'naturalism' to reinterpret American Legal Realism. We agree that Realism was caricatured by Hart and others, that most Realist views are compatible with positivism, and that there should be a close connection between conceptual analysis and empirical enquiry, with which we are both sympathetic. But Leiter's account is historically skewed in that he treats American Legal Realism as a theory about adjudication and reasoning about disputed questions of law, omitting entirely, for example, Frank's concern with questions of fact, the empirical studies of Moore at Yale and Oliphant and others at Johns Hopkins, Llewellyn's 'law jobs' theory, and other extra-judicial studies of law-related behaviour – in short, some of the most original and interesting products of the Realist Movement. It is odd to call an almost exclusive focus on judicial reasoning in hard (typically appellate) cases realistic. See further Chapter 16.3 below.

[133] Haack (1993) at p. 119.   [134] Leiter (2007) at p. 137, n. 2.

understanding of law. However, in this view, conceptual elucidation is still a necessary part of empirical and normative enquiries about law, but such analysis needs to be sensitive to advances in our empirical knowledge of the real world. Naturalism may have deflated the immodest role of conceptual analysis in philosophy without requiring that it should be abandoned. It still leaves a modest, but important, role for conceptual analysis in jurisprudence and supports the idea of continuity between analytical, normative, and socio-legal studies. In the next section I shall argue that analytical jurisprudence and empirical legal studies need to be more closely linked, but this is consistent with several different versions of moderate naturalism.

(b) Analytical jurisprudence and empirical legal studies: 'the olive branch thesis'

In the Preface to *The Concept of Law* Hart made the following statement: 'Notwithstanding its concern with analysis the book may also be regarded as an essay in descriptive sociology; for the suggestion that inquiries into the meanings of words merely throw light on words is false.'[135]

The phrase 'an essay in descriptive sociology' attracted an enormous amount of, largely adverse, comment. Two lines of criticism were based on a misunderstanding of Hart's claim. First, presumably, 'description' in this context was meant to be contrasted with evaluation and justification.[136] However, 'description' was sometimes taken to exclude interpretation and explanation, thereby downgrading sociology as a merely descriptive enterprise.[137] A second misunderstanding arose from the suggestion that Hart was claiming to describe actual phenomena. Some claim that he was describing the form and structure of legal systems, but this distracts attention from the significance of Hart's contribution: he was not claiming to *do* empirical description, but rather to provide *tools* for this purpose. Description, interpretation, and explanation all presuppose adequate concepts.

The central thesis of this book is that as the discipline of law becomes more cosmopolitan, jurisprudence as its theoretical part needs to broaden its reach to take more account of non-Western legal traditions, a wider range of legal phenomena, and different levels of normative and legal relations and ordering. It also needs a more empirical orientation at the core of legal scholarship. For many years I have argued that Herbert Hart and his followers revolutionised the

---

[135] Hart (1961) Preface.

[136] Of course, there has been controversy around the question of whether sociological description can ever be value free, on which see Tamanaha (2001) pp. xvi–xvii and 234–5; see Dixon (2001), MacCormick (2007) Chapter 16, with which I am in general agreement.

[137] Hart, however, who was largely responsible for pioneering 'the hermeneutic turn' in legal theory, could hardly be charged with indifference to or naivety about interpretation; in other contexts he clearly included explanation within the sociological and historical enterprise (see e.g. the discussion of explanatory enquiries in Hart and Honoré (1985)).

methods of analytical jurisprudence, but they tended to accept uncritically the agenda of questions they inherited, which in turn was based on a narrow conception of law that centred on legal doctrine and its presuppositions.[138] Although they treated law as a social phenomenon their work proceeded 'in almost complete isolation from contemporary social theory and from work in socio-legal studies, with little overt concern for the law in action'.[139] As an example of this, Hart himself continued to focus almost entirely on concepts of legal doctrine or its presuppositions ('law talk') but paid almost no attention to concepts of 'talk about law', such as dispute, group, function, institution, order, system and so on, which were as susceptible to and in need of the same kind of conceptual elucidation.[140]

I have sometimes suggested that the famous claim that *The Concept of Law* was an essay in descriptive sociology can be interpreted as an olive branch offered by Hart to socio-legal studies.[141] Nicola Lacey and David Sugarman have since persuaded me that this interpretation is historically incorrect in that for most of his career Hart shared the Oxford prejudice against sociology.[142] The argument is nevertheless analytically correct, for conceptual elucidation is as important for social scientific investigation as it is for legal exposition and the methods of conceptual analysis developed by analytical philosophy are applicable to important concepts in empirical legal studies and the social sciences generally. If this interpretation had been accepted, a quite unnecessary chasm between analytical jurisprudence and empirical legal studies might have been bridged. Hart and his followers might have directed their attention in a more sustained way to socio-legal concepts that were not normally considered the concern of analytical jurisprudence, and socio-legal scholars might have been more receptive to the methods and teachings of analytical philosophy.

Recently Nicola Lacey has advanced a more fundamental explanation of the narrow focus of most contemporary analytical legal philosophy.[143] Hart's conception of his enterprise came from working 'within a philosophical community … that conceived its own boundaries narrowly'.[144] Hart treated philosophical questions as quite distinct from historical and sociological ones and rejected any idea of continuity between them. He was relatively unmoved by

---

[138] Twining (1979) (reprinted in *GJB*, Chapter 4).

[139] *Ibid.*, 561 (*GJB*, p. 73). 'Empirical legal studies' is here used in a broad sense to include sociology of law and other aspects of the interface between law and the social sciences at both theoretical and more applied levels. See Chapter 8.2 below.

[140] *Ibid.*, at pp. 578–9 (*GJB*, 90–1). Several of these concepts are discussed below in Chapter 4 and Chapter 15.

[141] Twining (1997b) at pp. 168–9; (2005b) n. 27.

[142] Lacey (2004) at pp. 230–1, 260–1, 322; Sugarman (interview) (2005). In circles in which sociology is held in low esteem this conflation of sociology and the social sciences can be used as a not too subtle kind of put down. (See Lacey (2004) at pp. 149–50, 185, 260–1; See also Nagel (2005)).

[143] Lacey (2006). This is a development of arguments introduced in Lacey (1998) and her biography of Hart (2004).

[144] Lacey (2006) at p. 953.

historical and sociological criticisms of *The Concept of Law* because he thought that these raised different questions from those that he had set out to answer. As a result 'the social fact' dimensions of *The Concept of Law* were imperfectly realised. Joseph Raz and others followed Hart in trying to maintain a sharp distinction between philosophical and empirical questions.[145] As a result they failed to resolve the tension between emphasising that law is a social phenomenon and refusing to consider it empirically.[146]

Lacey suggests that the dilemma of trying to theorise law as genuinely normative yet grounded in social fact is even more acute in the context of particular (or special) jurisprudence. In a perceptive discussion of *Causation in the Law*, Lacey acknowledges that this thorough application of linguistic analysis to hundreds of cases greatly clarified the legal concept of causation and grounded a convincing critique of 'causal minimalism' of American jurists such as Wechsler.[147] Hart and Honoré gave a very rich account of the discourse of causation in the law, but they gave 'no systematic analysis of the institutional, practical, professional context in which the legal language was used'.[148] As a result the authors gave a very thin account of the very different social roles of contract, crime, and torts; law is analysed as a body of doctrine rather than as a social practice; and as a result 'law is implicitly (mis)represented as founded – actually or ideally – on a metaphysics: a moral or conceptual structure whose validity transcends space and time'.[149] Lacey further illustrates her thesis with reference to Hart's theory of responsibility and the social and institutional basis of corporate criminal responsibility.[150]

Two points about Lacey's argument deserve emphasis. First, her thesis is about 'a general commitment to theorising law as a *social* phenomenon'. This is separate from a more general argument about the need to theorise law sociologically.[151] Second, her thesis is not merely that linguistic analysis of legal

---

[145] Lacey attributes this to Raz's distinction between 'momentary' and 'non-momentary legal systems' (Raz (1970) at Ch VIII). The identity of the latter is determined primarily by their content, of the former by the criteria of identification of valid legal standards. 'Raz may be taken to imply that the social-theoretic analysis of law can be neatly bracketed off from the analytic.' (Lacey 2006 at p. 981).

[146] '[T]he richer the characterization of law's social basis – its institutional forms, its various types of rules, its role and its functions – the less plausible is any theoretical claim to universality. Hart wanted to maintain the claim to universality as well as descriptiveness. In doing so, he ended up with the worst of both worlds. On the one hand, he produced a theory whose commitment to a social fact dimension meant that it did indeed reflect certain features of institutionalization – a fact that already compromised its universality. His theory, after all, fits most comfortably with a centralized state legal order. On the other hand, in the grip of the ambition for universality, he failed to deliver any rich paradigm of law's institutional form.' (Lacey, 2006 at pp. 957–8).

[147] 'Causal minimalism claims that there is no *sui generis* concept of causation deployed in law beyond the "factual" idea of causation as a *sine qua non*...Beyond this...decisions about how to attribute causal liability are based on policy considerations such as efficiency or moral considerations such as fault'. (Lacey, 2004 at p. 212).

[148] *Ibid.*, p. 217.   [149] Lacey (2006) at p. 45; See Lacey (1998a).   [150] Lacey (1998a).

[151] *Ibid.*, p. 44, n. 80. See Cotterrell (1998).

discourse divorced from its institutional and social context is incomplete; rather that it is misleading. If *Causation in the Law* had included a richer account of the context in which legal language is used it would have been a quite different book:

> We could expect it to have explored questions such as the institutional factors which restrict the extent to which judges will appeal to pragmatic or policy arguments – their sensitivity to the need to legitimate their decisions, their (system-specific) understanding of their constitutional role and so on. As an empirical matter, these institutional factors shape not only the appeal to policy in causation cases but also the development of causal concepts themselves.[152]

Lacey's critique of attempts to draw a sharp line between philosophical and social perspectives on law elicited a sharp response from a philosopher, Thomas Nagel:

> Lacey seems to have a weak grasp of what philosophy is. Hart's work consists not merely in analysis of doctrinal language, but in the philosophical elucidation of institutions, practices, concepts, and forms of reasoning and justification that are the most basic and general elements of law and politics. He is acutely aware of the importance of institutions and power relations, but the questions he addresses cannot be answered by social and historical study... [F]or all philosophers, the understanding they seek has to be pursued primarily by reasoning rather than empirical observation, because it is concerned with concepts and methods that enable us to describe and think about what we can observe. These are not mutually exclusive approaches or forms of understanding: they address different questions, and they operate at different levels of abstraction and generality.[153]

Thomas Nagel takes Lacey to task for associating Hart's neglect of institutional and practical context with differences between J. L. Austin and Wittgenstein.[154] But he completely misses the point of her criticism, which is that legal concepts and legal doctrine can only be understood in the institutional and practical context of their use and that an account of causation or corporate responsibility in English law is likely not merely to be incomplete, but misleading if these contextual factors are ignored. For the same reason, abstracted accounts of 'legal reasoning' or 'adjudication' are likely to be over-generalised or inaccurate in other ways, if differences in institutional and procedural contexts are overlooked. The extent to which such contextual factors are similar or uniform both across and within jurisdictions is an empirical one. Philosophers who wish to understand legal phenomena need to equip themselves with local knowledge.

Many of us have argued for many years that law, including legal doctrine and concepts, needs to be understood in context. Recently there have been encouraging signs of a convergence between empirical and analytical approaches. For some time analytical jurisprudence was treated with hostility by many who

---

[152] Lacey (2004) at p. 218.   [153] Nagel (2005).

[154] If Lacey had implied that Wittgenstein would have actually undertaken empirical work this would be misleading, but she denies this (Lacey (2006) at n.39).

favoured contextual or socio-legal perspectives.[155] The disdain was mutual.[156] Recently, however, the mood has changed. Leading empirical legal scholars including Cotterrell, Griffiths, and Roberts have acknowledged that Hart's *The Concept of Law* made a significant contribution to social science.[157] Leiter has reinterpreted Legal Realism in terms of Naturalist philosophy, some versions of which treat conceptual analysis as continuous with empirical inquiry in the social sciences.[158] Lewis Kornhauser has recently elaborated a social scientific concept of governance structures (of which legal systems are a class) that explicitly takes its inspiration from Hart.[159] Especially significant are Brian Tamanaha's use of Hart's positivist premises as the starting point for his socio-legal positivist general jurisprudence[160] and the fact that some analytical jurists have sympathetically reviewed Tamanaha's work.[161]

2.5 Conclusion

A more cosmopolitan discipline of law needs to confront problems of generalisation – conceptual, normative, legal, interpretive, and empirical – across jurisdictions, levels of ordering, legal cultures, and traditions. This is a task for general analytical jurisprudence. This chapter explores one aspect of analytical jurisprudence in this context, viz., analysis of the concepts and presuppositions of legal discourse. It starts from the premise that globalisation raises questions about the adequacy of much of the present conceptual framework of legal discourse for discussing legal phenomena across jurisdictions, traditions and cultures. It is concerned with the usability of concepts and terms in cross-cultural and transnational legal discourses. It raises, but does not claim to resolve, a number of issues about the transferability of groups of concepts: which do or do not 'travel' far or travel well? The focus is broad in that it is concerned with all legal discourse (both law talk and talk about law) in widening geographical contexts. It is narrow in that it deals with clarification of concepts, which is only one aspect of most enquiries. The central point is that the heritage of techniques of analysis in the Anglo-American tradition of analytical jurisprudence is worth building on, but that such techniques need to be applied to a much wider range of issues and concepts than has been done by leading analytical jurists. In short, it is a plea for more middle order, general analytical jurisprudence.

---

[155] Early critics of Hart from a social science perspective included Edgar Bodenheimer (1955–56) and B.E. King (1963). More recent examples of hostility to analytical positivism include Peter Fitzpatrick (1992) and Morton Horwitz (1997).

[156] The patronising attitudes of Oxford philosophers towards lawyers at the time of Hart's election to the Chair of Jurisprudence in Oxford are vividly illustrated in Lacey (2004) at pp. 149–50. Hart it seemed was expected to colonise, educate and upgrade academic law.

[157] E.g. Cotterrell (1998); (Roberts (1998), (2005); Griffiths (2003).   [158] Leiter (2004) and (2007).

[159] Kornhauser (2004).   [160] Tamanaha (1997) (2001) discussed in Chapter 4 below.

[161] E.g. Bix (1995), (2000); Himma (2004).

Section 2.3 above reports on some preliminary case studies of groups of concepts in this regard: Hohfeld's analytical scheme represents one of the highlights of traditional analytical jurisprudence and has a high degree of transferability. The same applies to legal subjects or persons.[162] In an earlier study I concluded that concepts associated with legal education, legal professions, and lawyers on the whole do not travel well, even within the same 'legal family' or between contexts in a single jurisdiction. However, transnational discourse about prisons, especially in relation to conditions and treatment of prisoners, was selected as an example of a body of concepts that seems on examination to travel surprisingly well.

These pilot studies illustrate the artificiality of trying to maintain sharp distinctions between different branches of jurisprudence. Any transnational study of prison conditions or anti-corruption measures or legal education is likely to involve conceptual, normative, interpretive, and empirical dimensions. In the case of prisons the discourses have travelled as part of complex processes of diffusion. Hohfeld provided some powerful analytical tools for studying normative orders, but how well they fit 'radically different cultures' or all normative systems are questions that require further empirical and interpretive investigation.

These enquiries started from concerns about the health of law as an academic discipline as it is rapidly becoming more cosmopolitan. The concerns were initially theoretical, but this does not mean that the argument has no practical implications. In a period of accelerated diffusion of legal ideas, a good deal of academic attention has been paid to abstract, often contested, concepts such as development, human rights, democracy, good governance, and the Rule of Law. Rather less attention has been paid to the conceptual aspects of more specific programmes and measures by which these proclaimed values are meant to be implemented – such as constitution making, judicial reform, anti-corruption measures, penal reform, harmonisation of laws, and measures for promoting free and fair trade. Such activities reach a peak of intensity in situations involving reconstruction (as in Afghanistan and Iraq), structural adjustment, transitional justice, or systematic reform in 'countries in transition'. They are also an almost inevitable part of legal life as the world becomes more legally interdependent.

Whatever one's political views, these are important activities deserving critical scrutiny. A common criticism of transnational reform programmes has been that they are often driven by people who are ignorant of local conditions, traditions and cultures. Assumptions that 'one size fits all' are a common target of the critics. There is a conceptual aspect to these concerns. Where concepts such as court or constitution or corruption or lawyer have deep roots in local history or have acquired strong cultural or ideological baggage,

---

[162] See Chapter 15.2 on the web.

the dangers of ethnocentric projection are obvious. So it is worth asking, how much of our stock of concepts is local and context-specific?

This chapter has been written not so much in the spirit of Jeremy Bentham's universal legislative dictionary as of Clifford Geertz's cautions. Writing of international law, Geertz says: 'Whatever the uses certain features of such law... may or may not sometimes have in ordering relations between states, they are, those features, neither lowest common denominators of the world's catalogue of legal outlooks nor universal premises underlying all of them, but projections of aspects of our own onto the world stage. This as such is no bad thing (better, by my local lights, Jeffersonian notions of rights than Leninist ones), except perhaps as it leads us to imagine there is more commonality of mind in the world than there is or to mistake convergence of vocabularies for convergence of views.'[163]

---

[163] Geertz (1983) at p. 221.

Chapter 3

Mapping law: Families, civilisations, cultures and traditions

3.1 Introduction

> Until you behold it yourself, it is almost impossible to believe that here, inter-posed between the sea and the plains of Bengal, lies an immense archipelago of islands. But that is what it is: an archipelago, stretching for almost three hundred kilometres, from the Hooghly river in West Bengal to the shores of the Meghna in Bangladesh.
>
> The islands are the trailing threads of India's fabric, the ragged fringe of her sari, the *achol* that follows her, half-wetted by the sea. They number in the thousands, these islands; some are immense and some no larger than sandbars; some have lasted through recorded history while others were washed into being just a year or two ago. … The rivers' channels are spread across the land like a fine mesh-net, creating a terrain where boundaries between land and water are always mutating, always unpredictable. Some of these channels are mighty waterways, so wide across that one shore is invisible from the other; others are no more than two or three kilometres long and only a few hundred metres across. Yet each of these channels is a 'river' in its own right, each possessed of its own strangely evocative name. When these channels meet, it is often in clusters of four, five or even six: at these confluences, the water stretches to the far edges of the landscape and the forest dwindles into a distant rumour of land, echoing back from the horizon. In the language of the place, such a confluence is spoken of as a *mohana* – an oddly seductive word, wrapped in many layers of beguilement. (Amitav Ghosh).[1]

> Neither this book nor any other can say how a page *should* be read – if by that we mean that it can give a recipe for discovering what the page really says. All it can do – and that would be much – would be to help us understand some of the difficulties in the way of such discoveries. (I. A. Richards).[2]

In Chapter 2, I argued that one task of analytical jurisprudence is to develop a framework of linked concepts that can be used in studying legal phenomena from a global perspective. This framework can include familiar concepts such as legal relations, legal subjects (persons), social practice, rule (norm), institution, and system; there are some concepts that need further attention from this perspective, including normative order, legal order, legal system, group,

---

[1] Amitav Ghosh, *The Hungry Tide* (2005) at pp. 6–7.
[2] I. A. Richards, *How To Read a Page* (1967) at p. 1.

community, and society; and there are some less familiar ones, such as levels of law, social arena, surface law, interlegality, and invisible or unnoticed legal orders.

The purpose of this chapter is to explore some of the difficulties involved in constructing a reasonably inclusive conception of law from a global perspective as part of a revived general jurisprudence that is responsive to the challenges of globalisation. Such a conception of law may be useful for a number of purposes: First, it may serve as a starting point for constructing an overview or total picture of law in the world as a whole – a picture that delineates some broad patterns without concealing the diversity and complexity of legal phenomena. Second, it may serve as an organising concept for a framework of concepts that may be useful for giving general accounts of legal phenomena and analysing them from a global perspective. The process of constructing an overarching concept will identify a group of related concepts, not all of which will form part of the criteria of the identification of law, but which, taken together, may have heuristic value in investigating, interpreting, analysing, comparing, generalising about, and explaining particular legal orders and legal phenomena with some precision. Third, it can maintain continuity with our heritage of ideas by building on and refining an existing body of theory within the Anglo-American tradition and pointing to connections with other bodies of literature.

Chapters 3 and 4 proceed as follows. After a brief methodological introduction, we shall consider a series of approaches to constructing general accounts of law. First, a survey of some attempts to 'map' law in the world using quite simple geographical perspectives. These will illustrate some of the main difficulties in constructing reasonably comprehensive overviews. Second, a consideration of world history as a perspective in which civilisation, culture, and tradition are key concepts, which may be more helpful than 'legal families' and 'legal systems'. Chapter 4 takes a critical look at the work of three quite different jurists in the Anglo-American tradition who have given general accounts of law: Hart, Tamanaha, and Llewellyn.[3] Fourth, drawing on all of these, but going beyond them, I shall outline an approach to constructing a reasonably comprehensive and flexible conception of law that can serve as an organising concept for the kind of framework of analytic concepts that it is one of the tasks of general analytical jurisprudence to develop.

3.2 Four responses to the question: 'What is law?'

To construct a picture or overview of law in the world requires some conception of the subject of the picture. So one might be tempted to start by asking: 'What is

---

[3] Two important books published in 2007 – MacCormick (2007) and Galligan (2007) are discussed in the footnotes at appropriate places. While both focus mainly on state law, they generally complement rather than contradict the position put forward here. Twining (2009) contains a longer discussion of MacCormick's institutional theory of law.

law?' This question, variously interpreted, has been a central concern of most Western legal theorists. Indeed, so obsessive has been the quest, so extensive the controversies, and so varied have been the responses that it sometimes looks as if some jurists believe that this is the central question of legal theory and that jurisprudence is a one-question subject.

Within jurisprudence it is widely recognised that the question: 'What is law?' is ambiguous and potentially misleading.[4] In the present context it is useful to distinguish between four different types of enquiry in response to that question: the search for the correct or proper or agreed definition of the term 'law'; the construction of general theories about the essential nature of law; the construction of one or more broad concepts that give a broad overview of a field of study without necessarily defining its boundaries; and the development of a coherent framework of general analytic concepts.

Here, we are mainly concerned with the third and fourth types of enquiry. This chapter deals with constructing one or more conceptions of law as organising concepts. However, all four types of enquiry are relevant here. So it may be useful to begin by dealing briefly with the first two.

It is now widely accepted that within jurisprudence it is not sensible to interpret the question posed in the form 'What is law?' as a request for a general definition of the term – that is a semantic question about the meaning of a word.[5] It has been pointed out that words do not have proper or correct meanings; that the word 'law' is notoriously ambiguous; and that it has so many different associations and nuances of meaning that it is futile to expect widespread agreement about its definition or usage. If asked by a foreigner, or even a first year law student, the question 'What is law?' may be interpreted as a request for clarification of an unfamiliar term. But questions about abstract legal concepts such as law or right or justice are typically asked by jurists who are familiar with the terms but are nevertheless puzzled by them.[6] Within jurisprudence, the context is more like that of of an art critic wondering

---

[4] It may, for example, be based on some false assumptions about language (e.g. that words have correct or proper meanings or that all nouns stand for things (see Chapter 2, n. 112) or it may be a request for information or evaluation dressed up as a semantic or conceptual question. (Hart (1954)). For example, 'What is the correct or proper meaning of the word "law"?' assumes that there is only one meaning and that words have correct or proper meanings (the proper meaning fallacy) (See p. 34 above.) If the question is re-posed in such terms as: 'What is the essential nature of law?', this assumes that law has an essential nature (which is much contested) and it is unclear what that means. If the question is re-posed in such terms as 'What is law for?' it assumes that law (generally) has one or more definite purposes or functions and this raises problems about functional analysis that are discussed below. But underlying the question may be an unexpressed concern about political obligation: 'Do I have a moral obligation to obey the law?' Or: 'Under what circumstances is one justified in breaking the law?' Some jurists would insist that such questions presuppose a clear conception of law, but others maintain that one's conception of law has important implications for questions about political obligation and civil disobedience.

[5] See, however, MacCormick (2007) on 'explanatory definition', which is close to the approach adopted in this chapter.

[6] Hart (1954).

'What is art?' or a scientist pondering about the nature of science. 'What is law?' is typically asked by a jurist or lawyer who has an intimate knowledge of the subject and yet is troubled by it. The idea is familiar, the concept is abstract, and it is learned and intelligent people who are especially puzzled. No definition is going to resolve this puzzlement.

As with the introspective question 'Who am I?', the exact nature of the puzzlement may not be entirely clear. It may just be a question about how the term is being used in a particular context, in which case a simple stipulative definition may suffice; it may be an indirect way of asking about salient characteristics of law or the functions or legitimacy or origins of law – questions that presuppose that law itself has already been identified. Often, however, the question 'What is law?' is treated as a request for an answer to some such question as: 'What is the essential nature of law?' and this is interpreted as a request for a 'general theory of law'. It is often assumed that 'a theory of law' is an attempted answer to this question. For example, Kelsen's Pure Theory of Law,[7] Hart's depiction of the form and structure of state legal systems in *The Concept of Law*,[8] and Raz's concept of a legal system,[9] are often interpreted as theories about the nature or essence of state law. For some people this is *the* question of jurisprudence.

I shall draw on the ideas of Kelsen, Hart, Raz and other jurists, but it is not part of my enterprise to develop a general theory of law of this kind for three reasons: First, for the purposes of viewing law from a global perspective as part of a cosmopolitan discipline, a conception of law that is confined to state law (and maybe a few close analogies) leaves out far too much. There are many phenomena, which can be subsumed under the umbrella of non-state law, that are appropriate subject-matters of our discipline that would be excluded or distorted by so narrow a focus, such as various forms and traditions of religious or customary law. Second, to assume that law, or even state law, has a common nature or core involves reductionist and essentialist tendencies about which I am deeply sceptical. Rather, the picture that I wish to construct emphasises the diversity, the complexity, and the fluidity of the phenomena with which we are or should be concerned. Thirdly, I reject the conception of jurisprudence as a monolithic enterprise that centres on one or only a few 'core' questions.

The aim of this chapter is not to advance either a general definition of law or a general theory of law in the conventional sense. Rather it is the modest one of constructing an organising concept that may be helpful both in providing the base for a broad overview and for suggesting links with concepts, ideas, hypotheses, and theories that form part of our juristic heritage or those of other disciplines that bear on the enterprise of understanding law.

---

[7] Kelsen (1945).   [8] Hart (1961).   [9] Raz (1970) (1979).

3.3 Mapping law

(a) 'Mapping'

In trying to draw pictures of law, especially broad overviews, jurists often resort to spatial metaphors: panorama, landscape, field, country, locality, empire, domain, together with boundaries, strata, paths, routes, journeys and frontiers. In attempts to construct overviews or total pictures of law in the world as a whole, it has been quite common to talk about 'mapping law' – sometimes figuratively, but sometimes quite literally by producing geographical maps.[10] The Bengal archipelago, as described by Amitav Ghosh, presents some obvious difficulties to professional cartographers; these would be much greater for an amateur. I shall argue that constructing a useful overview of legal phenomena in the world as a whole shares some of these difficulties, but is even harder.

A cartographer of the Bengal archipelago would have to confront a number of difficulties from the outset: First, a map presupposes adequate concepts and reliable data: modern cartography has relatively well-developed conventions concerning concepts and symbols, but in this context it may be quite difficult to give precise meanings to river, channel, confluence, sandbar, island, or *mohana*. Similarly in law there are problems about individuating the units to be mapped: are we concerned with families of legal systems or legal traditions or particular legal systems or legal orders or normative orders of particular communities or groups or more dynamic phenomena, such as patterns of diffusion? What are the smallest units that can be sensibly included in a picture or map of world law? And how can historical changes and shifts in more ephemeral phenomena be indicated? What counts as one system, order, tradition or other unit? Second, while it might be possible to draw a rough outline of the edges of the archipelago, there are few other clear boundaries or divisions within it. Third, there are thousands of islands and sandbars, which greatly vary in size. These islands are of differing duration, some ancient, some very recent, some ephemeral. They vary in size, power and stability, rather like member states of the

---

[10] When one talks of 'maps' it is natural to think of physical maps of the kinds one finds in an atlas. But like 'travelling well' it is a mistake to over-emphasise the physical. Geographical maps are only one convenient way of presenting information in easily understood form. Mapping is a common metaphor for 'the mental conception of the arrangement of something' (OED). Physical maps are mainly useful for representing the spatial relations between phenomena in respect of their relative size, position, and distribution. Traditional cartography is best for depicting relatively stable spatial relations on a flat plane. Modern cartography has increased in sophistication, for example in depicting phenomena in three dimensions or charting movement over time, such as winds and fronts in television weather maps. In constructing mental maps or pictures we may also resort to other kinds of visual display, such as charts, graphs, images, and statistical tables. Enormous advances have been made in recent years in techniques of visual presentation of information, but legal scholarship has generally been slow to make use of them. (See especially Edward R. Tufte's wonderful *Envisioning Information* (1990), see also Tufte (1983) (1997)). Most of our pictures of law from a global perspective have been in conventional prose, nevertheless making rather free use of spatial metaphors. On geographical and mental mapping of law see further *GLT*, Chapter 6.

United Nations. Fourth, the islands are in constant interaction with flowing water. Some flows are individuated as channels or rivers, each with a name, even though some are immense waterways and others are only two or three kilometres long.[11] Next, our cartographer would find that the more details she included, the more inaccurate the map would be. How much detail is appropriate depends on its intended purposes. It is clear that a small scale map would have only limited uses and that it would be even harder to produce detailed maps that would be safe guides to navigation. Indeed, navigation requires considerable local knowledge of changing conditions so that visitors would normally rely on local boat people as guides rather than maps, even if these are well-developed.[12]

This analogy with the archipelago suggests just some of the obvious difficulties of constructing a reasonably comprehensive picture of law in the world. It suggests three further points that need bearing in mind.

First, it is dangerous to think of all normative and legal orders as having clear and precise borders. We are used to equating state law with relatively well-defined territory of countries, provinces and jurisdictions. Indeed, it would not be very difficult to construct a map consisting of the state legal systems of all the members of the United Nations. But it is trite that formal membership conceals great variations between states in respect of size, power, wealth, type of regime, stability, autonomy, democracy, political culture, and so on.[13] There are, of course, some disputes about territory or borders, and some issues about jurisdiction, but a map of state legal systems would be not very different from a standard world map of countries or nation states. As we shall see, there are difficulties about producing a satisfactory taxonomy of state legal systems, but that is not the main problem. National boundaries are more permeable than they were, so that it is increasingly artificial to treat countries, societies and nation states as fixed self-contained units that exist and can be studied in isolation. Here, too the difficulties can be exaggerated. Much more difficult is the point that there are real problems with regard to individuating non-state normative orders as defined units – many are more like Ghosh's currents and rivulets.

---

[11] One may ask about this analogy to mapping the Bengal archipelago whether it is more appropriate to treat law as being like water or land – which is law and which is context? My intention is to equate law with water here, in order to emphasise fluidity and to introduce the idea of surface law. But the question indicates the limits of the analogy.

[12] No doubt a professional cartographer armed with sophisticated techniques and modern technology could produce more sophisticated and even more useful maps. And drawing on the expertise of other specialists could produce a whole atlas dealing with the climate, ecology, hydrology, and zoology of the archipelago. In Ghosh's *The Hungry Tide*, Pira the heroine, a cetologist interested in dolphins spends the better part of a day charting one quite small pool using relatively sophisticated technology. She depends entirely on local boatmen for navigation.

[13] On the ephemerality of states, the permeability of their boundaries and variations in size see Glenn (2003) and Diamond (2005).

Second, as the archipelago's 'rivers' interact with each other and with islands and sandbanks, so do legal orders interact both with their immediate environment and with each other. We talk of studying 'law in its social, economic, and political context' and it is a truism of a contextual approach that it is one thing to study law in context, quite another to define law as context.[14] But as with Bengal's confluences, what is river and what is environment are often not clear-cut. Later we shall explore further the idea of interaction between laws, legal systems, and legal orders in relation to *diffusion*[15] and the useful concept of *interlegality*.[16]

Third, a further point, not emphasised in the quotation, is that such a description only deals with surface appearances. While outwardly a *mohana* may resemble a static lake, underneath the surface the terrain may be uneven, the flows of water more complex, the depths and shallows hidden, and the map will tell us nothing about the teeming life below. Similarly, many orthodox or official accounts of legal systems tell us little or nothing of what the submerged terrain is like and what is actually going on beneath the surface. They deal only with *surface law*. Moreover, like hidden currents or depths, many legal orders of varying significance are overlooked, marginalised or treated as invisible.[17]

All of the difficulties facing our amateur cartographer are shared by the legal cartographer.[18] But there are further complexities that need to be considered.

(b) Levels again

In Chapter 1 I introduced the idea of 'levels of law' using familiar spatial terms such as national, regional, global and other terms referring to patterns that could relatively easily be 'mapped' on plane surfaces, such as diasporas, empires, alliances, and networks. These geographical analogies were introduced to make some general points:

(1) For most purposes it is inadequate to theorise law solely in terms of two levels: municipal state law and public international law in the classical sense ('The Westphalian Duo').

(2) Rough geographical characterisation brings out the point that different levels are not nested in a single vertical hierarchy – diasporas, alliances, and empires cut across simple divisions into global – regional – national – local.

---

[14] Twining (1974b) at pp. 164–7.   [15] See Chapter 9 below.   [16] See Chapter 16.2 on the web.

[17] Most, but not all, maps depict surface relations between observable phenomena. So our amateur cartographer will probably tell us almost nothing about what lies beneath the surfaces of the archipelago. Similarly, I shall argue later that most orthodox accounts of state legal systems, for instance official accounts and textbooks, tell us only about what is meant to happen and almost nothing about methods of interpretation, interposed norms and what actually happens in practice. Chapter 10 develops the idea of surface law to depict this tendency. Related to this is the idea of 'invisible' or unnoticed legal or normative orders, for example, the non-state regimes of ordering in Brazilian *favelas* and the Common Law Movement, see nn. 27 and 28.

[18] See n. 12 above.

(3) Because of this many normative and legal orders co-exist in the same time-space context; hence the idea of normative and legal pluralism.

(4) Few of these patterns and relations are static. This is illustrated by the idea of concepts 'travelling' well or badly, migration of laws, diffusion, spheres of justice, and the complexities of interlegality.

Table 3.1 carries the geographical analogy further by listing a number of 'levels' of relations and of ordering and giving possible examples of each. This table was constructed for three main purposes: first, to illustrate how a geographical map or series of maps of law in the world might be organised; second, to list a number of obvious and not so obvious examples of candidates for inclusion in a reasonably inclusive picture; and third, to bring out some further difficulties in constructing such overviews.

In considering this table, it is important to distinguish between levels of relations and levels of ordering. All of the examples are of putative normative

Table 3.1 Levels of Law[1]

Law is concerned with relations between subjects or persons (human, legal, unincorporated and otherwise) at a variety of levels, not just relations within a single nation state or society. One way of characterising such levels is essentially geographical:

- global (as with some environmental issues, a possible *ius humanitatis*) and, by extension, space law (e.g mineral rights on the moon);
- international (in the classic sense of relations between sovereign states and more broadly relations governed e.g. by human rights or refugee law);
- regional (e.g. the EU, ECHR, and the African Union);
- transnational (e.g. Islamic, Hindu, Jewish law, Romani (Gypsy) law, transnational arbitration, a putative *lex mercatoria*, Internet law, and, more controversially, the internal governance of multi-national corporations, the Catholic Church, or institutions of organised crime);
- inter-communal (i.e. normative orders governing relations between religious communities, or Christian Churches, or different ethnic groups);
- territorial state (including the legal systems of nation states, and sub-national jurisdictions, such as Florida, Greenland, Quebec, and Northern Ireland);
- sub-state (e.g. subordinate legislation, such as bye-laws of the Borough of Camden) or religious law officially recognised for limited purposes in a plural legal system; and
- non-state (including laws of subordinated peoples, such as native North Americans, or Maoris, or gypsies) or illegal legal orders, such as Santos's Pasagarda law, the Southern People's Liberation Army's legal regime in Southern Sudan, and the 'common law movement' of militias in the United States.

Which of these orders should be classified as 'law' or 'legal' is essentially contested within legal theory and also depends on the context and purposes of the discourse.

[1] Adapted from *GLT*, Chapter 6 at p. 139. Recent studies of Romani (Gypsy) law have been pioneered by Walter Weyrauch. See especially, Weyrauch and Bell (1993) and Symposium (1997). The Southern Peoples' Liberation Army has operated a system of courts dealing with both civil and criminal cases in areas which they occupy in the civil war in the Southern Sudan. (Kuol (1997). On the Common Law Movement see Koniak (1996) and (1997). On Pasagarda see Santos (1995).

or legal *orders* – potential units to be mapped. But some of the categories also apply to levels of relations: for example, relations between states (international), relations within regions or within nation states, relations between legal persons that cross state boundaries (transnational), or relations within smaller communities or groups within one state (sub-state or local).[19] Relations and normative orders are not co-extensive in this respect: for example, my relations with a local shop may be governed by several legal and normative orders belonging to different levels, some interlocking, some quite distinct or even conflicting: United Kingdom law, English law, local bye-laws, European Community law (directly or indirectly), and possibly by international human rights law, religious law, or local custom (e.g. norms of the local 'black economy').[20] Or again, a contract between exporter X and importer Y may be governed by the law of country Z or by some more complex arrangement.

Although the table includes several examples of non-state orders, the territorial boundaries of nation states still play a major role, even if their hold is in the process of being loosened. Public international law and some other examples of 'official' orders use territorial boundaries to designate units (e.g. international, regional, national, provincial, or local government boundaries). However, non-state law can operate within a state or other official jurisdiction or without regard to national boundaries: 'transnational' implies transcending state boundaries, without necessarily totally disregarding them. States are clearly the main actors in creating regional and international human rights regimes, but some non-state alliances, diasporas, and networks are in practice wholly or mainly regional.

Some scholars have criticised the use of 'levels' of law in this context. For example, Goodale and Merry in *The Practice of Human Rights* substitute 'networks' for talk of geographical levels.[21] For the purpose of linking human rights practice to questions of structure, power and communication, this move seems appropriate, but it does not fit my present purpose. Like them, I have rejected the global/local, national/international dichotomies as too simple. We

---

[19] There are, of course, other ways of classifying legal relations: state–state; citizen (or subject)–state; citizen–citizen; subject–subject and so on. Relations are also classified in other ways (e.g. by subject-matter: personal, familial, commercial, employment and so on).

[20] On 'the informal sector', see Hansen (2001). Benton (1994) shows convincingly that sharp distinctions between informal and formal economic sectors and between state/non-state law do not reflect the perceptions of participants. It is wrong to assume that actors in the informal sector do not use or pay attention to state law. On 'rule density' see *HTDTWR*, pp. 142–3.

[21] Much more promising for our purposes are studies of transboundary social processes that drop the global/local: international/national dichotomy in favor of some version of network analysis. Network analyses emerged in large part to describe the changes in information technology and communications over the last fifteen years, the same period when transnational human rights discourses have become more prevalent and consequential. Networks describe the spaces that provide the 'material organization of time-sharing social practices' ((Castells (2000) at p. 442), practices which are determined by the imperative 'not just to communicate, but also to gain position' ((Castells (2000) at p. 71, citing Mulgan (1991) at p. 21)' (Goodale and Merry (2007) Introduction at pp. 17–18. See further n.22 and Riles (2001).

also agree that spatial metaphors, such as 'networks', are illuminating up to a point and that a vertical characterisation of legal relations gives a misleading impression of hierarchy, (e.g. in respect of authority, power, and importance).[22] But the idea of 'networks' does not catch some other complexities that cut across neat spatial pictures: diasporas, empires, alliances, trade routes, and traditions. Moreover, network analysis is most useful at lower or more specific levels of abstraction.[23]

Table 3.1 lists a number of candidates for inclusion in a reasonably comprehensive overview of law in the world. It assumes that these are all sufficiently discrete units to be treated as normative, and possibly legal, orders. But what counts as one order in this context? This problem of individuation is sometimes overlooked. For the purposes of this kind of mapping, deciding whether to differentiate United Kingdom law and English law, Northern Ireland law, Scots law, and possibly Welsh law should not be too difficult. But what should count as one 'order' in respect of Islamic law or Romani ('Gypsy') law is, as we shall see, a more puzzling issue.[24]

The table deliberately leaves open which of the listed candidates are to count as 'legal' in this context. That depends on the purpose of the enterprise. For example, a map of intellectual property regimes in the world might be confined to the Westphalian Duo.[25] A map of human rights regimes might be a bit more complex. A map of major examples of religious law in the world would be much more difficult to construct, partly because what counts as religious is problematic, partly because some states recognise some aspects of some religious laws, but not others, as part of municipal law, partly because what counts as one religion or a major religion is also debatable, and last, but not least, the availability of relevant data is at best uneven. Even with a single stipulated definition or set of criteria of identification of law there will almost inevitably be borderline cases or grey areas. How to resolve these difficulties depends on

[handwritten margin note: Most of Europe, Christianity rules as majority anyway.]

---

[22] Some theorists of legal pluralism (e.g. Pospisil) suggest that talk of 'levels of law' implies some hierarchical relationship. This can be misleading (Benton (1994)) and is not intended here.

[23] Goodale and Merry (2007) usefully apply network analysis to human rights discourse and also indicate some of the limitations of this perspective (at pp. 18–22). They do not entirely reject the simple dichotomies: the sub-title of the book is *Tracking Law Between the Global and the Local*. Glenn (2004), and in a very different way, the proponents of autopoiesis such as Teubner, also emphasise the communication of ideas as central to law. On diffusion of law as communication (or miscommunicaton) of ideas, see further Chapter 9 below.

[24] One would need to clarify how each candidate for inclusion is conceived: for example, 'Islamic Law' in this context is much broader than just those aspects of Islamic law that are officially recognised by Islamic states, such as Saudi Arabia, or within mixed municipal legal systems, as in Tanzania. The term 'Islamic law' is variously used to apply to a juristic tradition, a body of doctrine, which may or may not be geographically located, or to institutionalised phenomena in particular places. But what precisely would it include in this context? In other words, even for the minor task of compiling an atlas, quite difficult conceptual problems would arise. Moreover, the term 'Islamic law' (shari'a in a broader sense) obscures the important distinction between the path set out in the Koran (shari'a as 'the way' or 'path') and *fiq* (man-made law, including interpretations by jurists).

[25] See Wood (2005).

context, purpose, and what is at stake. We shall explore the borderland between 'the legal' and 'the non-legal' further below, but it is worth re-emphasising that the importance and difficulties of borderline cases can easily be over-estimated if the context is clear.

Another taxonomic question relates to the grouping of legal orders. Supposing we have agreed a list of units to be mapped as discrete legal orders in this context; can they be classified into larger groupings? Clearly there are patterns of varying significance relating to geographical location, state of economic development, types of polity, power relations, and so on.[26] But are there any characteristically legal categories that can be used as a basis of classification? This question has been much debated in relation to legal families and traditions, but many scholars consider the debate to be unsatisfactory and largely trivial. We shall consider the debate briefly, partly because it is useful to have some broad generic categories, but also because the reasons why these debates are generally unsatisfactory are themselves illuminating.

Table 3.1 is open to several lines of criticism: the various 'levels' are vague (e.g. what counts as a 'region?'); scholars disagree about the merits of the claims of some of the candidates to be counted as 'legal' (e.g. should we as jurists take Pasagarda Law[27] or the Common Law Movement[28] seriously?); and, anterior to this, are all the candidates in the table species of the same genus? (Are they all normative orders in the same sense?). These criticisms have some force, if one expects precision and conceptual refinement in such an overview. The table is only useful as a rough first step and to differentiate between three basic questions: First, what counts as one normative order? (the problem of individuation). Second, how should we distinguish the legal and

[26] One of the most useful forms of analysis in post-colonial situations, pioneered in relation to the world economy by Immannuel Wallerstein (e.g. (1979) (1991) (2002)), and nicely developed by Halme (2007) in relation to human rights actors, is the spectrum between centre and periphery in relation to power and influence.

[27] 'Pasagarda law' refers to the institutions and processes concerning housing and other matters dealt with by the Residents' Association in an urban settlement (*favela*) in Rio in the 1970s as described by Santos (1995). It is a nice example of 'squatters' law' contrasted with, but sometimes echoing, 'the asphalt law' of the state system. It is a relatively clear example of an institutionalised normative order oriented towards ordering internal relations within a community that largely fell outside the reach of the state legal system. Santos (1995). See further pp. 313–15 below. The situation has changed significantly since 1990. On 'illegal cities' see Fernandes and Varley (1996).

[28] 'The Common Law Movement' as described by Koniak (1996) and (1997) is the 'legal' arm of the militias in the United States. 'Common law courts' have been set up in many states, 'freemen' do not recognise Federal and State law for most purposes (including tax, social security, driving licences), and their activities (including harassment of officials) have from time to time been a matter of concern for state judges and law enforcement agencies. The Common Law Movement has a developed an ideology and body of doctrine, much of which is expressed in a legalistic form of discourse derived from traditional common law concepts. On Koniak's account it fits the category of an institutionalised normative order oriented to ordering relations both within these outlaw communities and with the outside world. It is an interesting example of a not insignificant phenomenon that is largely ignored, indeed almost 'invisible'. Over several years I have not encountered an American law student who had even heard of it, let alone studied it prior to my course. If it warrants the label 'law', it is in the view of some a rare example of 'a crazy legal order'.

the non-legal in this or similar contexts? (the problem of identification of the legal). Third, are there useful ways of categorising the candidates that have been identified for inclusion in this mapping exercise? (the classification of legal traditions, families, systems, and cultures). We shall deal with these questions in reverse order, by starting with attempts to construct simple overviews, then moving onto the vexed question of criteria of identification of legal orders, before dealing briefly with problems of individuation. But before that, it is useful to consider one objection to the very idea of 'mapping law'.

(c) Woodman on the impossibility of maps of law

In a thoughtful paper entitled 'Why There Can be no Map of Law', Gordon Woodman (2003) challenges the very idea of thinking literally or even meta-phorically in terms of mapping law.[29] The practice of relating laws to countries, societies, fields, or localities is, he suggests, a hangover from 'legal centralism', which treats state law as the paradigm. State law is typically defined in terms of relatively determinate territory, but many laws and legal orders are not. In the standard situation of legal pluralism, 'in which a population observes more than one body of law', there may not be settled choice of law rules, the population may be dispersed, membership of the population may be ambiguous, there may be variations and inconsistencies within a single 'system' or body of law, and an individual may observe different laws for different purposes, even in relation to a single transaction or relationship. For instance, much of Luo customary law in Kenya is personal, not territorial; the population of Luos is dispersed both across national borders and within Kenya; there may be indeterminacy about who is a Luo; some may categorise themselves or be categorised as Luos for some purposes, but not for others; there are variations within Luo law; and, as happened in the famous *Otieno* case,[30] the individual may have left the situation ambiguous (perhaps deliberately) with regard to the law that applied to the burial of his body.

It may be objected that Woodman underrates the sophistication of modern cartography and that some of the possibilities that he indicates are exceptional. Furthermore, maps may be useful for depicting broad patterns and distribu-tions without being overly concerned with details and exceptions. For example, Islamic law when it is institutionalised has many of the features that Woodman points out: there are significant variations within Islam; who counts as a Muslim is not always clear; interpretations and practices vary and change; there are uncertainties and choices to be made about the application of Islamic or other rules in particular situations; and the 'population' of Muslims is widely dispersed around the world, both between and within many countries. Nevertheless, there

---

[29] Woodman (2003) challenged by Marten Bavinck in an unpublished paper (2003). See now, Bavinck and Woodman (forthcoming) in which they explore their differences.

[30] *Wambui Otieno v Ougo and Siranga* (1986–7) see pp. 272–3 below.

are quite useful maps of religious diasporas indicating significant populations, movements, and rates of conversion.[31] Some deal broadly with the world as a whole, some deal in more detail with distribution in smaller geographical spaces. If we were to say that Islamic law typically exists as an institutionalised social practice wherever there is a significant population of practising Muslims, existing maps of religious diasporas would be adequate to obtain a general impression. Obviously such maps do not claim to locate every single devout Muslim.

This leads on to a further point: if we conceive of law in terms not only of ideas but also of social practices we are concerned with actual behaviour that takes place at particular times and in specific places. Islamic law is institutionalised as a social praxis by mosques, and khadis and actual ceremonies and dispute settlement processes. To find out about these requires further empirical enquiry about institutions, processes, and other concrete social practices. There would be practical problems about constructing maps of Islamic legal praxis in a given locality or region with a high degree of precision, there would be grey areas, and data might be hard to obtain.[32] But producing workable pictures is neither impossible nor mysterious. There is some potential for a cartography of law (provided that we have adequate concepts and data).[33] But it is not easy. There are problems about individuating 'legal orders' and 'systems', they may not be internally coherent or consistent, not all laws belong clearly to a specific system or order, law is constantly in flux, the boundaries can be fluid and permeable, laws operate at different levels of ordering and relations, and people are often subject to multiple legal orders, often without a clearly defined choice of law norms. To these obstacles in the way of simple mapping, Woodman has usefully added some further complicating factors.

As we have seen, ordinary academic discourse is riddled with spatial metaphors.[34] These metaphors are useful, so long as we bear in mind that they are just metaphors. In 'mapping' relations, for instance between members of a family, a picture of their geographical distribution may be less illuminating than an analysis in terms of kinship, or genes, or affection, or power, or conflicting or shared interests. So, too in mapping legal relations. Social practices involve patterns of actual human behaviour in particular places. Their spatial distribution and relations can in principle be mapped.

Legal ideas and practices vary in scope, scale and quantity; normative and legal orders are often difficult to individuate; some legal orders have ostensibly

---

[31] On religious diasporas see, for example, Chaliand and Rageau (1995) Barrett *et al.* (2001). On the unreliability of religious statistics see Jenkins (2007).

[32] Maps of diasporas are often made showing migration routes and established communities. For example, an excellent geography of the Jewish diaspora includes a map of the situation in 1890 that identifies settled Jewish communities of 20,000 or more and 'other significant communities' in 1890. (Chaliand and Rageau (1995) at p. 46). It would not be difficult to produce a similar map of Islamic law in the modern world using existing maps of the Islamic diaspora. For example, *The Oxford History of Islam* has a simple map of the distribution of Muslims in the world. (Esposito (1999) at p. x).

[33] E.g. Blomley (1994), Economides (1996), Holder and Harrison (2003).   [34] See p. 67 above.

well-defined boundaries, but many are more like waves or clouds than billiard balls; nearly everything is in flux, but at different speeds; there is almost continual interaction with other legal orders and other phenomena; and above all there is the brooding omnipresence of the question: 'What differentiates legal from other phenomena?' Bearing in mind these warnings, let us look briefly at some previous attempts to construct overviews of law in the world.

3.4 Families, civilisations, cultures and traditions

(a) Legal families

In *Globalisation and Legal Theory* I tell the story of various attempts to map law in the world and individual legal orders:[35] Wigmore's attempts to construct typologies of the legal families, and my own amateurish attempts at legal cartography in Khartoum in the late 1950s and again in Belfast ten years later. I suggested that all were unsatisfactory for much the same reasons that are outlined in the last section. But I also argued that some useful lessons could be learned from such attempts: first, if one accepts that legal relations and legal ordering take place at different levels, the phenomena are probably too complex to depict in a single map or chart – something more like an historical atlas is needed.[36] Second, geographical maps mainly depict spatial relations and distributions, and as such they have a restricted application to legal phenomena. Most maps depict what is on the surface and are uninformative about what lies beneath. Third, geographical maps presuppose mental maps – they are means of depicting pre-existing concepts and data: part of my argument is that such concepts and data are underdeveloped in general jurisprudence.

After World War II it was the practice in some Continental European law faculties to present overviews of 'Les Grandes Systèmes de droit contemporain', usually in terms of 'legal families'. This led to some modest textbooks[37] and to the revival of a long-running and unsatisfactory debate about how major systems, traditions, or families of law should be classified. It is not necessary here to repeat the details of this debate, but it may be useful to consider the least unsatisfactory of these attempts. Zweigert and Kötz's *An Introduction to Comparative Law*[38] was, for a generation, the leading student textbook on the subject. Rejecting single criteria such as race, ideology, geographical location, stages of economic development, or relations of economic production, they

---

[35] *GLT*, Chapter 6. Compare Robert Seidman's excellent attempt to illustrate state legal pluralism by a fictitious case modelled on Lon Fuller's 'The Case of the Speluncean Explorers' (Seidman (1967) Fuller (1949)).

[36] A good historical atlas of law in the world could be illuminating up to a point, if it was reasonably detailed and inclusive (i.e. going beyond state law). But it would probably have the limitations of all such works. The concern of this chapter is with mental or figurative mapping with an emphasis on what kind of conceptual apparatus is needed.

[37] E.g David (1964), Arminjon, Nolde and Wolff (1950–51), Derrett (1968), Zweigert and Kötz (1971, first German edition).

[38] Zweigert and Kötz (3rd edn, 1998).

focused on the 'styles of legal thought' of contemporary living legal systems and suggested multiple criteria for classifying them into families:

> (1) its historical background and development; (2) its predominant and characteristic mode of thought in legal matters; (3) especially distinctive legal institutions; (4) the kind of legal sources it acknowledges and the way it handles them; (5) its ideology.[39]

These multiple criteria led them to adopt the following classification of 'legal families' (i.e. groups of legal systems):

> (1) Romanistic family; (2) Germanic family; (3) Nordic family; (4) Common Law family; (5) Socialist family; (6) Far Eastern systems; (7) Islamic systems; (8) Hindu law.[40]

Although this scheme has attracted some criticism, it was probably adequate for an introductory student text and it had the merit of identifying some of the main difficulties underlying the problem of classification. For present purposes, it is enough to point out that, the eight categories do not refer to species of a single genus: the first five refer to state legal systems (but some have historic roots preceding the rise of the nation state); the sixth, 'Far Eastern Systems', is more of a rag-bag than a family, joined together mainly by geographical location;[41] (7) and (8) open the way for recognition of non-state law, for Zweigert and Kötz recognised that it would be a distortion to limit their account of Islamic law to Islamic states or even to those aspects recognised as a source of law in plural state legal systems. But this involved a shift of meaning of 'system' from existing state legal system to a system of thought. However, the label 'system' is dropped from Hindu Law, perhaps because there is no modern Hindu state. Analytically, this scheme is more like a muddle than a systematic classification, but, of course, that may not matter if not much depends on the classification anyway.[42]

Zweigert and Kötz's account of legal families may be the least unsatisfactory attempt to base an overview of law in the world on the basis of a taxonomy of legal families. However, it has two main weaknesses: it lacks a coherent organising concept and it downplays the importance of history. The best hope for developing a coherent picture of law in the world, it has been suggested, is to adopt an historical perspective. So let us now look at another intellectual tradition: world history and its neglected sister, historical jurisprudence, which use a different set of basic concepts.

---

[39] *Ibid.*, pp. 69–75.

[40] *Ibid.*, (1987 edn.) at p. 75 in the third edition the suggestion that this was intended as a comprehensive taxonomy was abandoned ((1998) at p. 73).

[41] See the criticisms of Patrick Glenn's category of 'Asian legal tradition' by Huxley, Palmer, and Stickings in Foster (ed.) (2006).

[42] See further the approach of Mattei (1997a) to develop a taxonomy on the basis of economic analysis.

(b) World history as a perspective: civilisation, culture, and tradition

World history as a genre is notoriously vulnerable to criticism especially about details; it can help to map areas of ignorance, but in its positive assertions it can only be as well grounded as the best available sources and it is constantly threatened by the pitfalls of generalisation. Some deny that such an enterprise can be intellectually respectable, let alone scholarly or objective. Others, myself included, take the view that, whatever their faults, scholars such as Vico, Toynbee, Braudel, and Wallerstein,[43] or in our own discipline, historical jurisprudence in the mode of Sir Henry Maine, Sir Paul Vinogradoff, Harold Berman, and Patrick Glenn have contributed much of value.[44]

History and geography are closely interrelated. Just as there are historical atlases, so most world history treats spatial factors as important. But as we move on to an historical perspective some concepts, such as countries, nation states and legal systems, become less central and others, such as civilisation and culture and tradition, become important, though elusive, organising concepts.

Each concept has changed over time and has been the subject of controversy. Each has sometimes acquired associations that are inappropriate here: 'civilisation' has often been used in colonial contexts to suggest the superiority of Western civilisation in respect of such matters as religion (Christianity), learning (science), technology, education, law (modernity) and even manners (civility). Civilisation is often contrasted with barbarism. Similarly, terms like 'culture' and 'cultured' are sometimes used narrowly, even snobbishly, to refer to 'high culture', or to 'higher' learning, the arts and literature, or manners. Conversely 'tradition' and 'traditional' sometimes carry suggestions of conservatism, inertia and resistance to change.

If these are to have any value as analytical concepts, we need to rid them of some of their stronger emotive associations. Here I shall argue that 'civilisation' as used by Braudel, 'culture' as elucidated by Kroeber, Kluckhohn and Bell, and 'tradition' as developed by Krygier and Glenn are all useful for present purposes.

The French historian, Fernand Braudel, in his *History of Civilizations* treated 'civilization' as the generic term for the totality of civilisations.[45] A major civilisation is a shared heritage of material and spiritual characteristics that has survived and evolved over at least three planes:[46] *la longue durée* of structures and traditions; the intermediate level of 'conjunctures' lasting no more than one or more generations (e.g. the rise of an empire); the more particular scale of 'episodes' (e.g World War I, the French Revolution) and 'events' (e.g. The Fall of the Bastille, the Battle of the Somme) which have been the main focus of traditional history. 'Civilization is the longest story of all.'[47]

---

[43] E.g. Vico (1744), Toynbee (1947), Braudel (1993), Wallerstein (1979, 1991).

[44] E.g. Maine (1870), Vinogradoff (1920–22), Berman (1983), (2003), Glenn (2004). See now Goldman (2007). On historical Jurisprudence see below p. 228.

[45] Braudel (1993) (trs. Richard Mayne), first French edition (1987).

[46] Braudel (1993) at p. 34.   [47] *Ibid.*

Braudel focused on Islam and the Muslim world, Black Africa, The Far East (China, India, and Japan), Europe, America (Latin America and the United States) and 'the other Europe' (Muscovy, Russia, the USSR and CIS) as 'major civilizations'. He compared and contrasted them largely in terms of geography, history, religion, tradition, and structures. He emphasised the stability of structures, the pervasiveness of change, and the persistence of interaction and exchange of ideas between civilisations. The scheme of classification used in this great work illustrates the fragility and arbitrariness of any attempt at description at this level of generality.[48]

Somewhat less general, but equally contentious, are the concepts of 'culture' and 'tradition'.[49] A much-quoted account of 'culture' is that of Kroeber and Kluckhohn:

> Culture consists of patterns, explicit and implicit, of and for behaviour acquired and transmitted by symbols, constituting distinct achievements of a human group, including their embodiment in artifacts; the essential core of culture consists of traditional (i.e. historically derived and selected) ideas and especially their attached values; cultural systems may, on the one hand, be considered as products of action, on the other hand as conditioning elements of further action.[50]

Although controversial, this is useful here in focusing attention simultaneously on ideas, practices, and tradition. Ideas constitute practices and give them meaning. Ideas include both values and beliefs about the human condition and the nature of the world (and beyond).[51] Praxis relates these to actual behaviour.

'Culture' has a lower order of generality than 'civilisation', because it can apply to a single human group. Civilisation is the total heritage of cultural artefacts (ideas and practices). The two concepts operate best at different levels of generality. We can talk of European or Western 'civilisation', but we are

---

[48] On Samuel Huntington's use of 'civilisation' see n. 58 below.

[49] Braudel (1993) makes some interesting observations on the history of the concept of 'culture' (kultur), and he links it closely to 'civilization': 'One can say, for example, that a civilization (or a culture) is the sum total of its cultural assets, that its geographical area is its cultural domain, that its history is cultural history, and that what one civilization transmits to another is a cultural legacy or a case of cultural borrowing, whether material or intellectual.' I prefer Kluckholn and Bell's more precise conception of 'culture' that explicitly links both ideas and actual behaviour and thus creates a bridge to the concept of social practice.

[50] Kroeber and Kluckhohn, (1952) at p. 181. The authors denied that this was a definition: 'We do not propose to add a one hundred and sixty-fifth formal definition … We think it is premature to attempt encapsulation in a brief abstract statement which would include or imply all the elements that seem to us to be involved…Without pretending to "define", however, we think it proper to say at the end of this summary discussion of definitions that we believe each of our principal groups of definitions points to something legitimate and important. In other words, we think culture is a product; is historical; includes ideas, patterns and values; is selective; is learned; is based upon symbols; and is an abstraction from behavior and products of behavior' (1952 ibid. at p. 157) cited in Berelson and Steiner (1964) at pp. 643–4.

[51] For an excellent development of Kroeber and Kluckhohn's conception in relation to 'legal culture' see Bell (2001) Chapter 1.

extending the term if we apply it to narrower groupings. Conversely we can talk of a local culture, of legal culture, and of multi-cultural societies and groups. But if we make statements about 'European' culture we are almost certainly going to over-generalise.[52]

The concept of 'tradition' is even more problematic. In a striking departure from the largely atheoretical *Grandes Systèmes* approach, Patrick Glenn's *Legal Traditions of the World* sets out to give an overview of law in world history on the basis of a coherent and sophisticated theoretical account of the idea of tradition.[53]

For Glenn, tradition involves the communication of information over time. The concept emphasises memory, communication, continuity, and selection. A tradition typically has a stable core, but no fixed boundaries. Major traditions are complex, constituted by traditions within traditions, which are often competing or conflicting with each other. They accordingly accommodate internal controversy and debate, provided that the core of ideas is stable or only changes slowly. If a tradition is undermined by doctrinaire lateral movements, such as fundamentalism or universalism, the tradition is corrupted and in extreme cases ceases to exist.[54]

Tradition is Glenn's organising concept. He rejects the more fashionable 'culture' for several reasons:[55] it is vague and ambiguous; in some usages it combines both ideas and behaviour, whereas tradition focuses only on information (ideas); interpretations of 'culture' are often driven by the Western tendency to stress the internal unity of groups and systems and thus to emphasise separation and difference rather than permeability and continuity.[56] 'Culture' and 'system' tend to be used to de-emphasise history, whereas tradition draws attention to the normative survival of the past in the present.[57]

---

[52] Bell (2001) argues that the French legal system has several distinct legal cultures. For a useful discussion of the problems of using the terms 'culture' and 'legal culture' as analytic concepts, see Cotterrell and Friedman in Nelken (ed.) (1997). See now Örücü and Nelken (eds.) (2007) *passim*. Friedman (1997) at p. 34 claims that his usage of the term refers to 'ideas, values, expectations, and attitudes towards law and legal institutions', that is to measurable phenomena that can be studied from the outside, as opposed to 'ideology' which is confined to ideas. This is, however, somewhat narrower than the concept adopted by Kluckholn and Bell. See also Nelken in Örücü and Nelken (2007) Chapter 5.

[53] This section is based on Glenn (2004). The third edition, Glenn (2007) was published too late for consideration here.

[54] For example: 'Fundamentalism, and violence in pursuit of it, is...not inherent in tradition, but represents a departure from its most important characteristic.' (Glenn (2004) at p. 23).

[55] This summary of Glenn's caution about, if not antipathy to, 'culture' as an analytic concept is based on several of his writings and a conversation with him in 2003.

[56] Glenn is clearly uncomfortable with systems theory (e.g. Glenn (2004) at pp. 50–1,153–4). He points out that French legal scholarship has moved away from its former emphasis on 'legal systems' (*ibid.*, pp. 153–4) and he emphasises the duality of formal and informal legal orders. He even goes so far as to say: '[A] state (or national "legal system") is only an institutionalised recognition of the ascendancy of a particular tradition at a particular time, which is unlikely to have obliterated other, competing traditions even within its territory.' (*Ibid.*, at p. 53).

[57] Glenn (2004) Preface at p. xxv.

Furthermore, in recent times 'culture' has sometimes been used as a euphemism for race, in much the same way as 'civilisation' was used to justify colonialism, racial superiority, or technocratic modernisation.[58]

There are some who resist the idea of tradition. The adjective 'traditional' sometimes carries suggestions of static, conservative, old-fashioned, or out-of-date. It is often used pejoratively in contrast with 'modernisation'.[59] It is sometimes contrasted with 'rational', but rationalism, Glenn suggests, is itself a tradition which cannot escape from itself.[60] It is true that emphasising tradition directs our attention to the past and that inertia and routine are familiar aspects of tradition; but traditions are rarely static – ideas about change are often a distinguishing characteristic. No tradition can exercise full control over what information is preserved and captured in the future.

Glenn asserts that traditions contribute a sense of identity to societies and peoples, often more so than ethnicity or race or geographical location.[61] The extent to which law is constitutive of that identity varies between traditions.[62] Traditions typically precede the formation of political structures, such as the state, though subsequently they may be influenced by them.[63]

A focus on tradition raises questions about the forms and methods of communication of ideas over time: which ideas are transmitted how, when, and by whom is an essential part of the story of any tradition. It also raises questions about change within and between traditions. Glenn argues that the idea of tradition can provide a basis of comparison. Although different cultures may have different conceptual schemes, traditions are comparable[64] because every tradition has to address four issues: the nature of the core that constitutes its identity; its underlying justification; its conception of change; and how it

---

[58] Like 'culture', 'civilisation' is a Western concept that presupposes tradition. It is closer to tradition in that it emphasises continuity over time and points to relatively stable underlying structures rather than precise outer boundaries. But 'civilisation' gained currency as a concept of universal history used to justify colonial rule. In sharp contrast to Samuel Huntington's 'clash of civilisations' (1997), Glenn uses the more fluid, open concept of tradition as the basis for his vision of 'sustainable diversity'.

[59] On the common perception of tradition as inherently being a brake on development see Chapter 11.6 below.

[60] Criticised by Halpin (2006a) at pp. 116–7.   [61] Glenn (2004) at pp. 33–8.

[62] *Ibid.*, p. 40. Islamic law and Jewish law purport to regulate most aspects of life, Cthonic law and common law far less so. Glenn substitutes 'Cthonic' (meaning living in or in close harmony with the earth) for 'custom', 'native', 'aboriginal', or 'customary law', because of the negative associations these terms have acquired (*Ibid.*, pp. 73–4). This is strongly criticised by Woodman (2006).

[63] Glenn (2004) at pp. 35–8.

[64] Glenn enters into an elaborate argument about comparability and commensurabilty, (pp. 44–8, 354–5). but see especially 'Are Legal Traditions Commensurable?', Glenn (2001). This is criticised by Halpin (2006a). See now Glenn's reply to his critics (2007) and Halpin's reply to that (2007). It is questionable whether it is necessary to enter into the complex philosophical controversies for the purpose of asserting that legal traditions are comparable in respect of the 'shared problems' that Glenn attributes to them. In one view, not all comparable phenomena are commensurable.

relates to other traditions.[65] These four concerns provide the framework of analysis for Glenn's magisterial account of seven major legal traditions.[66]

In a deservedly well known article, Martin Krygier emphasised three themes which find echoes in Glenn: first, that tradition is central to understanding the nature and behaviour of law and, far from being peripheral, it is central to most legal systems; second, Krygier rejects the post-Enlightnment tendency to treat tradition and change as antimonies; and third, 'important traditions are a combination of inheritance and (often creative) reception and transmission'.[67] A broad concept of tradition is crucial to understanding law because it captures elements that tend to be missed by legal theorists who analyse law in abstract terms (such as command, norms, rules and principles) or social theorists who analyse it in terms of roles, interests, power, systems and so on. What they miss is 'pastness': 'tradition draws attention to the authoritative presence of the past, which is so pervasive in almost all legal systems'.[68]

Glenn accepts all this, but he goes further on several points: First, he emphasises that tradition involves the communication of information rather than the handing down of practices and institutions. Second, tradition is not a matter of passive acceptance. Rather, even when there is little or no resistance, there is a process of 'massaging', involving selection, refinement and the filtering out of 'noise'.[69] Third, Glenn emphasises that in the long-term adherence to a tradition depends more on persuasion than domination or repression. 'The great and powerful traditions are those which offer great and powerful, even eternal and ultimately true, reasons for adherence.'[70] Fourth, as we have seen, unlike Krygier, he is resistant to ideas of culture and system, insofar as they suggest enclosed, self-contained units.

Glenn's picture of a tradition is of a continuous, constantly changing flow of ideas over time that contains a relatively stable core, but no precise boundaries. His general vision is captured quite well in the following passage:

> Traditions and hence communities, thus come to be defined by the totality of the flow of information in the world, including its quality and meaning. In the past the flow of information from tradition to tradition was largely that of formal learning (*translatio studii*), since contact between traditions was less frequent. Evolutionary (autonomous) or multi-independent theories of social development thus enjoyed considerable support. Today such theories have become increasingly hard to defend, at least in contemporary contexts, since it has become

---

[65] Glenn (2004) Preface at p. xxvi.

[66] Although Glenn is reluctant to draw on abstract theory, there is a distinguished tradition of theorising about tradition by Carl Friedrich (1972), Edward Shils (1981), Harold Berman (1983), and Martin Krygier (1986), (1988). See now Goldman (2007). See also the more sceptical approach of Hobsbawm and Ranger (eds.) (1983).

[67] Krygier (1986).   [68] Ibid.   [69] Ibid., pp. 16–18.

[70] Glenn (2004) at p. 41. This theme is developed in his important article on 'Persuasive Authority' Glenn (1987). On the controversial thesis that no receptions are imposed see Chapter 9 below.

increasingly hard to identify any tradition which maintains itself through exclusively internal reflection and debate. All of the legal traditions discussed here, which cover the greater part (if not the totality) of the world's population, are in constant contact with one or more of the other legal traditions. There is thus the possibility of transmission and exchange of all forms of tradition, and of all or most of their content. Formal learning is now accompanied by other forms of diffusion.[71]

Whether or not Glenn has constructed a full-blown general theory of traditions, he has produced a rich set of ideas on which to base a bold account of legal traditions.[72] *Legal Traditions of the World* adopts and maintains a genuinely global perspective; by treating 'tradition' as the core concept it puts history at the centre of comparative law. It presents a sustained argument based on an explicit theory. Glenn's thesis has implications for some issues of contemporary concern that have hardly featured in the orthodox texts on comparative law: economic and cultural globalisation; 'the clash of civilisations'; corruption; fundamentalism; diffusion and convergence; nationalism and identity politics; universalism, relativism and incommensurability; multivalent logic; and even chaos theory. He has largely succeeded in his main aim of constructing a broad framework for mutual comprehension and dialogue across major legal traditions.

In the present context three points bear directly on my central argument. First, as an organising concept, 'tradition' clearly serves Glenn's purposes better than 'civilisation', 'culture', 'legal system', and 'legal family'. In particular, it captures pastness, normative authority, and active involvement of the recipients ('massaging') that are central elements in his picture. 'Civilisation' is too general for Glenn's purposes, and 'culture' and 'legal system' are too specific. However, Glenn is perhaps too dismissive of these other concepts, some of which are useful at different levels of generality. For example, 'culture' is admittedly both vague and ambiguous and susceptible to reification. It needs to be given a precise meaning that has analytic value in a given context. But for some theorists, 'culture' captures some elements better than 'tradition' – for example, attitudes, expectations, institutions, habits and actual practices, which can be studied empirically.[73] It is useful where it is important to treat these elements and their interrelations together. Glenn's conception of tradition implies a quite sharp distinction between information (ideas in a broad sense) and actual

---

[71] Glenn (2004) at p. 41.

[72] Citing Popper, Glenn denies that he is advancing a general theory of tradition. He does this in order to distance himself from *à priori* theorising and concept construction that he attributes to Western rationalism. Instead, he claims he arrived at his central themes by immersing himself in each of several legal traditions and identifying shared concerns. However, Glenn cannot escape from using a coherent framework of analytic concepts – including information, communication, selection, normative, justification, history, corruption, and legal.

[73] See, for example, Bell (2001) Chapter 1. See also Nelken (ed.)(1997).

behaviour.[74] Tradition involves the transmission of information (i.e. ideas).[75] Although they overlap, ideas may not be implemented, practice may not be based on articulated ideas. By confining his focus to ideas, rather than to their application in practice, Glenn makes his enormous subject more manageable. His thesis is best interpreted as a contribution to the history of ideas rather than as a history of actual legal processes, institutions, and power relations – a much larger and more complex subject.

Second, Glenn has been criticised for refusing to indicate how he characterises specific traditions as 'legal'.[76] How, in his account are legal traditions differentiated from other kinds of tradition – for example, political, religious, moral, literary, or culinary? Glenn seems deliberately to beg such questions: he points out that such differentiations vary between traditions and, as in the case of our own distinctions between law, morality, politics, and religion can be regularly, perhaps essentially, contested within a tradition. He is also dismissive of attempts to construct a general definition of law.[77] I am generally sympathetic with such impatience, and prefer to use different conceptions of law in different contexts.[78] However, it could be argued that Glenn needs a definition in the context of his argument, for he treats legal traditions as the main unit of comparison. If law is conceptualised differently within traditions (or is the subject of endless debate) that tells us about 'law' as a folk concept; but in order to transcend and compare legal traditions, Glenn needs an analytic concept of the 'legal'.[79] Like it or not, Glenn is working within the Western intellectual tradition and his main background is in law.

Glenn's response to this argument is that he is trying to break out of the iron cage of Western rationalism and to interpret each tradition on its own terms and that his method is to look for patterns by immersing himself in different traditions without the aid of a comparator (or *tertium quid*),[80] in this case an abstract criterion of identification of 'legal traditions'. In Glenn's defence, it can

---

[74] 'A tradition is thus composed of information, and it would be inappropriate to see it', as mooted by J. G. A. Pocock, as 'an indefinite series of repetitions of an action'. This would be to confuse the results or impact of the tradition, its immediate manifestation with the tradition itself (at p. 13) (citing Pocock, (1968) at p. 212).

[75] John Bell (2006) is probably right in suggesting that this leads to a quite narrow conception of law, because it leaves out institutions, praxis, the law in action. However, I disagree that it commits Glenn to equating 'law' with legal rules or doctrine. The 'information' that is transmitted through tradition is much broader than that: it can include stories, concepts, beliefs, facts, symbols, values, political theories, heuristics and, if not actual institutions, at least ideas about institutional objectives, design and significance. Moreover, Glenn emphasises that what kinds of information are selected not only varies between traditions, but is also fundamental to the tradition itself.

[76] This issue was raised by several reviewers in the Symposium on *Legal Traditions of the World*, Foster (ed.) (2006). Glenn replied (2007a)

[77] See especially the discussion of 'Cthonic law' at p. 69.   [78] See p. 117 below.

[79] On 'folk concepts' see p. 41 above. For criticism of Tamanaha's 'labelling theory' as an attempt to use 'folk concepts' to provide the basis of a general (analytic) conception of law, see Twining, (2003a) at pp. 223–43.

[80] Glenn (2004) at pp. 47, 353–5. Cf. Glenn (2007a).

be said that his selection of the phenomena to be studied could be said to rely on convention: he is giving an account of, and comparing seven examples of what are widely recognised (by Western scholars) as major traditions. However, and third, this leads on to a further question that threatens to revive the sterile taxonomic debates about 'legal families': how can legal traditions be classified? Five of Glenn's seven categories are recognisable: three religious traditions – Talmudic, Islamic, and Hindu; and two familiar Western traditions (a common law and a civil law tradition). Unfortunately, two of his categories – 'Cthonic' and 'Asian' – are not conventional; rather they are quite novel.[81] Both have attracted sharp criticism.[82]

If these criticisms are justified, as I believe they are, then Glenn's list of traditions seems no more satisfactory than Zweigert and Kötz's list of families of legal systems. Nor are their lists very different.[83] Neither Zweigert and Kötz nor Glenn make their taxonomies bear much weight. Both admit that their categories are only rough indicators of large-scale phenomena that overlap and interact in complex ways.

Zweigert and Kötz and Glenn represent the main contemporary attempts in the tradition of comparative law to produce broad overviews of law in the world. At the very least, they illustrate some of the difficulties of producing simple taxonomies of large-scale legal phenomena. Neither makes a serious effort to maintain a clear distinction between legal and other phenomena. Their main contributions lie not in their schemes of classification, but what they say about their subject-matters. Zweigert and Kötz give a generally descriptive introduction to the salient styles of thought of the 'families' they deal with. Glenn is equally selective, but more intellectually ambitious in trying to identify and compare the salient characteristics of major legal traditions.

I shall follow Braudel in respect of civilisation, and Glenn in respect of tradition here, because this provides a convenient way of setting a context for constructing a picture of law in the world today. Braudel emphasises geography as well as history, Glenn emphasises the past and transmission of ideas across time. Both try to point to broad patterns, while being acutely aware of the diversity of human experience, the importance of particularity in giving an account of that experience, and the pitfalls of generalisation. However, the concept of 'culture' constructed by Kroeber and Kluckhohn, and developed

---

[81] The third edition of Zweigert and Kötz has separate chapters on Chinese law and Japanese Law, under the heading 'Law in the Far East'.

[82] E.g. Woodman, Huxley, and Palmer in Foster (ed.) (2006). See Glenn's reply (2007a).

[83] Both use common law, civil (or Romanist) law, Islamic law, and Hindu law as categories. Both treat Asia as problematic, both are explicitly selective. Glenn says almost nothing about Scandinavian law (see critique by Andersen in Foster (ed.) 2006 at pp. 140–1), nor about socialist, soviet, or Russian law (see the sharp critique by W E Butler in Foster (ed.) (2006) at pp. 142–6); Glenn has separate chapters devoted to Cthonic (customary) law and Talmudic Law. See Glenn (2007b).

by Bell, is also useful because it explicitly links both ideas and actual behaviour in a single concept and provides a link to the idea of social practices.

In Chapter 1, I discussed Ronald Dworkin's distinction between a 'doctrinal' and a 'sociological' concept of law.[84] While criticising his characterisation and downgrading of 'the sociological concept', I accepted the basic distinction and indicated that, in my view, both perspectives – and many others – are needed in general jurisprudence. The distinction between tradition and culture suggested here, roughly reflects that distinction. Dworkin's doctrinal concept and Glenn's idea of tradition are confined to ideas and are normative;[85] Kluckhohn's conception of culture combines ideas and practices, ideas about how people ought to behave and how they actually behave. Friedman emphasises that culture consists of 'ideas, values, expectations and attitudes towards law and legal institutions' that are measurable and can be studied directly (what people think) and indirectly through how they behave (practices).[86]

In my view, 'culture' is too volatile a term for present purposes.[87] Here, the key concept is social practice, which similarly combines actual behaviour and the ideas behind that behaviour (the internal point of view). There is a difference between an account of the Islamic legal tradition(s) in terms of doctrine (the interpretations of jurists – and individual believers – about what the Holy Qu'ran and other sources prescribe), and how Islamic law has been institutionalised as a form of social practice, involving both ideas and actual behaviour by real people at particular times and places. It is part of my thesis that in order to understand law we need to view it both doctrinally and empirically and that conceiving of it as a form of institutionalised social practice combines both elements.

Chapter 4 explores three attempts to construct a general conception of law as a species of institutionalised social practice. The problem of constructing criteria of identification of law that clearly differentiate the legal from the non-legal has attracted some of the best minds in jurisprudence. We shall consider Hart's account of the concept of a municipal legal system, and Tamanaha's bold attempt to broaden a positivist conception of law to include significant forms of non-state law, while staying true to Hart's basic premises

---

[84] Above pp. 27–30.

[85] Glenn is very emphatic about the normativity of tradition (Glenn, 2007b at pp. 72–4). Of course, accounts of legal doctrine can be accurate or inaccurate, true or false. For example, it is true to say that Islam is a monotheistic religion and false to say that the English law allows polygamy. But the ideas of a tradition are primarily prescriptive. Dworkin's point is that for participants in a legal order interpretation of its doctrine is essentially normative and argumentative.

[86] Friedman (1994) at p. 119. See Friedman (1997) at pp. 33–9. See above n. 52.

[87] Culture can be useful as a broad umbrella concept, referring to ideas, values, expectations, and attitudes. To these some theorists add actual behaviour. Podgorecki and his followers focused on knowledge and opinion about law. (Podgorecki (1973)). All of these can be studied empirically, but different authors focus on different aspects. However, 'culture' is too vague to be of much use as an analytical concept, unless it is operationalised with precision in a particular context. For a contrary view see Friedman (1997) and Nelken (2007).

and differentiating legal from other phenomena. Next we consider the significance of Llewellyn's law-jobs theory, which he claimed could be applied to the social ordering of any human group. Finally, I shall develop one way of constructing a conception of law that can serve as a flexible organising concept and as the basis for a framework of analytical concepts that can be useful for giving an account of legal phenomena from a global perspective. This framework draws on Hart, Tamanaha, and Llewellyn, modifies, refines, and supplements some of their concepts, and indicates links to other significant bodies of literature in both jurisprudence and the social science.

Chapter 4

Constructing conceptions of law: Beyond Hart, Tamanaha and Llewellyn

4.1 Tamanaha on Hart

(a) *The Concept of Law*

Hart's *The Concept of Law* is the standard starting-point for considering conceptions of law. According to Tamanaha:

> 'Hart's core analysis has survived relatively unscathed following forty years of critique. With the notable exception of Ronald Dworkin's engagement, much of the discussion today consists of refinements and modifications of Hart's theory, rather than outright repudiations.[1]

Hart's project was to advance and defend a general descriptive theory of law.[2] Hart employed methods of conceptual elucidation that were derived from Bentham and modern analytical philosophy. These methods are still widely, but not universally, accepted today and they form the basis for the approach adopted in this chapter. Although he used some of the tools of analytical philosophy developed in the heyday of J.L. Austin, I do not accept that it is merely 'a semantic theory' or an exercise in 'linguistic analysis'.[3] It both elucidates basic concepts and uses them to describe common features of the form and structure of all state legal systems. It is presented and has been largely interpreted as a general analytical theory of law – a set of answers to some basic puzzlements about the nature of law in general. It makes few claims for being useful in guiding detailed research or in assisting judges or lawyers in dealing with practical problems and it has not been used much for such purposes.

For the purpose of this chapter I have accepted as a starting point two basic tenets of positivism: the separation thesis and the social sources thesis.[4] Hart can take much of the credit for clarifying these theses in their modern form.

---

[1] Tamanaha (2001) at p. 132. This section is a substantially shortened version of Twining (2003a). Some passages are reproduced here by kind permission of the Editors of the *Law and Society Review* and Blackwell Publishing Ltd.

[2] On Hart's claim to be contributing to descriptive sociology see Chapter 2.4(b) above (the olive branch thesis).

[3] On the debate about the 'semantic sting' see Hart, (1994) *Postscript* at pp. 244–8 and Raz (1998), Dworkin (2006b) Chapter 8.

[4] See pp. 25–7 above.

I also accept that elucidation of concepts is an important part of understanding law and that his methods of conceptual analysis were appropriate for his purposes.[5] However, I shall not follow him in treating state law as the core or paradigm case of law even though this assumption is quite common in academic and ordinary English usage. For this tends to restrict attention to forms of normative ordering that are closely analogous to state law.[6]

The bare bones of Hart's model or conception of law can be summarised as follows:

It is true to say that a law exists under the following conditions:

1. This law satisfies the criteria of validity of the legal system of which it is a part.
2. This legal system is formed of a combination of primary and secondary rules;
3. These rules derive their validity from a basic rule of recognition;[7]
4. The rule of recognition is as a matter of social fact accepted as such by the officials of the system; and
5. The legal system is effective in the society to which it belongs.

Each of the elements in this model has been subjected to intensive scrutiny and analysis. Hart treated all municipal legal systems (sovereign state and subordinate state) as fitting this model. He interpreted classical public international law as sufficiently analogous to be included, but in one of the weakest sections of the book he treated so-called 'primitive' legal orders as pre-legal.[8] With the exception of public international law as it was conceived in 1960,[9] this model is confined to state or municipal law.

(b) Brian Tamanaha

Can Hart's model be modified to accommodate a broader range of phenomena, including at least important manifestations of non-state law, without becoming so broad as to include almost all social institutions and practices? This question is addressed by Brian Tamanaha in his important book *A General Jurisprudence*

---

[5] See Chapter 2.4(a) above.
[6] The classic attack on 'state centralism' is Griffiths (1983).
[7] It is important to distinguish here between *criteria of validity of laws* (particular to a given legal system) and *criteria of identification of law(s)*, which are part of a general concept of law. (Wollheim (1954)).
[8] *CL*, pp. 91–9. For criticisms see A. Allott (1980) Chapter 2.
[9] Public international law has changed and developed in the past half-century. Like his near-contemporary John Rawls, Hart relied on a picture of the field that is now considered to be out-dated. For recent surveys of conceptions of and developments in International Law see M. Evans (2006) and P. Allott (2002). On Rawls see *GLT*, pp. 69–75, Allan Buchanan, 'Rawls's Law of Peoples: Rules for a Vanished Westphalian World', *Ethics*, 110, (July 2000).

of Law and Society.[10] This is one of the first efforts to develop a post-Westphalian theory of law.

Brian Tamanaha, Professor of Law at St John's University, New York, was raised in Hawaii and educated in the United States. Early in his career he served as assistant Attorney General of Yap in Micronesia. This experience made a profound impression on him:

> Law in Micronesia was remarkably unlike what I learned law was, and should be, in the course of my [American] legal training…. Micronesian law was trans-planted in its entirety from the United States; even the majority of the legal actors, like myself, were American expatriates. Their customs and values could hardly have been more different from the legal system and its norms. To cite a few examples, from Yap in particular: they had a thriving caste system, yet the law prohibited discrimination; their culture was consensual in orientation, but the law was based upon the adversary model; their understanding of criminal offences required a response by the community itself (literally), but the state insisted that it has a monopoly on the application of force, and any direct community reaction is illegal vigilantism; property ownership was a complex mixture of possession rights, use rights, consultation over use and possession, and community ownership simultaneous with chief ownership, whereas the property and mortgage laws were based upon common law notions of fee simple, life estate, and remainders; their political system was democratic, but for most elections candidates stood unopposed because the approval of traditional leaders was *de facto* required of anyone who wished to win; the law was written in English legal language, while many people had a rudimentary command of English, and others could not speak it at all (never mind the more complex and inaccessible legal language); court decisions were filled with legal arguments based upon U.S. common law and constitutional analysis which simply had no parallel or groun-ding in Micronesian society; many people were ignorant of the law, and feared or avoided it; state law was a marginal force in the maintenance of social order. The law in Micronesia was like an alien presence in their midst, mostly irrelevant, taking care of tasks related primarily to the operation of the government, occa-sionally intruding on their lives in various unwelcome ways.[11]

Tamanaha's second book, *Realistic Socio-legal Theory: Pragmatism and a Social Theory of Law* (1997) set out to provide a basis in philosophy and social theory for a 'thoroughly social, non-essentialist, behaviour-based view of law'.[12]

---

[10] Brian Tamanaha, *A General Jurisprudence of Law and Society* (2001) (hereafter *GJLS*). This was preceded by *Understanding Law in Micronesia: An Interpretive Approach to Transplanted Law* (1993) (hereafter *ULM*) and *Realistic Socio-Legal Theory: Pragmatism and A Social Theory of Law* (1997) (hereafter *RSLT*).

[11] *GJLS*, pp. xi–xii

[12] *RSLT*, p. 245. The main use of 'isms' in jurisprudence is to caricature the views of those whom one seeks to criticise. However, Tamanaha goes in for self-labelling, characterising himself as a legal positivist (following Hart), a pragmatist (Dewey rather than Rorty) an interactionist (Mead, Goffman, and Geertz), an interpretivist (Weber, Mead, Schutz) and a conventionalist (again following Hart). These labels at least give a general indication of where the author is coming from and signal likely points of departure for those with different views or perspectives. (On isms see Chapter 16 on the web.)

This provided a very solid basis of analytical concepts for his third book, *A General Jurisprudence of Law and Society* (2001) in which his aim was to revive the idea of general jurisprudence. For him this means constructing a single framework for a universal jurisprudence as a basis for a theoretical understanding of law anywhere.[13] In particular, he wishes that framework to embrace the realities of law in transitional and developing countries and at transnational levels as well as in post-imperial countries that are sometimes referred to patronisingly as 'advanced', 'parent', 'civilised' or 'mature'. His experience in Yap, a colonial situation which he soon learned was 'not that unusual',[14] led Tamanaha to develop a powerful critique of some commonly held views. He argues that standard Western legal theories fail to capture this kind of situation not only in colonial and post-colonial states, but also in major Western cities and in industrialised societies. The people of Yap clearly considered their own traditional mores, processes and institutions to be 'law'.

For Tamanaha, the challenge for legal theory is to accommodate all of these complexities and variety within a single framework:

> Without one, there is no hope of understanding law in situations like those in Micronesia, together with those in the West, as well as everywhere in-between, and no hope of comparing these situations in ways that will be fruitful for all.[15]

Here I shall concentrate on only one aspect of these two important books – the attempt to construct a 'core concept of law'[16] as a basic building block for his version of General Jurisprudence. For this purpose Tamanaha adopts a two-stage strategy. First, he criticises some views and assumptions that he claims have been central themes in much of Western legal thought. Second, he applies Occam's Razor to Hart's conception of law, ending up with a radically slimmer version that encompasses a much wider range of phenomena.

The first stage involves a very extended critique of two related visions of the relationship between law and society: (a) 'mirror theories', which in various ways claim that law mirrors or reflects society; and (b) 'the social order thesis', which claims that law maintains or contributes to social order. The two sets of ideas are related and can be combined in the single succinct sentence: 'Law is a

---

[13] My current enterprise is also labeled 'general jurisprudence', but this seems to be largely coincidental. In particular, I have a broader conception of the functions of theorising about law. We also attach different meanings to the term: by 'general' Tamanaha means 'universal', whereas my concern is with the extent to which it is feasible and desirable to generalise about legal phenomena across two or more legal traditions or cultures. (See Chapter 1 above.) In short, Tamanaha's bias is universalistic (with a tendency to science), my starting-point is particularistic, with a bias towards 'softer' humanistic disciplines. Despite these differences our enterprises and ideas are converging.

[14] *GJLS*, p. xii.   [15] *GJLS*, P p. xii.

[16] I shall follow Hart and Tamanaha in using the word 'concept' rather than 'conception' to characterise their focus, but the latter is more apt. Tamanaha acknowledges that his is only one of many possible ways of conceptualising law and the title of his book (*a general jurisprudence of law and society*) indicates some explicit limitations. On whether the title of Hart's book was a misnomer see Twining (2006a) at pp. 125–6.

mirror of society which functions to maintain social order.'[17] Tamanaha sets out to show how pervasive both of these views have been in Western legal, social and political thought, sometimes as explicit theories, but more often as undeveloped, but influential, assumptions. He then argues that most versions of these views conflate criteria of identification of law (what law is) with its functions (what law does) and that they have been at the root of two great myths – the progressive evolution myth and the social contract myth – which are both used ideologically to legitimate law. According to Tamanaha they are based on wishful thinking rather than on evidence.

It is not Tamanaha's aim to show that the mirror thesis and the social order thesis are both empirically false. Indeed, he acknowledges that law sometimes reflects social conditions (but often it does not) and law may sometimes contribute to social order (but often it is ineffective, or marginal in this respect, and sometimes it may promote conflict). Rather the point is that these ideas oversimplify,[18] over-generalise,[19] and conflate criteria of identification with actual effects or functions.[20] Rather than make any such assumptions about relations between law and a given society and about the functions of law, socio-legal scholars should make such matters the subject of systematic empirical enquiry. But this requires adequate conceptual tools for description; it is the job of general jurisprudence to provide such tools.[21]

We need not here concern ourselves with the extent to which either the mirror thesis or the social order thesis in fact represent the views of those to whom Tamanaha attributes them, nor with issues about their validity or truth, nor the claim that they have been widely used to legitimate unsavoury regimes. Tamanaha's objective in attacking mirror theories and the social order thesis is to remove any empirical and functionalist assumptions from his core conception of law and thereby to separate conceptual questions about criteria of identification from empirical questions about how law functions in fact and its relationship to any particular social context or arena. For example, he converts the mirror and social order theses, which he attacks as being empirically dubious, into open-ended questions which he acknowledges as 'core initial inquiries for general jurisprudence':

---

[17] *GJLS*, pp. 1, 36.

[18] For example law's functions can be quite diverse and vary from context to context (e.g. *GJLS*, p. 179. cf. *RST*, p. 109).

[19] For examples see p. 113 below.

[20] In this context Tamanaha uses 'function' to refer to contributions [to society] or effects rather than to purpose, motive or point. (See Section 3(a) below.)

[21] Tamanaha's argument is too long and complex to consider in detail here. His critique of the two theses is cogent, but there is room for disagreement about his claims that many leading theorists have held strong versions of one or other of these views. In particular, he does not pay much regard to the variety of different concerns underlying 'mirror theories'. Some may also think that he accepts Alan Watson's 'transplants thesis' too uncritically and so does not allow sufficiently for the interaction of imported law and local conditions over long periods of time. These points are considered in detail in Twining (2003a).

To what extent is (state, customary, international, religious, natural, indigenous etc.) law a mirror of prevailing customs and morals? (2) to what extent does (state, customary, international, religious, natural, indigenous etc.) law contribute to the maintenance of social order?[22]

The second stage of Tamanaha's argument takes Hart's *The Concept of Law* as its starting point. He accepts Hart's positivism, his rooting of law in social practice, and his methods of conceptual analysis, but subjects the rest to a sustained critique. If Hart's theory is interpreted as being confined to modern state law (and by analogy public international law) this is too narrow for a 'globalised' general jurisprudence that covers both non-Western and Western law, different levels of transnational relations,[23] and various manifestations of 'non-state law'.[24] The objective is to construct a much more inclusive conception of law that is nevertheless distinguishable from other phenomena.

In constructing his 'core concept of law' Tamanaha's method is to pare away as far as possible all empirical, functionalist, and normative assumptions from his basic concept of law and related concepts. Thus he converts the 'social order' and 'mirror' theses from empirical assumptions into open-ended questions, using the same concepts: To what extent does law mirror society in this context? For some concepts he goes so far as to empty them of any general content. Thus having decided that the concept of 'society' no longer has any analytical value, he substitutes 'social arena' as an 'orienting concept' delimiting the field of study, but leaves its boundaries to be defined '*in any way desired*, as determined by the purposes of study'.[25] This use of 'empty' concepts involves deferring the precise definition of some concepts to much more specific contexts. Strangely, as we shall see, he does not use this technique with his 'core concept of law'. One may cavil about some particular examples (How does one know if law is mirroring society in a given context?), but the strategy of constructing his basic conceptual framework out of deliberately 'thin' concepts is one that I shall follow.

Tamanaha's method is to cut away large parts of Hart's model of law, while retaining 'the core' which, ironically, provides the basis for a non-essentialist conception of law. This ruthless pruning of Hart can be restated as follows:

---

[22] At p. 231 (original italics).   [23] *GLT*, pp. 139–40.

[24] Why include 'non-state law'? A short answer is that a picture of law in the world which excludes, for example, Islamic law, European Community law, human rights law, and all non-state custom would be radically impoverished; but to try to subsume these and other examples under the Westphalian duo of municipal law and public international law would involve both distortion and extension. Of course, municipal law remains the most important concern of most practicing lawyers in the West, although that is changing quite rapidly. See further Chapter 12 below and *GLT*, Chapter 6 and *GJLS*, pp. 224–30.

[25] *GJLS* at p. 207.

(1) Tamanaha accepts the 'social sources thesis' of Hart and Raz,[26] but extends it beyond state law 'to all manifestations and kinds of law'.[27] In other words, the source of law is the acceptance of social practices as law by those subject to them.

(2) Like Hart, Tamanaha rejects any necessary conceptual link between law and morality, but he also rejects any such link between law and any social functions, such as social control, social order, or dispute processing.[28] He boldly extends the separation thesis to read:

> There is no necessary connection between law of whatever manifestation or kind and morality *or functionality*.[29]

(3) Since the link between law and function has been severed, so has any requirement of effectiveness in performing any function.[30]

(4) Tamanaha retains as illuminating the idea of the union of primary and secondary rules, but confines it to state law and drops it as a necessary element in his core concept of law.[31]

(5) Tamanaha rejects as essential or necessary any link between law and state, any idea of institutionalised norm enforcement,[32] or claims to comprehensiveness, to supremacy or to monopoly of power within a particular geographical territory or to exclusivity or openness.[33]

---

[26] *Ibid.* at pp. 159–61.   [27] *Ibid.* at p. 159.

[28] In the Postscript Hart appeared to deny that he was a 'functionalist' (*CL*, pp. 248–9). But Tamanaha points out that the condition of efficacy implies that it has to be an effective mechanism of social control and is therefore functionalist. He also treats functionalism as being in conflict with conventionalism. He follows Marmor (1998) in seeing a profound tension between Hart's conventionalism and his (alleged) functionalism (pp. 148–9, 189). Galligan disagrees '[A]lthough Hart has much to say about law's functions it is not central to his analysis'. Galligan (2007) at p. 17, see further pp. 198–204.

[29] Tamanaha (2001) p. 157 (original italics).   [30] *Ibid.*, at pp. 143–8.

[31] Tamanaha points out that since a union of primary and secondary rules can be found in the internal governance of some institutions, such as corporations and universities, this can hardly be a distinguishing characteristic of 'law' (p. 138).

[32] Tamanaha (2004) at pp. 138–40.

[33] In paring away these 'essentialist' elements Tamanaha criticises Raz (especially the views expressed in Raz (1979)) and Kelsen (1945) at some length (pp. 138–48). Most of these elements are connected to the idea of state law, but some religions claim to be comprehensive and supreme. Galligan identifies seven specific features of modern state law: (a) the dominance of enacted law; (b) 'specialized organizations and institutions of officials with authority to make, apply, and enforce the law'; (c) coercion – but in many contexts regulatory compliance is more significant than coercion (*ibid.*, Chapter 17); (d) claims to final authority; (e) regulation; (f) standards constraining officials in their relations with citizens; (g) a distinctive normative structure based on rule of law ideas and a distinctive role for government institutions. Galligan allows for conceptions of 'non state law', but argues that these features distinguish modern state legal orders from other forms of law (descriptive) and provide a basis 'for ideas and values that ought to win support and protection' (normative). (Galligan (2007) at pp. 20–2) This useful characterisation does not challenge ideas about the significance of non-state law and the continuities between 'official' and 'unofficial' law. See further Chapter 12 below.

(6) Tamanaha drops the ideas of normativity, of institution, and of 'system' as necessary features of the core concept of law.[34]

(7) Tamanaha extends the rule of recognition beyond officials to include all social actors. But he retains 'the internal point of view' as crucial.[35]

On Tamanaha's interpretation, Hart is an 'Essentialist' in that he specifies necessary conditions for the application of his conception of law, and a 'Functionalist' in that he assumes that law is effective and hence performs certain functions of ordering. Hart is also a 'Conventionalist' in two senses: first, he roots the rule of recognition in social practice, so the source of law is social convention; and, second, he uses conformity to ordinary linguistic usage as the main justification for treating municipal state law as the central or paradigm case of law; this provides a relatively clear criterion of identification of the core, if not the penumbra, of the concept.

On the basis of this interpretation, Tamanaha ruthlessly lops off all 'Essentialist' and 'Functionalist' elements, while retaining both aspects of Hart's 'Conventionalism'. Out go, as criteria of identification, the ideas of legal system, social control, social order, efficacy, the union of primary and secondary rules, sanction, rule of recognition, acceptance by officials, and even institution and rules. These may be contingent features of particular instances of law, but they are not essential elements of Tamanaha's core concept. 'Social arena', a broader and more flexible term, is substituted for 'society'.[36] The classic 'separation thesis' is extended to include functionality as well as morality. All that is left is a legal positivist premise, the idea of a social practice, and how people in a given social arena use the term 'law' (or its equivalent in another language). The result is the following formulation:

> Law is whatever people identify and treat through their social practices as 'law' (or droit, recht, etc.).[37]

In short, law is whatever social practices people label as 'law'. Thus, law can be said to exist even if it has no functions, is ineffective, has no institutions or enforcement, involves no union of primary and secondary rules, and even if there is no normative element. This thin set of criteria of identification enables Tamanaha to include within a single conception of law, state law, customary law, religious law, international law, transnational law, and even natural law (secular as well as religious).[38] 'All of these manifestations and kinds of law are social products. The existence of each is a matter of social fact.'[39]

---

[34] On system, see Chapter 15.4 on the web.

[35] For a good discussion of acceptance by officials see Galligan (2007) pp. 128–30.

[36] *GJLS*, pp. 206–8.   [37] GJLS, pp. 166, 194 (original italics).

[38] '*Natural Law*. Of all of the kinds of law set out herein, this is the most inchoate and diverse in its specific manifestations. Unlike the others (except indigenous law), it often has no institutional presence, though it may be supported and perpetuated by institutions (like academic philosophy departments and Church-taught Sunday school). In social arenas, natural law is believed and acted upon, and thus has a measurable influence, a social presence.' (*GJLS*, p. 230). See further Twining (2003a) at pp. 221–23.

[39] *GJLS*, p. 159.

Tamanaha summarises the relationship of his theory to Hart's as follows:

Socio-legal positivism remains true to Hart's conventionalism and his focus on social practices, but to a greater extent even than Hart did, because it discards the essentialist and functionalist aspects of his approach, which often came into conflict with his conventionalism. To Hart's account, it adds the conventional identification of legal actors qua actors. It retains Hart's abstraction of primary and secondary rules at the (most reductive) core of state legal systems. However, it eliminates from Hart's account the requirement that the primary rules must be generally obeyed by the populace, and it eliminates the requirement that the legal officials accept the secondary rules. It makes no presuppositions about the functional effects that law might have, if any. It makes no presuppositions about the normative aspects, if any, that law might possess. It re-characterizes Hart's account to be an abstraction of state law, not a concept of law as such. State law is one among several types or kinds of law, and a multitude of specific manifestations of law. Other kinds of law, each of which can be conceptualized in more abstract terms based on their focal meanings, need not necessarily involve institutions and they need not necessarily qualify as 'systems'.[40] Finally, the elements discovered in the course of this abstraction are simply features – features that can change, features of which there may be variations within a given kind of law – not essential elements. This bare – some might say impoverished – view of legal phenomena is well suited to achieving the positivist goal of constructing a general jurisprudence.[41]

At first sight Tamanaha's thinning of Hart may seem quite radical, but this is misleading.[42] By excising all essentialist elements from his core concept of law, Tamanaha has not expelled these concepts from empirical legal studies. He does not suggest that concepts such as institution, dispute, sanction, social order, authority, or rule system are unimportant or useless. They are not deleted from the vocabulary of socio-legal theory. Indeed, each of them may be characteristic elements of many examples of legal phenomena. Tamanaha undertakes functional analysis (while trying to avoid the pitfalls of traditional Functionalism);[43] and he uses all of these concepts when discussing particular

---

[40] On 'focal meaning' see n. 100 below.   [41] *GJLS*, p. 155.

[42] This bold, seemingly radical, adaptation of Hart is calculated to draw sharp reactions from both Hart's followers and his critics. Some of the interpretations of Hart are controversial; Tamanaha's robust positivism will not satisfy anti-positivists; some socio-legal scholars may contest his account of 'mirror theories' and his espousal of a version of Watson's 'transplants thesis'; and some may just ignore his work as too radical or too threatening to warrant a response. These are important issues, but most of them are beyond the scope of this chapter. For more detail see Twining (2003a).

[43] Tamanaha distinguishes between Functionalism (exemplified by Durkheim, Malinowski, and Luhmann) and functionalism (with a small f). The former position, Functionalism, postulates that law is characterised by 'the necessary functions that law satisfies as an integral element within society'. (*GJLS*, pp. 35, 187; see also *RSLT*, pp. 105–7). 'The second version of functionalism (with a small f) … says that law is what law does and what it does is maintain order.' Malinowski was a Functionalist, Ehrlich was not (p. 187). Tamanaha's critique applies to both groups (i.e. anyone who maintains a necessary conceptual connection between law and social order or who makes strong general claims about law's actual effects). However, he leaves the door open for functional analysis and allows for the fact that manifestations of law often can and do satisfy certain kinds of functions (here meaning effects, see below), but that is a matter for empirical enquiry.

manifestations of law. For example, he argues that the idea of a 'union of primary and secondary rules' is useful in elucidating the form and structure not only of state legal systems, but also the governance of some organisations, such as universities, sports leagues or corporations, even if they do not attract the label 'law'.[44] He is even willing to accept 'dispute processing', 'institution-alized norm enforcement' and 'normative orders' or 'rule systems' as useful categorisations for orienting or limiting or focusing particular lines of enquiry, provided that they are kept conceptually distinct from his more abstract core conception of law.[45] In short, what Tamanaha has done is to remove a signifi-cant number of features that are often incorporated into the concept of law and to treat these as contingent, possibly salient or characteristic features of some, many, most or even nearly all types of legal practices without treating them as necessary or defining elements.

In my view, Tamanaha's arguments for thinning down Hart's model in this context are valid, but his pruning goes too far in two specific respects relating to the concept of social practice. A third difference is that I do not think that his 'labelling test' can be made to work.[46] The next sections revise Tamanaha's concepts of order and ordering and reinterpret the concept of social practice so that it includes at least minimal elements of normativity and institutionalisa-tion. Later, I reintroduce an element of 'thin functionalism' to remedy the defects of his labelling test. These modifications will also serve to narrow the gap between Tamanaha and mainstream positivist theories such as Hart's.

(c) Excursus: Control, order, and ordering

Tamanaha's second target is the proposition that 'law functions to maintain social order'. 'Function' in this context refers to effects, consequences, or contribution to society rather than purpose or point.[47] At this stage, it is useful to clarify what is meant in this context by the ideas of social control, social order, and ordering (or patterning) of relations.

In ordinary usage 'order', 'ordering', 'orderly' have many different meanings; some of the differences are quite nuanced. According to Wrong 'The "problem of order" has come to be widely recognized as a major, often the major, perennial issue of social theory.'[48] In this context it is useful to distinguish between three main usages which differ from each other mainly in respect of scope: (i) social control; (ii) social order; and (iii) ordering of relations between legal persons or units (legal subjects).[49]

---

[44] E.g. pp. 178, 183–4.   [45] E.g. at pp. 185, 198, 204.
[46] See Twining (2003a) at pp. 223–31. Cf. Himma (2004).
[47] See n. 43 above; Chapter 4.3(d) below.   [48] Wrong (1994) 37 cited in *GJLS*, p. 208.
[49] 'Ordering' (i.e. patterning) is used here as a broad residual category to include constituting, facilitating, defining, legitimating and all other supposed 'functions' of law not covered by social control and social order.

Often, but not always, 'social control' carries associations of authoritarian/ dominant direction and supervision by the state or other authority. Although it may include some factors that have the effect of controlling behaviour without human agency, it is often difficult to sever the association of 'control' from ideas of purpose and agency.[50] For this reason the term often has a negative connotation, implying 'coercion, manipulation, labeling, and stigmatisation'.[51]

A great deal of literature on law has been directed against the quite common assumption, suggested by the phrase 'law and order', that the sole or main function of law is coercive social control by authority of deviant behaviour. This assumption treats criminal law as the paradigm case of law and punishment as the characteristic form of sanctioning. Today, within legal and social theory this narrow 'social control' model of law can be considered a soft target, for it is generally agreed that the prevention and punishment of deviance is only one of the typical concerns of state law.[52] Most jurists accept that in addition to contributing to group survival, co-ordination and flourishing, law's functions can be and often are constitutive, symbolic, regulatory, benefit conferring, facilitative, condemnatory, educative and so on.[53]

When Tamanaha attacks 'the social order function', he clearly intends something wider than, but inclusive of, social control.[54] However, in several places he asserts that law can have other functions besides 'social ordering' or 'contributing to social order'.[55] Tamanaha therefore seems to be making a distinction between 'social order' on the one hand and other functions, which include

---

[50] Cusson (2001) at p. 2730 citing (Gibbs (1989).

[51] Functionalists have often been criticised for assuming that maintaining order is always good; Tamanaha and Llewellyn explicitly distance themselves from any such assumption (*GJLS*, pp. 211–12; for a charitable reading of Llewellyn in this regard, see *GJB*, p. 192 n.50).

[52] Tamanaha criticises Donald Black (1976) (1989) for making the essentialist claim 'that law is governmental social control', thereby excluding other functions of law from his enquiries and eliminating the possibility that government has access to other forms of social control (*RST*, p. 127).

[53] For example, Hart speaks of 'the diverse ways in which the law is used to control, guide, and plan life out of court.' (*CL*, p. 39). In this and other passages Hart talks in terms of 'social control' (*ibid.*, pp. 165, 188, 208) but he probably intended in it in a broader sense than is suggested in the text. Tamanaha's formulation: *RST*, p. 109 'Law performs many functions besides social control, including, *inter alia*, enabling or facilitative, performative, status conferring, defining, legitimate, integrative, distributive, power conferring and symbolic; and there are many forms of social control besides law.' (*RST*, p. 109) See further, Summers (1971), *HTDTWR*, pp. 147–56.

[54] In *RST*, 109-11 Tamanaha differentiates between a narrow (conformity/deviance) conception of 'social control' and a broader (social order) sense of social control. In *GSLS* he mainly uses 'social order' in sense (ii) in the text, but draws a not entirely clear distinction between the social order and other functions of law.

[55] In a passage that needs clarification he gives examples of law that has 'little to do with general social order', including law as the formal structure underlying the market and transactions, constructing the infrastructure of government bureaucracy and law as a form of instrumental action by users and other agents which is different in operation from law as the enforcement of norms. 'Law as a means and form of government action is a different animal – in purpose use and function – from law governing everyday social life' (*GJLS*, p. 238) '[The social order] view of law blinds us from seeing the many other things that law (in all of its various kinds) does and is used to do' (p. 209).

providing infrastructure for market and governmental activity.[56] But most of his examples are concerned with contributing to and maintaining orderly relations. Some of these may contribute significantly to group life, but some may merely promote orderly relations between individuals and other subjects, including relations with and between outsiders and relations between groups in contexts in which these groups cannot be said to be part of a larger group or community.[57]

For our purposes it will be useful to adopt a broader interpretation of 'ordering' than Tamanaha's, while confining it to social relations and excluding primarily individual habits and practices.[58] If ordering means patterning rather than just controlling, it can include constituting relationships (e.g contracting, forms of commercial organisation, kinship systems), defining (e.g. marriage, status), regulating (e.g financial markets), constraining relationships (e.g. disputes, kinship taboos, conduct of wars) and so on. In this sense it is a broad residual category covering all supposed functions of law.

If a broad conception of law for purposes of study is concerned with the ordering of relations between subjects (human, legal, etc.) both within and between groups, this does not involve commitment to any of the following:

(a) *That law is the only institution that contributes to ordering.*
(b) *That ordering cannot occur without law.*
(c) *That law in fact always promotes ordering.*
(d) *That the only functions of law relate to dispute-processing or social control or order in a narrow sense.*[59]

(d) Social practices, rules, and institutions

Tamanaha's excision of rules from the criteria of identification of law is surprising, not least because it deliberately opens the way for the re-entry of the idea that law can be solely a matter of brute force – 'the gunman writ large', whom Hart had been concerned to expel.[60] Tamanaha accepts that rules will usually, perhaps nearly always, be an important element in most manifestations

---

[56] *GJLS*, pp. 236–40.
[57] On subjects ('persons') see Chapter 15.2 on the web; On the question 'are all laws the laws of a group?', see Chapter 15.4 on the web.
[58] Tamanaha treats Parsons's purely 'factual order' (i.e. 'regularity of conduct, patterns of behaviour, predictability' (p. 210)) as too wide, because many observable patterns of human behaviour (e.g. eating and sleeping) are not meaningful for social investigators. (*GJLS*, p. 211) On the other hand, the idea of 'normative order' is too narrow, because it excludes sources of order that are not normative (*ibid.*). Tamanaha settles for a bald statement that 'to say that a social arena is "ordered" is to assert that that arena reflects *a substantial co-ordination of behaviour.*' (*Ibid.*, italics in original).
[59] See further Twining (2003a) at pp. 217–18.
[60] *GJLS*, p. 66, *CL*, pp. 18–20. Hart was attacking the *equation* of law with the idea of a gunman; Tamanaha merely allows for the *possibility* that a gunman situation (i.e. a regime relying on brute force alone) could count as law. See further Twining (2003a) n. 21.

and kinds of law. However, he emphasises that there are many historical and contemporary examples of regimes and orders that have attracted the label 'law', yet are no more than social practices established or maintained by brute power, and obeyed out of fear or self-interest alone, without any voluntary consent or normative acceptance by those subject to them.[61] Tamanaha's concern is to eradicate any normative element and any conceptual link to legitimacy from his core concept. Questions of evaluation, justification and legitimation must be kept strictly separate from 'description'.

There is an apparent consistency in this ruthlessness. However, quite apart from those who consider the strict separation of law from morality to be misconceived, there is a question whether it is possible to hold the line quite so rigorously. Tamanaha treats law as a species of social practice. But can a social practice be said to exist without any normative element? At first sight Tamanaha's response seems to be negative:

> A social practice involves an activity that contains integrated aspects of both meaning and behaviour, linked together by a loosely shared body of (often internally heterogeneous) norms and patterns of action.[62]

However, in some other passages he rules out any necessary conceptual connection between the idea of social practice and normative ideas such as authority, validity, or approval. In my view, it is unnecessary to eliminate any suggestion of normativity from the criteria of identification of law, provided that it is clear that 'normative' in this context does not necessarily imply approval, but can include an acknowledgement of the existence as a matter of fact of a rule, convention, protocol or other prescription. Although it is hard in practice to differentiate between folkways and mores, habit and custom, it is useful to treat folkways and habits as external descriptions of observed behavioural patterns, whereas mores and customs involve an element of internal conception of the normative: 'we do this and it is right, proper, appropriate, prescribed, or conventional'. In ordinary usage the concept of 'social practice' may hover between the descriptive and the normative, but in legal theory the idea of norms or rules is so central and so much a part of intellectual tradition that it is useful to include normativity as a necessary element of the idea of social practice in this context.[63] It is also important to underline the point that normativity, like patterning, and efficacy are relative matters.[64]

---

[61] *GJLS*, pp. 65–71.

[62] *GJLS*, pp. 164. He goes on to cite passages from Alastair MacIntyre and Stanley Fish that overtly contain concepts – authority, standards, and appropriate – which in this context are clearly normative. (*Ibid.*). See p. 66 (discussion of the belief of some that power itself confers authority).

[63] On Tamanaha's treatment of normativity in relation to the concept of social practice see Twining (2003a) at pp. 233–7.

[64] See the discussion of degrees of law in Finnis (1980) at pp. 276–81; contrast Dixon (2001) at p. 77.

It is also useful to link the idea of institution with social practice. Tamanaha virtually equates 'institution' with 'organisation' and distinguishes between social practice and social institution. For him, chess is a social practice; a chess club is an institution. But a weaker usage of 'institutionalised' means established or settled. For a social practice to exist it needs to be relatively established – to be institutionalised in this sense.[65]

Thus one can build weak senses of both norm and institution into the concept of social practice. For instance, we can say that a social practice exists when a pattern of behaviour is established and that pattern has a broadly shared intersubjective meaning for the participants that includes some notion of obligation, rightness, appropriateness, prudence, or convention.[66] This move slightly narrows the scope of social practice and hence Tamanaha's conception of law, but not to the extent of excluding any of his main categories.[67]

These modifications still do not, on their own, provide criteria for differentiating 'legal' practices from other social practices. Like many legal pluralists and other proponents of the inclusion of non-state law, Tamanaha is anxious to differentiate 'law' from table manners, the rules of etiquette, and the rules of organisations such as hospitals and sports leagues.[68] However, by eliminating all 'essentialist' and 'fundamentalist' criteria of identification he is left with no analytical basis for differentiating legal from non-legal social practices and institutions. He is accordingly driven to rely on the vagaries of local usage, so that only those social practices that are labelled 'law' by those subject to them count as law. I have argued elsewhere that this labelling test cannot work for several reasons.[69] In brief, the idea that analytic concepts are part of the equipment of an external observer or scientist are useful precisely because they can get round problems arising from the absence of local conceptual equivalents, idiosyncratic or contested local usage, or difficulties of

---

[65] See Raz (1979) at pp. 115–16 (acknowledging that institutionalisation is a necessary, but not a sufficient condition for differentiating legal systems from other social phenomena, some of which may have primary institutions and structural features shared with municipal legal systems).

[66] *RSLT*, pp. 150–1, 157. See further MacCormick (2007) Chapter 1.

[67] Indeed, restricting the core concept of law to relatively established social practices sidelines conceptual chestnuts about momentary legal systems, one-person legal orders, post-coup regimes, and governments in exile that are best treated as borderline cases. Including institutionalisation and normativity as elements in the concept of social practice brings us closer to mainstream theories, without undermining the point that we need a conception of law that includes non-state law.

[68] On the distinction between the 'point' of an organisation , such as a school or hospital, and its internal governance, which in some contexts may qualify as non-state law see p. 374.

[69] Twining (2003a) pp. 223–31. For example, why do we talk of 'the Laws of cricket', but 'the rules of association football'? Using Tamanaha's test, cricket is subject to law, but football, and most other sports, are not. This may reflect the different class origins of the two sports, but it is hardly a satisfactory basis for an analytic concept of sporting rules.

translation.[70] In short, Tamanaha is trying to use folk concepts for analytic purposes in a way that may create confusion.

There are three possible ways of rescuing Tamanaha in this context. One alternative is to apply Wittgenstein's method of 'family resemblances' to the concept of law. Wittgenstein showed that in ordinary usage the idea of a game cannot be adequately analysed either in terms of core and penumbra or by stipulating a set of necessary and sufficient conditions for its use, or even in terms of a jointly sufficient set of conditions. But 'game' can be elucidated in terms of activities that have overlapping characteristics linking them in ways that members of a family may be linked.[71] This is a valuable technique that can be applied to law, which is an even more complex concept than game. Law conceived in such a fashion can serve as a flexible orienting concept, leaving open the possibility of drawing more precise boundaries for the purposes of a particular study. However, there is unlikely to be any consensus about which conditions to select as criteria of identification outside a specific context. It would re-introduce all the problems of selection of features as 'significant' that Tamanaha had rejected for not being 'essential', such as effectiveness, sanctions, and the union of primary and secondary rules. Analysis of law in this way can be illuminating, but the outcome would lack the simplicity and elegance that Tamanaha is seeking.

A second possibility is to suggest that Tamanaha has indeed successfully eliminated all plausible candidates to be general criteria of identification of law. In short, his argument is a *reductio ad absurdum* of the quest for such criteria. I am sympathetic to this view, because I believe that setting up appropriate differentiae is best left to specific contexts, when context and purpose can provide more specific and clearer criteria for drawing such boundaries.[72]

A third possibility is to revert to 'thin functionalism'.[73] For many people the idea of purpose, point, or function is an inherent part of their conception of law, but at first sight this may appear to be inconsistent with positivism or it may be vulnerable to some of the standard objections that are raised by critics of 'Functionalism'. However, in the next section I shall consider a third possibility in connection with Karl Llewellyn's law-jobs theory and the concept of institution. I call this 'thin functionalism' and argue that it has some merit in the

---

[70] Tamanaha is rather dismissive of problems of translation, p. 203, *GJLS*, See also pp. 168–70, discussed in Twining (2003a) at pp. 225–6. See also on translation, Tony Allott: 'There is a simple test to decide whether we are arguing about something fundamental in the nature of LAW or are discussing a fine point of English usage: translate the queried sentence into several foreign languages, preferably not near ones such as French or German, but remoter ones such as Chinese or Swahili: does the purported discrimination or argument still stand up? If it does not, it suggests that the argument is a linguistic one about English usage.' (A.N. Allott (1980) at pp. 4–5).

[71] Wittgenstein (1969) at p. 17; (1974) para. 66. *HTDTWR*, pp. 194–5, 396–9; See also Waldron (1994) at pp. 517–20, usefully discussing 'religion', which is here relevant to analysing the concept of 'religious law'.

[72] For a more detailed discussion see Twining (2003a) at pp. 223–5.   [73] See p. 103 below.

particular context of trying to construct a broad overview of law from a global perspective.

It does not follow that Tamanaha's efforts have been a waste of time, for he has provided a wealth of provocative arguments and ideas that challenge our existing stock of concepts and theories. Furthermore, he has, perhaps inadvertently, made a cogent case for abandoning the quest for a single, usable worldwide conception of law and for focusing attention on a whole group of concepts at a slightly lower level of abstraction, including functionalist ideas such as dispute processing, norm-enforcement and various kinds of regulation. In respect of the candidates that were eliminated as necessary conditions he has at least indicated some of the considerations that bear on their suitability as organising or working concepts at a lower level of abstraction for specific enquiries.

An additional reason for refusing to specify general criteria for differentiating law from other social practices is that we are dealing with phenomena that involve continuous variation along several axes: institutionalisation, normativity and effectiveness/efficacy are all matters of degree. 'Bright line' criteria tend to be artificially sharp and hence arbitrary in the grey areas. If one postpones such determinations until one has identified a clear context and purpose of an enquiry, that context and purpose can provide more specific criteria for less arbitrary inclusion and exclusion.

The last section of this chapter includes a formulation that will serve as a reasonably inclusive concept for the immediate purpose of constructing total pictures of law in the world and as the basis of a framework of useful concepts for such enterprises. This may work better than Tamanaha's test, but it is important to emphasise that this is not intended as a general definition or conception of law outside this specific context. I prefer to use different conceptions of law in different contexts.

4.2 Refining Llewellyn: the law-jobs theory

The purpose of this chapter is to suggest a way of constructing one or more general conceptions of law that may be useful for looking at legal phenomena from a global perspective. So far we have considered the strengths and limitations of historical and comparative law perspectives on legal traditions and legal cultures and of the general descriptive theories of Hart and Tamanaha for this purpose, building on some aspects and putting aside others. I have accepted Hart's positivist premises, his methods of conceptual elucidation, and his idea of a general descriptive theory of law; but I agree with Tamanaha's argument that a broad conception of law needs thinner criteria of identification and that several of Hart's important concepts – including rule of recognition, acceptance by officials, efficacy, and union of primary and secondary rules – need to be pared away as general criteria of identification, although they may be useful at lower levels of generality, for example in analysing state law.

While Tamanaha has done an important critical exercise in ground-clearing, his central thesis in *A General Jurisprudence of Law and Society* has three important limitations: first, his labelling test fails to provide a workable set of criteria for identification of law; second, although it makes some valuable connections with various strands in modern legal and social theory, his conceptual framework is too abstract to have much purchase or to give much guidance for empirical legal research; and, third, his strongly positivist socio-legal thesis restricts his contribution to only one aspect of a rounded general jurisprudence of the kind that is needed to underpin a healthy cosmopolitan discipline of law.

A broader and more comprehensive vision of general jurisprudence was outlined in Chapter 1. This chapter is concerned mainly with one aspect of analytical jurisprudence: whether we can usefully construct a general core conception of law. This section explores to what extent Karl Llewellyn's law-jobs theory, charitably interpreted, can be used to meet the first two deficiencies in Tamanaha's general jurisprudence. The final section argues that a synthesis of selected parts of the theories of Hart, Tamanaha, and Llewellyn can provide a useful foundation for this enterprise, but that they need to be further supplemented and refined.

I have written about Llewellyn's law-jobs theory at length elsewhere, especially in relation to his ideas about realism and to the American Realist Movement.[74] In the past I have mainly treated the theory as a useful heuristic for analysing the internal ordering of institutions and groups.[75] This section considers the theory as a contribution to the kind of general descriptive jurisprudence advanced by Hart and Tamanaha, comparing some key aspects of Tamanaha's and Llewellyn's conceptual schemes, with particular reference to the concepts of function and institution. The argument can be summarised as follows: like Tamanaha, Llewellyn's general picture of law is positivist, analytical rather than empirical, and compatible with a global perspective. Like Hart and Tamanaha, Llewellyn roots law in social practices and institutions. Unlike them, Llewellyn explicitly refused to construct a general conception of law that could be clearly differentiated from other social institutions and practices. He gave some interesting reasons for this refusal. However, the law-jobs theory can be interpreted as assuming some implicit, but vague, criteria of identification that are rooted in a defensible form of 'thin functionalism'. I shall argue that not

---

[74] See especially *Karl Llewellyn and the Realist Movement* (1973) (hereafter *KLRM*) and 'Karl Llewellyn's Unfinished Agenda: The Job of Juristic Method' (1993) (hereafter *JJM*) (reprinted in *GJB*). This section draws heavily on these two works.

[75] As a heuristic theory, it provides a useable framework and a set of questions that can be asked about the internal ordering of any group or institution. The central question is: how are the law jobs done in this group? Not does this group have law? Nor: to what extent are the law jobs done by 'law'? Allied to Llewellyn's version of 'the case method' or subsequent variants on it, it provides a route into constructing a detailed, down-to-earth account of how the law jobs are in fact tackled in a particular context.

only can Llewellyn's theory be defended against standard criticisms of Functionalism, including Tamanaha's,[76] but that it provides a more workable criterion of identification than Tamanaha's labelling test and it opens up a direct way into some kinds of specific empirical legal enquiry. In short, Llewellyn provides a remedy for two of the main deficiencies in Tamanaha's account. However, the law-jobs theory was developed over fifty years ago, it was conceptually a bit crude, and it did not deal with many of the issues addressed by Hart and Tamanaha. Accordingly, it needs to be refined, updated and synthesised with those aspects of their contributions that I have accepted.

The bare bones of the law-jobs theory can be restated as follows:[77] All of us are members of groups, such as a family, a club, a teenage gang, a sports team, a school, a commercial organisation, a trade union, a political party, a nation, a nation state, an international NGO, UN agency, the world community. In order to survive and to achieve its aims, in so far as it has aims, any human group has to meet certain needs or ensure that certain 'jobs' are done. These, for the purposes of study, can be broken down into five or six rough categories.[78]

First, is adjustment of the trouble case (dispute, grievance, offence).[79] When conflict or other trouble arises, it has to be resolved or, at least kept to a tolerably low level, otherwise the group will disintegrate or its collective objectives will be frustrated or impaired. The second, and perhaps the most important, job is the preventive channelling of conduct and expectations to avoid trouble. Third, as needs, conditions, and relations change, so the conduct and expectations of the group have to be re-channelled. Fourth, there is the job of 'Arranging for the Say and the Manner of its Saying' (i.e. the advance allocation of authority and development of authoritative procedures for decision). This job is proto-typically the primary function of a 'constitution' of a club, or organisation or a nation state. Where power and authority diverge there tends to be a gap between what actually happens and what is meant to happen. Giving a realistic account of a constitution as a kind of institution is accordingly problematic.[80]

---

[76] On the distinction between Functionalism and functionalism see n. 43 above.

[77] Adapted from JJM; for longer discussions see *KLRM*, pp. 15–84. Llewellyn's main accounts are in *The Cheyenne Way* (1941) (hereafter *CW*), 'The Normative, the Legal and the Law-Jobs' (1940) (hereafter *NLLJ*), 'Law and the Social Sciences, Especially Sociology' (1949) (hereafter *LSS*) reprinted in *Jurisprudence: Realism in Theory and Practice* (1962) Chapter 15 and *Law in Our Society* (unpublished, 1950 edn) (hereafter *LIS*).

[78] See Chapter 15.3 on the web.

[79] Llewellyn's choice of 'trouble' is a good example of his use of deliberately vague terms in some contexts to avoid definitional problems. 'Dispute' is a concept that has given rise to difficulty in legal anthropology and in discussions of 'alternative dispute resolution' because there is pressure to extend the term to include such diverse phenomena as welfare claims, criminal prosecutions, and clashes of interest of which one or more of the parties may not be aware. The broader 'trouble' avoids these difficulties and points to links with the idea of 'problem solving'. See further Twining (1983). In *The Cheyenne Way*, 'claim' is anterior to 'dispute': divergent urges or desires among members of a group give rise to claims that may result in disputes (*CW*, p. 274) 'Trouble' is more inclusive than any of these. See John Griffiths ((1983) (substituting claim for dispute as the focal concept), discussed in Twining (2006a) at pp. 249–52.

[80] Llewellyn (1934). See further, Twining (1993b); MacCormick (2007) Chapter 3.

Fifth, there is the job of 'providing Net Positive drive: Integration, Direction, Incentive for the whole'. Llewellyn, like Bentham, explicitly linked positive and negative sanctions (e.g. rewards as well as punishments) within his conception of law-government. Finally, in any group, but especially in complex groups, techniques, skills, devices, practices, procedures and traditions need to be developed, institutionalised, and adjusted if the first five needs or jobs are to be dealt with adequately or well. This is what Llewellyn called 'the job of juristic method'.[81]

The law-jobs theory was first developed to solve a research problem.[82] In the 1930s some social anthropologists maintained that the American 'Plains Indians', such as the Shoshones and the Cheyennes, had no law because they had no sovereign and no courts, and because they were perceived as being uncommunicative about their social norms either through reticence or inarticulateness or because they just did not think in terms of rules. Llewellyn's response was to point out that all human groups have conflicts and one way into studying indigenous law would be to enquire in detail how actual disputes were handled within a particular group. The law-jobs theory provided a working framework of enquiry and the case method provided the basic technique of investigation. Llewellyn was generally sceptical of 'Grand Theory' and resistant to constructing a general definition of law outside a particular context and purpose, but over time he developed the law-jobs theory as the most general part of his 'working whole view' of law. Thus the law-jobs theory was originally conceived as a heuristic for a particular kind of enquiry, but it is here being considered for its value in constructing a general organising theory.

4.3 Tamanaha and Llewellyn compared

(a) Some affinities

There are some important affinities between Tamanaha and Llewellyn. First, they are both law-trained sociologists of law, with a particular interest in the empirical study of the law in action. Second, they are both legal positivists. Tamanaha is arguably a rather strong positivist. Llewellyn personally was

---

[81] The term 'juristic method' should not be conflated with 'legal method', a much narrower category in ordinary legal usage. 'Juristic method' encompasses all aspects of institutional machinery, which, said Llewellyn, includes 'ways *and* personnel *and* ideology about both.' *NLLJ* at p. 1392. It is not confined to the skills and techniques of individual specialists (the crafts of the lawyer, styles of judges, the skills of different kinds of negotiator). It includes craft-traditions; legal inventions; institutional design; and any kind of machinery or institutionalised way of doing any of the law-jobs. Juristic method is 'the *ways* of handling "legal" tools to law-job ends and of the ongoing upkeep and improvement of both ways and tools'. *Ibid.*, p. 1392. The ideas of juristic method and legal technology are discussed at length in *JJM*.

[82] Hoebel (1964), *JJM* in *GJB*, pp. 157–60.

a rather weak legal positivist,[83] but he worked within that tradition and the law-jobs theory can be interpreted as being compatible with sophisticated versions of the separation thesis and the social sources thesis. Third, Tamanaha is concerned with law in the world as a whole. The law-jobs theory also fits a global perspective in that it claims to be applicable to all human groups, from a temporary two-person unit to all humankind. Fourth, the law-jobs theory is inclusive, in that it goes beyond state law to include any form of institution that is oriented to doing the law jobs. However, it is not so extensive as to cover all institutions. At a very general level, Llewellyn distinguished between law and other social institutions such as those concerned with medicine and education.[84] He explicitly stated that law was not the only, nor necessarily the main, institution that in fact contributed to doing the law jobs in any given situation. Thus he did not fall into the trap of treating all functional equivalents as law. Finally, both Tamanaha and Llewellyn realise the importance of the phenomena of normative and legal pluralism, but recognise the difficulties in conceptualising them.[85]

(b) The law-jobs theory as an analytical theory

The law-jobs theory has sometimes been interpreted as making some rash empirical claims (or as being a general theory of dispute settlement). This is a mistake. One reason for the broad reach and flexibility of the theory is that it is almost devoid of empirical content. It is not falsifiable. Rather it is an analytical theory like those of Hart and Tamanaha, providing concepts for asking questions, framing hypotheses and pursuing empirical enquiries. Like Tamanaha, Llewellyn has excised almost all empirical and normative content from his basic conceptual framework.[86] On one interpretation the sole empirical claim is that human beings live in groups,[87] but they have 'divisive urges' that can lead to

---

[83] On 'strong' and 'weak' positivism see Chapter 1.7 above. In the much-quoted statement of a positivist starting point for legal realism, Llewellyn includes two qualifiers. 'The *temporary* divorce of Is and Ought *for purposes of study*' (Llewellyn (1962) at pp. 55–7. His later statements of a legal positivist position are even more guarded. Llewellyn was never as unequivocal a positivist as Holmes or Hart or Tamanaha. But it is fair to say that he belongs to that tradition.

[84] *NLLJ*, pp. 1389–90.   [85] *GLT*, pp. 82–8, Twining (2003a) pp. 248–50.

[86] While group survival and flourishing (achievement of ends) depends on the law-jobs being done, the theory does not assume that group survival or flourishing is necessarily desirable – the theory can apply to groups about which the analyst is hostile or indifferent. Similarly, Llewellyn did not make any assumption that conflict is always undesirable. He explicitly recognised that conflict can be an engine of change (see more generally, Coser (1956)).

[87] Llewellyn and Hoebel identified groups, divergent urges, and (rightful) claims as the basic elements of the law-jobs theory. On 'groups' they wrote: 'There is first the relevant entirety or group or Whole. By this is meant two or more persons who are engaged in some kind of observably joint and continuing activity, and who recognize themselves in some fashion as being parts of a Whole. Given in the same concept is some type and degree of actual patterning of behavior-in-the-group, a patterning which affords an interlocking of the behavior of individuals, a back-and-forth, a building of this one's behavior together with that one's into a working whole. And given in that is, in turn, some quantum of those advance adjustments by one person to the anticipated behavior of another which we call expectations.' (Llewellyn and Hoebel, 1941) at pp. 273–4). See further Chapter 15.3 on the web.

'trouble' that threatens group survival and co-ordination.[88] There may be some secondary empirical assumptions, especially relating to juristic method, but the nature of the law-jobs theory is to provide a set of linked concepts as tools for analysis that involve minimal empirical, normative or functionalist assumptions. There is no assumption that conflict is necessarily bad, that order is necessarily good, nor that the law-jobs are in fact done by law-government.

(c) The importance of rules

Hart treated legal systems as systems of rules; Tamanaha treats rules as a contingent rather than necessary element in his conception of law, but he is careful to emphasise their importance. Llewellyn is sometimes criticised for being a 'rule skeptic', who believed that 'talk of rules is a myth'. As an interpretation of his general position, this is a travesty.[89] He was Chief Reporter of the Uniform Commercial Code, he wrote but never completed a book on 'The Theory of Rules',[90] and he regularly argued for 'Grand Style rules'. In fact the law-jobs theory gives a more emphatic place to rules than does Tamanaha. It treats rules and other norms as an important element in legal phenomena without making them paramount. It is always an open question: to what extent are the law-jobs in fact being done by rules or other norms (paper or real) and/or by other means?[91] It is not clear that Llewellyn consistently treated rules as a necessary feature of law or of social institutions generally, but the law-jobs theory can easily be interpreted as including weak normativity as an element in the idea of a social practice, as was argued above.[92] Similarly, if one treats a degree of institutionalisation as being a necessary condition for the existence of a social practice, this fits the law-jobs theory. Law consists of social practices institutionalised around doing the law jobs.[93]

---

[88] On my interpretation, the other theses about group survival and group functioning are best treated as tautologies. When Llewellyn says 'the jobs get done always – or the group simply is no more', (*NLLJ*, p. 1382) what this means depends on the meaning of 'group' in this context. If the term is defined in terms of co-operation and absence of conflict, then by definition if the level of conflict rises to a certain level there is no longer a 'group'. See further *KLRM* at pp. 180–2 and Chapter 15.3 on the web.

[89] *KLRM, passim.*   [90] *KLRM*, Appendix B.

[91] On 'paper rules' see Chapter 10.2(b) below.   [92] See above pp. 100–1.

[93] Like Hart, Llewellyn treats law as a species of social institution (i.e. 'organized activity built around the doing of some a job or cluster of jobs' (*LIS*, p. 21). This is compatible with the idea of law as a social practice that is relatively institutionalised, as was suggested above. Llewellyn's conception of institution was influenced by Walton Hamilton (1932). The law-jobs theory provides a potentially fruitful bridge between jurisprudence and modern organisation theory (e.g. Scott (1995), (1998), (2001) and the 'new institutionalism' (e.g. North (1990)).

(d) Thin functionalism

There are two major points at which the law-jobs theory and Tamanaha's position appear to diverge: functionalism and Llewellyn's explicit refusal to produce a general definition of law.

Historically, the law-jobs theory emanated from the strong Functionalism of the 1920s and 1930s. Llewellyn is sometimes branded as an 'extreme functionalist'.[94] Certainly he used functional analysis, he conceived of law as having 'jobs' or tasks and, although he recognised the role of conflict in social change, it is fair to say that he was nearer to the consensus end of the conflict-consensus spectrum of social theories.[95] However, he was much closer to Robert Merton, a sophisticated defender of modified functionalism, than to Talcott Parsons, who has been the prime target of the critics. For example, it is reasonably clear that, in relation to law, Llewellyn was not guilty of committing any of the main fallacies dealt with by Merton: the postulate of functional unity of society (i.e. strong organic integration); the postulate of universal functionalism (that all institutions and practices necessarily have functions) and the postulate of indispensable items (that some [legal] institutions are indispensable).[96] More important than Llewellyn's personal biases, however, is the question of whether the law-jobs theory can be interpreted or adapted today to meet the most significant objections to functionalism. I believe that it can.

First, as we have seen, there is nothing in the theory that involves commitment to the idea that group survival is necessarily desirable or that conflict is always undesirable. All that it suggests is that for any group to survive and to further its ends, certain conditions need to be satisfied. This applies to controversial, anti-social, or evil, or opposing groups and to both sides in a war or other conflict. The theory involves no ideological commitment to the status quo or to the survival or flourishing of any given group.

Second, a great deal of criticism of classical Functionalism is directed to statements of the kind 'the function of law is to maintain order'. 'Function' is a highly ambiguous term: it can refer to purpose, role, consequences or effects or to a combination of these (e.g. the purpose of x is to have effect y and it in fact has that effect). If 'function' here means consequences (or purpose(s) plus consequences) this kind of claim can be shown to be empirically false or greatly exaggerated in many contexts. This is the core of Tamanaha's attack on the twin 'social order' and 'mirror' theories.[97] In my opinion, Llewellyn can be defended from this attack.

Tamanaha's criticisms are justified if statements of the kind 'the function of law is to maintain order' refer to actual effects (or to purpose plus effects). Such statements are too simplistic because laws are made and used for many different purposes and have many different effects. Similarly, this kind of functionalist

---

[94] E.g. Hunt (1978) Chapter 3.   [95] *KLRM* pp. 219–26; *JJM*, p. 44, n. 50.
[96] Adapted from Merton (1949/1967) Chapter III (above pp. 97–9).   [97] See above p. 99.

claim does not work as a differentiating feature, if true, because many other social practices can and often do contribute to order.

So far as purpose is concerned, if this implies conscious human choice, it is easy to point to many examples of laws that developed incrementally or without thought or were instigated or maintained by a mixture of different motives and interests. Attributing 'purpose' to particular laws and law generally runs into very similar difficulties to those surrounding 'legislative intent'.[98] One can accept that whether in any given context law (or specific laws) contribute to any given outcome is best treated as an open question requiring empirical investigation.[99]

However, 'function' can also mean 'point', which is much more flexible than purpose on its own.[100] 'Point' is broader, for it can include the idea that a practice is valued or justified or observed, whatever its historical origins, as in Ronald Dworkin's account of the social practice of doffing one's hat as an example of courtesy.[101] The point of the practice is to show respect. Here point includes purpose, but can also refer to any motive, value or reason that can be given to explain or justify the practice from the point of view of the actor. It can refer to origins or equally well to the meaning of the practice as it now stands. The key idea is that 'the point' is part of the concept – one cannot explain the practice of doffing one's hat without reference to courtesy and hence to respect. In this example, showing respect is a moral value; but 'point' is not restricted to morals. For example, the point of the electric chair is to kill people sentenced to death; the point of a hammer is to knock in nails; the point of a confidence trick is deception. Doffing one's hat may make observers laugh; an old electric chair may be used for sitting on; a hammer can be used to kill someone. One might

---

[98] The sixteen American scholars who contributed to the collection entitled *My Philosophy of Law* (Kocourek (ed.) 1941) were invited to discuss the origin, the nature and the purpose of law. Nearly all of them did and most jurists conceive of law as being purposive in some sense. Critics of functionalism have brought out why on its own this is too simple – a social practice may arise without any clear conscious purpose; the purposes for which a law is used are many and various; they may change over time; what is the point or purpose of law is contested by jurists and so on. Clearly statements of the kind 'the purpose of law is social control' are too simple. Besides being too simple – suggesting there is only one purpose – this idea has rightly been criticised as treating criminal law as the paradigm case of law – associated with a Hobbesian sovereign maintaining law and order. But this neither fits the complexities of modern law, nor the standard picture of pre-literate societies without centralised rulers, like East African 'societies without Chiefs' (Mair 1962), nor modern public international law. Few, however, would want to create a complete break between the concepts of law and of social control – nor the broader idea of 'social order'. See further Chapter 4.1(c) above. See also Tamanaha's wide-ranging attack on 'instrumentalism' in the United States (Tamanaha (2006) discussed at Chapter 16.4).

[99] On the difficulties of treating legal rules as independent variables in respect of consequences, see Griffiths (1978) and (2003).

[100] This is close to John Finnis' influential idea of 'focal meaning', Finnis (1980) at pp. 12–18, citing Weber. Cf. MacCormick (2007) at pp. 294–7. It differs in that it substitutes a more abstract 'point' for law than such specific values as justice, reasonableness, or rights. Since 'ordering' in the sense of patterning is not tied to any specific *moral* values, it is consistent with a weak positivist version of the separation thesis. See further Twining (2008b).

[101] Dworkin (1986) at pp. 47–60, 68–73.

say that a practice of courtesy developed for the purpose of, or in response to, a felt need for a way of showing respect. If it was sometimes followed or viewed ironically or mockingly, this was parasitic on the meaning of the practice. When a practice declines, it may begin to lose its original point and become considered quaint or out-dated. A social practice or institution can be used for purposes or with effects outside 'the point' that is part of the concept.[102]

'Point' is preferable to purpose as it allows for the idea of social practices emerging, developing, becoming entrenched, or changing in response to complex processes of interaction that cannot be accounted for in terms of deliberate purpose, consensus or conscious choice. The law-jobs theory allows for the full spectrum of possibilities from deliberate, conscious, purposive, rational problem solving and action, through different forms of collective decision making (which may involve compromise, manipulation, etc), to various kinds of semi-conscious or unconscious shifts in patterns of behaviour or expectations in response to various stimuli.

Here again, the concept of 'institution' is useful. On one interpretation of the concept, a social practice becomes institutionalised in response to certain perceived needs or problems. What is special about the practice is that it is *oriented towards* or specialised to those problems. Thus for Llewellyn what is special or peculiar about law is its orientation towards the doing of a cluster of jobs – dispute prevention, dispute settlement, allocation of power and authority and so on. What differentiates law from other social practices is this special orientation. For Llewellyn, the jobs or needs are all related to group survival and flourishing, but we can build a wider range of jobs into our conception.[103]

'Orientation towards' does not imply a monopoly. No claim is made that law is the only practice or institution concerned with these jobs – morality, religion, education may have overlapping concerns and may be as important in terms of effects. But just as the point of education is learning not social ordering; the point of medicine is health; the point of the institution of law is doing the law-jobs. The law-jobs are not the only jobs law is used for; law is not the only institution concerned with the law-jobs. But the idea of 'orientation towards' is part of the concept of education, medicine or law.

Law may be an even more elusive concept than education and medicine. For, while all social practices have borderline cases and overlaps, for some there is

---

[102] On 'focal meaning' see n. 100 above.

[103] See *GJLS* pp. 236–40 on the role of law providing a formal infrastructure for the market and transactions and for government bureaucracy, both of which 'have little to do with social order'. One objection that may be raised is that the law-jobs theory does not provide any clear criteria for differentiating between law (law-government) and 'non-legal' institutions and practices. This is only half-true: law as an institution becomes differentiated as it becomes established as an institution *specialised* to doing the law jobs. As emphasised above, this involves no claim to monopoly, or effectiveness, or necessity (the law-jobs can be done by other means) or limited focus (law can have other functions). However, this criterion is quite vague. How well-established? How specialised? Outside a more specific context, this vagueness can be claimed as a virtue. Specialisation, institutionalisation, and differentiation are relative matters.

usually one core idea – in medicine it is health, in education it is learning – whereas with law there is a complex set of ideas – dispute processing, allocation of authority, provision of 'net positive drive', creating infrastructures for commerce – which are not necessarily linked. It is quite possible to conceive of a society or social arena which keeps the maintenance of group survival and of basic order quite separate from the provision of 'net positive drive' for the group as a whole and for its members. Indeed, the model of minimal government, underpinning a free market economy in conjunction with the 'invisible hand' almost fits that idea.[104]

The 'thin functionalist' pares away the aspects of functionalism that have attracted most criticism, makes no claims with regard to success in achieving purposes or actual contributions, effects or consequences, but retains the idea of 'point' – which includes the purposes and motives of institution-builders, managers and users, without suggesting that these purposes are necessarily moral or for the general welfare.[105]

(e) From concepts to hypotheses

Law-government is oriented towards the performing of some jobs or responding to some 'needs';[106] this does not involve any implication that it succeeds in or contributes to doing the jobs in any given situation. Nor does it involve denial that it may have side-effects or consequences that are different from what they were supposed to be. 'Law-jobs' refers to orientation not to actual impact. This is clearly illustrated with reference to Tamanaha's criticisms of 'the social order thesis', where he treats the following propositions as fallacies:[107]

---

[104] In Tamanaha's account of Yap the state legal system barely impinged on the lives of ordinary peoples. One day his superior (the Attorney-General) suggested that as Tamanaha seemed under-employed he might like to draft a general corporations law, including banking. 'But there aren't any corporations or banks' said Tamanaha. 'That does not matter,' replied his superior. (ex rel. Brian Tamanaha). This is a nice example of the constitutive function of law. History does not relate if subsequently any banks or other corporations were in fact set up under Tamanaha's law. If they were, this would then have been a good example of law having functions that are only indirectly related to basic social ordering.

[105] The 'thin functionalist' analysis of law is similar to the 'focal meaning' approach pioneered by Weber and developed in different ways by Finnis (1980), Dworkin (1985) and, most recently, MacCormick (2007). It differs from these in that it substitutes a more abstract 'point' for law than such values as justice, reasonableness, or vindication of rights. Since ordering in the sense of patterning is not tied to any specific moral values, it is consistent with a weak positivist version of the separation thesis. See further Twining (2009).

[106] The concept of 'needs' is of great significance in the theory of human rights (See Chapter 6 below). In that context, needs is clearly a normative concept. Perhaps Llewellyn substituted the more down-to-earth jobs to suggest an empirical notion: if a group is to survive and flourish according to its own values, the following jobs have to be done somehow. Llewellyn was not committed to any assumption that group survival and flourishing are necessarily desirable.

[107] These propositions arise largely from Tamanaha's extensive critique of Functionalism, which is spread throughout both *RSLT* and *GJLS* (see especially pp. 175–81 and the index). References in the footnotes are just illustrative.

(a) that law is the only institution that contributes to ordering;[108]

(b) that ordering cannot occur without law;[109]

(c) that law in fact always promotes ordering;[110]

(d) that the only functions of law relate to dispute processing or social control or social order in a restricted sense;[111]

(e) that law is generally effective;[112]

(f) that law is effective in the maintenance of social order by virtue of its reflective quality;[113]

(g) that law never promotes conflict or disorder.[114]

These are 'fallacies' in the sense of dubious empirical assumptions that cannot be taken for granted. They all refer to factual consequences – what law *does*. But if 'function' refers to orientation rather than impact, the law-jobs theory involves no commitment to any such assumptions. Like Tamanaha's core conception, its criteria of identification are free of all such empirical assumptions.

Tamanaha also makes some bold generalisations that are counterparts to the 'fallacies' that he criticises. For example that:

1. Law is only one of the sources of social order.[115]

2. Primacy for maintaining social order usually lies in the other sources of social order.[116]

3. *The natural social condition is one of order, permeated at various levels with regular episodes of conflict.*[117]

4. 'The traditionally assumed relationship [between law and social order] gets things precisely upside down. It is state law that is dependent on those other sources of social order if it is to have a chance of exerting an influence.'[118]

These propositions are best treated as hypotheses that can be translated into open questions in particular contexts. The law-jobs theory as an analytical theory neither supports nor denies any such empirical claims. It is compatible with treating these in the form of questions or as hypotheses to be tested in particular situations or more generally. Since the time of Maine such very broad generalisations have been out of fashion – the sociologist Donald Black is a striking exception[119] – and most socio-legal scholars prefer to work at a less abstract level. Tamanaha deserves credit for boldly sticking his neck out in this way, and his list of 'fallacies' helps to identify some dubious assumptions that

---

[108] *GJLS*, pp. 137–8, 176–7, 211–23.

[109] *Ibid.*, at pp. 35–6, 145–6, 208ff. See also Merton's indispensability fallacy.

[110] *Ibid.*, at p. 240.   [111] *Ibid.*, at pp. 36–7, 179, 237–40. See also *RSLT*, p. 109.

[112] See p. 94 above.   [113] Chapter 5 *passim*.   [114] *GJLS*, p. 240, *RSLT* see also, p. 128.

[115] Others include the Unarticulate Substrate; shared norms and rules (not only legal); Self-interested social behaviour; Consent; and a catch-all category: Love, Altruism, Sympathy, Group-Identification; Social Instinct; Coercion and Threat of Coercion (not only legal sanctions). (pp. 213–21) I shall not attempt to analyse this preliminary typology here.

[116] *GJLS*, p. 236.   [117] *Ibid.*, 223 (Original italics).

[118] *Ibid.*, p. 224.   [119] See Chapter 8.9 below.

dimension, such as international law, comparative law, and environmental law.[3] Furthermore, increasingly some of our canonical texts have been translated into other languages where they have been read and looked at with fresh critical eyes. Second, there has been continuous interaction between different legal traditions at many levels. In this respect practice has often been ahead of theory. Third, Western ideas have been dominant, but not unchallenged, in international arenas such as the United Nations (UN) system, the World Trade Organisation (WTO), international financial institutions (IFIs), various human rights regimes, and transnational NGOs. The interests of non-Western governments and peoples have often been articulated in the language of utility or rights or justice. As we shall see the Universal Declaration of Human Rights (UDHR) is often treated as an emblem of 'universally' accepted values, but its origins, wording, and interpretations raise questions about its significance and whether it represents a genuinely worldwide consensus.

Issues about universality and generality in respect of values have concerned philosophers throughout history. Western jurisprudence has a long tradition of universalism in ethics. Natural law, classical utilitarianism, Kantianism, and modern theories of human rights have all been universalist in tendency. These have, of course, been subjected to persistent challenges from various forms of scepticism, relativism, subjectivism and, lately, in a different way, communitarianism. During the last half-century, debates about legal positivism and liberal political theory have dominated our legal philosophy, especially in the Anglo-American tradition. Thus, at first sight, there seems to be less need of a revival in respect of general normative jurisprudence than in respect of analytical and empirical approaches. However, this is only partly true, for three main reasons.

First, in jurisprudence, most juristic discussions of justice, positivism, law and morals, and obedience to law have been almost exclusively concerned with the municipal law of nation states. For the most part they barely address questions of value in relation to other levels of legal ordering (public international law is a partial exception) nor in relation to the phenomena of normative and legal pluralism.[4] As we shall see, a particularly clear example is Rawls' theory of justice. This is explicitly, and unconvincingly, limited to nation states as notionally self-contained communities, and, as a secondary matter, to relations between such states.[5] It is difficult to defend a theory of justice

---

[3] On international law and comparative law see Chapter 1, n. 28 above; on environmental justice Bullard (2005), Ebbeson and Okowa (2008); on transitional justice e.g. Teitel (2000), Bell, Campbell, and Ni Aolain (2006) and publications of the Transitional Justice Institute, University of Ulster.

[4] On normative and legal pluralism, see *GLT*, pp. 82–8 and 224–33 and Chapter 16.2 on the web.

[5] Rawls uses such phrases as 'more or less self-sufficient' (1971) at p. 4), 'self-contained national community' (*ibid.*, p. 457), and 'a closed system isolated from other societies'. (*ibid.*, at p. 8). The fullest critique of this aspect of his theory is Pogge (1989), see also (2001b). See *GLT*, pp. 69–75. Since then, Rawls has defended and refined his position in *The Law of Peoples* (1999c), but very few find his arguments any more convincing.; see for example, the Symposium in 110 *Ethics* (2000) 669ff. (See section 5(6) in this chapter.)

restricted to liberal, self-contained societies, when no such entities exist. Just because Rawls's theory is concerned with basic practical principles of institutional design, questions about its extension or adaptation to institutions concerned with ordering at other levels are of particular significance. For example, Rawls seems to have almost nothing to say about regional integration or the just regulation of exploitation of unappropriated minerals on this or other planets.[6]

Second, in the face of challenges from multi-culturalism, pluralism, and various kinds of relativism, some leading liberal thinkers have beaten a partial retreat into a kind of particularism.[7] In recent times liberal democratic political and legal theorising has tended either to be geographically indeterminate or to place some limits on their geographical claims. A great deal of recent Anglo-American normative jurisprudence has been relatively local in respect of provenance, audience and even focus.[8] For example, most writings about the new communitarianism, critical race theory, and republicanism have been explicitly or implicitly or unselfconsciously American or at least American-influenced.[9] Feminist jurisprudence has only recently begun to be genuinely transnational.[10]

Thirdly, nearly all Western modern normative jurisprudence is either secular or explicitly Christian. Post-Enlightenment secularism has deep historical roots in the intellectual traditions of Western Christianity.[11] Even those theories that claim universality have proceeded with only tangential reference to, and in almost complete ignorance of, the religious and moral beliefs, values, and traditions of the rest of humankind.[12] When differing cultural values are discussed, even the agenda of issues tends to have a stereotypically Western bias.[13] When such issues

---

[6] On *ius humanitatis* see p. 171 below and *GLT*, p. 240.

[7] There are some important exceptions to the trend towards greater geographical particularity. The field of international ethics, exemplified by Peter Singer, Brian Barry, Henry Shue, Onora O'Neill, Martha Nussbaum, Amartya Sen, and Thomas Pogge, among others, addresses transnational issues from a global perspective. There have been lively debates about human rights and cultural relativism, and about universalism versus contextualism, and I discuss these below. In practice, the most politically influential ideas, are probably still the ideological assumptions underlying the 'Washington Consensus' which links free market economics to the seductive catch-phrase 'human rights, good governance, and democracy'. However, this is sometimes interpreted as a cover for unfettered capitalism. See Chapter 11.3(c) below.

[8] *GLT*, pp. 128–9.

[9] *GLT*, pp. 58–60. Critical legal scholars have recently turned their attention to comparative law, Latin America ('Lat-Crits') and issues of globalisation, but it is too early to assess the significance of these developments. On 'New Approaches to International Law' (NAIL) see Riles (2004), Rajagopal (2003).

[10] E.g. Okin (1999), Nussbaum (2000), Wing (2000), Mukhopadhyay and Singh (eds.) (2007), Stewart (forthcoming 2009).

[11] Siedentop (2000).

[12] It is notoriously difficult to estimate the numbers of adherents of world religions. With the normal *caveats*, *The Oxford Atlas of the World* (1994) estimates that Christian 'adherents' represent about 40–43 per cent of the world population, Muslims about 25 per cent, and other religions the rest. No figure is given for atheists and agnostics.

[13] This tendency is well caught by the quotation from Ahdaf Souief's novel *The Map of Love* (1999 at p. 6), cited at the start of Chapter 13.

as the relationship between law and morals (positivism), multi-culturalism, religious toleration, and cultural relativism have been discussed, the enquiries and debates take place largely within the framework of Western traditions of thought, often with explicit or implicit reference either to Western societies or to international relations as perceived from Western points of view. A genuinely cosmopolitan general jurisprudence will need to do better than that.

Before considering two central strands of our Western heritage in detail, let me touch briefly on three matters that I shall treat as tangential to my argument: legal positivism, universalisability, and debates about universalism and cultural relativism.

5.3 Positivism, universalisability, universalism and relativism

(a) Positivism revisited

Here, I shall deal briskly with issues of legal positivism. As explained in Chapter 1, I am prepared to accept the label of a legal positivist in the tradition of Bentham, Hart, Llewellyn, and MacCormick.[14] I subscribe to a version of the separability thesis, that is to say that in some contexts it is useful for clarity of thought to hold to a distinction between law as it is and law as it ought to be. I probably count as a 'weak' positivist, in that I accept that there are some contexts in which a sharp distinction between 'is' and 'ought' breaks down – for example, in some kinds of argumentation about questions of law and questions of fact.[15]

Nor is it necessary here to dwell on fallacious views that suggest that this kind of legal positivism is immoral or amoral or indifferent to questions of morality or justice, or commits one to rejection of values associated with human rights or the rule of law. On the contrary, for many positivists, including myself, a positivist position arises in large part out of moral concerns. Bentham distinguished the 'is' and the 'ought' for the sake of the ought – in order to criticise and construct. Herbert Hart emphasised the distinction for the sake of clarity of thought both in respect of a descriptive theory of law and in dealing with issues of political morality.[16] I agree with positivists such as Joseph Raz and David Lyons that questions about fidelity to law, political obligation, and civil disobedience are important moral issues, but that these issues can be addressed and argued about more clearly if one starts with a distinction between law and morality.[17]

---

[14] *GLT*, Chapter 5. On MacCormick's move away from positivism in *Institutions of Law* (2007) see Chapter 1 above, n. 96.

[15] 'Weak' is not used here in the sense of the recent debate about the rule of recognition. See p. 27 above.

[16] On the underlying concerns of Hart's positivism, see Lacey (2004) 196–209. On Hart as a modified utilitarian see Chapter 5.7 below.

[17] *GLT*, p. 118 (see *GLT* for references).

For me the crucial point is one of vocabulary: understanding law needs to encompass ideals and aspirations on the one hand, and what actually happens on the other. We need to have vocabularies for both aspiration and reality and that requires a distinction between ought and is in some contexts. One needs a vocabulary that describes actual institutions and practices, not least because of the many awful things that are done in the name of law by those who exercise power. This is partly a matter of standpoint: it may be appropriate for a judge to expound and justify interpretations of the law in terms of Dworkinian principles, but this mode of discourse will not do for Amnesty International, Human Rights Watch, local reformers, or other observers and critics, for they need clear distinctions between aspirational standards and descriptions of actual practices.[18] Suffice to say here, it is my view that moral concerns are an essential, but not a sufficient, part of the enterprise of understanding law.

(b) Universalisability

It is important to distinguish between universalisability, a technical term in ethics, and the highly ambiguous terms, 'universalism' and 'relativism'. A simple version of The Golden Rule 'Do not do unto others, what you would not have them do unto you' is often expressed in terms of 'universalisability', suggesting that moral terms imply 'universal' application to any relevant similar situation. The central point is that morality is a matter of following rules and that it involves consistency in moral decision making.[19] Principles such as 'treat like cases alike' leave scope in theory and in practice for very restricted interpretations: for example, a 'principle' that there shall be no discrimination in employment in respect of locals, which excludes aliens or immigrants. While some versions of universalisability explicitly cover all human beings, the precise scope of most versions of The Golden Rule is not a central concern. It typically leaves open such questions as: What cases are relevantly similar? Who count as others? – Members of one's own family or community or race? All humankind? Animals? All sentient beings? And so on. Here I shall treat it as a purely formal requirement of most ethical theories.

(c) Universalism

The *Oxford English Dictionary* lists seventeen primary meanings of 'universal', apart from its technical usages in logic and philosophy. Here we are mainly concerned with claims that certain basic values or moral principles are applicable at all times and in all places, for example the claim that natural law

---

[18] *GLT*, pp. 46, 114, 120, 134.

[19] Wattles (1996) at 129; see Hare (1981). I shall not pursue here the complex topic of the relationship between Kant's Categorical Imperative and the Golden Rule. On universalisability in legal reasoning see Feteris (1999).

principles, derived from universal human nature, are unchanging and invariant; or the claim that human rights exist for all humankind by virtue of their humanity.

It is important to distinguish this usage from other usages and to recognise that there are varieties of universalism in this sense. For example, Jeremy Bentham is sometimes interpreted as a universalist utilitarian in contrast with egoistic utilitarianism.[20] For the egoistic utilitarian the only relevant consequences are those that affect one's own happiness directly or indirectly; the universalist, on the other hand, should always weigh the consequences for the whole community in question or for humankind or for all sentient beings.[21] Both egoistic and universalistic utilitarianism treat utility as a universal principle in the sense used here. There are other logical, theological, and philosophical usages that do not apply here.

Claims to universality also take different forms. In the present context it is useful to distinguish between five varieties:

(a) *Normative universalism*: a claim that there is one, and only one, set of correct or true or valid moral principles or values applicable at all times and in all places.

(b) *Descriptive universalism*: a claim that the same fundamental values or moral principles are in fact shared by (nearly)[22] all cultures. For example, that all known cultures have incest taboos or prohibitions about killing. This contrasts with the idea that it is a social fact that there are fundamental differences and disagreements about values across and within cultures (belief pluralism).[23]

(c) *Consensual universalism*: a claim that there is a consensus in fact about certain values or principles at a given time. Such a historically contingent consensus may be arrived at by negotiation or convergence or persuasion or even by acceptance brought about by coercion or imposition.[24] For example, the fact that almost all the members of the UNs have subscribed to the Millennium Development Goals; that genocide is 'universally' accepted as prohibited by *ius cogens* as part of public international law; that 'dignity' is universally treated as a fundamental human value; and more controversially, that gender equality is 'universally' accepted in principle, even if it is interpreted differently in different societies and cultures.

---

[20] Smart (1967) at 207.

[21] The interpretation of Bentham as a universalist in this special sense is historically correct and, in my view, part of the least vulnerable interpretation of utility. See p. 135 below and Dinwiddy (2004) Chapter 3.

[22] Descriptive and consensus universalism are more easily defended if allowance is made for some deviants and exceptions. It is reasonable to allow universalist claims some margin of appreciation.

[23] This formulation assumes that cultures are sufficiently monolithic to be treated as comparable units. This simplifies exposition, but of course beliefs can vary considerably within a culture.

[24] J. Cohen (1992).

(d) *Ethnocentric universalism*: a claim or assumption that one's own values and moral principles are either superior to those of others or are shared by them.[25]

(e) *Surface universalism*: this applies to a situation where (nearly) all relevant parties have agreed to a verbal formulation that is so ambiguous or vague that it probably conceals profound differences beneath the surface. A claim that gender equality is universally recognised as an aspiration is often given as a standard example of surface universalism. More controversially, some maintain that the Universal Declaration of Human Rights falls within this category. The converse of this is surface diversity – where apparently different beliefs/values can be shown to be fundamentally similar.[26]

These categories overlap. There are distinctions and refinements within each of them. For present purposes, the most important distinction is between empirical and normative claims and those that combine the two elements, such as claims about moral principles derived from the nature of man.

(d) Relativism

In normative jurisprudence, universalism is most often contrasted with relativism. Ethical relativism also takes many forms. Here I shall focus on cultural relativism, that is to say the view that there are no universal values or moral principles independent of context, because beliefs about such matters are relative to culture and historical context and that there are no criteria for evaluating cultures from the outside.

In any discussion of 'relativism' it is important to ask what is relative to what? As Haack puts it, "'relativism' refers not to a single thesis, but to a whole family".[27] In the present context we are primarily concerned with moral values (as opposed, for example, to meaning or truth or reality) in relation to beliefs of a culture or community or individual. A universalist claim that some values or moral principles are universal can be interpreted as a claim that they are applicable at all times and in all places. The converse is a moral relativist claim

---

[25] In ordinary usage 'ethnocentrism' means 'Culturally biased judgment' (Levine (2001)). William Graham Sumner employed the term as an explicitly sociological concept as part of a theory about internal and external relations:

> *Ethnocentrism* is the technical name for this view of things in which one's own group is the center of everything, and all others are scaled and rated with reference to it.
> Folkways correspond to it to cover both the inner and outer relation. (Sumner (1906) at 12–13).
>   Sumner's view has been criticised as being too broad and for drawing boundaries between groups too sharply. In a weaker form, ethnocentrism is the tendency to look at other cultures through the filter of one's own cultural presuppositions Barfield (1997) p. 55. On ethnocentrism and human rights, see pp. 204 and 215 below.

[26] On dignity as 'a placeholder concept', see McCrudden (2008); on 'surface law' see Chapter 10 below.

[27] Haack (1998), p. 149.

that 'there exist diverse, incompatible moral systems and there are no over-arching criteria to decide between them'.[28] But there are several different kinds of moral relativist claim, some of which are the converse of normative, descriptive, and consensual universalism. For our purposes, it is important to distinguish between descriptive and normative kinds of moral relativism and between strong and weak versions of each type.

Descriptive moral relativism takes the form of claims that beliefs and judgements about moral values and their application differ from culture to culture and time to time. This diversity of beliefs is an empirical fact, and even when there seems to be some convergence, as in relation to prohibitions against incest or killing human beings, these can be shown to be open to different, often incompatible, interpretations in different cultures. The converse position is empirical moral universalism, which claims that behind apparent diversity there lie shared values, many of which are grounded in facts about human nature. For example, all human beings *need* food, water, and shelter in order to survive; and that human beings have shared sexual, aggressive, and altruistic urges and possibly spiritual needs, even if these are realised in different ways in different cultures; and that there is almost universal agreement that 'dignity' is an important value.

Such descriptive claims are *au fond* empirical and interpretive. But they are of different kinds. That food is a precondition for survival is an uncontroversial biological fact about human beings. However, some interpretations of 'human nature' are highly controversial, typically involving a mixture of scientific 'truths' (e.g. about sexual urges), contested theories (e.g. nature versus nurture), and interpretations that involve a strong normative element (e.g. about the ends or the 'perfectability of man').[29] Furthermore, there is considerable room for disagreement about the relevance of empirical findings about human beings to ethical beliefs. For example, it is a widely held view that one cannot validly infer normative principles from empirical facts ('the naturalistic fallacy'): if one accepts that human beings have both aggressive and altruistic urges, what follows from that in relation to both individual and political morality? But others maintain that there is no fundamental dichotomy between human beings as they are and as they ought to be.[30] Empirical universalism and relativism have stimulated extensive research about beliefs and values.[31] And, of course, exploration of 'human nature' is a central concern of cultural

---

[28] Baghramian (2001) at pp. 13025–6.   [29] Passmore (1970).

[30] For a recent example, based on modern interpretations of Darwin see Gearty (2006) Chapter 1, (discussed Twining (2007) at pp. 215–16). For a subtle account of 'the illicit inference from facts to norms' see Finnis (1980), pp. 33–42 (reconciling Human dualism with Natural Law). On the naturalistic fallacy see Chapter 6 at pp. 202–3 below.

[31] Useful overviews are Peacock (2001) and Rezsohazy (2001). A central theme in the history of social anthropology has been the search for cultural universals and responses to it. A classic example is The Royal Anthropological Institute's *Notes and Queries in Anthropology* (6th edn., 1950) which for a period became a handbook for fieldwork. Some Natural lawyers, for example, Father Thomas Davitt SJ, sought to base natural law principles on generalisations about

anthropology, psychology, biology, socio-biology, and other life sciences. But there continue to be profound disagreements both about 'human nature' and about the appropriateness of grounding ethical theories on purportedly empirical assumptions about it.[32]

These are matters of perennial controversy in Western moral philosophy. Here I shall confine myself to two observations.

First it is difficult to deny that belief pluralism is a fact.[33] There may be strong disagreements about both the extent and the significance of such diversity and whether such divergences in respect of values are 'fundamental'[34] or 'incommensurable'.[35] There may also be disagreements about the prospects, the processes, and the desirability of convergence. I shall proceed on the assumption that at this period in history one of the major issues facing mankind as a whole is how to work out frameworks, institutions, and processes that support co-existence, co-ordination, and co-operation in a situation where there are extensive and deeply rooted differences of belief that are not amenable in the foreseeable future to consensus being arrived at by rational debate and persuasion. Acceptance of this fact as a working assumption does not necessarily involve commitment to a sceptical epistemology. This assumption, which is open to challenge, tends to point to placing due weight on tolerance and open mindedness and on agreement about fair procedures for negotiation and decision rather than attempting to try to reconcile irreconcilable substantive beliefs.[36]

Second, each version of relativism and universalism varies significantly in terms of strength and weakness. There is a long tradition, especially with regard to human rights, to talk of a divide between universalism and cultural or other relativism.[37] But there is also a widespread tendency to treat such talk as

human nature derived from anthropological findings (Davitt (1964)). A contemporary example is empirical justice research pioneered by Peter H. Rossi (Rossi and Nock (1982), Rossi and Berk (1997)) and continued by Guillermina Jasso and associates whose stated aim is 'To describe and understand the human sense of (in)justice theoretically and empirically'. (e.g Jasso and Wegener (1997) and (1998)). This work is interesting, but it raises conceptual, interpretive and methodological problems that are not pursued here.

[32] See n. 30 above.

[33] John Tasioulas has usefully characterized value pluralism as 'an ethical doctrine, one that claims objective correctness, according to which: (i) there are many irreducibly distinct values; (ii) these values come into conflict in particular situations; (iii) some of these conflicts are incommensurable in that responses to them are not subject to a complete ranking (i.e. they cannot all be ranked as better or worse than each other, nor yet as equally good) and (iv) at the level of individual and collective forms of life, there are many different ways of responding to these values, which also are not subject to a complete ranking. An implication of (iv) is that the idea of the single best way of individual or collective life, even given "ideal" conditions, is a chimera.' (Tasioulas, (2008) at n. 14.

[34] Brandt (1967) pp. 75–8. Recently Ronald Dworkin (2006b) Chapter 4, has subtly defended the holistic ideal (integrity) against moral pluralism as advanced by Isaiah Berlin.

[35] On incommensurability see p. 81 above.

[36] Hampshire (1989). See further below the discussion of Rawls on overlapping consensus at p. 158 and Sen on discourse ethics at Chapter 7.4 below.

[37] See generally, Richard A. Wilson (ed.) (1997)

involving a false dichotomy. Aristotle, and modern Aristotelians such as Nussbaum, quite explicitly allow for differences between cultures; they merely insist on the universality of underlying principles.[38] Another universalist, Alan Gewirth, argues that universalism can justify certain kinds of ethical particularism, in the sense that 'one ought to give preferential consideration to the interests of some persons against others, including not only oneself, but also other persons with whom one has special relationships.'[39] Similarly, Joseph Raz, a committed universalist, has written sensitively and illuminatingly about the 'truth in particularism' and about the important challenges presented by multiculturalism to moral understanding.[40] He sees 'the universal and the particular to be complementary rather than antagonistic' and 'at the heart of multiculturalism lies the recognition that universal values are realised in a variety of different ways in different cultures and that they are all worthy of respect'.[41]

Indeed, among serious thinkers there seem to be very few strong universalists or extreme cultural relativists. And, of course, 'relativism' is a highly ambiguous concept.[42] There is a widespread view that polarising the debate merely serves to obscure a complex variety of issues that need to be differentiated. So are we faced again with the problem of a soggy middle ground? Happily, I think not. In respect of human rights there is a rich body of literature that explores important issues in detail and depth and these will be dealt with in Chapters 6, 7 and 13.

Against this background, we can now consider the implications of adopting a global perspective for two of the dominant normative theories in mainstream Anglo-American jurisprudence: classical utilitarianism and Rawlsian Justice.

---

[38] E.g. Nussbaum (2000).

[39] Alan Gewirth, in an important paper on 'Ethical Universalism and Particularism' states: 'The ethical particularism with which I am concerned here, then, is confined to preferences for or partiality towards various *groups*, ranging from one's family and personal friends to larger pluralities of one's community, nation, and so forth.' (Gewirth (1988) at p. 286). Gewirth sums up his argument respecting 'country and compatriots' as follows: 'This justification can be summarized in three steps. First, the universalist principle of human rights, in its component of basic well-being, justifies the general moral principle that minimal states, each operating within a particular territory, may be established. Second the subprinciple justifies that the state provides equal protection of the basic well-being of all persons within its particular territory. Third, this protection, in turn, justifies the particularistic, preferential concern that each of the state's members has for its particular interests, in recognition of the protection which he or she receives from the state.' (Gewirth (1988) at p. 301). Gewirth treats this as involving a different justification from preferential concern with voluntary associations. On utilitarianism and loyalty see *GLT*, pp. 66–7 and 131; cf. Fletcher (1993).

[40] Raz (1998) and (1999) Chapters 7 and 10.

[41] Raz (1998) at p. 204 (citing earlier writings). Raz acknowledges that morality can change, but not radically, and only against an unchanging background of continuing moral principles that explain the change. 'Since ... radical moral change is impossible, it follows that social relativism is untenable.' (1999) at p. 180. An even stronger universalist might argue that it is not fundamental moral principles that change, but our understanding of them.

[42] Haack (1998) Chapter 9 entitled, 'Reflections on Relativism: From Momentous Tautology to Seductive Self-contradiction'.

5.4 Classical utilitarianism: Jeremy Bentham[43]

(a) Utility

Utilitarianism is a species of consequentialism – the kind of moral theory that makes evaluations entirely (or almost entirely) by reference to factual outcomes.[44] There are many kinds of utilitarianism. I shall focus on Jeremy Bentham's version of what is often called 'classical utilitarianism', but in the process of interpreting Bentham I shall refer to distinctions that indicate some of the differences among utilitarians: utility as a principle of individual ethics ('morals') or public morality ('legislation'); the ambiguity of 'pleasure' (desire, satisfaction, and choice or preference)[45]; average and aggregate utility; the differences between egoistic and altruistic utilitarianism; and between act- and rule-utilitarianism.[46]

I have chosen Bentham because he is widely regarded as the most important jurist in the Anglo-American tradition: Bentham's views are nearly always challenging and percipient; sometimes they are persuasive, sometimes they are out-dated or just plain wrong. He wrote on a vast range of topics. Throughout this book he features as a reference point on particular issues that are topical: general jurisprudence, the concept of law, sovereignty, the extent of our moral concern, corruption, torture, capitalism and the welfare state, security, democracy, and his critique of non-legal rights. Some of the less well-known works – on international law, codification, and matters of place and time in legislation – are directly relevant to matters that we shall be considering. Despite the breadth of his interests, almost everything that he wrote had the same starting point: utility.

A particular reason why Bentham is interesting is because there are some illuminating tensions and ambiguities within his utilitarian theory.[47] Some of these have led to radically different interpretations that illustrate the variety and

---

[43] Some of the themes in this section are explored at greater length in *GJB*, Chapters 7 and 8. Bentham's views on utility are scattered throughout his writings. The most studied work, *Introduction to the Principles of Morals and Legislation* (*CW* (1970) ed. J.H. Burns and H.L.A Hart, 2nd edn 1996) (hereafter *IPML*) is less sophisticated than later expositions, especially *Deontology* (ed. Amnon Goldworth, CW, 1983). Of the immense secondary literature on Bentham as a utilitarian the following are especially recommended: Rosen (1996); Dinwiddy (2004) Chapters 1, 2 and 3; Harrison (1983); Schofield (2006).

[44] 'Consequentialism differs from utilitarianism, one of its species, mainly in the greater breadth of its value theory. Utilitarians assess outcomes by looking at individual well-being. Consequentialists look either at well-being or at moral goods such as equality, respect for rights, fidelity to one's word, and so on, or, indeed, commonly at both.' Griffin (1996) at p. 161, n.7 This long note contains an excellent discussion of consequentialism in general (*ibid.*, at pp. 161–6).

[45] On 'satisfaction', 'preference', 'desire' and choice, see n. 52 below.

[46] Bibliographical note: The best source for Bentham's original writings is the ongoing edition of his *Collected Works* (hereafter CW). For works not yet covered by this edition, the standard source is *The Works of Jeremy Bentham* (ed. John Bowring, 1838–43) (hereafter cited as *Works*).

[47] On 'Benthamic ambiguity' see *GJB*, pp. 214–5 and 262–3.

complexity of utilitarian ideas. Bentham advanced the principle of utility – the greatest happiness principle – as the sole criterion for evaluation of both individual behaviour (morals) and of political practices, policies, institutions, and laws (legislation).[48] The principle serves as a guide to decision and action and as a criterion for evaluation (including retrospective assessment) of decisions, actions, practices, institutions and laws. Here we are mainly concerned with utility as a principle of political morality and only incidentally as a principle of individual ethics. The salient and most controversial features of the theory are that it is generally forward looking, it is only concerned with actual or likely consequences, and that it claims to be the *sole* test of good and bad, right and wrong.[49]

The principle of utility prescribes that the right action is to promote pleasure or to avoid or reduce pain so that the outcome is the maximisation of happiness, (i.e. an aggregate surplus of pleasures over pains). 'It is the greatest happiness of the greatest number that is the measure of right and wrong'.[50] A particularly revealing formulation of utility from the point of view of the legislator is as follows:

> The only right and proper end of government is the greatest happiness of the members of the community in question: the greatest happiness – of all of them without exception, in so far as possible: the greatest happiness of the greatest number of them, on every occasion on which the nature of the case renders the provision of an equal quantity of happiness for every one of them impossible, by its being a matter of necessity, to make the sacrifice of a portion of the happiness of a few, the greater happiness of the rest.[51]

---

[48] This distinction is explicit in the title *Introduction to the Principles of Morals and Legislation*. A very high proportion of the literature on utilitarianism, and much of the criticism, focuses on utility as a principle of individual ethics. Jurisprudence is mainly concerned with utility as a principle of public morality. It is important in this context to bear in mind that 'legislation' is interpreted broadly to refer to all aspects of societal management, not solely to making positive laws. In a famous essay A. J. Ayer argued that the principle of utility as a guide to the legislator is less vulnerable to criticism than utility as a guide to the individual actor. (Ayer (1948) at pp. 245–59). However, this assumes that the principle has a different meaning in each of the two contexts.

[49] 'The principle of utility once adopted as the governing principle, admits of no rival, admits not even an associate.' (*Comment on the Commentaries* 27 (ed. Burns and Hart, *CW*, 1977).

[50] Jeremy Bentham, *A Fragment on Government*, Preface in *A Comment on the Commentaries and A Fragment on Government* (ed. Burns and Hart, *CW*, 1977) at p. 363.

[51] *Parliamentary Candidate's Proposed Declaration of Principles* (1831) cited by Dinwiddy (2004) at p. 31. Dinwiddy uses this passage, first as an example of Bentham adopting a social standpoint, and to make the point that although Bentham sets up *aggregate* happiness as the criterion, and seemingly is prepared to sacrifice the happiness of a minority, he considers the optimal goal to be 'the provision of an equal quantity of happiness for everyone'. Thus equality is linked (albeit subject to exceptions) to distribution of happiness. This point is bolstered by Bentham's recognition of the operation of diminishing marginal utility (discussed below). It is fairly clear that Bentham did not favour a principle of average utility (which directs maximising the average utility per capita rather than the aggregate – an important issue in relation to issues concerning (over)-population). For a sustained critique of average utility, see Rawls (1971) at pp. 161–75.

Some interpretations and criticisms of Bentham involve misunderstandings, even caricatures. Other interpretations are still contested by Bentham scholars. For example, Bentham is sometimes referred to as a 'hedonistic' utilitarian, only interested in self-regarding pleasures of the flesh. This is a caricature, for Bentham included in his list of 'pleasures' benevolence, amity, power, and revenge – in short anything that can form part of the motivation ('the springs of action') of human beings. However, there is a fundamental ambiguity about 'pleasure' in this context – does it refer to desires, preferences, or satisfaction? This leads to three significantly different interpretations of the basic principle: (i) 'Give as many people as possible as much as possible of what they desire'; (ii) 'give as many people as possible as much as possible of what they in fact (or would) choose or prefer'; or (iiii) 'give as many people as possible as much as possible of what will in fact satisfy them'. These are three different, though overlapping ideas.[52] Here, I shall treat Bentham as a preference utilitarian (i.e. 'maximise choice'), but acknowledge that there is scope for other interpretations or for charging him with inconsistency.[53]

Another misreading of Bentham, advanced by some scholars, is that his principle was self-regarding or selfish (egoistical): that the principle prescribes that the right action for the agent is to maximise his own self-interest.[54] In this view even amity and benevolence are self-interested. The better interpretation, which is also less vulnerable to criticism, is that utility prescribes that the goal for individual actors as well as legislators should always be to maximise the aggregate happiness of the whole community in question (i.e the general welfare rather than individual self-interest).[55]

A distinction sometimes drawn by modern commentators (but not found in Bentham) is between act- and rule-utilitarianism.[56] In the context of discussions of punishment, for example, it has been suggested that utility provides a general justification for the institution of punishment (deterrence, prevention etc.) but not for the punishment of the individual (why punish this man? – because he is guilty). This purported limitation of utility to justifying general

---

[52] 'Satisfaction' can occur with or without prior desire; 'preference utilitarianism' is ambiguous in that it can refer to an attitude or to actual choice. The important distinctions are between, desire, actual satisfaction, and choice.

[53] Ayer (1948) treats Bentham as a 'preference utilitarian', but this does not fit all of the texts.

[54] Lyons (1973/1991); see also Richard Layard (2005a) and (2005b) (arguing that happiness is measurable and that the best route to individual happiness is to be concerned for the happiness of others). Gearty criticises Layard in that having suggested that individuals seek their own happiness, he makes a number of prescriptions about what individuals ought to do in regard to respect for others, empathy for the stranger, and concern for the community that would lead to their own happiness. (Gearty (2006) at pp. 51–54.)

[55] See the debate between David Lyons (1973/1991), and John Dinwiddy (2004) Chapter 3. Here I follow Dinwiddy.

[56] The distinction can be traced back as least as far as John Rawls' classic article 'Two concepts of rules' (Rawls (1955), but some trace it to earlier debates. On the history see Smart (1967). Bentham scholars disagree as to whether Bentham was a consistent act- or rule-utilitarian, see the next note.

rules, institutions and practices would meet some standard criticisms, for example, that utilitarianism justifies too much in respect of punishing the innocent and promising; but, in my view, this distinction is both historically and analytically dubious. Act-utilitarianism has a place for rules, as guidelines and rules of thumb, but these are pragmatic rather than absolute principles.[57] There is no room for absolute or exceptionless rules in utility.[58]

Bentham outlined seven dimensions of pleasure and pain: the *intensity* as experienced by an individual; its *duration*; its *certainty* or likelihood in the future; its *propinquity* in point of time;[59] its *fecundity*,[60] its *purity*,[61] and its *extent*, (i.e. the number of people whose pleasures and pains are to be taken into account in making a calculation). Of these dimensions of value, Bentham felt that four were quantifiable, but he acknowledged that intensity was 'not susceptible of precise expression; it not being susceptible of measurement'.[62] For our purposes, the most significant is *extent*, because this relates to the range of our moral concern, especially to strangers and others who are not members of one's immediate community.

The Benthamite utilitarian calculates by 'weighing' pleasures and pains and aggregating the total with 'happiness' as the bottom line. This 'felicific calculus' has attracted much criticism, but it was also the starting-point for sophisticated forms of cost–benefit analysis.[63] If one takes the calculus literally, it is open to some obvious objections: First, how can one measure pleasures and pains? Some of the dimensions of utility – extent, duration, propinquity, are in principle measurable, but others, especially intensity, are not. Second, there is the problem of inter-subjectivity: how can one compare one person's pleasures and pains with another's? Third, are not many pleasures and pains of different

---

[57] Gerald Postema has argued that Bentham was an act-utilitarian, in that in the last resort judges should decide individual cases directly on the basis of utility even contrary to codified law (Postema (1986)). However, Paul Kelly has argued strongly that Bentham was an indirect (i.e. rule-) utilitarian as evidenced by his writings on civil law (Kelly (1990)). Both scholars may be correct in relation to the texts on which they concentrated, but Postema has been criticised for ignoring the context of *Equity Despatch Court*. See Dinwiddy (2004) at pp. 155–62. In my opinion, the distinction is not tenable analytically and the debate involves an anachronistic reading into Bentham of a dubious distinction that was developed after his time. So here I treat Bentham as an act-utilitarian, but the historical issue has yet to be resolved.

[58] On a utilitarian argument in support of the 'absolute', (i.e. not subject to suspension or exceptions) prohibition on torture in Article 3 of the European Convention on Human Rights, see p. 212 below.

[59] 'The magnitude of a pleasure, supposing it present, being given , – the *value* of it , if not *present*, is diminished by whatever it falls short of being present, even though its *certainty* be supposed entire.' *Codification Proposal* (1822/in Bentham 1998b) at 251. This argument is analogous to the idea that a bird in the hand is worth two in the bush.

[60] 'Its *fecundity*, or the chance it has of being followed by sensations of the *same* kind: that is pleasures, if it be a pleasure; pains if it be a pain'. (*IPML*, p. 39).

[61] 'Its *purity*, or the chance it has of *not* being followed by sensations of the *opposite* kind: that is, pains, if it be a pleasure: pleasures, if it be a pain.' (*IPML*, p. 39).

[62] Bentham, 'Codification Proposal' (1822) in Bentham (CW 1998) at pp. 250–54. For a good discussion of this political arithmetic, see Dinwiddy (2004) at pp. 48–51.

[63] Adler and Posner (eds.), (2001), especially Nussbaum (2001) at pp. 169–200.

kinds, so that they are incommensurable?[64] Is this not like weighing apples and oranges?

Bentham was well aware of these difficulties.[65] He acknowledged that intensity cannot be measured. He discussed how far pleasure and pain in general could be measured by a common metric, such as money. He recognised that people measure money differently in different circumstances and that each addition to a rich man's wealth is less valuable than the previous one – what later was labelled the principle of diminishing marginal utility.[66] However, from the point of view of the legislator some assumptions have to be made about the similarities of people's preferences:

> This addibility of the happiness of different subjects, however, when considered rigorously may appear fictitious, is a postulatum without the allowance for which all political reasonings are at a stand.[67]

In short, we have to proceed as if such comparisons and calculations are possible, while recognising their artificiality and fallibility. On this view the idea of a calculus is a metaphor. It may not be an exact measure, but the dimensions of utility provide a checklist of factors that are relevant to making judgements about the consequences of different courses of action. This may be rough and ready, but what is the alternative? In short, the calculus is a metaphor that models the nearest that we can come to rationality in making practical decisions. The admitted difficulties have continued to plague the theory of cost–benefit analysis, but have not inhibited its extensive use and abuse in practical life.

(b) Principles subordinate to utility

It is sometimes objected that the principle of utility is too abstract to give clear guidance in particular situations. This hardly applies to Bentham, who was given to drawing up lists that concretised the applications of utility, sometimes in relentless detail. His most important list deals with the 'subordinate ends of government': subsistence, abundance, equality, security.[68] These refer to intermediate goals to be pursued to maximise the greatest happiness of the greatest number. Prioritising these goals is still one of the main battlegrounds of political economy.

---

[64] On incommensurability see D'Agostino (2003), Espeland and Stevens (1998), and in relation to legal traditions, the exchange between Andrew Halpin (2006a) (2007) and Patrick Glenn (2007).

[65] See Dinwiddy, (2004), at pp. 48–51 for a good discussion of the problems of quantification. For a less sympathetic analysis see Griffin (1996) at pp. 103–7. See also Harrison (1983) at pp. 246–9.

[66] See pp. 138–9 below.

[67] Manuscript, UCL xiv 3, quoted by Dinwiddy (2004) at p. 49.

[68] This list is discussed in several places, including *Principles of the Civil Code* (1838–43) 1 *Works* 302–13 (1843) (trs. From Dumont's *Traité* with additions) and *Pannomial Fragments* (3 *Works* at 224–30). There are good discussions of the subordinate ends of government in Harrison (1983) at pp. 244–60 and Quinn (2008).

By security Bentham meant more than what is commonly referred to as 'law and order'. Security, sometimes called 'the non-disappointment principle', differs from other objects of law in that it concerns the future as well as the present ('extension in point of time')[69] and it covers all interests protected by law, including life, person, reputation, property, and status.[70] Thus vested property is an aspect of security, so is liberty – an enclave of individual choice created and protected by law.[71] Subsistence refers to the bare necessities of existence; the goal of abundance refers to wealth creation; and equality refers to amounts of happiness.[72]

Bentham recognised that the subordinate ends of government regularly compete with each other.[73] Perhaps surprisingly, he ranked them: other things being equal, subsistence and security are prior to abundance and equality:

> Without security, equality itself could not endure a single day. Without subsistence, abundance cannot exist. The first two ends are like life itself: the two last are the ornaments of life.[74]

Equality is important only insofar as it does not undermine the other three. Subsistence is an aspect of security, but it is sufficiently important to deserve separate treatment. These generalisations are more like rules of thumb than strict principles prescribing a form of lexical priority. For utility always requires the calculation of pleasures and pains in the circumstances of the particular situation.

Equality clearly comes last in this list, but its importance in Bentham's scheme is often underestimated. It comes into play in several ways. First, in the felicific calculus each person's happiness counts for one. There is no differentiation according to status, wealth, power, gender, race, age, or deserts. Second, *ceteris paribus*, equality is important itself when it is not in competition with other subordinate ends. Third, Bentham pioneered the idea that is now known as 'diminishing marginal utility':

> The effect of wealth in the production of happiness goes on diminishing, as the quantity by which the wealth of one man exceeds that of another goes on increasing: in other words, the quantity of happiness produced by a particle of

---

[69] *Codification Proposal*, 251–4.

[70] Dinwiddy (2004) at p. 85; Quinn (2008); Zedner, (2003) (exploring some of the ambiguities and complexities of the concept of security when it is invoked in contemporary political discourse). The concept of 'security' has also been problematic in development circles. For a good discussion see Busumtwi-Sam (2002).

[71] Bentham's treatment of liberty, especially his linking it closely to security, has been controversial. A good short discussion is Rosen (1983) at pp. 68–75. See now, Schofield (2006) at pp. 67–9, pp. 234–40).

[72] 'Subsistence' is variously interpreted: it can mean enough for physical survival or what at a given time are thought of as 'necessities' or sufficient to enable an individual to live as an autonomous agent (Griffin). See Chapter 6, n. 34 below. Cf. conceptions of poverty discussed in Chapter 11.

[73] E.g. *Principles of the Civil Code*, Chapter III. Relations between these objects. (1 *Works* pp. 302–3.)

[74] 1 *Works* p. 303.

wealth (each particle being of the same magnitude) will be less and less at every particle; the second will produce less than the first, the third than the second, and so on.[75]

Equality thus plays a significant role in Bentham's scheme, but it is subject to important limitations. He generally opposed compulsory redistribution of wealth because this leads to disappointed expectations; similarly, in his view, equality should not substantially reduce incentives for wealth creation (abundance). However, since inheritance need not involve vested interests and settled expectations, he supported the abolition of primogeniture and entails. He also suggested that where a person dies without any close relatives, 50 per cent should go to the public purse,[76] and he would probably have supported a much more radical scheme of limited inheritance than has ever existed in Britain.[77] He generally favoured other ways of bringing about relatively painless re-distribution and, in his later writings, he explicitly attacked the delusion that 'the maintenance of property was the only end of government'.[78]

Bentham had clear views on the role of law in respect of the subordinate ends of government. The primary role of law is to create and protect security;[79] it is less important for subsistence: as one of the most important modifications of well being, legislation is generally not needed.[80] However, as his writings on the Poor Laws show, Bentham favoured public support for the indigent, even at the expense of abundance.[81]

Bentham's views on the role of the legislator in promoting abundance are more complex. In some writings, notably *A Defence of Usury*, he went further than Adam Smith in opposing governmental intervention in the market. However, while maintaining that government had a limited role in directly promoting economic growth, he advocated intervention in a number of specific areas, and he regularly emphasised the indirect role of promoting abundance by providing stable conditions for economic activity (i.e. security).

Given the complexity and shifting emphasis of Bentham's writings on political economy, it is perhaps not surprising that he has been claimed as a precursor by proponents of laissez faire, of the modern welfare state, and of the

---

[75] 3 *Works* p. 229.

[76] *Supply Without Burden or Escheat vice Taxation* (1795) 2 *Works*, pp. 585–598; cf. Singer (2004) at pp. 42–3.

[77] 'After the death of an individual, how ought his property to be disposed of? The legislature should have three objects: – 1st. To provide for the subsistence of the rising generation; 2dly, To prevent the pain of disappointment; 3rdly, to promote the equalization of fortunes.' (*Principles of the Civil Code*, Chapter III Another Means of Acquisition – Succession 2 *Works* at p. 334; see *Supply Without Burden*.

[78] 9 *Works*, p. 77.

[79] On security he wrote: 'This inestimable good is the distinctive mark of civilization: it is entirely the work of the laws. Without law there is no security; consequently no abundance, nor even certain subsistence. And the only equality which can exist in such a condition, is the equality of misery.' (*Principles of the Civil Code* (1 *Works* at p. 307). Food Security is now an established term in development discourse, see e.g. Brown (2001), FAO (2005).

[80] On well-being see n. 85 below.   [81] Jeremy Bentham, *Writings on the Poor Laws* (2001).

idea of mixed economy.[82] Like Adam Smith, Bentham's views on political economy were much more complicated and balanced than his general image suggests.[83]

This scamper over some of the difficulties of interpreting utility does not do justice to the complexities of Bentham's thought, nor of utilitarianism in general. Here, I shall proceed on the basis that in discussing Benthamite utilitarianism we are referring to a form of universalist, prescriptive, aggregate, act-utilitarianism, concerned with the general welfare rather than egoism or egotism or narrowly hedonistic versions.

(c) Some standard criticisms of classical utilitarianism

Adopting the standpoint of the legislator, interpreting pleasure to mean preference or choice, making happiness refer to the aggregate of the welfare of the community rather than egoistic self-interest, and treating the felicific calculus as a metaphor all deflect some of the fiercest criticisms of utilitarianism. But there are still some standard objections to this version. One familiar critique is that of Rawls, which will be considered below, along with debates about utility and human rights.[84] Here it is relevant to mention the economist Amartya Sen, who over many years moved away from classical utilitarianism, without completely rejecting it. In Sen's view utilitarianism has two main strengths worth preserving:

(1) the importance of taking into account the *results* of social arrangements in judging them....
(2) The need to pay attention to the *well-being* of the people involved when judging social arrangements and their results....[85]

Sen identifies the main limitations of the utilitarian perspective to be:

(1) *Distributional indifference*: The utilitarian calculus tends to ignore inequalities in the distribution of happiness (only the sum total matters – no matter how unequally distributed)....
(2) *Neglect of rights, freedoms and other non-utility concerns*: The utilitarian approach attaches no intrinsic importance to claims of rights and freedoms (they are valued only indirectly and only to the extent they influence utilities)....

---

[82] 'He has sometimes been presented as a proponent of laissez faire, sometimes as a herald of the welfare state, sometimes as a harbinger of collectivism or "statism".' (Dinwiddy (2004) at p. 92.)

[83] On misuses of Adam Smith's ideas see, for example, Stiglitz (2002) Chapter 3. On the relations between Bentham's ideas and classical economics see the essays in Parekh (ed.) (1993) Vol. 4, Part I.

[84] On Rawls see pp. 154–5 below; on utility and rights see Chapter 6 at pp. 187–9 below.

[85] Sen (1999) at p. 60. For recent philosophical discussions of 'well-being' see Griffin (1986), debated in Crisp and Hooker (eds.) (2000).

(3) *Adaptation and mental conditioning*: Even the view the utilitarian approach takes of individual well-being is not very robust, since it is easily swayed by mental conditioning and adaptive attitudes.[86]

Sen is especially significant for our purposes for several reasons: first, he has been sympathetic to, but critical of, utilitarianism in relation to welfare economics, an area in which this kind of thinking has been especially influential. Second, although he has spent much of his career in the West, his roots are in India and in much of his work he adopts a global perspective. His is a very important 'Southern voice'. Third, much of his writing has been concerned with issues of development and rights; and, fourth, he finds merits and limitations in each of the main strands of liberal democratic theory, utilitarianism, libertarianism (exemplified by Nozick) and Rawlsian justice. This has led him to develop 'a capabilities approach', which has been very influential in recent development theory, in particular in relation to human development indicators and the Millennium Development Goals, which will be considered below in Chapter 11.

(d) Bentham and globalisation[87]

Besides being widely regarded as the greatest and most influential figure in Anglo-American jurisprudence, Jeremy Bentham is more directly relevant to globalisation than most other jurists. He was a universalist in ethics, and a near universalist in respect of constitution-making and the transplantation of laws; his criticisms of non-legal rights still have to be taken into account by any serious theory of human rights;[88] he pioneered general jurisprudence, and he often (but not invariably) explicitly adopted the standpoint of 'a (or the) citizen of the world', concerned with the welfare of humankind as a whole.[89] In 1831, not long before his death, he wrote in his Memorandum Book:

> J.B.'s frame of mind.
>
> J.B. the most ambitious of the ambitious. His empire – the empire he aspires to – extending to, and comprehending, the whole human race, in all places – in all habitable places, of the earth, at all future time.
>
> J.B. the most philanthropic of the philanthropic: philanthropy the end and instrument of his ambition.
>
> Limits it has no other than those of the earth.[90]

Apart from Bentham's utilitarianism and his theory of law, three works in particular are directly relevant when considering law from a global perspective.

---

[86] Ibid., at p. 62.   [87] For a longer discussion see *GJB*, pp. 237–42.
[88] See Chapter 6.5(a) below.   [89] Harrison (1983) at pp. 276–7.
[90] 11 *Works*, p. 72. The writings on international law (more extensive than in Bowring) are currently being edited for *The Collected Works*.

Nonsense Upon Stilts (until recently cited as *Anarchical Fallacies*)[91] is still the best-known critique of natural and human rights theories, which are in some quarters the dominant discourse of public morality today.[92] What is at stake here is not the underlying values (in criticising a right to food or development, a Benthamite is not denying that food or development are important); rather the thrust of the criticism is that such kinds of rights talk is unclear, misleading, meaningless or, in Bentham's words, 'pestilential nonsense'.[93]

Bentham introduced the term 'international law' to refer to relations between sovereign states. In his theory of law all law emanates directly or indirectly from the sovereign. Yet he was acute enough to recognise that there are difficult issues about the illimitability and indivisibility of sovereignty, and unlike some of our contemporaries he acknowledged that sovereignty could be split. He also posed, but did not resolve, an issue that is a key one in international ethics. Is the duty of a national leader or government to give priority to the interests of his own people or does it extend to humankind as a whole?[94]

Thirdly, a little known early work, *Essay on the Influence of Place and Time in Matters of Legislation* is potentially of great contemporary significance.[95] To what extent law is or should be context- and culture-specific is a central issue in the study and practice of transnational diffusion, harmonisation and unification of law and in local law reform, where foreign models and the experience of other countries are under consideration. Bentham posed the basic issues as follows:

> To give the question at once universal form, what is the influence of the circumstances of place and time in matters of legislation? What are the coincidences and what the diversities that ought to subsist between laws established in different countries and at different periods, supposing them in each instance the best to be established?[96]

Seldom have the basic issues been posed so sharply and addressed so systematically. In his later years Bentham aspired to be Legislator of the World. In some of his later writings on codification, which were connected with his

---

[91] Recently re-published in the *Collected Works* as 'Nonsense Upon Stilts' in *Rights, Representation and Reform: Nonsense Upon Stilts and Other Writings on the French Revolution* (CW, 2002).

[92] See Chapter 6.1 below.   [93] See Chapter 6.5(a) below.

[94] 'Would or would not the duty of a particular legislator, acting for one particular nation, be the same with that of the citizen of the world?' *Principles of International Law* 2 *Works* 561 (1786–9). Cf. Singer (2004), Preface (criticising the extreme prioritising of American interests in speeches by the Presidents Bush).

[95] Written circa 1780, the text first appeared in French in *Traité de législation civile et pénale* (ed. Dumont) (1802) but not published in English until 1838 in a truncated version in 1 *Works*, pp. 171–94 (Bowring (ed.)). Philip Schofield has recently edited the manuscripts for *Place and Time* (hereafter *OPT*) and has kindly made them available to me. This youthful essay is ebullient and discursive, with some interesting comments on a range of topics. Unfortunately, for the modern reader it is marred by some potentially racist and explicitly islamophobic passages, which may distract attention from the central argument.

[96] *OPT* at p. 1 (MS). The wording is only slightly different in the printed version, 1 *Works* 171.

unsuccessful attempts to sell his services as a codifier to a succession of foreign rulers and politicians, he gave the impression of being a near-universalist in legislation, a technocrat largely indifferent to local conditions and culture.[97] However, in *Essay on the Influence of Place and Time*, he gave some weight to Montesquieu's ideas on the importance of history, geography, and culture in the development of law, and advocated a quite moderate and gradualist approach to transplantation of laws. He argued that local sensibilities should be heeded and humoured, but that they should not be treated as insurmountable by the utilitarian legislator, who might need to rely more on 'indirect legislation' than direct imposition of new codes, at least in the short term. Bentham, like most modern exporters of law, concluded that 'universally applying circumstances' were much more important than 'exclusively applying circumstances',[98] but his arguments are interesting and incisive. Bentham's *Essay* is especially interesting in considering diffusion and harmonisation of laws, not least because it presents more of a challenge to modern contextualists, such as Lawrence Friedman and Pierre Legrand, than some of their standard targets.[99]

5.5 Peter Singer: a modern Benthamite[100]

Too much has happened since Bentham's time in respect of international law and global ethics for Bentham's relatively rudimentary texts on these topics to be a suitable starting point today. However, we have in Peter Singer an outstanding contemporary philosopher who has applied a form of Benthamite utilitarianism to a wide range of issues of practical ethics, many from a global perspective.[101]

Peter Singer was born in Australia in 1946. He has held positions in philosophy in Australia, the United Kingdom and latterly (since 1999) at Princeton. He is a respected philosopher, but he is more widely known as a public intellectual and political activist. One of his early works, *Animal Liberation* (1975), attracted a great deal of attention and made an immediate impact on the

---

[97] Bentham, *Legislator of the World* (1998a). This volume is concerned with late works and does not include the early essay on place and time.

[98] *Ibid.*, at pp. 291–2.   [99] See pp. 295 and 305 below.

[100] Bibliographical note: the main works discussed here are Singer *Animal Liberation* (1975), 2nd edn 1990/1; (numerous reprints and translations); *Marx* (1980), *Practical Ethics* (1979), 2nd edn (1993), *The Expanding Circle: Ethics and Sociobiology* (1983), (ed.) *A Companion to Ethics* (1991), *One World* (2002/2004) and two famous articles, 'Famine, Affluence and Morality' (1972) reprinted, with other contributions to the debate, in Charles Beitz *et al.* (eds) *International Ethics: A Philosophy and Public Affairs Reader* (1985) and in Peter Brown and Henry Shue (eds.) *Food Policy* (1977). A useful collection of essays about Singer is to be found in Dale Jamieson (ed.) *Singer and his Critics.* (1999), which contains a selected bibliography of Singer's writings from 1970–98.

[101] As a philosopher Singer was strongly influenced by R.M. Hare. On the similarities and differences in their positions on utilitarianism see R.M. Hare, 'Why I am Only a Demi-Vegetarian' and Singer's response in Jamieson (ed.) (1999).

animal movement.[102] The book is a sustained and powerful argument that one owes a duty to animals not to cause suffering or death unnecessarily. The starting point is Bentham's dictum: 'The question is not, Can they *reason*? Nor, can they *talk*? But, can they *suffer*?'[103]

The book exhibits three features that characterise much of Singer's work.[104] First, like Marx, Singer's concern is not merely to understand the world, but to change it.[105] In many of his writings Singer tries to persuade people to change their unconsidered beliefs and to act on their new ones. Indeed, *Animal Liberation* can claim many converts to vegetarianism[106] and to opposition to animal testing.

Second, Singer takes facts seriously. One of the attractions of utilitarianism is that it focuses attention on actual situations and empirical consequences. The power of Singer's arguments in *Animal Liberation* stems from combining simple principles with vivid pictures, detailed statistics, and other empirical data. Most of the book is taken up with marshalling evidence to support the thesis that current practices in carnivorous societies in fact involve immense cruelty to millions of animals and that this is unnecessary. The book is a straightforward application of the principle of utility to actual states of affairs and their consequences: Harming animals unnecessarily causes pain and is unacceptable; our practices harm animals unnecessarily; therefore, these practices are morally unacceptable.

Third, Singer believes that both individual ethics and informed, rational policy-making can bring about change. Singer's 'practical ethics' are immediately practical.[107] Much of his writing is concerned with individual ethics and he has generally shaped his life according to his beliefs: for example in his private life he is reported to be a vegetarian, to refuse to wear clothes made from animal skins, and to give a significant proportion of his income to causes in which he believes, especially those dealing with world poverty and animal welfare. In short, he acts as a role model for a particular kind of utilitarian.

---

[102] Singer does not use the term 'animal rights' for reasons discussed below.

[103] *IPML*, pp. 282–3n. The whole passage on 'Interests of the inferior animals improperly neglected in legislation' is well worth reading.

[104] Following Jamieson (1999) at pp. 6–7.

[105] Singer wrote a short book on Marx (Singer (1980)), but he was never a Marxist. Marx was scornful of utilitarianism, mainly in regard to the utilitarian conception of 'the general interest' rather than the idea of maximising happiness (at p. 63). Singer's judgement is that 'Marx saw that capitalism is a wasteful, irrational system which controls us when we should be controlling it. That insight is valid, but we can now see that the construction of a free and equal society is a more difficult task than Marx realised' (at p. 76).

[106] I do not have figures but I know a number of vegetarians who claim that it influenced them. Many commentators make similar claims about his influence. See Jamieson (1999) *passim*.

[107] *Practical Ethics* (2nd ed 1993) is a very successful textbook. It addresses a wide range of contemporary issues of individual ethics and social policy, some of which have 'global' dimensions (e.g. equality, rich and poor, development assistance, killing (including genocide), treatment of outsiders, and the environment). *One World*, discussed below, is his main work that focuses specifically on global ethics.

He also has 'the courage of his premises', in that he firmly adopts and campaigns for positions that follow from his arguments, even if they are very unpopular.[108]

In some of his works Singer advances pure utilitarian arguments and takes radical, often controversial positions that follow from robust premises. Like Bentham, Singer has been more concerned to use utility as a critical weapon rather than to justify it.[109] However, in his writings on famines and other 'global' issues and in his lectures on *One World* (discussed below) his concern is to persuade people with a wide range of ethical positions.[110] Here his arguments are more ecumenical and less philosophically sophisticated, but underlying them is a consistent quite simple utilitarianism.[111]

Singer has written about 'global' issues in many different contexts. For our purposes, two are of particular significance. First, in a well-known paper entitled 'Famine, affluence and morality' Singer stimulated a long-running debate around the question: who is my neighbour? – Bentham's dimension of 'extent'.[112] The article was specifically about the allocation of responsibility for famines, but it raised important issues about what should be the extent of the moral concern of individuals, associations, and governments. Building on empirical evidence that nearly all modern famines have been avoidable,[113] Singer argues that in an interdependent world utility imposes an obligation on all relevant moral actors to take measures to prevent famines:

> If it is in our power to prevent something bad from happening, without sacrificing anything of comparable moral importance, we ought morally to do it.[114]

This is a matter of duty, not charity. Famines are preventable and all involved moral agents have a duty to prevent them without regard to national boundaries, proximity, or distance. In today's world almost everyone is involved.[115] Singer acknowledges that the principle as formulated 'does seem to require reducing ourselves to the level of marginal utility'.[116] While he personally

---

[108] The best known example of this is his view that parents of seriously disabled newborn babies should be able to decide, with medical advice, whether the child should live or die. This position is part of a wider thesis on euthanasia. In respect of this Singer has been attacked not only intellectually, but personally, including the cancellation of events and even death threats, especially in Germany. (For a full account see the Appendix to the third edition of *Practical Ethics* (1993). Singer stood by his general position and fought for his right to debate it.)

[109] But see Singer (1979) and some of his early papers. He has acknowledged his debt to R.M. Hare and accepts much of his approach to moral issues in Jamieson (ed.) (1999) at p. 322.

[110] Ibid., at p. 302. Compare Thomas Pogge's use of 'ecumenical arguments' p. 172 below.

[111] As we shall see, other thinkers, such as Pogge and Sachs, have pragmatically stressed the relatively small costs involved in preventing famine and in mitigating global poverty and, like Singer, have also appealed to self-interest.

[112] See above and GLT, pp. 65–9. See Scanlon (1998).

[113] The *locus classicus* is Sen (1981), continued in writings collected in *The Amartya Sen and Jean Drèze Omnibus* (1999). The research is discussed in Attfield and Wilkins (eds.) (1992).

[114] Singer (1972) reprinted, with other contributions to the debate, in Beitz *et al.* (eds.) (1985) Part V.

[115] See p. 148 below on the idea of strengthening the perception of mankind as a community.

[116] Singer in Beitz *et al.* (1985) at pp. 258–59.

favours this strong utilitarian version, he points out that more moderate positions, which require less heroic sacrifices, would nonetheless result in 'a great change in our way of life.'[117]

Singer has dealt extensively with a number of objections to his thesis.[118] For example, it has been argued that it is unrealistic because it sets too high a standard, requiring sacrifices that the better off will not in practice be prepared to make.[119] Singer dismisses this objection as not being a moral argument.[120] But it is psychologically important and Singer has made some concessions to it. A second objection is that there are 'spheres of justice' or limits to our moral concern that justify drawing quite sharp distinctions between our duties to members of our own community (and those who are closely related to us) and our duties to outsiders, especially unidentified and distant strangers.[121] This raises very complex issues. A utilitarian may go some of the way towards meeting the objection by suggesting that families, friendship, close-knit communities, and other social institutions and associations probably generally promote aggregate happiness and this would justify giving some priority to friends, relatives, colleagues, club members, and fellow citizens. In the long run, utility is maximised by these arrangements. Similarly, one may be in a better position to make good calculations in respect of people one knows or one's own social situation, because one has better information. But Singer challenges the idea that proximity, either physical or relational, in itself is a relevant moral consideration.[122] Starting with an example of seeing a child drowning whom one could easily rescue at the cost of getting one's clothes wet, he suggests that one has a positive duty to act to save the child. The fact that he is a stranger is irrelevant. Sometimes, too, claims to relational ties can be forms of discrimination: justifying inclusion by claiming a blood relationship, or shared citizenship, for example, can be merely an excuse for discriminating on racial, gender, or xenophobic grounds. Moreover, among those who defend the idea of spheres of justice, loyalty to one's family is generally accepted to involve background constraints: in our culture, drugging the drinks of one's son's competitors in a tennis competition is generally condemned, paying for private education or schooling of one's children in a welfare state is contested, giving birthday

---

[117] *Ibid.*

[118] Especially, 'Reconsidering the famine relief argument', in Brown and Shue (eds.) (1977). Singer (1993) Chapter 8 deals with the issues in a broader framework.

[119] Beitz *et al.* (1985); Fishkin (1985).

[120] The fact that people will in practice be unwilling or reluctant to give up what they have because it is right to do so, does not affect the extent of their obligations. And, it has been pointed out, that many of the more extreme versions of human suffering in the modern world could be prevented or drastically reduced if, for example, individuals in rich countries gave a small part of their income to appropriate 'charities' or causes and all governments met the United Nations targets, modest and arbitrary as they are, for foreign aid, provided, of course, that the money was well spent.

[121] The *locus classicus* is Walzer (1983); see the debate between Luban and Walzer in Beitz (*et al.*) (1985), Part II.

[122] On Bentham's dimension of 'propinquity' (in time) see n. 59 above.

presents to one's family is generally accepted as a duty by utilitarians and non-utilitarians alike.[123] Similarly, to use reciprocity as a basis for preferring members of one's own group to outsiders, is not a coherent moral argument. Does it follow from this that we owe no duties to future generations? Once all the possible utilitarian considerations have been pared away the difference is that Singer is challenging the idea that 'friendship, loyalty, familial ties, self-respect etc. are important independently of their contribution to the best overall state of affairs.'[124]

A third line of attack is that Singer's thesis is based on premises that are open to many of the standard criticisms of utilitarianism. This objection has been confronted by Onora O'Neill who, in her well-known essay 'Lifeboat Earth', develops a non-utilitarian position that both by-passes criticisms of simple utilitarianism and meets the point that theories of rights tend to beg questions of allocating responsibility for realising rights.[125] Although O'Neill in fact agrees with many of Singer's arguments, she constructs a moral position about global responsibility for extreme evils (her main example is deaths from famine) that transcends different ethical theories. The argument goes as follows: 'any nonbizarre ethical theory which has any room for a notion of rights' will include a right not to be killed.[126] This right has a correlative obligation on everyone not to be involved in the killing of another without justification.[127] In brief, she lays the responsibility not to contribute to unnecessary deaths on anybody who is involved in the world economy, which in effect means all of us – both as individuals, as citizens, and as participants in associations or corporate bodies, for example as shareholders, managers, or directors of large business enterprises. Later, we shall consider a similar argument by Thomas Pogge to the effect that the responsibilities of the better off, both individuals and governments, can be based on a duty not to cause harm quite apart from any positive duty there may be to help tackle radical poverty.[128]

Several factors are combining to make this kind of thesis seem less utopian than it might have done even ten years ago: the rapid increase in interdependence; the immediacy of extreme problems such as famine, civil war, genocide,

---

[123] There have been a number of case of parents who overstepped the bounds of loyalty (e.g. the headline in *The Times* on July 20 2007 (News p. 3) 'Families to sue gymkhana mother accused of doping rivals' ponies'. In a recent German case a father was convicted of manslaughter in more tragic circumstances: he had drugged the drinks of his son's competitors at tennis, one became sleepy, withdrew and died in a car crash.

[124] Gruen, in Jamieson (ed.) (1999) at p. 141.

[125] O'Neill (1974) reprinted in Beitz *et al.* (1985); See also O'Neill (1986).

[126] O'Neill in Beitz *et al.* (1985) at p. 268, n.2.

[127] This duty applies even though we (a) do not kill single-handedly those who die of famine; (b) do not kill instantaneously those who die of famine; (c) do not know the individuals who will die as result of the pre-famine and famine policies we support (unless we support something like a genocidal famine policy); (d) do not intend any famine deaths. *Ibid.*, at p. 277.

[128] See Chapter 12 below.

and climate change; and the increasing scope of an overlapping consensus at world level about what constitutes intolerable situations in other countries.[129] All of these raise complex issues about sovereignty, the extent of our moral concern, and what constraints there should be on national leaders furthering national self-interest rather than broader concerns.

Singer addresses some of these issues in a book based on the Terry Lectures given at Yale in November 1999.[130] The central thesis of *One World* is that issues arising from globalisation have a moral dimension and that, in order to create a stable world community, national leaders 'need to take a larger perspective than of national self-interest'.[131] The facts of increased interdependence make it increasingly important that efforts should be directed towards making humankind with legitimated political institutions evolve in the direction, not of centralised world government, but of a federal structure, perhaps modelled on the European union.[132] For Singer, just as within a closed community the right action for individuals as for leaders is to promote the aggregate happiness of the community, so political leaders need to 'think outside the box' of short-term national interest. For this to happen the idea of humankind as a community needs to be greatly strengthened. Enlightened self-interest and charitable concerns may help in this regard, but on their own they are not enough. Singer roundly criticises President George W. Bush for such statements as 'We will not do anything that harms our economy, because first things first are the people who live in America.'[133] He is also highly critical of American protectionist policies and the US stance on such matters as the Kyoto Protocol, the International Criminal Court, and UN reform of fair trade.

From a global perspective, a modern utilitarian might argue that for every national leader the extent of his or her moral concern should be humankind as a whole, but the structure of international society is such that it is in the interests of humankind that (democratic) leaders should generally represent and seek to advance the interests of their own constituents, except where the utilities clearly require some sacrifice or tempering of those. The utilitarian can also point out that very often pursuing policies that will generally benefit mankind will also be pragmatic, statesmanlike examples of 'enlightened self-interest'. As we shall see, the proponents of the Millennium Development Goals have tended to emphasise this as well as pointing out how much can be achieved at relatively low cost.[134] But such arguments can only take one so far. For there will inevitably be occasions when national interests will clash with those of humankind or less well-off parts of it. Furthermore, a democratically elected leader risks not being

---

[129] On the consensus around the Millennium Development Goals see Chapter 11 below. On humanitarian intervention see Nardin and Williams (eds.) (2006).

[130] Singer (2002).   [131] Singer (2002), Preface at p. ix.   [132] Singer (2002), pp. 99, 199.

[133] *New York Times*, 30 March 2001, discussed in Singer (2002), Preface to 2nd edn. On American exceptionalism and its purported justifications see Koh (2003), Ignatieff (ed.) (2005), and Tasioulas (2008), section 3.

[134] See Chapter 11.4 below.

re-elected if she goes too far down the road of 'statesmanlike' concessions and sacrifices – human development strategies today are heavily dependent on mobilising public opinion in wealthier countries to support quite modest strategies, such as the Millennium Development Goals.

Singer discusses the arguments for and against 'first things first' stances. Many will disagree with his contention that sovereignty is of little or no moral significance.[135] More will agree with the idea of strengthening our vision of humankind as a genuine or robustly imagined community, but concede that there is a long way to go. Moreover, as many have pointed out, the current world order is far from democratic, but it is mainly wealthier democracies who are asked to bear the main financial burdens of poverty alleviation, peace keeping, international institutions and so on. Singer states that there is a strong ethical case against leaders giving absolute priority to national interests, but acknowledges that there is a case for giving 'some degree of priority' to them. However, he leaves open the question what does 'some degree of priority' amount to?[136] Like Bentham, Singer has posed the question how should national leaders behave, but also like Bentham he gives, at best, a vague answer. Nevertheless, he has made the case for taking the ethical dimensions of globalisation seriously and has identified some of the central issues.

Peter Singer is an outstanding example of a thinker who adjusts and extends classic arguments in the light of changed circumstances, including in relation to 'globalisation.' In Section 5.7, we shall see how Thomas Pogge has made a similar adjustment of the leading theory of justice of the twentieth century, but in a somewhat different fashion.

5.6 Modified utilitarianism

A modified utilitarian position accepts that utilitarian arguments can be valid, relevant, and cogent in making and assessing judgements of value, but rejects the claim that utility is the sole criterion of the right and the good. For example, Herbert Hart was generally sympathetic to utility as a principle of guidance and evaluation of legislation, but he also invoked 'principles independent of utility'. For example, utility can provide the main general answers to the question: Why prescribe punishments? For the institution of punishment is generally justified by its intended consequences (deterrence, prevention, rehabilitation, etc.). But it cannot provide satisfactory answers to the question of distribution: Who should be punished?[137] Classical utilitarianism is usually interpreted as justifying too much, such as collective punishments and punishing an innocent

---

[135] 'Sovereignty has no *intrinsic* moral weight' Singer (2002) at p. 148 and *passim*. See the right to national self-determination. Contrast Rawls (1999b).

[136] Singer (2002) at pp. 1–5. See Chapter 5.

[137] Hart (1968), Chapter 1. On the distinction between act- and rule-utilitarianism, see pp. 135–6 above.

individual in circumstances where the benefits outweigh the costs.[138] Similar arguments can be made about promising and torture.[139] Hart argued that punishment of the innocent involves a serious sacrifice of an important principle that is independent of utility: in this case an aspect of justice – punishment should be only inflicted on those who deserve it.[140] In short, utility provides the general justifying aim of the institution of punishment (forward looking reasons) but the distribution of punishment should be governed by independent justice-based principles of responsibility and proportionality. As Lacey put it, Hart worked within the tradition of Benthamite Utilitarianism, but gave a place to justice, rights and fairness.[141] Conversely, in discussing strict liability in criminal law, Hart argued that principles of responsibility place constraints on the general utilitarian aims of criminal justice, but in some circumstances – for example, in regard to some regulatory crimes – the benefits may sufficiently outweigh the costs to justify overriding these principles.[142] However, he suggested, 'such arrangements are always made with a sense that a principle is being sacrificed: that a compromise is being made.'[143]

A modified utilitarian position is different from one in which other values 'trump' utility. Natural lawyers and deontologists have not rejected all consequentialist arguments, rather they claim that there are values other than utility (even when broadly interpreted) and some of these values generally override consequentialist considerations. For example, when Ronald Dworkin asserts that rights 'trump' utility, he allows broad scope for arguments relating to the 'general welfare', for instance in regard to social policy and democratic legislation, but maintains that rights represent important enclaves of value that generally override utilitarian or other consequentialist arguments. Rights are not mere side-constraints, they are trumps.[144]

---

[138] Fred Rosen has argued that Bentham was not concerned with the problem of punishing the innocent and in discussing punishment for offences guilt is generally assumed and proportionality of punishment was built into the analysis. The issue came to the fore much later in connection with A.C. Ewing's *The Morality of Punishment* (1929) and in this context two false assumptions were made: first, that utilitarians justify punishment by deterrence alone, and second, that utilitarianism is a 'top down' theory in which pleasure alone is the only good and which has no principle of distribution; but classical utilititarianism, exemplified by Bentham, built up to utility from secondary principles which take issues of desert and proportionality into account. (Rosen (1997)). This interpretation is likely to be contested on the ground that punishing the innocent undermines security. On 'top down' theories, see below p. 153. If Rosen's historical argument is convincing, this is an important piece of revisionism, since he supports Paul Kelly's interpretation of Bentham as a rule utilitarian (Kelly, 1990). But for those who interpret Bentham as an act-utilitarian it does not quite meet the point that in some circumstances inflicting pain on the innocent (and torture) may be judged to be the lesser of two evils in some circumstances.

[139] On promising, see Sartorius (1969); on Bentham on torture see Twining and Twining, (1973/74). On recent debates see Levinson (2004) Greenberg (2006).

[140] Hart (1968) at pp. 19–24.   [141] Lacey (2004) at p. 7.

[142] Hart (1968), Chapter 1.   [143] Lacey (2004) at p. 282.

[144] The *locus classicus* of this famous metaphor is Dworkin (1977) at p. xi and Chapter 4. A good discussion is Guest (1997) at pp. 52–3, 189–90.

Some might argue that there is little difference in practice between the position of a modified utilitarian and of a rights theorist, who allows some space for utilitarian arguments. For example, Stephen Guest interprets Dworkin's position as saying 'that claims of right are not defeated by a simple appeal to a marginal increase of welfare'. But he continues: 'I say "marginal" to avoid the problems raised by the cases of catastrophe or emergency'.[145] But the modified utilitarian may only be prepared to sacrifice an important principle if the utilitarian benefits significantly or substantially outweigh the costs. Is there a difference? I think that there is, but it may not lead to great differences of outcome. First, take the situation of competing rights (or moral values independent of utility). The modified utilitarian may argue: 'Where rights conflict, utility determines'. Is the rights theorist committed to this? Well if she accepts some idea of lexical priority (such as Rawls' priority of liberty) probably not, but some followers of Rawls (and Hart as a modified utilitarian) reject lexical priority[146] – both involve dilemmas, but the non-utilitarian is not committed to only weighing consequences to resolve it. Similarly, in emergency situations or catastrophes, where the consequences are dire a rights theorist may be willing to sacrifice rights.

However, there are significant differences. For a modified utilitarian, utilitarianism has the following attractions:

(i) utilitarian arguments can be meaningful, valid and cogent;[147]
(ii) consequences are normally relevant considerations to take into account in practical decision-making;
(iii) utilitarianism is consistently concerned with actual or likely consequences;
(iv) Bentham's list of the 'dimensions' of utility helpfully pinpoints factors that are generally relevant in identifying and assessing consequences;
(v) the felicific calculus, interpreted metaphorically, approximately models the kind of practical reasoning involved in assessing consequences;
(vi) concepts such as 'the general welfare', 'well being', 'the public interest', and 'happiness', although vague, express important public and private goals.
(vii) value judgements are, up to a point, susceptible to rational appraisal and argument.

However, modified utilitarians have doubts about unconstrained utilitarianism such as Bentham's, in one or more of the following respects:

---

[145] Guest (1997), p. 65. On Dworkin's views on 'uncorrupted' (egalitarian) utilitarianism, see *ibid.*, pp. 186–90.
[146] E.g. Pogge (1989) *passim*, especially pp. 125–31, Hart (1983) Chapter 10. See Lacey (2004) at p. 283.
[147] For an example of a wholesale rejection of utilitarian arguments as moral arguments see Milne (1974).

(i) doubts whether all considerations relevant to making value judgements can be reduced to a single criterion;

(ii) doubts whether all valid reasons in evaluation are forward-looking, leaving no room for considerations such as desert, fair procedures, or retribution;

(iii) doubts whether unmodified utilitarianism can accommodate such values as dignity (respect for persons), distributive justice, fairness, and a virtuous disposition;

(iv) doubts about the feasibility and appropriateness of 'calculating' consequences in all situations.[148]

Such concerns are brought to the surface by examples of situations in which utilitarianism seems to miss the point. For example, on one interpretation, Bentham suggests that what is wrong with convicting the innocent is that it creates alarm in others[149] and that what is wrong with torture is its susceptibility to abuse.[150] If this interpretation is correct, it suggests a deficiency in utilitarianism. What is wrong with punishing the innocent is that it is unjust; what is wrong with torture is not solely or mainly its consequences, or the dangers of misapplication, but the intuitive idea that people just should not be treated in this way. These are but two instances where non-consequentialist arguments are felt to be needed, even by those generally sympathetic to utilitarianism. The modified utilitarian makes space for such considerations in terms of principles independent of utility, but may concede that such principles may sometimes have to be sacrificed in exceptional circumstances.

In his discussions of punishment and responsibility Hart treated considerations of justice and proportionality as being grounded in principles independent of utility.[151] In some instances utility must give way to justice, as in punishment of the innocent. However, in respect of strict liability utility considerations may be so strong as to override minor injustices, but even then there is a cost, the sacrifice of a principle independent of utility. As several commentators have pointed out, the trouble is that this form of modified utilitarianism gives no guidance on the scope or weight of the modifying principles. Lacey suggests that because utilitarian and justice-based principles 'float in different philosophical systems' Hart, unlike Rawls, 'cannot give us any clues about

---

[148] E.g. Griffin (1996) at pp. 106–7.

[149] Bentham's position on this issue is open to more than one interpretation: Compare e.g. p. vii, *Works* pp. 591–3 with *A Treatise on Judicial Evidence* (1825, (ed.) Dumont) at pp. 196–7. Denman (1824) at p. 180 attributed the interpretation in the text to Bentham and attacked it in the *Edinburgh Review*. Compare, however, Rosen (1997) discussed above, at n. 138. Of course, the pain involved in punishment or torture has to be taken into account.

[150] Twining and Twining (1973/4) at pp. 42–5, 79–90. Bentham's insight that *institutionalised* torture is susceptible to abuse has much support in history and provides another strong argument for an absolute prohibition of torture in opposition to arguments from 'the extreme case', which tend to be advanced in particularist terms.

[151] For a good discussion, see MacCormick (1981a) (2nd edn 2008).

how they should be traded off against each other.'[152] She concludes that Hart's treatment of punishment and responsibility was symptomatic of a general tendency to tentativeness in his later work. Tasioulas, in arguing for a less 'top-down' approach to punishment based explicitly on ethical pluralism, criticises such hybrid theories more forcefully:

> The resulting theory will be truly hybrid in character, assembled from the dismembered parts of incompatible general moral theories. But now a second defect is apparent, viz. that the theory arrived at is little better than an ad hoc compromise among radically different concerns. Proponents of hybrid theories can offer no coherent rationale for the principles they have combined – apart from the fact that they have been explicitly manufactured to yield results more attuned to our settled moral convictions – since one cannot at the level of underlying theory, endorse both consequentialism and deontology. They thereby violate the 'no-shopping' principle.[153]

Hart modified his utilitarianism to accommodate considerations of justice, rights, and fairness. But he acknowledged that, in his view, moral philosophy had yet to develop arguments in favour of rights that were 'comparable in clarity, detailed articulation, and appeal to practical men'.[154] In the next section, we shall examine first the attempts of Rawls and his successors to construct a well-grounded theory of justice for the modern world as an alternative to utilitarianism. Then Chapters 6 and 7 consider diverse attempts by theorists of human rights to meet Hart's challenge.

5.7 Theories of justice: Rawls and Pogge

(a) Rawls' Theory of Justice[155]

Rawls' *Theory of Justice* is generally regarded as one of the most important contributions to moral and political theory of the twentieth century. It stands to Anglo-American normative jurisprudence as Hart's *The Concept of Law* stands to analytical jurisprudence. It is regarded by many as having set the terms of

---

[152] Lacey (2004) at p. 283.

[153] Tasioulas (2006) at p. 281, citing Stuart Hampshire (1983) at p. 148.

[154] Hart (1982) p. 39. See his discussions of utilitarianism, rights, and justice in Hart (1983) Chapters 8–10.

[155] Bibliographical note: the main works by John Rawls cited in this section are as follows: John Rawls, *A Theory of Justice* (1971/1972) (hereafter TJ); *Political Liberalism* (1993) (hereafter PL); *The Law of Peoples* (1999c) (hereafter LP); *Collected Papers* (ed. S. Freeman, 1999b) (hereafter *Papers*). Especially important in the present context are four papers: 'Two Concepts of Rules', 64 *Philosophical Review* 72 (1955) (hereafter *TCR*); 'Kantian Constructivism in Moral Theory' (1980) (reprinted in *Papers* Chapter 16) (hereafter *KCMT*) (see now *PL* Lecture III); 'Justice as Fairness: Political, not Metaphysical' (1985) (reprinted in *Papers*, Chapter 18)(see also *PL* Lecture I 'Fundamental Ideas') and 'The Idea of an Overlapping Consensus' (1987) (hereafter *IOC*) (reprinted in *Papers*, Chapter 20). There are several useful symposia on Rawls, especially Norman Daniels (ed.) *Reading Rawls: Critical Studies of A Theory Of Justice* (1975) and Symposium on Rawls and the Law 72 *Fordham L. Rev.* 1380–2175, and a Symposium on *The Law of Peoples* in 110 *Ethics* (July, 2000); see now Martin and Reidy (eds.) (2006) on *The Law of Peoples*.

debate on justice and rights for nearly fifty years. I shall suggest that his two principles of justice (or some variant) are still strong candidates for providing widely acceptable standards for the design and appraisal of public institutions, but that Rawls' own attempts to transfer his theory of domestic justice to the supra-national arena were a sad failure. In this regard, it is more illuminating to focus instead on the work of his pupil, Thomas Pogge, as the best attempt to date to develop an essentially Rawlsian theory of global justice.

Rawls began his career as a moral philosopher in the late 1940s. Although his magnum opus, *A Theory of Justice* was not published until 1971, a draft manuscript was in circulation by 1960 and was progressively refined over a decade. World War II, Hiroshima and Nagasaki, the Cold War and anti-communism, the War in Vietnam, draft evasion, the civil rights move-ment, and other issues of social justice in the United States were all part of the backdrop during the long gestation period of Rawls' theory. During the 1950s and beyond, political philosophy was in a fallow period. Logical positivism, 'the revolution' in analytical philosophy, an atmosphere of general suspicion of both 'grand theory' and of Continental European philosophising, all discouraged engagement with substantive moral and political issues.[156] One of the achieve-ments of *A Theory of Justice*, an extraordinarily ambitious work for the period, was to reinstate substantive political philosophy as a reputable pursuit.

Initially Rawls seems to have been quite attracted to utilitarianism and, in a classic article published in 1958 entitled 'Two Concepts of Rules', he tried to meet some of the standard attacks on utility by distinguishing between justifi-cation of the legislator's question (justifying a decision to make a general rule) and the judge's question (Why punish this man?). Thus a rule prescribing punishment may be justified by its utilitarian purposes, but a decision to punish an individual under an established rule must be justified by a different non-consequentialist argument.[157] However, Rawls decided that utilitarianism could not be rescued, even though he continued to admire its scope and rigour and its progressive influence on reform.[158] So he developed his theory of 'justice as fairness' in the Kantian tradition of liberal individualism as a response and positive alternative to all forms of utilitarianism.[159]

He selected as his main target the version advanced in Henry Sidgwick's *The Methods of Ethics*.[160] Rawls interpreted this as defending the view 'that society is rightly ordered, and therefore just, when its major institutions are arranged so as to achieve the greatest net balance of satisfaction summed over all the individuals belonging to it'.[161] In short, the main object of his attack and, in his view the least vulnerable form, was an aggregate satisfaction version of utility as applied to the design of institutions. In Chapter 5 of *A Theory of Justice*

---

[156] See Chapter 2 above.
[157] Rawls (1955). This article was one starting-point for the contested distinction between act- and rule utilitarianism, that was discussed at pp. 135–6 and 150 above.
[158] Rogers (1999) at p. 50 (a useful introduction).   [159] *TJ*, p. 22.
[160] Sidgwick (1907).   [161] *TJ*, p. 22.

Rawls developed what is generally treated as the most important modern Kantian critique of classical utilitarianism. He argued that utilitarianism is inconsistent with the principles of justice as fairness in the following main respects:

(1) Justice as fairness requires that every individual has liberties and rights that take priority over the welfare of everyone else. By treating aggregate utility as the criterion, 'Utilitarianism does not take seriously the distinction between persons'.[162] Accordingly, it allows basic individual liberties and goods to be sacrificed to the general welfare.[163]

(2) In teleological theories the right is defined as that which maximises the good, whereas in justice as fairness the right takes priority over the good.[164]

(3) The priority of justice holds 'that interests requiring the violation of justice have no value'.[165] Utilitarianism, by contrast, does not distinguish between kinds or quality of satisfaction and allows pleasures of discrimination, or sadism, or a sense of superiority to be weighed favourably.[166]

(4) Utilitarianism and justice as fairness have different underlying conceptions of society:[167] the former treats individuals as means to maximise aggregate utility; the latter provides a structure which enables individuals freely to choose their own ends to the extent that these do not conflict within a basic structure of individual liberties.[168]

Rawls' central question was: What is the most appropriate moral conception of justice for a democratic society? Rawls considered other moral theories, but he developed his ideas primarily in response to utilitarianism. He insisted that 'justice is the first virtue of social institutions'[169] and that a theory of justice should be concerned with the basic structure of such institutions in a given society. Like Bentham, Rawls' primary interest is in institutional design.

Rawls summarised his original theory as follows:

---

[162] *TJ*, p. 27.

[163] 'Thus there is no reason in principle …why the violation of the liberty of a few might not be made right by the greater good shared by many' (*TJ* at p. 26).

[164] *TJ*, p. 24.   [165] *Ibid.*, at p. 31.   [166] *Ibid.*, at pp. 30–1.

[167] 'Implicit in the contrasts between classical utilitarianism and justice as fairness is a difference in the underlying conceptions of society. In the one we think of a well-ordered society as a scheme of cooperation for reciprocal advantage regulated by principles which persons would choose in an initial situation that is fair, in the other as the efficient administration of social resources to maximize the satisfaction of the system of desire constructed by the impartial spectator from the many individual systems of desires accepted as given.' (TJ, p. 33)

[168] Compare Amartya Sen's general critique of utilitarianism, cited above. Sen's pluralist capabilities approach claims to pay due regard to the motivations of utilitarianism, libertarianism, and justice as fairness, while maintaining a distance from them: 'In particular, the freedom-based perspective can take note of, *inter alia*, utilitarianism's interest in human well-being, libertarianism's involvement with processes of choice and the freedom to act, and Rawlsian theory's focus on individual liberty and on the resources needed for substantive freedoms.' Sen (1999), discussed further Ch. 7.4. below.

[169] *TJ*, p. 3.

My aim is to present a conception of justice which generalizes and carries to a higher level of abstraction the familiar theory of the social contract as found, say, in Locke, Rousseau and Kant. In order to do this we are not to think of the original contract as one to enter a particular society or to think up a particular form of government. Rather, the guiding idea is that the principles of justice for the basic structure of society are the object of the original agreement. They are the principles that free and rational persons concerned to further their own interests would accept in an initial position of equality as defining the fundamental terms of their association. These principles are to regulate all further agreements; they specify the kinds of social co-operation that can be entered into and the forms of government that can be established. This way of regarding the principles I shall call justice as fairness.[170]

The people in the original position would choose the following two principles:

First principle: 'Each person is to have an equal right to the most extensive total system of equal basic liberties compatible with a similar system of liberty for all.'

Second principle: 'Social and economic inequalities are to be arranged so that they are both:

    (a) to the greatest benefit of the least advantaged, consistent with the just savings principle,[171] ['the difference principle'] and

    (b) attached to offices and positions open to all under conditions of fair equality of opportunity.'[172]

These two principles have been variously interpreted, criticised and modified. Taken together they summarise Rawls' careful balancing of liberty and equality in a democratic society. Individual liberty takes priority, but only so far as it is embodied in certain basic liberties (rights).[173] Rawls' treatment of equality disturbed both strong egalitarians and anti-egalitarians: large disparities of wealth are not wrong in themselves, but any distributive arrangement must benefit the worst off as much as possible in respect of 'social primary goods' (including liberty, opportunity, wealth, and self-respect). Furthermore, wealth should not be allowed to distort the balance of political power that is required in a democracy.[174] The difference principle, based on game theory, is

---

[170] *Ibid.* at p. 1.

[171] 'The just savings principle can be regarded as the understanding between generations to carry the fair share of the burden of realizing and preserving a just society.' (*TJ*, p. 289) This allows for 'a suitable amount of real capital accumulation' (*TJ*, p. 285).

[172] *TJ*, p. 302. This formulation also contained two priority rules: The lexical priority of liberty and the Priority of Justice over Efficiency and Welfare. (*Ibid.*, 302–3).

[173] Nigel Simmonds illuminatingly contrasts this with the broader libertarian principle that 'liberty may be restricted only in order to maintain equal liberty': 'The first principle of justice differs from the classic liberal principle in that it protects, not liberty in general, but *certain specific liberties.*' Simmonds (1986) at pp. 48–9 (original italics).

[174] *TJ*, pp. 75–83.

sometimes referred to as 'maximin'.[175] It means that all inequalities should be arranged to benefit the least well off, subject to the priority of liberty. This has the effect of restricting the unfair 'natural' distribution of abilities, as well as wealth, and so limits the idea of equality of opportunity.[176] One suggested modification, that we shall encounter later, is to weaken or abandon the lexical priority of liberty in favour of a strengthened difference principle in order to make space for at least basic social and economic rights.[177] In *A Theory of Justice* Rawls controversially treated the state as neutral between forms of democratic government, but subsequently he became pessimistic about the idea of a capitalist welfare state, and suggested that his conception of justice could probably only be realised in 'a property owning democracy' or 'a market socialist regime'.[178]

A key to understanding Rawls' conception of justice is that it is silent about virtue or what constitutes a good life or the path to salvation. In other words it is only one aspect of morality. It is primarily concerned with the distributive aspects of the basic structure and not with other virtues for social arrangements (social ideals) such as efficiency or wealth creation.[179] In his later writings Rawls emphasised the idea of justice as a limited political concept concerned with fairness, reciprocity and public respect in the public realm as opposed to 'comprehensive moral theories', which must be confined to the private sphere in a diverse society.

The method by which Rawls derived these two principles has attracted a great deal of attention. Individuals decide on the basic structure of their society in the original position behind a 'veil of ignorance'. This device is intended to remove all considerations of self-interest from the identification of basic principles. The principles are arrived at by testing one's ideas and theories against one's basic intuitions and judgements in particular cases and vice versa until they form a coherent whole in 'reflective equilibrium'.[180] Despite some of the methodological and interpretive difficulties, many people, myself included, agree with Rawls' claim that most reasonable and reflective people would accept something like these principles, if they considered the issues free from vested interest and doctrinaire prejudices.

---

[175] 'The maximin rule tells us to rank alternatives by their worst possible outcomes: we are to adopt the alternative the worst outcomes of which is superior to the worst outcomes of the others.' (TJ, pp. 152–3).

[176] Pogge advances a powerful argument that both clarifies and modifies Rawls' opportunity principle. (*RR*, Chapter 4.)

[177] See Pogge and Sen, discussed below.

[178] Preface to the French Edition of *A Theory of Justice*, reprinted in *Collected Papers* (1999b) Chapter 19 at pp. 419–20.

[179] *TJ*, pp. 9–10.

[180] 'The process of mutual adjustment of principles and considered judgments is not peculiar to moral philosophy.' (Citing Goodman (1955) at pp. 65–8). (*TJ*, p. 20, n. 7) Goodman is sometimes given credit for coining the term, but it is clear that it was Rawls who gave it a wide currency.

A Theory of Justice was first published in 1971. It attracted a huge amount of attention. In the ensuing years Rawls clarified, modified and developed his position in a series of essays in response to numerous criticisms, but the core of the theory remained fairly constant. He then restated his position in *Political Liberalism* published in 1993. This version contains a number of ideas that are relevant to considering Rawlsian justice from a global perspective.

First, whereas in *A Theory of Justice* there is a consensus among its members about the appropriate moral basis for a well-ordered democratic society, *Political Liberalism* confronts the problem of belief pluralism. Its central question is:

> How is it possible that there may exist over time a stable and just society of free and equal citizens profoundly divided by reasonable though incompatible religious, philosophical and moral doctrines? Put another way: How is it possible that deeply opposed though reasonably comprehensive doctrines may live together and all affirm the political consequences of a constitutional regime?[181]

Second, in response to this new concern, Rawls insisted that 'justice as fairness is political, not metaphysical'.[182] It is a practical theory aimed at providing a moral foundation for political, social and economic institutions in a modern constitutional democracy in which the members have diverse, incompatible views. It is not a metaphysical or epistemological theory dealing with universal moral conceptions; nor does it apply to all societies.[183] It is a limited secular theory that can provide a basis for co-existence and co-operation in a diverse society independently of religious beliefs and ideologies. A key idea is that of an overlapping consensus: this does not refer to those doctrines that are common to the different belief systems in a given society, but rather to what free and equal citizens accept as a freestanding political view of society as a fair system of co-operation.[184]

---

[181] *PL*, p. xviii. Later Rawls restated the question as follows: 'How is it possible for those affirming a comprehensive doctrine, religious or non-religious, and in particular doctrines based on religious authority, such as the Church or the Bible, also to hold a reasonable political conception of justice that supports a constitutional democratic society? The political conceptions are seen as both liberal and self-standing and not as comprehensive, whereas the religious doctrines may be comprehensive but not liberal.' See also the formulation in '*Commonweal* Interview with John Rawls' (1998) reprinted in *Papers* (1999b) at p. 616, quoted at p. 162 below.

[182] *JF* at p. 226., PL *passim*. See. Joseph Raz: 'Four themes have to be distinguished, all of which are captured by the slogan "Justice as Fairness: Political not Metaphysical". First the theory is of *limited applicability*; second, it has *shallow foundations*; third, it is *autonomous*; finally, it is based on *epistemic abstinence*.' Raz (1994) Chapter 4 at p. 62. This important paper targets the element of epistemic abstinence in 'Rawls' modest conception of political theory' and suggests how the theory can be re-interpreted and adjusted to meet this line of criticism.

[183] See *JFPM*.

[184] *PL*, p. 40. Some critics have questioned whether such ideas can be kept separate from 'comprehensive doctrines'. See the discussion by Abdullahi An Na'im of whether, from a Muslim point of view, religious toleration should be viewed as a secular or a religious doctrine.

(b) The law of peoples

This last aspect of political liberalism is clearly relevant when we think about the institutions and practices needed for co-existence and co-operation in a world characterised by a diversity of belief systems, traditions, and cultures. On most interpretations of 'globalisation', which emphasise interdependence, the decline of sovereignty, and the permeability of borders, only one self-contained or closed society exists: the world.[185] And there is a need for a well-constructed political theory, which provides a coherent moral basis for the design of structures and institutions that can ensure stable, orderly and fair arrangements for co-existence, co-ordination, and co-operation between its diverse members. In light of the critical issues of radical poverty and increasing inequalities, a theory that claims to deal with global justice is especially welcome.[186]

Unfortunately, Rawls did not fulfil such hopes. His later works mark a retreat into a position that, from a global perspective, is a huge disappointment. *The Law of Peoples*, which contains the fullest statement of his views on global justice, has probably done more damage to Rawls' reputation than the posthumous Postscript of *The Concept of Law* has damaged Hart's. It is an embarrassment to many of his admirers and a soft target for his detractors. Here it is enough to summarise Rawls' main thesis in the *Law of Peoples* quite briefly. Instead of repeating the exercise in the original position with regard to principles of justice that individuals would choose to govern relations beyond their own society, Rawls constructed a more complex process in which representatives of peoples are substituted for individuals. If these representatives are from 'well-ordered' societies he suggests that they would choose the following principles:

'1. Peoples are free and independent, and their freedom and independence are to be respected by other peoples.
2. Peoples are to observe treaties and undertakings.
3. Peoples are equal and are parties to agreements that bind them.
4. Peoples are to observe a duty of non-intervention.
5. Peoples have the right of self-defense, but no right to instigate war other than for reasons of self-defense.
6. Peoples are to honor human rights.
7. Peoples are to observe certain specified restrictions in the conduct of war.
8. Peoples have a duty to assist other peoples living under unfavourable conditions that prevent their having a just or decent political and social regime.'[187]

Rawls presents these as 'familiar and traditional principles of justice among free and democratic peoples',[188] derived 'from the history and usages

---

[185] See n. 194–9 below.
[186] On issues of environmental justice from a global perspective see Ebbeson and Okowa (eds.) (2008).
[187] *TLP*, p. 37.   [188] *Ibid.*

of international law and practice'.[189] Rawls' principles only deviate from an uncritical rehash of classical positive international law in two significant respects: his list of human rights was considerably narrower than the rights recognised by the international human rights regime at the time (he deliberately omitted social, cultural, and economic rights) and he prescribed a limited duty of assistance to peoples living under 'unfavourable conditions'. Rawls' so-called Law of Peoples differs from his principles of domestic justice in two major respects: the subjects are peoples not individuals and the difference principle does not apply.

The Law of Peoples was heavily criticised by nearly all of the critics, including some of his disciples.[190] But for the huge respect in which he was held and the fact that he had suffered ill-health, the criticism might well have been harsher. In my view, *The Law of Peoples* is not worthy of the author of *A Theory of Justice* and is best forgotten. From a global perspective, it is bizarre to find a purportedly liberal theory of justice that rejects any principle of distribution, treats an out-dated conception of public international law as satisfactorily representing principles of justice in the global arena, and says almost nothing about radical poverty, the environment, increasing inequalities, American hegemony (and how it might be exercised), let alone about transitional justice or the common heritage of mankind or reparations or other issues that are now high on the global agenda.

Before considering whether any elements of Rawls' original theory of justice and its modifications as political liberalism can be rescued, it is worth looking briefly at the path of this retreat. The main ideas in *A Theory of Justice* were developed in the 1950s and 1960s, at a time when international ethics had not begun to develop in liberal circles. It was reasonable to assume that the main

---

[189] Citing Brierley (1963), and Nardin (1983). Rawls could be said to have had an outdated and simplistic view of international law. Even in *The Law of Peoples* (1999c), he continued to rely on the sixth edition of J L Brierley *The Law of Nations* (1963), which had first been published in 1928. This is especially unfortunate in that he claims to derive his Law of Peoples from 'the history and usages of international law and practice' (*LP*, pp. 41, 57). He did acknowledge that there had been 'a dramatic shift in international law since World War II', but mentions only limits on a state's right to wage war and limitations on sovereignty (citing a single Harvard doctoral dissertation). One cannot but feel that throughout his career Rawls did little reading about and was poorly advised on international law and relations.

[190] See Symposium in 110 *Ethics* (2000) especially papers by Charles Beitz and Allen Buchanan; Kuper (2000); Téson (1999), Pogge (2001b), and Tasioulas (2002b and c). More than one prominent contemporary has told me that they could not bring themselves to review the book they felt it was so bad. For a restricted defence, see Tasioulas (2005) (supporting a cut-off point for a duty of assistance (foreign aid), but raising it from subsistence to a right to an adequate standard of living). On foreign aid and subsistence see Chapter 11.4 below. Martin and Reidy (eds.) (2006) reached me too late to deal with here. It contains some attempts to defend *The Law of Peoples*, which make points worth considering (especially the chapter by Samuel Freeman), but these do not persuade me to revise the judgement that overall this is a very disappointing work. In mitigation, Tasioulas concludes: '[C]ompliance with Rawls's duty of assistance by wealthier and relatively well-ordered societies would amount to a colossal improvement on the intolerable conditions that prevail in the world today'. (Tasioulas (2005), p. 27).

arena for a theory of justice was a society roughly co-extensive with a nation state.[191] Rawls' book did, in fact, include a short section on international relations. In the context of considering the justification of civil disobedience, he acknowledged that 'It is natural to ask how the theory of political duty applies to foreign policy. Now in order to do this it is necessary to extend the theory of justice to the law of nations.'[192] In what has been widely recognised as one of the weakest sections of the book, he sketched out in a preliminary way some ideas that he later modified and developed in *The Law of Peoples*: that different principles of justice apply in the international arena, that the basic units of international relations are sovereign states, and that the moral basis of international law is that '[I]ndependent peoples organized as states have certain fundamental rights'.[193]

(c) Rawls as a citizen of the world

It could be argued that Rawls was not well placed to adopt a genuinely global perspective. He is distinctively American in a number ways. First, as a person he lived nearly all of his life in the United States. Culturally, he might be said to belong to the progressive wing of the American Puritan tradition. Second, nearly all of the political issues with which he was concerned while developing his ideas were either special local issues, such as race, the draft, and campaign contributions, or else they were directly connected to the United States' involvement in the wider world, especially in respect of wars: World War II (including Hiroshima), the Cold War and the War in Vietnam. Third, although his theory claims to apply to any liberal democracy, the most influential ideas are based on American constitutional history rather than other experiences of democracy. Fourth, in the period in which the idea of national borders was being eroded, Rawls increasingly emphasised the separateness of territorially defined societies. In *A Theory of Justice* he talked of the basic structure 'of society conceived *for the time being* isolated from other societies'.[194] Rawls is quite explicit about the domain of his domestic theory. It is restricted to a society, which is 'a self-contained national community',[195] 'more or less self-sufficient',[196] 'a closed system isolated from other societies'.[197] By emphasising sovereignty and the rights of people to self-determination he maintained this fiction in *The Law of Peoples*. One cannot but feel that his conception of the world outside the United States was distorted by viewing it through the prism of American culture and foreign policy. Finally, as part of his later retreat he placed increasing emphasis

---

[191] On recent scepticism about society as a viable analytic concept see p. 93 above and Chapter 15.3(b) on the web.

[192] *TJ*, p. 337.

[193] *TJ*, p. 378. On the issue of pacifism Rawls concludes that conscientious refusal is an affront to the government's pretensions, and in giving pacifists some leeway , 'states may even be seen to display a certain magnanimity' (*TJ* at p. 382).

[194] *TJ*, p. 8. (italics added).   [195] *TJ*, p. 457.

[196] *Ibid.*, at p. 4.   [197] *Ibid.* at p. 8. See *LP*, pp. 44, 46, 48, 56–7.

on the idea that: 'The aims of political philosophy depend on the society it addresses.'[198] In his later writings Rawls emphasised that his project is to develop a criterion of justice that would appeal to the common sense of reflective Americans because the ideas are embedded in '*our* history and the traditions of *our* public life.'[199]

In an interview in 1998 John Rawls was asked what was behind his shift in focus to religion in *Political Liberalism*, especially the essay on 'Public Reason Revisited'. His answer was solely in terms of the importance of religion in America:

> I think the basic explanation is that I'm concerned with the survival, historically, of constitutional democracy. I live in a country where 95 or 90 percent of the people profess to be religious, and maybe they are religious, though my experience of religion suggests that very few people are actually religious in more than a conventional sense. Still religious faith is an important aspect of American culture and a fact of American political life. So the question is: in a constitutional democracy, how can religious and secular doctrines of all kinds get together and cooperate in running a reasonably just and effective government? What assumptions would you have to make about religious and secular doctrines, and the political sphere, for these to work together?[200]

In respect of concerns, outlook, audience, and even his claims to the significance of his theory, Rawls' perspective was remarkably parochial.[201]

To emphasise Rawls' Americanness is not in itself a criticism. Any thinker's strengths and limitations are almost inevitably associated with a particular context and culture. Rawls' idea of reflective equilibrium involves appealing to intuitions and particular judgements that are, to a large extent, culturally based. But it is clear that he was not well suited to adopting a genuinely global perspective. His revival of social contract theory is quite abstracted from its European progenitors, Locke, Rousseau, and Kant. He was naïve about international relations and badly advised about international law.[202] A parochial and strikingly naïve picture of the 'other' pervades *The Law of Peoples*, as is illustrated by the paternalistic and offensive division of peoples into 'reasonable

---

[198] *IOC*, p. 1. Although this may not have been intended, this self-limitation has given succour to those like Walzer (1983) and Fishkin (1985) who wished to set robust limits to the sphere of justice. Rawls' limitation may be symptomatic of a more general conservative retreat, on which see Pogge (1989) at pp. 4, 9–11, 254, and *passim*. Ronald Dworkin makes a similar move, in order to emphasise the point that his kind of theory is concerned with right answers to specific questions of law within a particular system: '[I]nterpretive theories are by their nature addressed to a particular legal culture, generally the culture to which their authors belong.' Dworkin (1986), p. 102.

[199] *KCMT*, pp. 518–19, (italics added).

[200] *Papers* (1999b) at p. 616. The interview only makes reference to Christianity. The journal was *Commonweal* a liberal Catholic magazine. The editor refers to 'the relation of liberal society to the many religions that flourish within it.' (*ibid*). There is no mention of religious revival outside USA (on which see Jenkins (2007)).

[201] On parochialism see GLT, pp. 128–9.

[202] On Rawls' view of international law, see n. 189 above.

liberal peoples', 'decent peoples', 'outlaw states', 'societies burdened by unfavourable conditions', and 'benevolent absolutisms'.[203] He ends up in support of a scheme that, in the words of Thomas Pogge, his former pupil, 'arbitrarily discriminates in favour of affluent societies and against the global poor'.[204] One is tempted to dismiss the whole monumental scheme of Rawls' theory of justice as a culturally biased, parochial project, pandering to American isolationism, ethnocentrism, and self-interest, even among liberals.

This would be a mistake. For supporters and critics alike, Rawls' theory of domestic justice is still the almost inevitable starting point of any discussion of justice, at least in the West. It has stimulated over 5,000 articles and books and has been translated into over twenty languages. Few philosophical theories have been worked out with such care, patience, and precision. The crucial question is: how much of Rawls' concepts and arguments can be translated from the domestic context to the transnational arena in a way that meets the objections to *The Law of Peoples*?

Fortunately, this is essentially what Thomas Pogge, one of Rawls' own pupils, has done. He has ably defended and refined Rawls' original theory and has substituted his own quite radical theory of international justice and human rights. Mainly by changing one of Rawls' key conceptions – the postulate that justice as fairness is only concerned with the internal ordering of societies conceived as self-contained units – he has shown how much of Rawls' scheme can be converted from a parochial and quite conservative theory into one that could be of real value in providing a moral basis for a substantial critique and re-design of supra-national and international institutions. So rather than dwell on the weaknesses of *The Law of Peoples*, I shall focus on Thomas Pogge's attempts to construct a theory of international justice and human rights in a Rawlsian spirit.

(d) Rescuing Rawls: Pogge's first critique[205]

Pogge's writings fall into two distinct phases. First, *Realizing Rawls* might have been called *Rescuing Rawls*. It can be read as an attempt to rescue the core of his mentor's theory from his critics and from himself by responding to misconceived criticisms, by refining some aspects of Rawls's scheme, and by transferring Rawls' two principles, somewhat modified, to the supra-national

---

[203] *LP*, p. 4.   [204] *WPHR*, p. 108.

[205] Bibliographical note: this section draws mainly on the following works by Thomas Pogge: *Realizing Rawls* (1989) (hereafter *RR*); (ed.) *Global Justice* (2001a); *World Poverty and Human Rights* (2002) (hereafter *WPHR*) and numerous articles, some of which are discussed below Barry and Pogge (eds.) (2005), especially 'Rawls and International Justice' 51 *Philosophical Qrtrly* 251–53 (2001) at pp. 23–3. 'Real World Justice' 9 Journal of Ethics' (2005) at pp. 29–53 (a reply to critics of WPHR), 'Severe Poverty as a Human Rights Violation' in Pogge (ed.) (2007) Ch.1. A translation from German of a book on Rawls' life and work (Pogge (2007a), reached me too late to draw on here. In this book Pogge does not discuss Rawls' treatment of international relations because 'I could not construct a sufficiently convincing account of it'. (at p. x). This section concentrates on Pogge's writings about Rawls up to 2005, since when he has moved even further away from his mentor.

arena. Later Rawls developed his position in *The Law of Peoples* and, as we shall see, Pogge has significantly extended his arguments in relation to world poverty and in the process further distanced himself from Rawls.

The first two parts of *Realizing Rawls* defend *A Theory of Justice* against many criticisms, notably Nozick's extreme libertarianism and communitarian criticisms of Rawls' individualism. In this context, Pogge supports Rawls' core ideas especially the basic structure, the original position,[206] and concern for the least advantaged (the maximin principle). Pogge modifies Rawls' principles by weakening the priority of liberty, strengthening 'fair equality of opportunity', and giving more emphasis to basic social and economic rights.[207] But the first five chapters are essentially a sustained defence of *A Theory of Justice*.

In the third part of *Realizing Rawls*, Pogge is highly critical of Rawls' rudimentary treatment of international justice in *A Theory of Justice* and proposes a Rawlsian extension of Rawls' principles of justice to the global arena.[208] Pogge's argument, which was published before *The Law of Peoples*, could be restated as follows: There are no self-contained national societies in the modern world, nor are there likely to be. The only closed social system is humanity at large.[209] A theory of justice for any other kind of association,

---

[206] Pogge invokes the original position in several places, but he has been criticised for not attempting a methodological defence of Rawls, in particular against social contract theories in general (Review of *Realizing Rawls* by T.J. Norman (1990) at pp. 465 and 466. Norman, however, adds: 'Still, one has to welcome Pogge's predominantly normative discussion given a contemporary debate – encouraged by Rawls' recent writings – truly obsessed with abstract foundational problems. Surely the idea of modern liberalism and social democracy is based *at least* as firmly on a concern for the poor and disadvantaged as it is on a commitment to, say, neutrality or anti-perfectionism.' (*Ibid.*) Later Pogge abandoned the perspective associated with the original position (*WPHR*, pp. 226–7, n. 99). It is plausible to suggest that many people support Rawls' two principles (or variants on them) without being unduly concerned about the underlying methodology). On 'ecumenical arguments', see further pp. 171–2 below.

[207] Some commentators have suggested that Pogge's modified principles might represent a more plausible reconstruction of what reflective people would choose in the original position than Rawls' formulation. (e.g. Fuchs (1992)). I do not pursue this point here.

[208] *Realizing Rawls* (1989) was written before *The Law of Peoples* (1999c), but Pogge renewed his attack after 1999. One commentator suggested that if were there enough Rawlsians to classify, Pogge could be described alternately as: 'a *left* Rawlsian (one whose primary concern is with the plight of the worst-off, and who consequently believes that the USA is far from being a just society); a *middle* Rawlsian (identifying most with the "radical" Rawls of *A Theory of Justice*); and seeing in his recent developments an increasing conservatism and retreat into abstraction; a *political* Rawlsian (eager to retrieve and defend the moral and political content of the principles of justice, but relatively unconcerned with "issues in moral psychology, metaethics and moral epistemology",(i.e with "debates that are metaphysical in style if not in substance")… ; or a *globalized* Rawlsian (believing that a theory of justice must be developed in the first instance for a global rather than a national basic structure, and that familiar injustices in our societies, grave as they are, "pale in comparison" to those involved in the prevailing national institutional scheme.)' (Norman at pp. 465–6)

[209] Although Pogge talks of 'the global system' (about which I have reservations), not much would be changed by substituting some looser term, such as humankind. (On the concept of 'system' see Chapter 15.4 on the web). Pogge himself seems to envisage an extension of the Rawlsian model of a hierarchy of associations acting as systems within systems, whereas the picture that I

including the nation state, is dependent on background principles or 'ground rules' formulated at the global level.[210] Rawls' core ideas for a practical theory aimed at providing a criterion of justice for basic institutions can be applied to the global system with a few adjustments along the following lines: we live in an interdependent world, in which all are involved and from which 'we cannot just drop out'. This is a world of widespread deprivations and disadvantages, many of which have been promoted by existing transnational institutions; one test of basic institutions is the benefits and burdens they engender. The position of the least advantaged is one important measure of just institutions; it is highly probable that improved global institutions would help to alleviate at least some of the existing deprivations and disadvantages of the worst off. Rawls' two principles (modified and extended to give more weight to social and economic needs) and some of his basic ideas, such as the search for an over-lapping consensus, the individual as the ultimate unit of justice,[211] and the basic structure are more coherently applicable to 'the global system' than to artifi-cially bounded societies or states, not least because 'all institutional matters, including the ideal extent of national sovereignty, are now systematically addressed within a single framework'.[212] Pogge concludes, on the basis of this neo-Rawlsian approach, that 'our current global institutional scheme is unjust, and as advantaged participants in this order we share a collective responsibility for its injustice'.[213]

have suggested is a much more complex one of overlapping and cross-cutting semi-autonomous social spheres operating in a global context which is itself very complex. However, Pogge's theory can be interpreted as one which suggests that any theory of justice, including highly localised ones within families, societies, regional groupings, transnational associations and so on, has to be set in a much broader context which prescribes background rules and constraints for more localised spheres of justice. See *GLT*, pp. 72–5.

[210] See also Kant: 'The problem of establishing a perfect civic constitution is dependent upon the problem of a lawful external relation among states, and cannot be solved without a solution to the latter problem.' Quoted by Pogge from Kant's *Political Writings* (ed. H.Reiss (ed.) 1970). Rawls follows Kant (*Perpetual Peace* (1795)) in rejecting a centralised regime of world government on the grounds that it would either be a global despotism or else an unstable and fragile empire torn by civil strife. *LP*, pp. 54–5. This is a quite different point from the argument that the justice of any domestic political order needs to be set in a wider, transnational or global context, especially as societies become increasingly interdependent. (See *RR*, pp. 255–6.)

[211] Pogge, in *RR*, Chapter 2, defends Rawls against charges of atomism – (i.e of treating individuals as if they are socially and politically isolated and self-sufficient) but Rawls does treat the individual human being as the ultimate moral unit.

[212] *Ibid.*, 258.

[213] *Ibid.*, at 277. Also at p. 36: 'It is not easy to convince oneself that our global order, assessed from a Rawlsian perspective, is moderately just despite the widespread and extreme deprivations and disadvantages it engenders. Even if we limit our vision to our advanced Western society, it is hardly obvious that the basic institutions we participate in are just or nearly just. In any case, a somewhat unobvious but massive threat to the moral quality of our lives is the danger that we will have lived as advantaged participants in unjust institutions, collaborating in their perpetuation and benefiting from their injustice.' (*RR*, p. 36).

Despite the sharpness of Pogge's criticisms, it is worth emphasising how close his first book was to the early Rawls.[214] Pogge argues that Rawls' treatment of global justice is inconsistent with two of his own core ideas: the basic structure and his conception of all human beings as free and equal moral persons.[215] The core of Pogge's argument is that a sharp distinction between domestic and global justice cannot be maintained, especially in an increasingly interdependent world, and that societies can no longer, if they ever could, be treated as self-contained units. Rawls' two principles, or something very like them, can be applied directly to the critique and design of international and transnational institutions. By a relatively small adjustment of one part of Rawls' theory (which was undeveloped in *A Theory of Justice*), Pogge transforms a theory of justice that makes a mild critique of the domestic status quo in wealthy 'well-ordered' societies into a potentially radical critique of existing institutional arrangements at supra-state levels.[216]

Realizing Rawls was published in 1989. During the 1990s Pogge published a stream of articles, most of which focused on global poverty from the point of view of a philosopher who is passionately concerned to make a case for effective action that will have a broad appeal. Pogge's own position moved away from the Rawls of *A Theory of Justice* and even further from what he, with some justification, sees as a distressingly conservative retreat on Rawls' part. His criticisms of *The Law of Peoples* are far-reaching and harsh, concluding with the judgement that:

> Despite considerable vagueness in his treatment of economic institutions, it seems clear, then, that Rawls endorses double standards on three different levels: in regard to national economic regimes, the difference principle is part of Rawls' highest aspiration for justice; in regard to the global economic order, however, Rawls disavows this aspiration and even rejects the difference principle as inapplicable. Rawls suggest a weaker minimal criterion of liberal economic justice on the national level, but he holds that the global order can fully accord with liberal conceptions of justice without satisfying this criterion. And Rawls suggests an even weaker criterion of decency on the national level: but he holds that the global order can not be merely decent, but even just, without satisfying this criterion. Insofar as he offers no plausible rationales for these three double standards, Rawls runs afoul of moral universalism. He fails to meet the burden of showing that his applying different moral principles to national and global

---

[214] Pogge studied under Rawls and has an intimate knowledge of his mentor's texts. This has served him well in clearing away misunderstandings and unfair criticisms Although he is consistently critical of some details, Pogge defends and uses what he considers to be core Rawlsian ideas: the original position (which he later abandoned *WPHR*, n. 99); the conception of a theory of justice as political and practical rather than metaphysical; the focus on the basic structure and institutional design; the maximin principle, a consistent concern for the plight of the worst off; and the embodiment of these ideas in a relatively thin theory of human rights. Even more than Rawls, Pogge, while doing philosophy, is strongly committed to confronting real practical problems.

[215] *RR*, p. 240.   [216] Ibid., at p. 277. Also at p. 36 (quoted at n. 213 above).

institutional schemes does not amount to arbitrary discrimination in favor of affluent societies and against the global poor.[217]

(e) Pogge on radical poverty

The poorest 46 per cent of humankind have 1.2 per cent of global income. Their purchasing power per person per day [was] less than that of $2.15 in the US in 1993. 826 million of them do not have enough to eat. One third of all human deaths are from poverty-related causes: 18 million annually, including 12 million children under five.

At the other end, the 15 per cent of humankind in the 'high income economies' have eighty per cent of global income. Shifting 1 or 2 percent of our share toward poverty eradication seems morally compelling. Yet the prosperous 1990s have in fact brought a large shift toward global inequality, as most of the affluent societies believe that they have no such responsibility.[218]

We are all familiar with such statements. Often the statistics are concretised by particular stories or images. Few will disagree that something is badly wrong. But people differ as to precisely what is wrong about the situation. Why is this wrong? Surely, the facts speak for themselves – perhaps more eloquently than any articulated philosophy. If we focus on the situation of the poorest: there is widespread agreement that a situation of large-scale radical poverty is bad. But people may express their view of why it is bad in terms of utility (pain or unhappiness), basic needs, human rights, just deserts, equality, justice as fairness, humanitarian concern, or compassion, or a combination of these. They may also differ on what counts as 'poverty', on what are the main causes, where the responsibility lies, and what can be done to change it for the better or, more boldly, 'make poverty history'.

Such differences are at the root of debates within development theory.[219] They all have a moral dimension, but they also involve economic, political, psychological and cultural judgements about practicalities. What the potential contribution of moral philosophy is, is itself a matter of disagreement.[220] Most agree that it is an important, perhaps a necessary ingredient in such considerations, but few would claim that on its own it is a sufficient one.

In the West, nearly all theories of justice in the twentieth century focused on domestic justice, that is to say questions internal to a society treated as a more or less closed unit. Concern with supranational ethics has a long history, but in

---

[217] *WPHR*, p. 108.   [218] Jacket cover of Pogge (2002).   [219] See Chapter 11 below.

[220] Griffin, 'Discrepancies between the Best Philosophical Account of Human Rights and the International Law of Human Rights' (2001a), criticised by Tasioulas, (2002a). See Richard Rorty, who considers that a philosophical justification of the international human rights regime is neither necessary nor desirable (Rorty, (1989); (1993)]. In interpreting Pogge, Singer, An Na'im or even Rawls it is often difficult to sort out the abstract philosophical aspects from more pragmatic concerns of political persuasion, feasibility, and effectiveness in implementation. See n. 206 above and pp. 171–2 below.

recent times it was slow to develop in a sustained way until about 1980.[221] In the liberal tradition Brian Barry, Charles Beitz, Onora O'Neill, Thomas Pogge, Thomas Scanlon, Henry Shue, and Peter Singer are among those who have focused on important transnational ethical issues within the broad liberal tradition.[222] I have chosen to focus on Thomas Pogge because he is at once the best interpreter and the most persistent critic of Rawls in this respect. In some ways Pogge stands to Rawls as Tamanaha relates to Hart and Singer to Bentham: all three have built on and modified the ideas of their predecessors in translating them into a global context.

Since 1991, in many essays and several books Pogge has developed his argument in favour of effective radical reform of transnational institutions in order to implement the maximin principle.[223] It is worth considering Pogge's developed thesis briefly, because it represents one of the most sustained efforts by a contemporary philosopher to confront problems of distributive justice from a global perspective.

Building on his earlier critique of Rawls, Pogge rejects the idea that there should be a fundamental distinction between principles of domestic and transnational justice. If we use the device of the original position, then it should be individuals rather than representatives of peoples who should participate and they would need to make judgements as good Kantian cosmopolitan citizens, with the veil of ignorance hiding from them what kind of society they might find themselves in.[224]

Pogge's main argument is directed against two moral prejudices, that he considers to be widespread among 'nearly all our politicians, academics, and the mass media':[225] '[t]hat the persistence of severe poverty abroad does not require our moral attention, and that there is nothing seriously wrong with our conduct, policies, and the global economic institutions we forge in regard to world poverty.' [226]

---

[221] Significant early works in the revival include Barry (1972), Beitz (1979), Beitz *et al.* (eds.) (1985), O'Neill (1986), and Shue (1980). Neglected classics relevant to this revival include Kant's *Perpetual Peace* (1795) and Bentham's writings on international law.

[222] The term 'international ethics' is too narrow, because if used precisely it is restricted to the morality of relations between nations or states; on the problems surrounding 'global', 'cosmopolitan', 'supra-national' etc. See above pp. 69–72.

[223] See bibliography. This passage is based mainly on *WPHR* (2002). Pogge has continued to write and campaign in this area and in the process has modified some of his earlier positions.

[224] Of course, since the device of the original position is intended to provide a way to settle on principles that constitute the basic structure, the distinctions between democratic/hierarchical, decent/ non-decent societies that so concerned Rawls are part of what is in issue in constitutional design.Pogge tellingly mocks Rawls' argument that liberal societies should offer reciprocal recognition to 'decent' non-liberal societies: 'This is a strange suggestion because, in our world, nonliberal societies and their populations tend to be poor and quite willing to cooperate in reforms that would bring the global economic order closer to meeting a liberal standard of economic justice. The much more affluent liberal societies are the one blocking such reforms' (*WPHR*, p. 107).

[225] *WPHR*, p. 5.

[226] *WPHR*, p. 4. It is unclear whether 'our' in this context refers to Americans or cosmopolitan citizens or world leaders.

He argues that these prejudices are sustained by four 'easy assumptions': First, a belief that poverty prevents over-population and that efforts to reduce severe poverty will increase suffering and deaths in the long run. This is refuted by evidence, which suggests that reducing poverty and enhancing women's opportunities leads to falling birth-rates.

Second, that the problem of world poverty is so great that its eradication in a short period would involve such huge costs to the better off that it would meet with strong political resistance. Pogge's response that this greatly overstates the costs (Pogge's figure is 1.25 per cent reduction of aggregate gross national incomes).[227] Even if the point were true this would not justify neglect of the problem.

The third prejudice suggests that historical experience shows that 'throwing money at the problem' does not work and that most efforts at development assistance have failed. Here the response is more complex. Given the generally uneven record of development assistance, there is some truth in this belief. Pogge's response is that not all poverty eradication projects have failed, especially those that are used to increase the income of the poor. However, his main solution is not about spending and transfers. Rather it is to 'restructure the global order to make it more hospitable to democratic government, economic justice and growth in the developing countries', coupled with a willingness on the part of more affluent states to drive less of a hard bargain in international trade, investment and taxation.[228]

'A fourth easy assumption is that world poverty is disappearing anyway.'[229] This comforting idea is sustained by the desire to believe in it and by figures presented in such a way as to suggest that things are improving.

Pogge concentrates his fire on 'skilful defense(s)' built around the second assumption: a factual claim that existing institutional arrangements are not harming the global poor (the factual claim) and while causing severe poverty would be morally wrong, it is not seriously wrong to fail to benefit them by not doing all that we might.[230] Pogge's strategy is to challenge the factual claim by showing ways in which the existing structure maintains and contributes to severe poverty. This argument is developed at length in *World Poverty and Human Rights* (2002) and is continued in later writings.

---

[227] See also estimates cited by Sachs (2005), Singer (2004), Sen 1999) suggesting that the moral heroism argument is not a major threat as a great deal can be achieved within existing UN targets and by the Millennium Development Goals. Pogge devotes space to countering the argument that elimination of poverty is unaffordable, but places more emphasis on reforming supranational structures.

[228] *WPHR* at p. 9. This argument is developed at length in Chapters 4–7 of that book.

[229] *WPHR*, at p. 9. Complacency of this kind is associated with free market 'trickle down' arguments on the right and with optimistic belief in public initiatives such as the Millennium Development Project and the efforts of IFIs. See further Chapter 11 below.

[230] 'This defense combines two claims. Its factual claim asserts that we are not harming the global poor by causing severe poverty, but merely failing to benefit them by not eradicating as much severe poverty as we might. Its moral claim asserts that, while it is seriously wrong to harm the global poor by causing severe poverty, it is not seriously wrong to fail to benefit them by eradicating as much severe poverty as we might.' (*WPHR*, p. 12)

Many people, including Rawls, reject a sharp distinction between causing poverty and failing to reduce it – one version of the problematic distinction between acts and omissions. Utilitarians, including Singer, argue that if reducing poverty will increase aggregate happiness, that in itself is sufficient to ground duties to pursue this goal.[231] There may be room for differences about allocation of responsibility (whose duties?) and about the most effective strategies for achieving the goal. And, as we have seen, a pure utilitarian might make the duty an onerous one by insisting on a principle that 'if it is in our power to prevent something bad from happening, without thereby sacrificing anything of comparable moral importance, we ought morally to do it'.[232] This is a pure consequentialist argument. It has been criticised as involving 'moral heroism' or an 'overload of obligations' and in response to such resistance Singer himself has pragmatically been prepared to lower the ceiling of obligation; others have developed the further pragmatic argument that the costs of significantly reducing severe poverty involve only small sacrifices, but of course, this does not deal with eliminating all poverty and difficult questions about egalitarian considerations above some artificially prescribed poverty line.[233] In Benthamic terms, it is easier to reach consensus about distribution in relation to subsistence than in relation to abundance.[234]

Interestingly, in *The Law of Peoples*, Rawls rejects both the distinction between causing poverty and allowing it to happen and the idea that foreign aid is a matter of charity. Liberal and Decent Peoples have a duty to assist 'heavily burdened societies', whether or not they have contributed to their situation. But this duty is limited to enabling them to establish reasonably just or decent institutions.[235]

By choosing to rely on the causal argument that the basic structure of 'the global order' is contributing to poverty, Pogge has made a factual claim that invites controversy.[236] For the causes of underdevelopment and severe poverty

---

[231] Singer *et al.* in Beitz (ed.) (1985) Part V.

[232] *Practical Ethics* (1979/1993) 'Famine, Affluence and Morality' (1972).

[233] One of the attractions of the difference principle for some is that it does not put a ceiling on improving the lot of the worst off. Indeed, its operation does not depend on a definition of poverty. This is one reason why Rawls tried to set a limit on the duty of assistance (n.190 above).

[234] See p. 138 above.

[235] Rawls elaborates on this in *LP*, p. 55, 43n, pp. 106–19. He differentiates this from a global distribution principle, which he rejects. In this instance, he goes somewhat further than American foreign policy (but a liberal interpretation of the duty to assist can be used to support initiatives like the MDGs).

[236] For an interesting critique, the thrust of which is that Pogge overstates his case (international institutions have contributed to some amelioration but are open to improvement) see Risse (2005). Pogge responds in 'Real world Justice' Cf. Singer, *One World* (2004), judiciously advises caution on interpreting statistics about poverty and inequality and concludes that 'No evidence that I have found enables me to form a clear view about the overall impact of economic globalization on the poor' (at p. 89). He insists that the crucial question is how to promote the welfare of the poorest rather than the size of the gap between rich and poor (p. 84).

are a continuing matter of debate and disgreement among economists and development theorists. I do not propose to enter this controversy here.

Pogge has also devoted a lot of effort to advocating a particular strategy for attacking global poverty, what he calls 'A Global Resources Dividend'.[237] This is presented as a moderate or modest proposal, based on the idea that 'those who make more extensive use of our planet's resources should compensate those, who involuntarily, use very little'.[238] It is not necessary to go into detail about the desirability, feasibility, and political prospects of this proposal for it is one of a number of strategies that are on the table aimed at reducing or eliminating global poverty.[239]

For present purposes it is sufficient to make some points about the significance of Pogge's contribution: First, as a disciple of Rawls he has modified and refined the ideas in ways that many may agree represent a Rawlsian improvement on *A Theory of Justice*. Second, as an increasingly sharp critic of Rawls he has substituted a theory of international justice that is radically different from Rawls' own disappointing effort, but which is still Rawlsian in spirit. Third, by confronting in detail the facts of global poverty and some of the political practicalities it involves he has engaged with one of the major issues of our age from the point of view of a philosopher, who believes that abstract ideas are important in addressing practical problems. Whether on not one agrees with all of his arguments, the message is clear: if you are concerned about justice in relation to world poverty, read *World Poverty and Human Rights* rather than *The Law of Peoples*.

However, for our purposes Pogge's work has three limitations: first, it is highly focused on only one aspect of global justice, albeit a very important one. Pogge says little about environmental justice or transitional justice. He adopts a thin interpretation of human rights for his specific purpose. We need to consider more expansive versions. Second, Pogge is constructing an argument that is intended to have a broad appeal that transcends a range of positions. In particular, he does not rely on arguments that we owe a positive duty to help the worst off, as Singer does, but restricts his argument to a negative duty not to

---

[237] See especially *WPHR*, Chapter 8.

[238] *Ibid.* at p. 204.Pogge's proposal does not involve commitment to the idea that global resources are common property of humankind nor the more modest idea of *ius humanitatis* applying to hitherto unappropriated territories on this and other planets (discussed *GLT*, p. 240). Although the issues are mired in the realpolitik of international relations, especially in connection with the Law of the Sea and, more recently, the Arctic, it is a pity that so far philosophers, such as Rawls and Pogge, have not constructed the strongest theoretical foundation for this doctrine. The best work to date is Baslar (1998), which also has a quite comprehensive bibliography up to 1998 at pp. 383–417.

[239] Examples listed by Risse (2005) at p. 371 include the Millennium Development Project, discussed in Chapter 12 below; fulfillment of the UN target of 0.7 per cent of GNP devoted to state development aid; George Soros' proposal for 'special drawing rights' as development aid (Soros (2002)); various forms of tax on (e.g. carbon use weapons trading) or a general tax on financial markets. To these I would add the development of a more robust conception of *ius humanitatis* in international law (see n. 238).

support institutions that maintain or contribute to radical poverty. As Singer has modified his pure utilitarianism in order to broaden the appeal of his argument, Pogge appears to be have trimmed his philosophical views in order to persuade a broader political constitutuency, using in his own words an 'ecumenical approach'.[240] Thirdly, Pogge has devoted a great deal of effort to promoting one particular strategy for poverty alleviation; this is just one among many such proposals, some of which we will consider in Chapter 11. Before that we need to turn to turn to some broader aspects of human rights theory.

---

[240] Pogge (2005). On ecumenical arguments see further below pp. 353–4. See Abdullahi An Na'im's pragmatism in advancing arguments to persuade fellow Muslims. See Chapter 13.3 below.

Human Rights.[6] The rapid increase in human rights both transnationally and domestically has led to increasing attention being given to the compatibility of human rights values and ideas with belief systems, such as Islam and Judaism, that have not traditionally expressed such values in terms of rights.[7]

(c) *Discourse theories*: For those who accept deeply rooted diversity of beliefs as a fact, a standard move has been to shift from substantive moral theories, including theories of rights, into discourse ethics.[8] In this view, 'rights talk' is a form of discourse with varied and changing content, which provides a framework for argument, negotiation, interpretation, and articulating or making claims. For example, Amartya Sen grounds his moral theory of human rights not in substantive standards, but in the survivability of rights claims in open public reasoned discussions both within and across societies.[9] Yash Ghai, while sceptical of claims that human rights embody universal values, reports that he has found the discourse of rights invaluable in negotiating constitutional settlements between competing groups in multi-ethnic societies.[10] Some human rights theorists, who accept belief pluralism as a fact or who are otherwise concerned about claims to universality, have found inspiration in the work of Jurgen Habermas and the Frankfurt school.[11]

In different ways, some of the sharpest critics of human rights also attack it as *a mode of discourse* rather than challenging the underlying values or claims to universality. As we shall see, Bentham attacked the French Declarations of Rights as involving self-contradictory, ambiguous, nonsensical political rhetoric likely to encourage anarchy. Bentham's attack on talk of non-legal rights was comprehensive. Other commentators as different as Mary Ann Glendon (American Catholic, Republican) and Upendra Baxi (Indian secular, radical, public intellectual) have made the overuse and abuse of 'Rights Talk' their primary targets, while maintaining their commitment to human rights.

(d) *'Subaltern' perspectives: A body of political ideas and practices*, which has emerged not from abstract theorising nor conscious law making, but from the largely local experiences of suffering of millions of people and from struggles against poverty, injustice, colonialism and other forms of deprivation and oppression. In this 'subaltern' perspective the true authors of

---

[6] Jacques Maritain (1951) (1954). On the political context, see Glendon (2001).

[7] On Islamic Declarations and attempts to reconcile Islamic values with human rights, see Chapter 13.3 below.

[8] This view is associated with thinkers as diverse as Jurgen Habermas, Stuart Hampshire and Richard Rorty, and, in respect of human rights, Yash Ghai, Upendra Baxi and Sir Stephen Sedley.

[9] Amartya Sen (2004) discussed at Chapter 7.4 below.

[10] Ghai (2000b) discussed in Chapter 13.4 below.

[11] Especially, Habermas (1996). There is a good discussion of Habermas' contributions to Jurisprudence in Penner, Schiff, and Nobles (eds.) (2002). See also Dews (ed.) (1999).

human rights are said to have been communities in struggle.[12] In some versions of this view, modern human rights discourse 'gives voice' to and empowers the worst off, but underlying it is an emphasis on local and historically specific political battles against powerful interests – sometimes by individuals, or whole communities, or social movements, most of whom have not normally articulated their protests in terms of 'rights', at least until recently.

(e) *A Western colonial and neo-colonial ideology* that has been imposed by the West on the Rest. This view will be discussed in connection with 'the Asian Values debate'.

There are, of course, other perspectives on and visions of human rights, including various kinds of scepticism that we will consider below. In practice, these various perspectives have interacted, overlapped and sometimes competed with each other.[13] But their distinctiveness is illustrated by the different kinds of stories that they tell about their origins and growth.

Thus the story of Western ideas about human rights is often told in terms of histories of (mainly Western) ideas, starting with the Greeks and Romans (or before), continuing through medieval Christianity to the Enlightenment and social contract theories, culminating in philosophers in the Kantian tradition, such as Rawls, Nozick, O'Neill, and modern versions of Natural Law, exemplified by Finnis.[14] A variant of this, is to credit the intellectual origins in other traditions, but to claim that these have been replaced since the eighteenth century. For example:

> If the civilizations and ethical contributions of China, India, and the Muslim world towered over those of medieval Europe, it is equally true that the legacy of the European Enlightenment, for our current understanding of rights, supersedes other influences.[15]

By contrast, international lawyers generally tell a different story. While a few precursors are acknowledged, the history of the current international and regional human rights regimes begins after World War II. It is marked by the Universal Declaration of Human Rights as the founding document.[16] The story is then often told in terms of a split during the Cold War, with the Western powers supporting civil and political rights and the Soviet Bloc advocating social, cultural and economic rights. The story continues in at least two

---

[12] E.g. Baxi, (2006a); Rajagopal (2003). See further pp. 433–4 below.

[13] For example, Conor Gearty first opposed the introduction of the Human Rights Act in the United Kingdom, Ewing and Gearty (1990), then later advanced a prescriptive interpretive theory of the same Act, (Gearty 2004) and later still advanced a philosophical defence of human rights as moral rights (Gearty 2006).

[14] Some of these are explicitly limited to Western ideas (e.g. Kelly (1992), Morrison (1997), Ishay (2004)). Some combine the history of ideas about human rights as moral and political rights with accounts of the development of human rights law. There is, of course, an intimate relationship, but as is suggested in the text, it is important to keep them conceptually distinct.

[15] Ishay (2004) at p. 7.   [16] For a quite orthodox account see Steiner and Alston (2008) Chapter 2.

versions; first, that after the fall of the Berlin Wall, Western ideology triumphed and civil and political rights have been part of the ideological armoury of Western hegemony, combining or sitting uneasily with strong free market ideology. A second version is that 'the collapse of communism' made it possible to end the artificial divide between two types of rights and to emphasise the indivisibility and interdependence of human rights as a whole.[17]

The story of human rights discourse superseding other moral discourses is linked to these last stories. After 'the collapse of communism', symbolised by the fall of the Berlin Wall, some former Marxist and socialist intellectuals adopted the discourse of human rights. In this period there have been enormous advances in human rights law. Partly as a result, many other interested parties have jumped on the bandwagon. Indeed, one of Upendra Baxi's central themes is that human rights discourse has become commodified, professionalised by technocrats, and sometimes hijacked by powerful groups, so that it is in grave danger of losing touch with the experiences of suffering and the needs of those who should be the main beneficiaries – the poor and the oppressed.[18]

'Subaltern' perspectives on human rights do not yet have a developed historiography, but the outlines can be traced in stories of social movements, some before 'the era of Human Rights' such as the anti-slavery, suffragist, decolonisation, and workers' movements and more recent ones, including significant transnational NGOS and networks.[19] There is a growing number of particular studies, such as books about the role of slaves and 'free men' in the story of abolition.[20] Similarly, the picture of human rights as imposed Western ideology can be told in terms of resistance to Western hegemony and neo-colonialism and in the revision of colonial history.[21]

These stories are not so much alternatives as the founding myths of different perspectives on human rights. I am not here concerned about their validity, but to make the point that it is misleading to talk about theorising about human rights as if it is one kind of activity. In particular we need to maintain broad distinctions between human rights talk as forms of political rhetoric, of legal exposition and argument, and as moral discourses.

[17] On the Millennium Development Goals as an example both of recent emphasis on the indivisibility of basic rights and of shying away from explicit talk of rights see Chapter 11.4 below.

[18] Baxi, (2006a) discussed in Chapter 13.5 below.

[19] Baxi (2006d) at pp. 68–72 '[T]hus the ample terms of descriptive realism celebrate Mohandas Ghandi, Nelson Mandela, Frantz Fanon, Martin Luther King Jr. (amidst their equally luminous feminist others) that engaged 'agitation route' in ways that variously divested colonialism, racism, and patriarchy of the very last hegemonic/despotic vestiges and disrupted altogether the lineages of human rights idea in the European Enlightenment.' (Baxi, (2007a) at p. 60. See also Benton (2002).

[20] E.g. Linebaugh and Rediker (2000) (arguing that freed slaves were among the main originators of Western human rights ideas) cf. Schama (2005). On Baxi, see Chapter 13.5 below.

[21] An important example of this perspective is Balakrishnan Rajagopal, *International Law from Below: Developing Social Movements and Third World Resistance* (2003).

6.2 Human rights law and morality

Theories about human rights are of many different kinds. In much of the discourse about human rights, there is a tendency to conflate human rights law and human rights as moral or political rights. It is also necessary to distinguish between different kinds of theoretical issues within each sphere. There are also important questions about the relationship between human rights law and human rights as moral rights. There is in practice a close and complex interaction between them, but for our purposes it is important to keep them conceptually distinct. Even where the distinction is observed, both kinds of literature tend to be dominated by law-trained people.

The complex relationship between the various perspectives on human rights can be illustrated by reference to the legal protection of human rights. Since World War II the number of international human rights instruments has proliferated remarkably. It is a striking example of the diffusion of both ideas and law. In addition to the three basic instruments, the Universal Declaration of Human Rights (UDHR), the International Covenant on Civil and Political Rights (ICCPR), and the International Covenant on Economic, Social and Cultural Rights (ICESCR), there are scores of other instruments covering a wide range of areas, including Torture, Discrimination Against Women, Racial Discrimination, Refugees, the Rights of the Child, and the Rights of Mentally Retarded Persons.[22] In addition, customary international law has recognised some human rights to be part of *ius cogens*.

At least as significant as the global regime, has been the development of regional regimes. Of these, the European Convention for the Protection of Human Rights and Fundamental Freedoms and its several protocols is generally recognised as the most established, with the largest number of signatories, the most effective enforcement, and the most sophisticated jurisprudence. Other regional regimes have developed in the Americas, Asia, and Africa and, on one view, these arrangements offer the best hope for the future of human rights. An alternative view is that the European Convention may hold back development: narrowly conceived, based on outdated ideas, with cumbersome and expensive procedures, it is generally subject to rather cautious interpretation, and it is very difficult to amend.[23]

Furthermore there has been the spread of domestic regimes of human rights:

> Over the past twenty-five years, and particularly since the end of the Cold War, a commitment to judicially enforceable bills of rights has quite quickly become part of the legal mainstream in all democracies, even in those places whose deep democratic pedigrees might have been expected to have insulated them from this new human rights wave. The United States has long had its own indigenous code of human rights, of course, in the form of a Bill of Rights promulgated as a set of amendments to its constitution. But now Canada, New Zealand, and many of the

[22] For a general list see www.ohchr.org/english.   [23] Dembour (2006).

European countries such as Sweden and Ireland have embraced bills of rights. Post-colonial states have invariably taken the same road, with the most dramatic example being found in South Africa's post-apartheid constitution. The European Convention – replete with very general rights claims of various shapes and sizes – has been the driving force in wedding newly emerging post-Soviet Bloc states to the legal form of a general set of human rights guarantees. Not even that most established of elective democracies, the United Kingdom, has been immune to the Convention tide, with each of its constituent parts being required to abide by human rights law and with the Kingdom as a whole being also bound, since 2 October 2000, by the terms of the Human Rights Act, 1998. Australia is now one of the last remaining democracies where rights are not to be found.[24]

This ebullient statement by a former sceptic, illustrates why many people consider human rights to be 'the only show in town'. There is now a vast human rights 'industry', with an increasing body of specialists, activists, NGOs, agencies for monitoring and enforcement, and a booming literature. In many countries human rights regimes are sufficiently established at international, regional, and domestic levels that they will not be easily uprooted or curbed even if the general ideas behind them go out of fashion. In so far as there are discernible cultures of human rights, they tend to be dominated by lawyers – international lawyers at transnational (including regional) levels, and public/constitutional lawyers at local levels.

Explicitly or mainly juridical theories are of different kinds. For present purposes it is useful to distinguish between meta-theories, legislative theories, interpretive theories, and empirical theories. Meta-theories deal with a variety of matters such as whether Bills of Rights are generally desirable, whether a particular legal system should have a Bill of Rights and, if so, of what kind; or what methods of argumentation and justification are appropriate for discourse about such documents. Questions about the relations between human rights law and human rights as moral rights belong to meta-theory.[25] A human rights theory can be a 'legislative theory' recommending which rights should be recognised by law, on what conditions, and subject to what exceptions, as part of some particular regime or more generally.[26] These are different from interpretive theories, more or less particular, about how rights documents generally or a particular Bill of Rights or other legal regime should be interpreted. Conor Gearty's *Principles of Human Rights Adjudication*[27] could be

---

[24] Gearty (2006) pp. 64–5 (footnotes omitted). This passage contains some exaggerations: for example, Tanzania elected not to have a Bill of Rights after Independence in1961; when I last visited Australia I found some human rights law, but not as yet a Bill of Rights, although the possibility has been debated (see O'Neill, Rice, and Douglas (2004)).

[25] E.g. the views of Griffin, Tasioulas, and Sen on the differences in scope of human rights and legal rights, discussed in Chapter 7 below.

[26] E.g. Waldron (1999) (arguing against constitutional judicial review).

[27] Gearty (2004). Nothing in the text is intended to suggest that a sharp distinction can be maintained between legal and moral arguments in the context of interpreting specific human rights provisions.

read as advancing such a theory. Such juridical theories need to be distinguished from a theory that is essentially the articulation of a credo or a political manifesto that expounds a particular vision or conception of human rights without seeking to justify it. Empirical study of human rights law in action and theorising about the uses, limits, and social consequences of human rights law are relatively underdeveloped, but some advances have been made in recent years.[28] These are all different from a general philosophical justification (or critique) of a moral theory of human rights, which, in turn, can be of different kinds. The rest of this chapter is mainly concerned with such philosophical justifications.

Clearly moral and political arguments can play an important part in legislative, interpretive, and other theorising about human rights law. But there are two common fallacies in human rights discourse that need to be avoided. First, there is a not uncommon assumption that the international, regional, or domestic human rights regime can and should be founded on a coherent philosophy or ideology, based for example on a particular view of human nature or on ethical norms that are universally applicable in all times and places. In its most naïve form human rights instruments are viewed as the straightforward embodiment of some moral philosophy. But such universalism does not fit the history, present state, and likely future trajectory of the international human rights regime or of most other domestic regimes. That history is a complex story of reaction to particular historical contingencies, genuine idealism, opportunism, protracted negotiation (not always unpressured), compromise, adjustment, and power politics. Such histories can rarely plausibly be told as a simple story of unilinear evolution and progress.[29] And strong moral universalism does not allow for change over time.[30] Nearly all human rights law is the result of hard-won political consensus and compromise at particular moments in history. Of course, moral beliefs and philosophies have been an important motivating force in the development of human rights law, but they have not been the only, sometimes even the main, contributing factor. And in a world of belief pluralism, and in multi-cultural and multi-ethnic societies, one cannot expect to find much scope for a single universalist ideology or moral system – unless through domination and imposition.

A second related fallacy or false assumption is that human rights as moral rights are necessarily anterior to human rights law. The assumption is that ideas about human rights as moral rights have driven human rights law rather than vice versa. In other words, human rights law has developed through the application of pre-existing moral ideas. Historically, this view can at best only be partially true. As in other contexts, issues raised and argued about in the

---

[28] Lustgarten, (2006) at pp. 847–54 (e.g Jabine and Claude (1992), Peerenboom *et al.* (2006); Goodale and Merry (2007)). See further Chapter 8, n. 143 below.

[29] Standard overviews tend to tell the story of the evolution of the international human rights regime in terms of 'generations of rights'. For a more complex story, see Steiner and Alston (2008) Chapter 2.

[30] See Raz (1999) (2001).

crucible of litigation can be as much a stimulus to moral theorising as moral theory can help in addressing such issues. Legal experience can stimulate and enlarge moral imagination.

Assumptions that moral theory is anterior to human rights law underlie much conventional human rights discourse. However, there are other ways of interpreting the phenomena of international human rights that make greater allowance for pluralism and diversity. One such view is that human rights discourse can provide a flexible and relatively stable framework for constructing and developing norms, processes, and institutional arrangements on a basis of a negotiated consensus that accommodates rather than represses change or irons out diversity.[31] In this view the potential scope for both domestic and transnational regimes of rights is greater than any substantive philosophical theory of 'fundamental' or 'moral rights' can support.[32]

What is striking about the international human rights regime, and perhaps more controversially about domestic Bills of Rights, is that the embodiment of concepts of rights into positive law allows for rather more flexibility and open-endedness in respect of content, scope, and derogations than timeless moral or political theories.[33] No one can doubt that the international regime of human rights has evolved significantly over time; it has developed a sophisticated apparatus for distinguishing between aspirations, non-binding standards, other soft law, and legally binding conventions; and it is evolving more effective procedures for monitoring and enforcement. The process is one of gradual, sometimes uneven, often piecemeal, positivisation; the content is determined by the historically contingent construction of consensus – and sometimes what is incorporated in worldwide instruments is a good deal broader in scope than many political philosophers would dare to include in a fundamental theory.[34]

---

[31] E.g. Sen (2004) discussed below Chapter 7.4.

[32] I have argued elsewhere that Bentham would not necessarily have been opposed to the UK Human Rights Act (which indeed contains some Benthamic restraints on the power of the judiciary). (*GJB*, pp. 277–8) His main attack was against loose talk about non-legal rights (see below). As soon as rights get embodied in positive law most of his objections fall away. He might have quibbled about some of the drafting as being too vague, but the tradition of using abstract terms such as those found in the Universal Declaration or even the European Convention is readily defensible, not least because they allow for a margin of appreciation in relation to local differences. Part of his argument was that, if documents like the French Declarations were to serve any useful purpose, they needed to be developed out of the details of particular laws rather than constructed *a priori* in a 'top-down' fashion. This is part of a general thesis about the distinction between demonstration ('top down') and invention ('bottom up') (e.g. Bentham (2002) at pp. 181–6; Schofield (2006), pp. 60–2). See also Griffin and Tasioulas on the modest view of the role of philosophy as making sense of existing social practices (pp. 106 and 215 below).

[33] In respect of derogations from human rights law in times of emergency moral arguments are relevant, but so are detailed pragmatic, political, and other arguments about the necessity, usefulness, and acceptability to public opinion of particular derogations. On post 9/11 debates and derogations see Gross and Ní Aoláin (2006).

[34] 'We should be neither surprised nor troubled by some discrepancy between the list of human rights that emerges from a theorist's account and the lists that are enshrined in the law.' Griffin, (2000) at p. 1. See Chapter 7.2 below.

The outcomes are reached through various forms of political action, negotiation, learning, socialisation and forms of pressure that might not be easily justifiable within a single coherent theory. The jurisprudence of the international human rights regime worked out in detail over time by judges, commentators and diplomatic action is in some respects remarkably specific. When human rights norms are abstract or vague this is often appropriate, not least in allowing for 'a margin of appreciation' that takes account of local conditions and values; but they are also are capable of being quite precise, as is illustrated by international conventions and standards on children and prisons.[35] It shows that declarations, conventions, non-binding standards, as well as binding instruments can be meaningful, workable, and lawyerlike.

There is widespread agreement that human rights law and human rights morality are not and need not be co-extensive: it is perfectly understandable that not all moral rights should be incorporated in binding law, and conversely that a legal regime of human rights may extend beyond moral minima, but nevertheless be based on consensus. A coherent moral theory of human rights may include rights that may not be immediately enforceable or claimable or which may not be suitable for being legalised for other reasons. There may be good political or pragmatic reasons for not legislating (lack of consensus, feasibility, social or economic costs etc.); conversely a political consensus may justify extending a given regime of rights, in respect of detail, scope, or practical implementation, as has happened for example with the details of labour and welfare rights One of the values of legal arenas is that actual situations and stories change our perceptions – some of the stories of human rights are about recognition of claims that were beyond the imagination of abstract theorists. In short the criteria for the *legalisation* of moral and other rights are separate from the criteria of *identification* of moral rights within a given belief system.

The distinction between theorising about law and theorising about human rights as moral rights is convenient for exposition. It underlines the points that the two categories are not co-extensive, and that not all human rights should be embodied in legislation, which may in turn be more extensive in scope than is required by moral theory. However, we should not forget that the is/ought distinction is perennially contested within jurisprudence. In particular, in the context of legal and constitutional interpretation, many jurists maintain the position that moral principles and concerns are and should be a part of argumentation about disputed questions of law – not just as add-ons and gap-fillers. Ronald Dworkin's interpretive theory is most persuasive in this kind of context. A Dworkinian can quite consistently consider a theory of human rights as moral rights independently of law, can agree that moral rights

---

[35] On the Standard Minimum Rules for the Treatment of Prisoners, see Chapter 2.3. On vagueness in law see Waldron (1994), Endicott (2000).

and legal rights are not necessarily co-extensive, but insist that morality is an essential part of human rights law.[36]

6.3 Human rights law as 'universal': moderate scepticism

That human rights law has developed remarkably in recent years can hardly be denied. But there are nevertheless 'sceptics', 'realists', and 'nihilists', who doubt many of the optimistic claims made about these advances. Some point to great gaps between aspiration and reality; others emphasise the gaps between appearance and reality; yet others doubt the value of this 'legalisation' of what are essentially political questions and conflicts; and others argue that too often human rights law is used against the interests of those it is intended to protect.

The international human rights regime is nearly 'universal' at state level insofar as almost all members of the United Nations subscribe or are signatories to many, most or all of the main documents. A high level of formal acceptance by nation-states of much of the developing international human rights regime, including both 'hard' and 'soft' instruments, is indeed a remarkable achievement. But to treat this on its own as strong evidence of the universalisation of human rights is too simple. In the view of some, most of the regime does not go beyond optimistic aspiration and surface law. Commentators regularly point to the facts that formal acceptance is not universal, reservations are extensive, ratification is patchy and often cynical, monitoring is selective, and enforcement is, at best, uneven.[37] Kent suggests that there is a continuum of at least five stages of international and domestic compliance:

> (1) accession to human rights treaties, the acceptance of the norms that this entails, and acceptance by the target state of the right of UN bodies to monitor conditions and of its obligation to respond; (2) procedural compliance with reporting and other requirements; and (3) substantive compliance with the requests of the UN body, exhibited in international or domestic behavior. At the domestic level, the continuum extends to (4) *de jure* compliance, or the implementation of international norms in domestic legislative provisions; and (5) *de facto* compliance, or compliance at the level of domestic practice.[38]

This list could be extended. An optimistic universalist might reply: 'All of these points refer to a gap between aspiration and reality, which we readily concede. The important point is that there is a very broad worldwide consensus about the aspiration and this is based on values which are broadly, if not

---

[36] The development of Dworkin's views on rights can be traced through Dworkin (1977) (1985) (2006b). He has written remarkably little about international human rights.

[37] E.g. Kent (1999) at pp. 23–5. For a more detailed account and references see Chapter 10.2(a) below.

[38] Kent (1999) at p. 7. On compliance Kent follows the pioneering work of Abram and Antonia Chayes (e.g. Chayes and Chayes (1995)).

universally, shared and which are gradually converging towards a common set of standards that can be accepted and enforced.'[39]

However, some commentators doubt whether high-minded aspirations are, or should be, reflected in the realities of human rights practice. For example, what was originally intended as a bulwark against the state, is in fact often used to secure and advance state interests. An example of such 'realist' approaches is the detailed study of the jurisprudence of the European Court of Human Rights by Marie-Bénédicte Dembour. The European Convention on Human Rights is considered to be one of the most stable, deeply entrenched, and closely monitored human rights instruments. But Dembour argues that apart from any shortfalls in respect of compliance and enforcement, the European Court is enmeshed in state interests[40] and in practice 'the Commission and the Court have proved strong allies of government and order right from the beginning'.[41] Her study advances the following 'somewhat predictable arguments':

> [F]irst, state interests play a major role in the development of human rights law, though the Court can also come down hard on the state; second, the Court endlessly engages in trade-offs and compromise, gauging the potential consequences of its position even while creating the impression that human rights prevail over all other considerations; third, a privileged applicant has far greater chances to be heard by the Court than an underprivileged one, though even the latter can be heard; fourth, the *prima facie* objective of establishing common standards while acknowledging the need to respect social diversity, means that the Court cannot pursue an uncontroversial path; fifth, the Convention system remains biased towards men in many respects even if it is on the face of it, gender-neutral and equally open to women.[42]

Some may think that Dembour places too much emphasis on derogations and on the concepts of 'margin of appreciation' and 'proportionality' as devices for giving space to state interests, but her argument that the European Convention acts as a very limited brake on state power is widely accepted.

A third line of scepticism about the beneficial effects of human rights law concerns its tendency to formalise and rigidify approaches to issues that more appropriately belong to the sphere of democratic politics. An eloquent, much

---

[39] On hypocrisy in this context see Chapter 10 below at pp. 297–8, see also Chapter 11.3(b).

[40] Dembour (2006) p. 272.

[41] *Ibid.* at 47. Dembour calls herself 'a human rights nihilist'. In fact, far from being a moral sceptic, she considers human rights 'to be the vehicle for useful values in our contemporary world' (p. 2). She is ambivalent about human rights because she is sceptical of foundationalist and universalist claims, is dismissive of the idea that there is a single concept of 'human rights', and has a more than sneaking attachment to utilitarianism.

[42] Dembour (2006) at p. 9. Elsewhere, she sums up her argument as follows: 'I have shown how human rights remain enmeshed in state interests; allow us to evade important moral dilemmas which must be confronted; fail to include in their ambit everyone irrespective of social position; trumpet universal truths which do not hold in the face of social diversity but nonetheless stand because of the prevalent basis of power; and ignore women's concerns without even realizing it.' (*Ibid.* at p. 272).

quoted, statement of this view is by the Finnish international lawyer Martii Koskenniemi:

> [W]hile the rhetoric of human rights has historically had a positive and liberating effect on societies, once rights become institutionalised as a central part of political and administrative culture, they lose their transformative effect and are petrified into a legalistic paradigm that marginalizes values or interests that resist translation into rights-language. In this way the liberal principle of 'the priority of the right over the good' results in colonization of political culture by a technocratic language that leaves no room for the articulation or realisation of conceptions of the good.[43]

The dangers that are frequently cited include the politicisation of the judiciary, the legalisation of politics, the weakening of democratic processes, and the substitution of confrontation or all-or-nothing claims for the give-and-take of political negotiation, compromise, and the substitution of dogma for argument. Critics who take this line either oppose human rights legislation altogether (probably a minority) or favour only weak forms. For example, Conor Gearty was a leading opponent of the incorporation of the European Convention into English Law, but later became a strong supporter of the Human Rights Act just because it can be repealed by Parliament, is subject to exceptions and derogations, and the ultimate power to determine conflicts between the judiciary and other branches of government is given to the legislature by the provision for declarations of incompatibility. Gearty favours the HRA just because it lacks the power of judicial review.[44]

Many of these expressions of disillusion or scepticism or pessimism can be read as *internal* criticism and doubts about the achievements, scope, practices and uses made of human rights law. Dembour and Gearty are examples of human rights activists who are committed supporters of human rights law, but who see it as an arena of perpetual debate and contestation rather than the simple application of a set of universal standards.

6.4 Human rights as moral rights: comprehensive and selective scepticism

Many people who believe in human rights ground their conception and justifications in wider religious views. But others seek to advance conceptions and justifications that are both secular and universal, claiming to transcend belief systems and cultures. In this view, human rights are the rights that all human beings have by virtue of being human. The terrain is vast, and I propose to be

---

[43] Koskenniemi (1999). On scepticism about rights-based approaches to development, see Chapter 11.3(e) below.

[44] '[I]f the Human Rights Act does ultimately succeed, it will be because – not in spite of – the weak version of "rights", riddled with exceptions, that it seeks to guarantee' (Gearty, 2004) at p. 14; See also p. 96.

quite selective. We have already encountered rights theories in the Kantian tradition in the work of Rawls and Pogge both of whom, for different reasons, adopt quite narrow conceptions of the scope of human rights. This section begins by considering some of the main general challenges to any human rights theory and some more specific challenges to aspects of human rights discourse, some of which are advanced by supporters of (typically narrow) conceptions of human rights. Chapter 7 considers three recent attempts to give an account of and to justify belief in human rights as moral rights in the face of widespread scepticism and criticism from a variety of angles: James Griffin, John Tasioulas, and Amartya Sen. All three are concerned by the seemingly random proliferation of human rights claims and by problems concerning ethnocentrism and universalism in relation to such claims.

6.5 Comprehensive sceptics

Scepticism comes in many forms.[45] Amartya Sen usefully distinguishes between comprehensive dismissal and discriminating or selective rejection.[46] Comprehensive sceptics challenge the very idea of human rights; most 'discriminating' critics of human rights attack one or more aspects of human rights ideas, discourse, or practice in order to preserve what they consider to be a defensible conception – they are critics from within, many of them strongly committed to some version or vision of human rights. Before considering some of these debates within human rights theory, let us look briefly at more sweeping forms of human rights scepticism.

Comprehensive scepticism challenges the very idea of human rights. Some scepticisms may be based on one or other versions of a general ethical scepticism. One may reject the idea of human rights if one believes that judgements of value are merely expressions of individual preference (subjectivism) or that such judgements cannot be rationally justified or reasonable, (anti-rationalism); or one may reject all claims to universality of human rights if one believes that all values are culturally determined (strong cultural relativism).

More interesting for present purposes are forms of scepticism about human rights that are based on different ethical positions, such as utilitarianism or virtue ethics or forms of religious belief that do not involve the discourse of rights. We need to tread carefully here, because many such positions allow a limited or a subordinate role to the idea of moral rights or can be interpreted in such a way that they can be said to be basically compatible with human rights ideas, even if the mode of discourse has been different. For example, some consequentialists, including Peter Singer, are prepared to treat the realisation of human rights as representing desirable goals and consequences – they can be represented as intermediate goals subordinate to utility. Dr Francis Deng argues

---

[45] *RE*, Chapter 4, see Campbell, Ewing and Tomkins (2001).
[46] Sen (2004) discussed at Chapter 7.4 below.

that basic values of the Dinka of Sudan are fundamentally compatible with the values underlying the Universal Declaration of Human Rights.[47] Using different methods, Abdullahi An Na'im has sought to show the compatibility in most, but not all, respects between a liberal interpretation of Islam and basic human rights.[48] Several African thinkers have argued that traditional African culture recognised basic human rights before the advent of colonialism.[49] There are many other examples of debates within ethical and religious traditions about the compatibility, status, and role of ideas about human rights within a given tradition. Here we are more concerned with ethical positions that challenge the very existence of human rights or the utility of human rights talk.

There is long history of comprehensive scepticism about human rights. Nowhere has there been a more persistent tradition of scepticism than England. In the Western tradition, classic enunciations have been countered by classic attacks. The French and American Declarations and their theoretical underpinnings, or lack of them, were the subject of powerful attacks by Jeremy Bentham, Edmund Burke and Karl Marx.[50] So we have significant classic critiques from revolutionary, radical and conservative, even reactionary, standpoints, and, more recently, from some communitarians and post-modernists. Rather than attempt to be comprehensive, I shall focus on six major lines of attack that do not depend on general ethical scepticism:

(i) that talk of human rights is meaningless;
(ii) that, even if talk of human rights is meaningful, the existence of human rights has no foundation;
(iii) that, even if some human rights exist, human rights discourse adds nothing to our moral understandings: it is redundant, it cannot be a satisfactory basis for a moral theory; and it can be misleading or obfuscatory;
(iv) that human rights theories are excessively individualistic, atomistic, or egoistic;
(v) that human rights theories and discourse do not adequately accommodate feminist concerns;
(vi) that claims to the universality of human rights are unsustainable, in particular that human rights represent a colonial or neo-colonial ideology that the West has sought to impose on the Rest.[51]

(a) Talk of human rights is meaningless or mischievous nonsense

The most comprehensive attack on human rights (and other non-legal rights) was by Jeremy Bentham. The classic text is *Anarchical Fallacies*, variously

---

[47] See Chapter 13.2 below.   [48] See Chapter 13.3 below.
[49] See Chapter 13 below.   [50] A very useful source is Waldron (1987).
[51] A further challenge, that a great deal of human rights discourse involves unwarranted extensions and perversions of 'real' human rights, is advanced by both comprehensive and selective sceptics and is dealt with in Chapter 6.5 and 6.6 below.

known as *Pestilential Nonsense Unmasked* or *Nonsense Upon Stilts*.[52] The central thrust is that talk of non-legal rights (whether natural, moral, or human) is meaningless, but in the course of his critique Bentham also challenged ideas about absolute and inalienable rights. It is worth revisiting this text briefly, because it still presents a direct and powerful, essentially utilitarian, challenge to contemporary moral rights discourse.[53]

Bentham's argument can be restated as follows: To say that 'X has a right' logically implies some existing general rule or command; 'X has a legal right' presupposes a law commanded by a sovereign and backed by a sanction. Legal rights are creatures of positive laws. To talk of non-legal rights is nonsensical. Since natural law does not exist, the idea of natural rights is nonsensical, like the idea of a son without a father. Utility is the only moral principle and, if as Ronald Dworkin has subsequently argued, rights represent important enclaves of value that 'trump' utility, then it would be paradoxical for a utilitarian to recognise utility rights.[54] To talk of imprescriptible (i.e. unalterable) rights is also meaningless, for the sovereign's power cannot be legally limited. Such talk is nonsense piled on nonsense, 'nonsense upon stilts'.[55] Since rights conflict, talk of absolute rights is contradictory. Talk of non-legal rights is also mischievous and pestilential, raising expectations that cannot be fulfilled, inviting anarchy.

Bentham's objections relate to a mode of discourse, rather than to the values embodied in modern rights documents. A modern Benthamite can argue that to talk of 'a right to food' or 'a right to work' or 'a right to development' refers to important aspirations, but begs questions about the allocation of correlative duties, about enforcement if not legally binding, and about the feasibility of implementing such 'rights'. They represent wishful thinking. As Bentham put it: 'Want is not supply, hunger is not bread.'[56] Furthermore, the word 'right' is ambiguous, because as Bentham first argued, and Austin and Hohfeld developed the analysis, the word 'right' can refer to claims with correlative duties ('others ought or must'), or to privileges ('I may'), or to immunities ('others

---

[52] See now the new edition in the *Collected Works*: Jeremy Bentham, *Rights, Representation and Reform* (2002). On which, see Schofield (2006) at pp. 59–72. Bentham's preferred title was *Nonsense Upon Stilts*, but the work is more widely known today as *Anarchical Fallacies*.

[53] There is an extensive literature on *Anarchical Fallacies/Nonsense Upon Stilts*. Schofield (2006) Chapter 3 contains a careful exposition. See also Burns (1966), Twining (1975), Postema (1989), Bedau (2000). Several of these are collected in Parekh (ed.) (1993) Vol. 3.

[54] On Bentham's rejection of the idea of non-legal utility rights, especially on the grounds that that they are not peremptory see further Hart (1982), pp. 85–94; Postema, (1986) pp. 321–8.

[55] The phrase 'nonsense upon stilts' is open to several interpretations. It could mean nonsense piled on nonsense or even further out of touch with the ground. Catherine Pease-Watkin suggests that in this context 'on stilts' means inflated, puffed up, overblown (conversation with the author). This is supported by the context: the whole sentence reads: 'Natural rights is simple nonsense: natural and imprescriptible rights, rhetorical nonsense, nonsense upon stilts.' (Bentham (2002) at p. 330.

[56] The preferred wording in the 2002 edition (CW) is 'wants are not means: hunger is not bread' (at p. 330).

cannot') or to powers ('I can').[57] All of these words refer to relations between persons.[58] To say in a famine situation: 'A has a right to food' could mean that A has a claim to food, but the statement does not specify who has the duty to provide it. If it only means 'A may have food, if he can get it', it trivialises and obfuscates the problem. Such talk begs the crucial question of allocation of responsibility. Bentham's objections relate to a mode of discourse, rather than to the values embodied in modern rights documents.

My own view, which is fairly orthodox, is that some of Bentham's arguments are wrong, but others pose a serious challenge to loose talk about rights.[59] First, one of Bentham's arguments was that the only source of rights is positive law and to talk of non-legal rights – natural, moral, human – is meaningless. One can concede the logical point that sentences of the kind 'X has a right' indicate a relation between X's position and a rule or principle that is its source, but argue that there are moral principles that can be the source of moral rights.[60] For the utilitarian there are no moral principles independent of utility and utility is not a source of rights in any strong sense (e.g. that rights trump utility). But deontologists, natural lawyers, and even modified utilitarians, maintain that there are moral principles independent of utility and, if so, Bentham's point fails.

Second, what types of rights are human rights? Bentham began the line of analysis that culminated in Hohfeld's analysis of legal rights into claims, privileges (or liberties), powers and immunities.[61] This analysis is very widely accepted by philosophers as well as jurists, many of whom agree that the basic terms can be applied to moral as well as legal discourse.[62] Most candidates for being called human rights take the form of claim rights (e.g., a right not to be tortured, a right to life, a right to food, and procedural rights) or liberty rights (e.g freedom of speech, freedom of association).[63]

In legal analysis two points about claim rights have caused difficulty. First, Hohfeld suggested that all claim rights have correlative duties; 'X has a claim

---

[57] On Hohfeld, see Chapter 2.3(d) above.

[58] Rights are 'words of relation' both in respect of derivation from norms and referring to relations between persons. On evidence as a word of relation, see Bentham (1827) Book 1, Chapter 1.

[59] Twining, (1975) at p. 315. In response, Melvin Dalgarno (1975) argued that all of Bentham's arguments were valid, *ibid.*, p. 357.

[60] Similarly, we can drop the ideas of sovereign, command, and sanction from our theory of law, yet agree, as does Hart, that legal claims, duties etc. presuppose valid rules within an existing legal system (the logical point).

[61] On differences between Bentham and Hohfeld, see Hart (1982) Chapter VII. On the application of Hohfeldian analysis to games, such as chess, see Chapter 2.3(d) above.

[62] Moral philosophers including Wellman, Gewirth, Finnis, and O'Neill, argue that the Bentham-Hohfeld analysis can illuminate moral discourse (see Chapter 2 above at pp. 52–3) Griffin comments on Hohfeld as follows: 'Helpful as it is to have the variety of such conceptual relations plotted, they do not give us what we need to decide what rights there are, what their boundaries are, and how we resolve conflicts between rights themselves and other kinds of value.' Griffin (2001b) at p. 308.

[63] Others such as freedom of expression or religion may be interpreted as liberty rights, but for the sake of simplicity let us leave them aside.

against 'Y' means that 'Y owes a duty to X' and vice versa. But it has been pointed out that some legal duties do not have correlative rights (called 'absolute duties' by John Austin) and that sometimes the discourse of rights includes statements about rights where no correlative duty is indicated (rights of imperfect obligation). The first category need not cause difficulty. Duties not to be cruel to animals or to avoid unnecessary damage to trees or the environment are widely accepted as moral duties without correlative rights – they fall outside the sphere of human rights.[64] On the other hand, there is continuing controversy among human rights theorists about rights of imperfect obligation (i.e. rights without correlative obligations). On a Benthamite or Hohfeldian view such talk merely obfuscates the issues; but there is a different view, viz. that talk of 'a right to food' or a 'right to work' is a vehicle for giving voice to important claims even if responsibility for meeting these claims is not clearly allocated. We shall return to this controversy in due course.[65]

Third, most rights theorists accept that principles and rights regularly conflict, and so drop any strong version of the idea of absolute rights.[66]

Fourth, we can question the idea of unlimited sovereignty (Bentham himself accepted that sovereignty is divisible),[67] but agree that fundamental constitutional rights are subject to change. Whether fundamental moral or human rights are susceptible to change is a more complex philosophical problem, though not for a Benthamite.[68]

Finally, we can also question on empirical grounds Bentham's claim that loose rights talk in fact promotes anarchy and threatens the sum total of human happiness. My hunch is almost the opposite: on the whole, it seems to me that the twentieth century rights movement has generally promoted the welfare of humankind and strengthened respect for the Rule of Law. But that is just a hunch. An alternative, typically Marxian view, is that rights discourse is often dangerously mystifying window dressing.[69]

Thus, if one pares away the weaker parts of Bentham's argument, one is left first, with the logical points about the discourse of rights presupposing rules or principles; that such terms indicate typically bipolar relations between persons, and that both parties need to be specified; second, that talk of absolute rights is often self-contradictory; and, third, that difficult questions arise about the universality of rights over time and space. All of these are challenges that need to be faced not only by a coherent moral-political theory of rights, but also by the drafters of human rights documents and those who invoke rights in practical argument.

Of course, Bentham was not the only thinker to challenge the discourse and substance of the French Declarations. From different political starting points

---

[64] On 'animal rights' or 'the rights of trees', see below Chapter 7, n. 47.
[65] See p. 213 below.   [66] E.g. Dworkin (1977) pp. 81–4.   [67] Burns (1973).   [68] See n. 35 above.
[69] See Baxi (1998) at pp. 430–1 below. On the differences between Bentham and Marx on rights see Waldron (1987) and Hart (1983).

both Karl Marx[70] and Edmund Burke[71] launched powerful attacks on eighteenth-century rights documents and their theoretical underpinnings. They, too, made points of substance. Most of these criticisms have to be confronted by defenders of human rights and to a large extent they have framed the philosophical debates.[72]

(b) Anti-foundationalism

Ethical sceptics deny that human rights exist, because no values have an objective existence. Many religious people believe that human rights cannot be grounded on secular premises and seek to justify support of human rights on broader religious or spiritual beliefs. Utilitarians accept that there are universal (objective) values, but reject any idea of rights grounded on principles independent of utility. There are others again who are committed to supporting and strengthening human rights as a matter of faith. Some of these maintain that any attempt to provide a philosophical foundation or justification is misconceived and could possibly be harmful.

Perhaps the most influential proponent of this 'anti-foundationalist' view is Richard Rorty, whose position on rights is part of a broader post-modernist epistemological scepticism.[73] For Rorty, 'truth' is a matter of consensus or solidarity within a particular epistemic community: 'There is nothing to be said about either truth or rationality apart from descriptions of the familiar procedures of justification which a given society – *ours* – uses.'[74]

Following an Argentinian jurist, Eduardo Rebossi, Rorty argues that seeking foundations or philosophical justification for commitment to human rights is irrelevant and outmoded. Historically, attempts at justifying human rights were bound up with the search for distinguishing human beings from other creatures. But, since Darwin, we have come to think of ourselves 'as a flexible, protean, self-shaping, animal rather than as the rational animal or the cruel animal.'[75] Rorty defends 'the claim that nothing relevant to moral choice separates human beings from animals except historically contingent facts of the world, cultural facts.'[76] In short Rorty embraces a form of quite strong

---

[70] On the European Convention on Human Rights in a Marxist light, see Dembour (2006) Chapter 5.

[71] Waldron (1987).

[72] For example, we have a careful, thorough, and appealing attempt to do just that by Jeremy Waldron in the last chapter of his book *Nonsense upon Stilts* (1987), which deals directly with the criticisms by Bentham, Burke, Marx and modern communitarianism in the twentieth-century context. However, in making some important concessions to the critics, as Waldron does, one is left with a theory of human rights that is quite limited in scope.

[73] Rorty (1993). See also Rorty (1987) (1991). Susan Haack suggests that in following Rorty jurists have fallen into the twin traps of conflating 'anti-foundationalism' (itself an ambiguous term) in epistemology and ethics and of failing to differentiate between classical pragmatism (Peirce, James, and Dewey) and neo- or pseudo-pragmatism spearheaded by Rorty (Haack (2005)). On Rorty's epistemology and 'pragmatism' see Haack (1998) Chapter 2.

[74] Rorty (1987) at p. 42.   [75] Rorty, (1993) at p. 115.   [76] *Ibid.*, at p. 116.

cultural relativism.[77] Rorty, as a supporter of contemporary 'Eurocentric' human rights culture, suggests that this culture provides a more settled and persuasive basis for commitment to rights than can be provided by any attempt at philosophical justification. Philosophy can summarise and try to make coherent our culturally influenced intuitions rather than justify them.

Many find Rorty's argument attractive.[78] The message seems to be: 'Accept the current human rights culture and get on with the job of supporting and strengthening it.' However, in addition to any general objections to post-modern scepticism and this peculiar form of cultural relativism, Rorty's position begs some of the difficult questions within human rights theory. First, under the label of 'human rights' culture he conflates human rights morality, human rights law, and the politics of human rights. He provides no criteria for assessing and criticising the adequacy of any given regime of human rights law. Second, Rorty says nothing about the relations between 'our' human rights culture and other belief systems. Third, he seems to treat 'our' human rights culture as monolithic, settled, and non-contentious. He assumes a non-existent consensus. John Tasioulas puts the point well:

> The implication is that we, Eurocentric intellectuals, already *know* how to discriminate between genuine and bogus claimants to the title 'human right', how to interpret the rights that feature on our list, how to weigh them against competing ethical considerations, including other human rights, what human rights are rights *to*, whether and upon whom they impose duties, how they are best institutionalized and enforced, and so on. In light of this, what contribution could philosophy hope to make? But of course, the question is based on a false premise as no settled agreement exists on any of these questions. In neglecting the persistence of these extensive and ongoing controversies, Rorty shows himself to be disengaged from the human rights culture he purports to champion.[79]

In short Rorty begs almost all of the questions on the agenda of human rights theory, including those aspects to which a well-developed philosophical account might contribute. He does, however, pose in a sharp form questions about whether any philosophical *justification* is possible; and what can *philosophers* add to human rights theory? We shall consider both issues below.

(c) Some illusions of human rights discourse[80]

There is a philosophical view that the language of rights adds nothing to our moral understanding and that this language often obscures moral issues. Clearly, if one thinks that all talk of moral or human rights is meaningless

---

[77] *Ibid.*

[78] Conor Gearty is an example of a prominent human rights scholar and activist who found Rorty's anti-foundationalism attractive; but in the end he rejects it. (Gearty (2006) at pp. 20, 42, 56).

[79] Tasioulas (2002a) at p. 82.

[80] This heading echoes an unpublished paper by Joseph Raz, entitled 'The Illusions of Human Rights' (2003). I focus on Raz because James Griffin uses him as his main foil in trying to

and dangerous, one is likely to agree. But this view goes beyond Bentham in claiming that even if a particular theory of human rights is clear, coherent and precise it is redundant and likely to be obfuscatory or misleading. This is a philosophical argument, which is quite separate from the idea that talk of rights as political rhetoric can be a powerful weapon in empowering the less advantaged and for advancing political goals.

The redundancy argument is related to, but needs to be distinguished from, scepticism about the existence of rights, scepticism about the universality of human rights claims, and misuse and abuse of rights discourse. Each of these presents a challenge to contemporary theorists of human rights.

(i) Are human rights illusory?

Perhaps the biggest challenge facing contemporary human rights theory is to *justify* a claim that any human rights exist. If one is dissatisfied with Rortyian anti-foundationalism, then some basis for the very idea of human rights has to be put forward. The standard claim is that human rights are those rights we have by virtue of being human. Two main challenges are typically aligned against this view: first that one cannot logically derive an ought from an is ('the naturalistic fallacy'); second, to doubt that human nature is universal in any meaningful sense. As we shall see, some theorists side-step the first objection by acknowledging that 'human nature' is itself a normative concept.[81]

The second objection opens up a Pandora's box of philosophical disagreements. To keep matters simple let us focus on one specific argument of this kind. Joseph Raz, who claims to be an agnostic about the existence of any human rights, challenges any strong claims to universality. The argument may be restated as follows:[82] Universality is an essential feature of human rights. Few, if any, supposed rights are universal and therefore genuinely human rights. Most of the standard catalogues of alleged human rights are not universal and so are not real human rights. If there are any universal human rights, they are unimportant because they are too abstract and vague.[83] Some of the most important alleged human rights are historically contingent. Raz uses freedom of expression to illustrate the general point. In many circumstances, for example in complex modern societies, a right to freedom of expression is very important, but this is not true of all societies. For example, for Stone Age cave-dwellers and inhabitants of small medieval hamlets freedom of speech

---

construct his philosophical theory of human rights that is considered below. This section owes much to the ideas of Joseph Raz, but does not purport to restate his position, which is extremely subtle and which has developed over time and cannot be fully explicated in short compass. See Raz (1984), (1994), (2001), (2003) and Meyer, Paulson and Pogge (eds.) (2003).

[81] See pp. 202–3 below.

[82] Raz (2003). See also Griffin's reply in Griffin (2001a) n. 30 (arguing that freedom of expression is necessary for agency).

[83] Thus, one may accept that a suggested 'right to life' is a universal value, but it is open to so many interpretations, refinements, derogations and exceptions that the concept has limited value at this level of abstraction.

of solidarity or concerns about ecology, endangered languages or artistic heritage. But it is possible to subscribe to a theory of human rights without claiming that it is a comprehensive theory of political morality, rather one that highlights the importance of one group of interests. Jeremy Waldron puts it this way:

> The modest function of a theory of rights is not to claim completeness but to draw attention to these important individual interests. One is not guilty of any crass or misguided individualism simply for expressing moral concern about certain of the ills that may befall individual men and women, or the harm and neglect that individuals may inflict on one another. It is *awful* to be locked up or silenced, *terrifying* to be beaten or tortured, and *appalling* to be left to starve or vegetate when resources are available for food and education; and one may think these ills so bad that their avoidance should be an overriding aim of any decent society. To hold such a view and base it on the moral significance of what it is like, as an individual, to suffer these evils, is to embrace a theory of rights.[93]

Even if it is conceded that there are communal goods as well as individual interests, it can be objected that assertions of right tend to override communal goals. For example, individuals who are assertive about their rights can wreck a marriage, a family, or a team. The discourse of rights can be overbearing or divisive. The rights theorist can make a dual response: first, there is a difference between *having* rights and *asserting* them. The emotive phrase 'standing on one's rights' correctly suggests that there are occasions when a claim of right is likely to be disruptive or otherwise inappropriate. Waldron suggests that in such contexts rights are important as a fall-back when fragile communal relationships break down.[94] However, a stronger argument is that a thin theory of rights only concerns basic needs and interests for survival, well-being, and leading a worthwhile life. Where a marriage or family or community threatens or suppresses really important individual interests, one is justified in asserting one's autonomy. Standing up to an oppressive father, a dominant spouse, or an authoritarian superior may be necessary to protect one's autonomy. The nuances suggested by the difference between 'standing up for' and 'standing on' one's rights indicates many of the dilemmas that arise in relations between an individual and a group. A thin or modest theory of rights can meet this standard communitarian objection; more dogmatic versions may not.

A second charge under the heading of 'individualistic' is that human rights theories take an 'atomistic' view of individuals ignoring the social dimensions of the self.[95] Here the standard response is to confess and avoid. Utilitarians, Kantians, and human rights theorists make the individual an important focus of attention. For Bentham the individual sentient being is the basic unit in the felicific calculus.[96] For the Kantian, the autonomous individual person is the

---

[93] *Ibid.*, at p. 187.   [94] *Ibid.*, at pp. 188–9.   [95] E.g. Taylor (1979).   [96] See Chapter 5.4 above.

core focus of morality. Human rights are rights we have by virtue of being individual human beings. In that sense, all of these are 'individualistic' theories. But none of these positions necessarily involves a denial that we are social animals, if that means we are dependent on, formed by, and both liberated and constrained by social relations. Social relations are important, but how important is a matter of debate in different contexts.

Nor do these positions necessarily involve the view that morality only concerns the duties and rights of individual persons. The jurisprudence of legal personality allows that many kinds of entity can be legal subjects, some with both passive and active capacities, others only passive.[97] There are, of course, both conceptual and substantive difficulties about attributing a full range of capabilities to collectivities such as corporations, states, or trade unions and even more so to rats, ancestors, the unborn, and gods. Similar, but not identical, issues arise in relation to 'moral personality.' In human rights theory there are contested issues about the rights of peoples, group rights, animal rights, and a right to development. Can corporations claim to have *human* rights? Do members of future generations have *rights*? For many rights theorists extending the idea of moral rights to subjects other than individual humans is an unnecessary extension.[98] But to say that rights of individual human beings are important does not of itself involve commitment on any of these issues.

Criticism of, or unease about, the 'individualism' of human rights theory is sometimes interpreted as meaning that emphasising rights is selfish or egoistic in tendency. This raises issues too complex to pursue here. Waldron gives a succinct response to three versions of this criticism:

> The first charge is that to say a person has a right to something is to encourage her to exercise that right selfishly without regard to others. The second charge is that rights are characteristically claimed and enforced in an unpleasantly adversarial and self-centred manner. And the third is the charge that, behind these issues of exercise and enforcement, lies a deep and pervasive exaggeration in rights-theories abut the ineliminability of self-interest from social life. I want to reply to each of these charges in turn, arguing that the first is downright false, the second not necessarily true, and the third fair in the sense that rights-theorists do emphasize the importance of self-interest but false inasmuch as such an emphasis is not necessarily an exaggeration of the role that it plays in social and moral activity.[99]

Waldron deals with each of these charges convincingly and in detail. Suffice to say here that if one accepts the individual human being as the basic unit of morality, such 'individualism' involves no necessary commitment to selfishness, egoism, or an atomistic view of human nature. Nevertheless, there are

---

[97] MacCormick (2007) Chapter 5.
[98] The concept of legal subjects ('legal persons') is explored in Chapter 15.2 on the web.
[99] Waldron (1987) at p. 191.

theories point to a narrow range of human interests that are so important that one is justified in claiming that they generally 'trump' other values in most circumstances.

Fifth, the charge that human rights talk tends to be loose, abstract, and open to overuse and abuse can readily be conceded. Indeed, this is a central concern of many contemporary rights theorists, who seek to resist the proliferation of human rights claims by constructing criteria for distinguishing between genuine claims and those that are bogus or unjustified extensions.

Sixth, the charge that human rights represent Western values imposed by the West on the Rest can be met by the response that (a) the origin of an idea says nothing about its validity; (b) that human rights are rights we have by virtue of a universally shared humanity that has a moral core in respect of fundamental needs and interests which go beyond biological imperatives for survival and subsistence to include conceptions of well-being and self-realisation. This moral core applies to all human beings independently of what they believe. However, (c) human rights theories have mainly developed within a particular broad intellectual tradition and have spread without much regard to and in ignorance of other belief systems and cultures that may be based on different cosmologies and conceptions of human nature. Accordingly, there are real dangers of ethnocentrism that need to be countered by reducing the ignorance, exploring the extent to which there are or could be shared values, and being prepared to learn from other cultures and belief systems.

Not all rights theorists are willing to make such concessions. However, my argument is that these concessions can be made without surrendering a belief in human rights. In order further to focus the discussion, let us consider a particular standpoint to which contemporary human rights theories are commonly addressed. Imagine someone, perhaps a human rights activist, who is attracted by the idea of human rights and who is generally committed to human rights law as a good thing, but who is also concerned about the meaning, justification, scope, and coherence of ideas about human rights as moral rights. In other words, she is seeking to clarify and justify her beliefs in a social practice to which she is politically and emotionally committed.[5] For the sake of simplicity, let us assume that she accepts the following working assumptions:

- She does not accept strong versions of ethical scepticism or subjectivism, so these comprehensive challenges can be set on one side.[6]
- She is not religious, so religious-based theories of human rights do not appeal.[7]

---

[5] She is seeking in Tasioulas' words 'the presuppositions of certain social practices to which we are ineluctably committed'. (Tasioulas (2007a) at p. 83.)

[6] The reply to general moral scepticism is to articulate a coherent and cogently argued moral theory.

[7] Alternatively, whether or not she is religious she seeks a philosophical basis for human rights independently of religion.

- She recognises that some human rights theories claim to transcend religions and to provide a consensual basis for co-existence and co-operation between believers in different religions and non-believers alike.
- She accepts the distinction between human rights law and human rights as moral rights.
- She rejects the anti-foundationalist challenge that human rights culture provides its own justification, because what she is seeking is a human rights theory that can *independently* justify, evaluate, and guide human rights discourse and human rights law.

Any one of these assumptions could mark a point of divergence from the kind of philosophical theory that she is seeking. But even if these are granted, such a theory needs to confront several central challenges to beliefs in universal human rights as moral rights:

- the 'nonsense' challenge – to the very conception
- the challenge to grounds for existence
- the proliferation challenge: that there are no criteria for determining the scope of human rights or for distinguishing between genuine human rights and those that are bogus or unwarranted extensions
- challenges to universality claims
- the ethnocentrism challenge: that human rights ideas evolved in one intellectual tradition largely without regard to and in ignorance of other belief systems and cultures for many of which the language of rights is an alien form of discourse.

We may add a further general challenge, echoing Herbert Hart, that even if all these challenges are satisfactorily met, philosophers have not yet constructed a philosophical theory of human rights comparable to utilitarianism in its clarity, specificity, and practical appeal.[8]

With these challenges in mind, let us consider three recent attempts within the Anglo-American tradition to provide a coherent philosophical justification for a non-religious theory of universal human rights from a global perspective: by James Griffin, John Tasioulas, and Amartya Sen. James Griffin is an example of a moral philosopher who has attempted to construct a general substantive theory of human rights on the basis of two core values related to agency (autonomy and liberty); this differs from the somewhat broader thesis of John Tasioulas, who grounds his rather more expansive theory on an explicit theory of moral pluralism. Both of these are substantive theories that purport to provide criteria for determining any particular claim that this or that kind of human right exists. By contrast, Amartya Sen has recently advanced a 'discourse theory' of rights. This view treats human rights discourse as involving an

---

[8] See p. 173 above.

ongoing search for consensus through rational public debate in the face of belief pluralism and scepticism about universality.

7.2 James Griffin: a dualist substantive theory[9]

James Griffin was the holder of the White's Chair in Moral Philosophy at Oxford from 1996 to 2000. In a highly regarded work on *Value Judgement*,[10] Griffin criticised the three main strands of ethical theory in the Western Tradition – utilitarianism, deontology, and virtue ethics – for being too ambitious, demanding too much of moral agents. Instead, he suggested a more modest, 'bottom up' approach that starts with existing practices and bases ethical thinking in beliefs 'of high reliability' including well-grounded beliefs about interests, facts, and ideas that are deeply embedded in our language and that affect our core interests (e.g. pain).[11] Prudential and moral beliefs should be formed by taking into account facts about human interests, agents and social organisation.[12] Ethics' picture of agents should be realistic and the role of philosophy in developing ethical norms is quite modest.

Griffin turned his attention to human rights quite late. He was concerned about a widespread cynicism about them, especially the debasement of much human rights talk and the proliferation of human rights claims. Griffin boldly proclaimed that his aim was to 'complete the Enlightenment Project by making the concept of human right considerably more determinate than the Enlightenment left it.'[13] Building on the tradition of linking dignity and freedom in relation to personhood and agency, Griffin summarised 'the best account' of human rights as follows:

> What seems to me to be the best account of human rights is this. It is centred on the notion of agency. We human beings have the capacity to form pictures of what a good life would be and to try to realize these pictures. We value our status as agents especially highly, often more highly even than our happiness. Human rights can then be seen as protections of our human standing, our agency. They are protections, then, of that somewhat austere state, the life of an agent and not of a good or happy or perfected or flourishing life. It is not that what human rights protect is clearly the most important aspect of our life; the nature and degree of its importance remains to be seen. But it is what various Renaissance and Enlightenment philosophers have marked off with the notion of 'human dignity'. We attach special importance to it, and that is reason enough to mark it off, too,

---

[9] 'Dualist' because the theory is based on two values: autonomy and liberty. This section is based on James Griffin, *Value Judgement* (1996), (2001a) ('Discrepancies', Presidential address) (2001b) ('First Steps') (2003b) ('Group Rights') and (2003a) ('A short intellectual biography'). (See also Crisp and Hooker (eds.) (2000) including Griffin's 'Replies'). Griffin, *On Human Rights* (2008) reached me too late for consideration. John Tasioulas' article on 'Retracing Griffin's Steps' (2002a) has been of great help in preparing this section.

[10] Griffin (1996).   [11] *Ibid.*, at pp. 125–8.   [12] *Ibid.*, at 129.   [13] Griffin (2001a) at p. 2.

with the language of human rights.[14] .... Briefly an agent is someone who chooses goals and is then free to pursue them. Both choosing and pursuing, both autonomy and liberty, are values we attribute to agency.[15]

For a human right to exist it must satisfy the tests of personhood (liberty and autonomy) and of 'practicalities', that make a human right 'an effective, socially manageable claim on others'.[16] Based on these tests Griffin's preliminary list of human rights comes quite close to the standard rights protected by international human rights law:

> Out of the notion of personhood we can generate most of the conventional list of human rights. We have a right to life (without it, personhood is impossible), to security of person (for the same reason), to a voice in political decision (a key exercise of autonomy), to free expression, to assembly, and to a free press (without them, exercise of autonomy would be hollow), to worship (a key exercise of what one takes to be the point of life). It also generates, I should say (though this is hotly disputed), a positive freedom, namely a right to minimum learning and material resources needed for a human existence, something more, that is than mere physical survival. It also generates a right not to be tortured, because, among its evils, torture destroys one's capacity to decide and to stick to the decision. And so on. It should already be clear that the generative capacities of the notion of personhood are quite great.[17]

Griffin builds on the tradition of human rights law, especially the concept of dignity,[18] but his list is confined to those rights that are well-grounded according to his tests. And he uses these tests to doubt or exclude other familiar claims to be human rights. For example, he treats as doubtful, but understandable extensions, compensation for a miscarriage of justice and some employment rights (e.g. equal pay for equal work, promotion on merit, healthy and safe working conditions). He treats a whole range of other claims as unjustifiable extensions, including some which are aspirations not rights (a right to peace, the highest standard of health), or too broad (a right to work, honour and

---

[14] This is the formulation in Griffin (2003b), at p. 162. The wording is only slightly different from that in Griffin (2001a) at p. 4. This is a summary of a thesis developed at greater length in 'First Steps' (2001b). Griffin attacked the idea of 'group rights' which are not reducible to individual rights on the grounds that such talk is 'part of a widespread movement to make the discourse of rights do most of the important work in ethics, which it was neither designed to do nor should now be made to do.' (2003b at p. 161).

[15] Griffin (2001a) at p. 4.

[16] Griffin (2001b) at p. 315. Tasioulas describes these 'practicalities' as 'a very diverse group of considerations that includes (i) general facts about human nature, (ii) general facts about social life, (iii) social utilities, (iv) traditions and socio-economic conditions of particular societies.' (Tasioulas (2002a) at p. 84.

[17] See now Griffin (2008) at pp. 37–9. Griffin (2001b) at p. 311. Griffin makes it clear that this is not a closed list.

[18] On dignity see McCrudden (2008) and Deng (1971) (1986), An-Na'im and Deng (1990) discussed in Chapter 13.2.

reputation) or ill-conceived (a right to inherit, freedom from propaganda favouring war, a right to happiness).[19]

Griffin emphasises that human rights based on personhood protect one enclave of values, agency, but this is not the only, nor necessarily the most important aspect of life.[20] In short, human rights compete with other values as well as with each other. What are these other values? He explicitly mentions in the passage quoted above 'a good or happy or perfected or flourishing life' as separate ideas. In discussing some particular examples he suggests that some fall under justice rather than rights (e.g promotion on merit), because justice is in some respects broader than rights.[21] He is quite clear that not all moral values should be subsumed under rights, but he is less clear whether human rights are one aspect of justice or a separate category which overlaps with it.[22] By basing human rights on liberty and autonomy, Griffin's list is largely restricted to rights associated with civil and political (largely negative) rights but there is some provision for (largely minimalist) social and economic rights in respect of education and material resources for subsistence.

Griffin's relatively thin theory of human rights as moral rights is a brave effort to meet the main challenges to moral theories of human rights. It meets the 'nonsensical' challenge by providing a meaningful account based on a version of liberal democratic theory. It meets the challenge of 'the naturalistic fallacy' by including an explicitly normative element (based on dignity) into its assumptions about human nature/personhood; it provides a counter to Rortyian scepticism first by providing an account that is at least as solidly grounded as Rorty's assumptions about a single stable human rights culture and, second, by showing that such a theory can be useful as providing a template for evaluating and guiding human rights law. Griffin's response to the redundancy ('no value added') challenge is that his account of rights does not purport to replace, take over, or modify our general understandings of morality; rather it serves the more modest aim of drawing attention to and refining an important aspect of moral concern that deserves to be taken seriously.[23] Griffin's achievement is to construct a clear, coherent and cautious theory of human rights which has roots in a recognisable philosophical tradition and which provides some criteria for the existence and scope of human rights as moral rights. That leaves open the question of its claim to universality, which will be considered below.

Griffin's account is unlike many contemporary theories in several important respects: first, his theory is *substantive*. It maintains that human rights are

---

[19] Lists of acceptable, unacceptable and debatable rights are considered at length in Griffin (2001a) at pp. 8–26.

[20] Griffin (2001a) at p. 4.   [21] Griffin (2001a) at pp. 14–16.

[22] Tasioulas (2002a). Griffin (2008) (e.g. at pp. 41, 65, 276) clearly treats them as separate, but overlapping concepts and allows for rights-justice conflicts.

[23] Griffin can rightly argue that his theory sharpens our perceptions of some moral issues; whether his ideas could be rendered without resort to the language of rights is a separate question.

values of personhood and that these are universal and can be identified. Second, it purports to *justify* belief in human rights in general and in particular human rights on the basis of a general moral theory. It therefore rejects both the kind of anti-foundationalism promoted by Rorty and Rawls' avoidance of 'comprehensive doctrines' by claiming that his theory of justice is political, not metaphysical.[24] Third, by relating rights to human goods Griffin conceives of human rights as a species of human interests that can be identified in an intelligible way. These claims are bold rather than modest, not least because they confront problems that many contemporary theories try to sidestep.

7.3 John Tasioulas: a pluralist substantive theory[25]

In 'Retracing Griffin's Steps', John Tasioulas builds on Griffin's account of rights in several important respects, makes a few criticisms on points of detail, and then questions the claim to universality of his theory. The main divergences from Griffin are to substitute a pluralist theory of human interests for Griffin's dualist criterion of liberty and autonomy and to weaken the claims to universality. Subsequently, Tasioulas has defended his theory against charges that any general theory of human rights represents hopelessly Utopian aspirations unless it includes enforceability and clear allocation of responsibilities as part of the existence conditions of human rights.[26] Here we are mainly concerned with the challenge to claims of universality, but I shall touch on other aspects of Tasioulas' position.

A reconstruction of the theories of Griffin and Tasioulas suggests that they agree on the following points:

1. That human rights are possessed by human beings simply in virtue of their humanity.[27]
2. That human rights as moral rights should be kept conceptually distinct from human rights law and human rights culture.[28]
3. That philosophy can contribute in a modest way to the evaluation, interpretation, and development of human rights law and culture.[29]
4. That human rights are derived from moral theory rather than providing a basis for it.[30]
5. That human rights discourse should not be used to do the work of all moral discourse; human rights, justice, human flourishing, and other important values need to be kept conceptually distinct.
6. That human rights should be based on central human interests.

---

[24] See Chapter 5 above.
[25] This section is based largely on Tasioulas (2002a) (Retracing) and (2007a) (Moral reality). See also Tasioulas (2002b), and (2005). I am also grateful for some clarification of points in discussion with Tasioulas.
[26] Tasioulas (2007a).   [27] Tasioulas (2002b) at p. 89, (2007a) at p. 76.
[28] Griffin (2001a); Tasioulas (2002a).   [29] Tasioulas (2002a) at pp. 80–1.
[30] Taken together points 3–5 are a response to the 'no value added' argument.

7. That a theory of human rights should provide an account of existence conditions and criteria for distinguishing 'real' rights from unwarranted extensions and bogus claims.

8. Such a theory can provide a substantive account of human rights norms.

9. Human rights theory is moral rather than political in a Rawlsian sense.[31]

10. The best approach to constructing a theory of human rights as moral rights is 'to start with human rights as used in our actual social life by politicians, lawyers, social campaigners, as well as theorists of various sorts, and then to see what higher principles one must resort to in order to explain their moral weight, when one thinks they have it, and to resolve conflicts between them'.[32]

Tasioulas, building on Griffin, significantly departs from the latter's theory of human rights in two ways. First, he substitutes a pluralist justification for one based solely on personhood. Second, he significantly weakens any universalist claims.

The relationship between Griffin's and Tasioulas' positions is illustrated by the latter's independent justification of a Human Right to be Free from Poverty (HRP):

(1) For all human beings, poverty consists in a significant level of material deprivation that poses a serious threat to a number of their interests: health, physical security, autonomy, understanding, friendship etc.

(2) The threat posed by extreme poverty to the interests enumerated in (1) is, in the case of each human being, *pro tanto* of sufficient gravity to justify the imposition of duties on others, for example to refrain from impoverishing them, to protect them from impoverishment, and assist those already suffering from severe material deprivation.

(3) The duties generated at (2) represent practicable claims on others given the constraints created by general and relatively entrenched facts of human nature and social life in the modern world. Therefore:

(4) Each individual human being has a right to be free from severe poverty.[33]

This is in the spirit of Griffin and accords with his theory in the following respects: HRP is an individual human right; it is interest based; it is restricted to severe material deprivations that threaten autonomy and liberty of individuals;[34] it includes a condition of feasibility ('practicability'). However, it differs

---

[31] Tasioulas (2007a) at p. 78.

[32] This 'bottom up' approach accords with the concerns of the human rights activist wanting to make philosophical sense of her commitments (see pp. 204–5 above). Griffin (2001b) at p. 308. Cf. Tasioulas (2002a) at pp. 82–3.

[33] Tasioulas (2007a) at p. 78. Compare the interesting argument by Tom Campbell in the same volume that the idea of poverty as a violation of human rights is more soundly based on a principle of humanity and only secondarily on justice (Campbell 2007).

[34] Tasioulas leaves open the possibility of human rights above the minimum definition of poverty (i.e. subsistence but less than abundance). (Tasioulas (2005).

from Griffin (i) in not making the justification for the right (or for human rights in general) solely dependent on personhood values, but rather than on the deprivation of core interests that are valuable in themselves and (ii) in specifying that the imposition of positive duties on others is an existence condition of the right.[35]

Tasioulas' argument about pluralism is quite complex, but at its core it is based on two objections to Griffin's monism. The first relates to universality. Griffin is avowedly working in the Western tradition of ethics and his aim is 'to complete the Enlightenment project'.[36] Tasioulas, on the other hand, is concerned with poverty – and human rights generally – from a global perspective. Accordingly he has to confront the fact of belief pluralism.

> Some cultures may not accord the same significance to autonomy and liberty as Western societies, perhaps attaching greater importance than we do to living harmoniously with others (including other species), avoiding the infliction of pain and suffering, cultivating highly refined aesthetic and religious sensibilities and so on. With respect to such cultures, we may be hard-pressed to show that judging them by reference to the familiar schedule of human rights is anything short of cultural imperialism, especially if it has a detrimental effect on their capacity to sustain valued ways of life. Are we forced to conclude that such cultures are mistaken in failing to prize autonomy and liberty sufficiently highly? Or should we, like Rawls, prune back the list of human rights in the hope of accommodating them? Or is some other response available . . . ? An example of the latter would be the claim that legitimate value-pluralism within a historical epoch affects the interpretation and application of human rights norms but not their existence.[37]

Tasioulas wishes to preserve a substantive theory of human rights that confronts the challenge of value pluralism. His first step is to substitute for Griffin's monist idea of personhood a pluralist conception of human interests, which both acknowledges that rights can be based on a wider range of goods than liberty and autonomy and that recognises that different cultures and belief systems may have different conceptions of what human interests are important.

Tasioulas supports this move from monism to pluralism by a further argument: even within our own culture personhood values are not the only goods relevant to the justification of human rights.[38] Griffin's monist test leads him not only to curtail his list of human rights, but also to limit or even distort the reasons that can convincingly be given to justify particular rights. Tasioulas and Griffin would agree that within our tradition, and more generally, there is a strong case for justifying the existence of a right not to be tortured.[39] What is

---

[35] Tasioulas explains the difference as follows: 'Unlike Griffin, I don't think that any category of interests (subject to practicality constraints) immediately brings human rights into play; instead, even if you have a universal interest, you have to ask whether it generates a duty. Griffin omits this, to me, crucial second step.' (Communication to author, 29 June 2007).

[36] Griffin (2001b) at p. 2.   [37] Tasioulas (2002a) at p. 88.

[38] Tasioulas (2002a) at p. 8.   [39] Tasioulas (2002a) at p. 3.

wrong with torture? Griffin's justification emphasises the ground that the pain of torture undermines agency – 'the capacity to decide and to stick to the decision'.[40] That is one good reason; but surely it is not the only one. The infliction of severe pain on an individual is in itself a violation of a basic human interest, independently of questions of autonomy.[41] Griffin makes some justifications unnecessarily indirect and leaves out strong reasons for recognition/ existence of a right.

In addition to broadening the range of interests that can ground human rights, Tasioulas makes a major concession to critics of universalist claims by heavily qualifying the requirement 'at all times and all places'. Instead of treating human rights as atemporal, he suggests that they are contingent on a broadly defined historical context, which can currently be specified as the conditions of modernity.[42] This meets the objection that lists of human rights change over time – there are 'generations' of human rights not only in international law, but also in political and moral discourse – as is illustrated by the growth of anti-discrimination principles in respect of race, gender, age, sexual preferences and so on. In this view:

> For people today and the foreseeable future, human rights are possessed in virtue of being human and inhabiting a social world that is subject to the conditions of modernity. This historical constraint permits very general facts about feasible institutional design in the modern world, for example, forms of legal regulation, political participation, and economic organization, to play a role in what human rights we recognize. But this is different from making the existence of human

---

[40] Griffin (2001b) at p. 311. Griffin acknowledges that this is one 'among its evils' of torture (ibid), but seems to make this the main point. See further Griffin (2008) pp. 52–3.

[41] A utilitarian would take into account both the intense pain and the consequences not only for the victim and those close to him/her, but also for the torturer and the public at large (e.g. alarm) and the fact that experience shows that institutionalised torture is endemically subject to abuse (i.e. once established it is almost inevitably used beyond any situation in which its infliction could be justified). In my view this point supports a consequentialist argument for an 'absolute' prohibition, such as that under Article 3 of the EHCR. However, even for Bentham, the interference with autonomy and liberty is central: as a conceptual matter the point of torture is the infliction of pain for purposes of coercion. (Bentham in Twining and Twining (1973).) Situations where extreme pain and humiliation are inflicted on victims by means similar to those used in paradigmatic situations of torture, but the infliction is for reasons other than coercion (e.g. sadism or revenge) or the infliction is pointless (e.g. part of a routine in which the original purpose has been forgotten) are strictly speaking extensions of the concept of torture. Similarly, painless coercion (e.g. by administration of 'painless' truth drugs or disorientation) is not strictly speaking 'torture' for Bentham. Discussions of torture often oversimplify by failing to recognise the ambiguity of the concept and the variety of purposes and motives for which this kind of extreme treatment is used in practice. Of course, some types, (e.g. purely sadistic or pointless inflictions) do not raise moral *dilemmas* for reasonable people. On the background to controversies surrounding the authorisation by the Bush admnistration of 'coercive interrogation' (including water boarding) see Lichtblau (2008). Whether or not some of these techniques amounted to 'torture', several of them clearly amounted to inhuman or degrading treatment under public international law.

[42] Tasioulas (2002a) at pp. 87–8; see Tasioulas (2007a) at pp. 76–7.

rights turn on the specific institutional arrangements that obtain at any particular time and place.[43]

In a recent paper entitled 'The Moral Reality of Human Rights' Tasioulas develops his position with regard to two further challenges.[44] The first challenge, attributed to Raymond Geuss,[45] argues that enforceability should be an existence condition of human rights. Assertions of human rights are Utopian, misleading, and useless if they cannot be enforced. What is the value of a 'right not to be tortured' when around the world torture is as prevalent as it ever was? What is the point of 'a right to freedom from poverty' (HRP) when poverty has always been with us and in many respects is becoming more prevalent? Tasioulas' response might be rendered as follows: the existence of a right is a moral question; the prospects for enforcement depend on institutional arrangements. Human rights are moral rights possessed by all simply by virtue of their humanity. Rights concerning slavery, poverty, race or gender discrimination exist independently of any special relationship or existing social and political conditions. Their realisation and enforcement depend on institutions and practices that are historically contingent.[46] Very few universally enforceable entitlements exist today. Insofar as some progress has been made, for example in respect of slavery and racial and sexual discrimination, it is in part due to the force of compelling moral ideas. A distinction needs to be drawn between 'feasibility' in principle and actual enforcement. Griffin and Tasioulas both include a condition that there are no ineradicable facts about human capacities, and/or other constraints, that make them in principle unattainable (ought implies can). It is quite another thing to require that rights should be realisable in the short or medium term.

Tasioulas has also taken a strong position on the issue of 'rights of imperfect obligation'. Most candidates for being called human rights take the form of claim-rights (e.g. a right not to be tortured, a right to life, a right to food, and procedural rights) or liberty rights (e.g freedom of speech, freedom of association). As we saw in Chapter 2, Hohfeld suggested that all claim rights have correlative duties; 'X has a claim against Y' means that 'Y owes a duty to X' and vice versa.[47] However, there is continuing controversy among human rights

---

[43] Tasioulas (2007a) at pp. 76–7.   [44] Tasioulas (2007a).
[45] Geuss (2001).   [46] Tasioulas (2007a).
[47] Some legal duties do not have correlative rights (called 'absolute duties' by John Austin). Similarly, duties not to be cruel to animals or to avoid unnecessary damage to trees or the environment are widely accepted as moral duties without correlative rights – they fall outside the sphere of human or moral rights. To talk of 'animal rights' or 'the rights of trees' is generally considered to be an unnecessary extension that is not analytically helpful. See, however, the controversy provoked by Christopher Stone, *Should Trees Have Standing*? (first published in 1972, – see now Stone (1996).) An interesting example of duties without correlative rights arises in connection with 'principles of directive state policy' in the Preamble of the Indian Constitution (sometimes referred to as 'imperfect norms'), which although generally considered non-binding have been held in a few instances to be justiciable (and possibly enforceable) by the courts. (See e.g. Baxi (2007a) at pp. 62–3n.)

theorists about rights of imperfect obligation (i.e. claim rights without correlative obligations). On a Benthamite or Hohfeldian view such talk merely obfuscates the issues; but there is a different position, viz. that talk of 'a right to food' or a 'right to work' is a vehicle for giving voice to important claims even if responsibility for meeting these claims is not clearly allocated or they are not enforceable in practice.

The idea of 'rights' of imperfect obligation has been criticised by Onora O'Neill:

> [T]he correspondence of universal liberty rights to universal obligations is relatively well defined even when the institutions are missing or weak. For example, a violation of a right not to be raped or of a right not to be tortured may be clear enough, and the perpetrator may be identifiable, even when institutions for enforcement are lamentably weak. But the correspondence of universal rights to goods and services to obligations *to provide or deliver* remains entirely amorphous when institutions are missing or weak. Somebody who receives no maternity care may no doubt *assert* that her rights have been violated, but unless obligations to deliver that care have been established and distributed, she will not know where to press her claim, and it will systematically obscure whether there is any perpetrator, or who has neglected or violated her rights.[48]

O'Neill's position, and that of Hohfeldians (every claim has a correlative duty) involves contested distinctions between positive and negative duties and between welfare rights and civil and political rights. Tasioulas' thesis is that rights, as embodiments of central human interests, are conceptually distinct from ideas of *claimability* (O'Neill) as well as *enforceability* (Geuss).[49] To require the institutional allocation of duties or their effectiveness as conditions of the existence of human rights unduly constrains the 'great critical power' of human rights discourse in setting standards, expressing aspirations, and evaluating existing regimes, even if there are short- or long-term obstacles to their realisation on the ground.[50]

My own view is that it is possible to have a meaningful concept of a claim right with no clear correlative obligation, provided the conditions for its use are reasonably clear (as they are in Tasioulas' interest-based theory). Nevertheless the distinction between rights with correlative obligations and rights of imperfect obligation is important both in theory and practice. Similarly, clarity of thought is assisted by the idea of 'absolute' duties (duties without correlative rights) such as duties of all citizens not to be cruel to animals and to refrain from acts that unjustifiably damage the environment.

---

[48] O'Neill (2000) at p. 105. See O'Neill (1986) at p. 100: 'Once we talk about *rights* we assume a framework in which performance of obligations can be claimed. Holders of rights can press their claims only when the obligations to meet these claims have been allocated to specific bearers of obligations'.

[49] Geuss (2001) above.

[50] Tasioulas distinguishes 'feasibility', within a broad historical context ('ought implies can'), from actual institutionalisation and immediate effectiveness.

Tasioulas rejects the enforceability and claimability criteria of identification of rights; human rights exist by virtue of our humanity, irrespective of practical enforcement and clear allocation of corresponding or correlative duties. Like Griffin and many others he draws a sharp conceptual distinction between human rights law and human rights as moral rights and he rejects any suggestion that human rights play a foundational role in ethical thought; rather they are derived from important interests that can be specified independently of the concept of a right.[51] He combines these four ideas into an significant conclusion about the status of human rights:

> [R]ights occupy an intermediate position in our ethical thinking, standing between the ultimate values that ground them and the normative implications they generate, including the institutions and policies that best embody and give effect to those implications.[52]

At the very least, Tasioulas, building on Griffin, has tried to tackle head on the main challenges to any contemporary theory of human rights as moral rights. He treats as important issues the specification of existence conditions for 'real rights' and the criteria for distinguishing 'real rights' from false or doubtful pretenders. He also confronts the problem of proliferation, conceptual issues about enforceability and rights of imperfect obligation, the limits of distributive justice, and the problem of claims to universality in a context of belief pluralism, radically different social, cultural, and economic conditions, and change over time. The method of starting from existing human rights practices and commitments is contextually sensitive and gives a distinct, but modest, role to philosophical analysis.

Tasioulas' answers to his own questions will inevitably be controversial in so extensively contested a field. By allowing for a plurality of interests to be the basis of human rights, Tasioulas has opened the door for expanding the range of justifications for human rights claims and, perhaps, for supporting a longer list of 'real' rights than Griffin's.[53] This also allows for some more direct justifications of particular rights than Griffin's monist premise. By allowing that different cultures will interpret ideas of human interests and their relative importance differently, Tasioulas has gone some way to meeting charges of ethnocentrism. And by limiting claims to universality to broad historical contexts, he allows for the development of thinking and acceptance of human rights over time. By rejecting enforceability and claimability as existence conditions he provides a conceptual basis for making human rights discourse a resource for criticising existing institutions and practices. He also provides a philosophical basis for claiming that at least some social and economic rights exist, although he sets limits to duties of assistance across national or community boundaries.[54]

---

[51]   Tasioulas (2007a) at, pp. 82–9.   [52]   *Ibid.*

[53]   If some kind of consensus about the existence of a right is one criterion for its existence, expanding the list remains an option.

[54]   Tasioulas (2005) arguing that the cut-off point for international distributive justice should be an adequate standard of living rather than subsistence.

Tasioulas asks good questions and provides robust answers. Naturally his answers will not please everyone. They will not please moral sceptics, utilitarians, strong communitarians, and most Kantians. Even for those starting with broadly similar premises about objective moral theory, there are some grounds for doubt or disagreement. First, with regard to 'existence conditions' there may be an objection that by being so accommodating, Tasioulas has sacrificed too much of Griffin's specificity. 'Important human interests' is quite vague compared to Griffin's personhood test. By allowing for different cultural interpretations of what count as basic human interests and of criteria of importance, has he not re-opened Pandora's box? How might his theory accommodate interests treated as important by some 'radically different cultures' – for example, the rights of ancestors which involve the subordination of women?[55] By substituting a pluralistic conception of the grounds of existence for rights for Griffin's monistic criterion, is not Tasioulas left with as many unanswered questions as Hart's unspecified 'principles independent of utility'?

Second, in respect of cultures that do not think or speak in terms of 'rights', is this theory not just as ethnocentric as other rights theories in the same intellectual tradition? Do we not need to know much more empirically and interpretively about the compatibility of other belief systems with both the underlying values and the ways of thought of modern rights discourse? Suppose that we find a significant number of points at which some significant belief systems or value systems are incompatible and incommensurable?

Third, Tasioulas accepts that human rights can vary according to broad historical context – in his case the current conditions of modernity. However, 'modernity' is a strikingly vague term.[56] And, in what sense is it true to say that all human beings currently live in conditions of modernity?[57]

Fourth, in respect of rights of imperfect obligation, some (neo-Hohfeldians) will maintain that asserting rights without broadly allocated duties obfuscates the real problem. It may raise expectations that will not be realised. For example, in Darfur by almost any standard the ethnic cleansing, widespread rape and murder, and displacement of hundreds of thousands of people involve massive violations of moral norms. Calling them violations of rights adds nothing. The key practical problem is assigning and willing responsibility to take effective action. The important moral question – not an easy one – is *who has a duty to act*? Tasioulas' reply is that this is an important question, but it is best kept conceptually and rhetorically separate from questions as to whether Darfurians have rights and are they being violated.

Tasioulas has raised important questions, attempted brave answers and is still developing his theory. My own view is that within a recognisable

---

[55] See Chapter 13.2 below.

[56] On the vagueness of 'modernity' and Boaventura Santos' treatment of modernity and post-modernism see *GLT*, pp. 197–204 (reprinted *GJB*, pp. 286–93).

[57] For example, what are the implications of the fact that today there are many communities, groups and individuals who are not living in 'conditions of modernity'?

philosophical tradition Tasioulas has identified and confronted important philosophical questions and has advanced the debate in significant ways. One might dicker over some specifics but the effort deserves attention. However, adopting a global perspective I doubt whether he has gone far enough in taking account of the ways of thought and modes of discourse of other belief systems and cultures and how they perceive and evaluate their own interests in their own terms. This still remains a crucial challenge for human rights theory.

7.4 Discourse theories

(a) Ghai and Sedley

Griffin and Tasioulas are relatively rare among contemporary rights theorists in proposing substantive criteria for human rights. In the face of belief pluralism and criticisms of universalist claims, others have shifted to the position that human rights discourse provides a 'framework' or 'an arena' or 'a meeting ground' for dialogue, debate, or conversation about important values between people with different belief systems. Rawls' invocation of 'public reason' and An Na'im's emphasis on internal and external dialogue, represent moves in that direction.[58] But some rights theorists abandon any claims to universality about the substance of rights (existence conditions, criteria for recognition/accept- ance, and temporality) and try to substitute ideas of 'process' and 'discourse' for substantive theories.

There are many ways of making this kind of move. Once again, it is relevant to distinguish between human rights law and human rights as moral rights. However, it is useful to consider briefly two examples of lawyers who have made this move in respect of constitution-making and adjudication respec- tively. Yash Ghai on the basis of his extensive practical experience of negotiat- ing and drafting constitutional settlements and other agreements,[59] reports that he has found that a fairly orthodox discourse about basic 'constitutional rights' provides a workable, often effective framework for negotiating and mediating conflicting interests to reach constitutional settlements in multi-ethnic soci- eties. Recently he has also argued that the concept of 'a right to development' (highly controversial among human rights lawyers) is a useful way of framing basic constitutional principles for societies in which development (broadly conceived) is a high strategic priority.[60] Although clearly politically committed to certain values, Ghai has adopted an agnostic, somewhat sceptical, position on claims to universality of human rights as moral rights. Rather he emphasises the value of human rights discourse as a pragmatic tool in the kinds of political and constitutive processes in which he has been involved. Significantly, he reports

---

[58] On 'civic reason' see An Na'im (1990) and (2008) *passim* discussed in Chapter 13.3 below.
[59] Ghai (2000b). See further Chapter 13.4(a) below.   [60] Ghai (2008).

that in his experience material interests are at least as important as differences of culture and belief in this kind of process.

A similar path is followed by a distinguished English judge, Sir Stephen Sedley, who like Ghai has a Marxian background.[61] Sedley's concern is to steer a path between conventional doctrinaire universalism and [hopeless] relativism:

> To accept that what people collectively believe to be their fundamental rights changes [vertically] over time and varies [horizontally] from place to place is to do no more than recognise reality.[62]

Does this mean sacrificing what is valuable in human rights ideas?[63] Not so, says Sedley:

> [F]ew universalists claim to be travelling towards a promised land or even a defined goal. They would say, rather, that the process of arguing, urging, campaigning, denouncing, encouraging and asserting advances the world's understanding of human rights and spreads acceptance of them . . . You go, I suggest, back to the slow task of adjusting the tabulation and enforcement of human rights to the changing vertical consensus, and to making the case for a larger and better horizontal consensus. There is no place in this for the imposition of one society's standards on others, but there will be – as there already is – a process of pressure and example as more successful societies attract the emulation, or at least the acquiescence, of others.[64]

Ghai and Sedley are examples of two lawyers who have abandoned strong universalism in respect of substantive human rights, have stayed with some basic humanistic values, and shifted the focus to argumentation and negotiation in practical contexts, Ghai as a constitution-maker and law-reformer, Sedley as a judge interpreting human rights law, but also more broadly

---

[61] Sir Stephen Sedley, 'Are human rights universal and does it matter?' Holdsworth Lecture University of Birmingham, (2005). Sedley was for a time a member of the British communist party. He has in recent years been a staunch supporter and reflective interpreter of the UK Human Rights Act 1998. On Ghai's early engagement with Marxism and his ambivalence towards it see Chapter 13, p. 408 below. Sedley and Ghai are prime examples of intellectual lawyers who moved over time from Marxism to support for human rights without abandoning core concerns for the less well off.

[62] Sedley (2005) at p. 13.

[63] What is valuable: 'In contending, as I do, for a quite different understanding of human rights, I recognise how much is forfeited in abandoning the claim to universality. The adjective "human" can lose its meaning. Fundamental rights become the property of those lucky enough to live in societies which both recognise and enforce them. This is no doubt unpalatable, but it is at least closer to reality. The big question is where one goes from here. Universalism argues that you can go nowhere except into a mire of relativism which accepts that each society and each era will define human rights in whatever way suits it – or, rather, suits those who hold power. I don't doubt that that can happen: indeed the "margin of appreciation" accorded by the Strasbourg court to – in practice – intolerant decisions of member states on issues of blasphemy and obscenity is on one view a capitulation to exactly this kind of relativism. But does it have to happen?' (Sedley (2005) at p. 5).

[64] Sedley (2005) at pp. 2 and 13.

supporting commitment to the more general promotion of human rights. Both emphasise the value of human rights discourse as a process in particular legal arenas, with general acceptance as the pragmatic pay-off.

What of philosophers? For the past fifty years belief pluralism has been a central concern of many moral philosophers. Among those who have switched from an emphasis on substance to a focus on procedure, perhaps Stuart Hampshire and Jurgen Habermas are the best known.[65] Rawls' emphasis on the political rather than the metaphysical conception of justice as fairness and his emphasis on the importance of 'public reason' can be interpreted as representing a half-way move in this direction.[66]

(b) Amartya Sen[67]

Among several candidates who might illustrate a discursive, as opposed to a substantive theory of human rights I have selected that of Amartya Sen, partly because it is very influential, but also because Sen's ideas feature in several places in this book. As we have seen, he is an economist who has made important contributions to thinking about famines, poverty, and development theory. He is also a substantial moral philosopher. In his earlier writings he has both built on, rejected, and gone beyond elements in classical utilitarianism, libertarianism, and Rawlsian justice, while working in that general tradition.

During the 1990s Sen expounded 'a capabilities approach to development', which has four central themes: (1) poverty is not just a matter of low income, but rather a deprivation of basic substantive freedoms – a deprivation of elementary capabilities; (2) the approach shifts the focus of attention from states of affairs to agency – to what a person can do or be rather than what she has; (3) while wealth is important, it is not the measure of all things. This opens the way to including health, nutrition, education, non-discrimination, and liberty itself in concepts of development and poverty eradication; (4) there is a strong instrumental link between freedom and democracy.[68]

We shall encounter the capabilities approach again in the chapter on law and development. Here it is important to bear in mind that Sen is a consequentialist

---

[65] See, for example, Hampshire (1989); Habermas (1996).

[66] See Chapter 5 above. On the difference between Rawls and Habermas see Habermas (1995) and the reply by Rawls (1995). Rawls identified the main differences as being (i) that Habermas' position is 'comprehensive' while PL is an account of the political; and (ii) they use different devices of representation: Habermas' ideal discourse situation and Rawls original position 'have different aims and roles, with different distinctive features serving different purposes'. (*Ibid.*, at pp. 132–3).

[67] On Sen see Vizard (2006).

[68] In many of his writings, Sen uses the concept of entitlements instead of rights. Halpin criticises this on the ground that it conflates economic and social rights and in the process plays down the importance of law in *coercing* resolutions of conflicts between rights and interests. (Communication with the author.)

(a goals-rights approach includes treating actual enjoyment of rights as an important goal and outcome), working within the liberal democratic tradition, who treats basic individual freedoms, rather than utility or justice, as the main concept in his political theory. His theory of rights is part of, and a recent extension of, this broader theory of political economy.

In an important paper, published in 2004, Sen outlined 'The Elements of a Theory of Human Rights'.[69] The starting-point is the tension between the strong intuitive appeal of the idea of universal moral rights and the fact that there is widespread scepticism about the central idea. In particular, a theory of human rights needs to address two kinds of scepticism: comprehensive dismissal of the idea that human beings have rights simply by virtue of their humanity and selective or discriminating scepticism about certain kinds of human rights claims and demands, especially the inclusion on lists of human rights of economic and social rights.[70]

Sen's theory is clearly a contribution to the *philosophy* of human rights, particularly in respect of conceptual clarification and justification. He summarises his agenda for such a theory as follows:

A theory of human rights must address the following questions in particular:
(1) What kind of a statement does a declaration of human rights make?[71]
(2) What makes human rights important?
(3) What duties and obligations do human rights generate?
(4) Through what forms of actions can human rights be promoted and in particular whether legislation must be the principal, or even a necessary, means of implementation of human rights?[72]
(5) Can economic and social rights (the so-called second generation rights) be reasonably included among human rights?

---

[69] Sen, (2004) (hereafter 'Elements').

[70] Sen (2004) at p. 316. Comprehensive scepticism is exemplified by Bentham; discriminating scepticism by Maurice Cranston, Onora O'Neill, and Michael Ignatieff (Sen (Elements) n. 4). Sen does not deal directly with ethical relativists and strong subjectivists, nor with Rorty's view that human rights theory is better off without any philosophical justification. However, this article and his other writings clearly reject these positions.

[71] 'Declaration' is unclear in this context. It refers to pronouncements and proclamations and is clearly wider than formal documents such as the Universal Declaration of Human Rights, for it includes any assertion or claim that a given set of rights or even a single such right exists. But Sen seems mainly to have in mind public pronouncements and, interestingly, does not allow for some formal declarations being treated as 'soft law'. (See Chapter 4, n. 132 above.) Rather he asserts that 'pronouncements of human rights are quintessentialy ethical articulations, and they are *not*, in particular, putative legal claims'. (Sen (2004) at p. 321.) On the UDHR and the Standard Minimum Rules for the Treatment of Prisoners see p. 45 above. Baxi (2007a) Ch. 2, in a critique of Sen's article, discussed below at p. 272, makes some interesting remarks about such formal declarations, including by non-state agents.

[72] Sen seems to use 'legislation' in a broad, almost Benthamite sense. I interpret it in this context to refer to any kind of (official) law, but later raise some questions about whether his conception of law is adequate for his purposes (see pp. 222–3 below).

(6) Last, but not least, how can proposals of human rights be defended or challenged and how should their claim to universal status be assessed, especially in a world with much cultural variation and widely diverse practice?[73]

Sen gives crisp answers to these questions:

(1) Human rights are primarily ethical claims or pronouncements. A theory of human rights is a moral theory, independent of any juridical theory of rights.[74] Generally speaking, these moral rights are pre-legislative.[75]

(2) Human rights are grounded in important freedoms.[76] To qualify as the basis for human rights claims the relevant freedoms must satisfy two threshold conditions: '(i) special importance and (ii) social influencability'.[77] A freedom is sufficiently important if it justifies the conclusion 'that others should be ready to pay substantial attention to decide what they can reasonably do to advance it.' A claim to a human right can hardly be considered important if it can be shown that 'it is unlikely to survive open public scrutiny'.[78] This clearly put him in the camp of 'discourse theorists' rather than 'substantive theorists'. Apart from this requirement of survivability, Sen avoids laying down clear criteria of importance or listing the freedoms that satisfy this test.[79] The 'social influenceability' condition requires that it should be plausible that others could make a material difference by supporting such a right. For example, freedom to achieve tranquillity may be an important freedom, but it may not be a good subject of a human right because of 'the difficulty of guaranteeing it through social help.'[80]

---

[73] Sen (2004) Elements, pp. 318–19. Compare Griffin's implicit agenda in commenting on Hohfeld: 'Helpful as it is to have a variety of such conceptual relations plotted, they do not give us what we need to decide what rights there are, what their boundaries are, and how we resolve conflicts between rights themselves, or between a right and other kinds of value. What we mean by a substantive account would apply to all that.' (Griffin (2001a) 'First Steps', at p. 308). As we shall see, Sen deliberately avoids attempting such a substantive account and for this reason has a different agenda of questions.

[74] 'Even though human rights can, and often do, inspire legislation, this is a further fact, rather than a constitutive characteristic of human rights' (p. 317).

[75] Elements at p. 318. Sen rightly argues that human rights claims can be influential even if they do not have the force of law. He does not emphasise the influence of human rights law on human rights theorising.

[76] 'Note that while rights involve claims (specifically claims on others who are in a position to make a difference), freedoms, in contrast, are primarily descriptive characteristics of the conditions of persons' (p. 28) '[T]he ethical force of freedoms can help to generate claims in others' (ibid, n. 23 discussing the relations between fact and value in this context).

[77] Ibid at p. 319.   [78] Ibid at p. 349.

[79] Sen explicitly distances himself from Martha Nussbaum's 'list of capabilities' (Nussbaum (2000), pp. 70–86): 'My own reluctance to join the search for such a canonical list arises partly from my difficulty in seeing how the exact lists and weights would be chosen without appropriate specification of the context of their use (which could vary), but also from a disinclination to accept any substantive diminution of the domain of public reasoning.' (Elements, p. 333, n. 31.) The apparent weakness of the obligation, the concept of 'survivability', and the vagueness of the criteria of importance will be commented on below.

[80] Ibid., at p. 330. Survivability is different from Tasioulas' concept of 'feasibility' (Tasioulas, 2007a) discussed at pp. 213–14 above): the former refers to the likelihood of surviving robust debate, the latter to limiting human rights claims to actions of which duty holders are capable ('ought implies can') (see Sen (2004) Elements at p. 348, n. 55).

(3) 'Human rights generate obligations in others, that is reasons for action for agents who are in a position to help in the promoting or safeguarding of the underlying freedoms.'[81] I shall comment below on the apparent weakness of Sen's formulation of this kind of obligation.

(4) Human rights can be promoted and implemented by many kinds of means (e.g. public discussion, advocacy, law) and via different routes (e.g. agitation or public recognition, not necessarily through law). Legislation (i.e. embodiment in law) is only one means among many. This point further emphasises the distinction between moral and juridical theories of rights.

(5) Some rights are based on economic and social freedoms that cannot be immediately realised because of inadequate institutionalisation. Human rights exist independently of whether responsibility for realising these rights has been allocated. For example, everyone has a right to food, even though it is unclear who has primary responsibility for its provision. The fact that political or institutional change is required does not *ipso facto* make it a non-right. Thus Sen comes firmly down on the side of those who treat at least some social and economic rights as full human rights.[82]

(6) The universality of human rights relates to the idea of survivability in unobstructed discussion ... across national boundaries ... through an interactive process.[83] Concerned about pluralism of beliefs and the difficulties of articulating genuinely universal substantive norms of human rights, Sen follows Rawls and Habermas in rooting the acceptability of human rights claims in the opportunity for informed and open public discussion rather than in substantive universality. In order to fit in with his global perspective he extends Rawls' idea of public reason to 'global public reasoning'.[84]

Sen is an economist and he seems to have a rather simplistic, positivist, almost Benthamic view of law. He refers to laws as commands,[85] he conceives of human rights law almost entirely in terms of legislation,[86] he gives almost no attention to non-state law or customary law,[87] he ignores 'soft law', and in drawing a sharp distinction between human rights as moral rights and human rights law, he glosses over the difficulties of maintaining a sharp is/ought distinction in human rights discourse within legal contexts. I agree with Baxi's comment that '[t]he "legal" from which the ethical idea of human rights is to be distinguished stands poorly described or understood in [Sen's] "Theory".'[88] However, in the present context Sen's focus is on human rights as moral rights and his version of discourse theory could still be compatible with a more nuanced jurisprudence.

A striking feature of Sen's theory, and of some discourse theories, is the weakness of the obligations that it imposes. Duty-holders have an obligation to give reasonable consideration to,[89] 'to pay substantial attention to',[90] and to

---

[81] *Ibid.*, p. 319.   [82] On 'rights of imperfect obligation' see pp. 213–14 above.   [83] *Ibid.*, p. 320.
[84] *Ibid.*, p. 320.   [85] *Ibid.*, p. 319.   [86] *Ibid., et passim.*
[87] The index of *Development as Freedom* (1999) contains no references to law, adjudication, or any forms of religious law.
[88] Baxi (2007a) at 58n.   [89] Sen (2004) at pp. 319, see also 321, 322.   [90] *Ibid.*, p. 329.

engage in reasoned public debate about the existence and scope of human rights and about their deprivations and violations. Sen distinguishes between reasons for action, duties to consider action, and duties to act. He is concerned that recognition of obligations should not 'be translated into preposterously demanding commands.'[91] But this makes the correlative duties of human rights rather weak. Gearty treats Sen as 'emblematic of a drift of foundationalism from truth to discovery – a passive foundationalism, one that is rooted in thinking, not action.'[92] This is part of a wider unease with 'discourse' theory as lacking passion and as being naïve about the realities of political struggles in which rational persuasion needs to be backed by political mobilisation, hard bargaining, and, where necessary, legal coercion. A partial defence of Sen's version is that his is a philosophical theory seeking to provide a theoretical basis for human rights through reflection and reasoned discourse rather than a working theory for activists.

In his criticism of the 'Asian Values' debate, Sen charged the protagonists of Asian values with invoking highly selective, monolithic readings of South Asian intellectual traditions, emphasising the authoritarian strands and glossing over other more freedom-oriented perspectives.[93] Like Glenn, Sen envisages cultural traditions as arenas for perpetual internal debates rather than as monolithic, unchanging ideologies which provide the starting-point for 'clashes of civilisations'.[94] One of the attractions of discourse theories is that they substitute a conception of values requiring perpetual argumentation and debate for a picture of values being embodied in static doctrines.[95] Debates are a part of the discipline of human rights, which allows for considerable internal diversity, indeterminacy, and disagreement. This should be a source of strength rather than embarrassment.[96]

A great deal of Sen's work has been concerned with 'development' especially in poorer countries of the world. His perspective is more genuinely global than either Rawls or Habermas, whose main focus has been on internal issues of justice and democracy within relatively bounded communities.[97] Sen is

---

[91] *Ibid.*, p. 340.

[92] Gearty (2006) at p. 38. Gearty further dismisses Sen's 'Elements' as 'a foundationalist ethic disguised in contemporary jargon, an old-fashioned view of the world dressed in a new-fangled fashion that everybody is wearing these days'. (*Ibid.*, at p. 39). This seems to me to be unduly harsh. Sen's version of discourse ethics is a reflective response to belief pluralism from a genuinely global perspective and if a capabilities approach is now fashionable, it is largely thanks to Sen.

[93] Sen (1997). 'The real issue is not whether these nonfreedom perspectives are *present* in Asian traditions, but whether the freedom-oriented perspectives are *absent* there.' (Sen 1999), p. 234.

[94] On Glenn see Chapter 3.4 above. On Huntington see Sen (2004) at p. 351.

[95] See Ronald Dworkin's view of law as an argumentative enterprise (Guest (1997), pp. 6–9).

[96] Sen (2004) at p. 323, citing Waldron (2003) at p. 311. On the idea of a discipline of human rights see Baxi (2006a) discussed below.

[97] 'The methodology of public scrutiny draws on Rawlsian understanding of "objectivity' in ethics, but the impartiality that is needed cannot be confined within the borders of a nation.' (Sen (2004) at p. 356.) On Habermas see Dews (ed.) (1999) especially the paper by Pensky.

naturally sensitive to problems of ethnocentrism, but like nearly all other rights theorists he does not really address the issue of whether the language of rights is a suitable medium for the kind of public debates and conversations he envisages both within and between different traditions and belief systems.

Sen's theory of rights can be read as a philosophical addendum to his much more fully worked out ideas on development as freedom and the capabilities approach. Some aspects of Sen's particular formulation are quite widely shared with other contemporary theories: the insistence that this is a moral theory separate from a juridical theory of human rights; the focus on agency; the anchoring of universality in free, rational, public discussion and debate; the insistence that human rights extend to 'rights of imperfect obligation', including some important economic and social rights; the emphasis on cross-cultural dialogue; and the explicit and implicit rejection of strong forms of scepticism are all familiar features of some other theories of human rights. All are contested. The main claim to originality lies in linking this to 'the capabilities approach', in its practical influence on thinking about development and aid, and in steering a path through and beyond familiar debates about utilitarianism and Kantianism, universalism and relativism, and free market and welfare state ideologies.[98]

---

[98] The capabilities approach has influenced thinking about labour rights in Europe especially the Supiot Report (1999); see Deakin (2005) and works cited there.

Chapter 8

Empirical dimensions of law and justice

8.1 Introduction

In the first chapter I suggested that by and large Western traditions of academic law have been unempirical and narrowly focused, mainly concentrating on domestic state law of particular nation states and proceeding largely in ignorance of other legal traditions and cultures. This chapter deals with empirical understandings of legal phenomena. For reasons which will be explained below, I shall refer to this general area as empirical legal studies.

In earlier chapters we have already encountered some themes relevant to empirical perspectives on law and justice: the argument that there is a need for a closer connection between analytical jurisprudence and empirical legal studies especially in strengthening our stock of analytic concepts;[1] we have seen that 'the naturalist turn' suggests (in different versions) a philosophical basis for continuity between analysis of concepts and empirical enquiries.[2] In Chapters 1 and 3 we considered Dworkin's distinction between doctrinal and sociological conceptions of law and assessed theories that view law in terms of families, tradition (Glenn, Krygier) or culture (e.g. Friedman, Nelken, Bell, Cotterrell);[3] Chapter 4 analysed attempts to construct general conceptions of law as a social institution (Hart, Tamanaha, Llewellyn, MacCormick, Twining), including the suggestion that these can be defended in terms of 'thin functionalism'. We have also noted utilitarianism's concern with evaluating actual social consequences[4] and recent attempts to bring empirical perspectives to bear on human rights and justice.[5] It is now time to look more generally at empirical perspectives on law.

The purpose of this chapter is to consider the implications of globalisation for this broad and diverse field. After touching on the associations of the different labels used to designate these activities, the chapter considers the historical and theoretical background, and the current state of the field in 2007. It then examines some examples of ways in which quantitative and comparative empirical legal studies are responding to globalisation, and the prospects for and scepticism about an evidence-based, explanatory and

---

[1] See Chapter 2.   [2] See Chapter 2.4 above.   [3] See Chapter 3.4 above.
[4] See Chapter 5.4 above.   [5] See p. 180 above and p. 256 below.

cumulative social science of law. The chapter concludes with a consideration of the conditions that need to be met for the healthy development of the empirical dimensions of a cosmopolitan discipline of law.

8.2 A note on terminology

This book has followed tradition by dealing separately with analytical, normative, and empirical dimensions of law and justice.[6] I have emphasised throughout that these broad categories are merely for convenience of exposition, that the distinctions cannot bear very much weight, and that most scholarly enquiries in law involve a combination of analytical, normative and empirical elements. Concepts, values, and facts are not straightforward ideas and the relations between them are notoriously problematic.

Empirical understandings of legal phenomena are variously referred to as 'the law in action', 'law in the real world', 'socio-legal studies', 'law and society', and 'sociology of law'. I shall use 'empirical legal studies' generically to cover this very broad and diverse area. In some contexts 'empirical' is a contested concept. Here 'empirical dimensions of law and justice' is a rough category that covers theorising and enquiries about legal phenomena in 'the real world', while recognising that few enquiries can be 'purely empirical'. The term is used broadly to include theoretical, interpretive, and factual enquiries into legal phenomena, without commitment to any particular epistemology or perspective.[7] Here I shall side-step thorny issues about the extent to which empirical enquiries can be value free, their epistemological foundations, and perennial questions about legal positivism.[8] In short, my approach involves a broad conception of law and a pluralistic vision of what is involved in understanding law empirically.

Several of the adjacent terms are often used loosely to indicate this general area, but sometimes they have acquired specific associations. For example, 'Sociology of Law' is sometimes used in a narrow sense to refer to rigorous scientific work that applies theories and methods derived from the discipline

---

[6] 'Empirical dimensions of law and justice' is here preferred to 'empirical jurisprudence' for two reasons: first, it emphasises the close connections between normative and empirical legal theory and, second, 'theory' in this general area is more fragmented than is the case with analytical and normative jurisprudence. The chapter heading echoes Julius Stone (1966), who insisted on the interdependence of analytical, empirical, and normative concerns.

[7] See Chapter 1.3(d) above. 'There are almost as many empiricisms as there are empiricists, but what these views or approaches have in common is an emphasis on the importance of experience in the formation of concepts and to the acquisition of knowledge. The foil to empiricism is rationalism, which emphasizes instead the importance of thought and knowledge of material that is in some sense independent of experience.' (Lipton (2001) at p. 4481 (a useful brief history of the philosophical debates). Anyone who agrees that understanding law requires knowledge of what it is like in 'the real world' is an empiricist in this broad sense (Lipton is isolating *a priori* analysis of concepts). On the continuities between analytical jurisprudence and empirical legal studies see Chapter 2.4 above.

[8] See p. 13 above.

of sociology to legal phenomena.[9] The term is also used in a broad sense to cover all kinds of empirical legal studies, but this can be misleading for two reasons. First, as we have seen, 'sociology' is sometimes used disparagingly by analytical jurists and black letter lawyers, implying that the subject is 'soft' and 'not really law'. Second, in some contexts terms like 'sociology of law' and 'sociological jurisprudence' may suggest that the main, or even the only, important relationship between law and social science is with sociology. That is, quite obviously, wrong. In the United Kingdom the term 'socio-legal studies' was originally coined for bureaucratic purposes to designate those kinds of cross-disciplinary enquiries about law that qualified for support from public funds in respect of research that involved perspectives, methods or concepts from any of the social sciences, including anthropology, business studies, criminology, economics, geography, linguistics, penology, politics, psychology, social history, and some aspects of statistics. Each of these disciplines has its own complex history, culture, feuds, traditions, external relations, and fashions. Their relations to law are correspondingly complex. For example, quite separate stories are told about legal anthropology,[10] law and economics,[11] law and psychology,[12] law and development,[13] and law and geography.[14] The histories of relations between law and politics and law and sociology are even more complex.[15] On the whole, such points have been well understood by those involved in empirical legal research, but this diversity has sometimes been obscured at the level of theory. In my view, 'socio-legal studies' indicates more clearly than 'sociology of law' that social theory, a broad range of interpretive and other perspectives, and all social sciences are covered by the label. However, some consider the term to be specifically

---

[9] See further p. 231 below.

[10] E.g. Merry (2001), Nader (2002). On recent anthropological interest in international law and human rights, see Wilson (1997), Halme (ed.) (2004), Dickinson (2007), and Goodale and Merry (2007).

[11] E.g Duxbury (1995) Chapter 5 (for a brief update see Duxbury (2003) at 960–63). See Posner (2007), Ogus (2006); Brewer and Williams (2005); Mercuro and Medema (2006).

[12] During the 1980s Sally Lloyd-Bostock of the Oxford Centre organised a series of conferences on Law and Psychology that attracted a lot of interest from psychologists, practising lawyers, and judges. (e.g Lloyd-Bostock (1981) (1988)). But as the 'field' expanded it fragmented into different specialist areas. For overall surveys see Carson and Bull (1995), Memon *et al.* (2003), Brewer and Williams (2005), Brooks-Gordon and Freeman (eds.) (2006), Carson et al. (2007) (emphasising the applied nature of much 'law and psychology' work).

[13] On histories of 'law and development' see Chapter 11.2 below.

[14] See e.g. Blomley (1994), Holder and Harrison (2003).

[15] Some writers argue that sociology of law should be treated as a sub-field of mainstream sociology (e.g. Banakar and Travers (2002) at p. 349). Others argue that the sociology of law is not just a particular kind of applied sociology, such as medicine or work or migration, because law *constitutes* some of the main subject matters of sociology – for without law (and more generally social control) there would be no social groups, no social behaviour etc. (Griffiths' communication to the author Dec. 2007; see also Griffiths (2006)). These authors are making important points from the perspective of a narrow conception of sociology of law; my concern here is to emphasise the variety of relations between law and all social and behavioural sciences.

British and others, wrongly in my view, take it to refer only or mainly to policy-oriented empirical research.

'Law and society' has often been used in the United States in a broad generic sense to cover the whole range of socially oriented legal scholarship and theorising. However, several theorists of 'globalisation' have raised doubts about the continuing utility of 'society' as an organising concept.[16] Others have criticised the American movement, for parochial, positivist, or policy-oriented tendencies.[17] Given these associations, whether fair or not, I have resorted to a different label.

'Law in action' has a nice rhetorical ring, implying dynamism and contact with 'the real world'. When contrasted with 'law in books' it suggests practicality, concern with what actually happens as opposed to what is meant to happen, and with actual consequences.[18] The phrase has its uses, but it does not cover the full range of empirical legal studies, which also treat such matters as structures, institutional design, distributions of power, and attitudes to, and knowledge and opinion about, law.

Other theoretical lines of enquiry concerned with interpreting, describing, and explaining actual legal phenomena in 'the real world' are often assigned to historical jurisprudence or sociological jurisprudence. As we shall see, 'sociological jurisprudence' is sometimes used to refer to the ideas of socially oriented jurists, such as Ehrlich and Llewellyn. But the term came to be identified quite narrowly with the 'social engineering' perspective of Roscoe Pound and others and has gone out of fashion.[19] Similarly, 'historical jurisprudence' came to be associated almost exclusively with the idea of legal evolution, and in the Anglo-American tradition with the rather odd kind of history practiced by Sir Henry Maine.[20] This is an important tradition, but it is only one strand in the complex relations between legal theory and historiography. General jurisprudence also needs to take account

---

[16] E.g. Tamanaha (2001) at pp. 206–8.

[17] One example is Susan Silbey, who in her Presidential address to the LSA criticised state centralism, instrumentalism, scientism, determinism, and liberal reformism as faults of the Law and Society Movement and pleaded for critical empiricism (cited by Munger (1995/6); see Silbey and Sarat (1987), Sarat and Silbey (1988)). Some critical legal scholars have tended to dismiss 'Law and Society' work as uncritical and merely empiricist. On 'the pull of the policy audience' see n. 157 below.

[18] See further Chapter 10.2(b) below. The phrase 'law in action' has emotive appeal, but on its own it does not capture the full range of socio-legal concerns, which also covers the scale and distribution of particular phenomena (demographic realism), structures of power (Collier and Starr (1989)), knowledge and opinion about law (Podgorecki et al. (1973)), demand for law (Hendley (2001)) and so on.

[19] On 'instrumentalism' see Chapter 16.4 on the web.

[20] Peter Stein (1980) gives an excellent account of the rise and decline of 'the Historical School'. He makes the point that Maine's closest analogy was with geology rather than biological evolution. See Chapter 1, n. 77 above. For a broader interpretation of 'historical jurisprudence' which includes the work of Roberto Unger, Katherine Newman, and Bernard Jackson see MacCormack (1985). See now Berman (2003) and Goldman (2007).

of intellectual history, comparative and world history, as well as more particularistic kinds of historical enquiry.[21]

A further point that complicates the picture is that empirical studies of legal phenomena are not confined to enquiries that fall within the purview of the social sciences as these are bureaucratically defined. History, logic, literature, theology, and other subjects in the humanities have also had quite close links with law. For example, there is now a thriving law and literature movement; recently there has been a strong interest in law and culture at a time when cultural studies have been expanding; and there is a reviving interest in law and religion.[22] Indeed, there are potential relations, more or less developed, between legal scholarship and all of the humanities and social sciences. This expansion of 'law and …' relations does not stop there: for there is a direct interface with at least some of the physical sciences, such as genetics and socio-biology.[23] Furthermore, there are many kinds of inter-disciplinary and multi-disciplinary enquiries that are not easily labelled.[24] Insofar as these relations bear on empirical enquiries about legal phenomena, they are relevant in the present context.

This indication of the plethora of external relations between law and other disciplines is a reminder of the pervasiveness of law in social life; it also leads on to a further point: most academic lawyers are specialists and the actual and potential points of contact between legal specialisms and other disciplines vary tremendously. For example, macro-theoretical debates about law and development, micro-interactionist or ethnomethodological studies, research into witness psychology, and economic analysis of contract doctrine belong to different intellectual spheres at varied levels of abstraction and as part of quite different intellectual agendas and purposes. If they have anything in common, it is that they are all relevant to empirical understandings of legal phenomena. The difficulty of sketching this diverse and bewildering landscape should serve as

---

[21] Some would associate Patrick Glenn with 'historical jurisprudence', but his perspective is closer to world history. Compare Berman (2003) and Goldman (2007). The best prospects for a revival of historical jurisprudence, in my view, lie with closer relations with comparative history (see Haupt (2001)). Some aspects of the relations between enquiries in law and history are explored in *RE* (especially pp. 110–116 and Chapter 12).

[22] Some might cavil at linking 'humanistic' disciplines, such as literature and religion, with empirical legal studies. Insofar as relations between law and literature, culture, and religion are concerned with increasing understanding of what law is like and how it operates in 'the real world', I shall treat them as close to the general subject of this chapter. One of the justifications for studying law and literature, in particular, is that fiction in particular can provide social insights that the social sciences cannot, or in practice, fail to reach. For example, while some might dismiss Tom Wolfe's *Bonfire of the Vanities* (1988) as bad sociology, others claim that it gives an account of the experience of lower reaches of the criminal justice system in greater New York that is not rivalled in social science literature. However, although imaginative literature may be useful in suggesting insights and hypotheses, it is no substitute for an evidence-based testing of hypotheses.

[23] The interfaces between law and the physical sciences have received a great deal of attention recently in relation to expert and scientific evidence (e.g. Haack (2003) Chapter 9, Beecher-Monas (2007)), but that is largely separate from the subject of this chapter.

[24] On 'interdisciplinarity', 'cross-disciplinarity', and 'multi-disciplinarity' see Rowland (2006).

a warning against simple generalisations about inter-disciplinarity and attempts to subsume all lines of enquiry under a single master theory.

8.3 The historical context

For the last hundred years or so there have been protracted debates, introspection, and uneven advances in the relationship between law and other disciplines in the humanities and social sciences. Empirical legal studies have been largely driven by the intuition that understanding law requires that it should be studied 'realistically' and 'in context', drawing on the intellectual resources of other disciplines. Particular fields of law have tended to 'pair off' with different disciplines and perspectives in a rather fragmented fashion (e.g. torts with economic analysis, constitutional law with political science and political theory, family law with social policy and feminist perspectives). This makes it particularly difficult to generalise about theoretical aspects of empirical legal studies. For this reason it is necessary first to take stock of the historical background and current state of this very diverse field before considering the prospects for development in the context of globalisation.

The history of empirical legal studies has its roots in the intellectual history of law and social theory, the institutional history of projects and programmes, and in the long story of attempts to broaden the culture and focus of the institutionalised discipline of law from within. Most of these varied histories have been told at length elsewhere. Here, I shall comment briefly on each of these strands as they bear on the themes of this chapter.

(a) Law and social theory

The variety, fragmentation, and complex cross-cutting of empirical legal studies is to a large extent reflected in the diversity of the heritage of bodies of theorising considered to be relevant to particular enterprises. A common complaint is that much empirical legal research is 'atheoretical' (i.e it has not been based on some explicit overarching theoretical framework and methodology and its implicit assumptions have tended to be unsophisticated or incoherent).[25] More important is the point that there has not been a single dominant intellectual tradition and that most of the work has been done in specialist enclaves with their own specific, often local, intellectual histories. For example, nearly all economic analysis of law works within the tradition of Adam Smith, Friedrich Hayek, Milton Friedman, Richard Posner, and other free-market theorists or their critics. Law and psychology has a quite different,

---

[25] Baldwin and Davis (2003) at pp. 889–95. See Munger (1995) at pp. 33–4. Such criticisms are often overstated. Donald Black, John Griffiths, and Marc Galanter are among some notable counter-examples. On the general reluctance of academic lawyers to discuss methodology see McCrudden (2006).

and more varied, 'hall of fame' which includes behaviourists, and Freud, Jung, Piaget, and Bruner among others.[26] Empirical legal work on the family has drawn on an even more varied intellectual heritage from sociology, social history, social psychology, and feminist theory. 'The New Evidence Scholarship' has had unevenly sustained relations with epistemology, statistics, logic, argumentation theory, forensic science, forensic psychology, intelligence analysis, and artificial intelligence.[27] These cross-disciplinary relations are complicated by the fact that the relevant neighbouring disciplines often have their own fashions, feuds and sects. In short, it is very difficult to generalise about the relationship of empirical legal research to 'theory'.[28]

There are, however, some intellectual traditions that transcend more specialised cross-disciplinary relations. They are commonly referred to as 'social theory' and 'sociological jurisprudence'. Both categories are quite vague. Under the rubric of 'Law and Social Theory' there is something approaching a canon of classics, most of whom were 'grand theorists', not primarily interested in law, though some of them were law-trained. Such conventional lists nearly always include Marx, Weber, and Durkheim, who dominated social theory and macro-level studies for most of the twentieth century and beyond. The lists are often extended to include some of Parsons, Merton, Gurvitch, Luhmann, and Habermas. Further extensions encompass figures as varied as Selznick, Foucault, Derrida, Bourdieu, and Geertz.[29] Some, but by no means all of these, professed sociology as their main discipline and, for this reason, such groupings are sometimes given the label 'Sociology of Law'.[30] In relation to globalisation, Glenn, Santos, Tamanaha, and Teubner can be said to have contributed to law and social theory.

The term 'sociological jurisprudence', usually associated with Roscoe Pound, is sometimes used more broadly to refer to individuals whose primary discipline has been law, but who have been interested as jurists in the social dimensions of law. These are often sometimes accused by social scientists of eclecticism – that is 'cherry picking' ideas from outside law without reframing

---

[26] The recent turn to speculative psychiatry by Goodrich and others is yet another story (e.g. Goodrich and Carlson (eds.) (1998).

[27] *RE*, pp. 237–48.

[28] Frank Munger gives a thoughtful account of attempts to provide a general theoretical base for 'Law and Society' in the United States up to the mid-1990s. (Munger (1995/6) pp. 28–34).

[29] A useful survey is Banakar and Travers (2002). Cognate, but separate, are macro-theoretical perspectives on the world economy (e.g. the political economist Immanuel Wallerstein's 'World Systems Theory' which focuses on the spread of capitalism (e.g. Wallerstein (1984) (2002)), theories of development (see Chapter 11.2 below), and the extension of auotpoiesis to global ordering (e.g. Teubner (1996a)). Important thematic works develop such notions as 'the audit society' (Power (1997)), 'the risk society' (Beck (1992)), and 'the information age' (Castells (2000)).

[30] There is some justification for this in that nearly all of these individuals are treated as major figures in the history of sociology. However, in the context of empirical legal studies, it is important to emphasise that professional sociology is only one of the social sciences with which law has sustained relations and in many contexts it is not the most important.

their basic juridical perspectives.[31] Insofar as they can be lumped together in a single tradition, one might say that Montesquieu, Ehrlich, and Petrazycki were the most prominent pioneers – some might add Savigny and Maine. The best known twentieth-century figures include Roscoe Pound, some American Realists (notably Karl Llewellyn), Julius Stone, and Roger Cotterrell. It is tempting to suggest a distinction between jurists who looked at law from the inside (sociological jurists), and non-lawyers who approached it from the outside (sociologists of law). However, this just does not fit these lists, which mainly illustrate the futility of trying to classify thinkers.

(b) Institutional aspects

The institutional histories of the growth of empirical legal studies in the United States and the United Kingdom are quite well documented.[32] They are usually told in terms of initiatives as well as support by funding bodies, research institutes or programmes based on universities, the establishment of associations, journals, and series of books, and the leadership of outstanding individuals. Rather than repeat some quite familiar stories, I shall confine myself to a few general observations.

First, the history of criminology is largely separate from the rest of empirical legal studies. With roots that go back at least to the nineteenth century, criminology became established as a sub-discipline of sociology. Even today sociology is still the main field of most criminologists.[33] This contrasts with most other aspects of empirical legal studies for which law schools in recent years have been the main site of intellectual ferment and development. The systematic study of criminal justice administration and policy developed later than and largely separately from criminology and it is often treated as a hybrid sub-discipline, hovering somewhere between sociology, law, and public administration.[34]

Second, despite the intellectual roots of sociology of law in Continental Europe, the United States dominates the area.[35] American empirical legal research has a longer history, a grander scale, more generous funding, a more secure base, and a more consistently empirical orientation than in any other country. Some pioneers, such as Roscoe Pound and John Henry Wigmore,

---

[31] Such hostility is discussed by Banakar (2002).

[32] For the United States, good detailed accounts include Stevens (1983), Kalman (1986), Schlegel (1995), Duxbury (1995) and Hull (1997). A useful informal history and stock-taking of the field is Munger (1995/6). See also Cotterrell (1995) at pp. 73–90, Garth and Sterling (1998) and Garth (2001). For the United Kingdom see Galligan (ed.) (1995), *BT* Chapters 6 and 7.

[33] Short (2001) at pp. 2935–6.

[34] For a potentially controversial account see Szabo (2001), pp. 2954–8.

[35] Munger (1995/6 at n. 65) estimated that there were over forty law and society journals world-wide, about half of which are published in the United States and Canada. Since then the number has grown. A notable recent addition is the *Journal of Empirical Legal Studies* (2004–) based at Cornell.

preceded the efforts of the 1920s at Columbia, Yale, and Johns Hopkins to establish an empirical social science of law. These initiatives were closely associated with the rise and decline of the American Realist Movement, but the story is broader than that.[36] It is a complex one, in parts contested, but the crucial point here is that, although the pre-War efforts to develop law as a social science were written off as failures, the intellectual groundwork had been laid, and not long after 1945 these efforts were revived in a number of centres. Commonly referred to as highlights of the development of empirical legal studies in the United States are the establishment of the American Bar Foundation in 1952, the Ford Foundation's support of three major projects at the University of Chicago Law School from the early 1950s,[37] support for a number of later law school initiatives by the Walter E. Meyer Research Foundation and the Russell Sage Foundation in the 1960s,[38] the founding of the Law and Society Association (LSA) in 1964[39] and the *Law and Society Review* in 1966, and the start of National Science Foundation support in the early 1970s. Emphasis on these highlights probably understates the extent to which there was a widespread growing interest in inter-disciplinary research in both law schools and social science departments from the 1950s.[40] The field has grown and diversified ever since.

One aspect of empirical legal research in the United States is that, at least until the mid-1990s, and to some extent continuing, the great bulk of work focused on aspects of 'law in action' within the United States, relying almost entirely on American literature, with little interest in comparative work and developments abroad.[41] There were some important exceptions to this isolationism. From the early 1960s until the 1980s the Ford Foundation funded the 'law and development' programmes at Chicago, Yale, and Stanford, as well as

---

[36] For example, 'The achievements of the law and society movement have been steady and unspectacular; yet when we look back over what the movement achieved in the second half of the twentieth century, it seems fair to say that it moved beyond that planning stage which represented the pinnacle of the realist interdisciplinary project.' (Duxbury (2003) at p. 960).

[37] The Ford Foundation provided funds for three studies at the University of Chicago Law School on tax policy, commercial arbitration and the jury project, only the last of which was completed. Also at the University of Chicago, Aaron Director started teaching a course on the 'General Theory of Price', an extreme version of free-market ideology presented as a scientific method of analysis from which the powerful law and economics movement developed over the years. On Director see Duxbury (1995) at pp. 339–48. On my clashes with Director, see Chapter 11, n. 49 below.

[38] The variety of perspectives in the main centres is illustrated by the different kinds of leadership exercised by Edward Levi, Harry Kalven, and Aaron Director at Chicago, Willard Hurst at Wisconsin, Harold Lasswell and Myres McDougal at Yale, and Philip Selznick at Berkeley.

[39] Interestingly, the first national meeting of the LSA did not take place until 1975 in Buffalo (Munger (1995/6) at. n. 65).

[40] For a useful brief overview of the main law school programmes see Garth (2001).

[41] There are many reasons for this, but one consequence was a lack of reciprocity with foreign colleagues. Linguistically lazy Anglophones (that includes the British) rarely read beyond the literature in English, whereas polyglot foreign scholars read and were influenced by the American literature as well as their own thereby reinforcing American dominance in the field.

scientists and that many tend to underestimate its importance, this is depressing, not only for 'legal nationalists' like myself who preach the significance, pervasiveness and interest of our subject, but also because it bodes ill for the future development of empirical legal research.[71] In law, even for contextually oriented scholars, detailed acquaintance with the heritages of social theory and training in techniques of empirical research are generally 'add ons' that have to compete with other demands on academic lawyers and law students.[72] The best hope for sustained development of empirical understandings of law lies in an increased interest in legal phenomena within a wide range of other disciplines. Interdisciplinary work should not be restricted to one-way traffic.[73]

The Genn Report highlights some real problems, but perhaps it presents an unduly pessimistic picture. It approaches empirical research more in institutional than cultural terms. Much more important than squeezing some direct teaching of social science theory and methods into already overstretched curricula, is how far 'core' and 'standard' subjects are conceived in ways that are empirically informed and politically aware.[74] Doctrinal and contextual or socio-legal perspectives are much better integrated than they were in academic law generally, although there is still room for improvement. This implies that scholarly 'understanding' of family law or torts or criminal law or environmental law involves familiarity with materials from other disciplines. This is a general *expectation*, not an optional extra.

The title of the report – *Law in the Real World: Improving our Understanding of how Law Works* – may be rhetorically astute in making the case for increased funding for civil justice research in the United Kingdom. But the rhetoric is misleading insofar as it implies that structured empirical research is the only, or the main, route to understanding 'the law in action'. It is misleading in two ways: it suggests, first, that most theoretical and text-based academic work takes place in an ivory tower out of touch with 'the real world' and, second, that

what extent the UK is exceptional when compared to those other countries where empirical legal studies are reasonably well-established. The Genn Report may be unduly pessimistic about the amount of law-related research that is carried on by social scientists without being recognised as 'socio-legal'. For example, see Carson and Bull (2003), and (Carson *et al.* (2007)) on the range of work done by psychologists and forensic scientists. Economic analysis of law is not usually treated as 'socio-legal'.

[71] 'The case for law' and differing perceptions of the importance of law in the context of 'development' are discussed in Chapter 11.3.

[72] It may be unrealistic to expect all undergraduates and postgraduates to have specific instruction in techniques of empirical research because of curriculum overload, although some such instruction is desirable. Some teachers claim that methodology courses are unpopular with undergraduates. In my view, academic lawyers are too few in number and subject to too many diverse demands to be able to take on the main responsibility for doing empirical research (Twining (2003c). In many instances they may be best suited to serve as local guides and recruiters, rather than the foot-soldiers, who do the bulk of the detailed empirical work.

[73] Christopher McCrudden (2006) at pp. 645–50 makes the case strongly for greater interest in law by social scientists. See also McAuslan (2003), Banakar and Travers (2002) at p. 352.

[74] On different ideas about 'the core' of law as a discipline see *BT*, Chapter 7.

nearly all empirical legal research and data creation is or should be undertaken by university-based academic lawyers.

Law is a participant-oriented discipline.[75] Even the staples of black letter exegesis, legislation and cases, are products of practical decision making, with academic lawyers as their main professional critics. More important, academic legal culture in common law countries has been closely tied to legal practice.[76] Its main economic base is the primary education of aspiring practitioners. In some countries in Continental Europe, and elsewhere, a common complaint is that many law professors spend too much time in practice. Of course, a practitioner's or consultant's perspective on 'the law in action' may be quite different from that of an empirical researcher, for there are many ways to contact with 'the real world'.

Furthermore, it should not be assumed that universities have a monopoly of empirical research into law. The Genn Report stresses the significance of work done by Government research units in the UK,[77] but the point is much wider than that. Apart from research that takes place in various parts of the private sector, two related factors are leading to increased demand for reliable information about how the law works: greater emphasis on quantification generally and the 'audit culture' that requires that nearly all public sector activities be evaluated in terms of actual consequences, preferably using measurable indicators. Both of these are especially relevant to 'globalisation'. A number of transnational agencies are working to reduce the deficit in global statistics relating to law and the World Bank and other international financial institutions are increasingly evaluating the programmes they fund according to the methods of Results-Based Management (RBM).[78] We shall return to these trends later.

---

[75] *LIC*, pp. 112, 126–8. The first Professor of English Law in London, Andrew Amos, a practising barrister, tried to bring 'the fire and thunder of litigation' into the classroom (Baker (1977)). Until the 1970s almost all full-time law teachers were professionally qualified and had some first hand experience of legal practice. Some 'kept their hand in' part-time. On C. P. Snow's Lewis Eliot, see Chapter 17 on the web. As law schools expanded and became more integrated into the university, the proportion of academic lawyers with this kind of background declined, but other opportunities for contact with 'the real world' opened up.

[76] The numbers of full-time law teachers with experience of private practice has eroded, but today in the United Kingdom most academic lawyers are involved in a wide range of practical activities, usually viewed as 'outside work'. Consultancies both in the UK and abroad, membership of law reform committees, including the Law Commission, voluntary involvement in law-related NGOs, participation in human rights activities, serving as magistrates or on tribunals or parole boards are all activities that count as 'outside work', but which are encouraged by most universities (Twining, 2003c). A small survey of *Who's Who* entries of Law Fellows of the British Academy showed that about 80 per cent reported involvement in such activities (*ibid.* at p. 924). This is an area that could benefit from more research. Unfortunately Cownie (2004) did not explore this aspect of academic lawyers in detail.

[77] Genn (2006a) at p. 5, para. 21.

[78] On the dearth of global statistics relating to law in 2000, see *GLT* at pp. 154–7. On the application of RBM to the Millennium Development Goals see Chapter 11.4 below. On expanding regional and global data compilation see pp. 254–7 below.

To sum up: Berlin 2007 suggests that the broad field of empirical legal studies is expanding, dynamic, and diverse. However, the Genn Report highlights two widespread worrying tendencies: first, the tendency within socio-legal studies to neglect detailed empirical research in favour of more comfortable theoretical and bookish pursuits. In some countries there appear to be more generals than footsoldiers. Second, the report highlights a striking lack of interest in law within social science departments. Insofar as there is a tendency among many social scientists to underestimate the political, economic, and social importance of law this should be of great concern to the academic legal community on whom, Genn suggests, the main responsibility falls. Chapter 11 returns to this topic and considers varying perceptions of the importance of law in relation to 'development'. However, the Genn report may be unduly pessimistic about the receptivity of 'contextualised' academic legal culture to empirical understandings.

8.5 The implications of globalisation: social theory and the transnationalisation of empirical legal studies

The transnationalisation of empirical legal studies depends to a large part on the extent to which neighbouring disciplines have been oriented in that direction. Some disciplines or sub-disciplines that have a 'scientistic' orientation, such as economics, psychology, and geography, have an inbuilt tendency to think across national boundaries. Others, such as sociology, were quite slow to break away from the idea of a 'society' as the basic unit of study. In a different way, social anthropology has combined an intensive focus on small localities with a tradition of theorising that has not been tied to particular countries or states.[79] Only in limited respects have comparative empirical legal studies moved away from treating the nation state as the basic unit of comparison.[80]

Academic interest in 'globalisation' began to surface in the late 1980s. There was a relatively short intellectual lag before law caught on. Using Law and Society (LSA) meetings as one indicator, there were several panels in 1995 that could be said to be related to globalisation, but at that time, Frank Munger said, with some justification: 'Neither the association nor the field has addressed the issues raised by global research in a direct or systematic way.'[81] At Berlin in

---

[79] See, e.g., Starr and Collier (1989), Riles (2001).

[80] On 'networks' see Slaughter (2004) and Goodale and Merry (2007); for a sceptical view of the concept see Riles (2001).

[81] Munger (1995/6) at p. 49. Perhaps the boldest attempt to date to set an agenda is Santos' magisterial overview of 'the transnationalization of the legal field' (Santos (1995) at pp. 268–373, (2002) at pp. 187–312). Santos' agenda was to some extent limited by his political thesis about counter-hegemonic v hegemonic forces, so a number of other salient topics can be added to it (*GLT*, pp. 239–42). See further pp. 447–8 below.

2007, only a tiny number of panels were concerned solely with American issues – nearly all sessions included papers dealing with more than one country, over thirty panels purported to be comparative,[82] and words such as 'transnational', 'international' and 'global' were bandied about fairly freely. In short this was a deliberately cosmopolitan occasion, but it was not clear how far Munger's call for a systematic approach had been met.

In considering the implications of globalisation for the discipline of law as it is institutionalised in a particular country or region, it is helpful to distinguish between: (a) established transnational fields that command increased attention; (b) new or developing subjects that have strong transnational aspects (e.g. Internet law); (c) established fields formerly perceived as domestic that have recently acquired increased transnational dimensions, such as family and criminal law; (d) the diffusion of religious law and customary practices associated with large scale migration; and (e) the interface with municipal state law in Northern countries of the religious and customary practices of ethnic minorities (both immigrant and indigenous).[83] Nearly all of these examples relate to state law, but globalisation also has implications for the diffusion of religion, custom, and other forms of non-state law and for the interaction of state and non-state law at different levels of relations and ordering. Similarly, as the discipline of law becomes more cosmopolitan there is a growing tendency in legal education, legal scholarship and, to a lesser extent, legal practice to refer to foreign sources and examples in the study of domestic as well as transnational subjects.[84]

Today most academic lawyers are specialists. Some fields of expertise have developed distinctive sub-cultures (e.g. the cultures of specialists in international law or international commercial arbitration or family law tend to be quite different from each other both within particular countries and transnationally). Many areas of specialisation have distinct intellectual traditions. Some are quite mono-disciplinary, others have close connections with one or more disciplines in the social sciences or humanities. As we have seen, the heritage of theorising in socio-legal studies has been quite fragmented and localised. Similarly, the extent to which realist or contextual ideas have impacted on particular specialisms is very variable (e.g. in the United Kingdom, family law and torts have been perceived to be more receptive to contextual perspectives than land law or human rights).[85] Accordingly, it is not sensible to attempt generalisations about the implications of globalisation for empirical legal studies in such a wide

---

[82] Nearly thirty panels explicitly claimed to be 'comparative', but many merely juxtaposed the situation in several different countries.

[83] See further pp. 446–7 below.

[84] The debate in the United States about citation of foreign sources in court can be interpreted as a reaction to this tendency (McCrudden (2007)).

[85] Some might challenge this perception: on contextual approaches to property and land, (see e.g. McDougal and Haber (1948), McAuslan (1975), Clarke and Kohler (2005), and Woodman *et al.* (2004)). On empirical and statistical approaches to human rights, see n. 143 below.

variety of specialised fields. Instead, I propose to focus on comparative law to illustrate how socio-legal perspectives can impact on a particular area in the context of globalisation.

8.6 Comparative empirical legal studies

I have argued elsewhere that comparative law has an important role to play in constructing a general jurisprudence because, as John Stuart Mill pointed out, comparison is an important step on the road to generalisation.[86] Comparative law provides both the building bricks and serves as a testing ground for generalisation. Comparative work in law should play a crucial role in the process of enlarging our understandings of legal phenomena beyond national boundaries en route to exploring problems of generalisability. The idea of general jurisprudence includes the study of two or more legal orders; so do comparative legal studies. Comparative law and legal theory should be conceived as interdependent. If ever there was a time when a serious legal scholar could concentrate entirely on a single jurisdiction in respect of sources and focus, that time is past. Almost all legal scholarship draws on transnational sources, is informed by ideas from other disciplines and legal traditions, and even when the focus is highly local, either implicitly or explicitly makes comparisons with legal phenomena elsewhere. In short, to a significant extent we are all comparatists now.[87]

In *Globalisation and Legal Theory* I explored the implications of globalisation for comparative law and argued that the underlying conception of mainstream comparative law in the 'Country and Western Tradition' was largely atheoretical, narrowly focused, unempirical, and based on a dubious form of functionalism.[88] However, in some respects practice had outrun theory and there is quite a rich heritage of diverse particular studies. Nevertheless, I agreed with critics who maintained that comparative lawyers have tended to be too unreflective about methodology. So, one task for legal theorists is to explore in-depth issues about comparability, false comparisons, commensurability, types of comparative work, and the dearth of usable comparators.[89] Rather than go over the same ground again, let us consider here some examples of qualitative comparative legal studies before addressing the development of quantitative comparative law.

---

[86] *GLT*, Chapter 7. J. S. Mill (1843) Book IV of Operations Subsidiary to Induction.

[87] *GLT*, pp. 255–6.

[88] *GLT*, Chapter 7. See further Twining (2000b) and (2007a), and Örücü and Nelken (2007). On functionalism in comparative law see pp. 41 above and 304 below.

[89] See *GLT*, Chapter 7, and, a longer version, in Twining (2000b) Some of these themes are taken up and developed in Menski (2006) Introduction and Chapter 1. The point about comparators is intimately linked to the need to develop analytical concepts that cross legal traditions and cultures, discussed in Chapter 2.2(b) above.

8.7 Qualitative comparative legal studies

In 1996 Lawrence Friedman, who has himself contributed much to the field, pointed out that comparative and genuinely transnational socio-legal studies were in their infancy.[90] This is still broadly true, but there are some notable exceptions. For example, comparative criminology is quite well established and the comparative study of constitutions and constitutionalism benefits from the relative sophistication of comparative politics and government.[91] In recent years there have been encouraging developments in the transnational study of other subjects, such as law and the family, regulation, dispute processing, and responses to terrorism.

(a) Comparative sociology of legal professions[92]

One of the most developed enclaves of transnational empirical legal studies is research on lawyers and legal professions. When in 1981 a working group for the Comparative Study of Legal Professions was set up,[93] it was able to draw on a small, but generally excellent body of empirical studies of lawyers in the United States.[94] By 1990 three substantial volumes edited by Richard Abel and Philip Lewis had been produced (on civil law countries, common law countries, comparative theories). These were supplemented by Richard Abel's substantial studies of the legal profession in the United States and England and Wales.[95] Study of lawyers and legal professions has continued to be a strong field both within particular countries and transnationally. Recently there has been a strong surge of interest, with research moving in a variety of directions: organisation theory, economic analysis, dispersal and diffusion of law firms

---

[90] Friedman (1996).

[91] A sample of significant recent writings on constitutions and constitutionalism is to be found in Walker (ed.) (2003), (2005), Joerges and Petersmann (eds.) (2006), Loughlin and Walker (eds.) (2007) and Tsagourias (ed.) (2007). See also Held (1995), and Ghai (2005).

[92] I am grateful to John Flood for comments on this section.

[93] This was initiated under the auspices of The International Research Committee on the Sociology of Law (founded as a section of the International Sociological Association). The project resulted in three volumes (Abel and Lewis, 1988–89) and related studies on the legal profession in England and Wales (Abel, 1988) and American lawyers (Abel, 1989). These have formed the starting point for many more particular studies. The recent work of Dezalay and Garth, although using a different theoretical framework, could be said to a continuation of that tradition: Dezalay and Garth (1995),(1996), (2002a), (2002b).

[94] Starting with the pioneering ABA Survey of the Legal Profession (summarised in Blaustein and Porter (1954)), there followed excellent studies by Carlin (1962), (1966), Smigel (1964), Weyrauch (1964), Heinz and Laumann (1982) and others. In the United Kingdom Abel-Smith and Stevens (1967) stimulated debate as well as further empirical work. Johnstone and Hopson (1967) could be said to mark the rise of comparative studies of legal professions. Nascent 'third world' studies were synthesised and extended in Dias *et al.* (1981) (see especially notes at pp. 22–4). A central theme of several of these studies was the stratification of the legal profession and the fragmentation of legal practice.

[95] Abel and Lewis (eds.) (1989) 3 vols. Abel (1988), (1989).

transnationally, and the history of legal professions are all dynamic fields.[96] Of particular interest is the current Bremen-based project investigating the transnational work of lawyers.[97]

It is worth making several points about the comparative sociology of legal professions. First, most of the transnational studies have explicitly drawn on particular bodies of social theory. For example, Abel and Lewis drew on Marx, Weber, Durkheim and theories of professionalisation.[98] This led them to focus on class, structure, power relations, control, and claims to monopoly of knowledge.[99] As they acknowledged, their studies tended to be more informative about who lawyers (and their clients) are and how they are organised than about the specifics of legal practice: what lawyers do and how they do it.[100] Nevertheless a sophisticated theoretical framework ensured that the Abel and Lewis studies were coherent, even though most were parallel studies rather than being strictly comparative.[101]

---

[96] By December 2007, Professor Bill Henderson of Indiana (Bloomington) had compiled a list of 160 active legal profession scholars, including economists, geographers, and management specialists. Two recent symposia in the *North Carolina Law Review* (2006) and the *Indiana Journal of Global Legal Studies* (2007) give a conspectus of the dynamism and variety of this flourishing field. See also Flood (1996), (2002).

[97] 'The Collaborative Research Center 597: 'Transformations of the State' at www.sfb597.uni-bremen.de/. See also Flood 1996 (2002).

[98] Especially Johnson (1972) and Larson (1977). Outstanding specialised one-country studies have dealt with barristers' clerks in London (Flood (1983)), large law firms (Galanter and Palay (1991)) divorce lawyers (Sarat and Felstiner (1995)), poverty lawyers (Alfieri, (1993)), co-operation within corporate law partnerships (Lazega (2001)), corporate lawyers in China (Liu (2006)), and lawyer jokes (Galanter (2005)).

[99] See Halliday and Karpik (1997).

[100] This is now changing (see n. 97 above). However, early neglect of the empirical study of what lawyers do left the door open for those advocates of skills training to maintain the fiction of unity of the legal profession in the United States and to produce lists of 'fundamental lawyering skills' (e.g. ABA (MacCrate report) (1992)), while ignoring sociological literature on the stratification and fragmentation of legal practice. (See *LIC*, pp. 331–3.) In Great Britain, Moorehead, Paterson and Sherr have done valuable work on problems of assessing solicitors' competence for purposes of legal franchising (e.g., Sherr *et al.* (1994), Moorehead *et al.* (2000), Moorehead *et al.* (2003)).

[101] On the distinction between explicit comparison *stricto sensu* and parallel studies, implicit comparison and studies of foreign law see Twining (2000a) at pp. 41–4. At this stage most transnational empirical legal work falls short of being genuinely 'comparative'. In the 1980s I participated in a Commonwealth project on access to legal education and the legal profession. We agreed on the scope and objectives of the project and I prepared a theoretical framework, defining 'access' and listing possible barriers and pitfalls at different stages of a notionally linear process of education, training, and professional development, including an ideal type set in a mythical country in which aspiring and qualified lawyers were filtered out at every stage from birth, primary education, through initial qualification to retirement. The country studies that resulted hardly proceeded 'in parallel' and the outcome produced little by way of comparison or generalisation, but at best a rough set of tools for diagnosing the situation in any common law country and a rich body of largely anecdotal experience from a variety of jurisdictions within the Commonwealth. This may have been of some use for activists in interpreting their own situation, but it fell far short of a genuinely comparative study. (Dhavan, Kibble, and Twining (1989)).

Second, as was noted in Chapter 2, comparative studies of legal professions have been beset by threshold conceptual problems. Largely because there have been different local histories and traditions about the division of labour, specialisation, and the foundation of distinct 'professions', it has been difficult to find or construct a framework of analytic concepts for use in making comparisons and generalisations. Terms like 'lawyer', 'advocate' and 'legal professional' do not travel well. 'Legal actor', 'law trained person', 'legal personnel' are too vague for most purposes. 'Profession' and 'professional' do not translate easily. The term 'law student' is both vague and ambiguous even within a single country.[102] 'Legal services' may be a more promising concept, except that there are significant differences between countries as to who are the main or exclusive providers of particular services relating to, for example, tax planning, notarisation of documents, matrimonial advice, land transfer, or insolvency. While the more sophisticated studies have navigated these initial conceptual and terminological difficulties,[103] this is a field that is still vulnerable to dubious comparisons and false or even meaningless generalisations.[104]

Third, since the late 1980s there have been major upheavals affecting legal practice both transnationally and for quite specific local reasons. Some of these changes relate to such matters as access to legal representation, challenges to lawyers' monopolies, and public accountability. However, 'transnationalisation of legal practice' and the changes associated with it are often attributed to 'globalisation'. Like other globalisation discourse this has often led to inflated, sometimes nonsensical, talk of 'global (or European) lawyers', 'global law firms', 'global lawyering' and 'global law degrees'.[105] However, there is no doubt that there have been major changes, exemplified by the growth of large law firms, mergers, transnational and cross-disciplinary partnerships, problems of recognition of foreign qualifications, talk of a global code of ethics, and moves to 'harmonise' legal education and training, especially at regional levels.[106] Richard Abel's book on *The Legal Profession in England and Wales* (1989) brought together for the first time a vast amount of quantitative and qualitative data up to 1985. About 1990 an English QC remarked to me that this was a magnificent and unprecedented achievement, but added: 'Isn't it a pity that the history of our legal profession began in 1986'. The changes in the past twenty

---

[102] See Chapter 2.3(b) above.

[103] Abel and Lewis diffentiated between 'jurists' (holding a law degree – mainly a civil law term), jurisconsults (state lawyers, e.g. in the Soviet Union) and private practitioners (Abel 2001, at p. 8553), generally avoiding the vague generic term 'lawyer'.

[104] On the 'debased debate' about overcrowding, see p. 47 above.

[105] This is not to deny that there are some law firms and lawyers, who are willing to undertake work almost anywhere in the world (but they are few), and that there is some genuinely 'global law', but most transnational practice operates at sub-global levels, rather in the way that Hirst and Thompson characterised most multinational businesses in the 1990s – widespread, but not truly global. Hirst and Thompson (1999). See p. 16 above.

[106] Most of these developments can be tracked in the *International Journal of the Legal Profession*. See also Lombay (2004), Terry (2007).

years have to some extent meant that this generally excellent body of literature rapidly became out of date in respect of detail. Recent scholarly work has had difficulty in keeping pace with the changes, but these events have stimulated a great deal of academic interest in several disciplines.[107]

Fortunately, this heritage of theoretically sophisticated, soundly empirical studies provides a solid starting point for interpreting events as they develop and viewing them from a broad historical perspective. In 2001, Richard Abel, who is better qualified than anyone to do so, advanced the following bold interpretation of likely trends:

> Having relinquished control over supply to universities, subcategories are trying to reclaim it, but through credentializing more than licensure. As these specialisms are increasingly differentiated and stratified, legal professions move towards fission. Lawyers find it more difficult to justify restrictive practices, especially as consumers become more concentrated and sophisticated, resorting indeed to flexing their own market power. Private efforts to stimulate demand provoke a backlash against litigiousness. States seek to control and even contract their legal aid budgets. Within law firms, productive relations are increasingly capitalist, as differences in control and rewards widen. The divisions and hierarchy among lawyers, often mirrored by ascribed characteristics, greatly complicate both self-regulation and governance – the hallmarks of a profession. The professional constellation, which lawyers successfully struggled to attain in the nineteenth and twentieth centuries, is gradually being rendered obsolete by the combined forces of market and state.[108]

It remains to be seen how far these magisterial generalisations (mainly about lawyers in Western societies) will prove to be correct. But at least there is probably a more solid basis for such pronouncements than in any other area of transnational empirical legal studies.

(b) Integrating comparative law and empirical legal studies: procedure as an example

Although the mainstream of comparative law has been quite narrowly focused, it includes many excellent studies, and it is the main repository of wisdom about the problems and methods of doing comparative work in law.[109] While relatively little detailed empirical research has been done within the tradition, there is a wide range of quite sophisticated scholarship on which such research can build. A field that has been particularly well served is comparative procedure, especially in respect of institutional design, and this can be used to illustrate how mainstream comparative law might be better integrated with transnational empirical legal studies.

One of the most widely admired works of comparative law since World War II is Mirjan Damaska's *The Faces of Justice and State Authority*.[110] This set out a

---

[107] See n. 96–8 above. But see Flood (2002) (2007).   [108] Abel (2001) p. 3558.
[109] Twining (2000a).   [110] Damaska (1986).

way of analysing and comparing systems of procedure in modern Western legal systems through three sets of Weberian 'ideal types' relating to systems of government, systems of state authority, and systems of procedure. Damaska's general thesis is that hybrids, examples mixing the ideal types, can and do co-exist in one system, but some combinations are more 'comfortable' than others: for example, a bureaucratic hierarchal system of authority sits better with a managerial or dirigiste type of government and an 'inquisitorial', policy-implementing type of procedure than it does with a co-ordinate system of authority exemplified by the jury, lay magistrates, oral procedures, and very limited appeals. Damaska argues that most procedural systems involve hybrid combinations. He uses his analytical tools to great effect in describing, comparing, and explaining particular phenomena such as the civilian dossier, 'perverse' jury verdicts, career judiciaries, the relative infrequency of appeals in common law systems, and different styles of justification for decisions. This is an outstanding example of analytical comparative law that combines the consideration of ideology, doctrine, and practical operation in an illuminating way. It also brings out the dangers of *a priori* generalising within a single 'legal family'.

Judith Resnick, in an excellent article focusing on 'the work of adjudicatory processes that are based in courts', catalogues the range of variables in procedural systems.[111] She emphasises that litigation is involved in only a small minority of disputes,: how small a minority varies between countries. Lawsuits have many configurations; venues are varied; there are different tiers of decision making; the demographics of participants in litigation (e.g. race, ethnicity, gender) is changing; and the role of resources is critical. She concludes that despite many variations, the basic problems facing any procedural system are shared:

> The Constant Questions
> Despite all the variations in the resources of litigants, the kinds of cases, the people and the problems involved, the courts systems, and the procedures themselves, the underlying problems that procedural systems have to solve are the same: Who can seek redress? For what kinds of injuries? Requesting what remedies? Based on what kind of information? Presented to what decision maker? With any review or possibility of reconsideration? Obviously these questions do not admit to easy, unvarying answers; ideas about procedure are value laden. The questions to be addressed include Why have process at all? Why care about how a decision is made? If process is required, how much should be provided? Are opportunities to be heard adequate? How formal should a procedure be? How expensive should it be? Who should pay? How free should the parties be to initiate lawsuits? Who gets to litigate and who is foreclosed? And what about the decision makers – what kinds of information should be required prior to decision? What remedies should the courts be able to order? How much power should judges have and when should that power be constrained? When

---

[111] Resnick (2001).

may decisions be reconsidered, and when should they be considered final? Over and over again, procedure returns to these basic issues.[112]

This is an example of functionalist comparative law at it best. It integrates technical legal, empirical, normative, and policy issues within a single framework of questions that can be asked about the design and operation of any procedural system – or at least a system of third-party adjudication in a modern state.[113] Provided these limitations are recognised, the assertion that the problems are shared though the 'solutions' are not is probably justified. But this template may not apply without adjustment to court systems that are endemically 'corrupt' or inefficient, to institutions in which third-party adjudication is not sharply differentiated from other means of dispute processing, or to other 'court like' tribunals such as khadi courts in Morocco or 'gacaca' processes in Rwanda.[114] Comparative study of civil procedure of modern state legal systems has flourished in recent years. The work of Damaska and Resnick, linked to the socio-legal literature on litigation[115] and dispute processing,[116] provides a model of how integrated comparative work might be done in other areas of law. Damaska provides powerful conceptual tools, Resnick supplements this with a framework of questions. Both are working in 'The Country and Western Tradition' in that they focus mainly on municipal procedural systems in modern nation states, but their work is highly suggestive for future comparative empirical work on procedural systems, including international, transnational, and non-state legal institutions and processes.

The subject variously known as reception, transplantation, or diffusion of law is a topic that is now central to comparative law. This refers to the processes by which laws, legal ideas, and other legal phenomena are exported and imported from one or more legal systems, orders or cultures to another (or others) and the consequences of such processes. The subject has a long, if uneven, history. It has been quite well studied, but largely within the more traditional framework of comparative law. It has recently gained considerable attention, first because of the work of Alan Watson and, since 1989, because of events in Eastern Europe. From a global perspective diffusion is important because almost no legal system or legal order has developed in a vacuum uninfluenced by ideas from outside. Indeed, in Watson's view, transplantation is the main engine of legal change and is much more important in practice than legal innovation. Thus comparison is complicated by the almost universal hybridity of legal systems and orders. In order to concretise how general jurisprudence can help to develop and guide a field, Part B includes an essay

---

[112] Resnick (2001) at p. 12140.

[113] Resnick does not explicitly limit her analysis to 'modern' legal systems, but her examples are all taken from Western common law and civil law systems. She is, of course, well aware of the complex relations between adjudication and other means of processing disputes.

[114] On Morocco, see L. Rosen (1989); on Rwanda, see Clark (2006).

[115] On theories of litigation see Griffiths (1983), *RE*, pp. 248–52.

[116] See e.g. Roberts and Palmer (2005).

(see Chapter 9), which critically evaluates the predominant model of diffusion of law in traditional comparative legal scholarship and suggests that it is based on a number of assumptions that mask the complexity of the processes of diffusion and their effects.[117]

8.8 Quantitative comparative legal studies

For the rational study of the law the black-letter man may be the man of the present, but the man of the future is the man of statistics and the master of economics. (Oliver Wendell Holmes Jr. 1897)[118]

One of the standard tensions within the social sciences concerns the relative merits and costs of quantitative and qualitative methods. These tensions surface at various levels reflecting differences between disciplinary cultures, within particular disciplines, and in respect of particular projects or lines of enquiry. Such tensions are inevitably reflected in empirical legal research.[119]

To date law and empirical legal studies have usually been closer to the 'qualitative', humanistic pole of the hard/soft spectrum. Of course, there are legal as well as socio-legal scholars who have made use of available statistics – Richard Abel is a good example – and some have used a mixture of qualitative and quantitative methods. But apart from criminology, and in a different way, economic analysis of law, there has been relatively little sustained 'scholarly' quantitative research into legal phenomena, and some of the best-known were written off as failures. This is especially true of comparative law. In the present context the most interesting example is the SLADE Project, which was based at Stanford Law School in the 1970s.[120]

Belief that law and legal institutions are an essential ingredient in nation building and economic development tends to move in cycles.[121] In 1970, the Law and Development Movement was at its height in the United States, optimism about the role of law and lawyers in development had been strong in the 1960s, but cracks were beginning to appear. John Henry Merryman and Lawrence Friedman of Stanford surveyed the field and concluded that one weakness in existing approaches was that they lacked a solid empirical base. Very little was known about the actual workings of legal institutions and processes in less developed countries, except that they were quite varied in

---

[117] See further Twining (2005a), which explores the vast heritage of diffusion studies in the social sciences and points out that legal scholars have largely ignored these studies and, conversely, social scientists have generally ignored the diffusion of law. This is both surprising and disappointing, given the importance of law as a social phenomenon and the shared historical roots of diffusion studies. This example of two bodies literature talking past each other could be replicated in other areas.

[118] Holmes (1897) at p. 469.   [119] See pp. 258–62 and Chapter 16.4 on the web.

[120] The following account is largely based on Merryman (1974), (2000b), (2003), Legrand (1999), and Macauley (1979).

[121] On different histories of 'law and development' see Chapter 11.2 below.

respect of legal forms, institutions and cultures. With the help of a number of distinguished scholars they planned a project designed to explore empirically relations and correlations between social indicators of change and empirical 'legal' data. They distanced themselves from existing approaches to comparative law by focusing on institutions and processes rather than legal rules and by restricting themselves largely to quantitative data. For this purpose 'law' was defined in terms of actual institutions, processes and personnel of national legal systems and 'development' was broadly interpreted to mean any kind of social change, rather than planned, programmatic or progressive development. They established indicators of legal systems and of social change that were in principle susceptible to quantification, but they recognised that a qualitative variable, 'legal culture', would be important in interpreting the data. They drew a potentially significant distinction between external and internal legal cultures, that is the deeply rooted and firmly held attitudes and perceptions of a given legal system by outsiders who played no regular role in it and the attitudes and perceptions of regular actors within it.[122]

The project leaders decided to focus on countries in Latin America and Mediterranean Europe which in important respects shared a relatively homogeneous culture. The project was ambitious and innovative, the design was carefully thought through, the leaders were respected scholars, and the project promised much.[123] A large grant was obtained from USAID and empirically minded legal scholars were recruited from seven countries.[124] These national scholars came to Stanford in 1972 for a period of intensive preliminary work and then returned to their countries for three years of field research and data collection. A wealth of social data was already available in each of the countries, but not always in standardised form and was usually based on national statistics that could conceal important regional variations within a country. Far less data were available in respect of the twenty-six legal indicators that were selected and here data collection had to start almost from scratch.[125]

By 1976, when the USAID grant expired, a vast amount of social and legal data had been collected and collated and a highly original study of internal and external legal cultures had been completed. However, the next

---

[122] This distinction was further developed by Lawrence Friedman (Friedman and Pérez-Perdomo (2003)); see the exchange between Cotterrell and Friedman in Nelken (1997).

[123] '[W]e hoped we could begin to map several great unexplored territories: the quantitative aspects of legal systems; quantitative comparative law; and the relations between social and legal change.' (Merryman (2000a) at p. 724).

[124] Chile, Costa Rica, Italy, Mexico, Peru, Spain. Later, Colombia replaced Mexico.

[125] The indicators were bunched around four categories – legal institutions, legal actors, legal processes, and resources consumed. Each of these categories was treated as an analytical concept that applied to all six countries, and indeed more broadly, because '[a]ll legal systems, indeed all social systems, have institutions, actors and processes and consume resources' (Merryman (2000b) at p. 718). It would be interesting to compare these indicators with those used subsequently by the EBRD, World Bank and other international institutions that have been evaluating the health of legal systems in recent years.

important step – to move from description and data to explanation had not yet been taken.[126] Unfortunately, an application for a further grant to analyse and interpret the data was turned down. The only published outcome of this huge project was one volume of undigested statistics and some disparate national studies.[127] In a frank post-mortem John Merryman brooded openly about this hugely disappointing outcome for an ambitious and potentially very significant enterprise.[128] Mistakes were made, especially in treating data compilation and interpretation as separate projects, rather than as essential components in a single process. By 1976 quantitative approaches in social science were becoming unfashionable and, perhaps more important, thinking in development circles had entered a period when law was not considered of much relevance – a view that changed once again during the heyday of 'the Washington consensus'.[129] Almost no attempt was made by outsiders to use or interpret the data.

This last point is relevant to interpreting the recent rise in interest of quantification of legal phenomena. Here the demand comes mainly from outside the scholarly community. Some of the products, which are often very crude, have significant practical and political uses, but seem to have passed largely unnoticed by the academic lawyers.[130] Particularly significant is the growing use of indicators of the 'health' of state legal systems and the 'success' of legal reform projects in countries in transition and the 'third world'.

Experience has taught some agencies that there is more to law reform than producing a model or draft law borrowed from elsewhere and adopting or imposing it in another country.[131] More sophisticated models of law reform recognise that a measure has to find space in the government's legislative programme, be approved and amended in a (preferably democratic) legislative process, enacted, promulgated, explained to key actors, and provision made for implementation. After that its impact needs to be monitored empirically. Problems may arise at every stage of this complex process.

Learning from past experience, agencies like the World Bank, IMF, and the European Bank for Reconstruction and Development (EBRD) have increasingly placed emphasis on implementation and monitoring of impact. The history of the sociology of law teaches that assessing impact is one of the more elusive forms of empirical enquiry. In recent years considerable effort has been invested in devising quantitative measures for assessing impact at reasonable

---

[126] Merryman (1974) emphasised that the ultimate aim was to produce explanatory generalisations.

[127] Merryman, Clark, and Friedman, (1979). The volume is out of print, but the legal cultural data is on CD-ROM. For details see Merryman (2000b).

[128] Merryman (2000b), see Macauley (1979).   [129] See below Chapter 12.

[130] An exception is Taylor (2007).

[131] Ramasatry (2002) argues that a successful legal reform project is one that adapts internationally accepted legal principles and standards to the local legal environment, focuses time and resources on implementation, and, most importantly, works through an open, transparent and inclusive process.

cost. An interesting early example is the EBRD's 'Legal Indicator Surveys'.[132] In the absence of other available data about the practical operation of reform measures in areas such as commercial law, financial regulation, and insolvency, the EBRD canvassed the opinions of practising lawyers familiar with the relevant area about the comprehensiveness and effectiveness of particular reforms. These perception-based surveys were used in assessing 'the success' of such measures. Some of the findings were tested in relation to other available data; (e.g., whether there is any correlation between insolvency laws for the volume of private sector bank credit and for flows of foreign direct investment).[133]

The World Bank, IMF, USAID, and other agencies have continued to develop similar methods for evaluating the implementation and impact of reform measures in countries 'in transition' and developing countries. The influence of economists is apparent on the form and style of these indicators, which have so far been used mainly to assess the effectiveness of efforts to bring about transition to a market-oriented economy. The approach is generally technocratic, instrumental, top-down, led by outside agencies (despite claims to 'local ownership'), and market oriented.

In *Globalisation and Legal Theory* I pointed out the relative dearth of regular, systematically compiled statistics about legal phenomena at regional, global, and other supra-national levels. At the same time nearly all public and private institutions are increasingly part of a 'performance culture', dominated by targets, benchmarks, indicators, and league tables and that, like it or not, these are probably here to stay. The relative lack of sophistication of many of these developments is illustrated by reference to the notorious *US News and Report* law school league tables, a relatively soft target. I suggested that it was for academics to assess the uses, limitations and dangers of such developments and to examine critically their intellectual foundations.

Since then these trends have continued. In the United States *US News and Report* league tables seem to have increased their power without much increase in sophistication.[134] Transparency International's *Corruption Perception Index* still attracts an inordinate amount of attention.[135] The Millennium Development Goals set out eight major goals, supported by eighteen targets

---

[132] Beginning in 1995, and continued thereafter by a series of sector-specific assessments (e.g. on corporate governance, insolvency, and secured transactions), these surveys assess and compare the situation in countries in transition. They are intended to identify continuing needs for law reform and to be used to help measure the level of legal risk for each country and to specific investment activities (website last visited 24/8/07).

[133] *EBRD*, p. 71 Some of the most sophisticated general and regional statistics are published by EUROSTAT. http://epp.eurostat.ec.europa.eu/portal/ (last visited 24/8/07). These are not classified by legal categories, but see, for example, the entries under good governance, health, and land use. At present (2007) there are no data on crime, but these are promised shortly.

[134] Espeland and Sauder (2007) see n. 146 below.

[135] GLT, pp. 158–61. On developments in the methodology of the Corruption Perceptions Index (CPI), see Lambsdorff (2007).

to be monitored against forty-eight indicators.[136] At the global level, two recent developments deserve a brief comment.

First, since 1999 the World Bank has been constructing a database on legal systems worldwide. It is described as follows:

'Legal and Judicial Sector at a Glance:
Worldwide Legal and Judicial Indicators'
The Legal and Judicial Sector at a Glance database provides access to legal and judicial information and comparative indicators on court systems across over 100 developed and developing countries. The database has been developed by the Legal Vice Presidency's Knowledge and Management Cluster (LEGKM) at the World Bank as a tool for global knowledge sharing and for assisting legal and judicial reform initiatives.[137]

This database, and others like it, needs to be the subject of careful scrutiny and analysis. Here I shall confine myself to some brief observations. First, this project is linked to the World Bank's judicial reform and Rule of Law programmes and the indicators and data are conditioned by the underlying ideology of these programmes. Second, in terms of ambition, this represents a major step forward, bearing in mind that it is intended that this should be extended and refined over time. It contains mainly statistical data and it claims to enable comparisons of one hundred legal (mainly judicial) systems over a relatively few indicators. Third, it is easy to access, easy to use, and easy to quote. Fourth, it is at present strikingly unsophisticated. This is clearly exemplified by the Glossary, which contains a number of simple definitions that ignore nearly all of the difficulties of comparing courts, lawyers, and legal cultures.[138] The potentially misleading nature of these

---

[136] These are made more challenging because poverty is no longer measured solely in monetary terms. On the futility of aggregated global figures for the MDGs and the problems of avoiding 'one size fits all' traps see Chapter 11.4 below.

[137] The description continues: '*As a tool for legal and judicial reform the database was first developed in 1999 to provide end-users with a well-designed set of baseline benchmarks and performance indicators for comparing court systems and measuring the progress of legal and judicial reform initiatives. As a tool for global knowledge sharing the database provides general qualitative and quantitative information. This includes an overview of the legal and judicial systems of countries, description of the organizations and institutions within each system and information on the judicial budget, legal education and the legal profession ...*'

'The database differs from existing websites which contain basic descriptive information on legal and judicial legal systems, but few statistics, or which contain only links to judicial and legal sector institutions and organizations. 'Legal and Judicial Sector at a Glance' is a publicly available database that provides comprehensive legal and judicial information and statistics for individual countries and which can be compared to different legal and judicial systems' www4.worldbank.org/legal/database/Justice/jMainRight.htm. When visited in July 2007 the site had last been updated on 2/26/2007 and contained figures for 2001 and 2002.

[138] Ibid. (Glossary). To give three examples: 'Judiciary' is defined as 'The branch of government set up to interpret and administer laws, including courts and all those associated with the practice of law.'; 'civil court' is defined as 'A trial court that hears disputes under the common law or civil law statutes'; and 'lawyer' as 'A person who is certified by training and examination to practice law at different levels and in different jurisdictions, often specializing in some branch of law, e.g. civil, criminal, commercial or family'. The Manual for 'Legal and Judicial Sector at a Glance' includes an interesting questionnaire, which attempts to elicit standard information and data about any legal system.

figures is exacerbated by the fact that only Federal courts are included for the United States. At this stage of its development the database raises questions of accuracy, comparability and, indeed, meaningfulness.

A second resource centre is the World Bank governance databank. This seems a bit more sophisticated and even more ambitious than the Legal and Judicial System Database.[139] A 2007 paper presents estimates of six dimensions of governance covering 212 countries and territories between 1996 and 2006.[140] These 'aggregate indicators are based on hundreds of specific and disaggregated individual variables measuring various dimensions of governance from 33 data sources provided by 30 different organisations. The data reflect the views on governance of public sector, private sector and NGO experts, as well as thousands of citizen and firm survey respondents worldwide'.[141]

So far as I can tell, few, if any, academic lawyers have been involved. Since law and development scholars were 'self-estranged' and went into voluntary exile nearly all of this kind of work has been undertaken outside the academy.[142] Some academics are rightly cautious about data compiled by government or private sector organisations for specific policy or practical purposes. The compilation of statistics and basic data bases may be primarily a government or business and financial sector function, but such compilations need to be the subject of sustained critical scrutiny, not only so that their limitations and dangers can be pointed out, but also so that they can be improved. A great deal of the material discussed here is almost the only data we have.

This kind of development is not restricted to economic reforms by international development agencies. Quantified methods of evaluation of the 'health' of a situation have been used by human rights agencies, Transparency International, and 'democratic audit'.[143] Some of the most sophisticated discussions have centred on methodologies for measuring progress (or the reverse) towards achieving the Millennium Development Goals.[144] Although individual

---

[139] 'Combining participatory action-oriented learning, capacity-building tools, and the power of *data* the World Bank Institute (WBI), in collaboration with many units in the World Bank Group, supports countries in improving governance and controlling corruption. Using a *strategic* and multi-disciplinary approach, we apply action-oriented methods to link *empirical diagnostic surveys*, their practical application, collective action and prevention. Concrete results on the ground are emphasized in our *learning programs*. The integrated approach is supported by *operational research* and a comprehensive *governance databank*.'

[140] World Bank (2007) *Governance Matters VI: Governance Indicators for 1996–2006*

[141] Kaufmann, Kray, and Mastruzzi (2007).   [142] Taylor (2007).

[143] Developments up to 2000 were discussed in *GLT* at pp. 153–65. Since then they have proliferated. For recent discussions on corruption see Transparency International (2007). On statistical approaches to human rights see Cingranelli (1998), Jabine and Claude (1992), Green (2001); on other empirical approaches to human rights see Halliday and Schmidt (eds.) (2004), Goodale and Merry (2007), Peerenboom *et al.* (2006); on empirical approaches to international law see Dickinson (2007), especially Hathaway (2002) ('Do treaties make a difference?'). On democratic audit see McCrudden and Chambers (1994) and Lord (2004). On comparative empirical studies of justice and the sense of injustice see, for example, Rossi (1997), Jasso and Wegener (1997), (1998).

[144] Black and White (2004), UN (2003), see p. 349 below.

academics have been involved as consultants or researchers in some of these projects, a striking feature has been the extent to which law schools have been by-passed by these developments.[145] The one major exception has been in respect of law school (and more broadly educational) league tables, where their own interests have been directly involved. In the United States the annual *US News and Report* league tables for professional schools has provoked a storm of protest from academic lawyers and a number of not disinterested criticisms of what is one of the cruder versions of this kind of measurement. This has at least given academic lawyers some experience of criticising this kind of indicator.[146]

Various reasons have been given for academic lawyers' aversion to statistics: that law is chosen by the innumerate; that legal phenomena cannot be measured or counted; that legal categories defy quantification; that lawyers are resistant to 'scientism'; that it is bad policy to set targets for conviction rates or cases disposed of; that the experience of quantitative studies, exemplified by SLADE, has been disastrous. These reasons are at best only partly true, and they can only help to explain the past.[147] Quantification is growing not only because of increased sophistication in the social sciences, but also because of the pressures of bureaucratisation and accountability: an audit culture requires measurable objectives, and targets, standards and indicators expressed in quantitative terms.[148] Psychometrics, biometrics, and bibliometrics are growing in influence and we may not be far off the day that a broadened conception of jurimetrics may become fashionable.[149] Holmes' prophecy has been slow in being realised, but the trend is as he predicted.

It is now widely accepted that quantitative versus qualitative is a false dichotomy. Quantification has an inbuilt tendency to homogenise and to

[145] Taylor (2007).

[146] A recent call for a more disciplined approach to evaluating and responding to law school rankings in the US is Espeland and Sauder (2007) in an article advocating an approach which 'demonstrates how increasingly fateful public measures change expectations and permeate institutions, suggesting why it is important for scholars to investigate the impact of these measures more systematically.' (Abstract). Espeland has also done important work on commensuration which is directly relevant to assessing the validity of measures of the kind discussed in the text. Espeland and Stevens (1998). On theoretical problems of commensurability in comparative law, see Glenn (2001) and (2004) at pp. 44–58, 354–5 and Halpin (2006).

[147] As Merryman points out, most nations keep regular statistics on judicial administration, police, budget for legal institutions and so on. (Merryman (1999) at p. 515). International standardisation of some of these has been steadily developing.

[148] On 'the audit society' see Power (1997).

[149] 'Jurimetrics', a term coined by Lee Loevinger in 1949 (Allen and Baade (1963)), has been defined as 'the empirical study of legal phenomena with the aid of mathematical models on the basis of rationalism' (De Mulder (2004)). This is given strong support by the ABA's Section on Law and Technology, which publishes the journal *Jurimetrics*. This has focused especially on legal informatics, symbolic logic, predictive analysis of judicial decisions, and practical applications of technology in legal contexts, but has sometimes ranged much wider. Like the Gruter Institute for Law and Behavioral Research (which emphasises biology), 'jurimetrics' has tended to be somewhat isolated towards the 'scientistic' end of socio-legal studies, but that may be changing.

simplify; it facilitates large scale comparisons and generalisations; it enables macroscopic overviews, but there is no substitute for qualitative interpretation and testing and refining.[150]

8.9 An empirical science of law?

During 2000–1, I was a Fellow at the Center for Advanced Study of the Behavioral Sciences at Stanford – as near as one can get to academic heaven. I was the only jurist among a community of forty-five scholars, nearly all of whom were social scientists or socially oriented historians. The ethnography of this community was fascinating. Within the social sciences and the humanities there are two familiar extremes that can be variously characterised in such terms as hard/soft; scientific/humanistic, quantitative/qualitative and, most significant in the present context, generalist/particularist. Although there were few extremists, there were clear patterns: the psychologists, economists, and most political scientists clustered around the 'hard' pole, while the historians and the anthropologists, the only philosopher, and the solitary novelist were at or near the 'soft' or particularistic end of the spectrum. Nearer the centre were one sociologist, whose background was in conversation analysis and interactionism,[151] some educationists (two of whom were uneasily concerned with measurement, standards, and performance indicators), and myself, the only jurist, a common lawyer conditioned by a legal culture that emphasises the tensions between general rules and concrete cases.[152]

Many of us were well aware of the contrasts between our academic subcultures and an attempt was made to develop a sustained conversation about this, especially in relation to historiography. The exchanges were quite genteel, but occasionally they acquired a sharp edge: 'If you can't measure outcomes, how can you ever talk of "success"?' met with the response: 'If it can be measured, it is almost certainly trivial or misleading or ideologically constructed, like most official statistics.' One political scientist asked: 'How can you "explain" an historical event outside the context of a universe of cases?' The

---

[150] On false dichotomies between quantitative vs qualitative, case-oriented vs variable-oriented, and holistic vs analytic see Berg-Schlosser (2001) at pp. 2431–32. On 'surface law' see Chapter 10 below.

[151] In the tradition of Cicourel, Latour, and Goffman, see Atkinson and Drew (1979). See now Molotch (2003).

[152] Arguing about and forming judgements about appropriate levels of generality are matters that lawyers are meant to be especially well equipped to deal with. In our conversations at Stanford I was particularly struck by the interest exhibited by both 'hard' scientists and 'soft' humanists with some standard ideas in theorising about case law such as reasoning by analogy, the *ratio decidendi* of a case, and ladders of abstraction – that is, the idea that a particular fact situation can be categorised and described truthfully at multiple levels of generality, especially when there is latitude for categorising a number of elements in a single fact situation each at different levels of abstraction (Stone (1959); *HTDTWR* at pp. 59–60, 331–3). A similar sophistication may develop over time in the European Union in respect of discussion of concepts such as 'subdsidiarity' and 'margins of appreciation'.

historians seemed to me to duck this question, instead countering with their own questions, such as: 'How can such thin descriptions, or such unreal assumptions (like rational economic man), be a basis for any significant empirical generalisations or true accounts?' The contrasts between vocabularies were striking: anthropologists and historians talked of 'thick description', uniqueness, complexity, incommensurability, layers of meaning, multi-factor causation, and the importance of local knowledge. By contrast, 'harder' social scientists, striving to generalise, invoked Occam's Razor, used simplifying assumptions, stressed indicators, measurability, dependent and independent variables, patterns, trends and correlations. The catchword of the particularists was 'granularity'; some psychologists talked of 'the hard-wired' aspects of the human psyche. The historians were concerned with understanding past sit- uations and events in terms that emphasised complexity, particularity, and even uniqueness. Some 'scientists' explicitly claimed to be aiming for generalisations that could reliably predict the future.

From the perspective of an ethnographer of knowledge, one might say that there seemed to be dominant standards and reference groups that exerted a strong gravitational pull within each academic sub-culture. There are quite different criteria of academic respectability and prestige for cognitive psychol- ogists and positivistic political scientists on the one hand and for mainstream historians and social anthropologists, on the other. There are different national traditions in the social sciences, but some of these patterns transcended national boundaries. Of course, there are commonly sharp disagreements and factions within disciplines and their sub-cultures, but even there a shared local academic conscience may exert a powerful influence.[153] After a time, continuing the conversation seemed as likely to reinforce local prejudices as to build bridges between disciplines. Almost everyone talked politely of complementarity or combining the quantitative and the qualitative, but for me the centre seemed disappointingly soggy.[154]

As we have seen, law and empirical legal studies have usually been closer to the 'qualitative', humanistic pole of the hard/soft spectrum. At Stanford I found myself instinctively siding with the historians and the anthropologists, but semi-consciously I could not help be impressed by the intellectual ambition as well as the rigour of some of my more 'scientific' colleagues. And I wondered whether legal scholarship could ever satisfy their standards.

What are these standards? They are, of course, contested within the philo- sophy of science and the standards are not uniform across disciplines. For present purposes suffice it to say that for any empirical enquiry into legal phenomena to aspire to meet these standards the findings should be warranted

---

[153] Becher (1989).

[154] A similar sogginess pervades much of the literature on globalisation. The strong globalisers do not suggest that everything is being homogenised; indeed, many emphasise the complex and interactive nature of the processes. Conversely, sceptics such as Paul Hirst have not denied that there are significant trends towards interdependence (see Chapter 1 at p. 16 above).

by evidence – generalisable, explanatory (not merely descriptive), testable, predictive, and preferably cumulative.[155] Scientific findings tend to be mutually supportive, 'more like a crossword puzzle than a mathematical proof'.[156]

Judged by such standards, we are a very long way from achieving an empirical science of law. There are many reasons for this, but the most obvious ones are that most legal scholarship to date has not been empirically oriented, much that passes as 'sociological' or 'socio-legal' is theoretical or text-based, and relatively little actual empirical legal research has *aspired* to be scientific in this way. To put it simply: a great deal of legal research with an empirical dimension has been oriented towards policy, or law reform, or other kinds of immediate practical decision making. Many such enquiries are particular rather than general, not illuminated by theory, do not claim to be explanatory or predictive, and their findings do not accumulate.[157] There is also a strong resistance to 'scientism' in some enclaves of academic legal culture.[158]

Is genuinely scientific research into law possible? Some think not, but there are others who are committed to such an aspiration. My personal bias is towards the vision of Italo Calvino, who emphasised the complexities and elusiveness of 'the real world', while accepting a clear distinction between what is (ontology) and our apprehension of it (epistemology).[159] That position is quite different from those 'post-modernists' and 'post-structuralists' who collapse or blur this distinction.[160] That position does not involve a denial that an empirical science of law is possible, in the sense that some explanatory, falsifiable, predictive empirical generalisations about some legal phenomena are feasible. In my view, this is an admirable aspiration, but we are a long way from attaining it. Not only do we lack global analytic concepts and data of the kind and quality required, but we have a meagre stock of precise, refined, testable general hypotheses that have the potential to be developed into evidence-based

---

[155] This is just one model of 'science' (see Black (1995)). On cumulation and progress in science, see Haack's cautionary observations at (2003) pp. 143–5.

[156] See Haack (2003) at p. 58.

[157] The hostility of some sociologists of law to policy-oriented studies and government-generated data is sometimes overdone. Policy and practical decisions and project evaluations need to be based on *reliable* data; not all official statistics and data banks are compiled with short-term goals in mind; and knowledge does not need to be 'scientific' to be useful and important (see above). In my view, the sharpness of distinctions between 'pure' and 'applied', policy-oriented and scientific enquiries is often exaggerated. For example: 'There is … an increasing tendency for empiricist, policy-oriented research to present itself as sociology of law. There is, however, nothing sociological about this literature, since it does not address wider questions about the role of law in society' (Banakar and Travers (2002) at p. 346. Those who share the scientific aspiration have to face hostility from several directions: that it is not law; that it is not practical, that it is 'positivistic' or 'empiricist' in some derogatory sense.

[158] On justified and unjustified resistance to 'scientism' see Chapter 16.4 on the web.

[159] This issue is explored at length in the essay on 'Santos, Calvino, and Haack' in *GLT*, Chapter 8 (reprinted in *GJB*, Chapter 9).

[160] 'Post-structuralism' is a vague term that includes 'post-modernism' and interpretive, critical, and relativist perspectives that reject simplistic (often caricatured) versions of 'empiricism'. For an interesting interpretation see Banakar and Travers (2002), section 5.

generalisations that would satisfy the kinds of standards required of an empirical science.

It is one of the tasks of general jurisprudence, and of social theory generally to construct such hypotheses. There is a continuous tradition within academic law, as well as in some social sciences, which has aspired to be genuinely 'scientific' in this way. This is different from 'dogmatic legal science' in the civil law tradition that is doctrinal rather than empirical.[161] It is also different from empirical enquiries that have more modest or local aims. There are many genuine scholars who have different aspirations (e.g. in legal history and legal anthropology). As we have seen, there are those who consider an empirical science of law to be misconceived and many more who respond to the 'pull of the policy audience',[162] or other demands that legal scholarship should be directly relevant to immediate practical concerns.

On the whole the culture and economic base of academic law is not very hospitable to the enterprise of developing an empirical science of law. However, there is a minority tradition, both within the discipline of law and in sociology, criminology, and some other enclaves of social science, that has persistently pursued empirical truth about legal phenomena in the scientific spirit. The efforts of the 'scientific' wing of American Legal Realism, especially in the 1920s and 1930s are well-documented.[163] So, too are some enclaves of criminology. Others, such as SLADE, are less well-known. Some ambitious efforts, the Johns Hopkins Institute, the Chicago jury, arbitration, and tax projects, as well as SLADE, like Moore's notorious parking studies, have been written off as 'failures'. A more charitable interpretation is that both sponsors and critics have underestimated the enormity of the task of developing an empirical science.[164]

There are several kinds of empirical work that continue this tradition. I am more persuaded by John Griffiths' carefully crafted hypotheses about the social working of legal rules[165] than by Donald Black's ultra positivist approach to the

---

[161] John Merryman (1974), while arguing for 'The Explanatory Approach' to comparative law, gave a sympathetic and illuminating account of this tradition, but concluded that this approach 'is largely discredited in Europe and elsewhere in the civil law world.' (*Ibid.* at p. 99.) On one interpretation, Kelsen's Pure Theory of Law, often cited as the foundation of a dogmatic 'legal science', can be used to show that such an aspiration is misconceived, because 'impurities' are inevitably involved in any exposition of substantive law (Tur and Twining (1986) Introduction).

[162] Sarat and Silbey (1988).

[163] *KLRM*, Chapters 3 and 4 and pp. 188–96. Different interpretations are advanced by Kalman (1986) and Schlegel (1995).

[164] This is the argument developed in *KLRM* in respect of the 'scientific' Realists.

[165] In an important article on 'The social working of legal rules' (Griffiths (2003)), John Griffiths sets out to explore rule-following behaviour from a detailed 'bottom up' perspective on 'the shop floor' of 'semi-autonomous social fields' (following Moore (1978)). The central idea is whether and how one rule is followed is 'to a very important degree a matter of how other rules bear on the situation' (at p. 75). With appealing modesty, Griffiths acknowledges that he has only got to the stage of establishing a point of departure for the formulation of propositions for a testable explanatory theory 'that makes it possible to predict and explain the social working of legislation [and other legal rules]' (*ibid.*, p. 74). In other words, after thirty years he has begun to formulate a testable general hypothesis. He has developed and applied this hypothesis in his work on

scientific study of 'the behavior of law'[166] or recent macro-level attempts to explore correlations between legal traditions and economic development.[167] The validity and viability of these and other enterprises involve issues that are too complex to pursue here. What brings them together is intellectual ambition to pursue large issues in a scientific spirit. These aspirations deserve encouragement and support. However, a central theme in this chapter has been that a necessary condition for the healthy development of an empirical science of law is a significant increase of interest in legal phenomena on the part of social scientists.

8.10 Conclusion

In 1995/6 Lawrence Friedman stated that transnational socio-legal studies were still in their infancy.[168] In 2005, he published a paper entitled 'Law and Society Comes of Age'.[169] Friedman was not contradicting himself, nor had he changed his mind, for he was writing mainly about Law and Society research in the United States. The focus of most empirical legal research is still local, and rightly so, but it is increasingly informed by ideas, insights, findings and fashions from other parts of the world. The empirical legal community is also responding to 'globalisation' in diverse ways, as is illustrated by the programme of Berlin 2007. The responses are not co-ordinated, for most involve extension of the geographical reach of specialised fields. The following examples of some of the transnational socio-legal writing that has reached me during the past few weeks further illustrate the point: a symposium on transitional justice;[170]

euthanasia (Griffiths *et al.*, 2008). Griffiths' conception has affinities with, but is different from, Hart's distinction between primary and secondary rules and with Galligan's notion of 'social spheres' in which rules operate (Galligan (2007) Chapters 2 and 6). In the process of developing his argument, Griffiths strengthens his critique of 'instrumentalism', but modifies his prior thesis that legal rules should not be treated as independent variables: 'The continuities between "legal" and "non-legal" rules are thus more manifold and more profound than one had realized' and a neat distinction between rules as dependent and as independent variables is 'ill-conceived' (*Ibid.*, at p. 1 (abstract)). It is not possible in short compass to do justice to this rich and potentially very significant thesis. On the movement to integrate economic analysis with informal social norms see Ellickson (1998).

[166] For more than thirty years Donald Black has advanced a theory of 'how law behaves', that conceives of law as governmental social control that can be studied in terms of observable, measurable behaviour without reference to rules or the internal point of view. (Black (1976), (1989), (1993), (1995)). The aim is to measure correlations between 'the behavior of law' and other observable social phenomena (e.g in respect of stratification and culture in order to achieve generalisations that will predict future patterns and developments). This approach is strongly 'positivist' in denying any room for evaluation, explicit interpretation, or even explanation. Accordingly, it is highly controversial, but has attracted a significant following (see Symposium on 'Donald Black and the Sociology of Law' (1995)).

[167] See e.g La Porta *et al.* (1996) (1998), (1999), Dam (2006a), (2006b). For criticisms, see e.g. Siems (2005) and Roe (2006)

[168] Friedman (1996).

[169] Friedman, 'Law and Society Comes of Age' (2005). This was an overview of the field for the first volume of the *Annual Review of Law and Social Science*.

[170] Bell *et al.* (2007).

a volume of socio-legal essays on the practice of human rights;[171] an empirical study of self-regulation of the Internet;[172] an ethnographic study of the culture of human rights activists in Scandinavia;[173] a comparative overview of studies of different degrees of harshness of punishments;[174] and a survey of trends in family relations and family law in Europe.[175] This is in addition to numerous studies of how legal institutions actually work, of how laws get made, of processes and patterns of diffusion, and rather fewer on the elusive topic of 'impact' – what difference some piece of legislation or other change in the law made on people's behaviour or attitudes.[176]

The transnationalisation of the field has been quite uneven: a few specialised areas (e.g. criminology, regulation, studies of legal professions) are relatively well developed;[177] others, such as empirical comparative law and private law, rather less so. For a long time, feminist jurisprudence and gender-oriented socio-legal work seemed quite slow to move out beyond national boundaries, but since the Beijing Conference of 1995 this has changed rapidly.[178] Similarly, there has recently been a rapid growth of empirical work on the enforcement of and reactions to the steady growth of the international regime of human rights and the proliferation of domestic bills of rights.[179] The tensions between Western feminist and human rights ideas and traditional religious and customary regimes under which women are or appear to be disadvantaged is likely to be a major political and theoretical focus of attention in the coming years.[180] So, too, are studies of the gender dimensions of transitional justice, genocide, and war.[181]

On the basis of the foregoing, I suggest that for the healthy development of studies of the empirical dimensions of law and justice as part of a cosmopolitan discipline of law, five conditions need to be met:

First, a disciplinary culture, which at its core recognises the importance of empirical work and integrates it into both specialised fields and different levels of theory.

---

[171] Goodale and Merry (eds.) (2007).   [172] Mifsud Bonnici (2007).

[173] Halme (2007); See now Halme (2008).   [174] Whitman (2005).   [175] Antokolskaia (2007).

[176] See Friedman (2005) at pp. 2–3. Environmental law is the area in which the conceptual and other difficulties of assessing impact is most developed. See e.g. Holder (2004).

[177] After criminology, regulation is perhaps the most theoretically developed field of socio-legal studies. A number of regulatory models have been distinguished: command and control, collective laissez faire, enforced collective regulation, rights-based approaches and 'reflexive regulation'. (Ayres and Braithwaite (1992)). Reflexive regulation is explained by Scott as follows: 'this approach recognizes the "inner logic" of social systems and sets law the challenge of seeking to steer those social systems. A key aspect of this approach is re-casting the function of law from direct control to proceduralization.' (Scott (2004) at p.151 cited by McCrudden (2007) at p. 259). For a survey of regulatory approaches see Morgan and Yeung (2007).

[178] See e.g. Nussbaum and Glover (eds.) (1995), Cook (ed.) (1994), Okin (1999), Nussbaum (2000), Wing (2000), Stewart (2009 – forthcoming).

[179] See n. 143 above.

[180] For an example of the tendency of some non-lawyers to make sweeping condemnations of customary law and tradition mainly on the grounds of gender discrimination, (but also as perceived barriers to development) see, e.g. Mackinnon (2006) discussed at Chapter 11.6 below.

[181] See, e.g., Bell *et al.*, (2007).

Second, recognition that empirically oriented, evidence-based comparative legal studies are central to understanding legal phenomena. Globalisation is a great stimulus to comparison, which is a first step on the road to sound generalisation. However, we still lack well-developed methodologies for comparing legal phenomena and adequate concepts and data for making well-grounded generalisations about them.

Third, the culture and economic base of academic law generally tends to be particularistic, participant-oriented, and concerned with immediate practicalities of problem-solving and short-term decision making. This is likely to continue, but a balance needs to be struck between practical and theoretical, short-term and long-term, and 'pure' and applied enquiries.[182]

Fourth, the study of law cannot thrive as a monopoly of lawyers and jurists. Because of the third point, it is especially important that scholars in neighbouring disciplines in the social sciences and beyond should be more persuaded than they have been that law is pervasive, interesting and important, and that there are significant legal dimensions to many of their concerns.

Fifth, the development of a genuinely scientific social science of law – informed by theory, evidence-based, generalisable, explanatory, cumulative and predictive – is one important aspiration of legal scholarship. For the most part, we are still at a pre-pre-science stage, as Karl Llewellyn called it in 1941;[183] but he added: 'Knowledge … does not have to be scientific to be useful and important'.[184]

What is the role of theory in relation to these developments? If it is true that the main responses to globalisation and the momentum for change come mainly from within specialised fields, then we can expect that scholarly practice will tend to outrun legal theory. However, there are still the basic jobs of jurisprudence: elucidating and refining useful concepts; constructing syntheses; critical development of general normative principles; framing and refining hypotheses and middle other theories; constructing working theories, intellectual history; and building bridges between disciplines.[185] There is the additional task of persuading colleagues in other disciplines of the significance of law.[186] This book has stressed the need for more usable concepts, well-rounded data, and interpretive frameworks to provide a basis for comparison and generalisation. It has also emphasised the continuities between analytical, normative, and empirical theorising. There is a place for 'grand theory' as Glenn, Tamanaha, and Santos have demonstrated with their pioneering efforts.[187] But the most important task for jurists remains the critical examination of assumptions and presuppositions underlying legal

---

[182] See Preface above.   [183] Llewellyn (1941) at p. 13.
[184] Llewellyn (1941) at pp. 20–25, especially p. 22, discussed in *KLRM* at pp. 188–96.
[185] *GLT*, p. 189.   [186] On 'the case for law' see Chapter 11.3(d) below.
[187] On Santos see *GLT*, Chapter 8; on Glenn see Chapter 3.4;. On Tamanaha see Chapter 4 above.

discourses, not just the abstract discourses of other theorists, but the specialised discourses of particular fields and subjects. This applies as much to
comparative law and particular enclaves of empirical legal studies as to
expositions of doctrines of municipal law (e.g. contract theory), international
law,[188] and transnational legal processes.[189]

---

[188] On recent critical appraisals of international law theory see p. 10 above.
[189] Likosky (2002). Chapter 9 is presented here as an example of critical analysis in relation to
orthodox talk about transplantation, reception, or diffusion of law.

Part B

Chapter 9

Diffusion of law: A global perspective[1]

9.1 Mapping law: a naïve model of diffusion

> Renewing initiatives stand as a starting point. They bring new needs and new satisfactions to the world, then spread or tend to do so through forced or spontaneous, chosen or unconscious, quick or slow imitation, always responding to a regular pace, as a light wave or a family of termites. (Gabriel Tarde 1979, p. 3)

In my early years of teaching in Khartoum in the late 1950s, I used to teach a first year course called 'Introduction to Law'. In order to set a context for the study of the Sudan Legal System, I began by presenting my students with a map of law in the world as a whole.[2] This map suggested that almost every country belonged either to the common or civil law family. It indicated that some civil law countries were socialist (this was the period of the Cold War) and that many countries, mainly colonies and ex-colonies, recognised religious and customary law for limited purposes, mainly in respect of personal law, such as family and inheritance.

This simple map served a useful purpose in setting a broad context for the study of Sudanese law, in interpreting legal patterns in Cold War terms, and especially in emphasising the impact of colonialism on the diffusion of law. It explained, but did not purport to justify, why we were mainly studying English-based law. It also identified the Sudan legal system as an example of state legal pluralism, and it provided a starting point for discussing the future development of local law.

Today that map would look primitive, partly because the world has changed in fifty years, but mainly because it was based on assumptions that were dubious

[1] This is a revised version of an essay which was originally published in 49 *Journal of Legal Pluralism* 1–45 (2004). It is reproduced here by kind permission of the editor and publisher. This essay builds on and extends themes developed in Twining 2000a, GLT, 2001; 2002b, 2003b. A sequel to this paper, on 'Social science and diffusion of law' was published later (Twining 2005a). Much of the research for this paper was undertaken at the Center for Advanced Study in the Behavioral Sciences at Stanford in 1999–2000. I am grateful for the wonderful support of the staff of the Center and for advice on the historical and social science literature from Carol Gluck, Harvey Molotch, and David Snow. I am also grateful for helpful comments from Deirdre Dwyer, Trisha Greenhalgh, John Griffiths, David Nelken, Esin Örücü, David Westbrook, Gordon Woodman, and participants in events at the Centre for Socio-legal Studies (Oxford), the Harvard Law School, the University of Westminster, and the University of Groningen.

[2] For a more detailed account see Twining (2000a) at p. 142ff.

even then. For example, in orthodox terms, as a depiction of municipal state legal systems it could be said to have exaggerated the importance of the civil law/common law divide; it underplayed the differences between legal systems within the common law and Romanist traditions; it had a private law bias; and it paid too little attention to hybrid systems.

My map depicted all the national legal systems of the world as belonging more or less fully to either the common law or the civil law 'families', largely from the perspective of exporters. This was a picture that assumed massive transplantation. But, in addition to being naïve about what I was mapping, I accepted uncritically an equally naïve model of legal receptions. We can reconstruct this as an ideal type of a reception based on some widely held assumptions, even if the model as a whole would be recognised as much too simple by most sophisticated scholars of diffusion of law.

A standard example might take the following form: In 1868 Country A imported from Country B a statute, a code, or body of legal doctrine and this has remained in force ever since.[3] If this example is taken as a paradigm case and generalised up into an ideal type it can be shown to contain a number of questionable assumptions and some significant omissions. It assumes that:

(a) there was an *identifiable exporter and importer*;
(b) the standard case of a reception is export-import between *countries*;
(c) the typical process of reception involves a *direct one-way transfer* from country A to country B;
(d) the main *objects* of a reception are legal rules and concepts;
(e) the main *agents* of export and import are *governments*;
(f) reception involves *formal* enactment or adoption *at a particular moment of time*;
(g) the object of reception *retains its identity without significant change* after the date of reception.

Other common, but by no means universal assumptions, include the following:

(h) the standard case is export by a *civil law or common law 'parent'* legal system to a less developed *dependent (e.g. colonial)* or adolescent *(e.g. 'transitional')* legal system;
(i) that most instances of reception are *technical* rather than political, typically involving 'lawyers' law';[4]

---

[3] This is an example of a 'small-scale' reception, but most of the assumptions also apply to standard accounts of 'large scale' receptions.

'There is agreement, however, that the phrase "legal transplants" refers to the movement of legal norms or specific laws from one state to another during the process of law making or legal reform'.
(Mistelis (2000) at p. 1067, discussing Watson and Kahn-Freund and their protagonists)

[4] On the vulnerable, but not entirely meaningless, concept of 'lawyers' law' see Twining (1957) (my first effort to sort out some of the puzzlements generated by my map).

(j) that the received law either *fills a legal vacuum or replaces* prior (typically outdated or traditional) law.[5]

Each of these assumptions has been challenged individually in the literature, usually without reference to social science sources. Nevertheless, these assumptions are still widespread in legal thought and discourse about receptions/transplants and they exert a constricting, and sometimes a distorting influence and reinforce the tendency to make unfounded generalisations. Yet there clearly are patterns relating to law that can be discerned. The problem is first, to identify patterns that are not false, superficial or misleading and, second, to explain them. This is what the study of diffusion of law sets out to do.

Since 1959 the study of diffusion of law has proceeded under many labels including reception, transplants, spread, expansion, transfer, exports and imports, imposition, circulation, transmigration, transposition, and trans-frontier mobility of law.[6] In this chapter I shall use the term 'diffusion' to cover all of these in order to underline its potential connection with the study of diffusion in other social sciences. The literature contains many valuable studies and some rather unsatisfactory polemics. My thesis is that the study of diffusion of law has been handicapped by a set of widely held assumptions that are shared with my primitive map and that, in an era of globalisation, we need a broader and much more complex picture and a flexible methodology as a basis for studying the processes of diffusion and their outcomes. A sequel to this paper argues that, although legal diffusion studies had shared origins in nineteenth-century anthropology and sociology; they have lost touch with the massive body of literature in other social sciences dealing with diffusion of innovations and of language, religion, sport, and music. The time is ripe for contact to be renewed.[7]

---

[5] Most of these assumptions are closely related to 'the Country and Western Tradition' of comparative law, an ideal type which until recently fitted much of the discourse, but by no means all of the practice, of mainstream Western comparative law (see p. 101 above). As we shall see, not all the leading accounts of diffusion of law belong to that tradition.

[6] On the various metaphors used in connection with diffusion see Nelken and Feest (2001) at pp. 15–20 and Örücü (2002). These terms are not all synonyms. In particular, some focus on the original source (export, transfer, spread, transmigration, diffusion, diaspora), while others direct attention to the recipient (reception, import, transposition). In ordinary usage 'diffusion' may imply the former, but I shall use it as a generic term to cover both perspectives, as it does in standard social science discourse: 'Diffusion is the most general and abstract term we have for this sort of process, embracing contagion, mimicry, social learning, organized dissemination, and other family members' (Strang and Soule (1998) at p. 266). However, one needs to be aware of the 'exporter' bias in much of the literature. In economic analysis there has been a contrast between adoption perspectives focusing mainly on the demand side (individuals choosing to adopt) and market and infrastructure perspectives (placing more emphasis on structures, opportunities, marketing, and supply). (Brown 2001). In the context of medical research, Greenhalgh *et al.* (2004) usefully distinguish between 'diffusion' (informal spread) and 'dissemination' (planned spread) as two points on a spectrum that extends from natural spread ('let it happen') to managerial change ('make it happen').

[7] Twining (2005a).

Legal systems and legal traditions have interacted throughout history. Indeed, isolation has been quite exceptional.[8] So it is hardly surprising that themes concerning interaction and influence among legal systems and traditions are often dealt with as part of broader concerns within legal history, comparative law, law reform, law and development, post-conflict reconstruction, transitional justice, legal theory, sociology of law, and so on.[9] In focusing on the history or characteristics of a particular legal system or tradition, concentrating on outside influence can be as sterile as a search for origins in history or for 'influence' in literature or art.[10] It may also lead to too much emphasis on the exporter, or to over-concentration on particular moments of time (such as a 'reception date'), and it may direct attention away from prior and subsequent events and interactions.

The famous Otieno burial case in Kenya is an example of concern that foreign influence can obfuscate issues that are mainly local. The case concerned a dispute over burial rights between the Kikuyu widow of a leading Nairobi lawyer and members of his Luo clan in 1987.[11] The widow claimed the right to bury her husband in their matrimonial home near Nairobi, the clan claimed that he should be buried in his true home, the clan's burial ground in Nyalgunga. The case involved clashes of interest, perception and values between rural and urban, traditional and modern, women and patriarchy, as well as colonial v indigenous law. Those who emphasised the colonial origins of state inheritance law obscured the fact that this was a struggle between Kenyans, some of whom supported imported national law because it was, in their view,

---

[8] Glenn suggests that there are no pure legal systems in the world (citing P. Arminjon *et al.* (1950) at p. 49). He continues: 'The mixed character of all jurisdictions is camouflaged today, however, by state institutions, taxonomic comparative law methodology which establishes distinct "families" of law, by nationalist historiography which emphasizes that which may be distinctive in national legal systems. To say that all jurisdictions are mixed is not to accede, however, to environmentalist or diffusionist theories of cultural variety or to engage in any way in causal explanations of the phenomena' (Glenn (1987) at pp. 264–65n.). On the interaction of common law and civil law see Reimann (ed.) (1993).

[9] A good example is the seminal comparative study by Pistor and Wellons (1999) of law in six Asian economies from 1960 to 1995, a period of remarkable economic growth. While the focus was on the role of law in economic development, it incidentally led to some significant observations on 'transplants':

> A key finding of this research project therefore is that law and legal institutions should not be viewed as technical tools that once adopted will produce the desired outcome…The finding cautions against the blind transplantation of legal institutions without due consideration for the relevant economic framework within which they shall operate. It also suggests that law reform projects should not be assessed in isolation, but within a broader context of economic policies. (Pistor and Wellons (1999) at p. 19.)

[10] This account is in tune with the conclusion of a useful article by Edward M. Wise: 'The international dimension of legal culture constitutes one of the contexts in which legal change occurs. But merely describing the itineraries of legal thought cannot be expected to explain such change'. (Wise (1990) at p. 22).

[11] The case attracted a great deal of public attention at the time and has generated an extensive literature including Ojwang and Mugambi (1989), Cohen and Atieno (1992), and Van Doren (1988). For further references, see Manji (2002).

more suited to modern urban lifestyles or because it challenged patriarchal elements in a tradition that was depicted as quintessentially African. Similarly, in 'the Asian values debate', those who defend the cause of human rights and democracy in Asia typically treat the origins of the contemporary international human rights regime and discourse as irrelevant. It is one thing to oppose Western hegemony, it is quite another to decry the justification of freedom and democracy because of its 'Western' associations and origins.[12]

9.2 Some landmarks in the study of diffusion of law[13]

For some purposes it makes sense to focus on diffusion. When that has happened the underlying concerns, the perspectives and methods adopted, and the immediate historical context have been quite diverse. The literature on diffusion of law does not belong to a single research tradition.[14] This can be illustrated by taking a brief look at some of the landmarks in the study of legal diffusion as such.

Reception studies by lawyers are extensive and quite varied. Historically they can be traced back to the writings of Gabriel Tarde, Sir Henry Maine, and Max Weber.[15] Diffusionism represented a reaction against the prevailing nineteenth-century view that there were natural laws of evolution governing human progress. To start with there was a close connection with diffusion theory in cultural anthropology, but law soon faded into the background. Since World War II there have been a number of landmarks, stimulated by rather different concerns. First, there are studies of the 'Reception' of Roman Law in medieval Europe, exemplified by the classic works of Koschaker[16] and Wieacker,[17] and debates that these have stimulated. Second, there are accounts of the importation or imposition of the laws by colonising powers.[18] Such studies overlap with the literature of legal pluralism and law and development. Third, a good deal of attention has been focused on largely exceptional

---

[12] See Chapter 6.5(e) above.

[13] Highlights of the legal literature are surveyed in more detail in Twining (2005a).

[14] Trisha Greenhalgh usefully suggests that much of the social science literature on diffusion of innovations does belong to a single research tradition, which went through several phases, despite being located in several different branches of sociology (Greenhalgh (2004); see Greenhalgh et al. (2005)).

[15] Less well know is Bentham's early essay on *Place and Time in Matters of Legislation* the full manuscript of which has recently been edited by Philip Schofield. This presents an incisive, export-oriented analysis of the conditions that a 'legislator of the world' must confront in introducing foreign models. See Chapter 5.4(d) above.

[16] Koschaker (1953). Paul Koschaker's best known thesis, taken up by many subsequent writers, was that the reception of Roman law in Central Europe and the spread of the Code Napoleon were more a matter of imperial power and prestige than of superior technical quality. See Zweigert and Kötz (1998), p. 100.

[17] Wieacker (1981), (1990), (1967/1995) discussed in Whitman (1995).

[18] For example, Burman and Harrell-Bond (1979), Chanock (1985). The term 'imposition' is sometimes criticised as being too vague in this context, because nearly all influence takes place in the context of relative disparities of power.

'voluntary' receptions, especially in Japan and Turkey and, to a lesser extent, Ethiopia. In this regard, the work of Esin Örücü, on Turkey is outstanding.[19] Fourth, there is Alan Watson's general 'transplants thesis', his debate with Otto Kahn-Freund, and the literature that these have provoked.[20] And, recently there has been a pronounced revival of both academic and practical interest in relation to law reform and harmonisation as part of European integration, structural adjustment programmes in developing countries, reconstruction in 'countries in transition' in Eastern Europe, and post-conflict reconstruction.[21] This interest has arisen from a variety of concerns in a variety of contexts and again, in many instances, discussion of reception or transplants has been incidental to some broader issues.

Much, but not all, of the literature has focused on relatively large-scale receptions – the reception of Roman law in medieval Europe, the 'spread of the common law', the importation of a series of codes in Turkey or Latin America. This may partly explain the lack of interdisciplinary contact, for much of the modern sociological literature has been concerned with more detailed examination of the pathways and processes of diffusion of particular products, techniques or ideas.[22]

If these are some of the main landmarks of scholarly and theoretical work that has made diffusion of law a special focus of attention, there clearly is not one single, continuous research tradition. Rather the historical context of each of these disparate examples belongs to the largely separate histories of loosely related academic specialisms: cultural anthropology (diffusionism); Roman law and legal history (Wieaker); comparative law (Kahn-Freund; Örücü; Legrand (1997)) and legal pluralism (Chiba); recently major academic contributions have come via systems theory (Teubner), sociology of law (Cotterrell, Nelken), historical jurisprudence (Glenn), European integration (Allison, Legrand) and law and development (Dezalay and Garth, Pistor and Wellons). In this context, Alan Watson seems like a wild card defying categorisation.[23]

Whereas the concerns of the early diffusionists and legal scholars such as Wieacker, Watson, Glenn and Örücü have been almost entirely academic, some of these recent developments raise questions of immediate practicality: policy makers in international financial institutions want to know why 'transplants'

---

[19] Örücü (1995, 1996a, 1999, 2000, 2002, 2004).

[20] Watson (1974). Kahn-Freund (1974), Watson (1976). Watson has continued to elaborate on the theme: his most recent variations include Watson (2000a) and (2000b) (reply to Legrand). See also Watson (2007). On whether Watson's thesis deals only with surface law, see Chapter 10.1 at pp. 295–6 below.

[21] For example in Rwanda, Sierra Leone, Afghanistan, Iraq and, in some ways *sui generis*, post-Apartheid South Africa.

[22] Rogers (1995).

[23] Wieaker (1981), (1990), (1995); Kahn-Freund (1974); Örücü especially (1992), (1996a), (2000) see also n. 19 above; Legrand (1997), (1999b); Chiba (1986), (1989), (1998); Teubner (1992), (1996a), (1996b); Cotterrell (1997); Nelken (1997), Glenn (2004); Allison (1996); Dezalay and Garth (2002a), (2002b); Pistor and Wellons (1999).

have regularly been perceived to have failed and what are the conditions for, and how to measure, 'success' of reforms involving importation or imposition of foreign models (questions discussed below in Section 4); local reformers want to know what factors to take into account when choosing between alternative models (when they are given a choice); judges want guidance on when it is appropriate to treat foreign precedents and other sources as persuasive authority; [24] resisters want to learn about the most effective strategies and techniques for lessening the impact or adapting unwelcome imports to local conditions and so on. One feature of some of these developments is that an increasing number of reform efforts have been put out to tender to private organisations that have little interest in the academic debates, especially where they emphasise the uniqueness of local cultures and long time-scales.[25]

There is now a huge amount of information, case studies, and fresh perspectives that is too important to ignore. All of these developments have put the assumptions in the naïve model under increasing strain. Not surprisingly, nearly all of the practical reform efforts focus on municipal law. Some of the more theoretical work of Teubner, Glenn, Chiba, and others ranges more widely. Individual assumptions have been challenged, but not in a systematic way.

9.3 A global perspective: diffusion, levels of law, and interlegality

When I constructed my map in the late 1950s, I unthinkingly adopted a global perspective. As part of post-war reconstruction, there was at the time a good deal of talk of 'World Peace through World Law', 'the Common Law of Mankind', 'world citizenship' and even 'transnational law'. However, sustained focus on 'globalisation' was still some way off.[26] Since then the world has changed, law has changed, and so have our perceptions of both. Looking at diffusion of law from a global perspective inevitably assumes some mental map or total picture of law in the world. But clearly we need something a bit more sophisticated than my first effort in Khartoum.

In Chapter 3 I argued that a reasonably inclusive cosmopolitan discipline of law needs to encompass all levels of legal ordering, relations between these levels, and all-important forms of law including supra-state (e.g. international, regional) and non-state law and various forms of 'soft law' and legal orders. If one adopts a broad conception of law and treats levels of law and strong legal

---

[24] Glenn (2004) at 230n; Slaughter (1994); Fontana (2001); McCrudden (2007).

[25] Taylor (2007).

[26] Significant works of the period include Jenks (1958), Jessup (1956), Northrop (1960), and L. Jonathan Cohen (1954). In the early 1960s I attended some meetings organised in Chicago by the Council for the Study of Mankind. During the early years of the Cold War the International Commission of Jurists promoted the Rule of Law and civil and political rights (e.g The Act of Athens 1955) in counterpoint with the International Association of Democratic Lawyers, who supported anti-imperialist movements and social and economic rights.

pluralism as significant ideas, this has important implications for the study of diffusion. Nearly all accounts of reception or transplantation of law focus on municipal law – legal phenomena originating in one nation state or jurisdiction being imposed on, imported to, or adapted by another. The reception of Roman law in medieval Europe is a significant exception. Of course, there are contexts in which it is reasonable to focus on interactions between two or more systems of municipal law (country–country relations). But if one is concerned with legal ordering at all levels from the very local to the intergalactic, including non-state local, regional, transnational, and diasporic then clearly borrowing, blending, and other forms of interaction can take place at all levels and between different levels; interaction can be vertical, horizontal, diagonal, or involve more complex pathways.

Cross-level diffusion deserves more attention. Consider, for example, the paths through which one would need to trace the origins of the UK Human Rights Act, 1998. It is a story of complex borrowing from theories of human rights, public international law, national laws, and the specific ideas of a British draftsman (David Maxwell Fyfe) followed by fifty years in Strasbourg, interaction with legal systems of the Council of Europe, then back to London, Edinburgh and Belfast.[27] Similarly, Santos' account of Pasagarda law shows how the internal regime of a squatter settlement in Rio adopted and adapted some of the legal forms and legal vocabulary of the 'asphalt law' (i.e. the official state law of Brazil).[28] The Vienna Sales Convention of 1980 and other international instruments draw from a variety of national laws, blend them with other materials, and then in turn have influenced municipal laws.[29]

Such examples highlight the close link between normative and legal pluralism on the one hand and diffusion on the other. When normative and legal orders co-exist in the same context of time and space there is always the prospect of more or less sustained interaction between them. Diffusion is generally considered to take place when one legal order, system or tradition *influences* another in some significant way. 'Influence' – a notoriously vague notion – is only one kind of interaction, what Santos usefully refers to as 'interlegality'.[30] So it may be illuminating to conceive of diffusion of law as one aspect of interlegality.[31]

In the early days of the study of legal pluralism there was a tendency to think of co-existing legal orders in oppositional terms – as conflicting or competing.[32]

---

[27] Simpson (2001).   [28] Santos (2002), Chapter 3. See p. 73 above.

[29] Goode (1998), Chapter 4, II.

[30] Of course, talk of interlegality, interaction, and influence between legal orders raises difficult issues of individuation, on which see Sally Falk Moore ('semi-autonomous legal fields') (Moore (1978) at pp. 54–81) and Tamanaha (2001) at pp. 206–8. See further Chapter 15.4 on the web.

[31] Santos (2002) at pp. 437 and 90–1, discussed Twining (2007).

[32] Antony Allott interpreted the interaction between customary law and imported law in Africa mainly in terms of 'internal conflicts of law' (i.e. choice of law) on an analogy with private international law (Allott 1970, Part II).

But that is a mistake. Rather, the possible kinds of relations between co-existing legal orders can be extraordinarily diverse: they may complement each other; the relationship may be one of co-operation, co-optation, competition, subordination, or stable symbiosis; the orders may converge, assimilate, merge, repress, imitate, echo, or avoid each other. To take just one example: Santos' account of Pasagarda law at first sight looks like an account of an illegal legal system, usurping or subverting or competing with the official law of the state. On closer examination the relationship was much more complex than that: unofficial peaceful ordering of relations and settlement of disputes may complement rather than challenge official modes of ordering. Santos describes relations between the Pasagarda Residents Association and state agencies as constantly shifting and 'a model of ambiguity'. The relations with the police were especially complex: on the whole the community avoided the police; the police offered their 'good services' to the Residents Association, who, anxious not to become closely identified with them, acknowledged the offer, occasionally used the police as a threat, but only exceptionally actually co-operated with them. From the point of view of the state authorities the existence of an alternative locus of power and authority may be interpreted as a threat, a challenge, or a convenience. [33]

9.4 Beyond the naïve model: some counter-assumptions

In discussing my early map, I suggested that it presupposed a naïve model of reception that included some dubious assumptions and treated something like the following as a simple paradigm case of a small-scale reception: In 1868 Country A imported from Country B a statute, a code, or body of legal doctrine and this has remained in force ever since.

This example involves a *bipolar* relationship between *two countries* involving a *direct one-way* transfer of *legal rules or institutions* through the agency of *governments* involving *formal enactment or adoption* at a particular moment in time (*a reception date*) *without major change*. Although not explicitly stated in this example, it is commonly assumed that the standard case involves *transfer from an advanced (parent) civil or common law system to a less developed one*, in order to bring about *technological change* ('to modernise') by *filling in gaps or replacing* prior local law. There is also considerable vagueness about the criteria for 'success' of a reception – one common assumption seems to be that if it has survived for a significant period *'it works'*.

If one constructs these elements into an 'ideal type', we can see that the mainstream literature on diffusion of law allows for some deviations from this

---

[33] Santos (2002) Chapter 4; See also 'No-go areas' in Belfast and other cities. John Griffiths rightly warns against reifying levels and relations when discussing interlegality: from a sociological point of view, the focus should be concretely on people doing things (communication to author, Sept., 2004). See also Griffiths (2003).

model and makes some important distinctions between types of reception and of transplants.[34] Nevertheless, all of these assumptions are widespread. In particular, nearly all of the literature treats diffusion of law as involving relations between municipal legal systems through the agency of governments. If one adopts a global perspective and a broad conception of law operating at different levels of relations and of ordering, and if one conceives of diffusion of law as an aspect of interlegality, one can construct a systematic challenge to each of these elements as a necessary or even a characteristic feature of diffusion of law. This suggests that a much more varied and complex picture of diffusion of law and interlegality needs to be constructed. The alternative picture that emerges cannot be captured by a single polar 'ideal type'; rather it is a series of possible variants to each of the elements in the simple model. Table 1 (opposite) illustrates this without claiming to be comprehensive.

In order to clarify and to illustrate this table, it may be useful to comment on each of the elements and to provide some examples. Some are familiar and can be dealt with briefly, but others require more extended treatment. Three preliminary points deserve emphasis: first, my purpose is to illustrate some of the complexities of the diffusion of law and to suggest a method of analysis of the processes involved; it is not to set up a single alternative model. The subject is too complex for that. Second, much of this analysis applies even if one adopts a narrower conception of law than I have suggested, or if one is mainly concerned with diffusion of state law. Third, taken singly, most of the points are not new and I shall use examples that are to be found in the mainstream literature to illustrate them. The object is to construct a systematic picture of the complexities.

(a) Sources

The sources of importation are often diverse. The standard colonial and neo-colonial situation postulates a single exporting country imposing legal rules or institutions on a single importer. But the process is often more complex than that. For example, an importer may choose eclectically from several foreign sources, as Turkey did deliberately in the case of its various codes so as not to be beholden to any one European country. What is imported may be an idea or model that did not originate in a single legal order (e.g. when instruments of harmonisation, such as the American Restatements, Uniform Laws and Model

---

[34] Within the mainstream literature a number of important distinctions are fairly standard: (i) large scale/small scale receptions; (ii) voluntary/imposed receptions; (iii) socio-cultural affinity or diversity between exporter and importer (see Rogers (1995) distinction between homophily/heterophily); (iv) receptions of lawyers' law and of personal law; (v) some scholars, in particular Esin Örücü, have introduced a further range of distinctions, but largely within the framework of assumptions about state law (see below). Several of these distinctions were anticipated by Albert Kocourek (1936). See further Patrick Glenn's potentially controversial distinction between reception as alliance and reception as construction (denying that receptions are 'imposed') (Glenn (1987), p. 265); and Miller (2003), suggesting a typology based on importers' motives.

Table 9.1 Diffusion of law: A standard case and some variants

	Standard Case	Some Variants
(a) Source-destination	Bipolar: single exporter to single importer	Single exporter to multiple destinations. Single importer from multiple sources. Multiple sources to multiple destinations etc.
(b) Levels	Municipal legal system–municipal legal system	Cross-level transfers. Horizontal transfers at other levels (e.g. regional, sub-state, non-state transnational)
(c) Pathways	Direct one-way transfer	Complex paths. Reciprocal influence. Re-export
(d) Formal/informal	Formal enactment or adoption	Informal, semi-formal or mixed
(e) Objects	Legal rules and concepts; Institutions	Any legal phenomena or ideas, including ideology, theories, personnel, 'mentality', methods, structures, practices (official, private practitioners', educational etc.), literary genres, documentary forms, symbols, rituals etc. etc.
(f) Agency	Government–government	Commercial and other non-governmental organisations. Armies. Individuals and groups: e.g. colonists, merchants, missionaries, slaves, refugees, believers etc. who 'bring their law with them'. Writers, teachers, activists, lobbyists etc.
(g) Timing	One or more specific reception dates	Continuing, typically lengthy process
(h) Power and prestige	Parent civil or common law >> less developed	Reciprocal interaction
(i) Change in object	Unchanged minor adjustments	'No transportation without transformation'
(j) Relation to pre-existing law	Blank slate / Fill vacuum, gaps / Replace entirely	Struggle, resistance / Layering. Assimilation / Surface law
(k) Technical/ideological/cultural	Technical	Ideology, culture, technology
(l) Impact	'It works'	Performance measures / Empirical research / Monitoring. Enforcement

Codes, are created with a view to their being adopted by multiple jurisdictions within the same country);[35] or in many countries, as in the case of the Vienna Sales Convention or the UNCITRAL Model Law on International Commercial Arbitration. Conversely, an exporter, such as a colonial or neo-colonial power, may produce standard form instruments for export to many destinations, as happened with the Indian Evidence Act, the Indian and Queensland Penal Codes, and many other measures. Often the processes of interaction are more diffuse or complex, as when a generation of students has been sent to study abroad in several different countries and they return home bringing aspects of different legal cultures with them as part of their intellectual capital. This is an important part of the story of the reception of Roman law in medieval Europe. Many regional and international instruments are new creations drawing in part from a variety of national sources, but also involving important new elements. Simple binary interaction between legal orders and traditions cannot be assumed. Often, Örücü's culinary metaphors – mixing bowl, salad bowl, salad plate, and purée – may be more appropriate.[36]

(b) Cross-level interaction

Cross-level diffusion is an important and relatively neglected phenomenon. The standard example postulates a direct one-way transfer between municipal legal systems. Diffusion can occur horizontally at other levels than the national (e.g regional–regional or sub-state local–local). More important, it takes place *across* levels of ordering.[37] For example, states often adopt international norms as part of domestic law. The European Convention on Human Rights was given 'further effect' by the UK Human Rights Act 1998.[38] The Standard Minimum Rules for the Treatment of Prisoners have formed the basis for much regional and domestic regulation, as well as being used as a template for evaluating particular prison regimes.[39] Consider further the recent transnational networking by NGOs concerned with women's rights and their impact on the law in South Africa.[40] Similarly, Santos has shown clearly how the internal regime of the squatter settlements in Brazil imitated 'the asphalt law' of the state, a fairly standard situation in the anthropological literature.[41] Glenn gives many examples of influence between religious traditions or between local custom and

---

[35] On the Restatements and European integration see Chapter 10.2(d) below.

[36] Örücü (1995).

[37] For example, international–national, sub-national–national, national–transnational or national/international/transnational–non-state local and so on. See the useful critique of 'Compartmentalization of political space' by Mertus (1999) at pp. 930–33. On the limitations of spatial metaphors see Woodman (2003) discussed in Chapter 3.3(c).

[38] On the cross-level aspects of the Human Rights Act, see p. 276 above.

[39] Stern (1998), pp. 195–7; Human Rights Watch (1993).

[40] A. Griffiths (1997); Fishbayn (1999); See Riles (2000).

[41] Santos (2002) Chapter 3. Similar mimicking and adapting of municipal law concepts (e.g. lien, equity, sovereign) is an important part of the discourse of the Common Law Movement (the almost invisible 'legal' off-shoot of the militias in the United States). (Koniak 1996).

religious law.[42] In short, *diffusion may take place between many kinds of legal orders at and across different geographical levels, not just horizontally between municipal legal systems.*

(c) Pathways and routes

The pathways of diffusion may be complex and indirect.[43] A nice example is the Indian Evidence Act 1872. This was drafted for India by James Fitzjames Stephen. It was a great simplification, but also an idealisation of the English law of evidence. After its enactment in India it was used as a model in many other parts of the British Empire. It also had some influence on evidence in England: when Fitzjames Stephen failed to get his Evidence Bill adopted by Parliament, he used the Indian Evidence Act as the basis for his influential *Digest of the Law of Evidence* on which several generations of English and Commonwealth barristers were trained at the Inns of Court (Stephen 1876).[44] Of course, *reciprocal influence* is not uncommon even at state level, for example, the mutual interaction between American states, between England and Scotland, and between the United States, the United Kingdom, New Zealand, and Australia. Reciprocal influences between religious, customary, and municipal legal orders are well documented.[45]

(d) Formal and informal diffusion

The paradigm example of reception involves a *formal act of adoption or enactment*, for instance by enacting a statute, adopting a constitution, the creation of an Independence Constitution by the decolonising power, or the enactment of a 'reception clause' in local legislation. It may take place somewhat less formally, by a specific executive or judicial decision. However, much diffusion is *informal* and protracted as when legal ideas are carried by colonists, missionaries or merchants or spread by influential legal or other writings. (See (f) below.)

Formal acts of reception may differentiate law from most other objects of reception. But there are, of course, degrees of formality and even where the main agents are the government or particular officials a great deal of influence may operate more or less informally.[46] Where the agents are individuals or non-governmental groups formal acts of reception are likely to be exceptional.

---

[42] Glenn (2004) *passim*. On the 'irreducible continuum' between Islamic law and local custom see Rosen (2000), especially Chapter 5.

[43] On 'influence research' (Einflußforschung) see Derrett (1999) cited in Menski (2000) at p. 52.

[44] On Stephen and the Indian Evidence Act, see Twining (1994) at pp. 52–7, and Radzinowicz (1957).

[45] See e.g. Glenn (2004) at pp. 356–7; Chanock (1985); Benton (2002).

[46] Pistor and Wellons (1999) report that:

> Despite the absence of major formal law reform in most [of the six Asian] economies, the legal systems changed significantly between 1960 and 1995. This change cannot be captured by focusing only on the enactment or amendment of major codes. Legal change over the 35 years was less visible because it often took place at the level of administrative rule making or practice rather than the enactment of new major codes. (Pistor and Wellons (1999) at p. 4.)

(e) What is diffused?

Any 'legal' phenomena or ideas can be the objects of diffusion.[47] In short, *rules and concepts and legal institutions, such as courts, are not the only or even the main objects of receptions*. This is generally acknowledged in the mainstream literature on diffusion of law. Some objects are quite visible such as institutional designs, or formal procedures, or dress, symbols and rituals, or literary genres (e.g. law reports, journals), or structures, methods and practices of legal education and training, or personnel (e.g. foreign judges or advisers), or documentary forms;[48] others may be less obvious, such as styles of drafting or of judicial opinions or legislation or of argumentation, or prison technology or architecture, or prescribed alternatives to imprisonment. Some are more elusive such as 'mentality', concepts, conventions, unspoken assumptions, ideology, or even principles.[49] Rogers usefully reminds us that 'a set of innovations diffusing about the same system are interdependent'. It may be easier to study the diffusion of each finite item as if it is an isolated event, but in reality diffusion tends to operate in 'technology clusters'.[50]

(f) Agents

While the most visible agents of import and export are governments, there have been many other *agents of diffusion*. Weber, Watson and others have identified legal élites (the *honoratiores*) as often playing key roles in diffusion. Colonists, missionaries, and merchants have throughout history 'carried their law with them'. So have slaves, refugees, believers, and jurists.[51] Law is spread as much by literature as by legislation. Commerce, education and religion may be as

---

[47] On law as ideas and law as social practices see Chapter 1.7 above.

[48] A largely invisible form of diffusion relates to legal instruments – for example, standard forms for the numerous types of agreements and transactions involved in transnational trade, investment, and finance. To take but one example: the 'Conditions of Contract for Works of Civil Engineering Construction' (informally known as 'The Red Book') is a standard form contract drawn up by the Fédération Internationale des Ingénieurs-Conseils (FIDIC). It is an important element in the emerging transnational *lex constructionis*, which can be interpreted as part of the *lex mercatoria*. See www.l.fidic.org/resources/engineeringourfuture/ (Last visited May 2004). I am grateful to Michael Douglas for this example. Another example is the *lex pacificatoria* ('the law of peacemakers') that Christine Bell argues is emerging from mutually interacting peace processes (Bell (2006)).

[49] Compare the following list of objects studied from a geographical perspective:

> Hence, diffusion phenomena cover a wide range that includes transportation modes, such as the automobile, farming techniques, family planning, credit cards, broadcast and cable television, shopping centers, production practices, such as assembly line and just-in-time inventorying, political movements, cultural practices, frontier development, modernization in Third World settings, epidemics, urban ghettoes, and urban areas themselves. (Brown (2001) at p. 3676.)

[50] Rogers (1995) at pp. 14–15; on the limits of a technological perspective on law, see pp. 286–9 below.

[51] David Nelken has suggested (communication to the author) that detailed empirical study of jurists as change agents could be a particularly rich field. I agree. On change agents the social science literature is particularly suggestive: see Rogers (1995), Chapter 9.

important conduits as governmental action in bringing about legal change. Where colonists or merchants or immigrants 'bring their law with them' the process of diffusion may be more closely analogous to the spread of a language, involving thousands or even millions of unrecorded individual choices over long periods of time without necessarily having any historic moments or defining events.[52] There are grounds for believing that in law, as in other spheres, persuasion at grass roots and other levels is likely to be more effective than top-down law-making, but this hypothesis needs to be explored by further empirical research.[53]

(g) Time scales

Reception usually involves a long drawn out process which, even if there were some critical moments, cannot be understood without reference to events prior and subsequent to such moments.[54] The more sophisticated accounts of famous receptions of state law that involved one or more specific reception dates, such as the Turkish story,[55] emphasise the historical continuities over long periods of time. Conventional wisdom has it that one cannot understand the story of the McArthur Constitution without reference to the prior tradition of constitutionalism in Japan before World War II and the subsequent history of its interpretation and development to the present day.[56] The later chapters of stories of diffusion tend to be accounts of local importers' history, but that can also be misleading.

(h) 'Parent' legal systems

There is a tendency in the literature to assume that most diffusion, at least in modern times, involves movement from the imperial or other powerful centre

---

[52] But law, like language, 'is a group-oriented innovation par excellence' (Cooper (1982) at p. 20).

[53] For a strong version of this view, see:

> [R]eception is the obvious instance of adherence, on a large scale to persuasive authority ... It is ... inappropriate to consider reception as either imposed, following conquest, or voluntary, since all reception which occurs is necessarily voluntary. (Glenn (1987) at pp. 264–5.)

This seemingly goes against major trends in the literature on the colonial experience. However, Glenn's conception of 'reception' includes some idea of acceptance and persuasion – law is not 'received' unless it is accepted. Nevertheless, this position is debatable: see, for example, Burman and Harrell-Bond (1979).

[54] During the period of British colonial rule in Africa, Sudan (a condominium) was exceptional in not having a specified reception date. See further Allott (1970) Chap. 2.

[55] Ataturk's reforms in Turkey were introduced within a relatively short time span, but to understand them, it is necessary to consider both the long period of gradual modernisation and secularisation prior to 1923 and the equally long period of implementation, interpretation, adjustment, and slow and uneven acceptance since 1926. It is also necessary to consider further waves of reception related to religious revival, participation in the world economy, and Turkey's continuing attempt to become integrated into Europe.

[56] See, for example: Upham (1987); Inoue (1991); Beer and Itoh (1996); Moore and Robinson (2004).

to a colonial or less developed periphery. The paradigm example is export by a *'parent' common law or civil law system* to a less developed dependent (e.g. colonial) or adolescent (e.g. 'transitional') system.[57] To be sure imperialism, and neo-imperialism form an important part of the picture. But this patronising view hardly fits the story of the spread of law as part of the baggage of colonists, migrants, refugees and others or of the great religious diasporas throughout history, nor of interaction within countries, regions or alliances. Exclusive concentration on the spread of state law tends to go hand-in-hand with a formalistic and technocratic top-down perspective, which underestimates the importance of informal processes of interaction.

(i) 'No transportation without transformation'

Bruno Latour's dictum may be an overstatement if applied to legal phenomena,[58] but no serious student of diffusion can assume that what is borrowed, imposed or imported *remains the same*.[59] This is not just a matter of the interpretation and application of received law, but also of its use or neglect, impact, and local political, economic and social significance. Sometimes, it is true, a particular legal institution may remain in force and operative because it is part of the intellectual capital of a legal elite,[60] but most stories of reception are at least in part stories of interaction between the 'imported law' and 'local conditions'. How and to what extent any particular 'import' retains its identity or is accepted, ignored, used, assimilated, adapted, rooted, resisted, rejected, interpreted, enforced selectively, and so on depends largely on local conditions. Such accounts at least allow for interaction between imported law and local

---

[57] See the discussion in Zweigert and Kötz (1998), pp. 41–2.

[58] Latour (1996). In cultural geography:

> a basic notion is that the diffusing item is both a stimulus to a new innovation and itself subject to modification as it spreads. The relation between diffusion, the item being diffused, and the human landscape is therefore complex and subject to continual change. (Brown (2001) at p. 3677; see Alter (2001), p. 3684.)

[59] In social science accounts of diffusion the term 'reinvention' is sometimes preferred to 'adaptation', emphasising the idea that local people often employ creative problem-solving in which borrowing or imitation is only one aspect (Rogers (1995) at pp. 17, 174–80).

[60] Take, for example, Stephen's Indian Evidence Act of 1872. It has survived for over 130 years in India with only a few minor legislative changes. It has been encrusted with Indian precedents. The Indian practitioners' treatises, such as *Sarkar on Evidence*, are almost as bulky as their American counterparts (Sarkar (1913) p. 1971; cf. Woodruffe and Ameer Ali (1979–81)). Students' works stay close to the text and the Indian precedents by and large do not seem to deviate very far from the spirit of the draftsman. The Indian Evidence Act might be cited as an example of Alan Watson's thesis that many transplants survive for long periods almost unchanged and without any significant relation to local social, economic and political changes and conditions, but it has clearly been integrated into the professional life of generations of the Bar in India and elsewhere and has become a stable part of their intellectual capital. I suspect the full story would be more complex than that, but to date there seems to have been little empirical study of its use in practice.

conditions, including local law. But that is still adopting the standpoint of the exporter who seems to be asking in effect: What happened to our law?

Things can look very different from local points of view, whether these are members of a political elite, their opponents, minority groups, or individual citizens confronted in daily life with a variety of regulatory orders. A leading critic of the top-down bias in most Western accounts of reception, the Japanese scholar Masaji Chiba, goes so far as to say: 'The whole structure of law in a non-Western society is, seen from a cultural point of view, formed in the interaction between received law and indigenous law.'[61] Chiba's detailed studies of legal pluralism in Japan, Sri Lanka, and elsewhere from a non-Western perspective are a useful counter-weight to the exporters' bias in many Western scholars' accounts of diffusion. Another important theme relates to how importation of and resistance to foreign legal ideas, laws, and institutions often forms part of some broader local political struggle.[62]

(j) Filling a vacuum: the blank slate fallacy

It is often assumed that law has been imported to fill a vacuum or to fill in gaps or to replace pre-existing laws:[63] either there was nothing to replace, or else legal change was a straightforward matter. Where exporters have been ignorant of, or indifferent or hostile to indigenous or other pre-existing law, they have often treated it as invisible or insignificant. They have tended to underestimate what Merry calls 'the forms of resistance to the penetration of state law'.[64] Nearly all modern detailed studies of reception recognise that it usually involves inter-action with pre-existing normative orders, even if their main concern is with state law; whether or not these are designated as 'legal', 'informal', 'traditional' or 'customary' by particular writers is a secondary matter.[65] A good example is Dezalay and Garth's detailed study of the interaction of imported American ideas about legal education and judicial reform with local practices, attitudes and power structures in Latin America.[66] As with earlier points, the important

---

[61] Chiba (1986, p. 7). This perspective is developed in Chiba (1989). In later writings Chiba has moved beyond focusing solely on countries and sub-state forms of law to include 'trans-state law' (e.g. Chiba (1998)).

[62] Compare, for example, Chua (2003) (arguing that the impact of economic globalisation fuels a backlash against market-dominant ethnic minorities in whose interests commercial law reforms are perceived to be) with Dezalay and Garth's (2002b) account of 'palace wars' in Latin America.

[63] This is referred to in the social science literature as 'the empty vessels fallacy' (Rogers (1995), pp. 240–2). Mistelis (2000) at p. 1065) characterises much foreign technical legal assistance in Eastern Europe as 'legal surgery', with foreign concepts being introduced 'as if they were legal transplants to replace malfunctioning organs'.

[64] Merry (1988), p. 882.

[65] For example, Berkowitz et al. (2003) are concerned with the transplantation of state law, but acknowledge that '[M]ost societies today have both formal and informal legal systems' (Berkowitz, et al. (2003) at p. 175). A central part of their argument is that imported formal law typically has to interact with pre-existing informal legal (or other normative) orders.

[66] Dezalay and Garth (2002b).

thing is that processes of diffusion are nearly always mediated through local actors.

(k) Technological, contextual-expressive, and ideological perspectives

Throughout the legal literature on diffusion of law there runs a tension between three underlying conceptions of the objects and processes of diffusion. These might be labelled the instrumentalist, the expressive/contextual, and the ideological views of law.

Enthusiastic diffusionists tend to assume that laws are generally discrete technological products, as transferable as widgets or other innovations, to be imported as instruments of legal and social modernisation. The instrumentalist view sees the process as being essentially one of problem solving in which solutions developed elsewhere are imported to solve local problems. In this view legal rules, institutions, and practices are essentially a form of technology. Typically, in the process of modernisation less developed countries import inventions and devices produced in more developed 'parent' or 'metropolitan' countries, especially modern industrialised societies. The imports are technically more advanced and suited to modern conditions. The standard metaphors are revealing: import, export, invention, adaptation, transfer, imitation, machinery, and even engineering, hardware, and software.[67] There is even talk of competition between exporting countries to obtain market share or niches for their legal products. The values and orientation are consonant with bureaucratic rationalism and ideas of economic efficiency. The emphasis is on technical means to taken-for-granted ends.[68]

The second view is ideological. The most important factors in a reception are the underlying values, principles and political interests that motivate it rather than the details of particular rules or provisions. In this view, legal materials are pervasively imbricated with political values and beliefs.[69] In colonial times imported law was primarily seen as an instrument of social control and exploitation by the colonial power. But it was also presented as part of the 'civilising' mission of colonialism: 'We bequeathed you the Rule of Law'. In post-colonial times 'democracy, human rights, and good governance' and 'the Rule of Law' are exported as part of a market-driven ideology. Critical legal scholars denounce this ideology as 'liberal legalism'.[70]

Ataturk's reforms were as much ideological as technological: they were part of his overall strategy to secularise, democratise, modernise, and above all, Westernise Turkey. In recent years a great amount of activity has centred round the efforts to use law to move a country from a command or managerial economy to a free market system and to reform legal systems to encourage

---

[67] On metaphors relating to legal transplants see n. 6. above

[68] On technology and 'the technical prejudice' see Twining (2002a) at pp. 176–82; see David Kennedy (2003). On 'instrumentalism' see Chapter 16.4 on the web.

[69] See e.g. Duncan Kennedy (1997), David Kennedy (2003).

[70] On 'liberal legalism' see Chapter 11, pp. 344–6 below.

foreign direct investment. Such structural adjustment and modernising pro-grammes tend to combine the ideology of the free market with a set of assumptions that are instrumental and technological.

In a quite different context, comparative lawyers, such as Gordley and Ewald, have stressed the importance of grasping 'philosophical' underpinnings as a necessary part of making sense of legal doctrine. Gordley's account of the origins of contract doctrine is a story of how the basic structure of concepts and principles of contract doctrine got cut off from its roots in neo-Thomist moral theory and became incoherent.[71] Ewald stresses the relevance of constitutional theory in understanding the German BGB and its profound differences from classical Roman law.[72] From an ideological perspective, treat-ing imported law as no more than a series of technical solutions to shared problems – for example, talking of 'lawyers' law' as apolitical[73] – or choosing one system over another because of its technical superiority, obfuscates the underlying purpose and pretends that the ends are uncontentious.[74]

An alternative view is more romantic.[75] Law is mainly an outgrowth of local society, values and traditions and in large part expresses or reflects local society.[76] Law is embedded holistically in local culture. This makes reception and assimilation of foreign ideas problematic. Of course, legal systems interact and influence each other, but the processes tend to be slow and complex. Here, the discourse employs analogies and metaphors that congregate around natural phenomena and organisms: the seamless web, transplants, assimilation, diges-tion, contagion, irritation, rejection, even penetration.[77] Transplant sceptics

---

[71] Gordley (1991) discussed in Chapter 10.2(c) below.

[72] Ewald (1995a).   [73] On 'lawyers' law', see n. 4 above.

[74] It is a mistake to treat the instrumental and romantic views as mutually exclusive rivals. For example, Bruno Latour presents the processes of technology in a romantic light: see especially Latour (1996). Similarly, not all problem-solving is conscious and rational (HTDTWR, Chapter 2).

[75] An excellent analysis and sympathetic critique of the 'Neo-Romantic turn' is James Whitman (2003).

[76] A strong version of the expressive view is the 'mirror thesis' – the view or assumption that law reflects or 'mirrors' society. This is usually put in opposition to Alan Watson's transplants thesis, viz. that the main engine of legal change is imitation. I think that there is some value in this juxtaposition, but that the contrasts tend to be painted in over-sharp colours – see Chapter 4.1(c) at p. 92 above and, in more detail, Twining (2003b) at pp. 206–13.

[77] A more sophisticated version of the romantic view as an aspiration can be depicted in terms of an analogy with the architectural vision of Frank Lloyd Wright. In this view, like Wright's 'natural house', a legal system should be made of local materials sensitively used; it should become part of the landscape rather than appear as an alien imposition; and it should embody and express local values in a coherent fashion. In short it should be in harmony with its context. The natural house merges into the landscape, but it does not merely mirror it. Although Wright was a self-proclaimed romantic, his vision of the art of building did not involve rejection of ideas of function, technology, and utility. Some commentators link it to a particular ideology – the frontier spirit – upholding freedom, democracy, and robust individualism (Hoffman (1995)). At first sight this analogy may seem somewhat fanciful. But it has strong echoes in quite varied enclaves of legal theory: for example, Savigny's idea of law as the expression of the spirit of the people; in Karl Llewellyn's idea of crafts and period style, in Nonet and Selznick's responsive law, and even in Ronald Dworkin's idea of law as integrity. In this view, a house must be in harmony with its context; so must law.

tend to treat laws as expressive of and rooted in local culture, context, history and tradition. Rather than see particular concepts, laws, or institutions as discrete units, they tend to treat them as integral parts of organic, coherent systems.[78]

There may be some truth in each of these views. When Kahn-Freund contrasted the 'transplantation' of a kidney and a carburettor, he was making the point that technical areas of law, such as contract and commercial law, may transfer more readily than areas that may be more closely related to political and social context, such as much of public and family law. His general point was that legal phenomena are very varied and exist along a continuum of trans-ferability.[79] A similar contrast is sometimes made between 'lawyers' law', which is generally thought to travel well, and 'personal law', which does not. The reason why the Kemalist reception in Turkey has generally been treated as exceptional is just because it included marriage and other important areas of personal law. There is some value in these distinctions, but they need to be treated with caution.

The problem goes deeper than that. Which metaphor best fits the processes of diffusion or transplantation – technology, ideology, or architecture? Asking this is about as sensible as asking whether a law is more like a widget, a house or a belief-system. Law is too vast and varied to fit any such reductionist move; so too are the processes of diffusion. The problem-solving, expressive and ideo-logical views are useful reference points for considering the processes of diffusion of law. They represent three different, but related, perspectives for viewing particular phenomena. But legal phenomena, the motives of the agents of diffusion, and the inter-relations between legal orders and cultures are so diverse and complex that it is absurd to expect one or other perspective to fit all examples. One cannot proceed far in law without considering underlying beliefs, values and purposes. It sometimes makes sense to see particular legal rules, devices or institutions in terms of inventions that usefully solved discrete problems. Conversely, there is much more to understanding processes of most kinds of legal change than asking whether a particular solution fits a particular problem.

One of the reasons why the continuing debates about transplantation are so unsatisfactory is that they tend to be presented either as confrontations between extremists (technologists versus contextualists, 'strong Watson' versus 'strong mirror theories')[80] or else as discussions between moderates, like Kahn-Freund,[81] who treat transferability as a relative matter and who make so many concessions that they do not seem to be disagreeing – one side

---

[78] A good example is Allison (1996). This is a detailed study of the public/private law distinction in English law as an unsuccessful transplant. A central theme of the work is: 'Because of the coherence of legal and political system, transplantation is hazardous.' (Allison (1996), at p. 236) see Teubner (1992).

[79] Kahn-Freund (1974).   [80] Discussed in Twining (2003b) at pp. 206–13.

[81] Kahn-Freund (1974) at pp. 8–13 and 300–5.

emphasising difference, the other side similarity – the familiar problem of the half-full cup. One way out of this dilemma is to recognise that there is a limit to discussing such a complex picture at such high levels of generality.[82]

(l) Evaluating impact: 'success' and 'failure'

There is a tendency in the legal diffusion literature to talk vaguely of receptions 'working' or 'failing'. However, since 1990 enormous sums have been spent by foreign agencies on law reform in 'transitional countries', especially in Eastern Europe, and in post-conflict societies, such as Afghanistan and Iraq.[83] International financial institutions,[84] Western aid agencies (e.g., USAID) have supported law-related projects and programmes in the name of 'the Rule of Law', 'good governance', 'legislative reform', 'judicial reform', and 'institution capacity-building'. The funds are often channelled through large bureaucracies that need to 'show results' and are themselves subject to modern procedures of accountability. This in turn has led to the development of tools for diagnosing 'the health' of a legal system, assessing the effectiveness, efficiency and sustainability of reforms, and evaluating 'the success' of particular projects and programmes. These tools are under continuous review and refinement.[85]

---

[82] Twining (2005).

[83] I am grateful to Veronica Taylor and Terry Halliday for instructing me about some of these developments. See Taylor (2007).

[84] By no means only the World Bank (IBRD) and the IMF. For example, the European Bank for Reconstruction and Development has played a pioneering role in developing assessment measures in relation to Eastern Europe. The Asian Development Bank sponsored, *inter alia*, the seminal study by Pistor and Wellons (1999). The Department of International Development (UK) has developed evaluation guidelines (e.g. DFID, 2002).

[85] For example, the USAID Commercial Law and Legal Institutions Reform Project in Eastern Europe and Eurasia (C-LIR) made the following self-assessment of its previous efforts:

> The success of ... early efforts – referred to here as *1st generation* commercial legal and institutional reform (C-LIR) – were mixed. New laws were drafted (sometimes copied verbatim from advanced market economies) and enacted, but with little lasting change ... During [the] second phase, practitioners' attention turned to rationalizing and strengthening the institutional framework for implementation and enforcement of commercial and other laws. This led to important advances in institutional and operational analysis, regulatory design, and capacity building ... While significant gains were achieved in certain substantive areas (e.g. GATT/WTO accession, customs administration, collateral registries, and capital markets), there was little progress in others – notably the enforcement of bankruptcy, antitrust, and intellectual property laws ... 'third generation' C-LIR [focuses on] the 'implementation-enforcement gap' [and] achieving sustainability in implementation and enforcement of legal and institutional reforms. (C-LIR Handbook 1999 p. 3, quoted by Taylor (2007) at p. 96).

> Taylor comments:

>> The vision of law encapsulated in these 'three generations' of USAID law reform is still predominantly the formalist view ... and the ultimate aim is instrumentalist – to deliver a technique for evaluating and ranking legal systems. (Taylor (2007) at p. 96.)

This audit culture is far removed from the vague references in the academic literature to the 'success' or 'failure' of transplants and receptions.[86] Performance indicators, efficiency criteria, benchmarks, compliance assessments, and even league tables have been and are being developed by various agencies and have been used in the allocation of funds. As has happened on a large scale, some of these law reform and evaluation tasks are contracted out to private sector organisations, who are often under further pressures to produce standardised, packaged, cost-effective proposals and evaluations within a strictly limited time-scale. And some of these processes lack the transparency that they are meant to be promoting.[87]

A striking feature of some of these relatively new activities is that the law schools have been largely by-passed. In the development of performance measures, economists and other non-lawyers seem to have been involved with practising lawyers, largely unaware of, or uninterested in, the controversies and accumulated learning, such as it is, of the scholarly heritage of comparative law, law and development, regulation, compliance, and transplantation. This is especially the case where academics emphasise the uniqueness of local histories and long time-scales. The assumptions underlying these measures tend to be technocratic, formalist, and strongly instrumentalist, paying scant regard to culture, context, and tradition.[88]

It is tempting for academic lawyers – especially comparative lawyers and socio-legal researchers – to dismiss these developments as crude, insensitive 'fairy tales' unworthy of the attention of serious scholars. Some may refuse to have anything to do with them on the ground that they are ideologically unacceptable. Many academics are averse to both audit and soundbites, especially when they are combined in league tables. All of the standard objections to educational league tables are immediately suggested: hard variables push out soft variables; they quantify the unquantifiable; they compare the incommensurable; their weightings are arbitrary; they often involve dubious or simplistic assumptions, false precision, hidden biases in weighting and 'one size fits all'.[89]

---

[86] For example, Watson (1974) at pp. 88–94 and Allison (1996) at pp. 15–16, 236 talk airily about success and hazards without specifying any criteria for evaluation. Berkowitz *et al.* (2003) usefully canvass recent empirical studies of the impact of legal change on economic development. They conclude their article with a broad generalisation: 'Yet, *after two hundred years of for the most part unsuccessful legal transplants*, more patience with the development of legal institutions seems to be in order' (Berkowitz *et al.* (2003) at p. 190; italics added).

[87] The EBRD has been more open about this, for example, through its bulletin, *Law in Transition*. See especially Ramasatry (2002).

[88] Taylor (2007).

[89] Twining (2000a) at pp. 161–5. In her BBC Reith Lectures Onora O'Neill (2002) argued that many criticisms of target setting, performance indicators and some forms of 'transparency' were justified in that they tend to foster a culture of blame rather than to mitigate the 'crisis of trust' they were supposed to remedy.

The trouble is that these new developments are very influential and they are here to stay.[90] Some of the early efforts may have been crude, but the methods are being continuously refined.[91] At the very least, these influential attempts to measure and evaluate programmes of law reform deserve to be subjected to sustained theoretical critique. Economic analysis, the 'New Institutionalism', and the imperatives of audit, however controversial they may be, are introducing genuinely new ways of profiling and analysing state legal systems. One might add that the shift from legislation to enforcement to concern with sustainability represent significant moves away from surface law to increasingly realistic concern with the law in action. In future comparative law will have to adjust to proliferating data banks, increased quantification, the concepts and paraphernalia of bureaucratic rationalism, and fundamental problems of incommensurability.[92]

9.5 Conclusion

To sum up: Diffusion processes as an aspect of interlegality are far too varied and complex to be reduced to a single model or ideal type. However, the above analysis suggests some cautionary warnings against making simplistic assumptions:

(1) Relations between exporters and importers are not necessarily bipolar, involving only one exporter and one importer. The sources of a reception are often diverse.

(2) Diffusion may take place between many kinds of legal orders at and across different geographical levels, not just horizontally between municipal legal systems.

(3) The pathways of diffusion may be complex and indirect and influences may be reciprocal.

(4) Diffusion may take place through informal interaction without involving formal adoption or enactment.

(5) Legal rules and concepts are not the only, or even the main objects of diffusion.

(6) Governments are not the only, and may not be the main, agents of diffusion.

---

[90] Many of these developments relate to commercial law and are relatively new. Academic attention has been directed to such matters as democratic audit and the use of statistics in human rights evaluation for rather longer. See, for example, on the Democratic Audit of the United Kingdom Beetham (1993), Klug et al. (1996). See further Chapter 8, n. 143 above.

[91] A bold attempt to apply macro-economic analysis to legal transplants is Berkowitz et al. (2003). See the controversial work of La Porta et al. (1996),(1998), (1999) and Balas et al,. (2008) and their critics, e.g. Siems (2005) and Roe (2006).

[92] On surface law see Chapter 10 below. On incommensurability, see Espeland and Stevens (1998), D'Agostino (2003), Chang (ed.) 1997. On theoretical problems of commensurability in comparative law, see Glenn (2001), (2004) at pp. 44–58, 354–5, criticised by Halpin (2006a).

(7) Do not assume one or more specific reception dates. Diffusion often involves a long drawn out process, which, even if there were some critical moments, cannot be understood without reference to events prior and subsequent to such moments.

(8) Diffusion of law often involves movement from an imperial or other powerful centre to a colonial, dependent, or less developed periphery. But there are also other patterns.

(9) The idea that transplants retain their identity without significant change is widely recognized to be outmoded.

(10) Imported law rarely fills a vacuum or wholly replaces prior local law.

(11) Diffusion of law is often assumed to be instrumental, technological, and modernising. But there is a constant tension between technological, contextual-expressive, and ideological perspectives on law.

(12) There is a tendency in the diffusion literature to talk of receptions 'working' or 'failing'. Only recently have attempts been made to evaluate and measure impact empirically. Many of the instruments that have been developed are suspect, but this is an area that needs serious academic attention.

These general propositions can serve as warnings of complexity. But such warnings should not stop at the big picture. There is a need for many kinds of detailed study of the phenomena. Any student of diffusion needs to ask questions about sources, levels, pathways, what is diffused and received and how it changes in the process, change agents, prior conditions and arrangements, formal acts of reception, time-scales, implementation and impact. This kind of analysis is standard in more developed social science diffusion studies. A second paper explores the gap between the legal literature on reception/legal transplants and the social scientific literature on diffusion and considers what might be learned from this more sophisticated and strongly empirical tradition that might be helpful or suggestive for detailed studies of processes of diffusion of law.[93]

---

[93] Twining (2005a).

Chapter 10

Surface law[1]

10.1 Sophie's problem

Once upon a time Sophie, a student of dispute processes, decided to investigate the handling of disputes in universities. Casual enquiry suggested to her that appointments and promotions of academic staff were a major source of regular and bitter conflicts in academic life. She decided to do a pilot study on the topic in the local university, an institution that broadly followed British patterns of academic governance.

Although her perspective was ethnographic, Sophie decided to start with the formal structure of authority and decision-making in the university. The annual calendar set out the texts of the Charter and Statutes of the University. A regularly updated 'blue book' collected the main regulations of the central administration. From these sources she learned that all appointments to academic positions were made by the Governing Body (the Council) on the recommendation of the University Appointments Committee, chaired by the Vice-Chancellor or his deputy. The Committee consisted of twelve regular members and for each appointment just two representatives of the relevant department or subject area. Under the university statutes all 'permanent' academic vacancies had to be advertised, with formal applications addressed to the Registrar of the University.

Sophie obtained an interview with the Registrar. Before she saw him she studied all of the formal rules governing appointments that were published in the University's calendar and 'blue books'. She was sceptical whether these told the whole story. The Registrar outlined the procedures in terms that followed

[1] This is a revised version of a paper published in Petersen, Kjeer, and Madsen (eds.) *Paradoxes of European Integration* (2008) and is reproduced here with permission of the publisher. The idea originated in a conversation with the late Henrik Zahle. We discussed what it meant to assert that Alan Watson's transplants thesis only dealt with 'surface law'. We moved on to relate the concept to convergence theories in comparative law and to projects for unification and harmonisation of laws. We planned to expand it to cover Henrik's ideas about polycentricity (Petersen and Zahle (1995)). Tragically, he died soon after this initial conversation. So this is hardly more than half a paper. It is dedicated to his memory. It is published here with the permission of Dartmouth Pubishing Company. I am grateful to Hugh Beale, Caroline Bradley, Andrew Halpin, and Neil MacCormick for useful comments and suggestions.

the published rules. He also showed her two sample files containing advertise-ments, referees' reports, and extracts from the minutes of the Appointments Committee. All seemed to conform to the rules. The Registrar expressed surprise that appointments might be considered contentious:

'The process works smoothly. The short-listed candidates are all interviewed on the same day. Decisions are made on the spot and, usually within 24 hours, the Vice-Chancellor contacts the preferred candidate with an offer, which is subject to confirmation by Council. In my ten years, Council has approved all such recommended appointments.'

The Registrar concluded: 'You are wasting your time. If you are looking for controversy or conflict, you would do better by looking at student discipline, salary disputes, or proposals for curriculum revision.'

Undeterred, Sophie went to see the Dean of the Faculty of Humanities and Social Sciences, who confirmed nearly everything that the Registrar had said and added little.

'But, have you not had any controversial appointments?' asked Sophie.

'Of course, not all appointments are popular, especially among the younger staff, but this is a University matter and we have succeeded in keeping it that way. There was one minor incident two or three years ago in one Department, when some of the staff tried to "democratise" the process. As soon as we learned about this, we clamped down on it.'

'How did you find out?' asked Sophie.

'A candidate who was not short-listed sent in a claim for expenses for an unauthorised visit', was the reply.

Sophie decided to move down to departmental level. But instead of contact-ing any more officials she chose to start with some of the younger members of staff. Borrowing from John Flood's approach to barristers' clerks, she met two of them in a pub.[2] When asked about the claim for unauthorised expenses, they laughed: 'Oh, we are careful not to repeat that mistake. When candidates come down for informal visits we pay their expenses on the spot from the fund for visiting speakers – we ask them to give a seminar as well as interviewing them.'

'Who interviews them?'

'The Departmental Appointments Committee (DAC), in addition to indi-vidual interviews by interested colleagues'.

As recounted by these two informants the DAC had been in existence for a decade and still continued. It consisted of six elected members and the Head of Department *ex officio*. Both elections to the DAC and decisions on specific appointments were regularly contested. The DAC controlled the short list. The Head of Department was mandated to press for the appointment of the candidate (s) chosen by the DAC, whatever his or her views. Careful 'official' records were kept. On gaining access to these files, Sophie found a rich documentary record of

---

[2] Flood (1983), Goffman (1959).

over a decade of disputes with the names of dozens of further potential candidates who had not reached the university's shortlists. Her project was viable.

This is a familiar example of an 'unofficial institution' with quite elaborate interposed norms.[3] The DAC had detailed written records of actual disputes, almost none of which reached the attention of the University authorities, who believed that they had a monopoly of power and authority over the whole process, when in fact they were nearly always merely rubber-stamping decisions taken at earlier secret, 'democratic' and disputatious stages of the same process.

If Sophie had followed the advice of Llewellyn and Hoebel,[4] or of John Flood, she would have started in the pub and asked questions along the lines of. 'Had any good disputes lately?'[5] With the co-operation of informants and access to records, she could have collected quite detailed case studies that would illustrate in a concrete way the existence of a highly institutionalised set of techniques, procedures, forms, and devices and their interaction with the 'official' system of governance.

The documentary material supplemented by further interviews provided enough material for a doctoral thesis. Sophie began by analysing her data in terms of some standard traditional dichotomies: appearance/reality; aspiration/reality; paper rules/real rules; law in books/law in action; back stage/front stage; official/unofficial; theory/practice.[6] What these seductive dichotomies have in common is that they are often used to identify a 'gap' between each of the contrasted pairs.

It is tempting to say of this example that the official accounts of the appointments procedures were superficial, incomplete, and misleading and that the University's Charter, Statutes, and other published rules were only 'surface law'. The starting point for this chapter was Alan Watson's thesis that imitation and transplantation of law are the main engines of legal change and that most law exists largely independently of local social, political and economic conditions.[7] In the process of the development of this thesis, Watson attacks the idea that law 'mirrors' society; he treats legal doctrine, especially private law, as a largely autonomous technical creation; he is highly critical of traditional comparative

---

[3] The *locus classicus* on interposition is Kadish and Kadish, *Discretion to Disobey* (1973). See the account of the local dispute process institutions tagged on to the colonial courts by the Basoga in Uganda in Fallers (1969).

[4] Llewellyn and Hoebel (1941).

[5] The Llewellyn-Hoebel 'case method', given classical shape in *The Cheyenne Way* (1941) was designed to learn about actual institutions and practices in the context of informants who were inarticulate, or secretive, or did not think in general terms about rules, institutions and practices. The uses and limitations of the case method in legal anthropology have been extensively canvassed in the literature, see, for example, Epstein (1967), and *GJB*, pp. 157–70 and 192, n. 50.

[6] She also considered using the Marxian distinction between base and superstructure, but decided that it did not fit her case study.

[7] Alan Watson has developed and modified his general thesis over more than thirty years, sometimes in moderate, sometimes in deliberately provocative form. (On 'weak' Watson and 'strong' Watson see Ewald (1995)). A useful short summary of his position in Watson's own words is included in Schlesinger *et al.* (1998). For a summary of my views, see Twining (2005), pp. 211–13. Watson's sharpest critics include Friedman (1996) and Legrand (1999).

law (especially the 'legal families' perspective); and he needles 'law in context' approaches generally. Without much empirical evidence to support him, Watson treats most law as a superficial gloss on society, provoking the riposte that 'perhaps Watson's generalisations about law are similarly superficial'.[8] Watson says little or nothing about enforcement, impact, or use of imported law and other aspects of the 'law in action', nor about the extent to which the 'transplants' are changed by interpretation, practice or local culture. In short, Watson only deals with 'surface law' and 'paper rules'. But what does that mean? For surely some processes of diffusion can and do make an enormous difference – transplants can be assimilated, fought over, used, enforced, and can even serve to constitute significant social, economic, and other relations.[9] What precisely is the impact and what differences they make is a matter for (quite difficult) detailed local empirical enquiry into particular examples. So what are the implications of saying that Watson deals only (or mainly) with 'surface law'?

On reflection it became clear that this puzzle has wider implications in relation to unification, harmonisation or convergence of laws across jurisdictions, diffusion, legal pluralism, and many other topics, including ultimately: what is involved in understanding law? It is also clear that this enquiry calls for a re-examination of some familiar dichotomies of the kind that bothered Sophie. This chapter is intended as only a modest contribution to these broad topics by suggesting that we need a more precise and sophisticated apparatus of analytic concepts and distinctions to give adequately differentiated accounts of some of these standard dichotomies and the relations between them.

10.2 Five case studies

In this context 'surface law' refers to formal statements of legal rules or doctrine enunciated in codes, treaties, regulations, textbooks, restatements and the like. Before analysing the concept in more detail, I shall introduce some examples that illustrate the standard dichotomies in a variety of contexts: (a) The gap between 'aspiration' and 'reality' in relation to the international regime of human rights; (b) Gaps between 'appearance' and 'reality' in discussions of legal realism and socio-legal studies; (c) Different conceptions of what constitutes 'depth' in relation to convergence in comparative law; (d) Unnoticed, secret, or 'invisible' legal orders; (e) The American experience of attempts at unification and harmonisation of law and its possible relevance to recent projects to harmonise or unify European private law.[10]

---

[8] Twining (2005) at p. 213.
[9] Much of the literature on Ataturk's 'legal revolution' focuses on the complicated story of the uneven acceptance of the new laws over a considerable period of time.
[10] On other contexts in which questions about surface law arise, see pp. 43, 68–9 and 129 above.

(a) Aspiration and reality: universalism and the international regime of human rights

The international human rights regime is nearly 'universal' at state level insofar as almost all members of the United Nations subscribe or are signatories to many, most or all of the main documents. A high level of formal acceptance by nation-states of much of the developing international human rights regime, including both 'hard' and 'soft' instruments, is indeed a remarkable achievement. But to treat this on its own as strong evidence of the universalisation of human rights is too simple.[11] In the view of some, most of the regime does not go beyond optimistic aspiration and surface law. Apart from the fact that formal acceptance and ratification is patchy and that significant reservations are common,[12] the following points are regularly made by commentators:[13]

(i) formal acceptance and ratification may have been pressured, insincere, cynical, or perceived as a meaningless formality;

(ii) the norms may be given different meanings by different signatories;[14]

(iii) there are well-known differences about the relative importance and priorities given to different groups of rights (e.g civil and political/social and economic), to balancing conflicting rights, or to balancing rights and economic and other considerations;

(iv) international monitoring and reporting, let alone enforcement, is selective and uneven. It allows great scope to more powerful states to pursue their own interests under the guise of human rights and democracy; on the whole, the monitoring of civil rights is, so far, much more developed than for social, cultural, and economic rights;[15]

---

[11] See pp. 183–4 above.

[12] On reservations, see J.P. Gardner (1997); Lijnzaad (1995); Sachleben (2006).

[13] A useful alternative formulation is by Ann Kent: 'A major source of contention is the universality of the human rights regime, in the sense of universal acceptance of its norms and principles, the scope of its monitoring and the impartiality of its application. Although there is no doubt that the regime exists and that it is both formally accepted and applied by states, it is not clear that it holds the same meaning for all. Obstacles to universality of interpretation include: (a) a lack of consensus about norms; (b) the need for norms to be processed and put in operation through institutions; and (c) the fact that the carriers of ideas in institutions are states.' Ann Kent in *China, the United Nations, and Human Rights: The Limits of Compliance* (1999), a work that I have found particularly helpful in writing this section. See also Rosemary Foot (2000).

[14] A common arena of contention is different interpretations of 'sovereignty' both in international law and in both internal and transnational political discourse.

[15] Kent suggests that there is a continuum of at least five stages of international and domestic compliance: '(1) accession to human rights treaties, the acceptance of the norms that this entails, and acceptance by the target state of the right of UN bodies to monitor conditions and of its obligation to respond; (2) procedural compliance with reporting and other requirements; and (3) substantive compliance with the requests of the UN body, exhibited in international or domestic behavior. At the domestic level, the continuum extends to (4) *de jure* compliance, or the implementation of international norms in domestic legislative provisions; and (5) *de facto* compliance, or compliance at the level of domestic practice.' Kent (1999), at pp. 23–5. Cf. Dembour (2006) esp. Chapter 5.

(v) the signatories of human rights instruments are nation states, who may not be democratic or truly representative of their people;

(vi) the international regime applies mainly to states, to a lesser extent to regional groupings, and only patchily to non-state actors such as refugees and displaced persons, freedom fighters, and transnational businesses;

(vii) there is often a large gulf between external acceptance of the international regime of human rights and internal law, attitudes, political and legal culture, and actual practices.[16]

This list of obstacles and shortfalls, familiar to human rights lawyers, can be extended. While some of the points relate specifically to treaties, the discourse of international lawyers is suggestive in considering surface law: acceptance, reservation, accession, ratification, enactment, implementation, enforcement, compliance, at both international and domestic levels, (procedural, substantive, *de jure*, and *de facto*),[17] uniform interpretation and application, reporting, and monitoring (to which one might add impact assessment) are familiar categories and distinctions which highlight points about the kinds of information that may often not be ascertainable from surface law.

(b) Appearance and reality: some 'realist' perspectives

Roscoe Pound and the early American Legal Realists are generally credited with developing a range of ideas around contrasts between 'appearance' and 'reality': law in books and law in action;[18] paper rules and real rules;[19] rules and results (outcomes in particular cases);[20] rules and consequences ('impact');[21] rules and predictions;[22] the idea of total processes; the distinction between process and outcome, and so on. Most of these ideas have been developed, refined and extended with some sophistication, mainly under the rubrics of 'Law and Society', 'Law in Context', 'Sociology of Law', and 'Socio-legal Studies'.[23] Concern with action, policy, process, impact, and so on is now commonplace in legal scholarship and legal discourse generally. In the present context it

---

[16] *Ibid*, p. 7. On compliance Kent draws heavily on the pioneering work of Abram and Antonia Chayes (e.g. Chayes and Chayes (1995)). 'Compliance' is now the central focus of empirical studies of regulation. See, for example, McBarnet (2004) (especially rich on 'creative compliance' in relation to tax avoidance), Morgan and Yeung (2007) Chapter 4, Galligan (2007) Chapter 17, and the literature cited there.

[17] Kent (1999) at p. 7, cited above.   [18] Pound (1910).   [19] Llewellyn (1930/1962).

[20] 'If rules were results, there would be little need of lawyers' (Karl Llewellyn, (1930, 1960)) at p. 9.

[21] Pound (1917). One of the common points of departure of Realists was, according to Llewellyn: '(8) An insistence on evaluation of any part of law in terms of its effects, and an insistence on the worthwhileness of trying to find these effects.' (1930)(1962) at pp. 42, 55–7.

[22] Insofar as some Realists conflated the concepts of rules and predictions, they have been rightly criticised; insofar as they emphasised the uses and limitations of rules as means to predicting and the importance of prediction in legal practice, their insights have often been ignored.

[23] On the meanings of these terms, see Chapter 8.2 above. On the misleadingly sharp dichotomy between 'sociology of law' and 'socio-legal studies', which became an arena of contention in the 1970s, see David Nelken (1981).

should be sufficient to make a few observations relevant to the standard dichotomies and the idea of 'surface law'.

Most generalisations about 'the Realists' are false or trivial or both.[24] But by focusing on specific individuals and texts, we can remind ourselves of some non-trivial points:

First, for early Realists, such as Corbin and Llewellyn, 'rule-scepticism' did not entail the belief that 'talk of rules is a myth'.[25] Rather they made the point that articulations of rules in texts and judicial opinions tended to be misleading because they were too abstract and too 'formal'. In particular, they did not catch the 'real' reasons that influenced judges or justified their decisions. In short, surface rules were often not the operative rules. Corbin put it this way in a letter to Llewellyn:

> Pared-down principles there must, of course, be – 'the law'; but it seldom struck me that the ones I found in print were *the* ones.[26]

Second, it was Llewellyn who in an early article drew his famous distinction between 'paper rules' and 'real rules'. This has often been misunderstood. His main concern was to distinguish between descriptions of judicial behaviour (what judges do and what influences them) and normative prescriptions (rules that guide and justify decisions):[27]

> 'Real rules' then, if I had my way with words, would *by legal scientists* be called the practices of the courts and not 'rules' at all....The concept of 'real rule' has been gaining favor since it was first put into clarity by Holmes. 'Paper rules' are what have been treated, traditionally, as rules of law: the accepted *doctrine* of the time and place – what the books say 'the law' is....'[28]

---

[24] Twining (2002) *GJB*, Chapter 5. On the distinction between [American] Realism and realism see Chapter 16.3 below (on the web).

[25] 'It may seem strange that the contention that rules have a central place in the structure of a legal system could ever be seriously doubted. Yet 'rule-scepticism', or the claim that talk of rules is a myth, cloaking the truth that law consists simply of the decisions of courts and predictions of them, can make a powerful appeal to a lawyer's candour'. H. L. A. Hart (1961)) at p. 133. Hart attributed 'rule scepticism' to Holmes and Llewellyn, but conceded that there were moderate versions of this position. On Llewellyn's attitude to rules see below.

[26] Arthur Corbin to Karl Llewellyn, letter 1 December, 1960 (quoted in *KLRM*, p. 32). See the longer quotation from Corbin *ibid*. On Llewellyn's mature account of 'the steadying factors' that made appellate judicial decisions reasonably predictable, see Llewellyn (1960).

[27] In his early 'Realist' writings Llewellyn, like most American jurists, was strongly court-centred; however, his law-jobs theory allows for a much wider conception of 'legal action'.

[28] Llewellyn (1962) at pp. 21–2 (originally published in 1930). Llewellyn was concerned to distinguish between authoritative prescriptions (rules for practice) and descriptions of practice (see the phrase, 'as a rule X does'). His main point is that the relationship between a prescriptive rule and the practice relating to it is unclear on its face. So one needs to be sceptical of any implicit or explicit claims that a practice conforms to the rule(s). This scepticism is not about the existence of rules, but about the idea that they describe practice. The 'realistic' jurist needs to know about the rules and the practice and their relationship with each other.

The idea of 'paper rules' has often been interpreted to refer to rules that are not operative at all or are merely a façade. That was not Llewellyn's point. Rather it was that such surface rules on their own are not very informative:

> Are 'rules of law' in the accepted sense eliminated in such a course of thought? Somewhat obviously not. Whether they be pure paper rules, or are the accepted patter of the law officials, they remain present, and their presence remains an actuality – an actuality of importance – but an actuality whose *precise* importance, whose bearing and influence become clear...First of all they appear as what they are: rules of authoritative ought, addressed *to* officials, telling *officials* what the *officials* ought to do. To which telling the officials either pay no heed at all (the pure paper rule; the dead letter statute; the obsolete case) or listen partly (the rule 'construed' out of recognition; the rule to which lip-service chiefly is paid, while practice runs another course) or listen to with all care (the rule with which the official practice pretty accurately coincides).[29]

Neither Corbin nor Llewellyn were strong 'rule sceptics'. Corbin worked on the first Restatement of Contracts. Llewellyn was Chief Reporter of the Uniform Commercial Code. He wrote a book (unpublished) on 'The Theory of Rules', and consistently argued for better, more informative 'Grand Style' rule formulations that 'carry their reasons on their face'.[30] If there is a core idea in Legal Realism it is that for most purposes in nearly all contexts talk of rules alone is not enough.[31] For Realists like Llewellyn and Corbin, the key feature of the idea of surface law is that on its own it is not very informative. The basic insight is that bare statements of legal rules are generally not self-enacting, self-interpreting, self-applying, self-invoking, self-enforcing, or self-legitimating. For most theoretical and practical purposes the study of rules alone is not enough.[32] Of course, what is considered 'enough' depends on context and purpose and is regularly contested; similarly, without more, the idea of 'reality' begs a lot of questions.

Third, contrasts between the law in books and the law in action, real rules and paper rules, front-stage and back-stage have sometimes led to a temptation to shift attention to one branch of the dichotomy and to neglect the other. For example, to claim to be only concerned with real rules or the law in action or what goes on backstage. A healthy counter-balance is a classic article by Doreen McBarnet in which she criticised socio-legal scholars and criminologists for ignoring legal rules or treating them as unimportant.[33] McBarnet's point was

---

[29] Llewellyn (1962), p. 23.   [30] *KLRM*, n.23, Appendix B.

[31] Twining *GJB*, Chapter 5 (arguing that nearly all other generalisations about the Realists are false or trivial or both).

[32] *HTDTWR*, Chapters 2 and 3. See Galligan (2007) and Griffiths (2003) on social spheres and background rules; see pp. 321–2 below.

[33] McBarnet (1978). More controversially, McBarnet argued that far from criminal justice norms embodying civil rights and due process, many of them subverted it: 'The operation of the law is not a subversion of the substance of the law, but exactly what one would expect it to produce: the law in action is only too close a parallel to the law in books; due process is for crime control.' *Ibid.*, pp. 30–1. This was criticised as overstatement by Roshier and Teff (1980) at pp. 16–17; See Nelken (1981) at pp. 41–2, n. 16.

that her colleagues had made a contrast between the proclaimed ideology of the criminal justice system and what went on in practice, ignoring the details of the law. Whereas, the more interesting contrast was between the ideological pretensions of the system and the detailed substantive rules on the other. Here legal detail was hidden behind surface ideology.[34]

(c) Comparative law: Three perspectives on convergence

> With the enactment of the Chinese Civil Code, systems of private law modeled on those of the West will govern nearly the entire world. Western legal systems, moreover, are much alike. Both 'common law' systems such as those of England and the United States and 'civil law' systems such as those of France, Italy and Germany have a similar doctrinal structure based on similar legal concepts. They divide private law into certain large fields such as property, tort and contract, and analyze these fields in a similar way….The organization of the law and its larger concepts are alike even if particular rules are not. Accordingly, though answers may differ, the problem of whether a boy is liable for injuring a playfellow or a seller is liable for defects in his merchandise is analyzed in much the same way in Hamburg, Montpelier, Manchester and Tucson, or for that matter in New Delhi, Tel Aviv, Tokyo, and Jakarta.[35]

This is the opening paragraph of James Gordley's *The Philosophical Foundations of Modern Contract Doctrine*. It is intended to be provocative and at first sight it succeeds. This looks like a rash and superficial generalisation about 'global law'. Apart from not providing evidence in support of this statement, it seems, on the face of it, to give a misleading account of how disputes and accidents are handled in different countries and cultures. Let us postulate a case in which a schoolboy seriously injures a playfellow in a school yard in Tokyo, or Jakarta or Montpelier or Tucson, Arizona. Can we assume that the reaction would be uniform in all places? Might not it be fatalistic in one place, the start of a family or clan feud in another, the basis for an insurance claim in a third, and an occasion for litigation in a fourth? Even if we think in terms of possible litigation, is it clear that questions about who might sue and who might be sued could be different (the playfellow or his parents, or his clan as plaintiff bringing action against the boy, his parents or clan, the school, a public authority, or an insurance company)? Would fault be an issue in all places and would similar distinctions be drawn between accident, negligence, recklessness, and intent? Would considerations of age, provocation, contributory negligence and

---

[34] A different, but related, theme is developed in Nelken (1981). This contains a brief, but useful, intellectual history of 'concerns about "discrepancies" or "disjunctions" between promises or claims held out for law and its actual effects (at p. 41) The significance of Nelken's paper in the present context is that 'the gap problem' refers to a variety of recurrent concerns, which are of considerable theoretical and practical significance, but which need to be differentiated. See also the good discussion in MacCormick (2007) at pp. 70–4.

[35] Gordley (1991) at p. 1.

so on be similar? And in respect of the People's Republic of China, to what percentage of the population is the Civil Code relevant as a practical matter?[36] In short, Gordley seems to be making a wildly misleading generalisation about both the law in books *and* the law in action.

A more charitable reading, however, suggests that Gordley's thesis may well be correct on its own terms. First, he explicitly states that he is not generalising about detailed rules, but about the underlying concepts of the law of obligations. Second, he is making no claims about enforcement, use, or litigiousness in different countries. Rather he is suggesting that if a jurist were presented with a hypothetical problem about a wrong, such as this, the basic conceptual tools for analysing the situation would be the same in most parts of the world.[37]

The Philosophical Foundations of Modern Contract Doctrine is an outstanding work of intellectual history. Gordley's thesis is that in the sixteenth and early seventeenth centuries Spanish neo-scholastics[38] achieved a synthesis of Roman contract doctrine and Aristotelian moral philosophy mediated by Thomas Aquinas. The result was a coherent system of contract based on the Aristotelian virtues of truthfulness (including promise keeping), liberality, and commutative justice. In the seventeenth century the Aristotelian basis for this theory of contract was undermined by the criticisms of post-Enlightenment thinkers, but the doctrines themselves survived. 'Legal doctrine and moral philosophy began to drift apart'.[39] The doctrines were reformulated by the early modern natural lawyers, first Grotius and then Puffendorf, Domat, and Pothier. Both the continental codes and common law cases drew heavily on these doctrines, shorn of their philosophical basis. Out of this evolved a positivistic and incoherent 'will theory' of contract detached from any theory of virtue or the Aristotelian idea of essences. In the twentieth century the inadequacy of the will theory has been widely recognised, but neither Kantian nor utilitarian theory nor economic analysis can provide a philosophical foundation for explaining 'why the law does not place the same value on all commitments or treat them in the same way'.[40] Many jurists are now pessimistic about the very possibility of discovering general doctrines that can explain the rules of positive law or the results most people regard as fair.

Gordley's elegant thesis is a powerful argument about the intellectual roots of modern contract doctrine, its shared origins in the synthesis of Roman law and neo-Aristotelian ideas by the Spanish scholastics, and its decline into incoherence in both civil and common law systems. Gordley explicitly claims to be writing about contract theory rather than a history of the law of contract or its practical operation, which for most of the time was hardly influenced by the

---

[36] Remoteness of state law from the general population in China may not be a significant break with tradition. See William C. Jones (2003). See Tamanaha's account of Yap in at pp. 90–1 above.

[37] However, he can be faulted for assuming that jurists in these scattered metropolitan centres all share the same *mentalité* (see below); See Pierre Legrand's critique of Gordley's 'reductionism' in another context. Legrand (1999b) at pp. 87–90.

[38] Vitoria and his school (Covarruvias, de Soto, and Molina).

[39] See Gordley (1991) at p. 121.   [40] *Ibid.*, at p. 214.

writers he discusses. Instead it is the story of the rise and decline of attempts to find a coherent philosophical foundation for the law of contract.

Gordley's generalisation is not about surface law. It is not about the rules of private law, but rather about the shared historical origins of some basic concepts and the sad story of their losing touch with their ideological roots. He emphasises structure, concepts, and ways of thought rather than detailed rules and actual practice. His concern is with the interdependence of doctrine and underlying ideology. This can hardly be treated as shallow or superficial. But what lies under the surface in this account is not social context or actual use or practical effects, but rather basic concepts and ideology at two or three removes from the 'surface'.

In the published version of his inaugural lecture at University College London in 2001 Professor (now Sir) Basil Markesenis contrasts differences between what is on the surface and what lies beneath from the point of view of a comparative lawyer.[41] His starting point is a rejection of the comparison of concepts (and by implication detailed legal rules):

> [C]omparison of systems through their concepts can lead to confusion and inaccuracies. For different concepts may conceal similar solutions and philosophies, and similar concepts may hide differences, which flow from other structural differences.[42]

The theme is a familiar one in comparative law, but Markesenis' interpretation is quite distinctive. First, he contrasts the 'surface' concepts and rules of legal doctrine with the concrete solutions to problems that are reached in particular cases.

Second, exhibiting the *mentalité* of a common lawyer, he argues that the best method of comparison of the operation of legal doctrine in practice is through careful study of actual judicial decisions.[43]

Third, he differentiates a number of 'levels' which need to be distinguished in teasing out similarity and difference. At the risk of over-simplification I shall restate these as follows: First, there is the level of abstract legal doctrine – rules and principles. This is not very useful in making comparisons between common law and civil law doctrine as it operates in adjudication, because common law judges are not given to making precise formulations of legal rules. A second level, the explicit reasoning of judges, is also not suitable, because of the generally more open style of common law judges in respect of policy arguments and the predominantly opaque style of most judges in the civilian tradition.

---

[41] Markesenis (2001). Some of the themes in Markesenis' lecture were developed at greater length in essays collected in Markesenis (1997).

[42] *Ibid.* at 595. See Kahn-Freund (1978) at pp. 285–7.

[43] Markesenis (2001) at p. 592: 'The study of a foreign legal system, especially through decisional law, has the advantage of putting one initially at ease. For invariably in such studies one is starting the journey of discovery by looking at litigated situations that are the same in most countries' (at p. 592).

Both exposition of legal rules and judicial reasoning are, for Markesenis, 'on the surface'.[44] A third level of enquiry is a search for policy reasons which may or may not have been made explicit in the reasoning of the judges concerned, but which may be inferred by careful analysis and some knowledge of the context. But there is a fourth level, which is to identify core issues of policy that any [modern] state must confront. 'At this level legal arguments become subservient to political, economic or moral ones, which now come to the fore'.[45] Markesenis concludes:

> [T]he core issues which confront our European systems are the same even though the answers they receive are different. The next realization is that if the answers differ it is not really because of the concepts or even the arguments used on the surface, but because of understandable and legitimate divergences at the core … [h]owever at the core we do not find legal, and certainly not legalistic, arguments. On the contrary, we here encounter political, moral, social and economic issues. Because these issues are of wider import, lawyers cannot solve them. Moreover, and this is just as important, they are not issues that can be described as typically French, German, or English: they appear across borders and thus their very nature encourages comparison. Finally, individual systems – for instance, the French – can and have vacillated over what kinds of answers are appropriate to these fundamental questions….'[46]

Markesenis's method is a sophisticated variant of the 'functionalist' tradition in comparative law, which treats law in terms of responses or 'solutions' to problems and often suggests that civil and common law systems converge by arriving at similar solutions to shared problems often by different conceptual routes. This approach has been much criticised, but I am not here concerned with that controversy.[47] However, Gordley and Markesenis may not be as

---

[44] Markesenis (2001) uses the word 'surface' explicitly several times (e.g at pp. 602, 604, 612 (twice)), 'deep' or 'deeper' (e.g at pp. 607 and 608), 'the superficial reader' (of judicial opinions) (p. 610) and 'levels' several times. As I read him, he treats explicit concepts, rule statements, judicial reasoning, and even particular fact situations as all being on the surface in the context of his argument that in doing comparative analysis of judicial opinions one needs to dig beneath all of these.

[45] *Ibid.*, at p. 608.

[46] *Ibid.*, at p. 612. The passage continues: 'So the real differences between the systems do not lie at the surface where sets of similar facts lead to litigation – I call this, the first circle – but at the core – which I call the third circle. What stops us from realizing this phenomenon and where necessary, addressing it in an intelligent way (especially if the harmonisation of laws is our aim) are the arguments that take place in the second circle where concepts, notions, and legal reasoning reign supreme. … The proper understanding of the systems thus requires us to reduce the importance of the second circle and to locate and define the real issues which lurk in the third.' Markesenis' three 'circles' differ from my rendering in the text, because I am concerned to treat explicit rule statements, concepts and explicit reasoning as all being on the 'surface' as well as the 'sets of similar facts' he refers to in this passage. That fits in better with the other contrasts discussed in this chapter.

[47] On 'the functionalist heritage' see *GLT*, pp. 176–7, Hyland (1996), Graziadei (2003), Örücü and Nelken (2007).

different as they appear. Gordley is arguing that the law of obligations in both civil and common law traditions has quite similar conceptual structures that have shared historical roots, but both have lost touch with the underlying ideology. Markesenis is arguing that conceptual differences are less important than underlying problems and that the 'deepest' level is basic issues of policy and ideological responses to these 'core' issues (the metaphor shifts) and that the ideology may be contested within, as well as across, legal systems. Both converge in treating ideology as lying 'deeper' than both detailed rules and basic legal concepts. Ironically they differ from McBarnet who in the 1970s treated the proclaimed ideology of the criminal justice system as being on the 'surface' for criminologists.

Gordley and Markesenis are also similar in emphasising convergence and underlying similarities. Here, they are part of the target of the fierce campaign by Pierre Legrand against 'traditional' comparative law. In a series of broadsides in papers with such titles as 'Legal Traditions in Western Europe: The Limits of Commonality',[48] 'European Legal Systems are Not Converging,'[49] and 'Against a European Civil Code',[50] Legrand has attacked plans for unification and harmonisation of laws in Europe and, more generally, the tendency in comparative law to emphasise similarity rather than difference:

> I argue that the constant repetition of the all-encompassing principle of sameness as a re-presentation of desire within the law is not innocent, that it conceals as much as it reveals, that it is analytically comparable to trauma. I argue that the seemingly inexorable logic of sameness – ultimately moving from *ipse* to *idem* (that is from 'similarity' which is after all a form of difference, to 'sameness') – hides an active subjectivity which, at the very least, takes the form of a love of order, of an affection for normativity (must not one assume responsibility for the tendency of one's political truth?). Yet, like all desire, the desire for oneness-in-the-law must ultimately fail because it focuses on the impossible object which can exist only in a condensed or abstract version of itself, that is, something which it is not in fact.[51]

For Legrand what lies beneath the surface of detailed legal rules, legal doctrine, and legal concepts is 'legal culture' and the *mentalité* of lawyers, which are so fundamentally different within the broad common and civil law traditions that any attempts to unify, harmonise and claim convergence between the two traditions are bound to be superficial.[52]

---

[48] Legrand (1995) at pp. 63–84.   [49] Legrand (1996).
[50] Legrand (1997b).   [51] Legrand, (2003) at pp. 304–5.
[52] I have argued elsewhere that as much as those he criticises Legrand falls four square within the 'Country and Western Tradition of Comparative Law' in that he largely confines his attention to state law in 'parent' common law and civil law systems and is still concerned with legal doctrine, although from an epistemic point of view, see Twining (2000a) at pp. 62–3.

(d) Unification and harmonisation of laws

(i) The American experience[53]

The American Law Institute (ALI), an alliance of leading judges, practitioners and academics, was founded in 1923 as a response by the organised legal profession to a number of perceived challenges to law in the United States: the need to adapt the common law to American conditions; the need to preserve the unity of the common law across a multiplicity of jurisdictions; the modernisation of the law in the wake of social, economic and technical change; and the simplification of the sources of law in the face of the burgeoning output of authoritative materials by Federal and state legislatures, courts and other agencies. The ALI was also seen by some as an attempt by the leaders of the legal profession to strengthen its control over the management and development of the administration of law by virtue of their technical expertise. The *Restatement* project offered academics, who would do most of the work, influence and status within the legal establishment.

The objectives were reformist, to improve, modernise and unify the common law, but they had to be presented as apolitical. The involvement of the judiciary, the desire to produce an authoritative text that would not be a code, and the desire to by-pass the state legislatures, required not only circumspection in describing the objectives but also procedures and a form that would not invite political criticism. For the enterprise to succeed it was essential that it should operate largely by consensus in a non-partisan mode, so that its products would be accepted by the legal profession and, if they were aware of it, by the general public as representing the agreed wisdom of experts on matters that were essentially technical.

Three main instruments were developed to further these ends: restatements, model codes, and (in co-operation with the Commissioners for Uniform State Laws) uniform laws, of which by far the most important has been the Uniform Commercial Code (UCC). In the early years the Restatement project was given the highest priority. A series of code-like texts was to be prepared, designed in the words of the first Director; 'to present an orderly statement of the general common law of the United States .... The object of the Institute is accomplished insofar as the legal profession accepts the restatement as *prima facie* a correct statement of the general law of the United States.'[54]

Three factors in combination virtually dictated the choice of some such solution: the first and overriding consideration was that the legislatures must be by-passed.[55] Second, practitioners and judges felt that they were drowning in

---

[53] This section is a condensed version of longer accounts in *KLRM*, pp. 272–6 and *BT*, pp. 132–5.

[54] William Draper Lewis, Introduction to *Restatement of Restitution and Unjust Enrichment* (1937) at p. 9.

[55] At the First Meeting of the ALI, John W Davis stated more frankly than most: 'None of us here, I fancy, certainly none of those who are familiar with Congress or the forty-eight legislatures of our states, anticipate that this labor shall be committed to their charge.' ALI, *Proceedings*, II at 112 (1923).

a sea of precedent and the courts, partly because of their complicated structure, were failing as instruments of harmonisation and simplification. What was wanted was a simple, clear, accessible text. Third, the *Restatements* would be authoritative only to the extent that they would in fact be used by the legal profession and the courts.[56] To this end any suggestion of utopian or radical reforms would need to be discounted. The acceptability of the *Restatement* would be enhanced by being primarily expository in form and style. 'The back stage' view was that the aim was simplification, unification, *and* improvement of American common law; 'the front stage' presentation was of an impartial and accurate distillation of existing uniformities.

Even those who accepted the main objectives, methods and underlying theory of the *Restatement* acknowledged that there were practical problems in providing a correct, simple statement of the common law of over fifty jurisdictions. What is the draftsman to do if there is no case in point, or the authorities are in conflict, or if there is no succinct judicial formulation of a rule? What if some states have changed the law by statute or if a recent case from a court of high authority in one jurisdiction purports to overrule or depart from previous authority? Or if local conditions are not uniform throughout the various states? When in doubt, is the conscientious draftsman to choose the predominant opinion or to predict what the courts are likely to do or to choose what s/he considers to be the 'best' opinion? And what if the law is clear, but the Reporter or professional opinion generally considers it to be bad for some reason?[57]

The *Restatement* form is a theoretical hybrid, glossing over the distinction between a neutral exposition (description) of what the law is and a statement of preference or recommendation as to what the law ought to be (prescription). One of the fundamental themes of realist jurisprudence is, of course, that the nature of authoritative legal materials is such that they do not always yield one correct answer as to what the law is, with the result that equating exposition of the law with a simple model of descriptions of the empirical world is misleading. The *Restatement*, while based on meticulous analysis of the authorities, recommends solutions with relatively few inhibitions when the authorities do not speak with a single tongue. The method is that of interstitial development of the law by simplification and by expressing choices between competing alternatives. Its value for practical purposes lies in its accessibility, its relative simplicity and its decisiveness. The two latter qualities reduce its value for the historian or for the theorist who is looking for a reliable contemporary

---

[56] Later editions of the *Restatements* could enhance their authority by citing precedents which cited the *Restatements*.

[57] Barton Leach, a Reporter, lamented: '[W]e can never adversely criticize a rule which we find we have to state. Such a by-law presents a very unpleasant dilemma to a Reporter. He must either state a good rule which he knows perfectly well is not the law; or he must state a bad rule and by his very statement entrench it further.' Leach (1938) at p. 519.

'description' of the state of the law at a particular moment in time, a quest which some would consider to be misconceived in any case.

The *Restatements* have come under fire from various quarters. To the radical reformer they are over-cautious as instruments of legal development since they only attempt to change in the absence of a consensus, and restrict themselves to choosing between alternatives that have already been adopted somewhere. The *Restatements* were also attacked for being undemocratic. In 1992 one Federal Judge wrote that the ALI was an unelected, unaccountable elite involved in quasi-legislation 'without obtaining any input from Congress and/or the State legislatures, without obtaining input from the broad-based representative interests of the masses of ordinary citizens, and without giving any meaningful consideration of any kind to the social, economic and political interests of the various minority groups in this country.'[58]

While some Realists, such as Corbin, were involved in the project, others, attacked the whole enterprise from the start, as being theoretically unsound. The most common criticisms were levelled at four underlying assumptions: (a) that it is possible to describe the law as it is in neutral terms; (b) that it is possible to declare the principles of common law independently of authority; (c) that it is possible to make meaningful statements of legal rules without reference to their rationales; and (d) that it is possible to make accurate and meaningful statements of legal rules without reference to the practical context of their operation.[59]

The value of the Restatements is still controversial. At the seventy-fifth Anniversary of the ALI much was made of its success, including over 110,000 citations by the courts.[60] Whereas immense efforts had been devoted to drafting uniform laws and persuading state legislatures to adopt them, successes were largely confined to commercial law.[61] On the other hand, Lawrence Friedman has lamented the enormous investment of effort by leading scholars in a misconceived enterprise – a waste of talent on 'toys of the trade'.[62] In 2002 he returned to the attack:

> Another project, dominated by the treatise writers, was the heroic (and probably foolish) attempt to 'restate' the common law ... But the draftsmen ignored, for the most part, the social and economic meaning of the working common law. They made it logical and orderly, but at the cost of ripping out the living, pulsing heart of the system.[63]

One may interpret the Realist sceptics and Lawrence Friedman as dismissing the Restatements as merely surface law: divorced from any social, economic, or

---

[58] Simmons (1992).   [59] A good survey of the early criticisms is Merryman (1954).

[60] The American Law Institute (1998).

[61] 'Uniform acts prepared by the Conference [of Commissioners on Uniform State Laws] not relating to commercial law have not been generally adopted by state legislatures' (*ibid.*, at p. 251).

[62] Friedman (1985) at pp. 674–6.

[63] Friedman (2002) at p. 488. See Friedman (1973) at p. 488. Friedman is one of Alan Watson's sharpest critics, see p. 295 above.

procedural context they were misleading as descriptions, uninformative about legal doctrine in action, feeble as attempts to modernise or reform, and of a limited practical value – an odd juristic hybrid, a common law quasi-code with at best limited persuasive authority. Perhaps the main objection was that the static code-like form was contrary in intention and spirit to the incremental development of the common law in the crucible of litigation.

Whether or not such criticisms are overdrawn, they apply far less clearly to American efforts to harmonise private law through uniform laws and model codes. The story of efforts to promote uniform laws through legislation is different from the Restatements in respect of juridical form, the politics of enactment, and practical impact. By far the most ambitious and influential project was the Uniform Commercial Code (UCC), which was jointly sponsored by the ALI and the Commissioners for Uniform State Laws. Hardly anyone thinks of that as merely 'surface law'. Of course, if one reads the UCC solely as text, it counts as such, even though it includes explicit guides to interpretation, statements of purpose, and extensive comments normally presented as part of the text. But this is not how the UCC is read and used by American judges, practitioners, academics, and students. The culture of the UCC is underpinned by a vast literature that recounts its origins, underlying jurisprudence, legislative history, judicial interpretation, and scholarly expositions, critiques, and controversies. No more than 'The American Constitution' or 'the European Convention on Human Rights' refers solely to a document, the referent of 'the UCC' is not a bare legislative text. If outside the United States it were treated as such by students of comparative law or law reformers looking for legislative models, it would be subject to the same dangers of misunderstanding and misuse as unadorned surface law. The style of drafting, the form, the idea of a common law 'code', the underlying assumptions about judicial interpretation and the code's relation to commercial practice, all belong to the culture of common law, with a few Llewellynesque glosses.[64]

(ii) Projects for unification and harmonisation of European Private Law: the 'Restatement' model[65]

Interestingly, in efforts directed towards unification and harmonisation of private law in the European Union, the Restatements have been used as an ostensible model in several leading projects.[66] To what extent do these classic American projects have any relevance to the contemporary European context?

---

[64] More generally, Andrew Halpin argues for 'a richer notion' of legal doctrine, which includes not only formulations of rules, but also principles, differentiated conceptions of interpretive roles, and sophisticated conceptions of the nature of legal materials – all of which are usually 'beneath the surface'. Halpin (2004), Chapter 1.

[65] An excellent introduction to this topic is Smits (2007); see also Fazio (2007). On the Trento Common Core Project see Gerber (2004) and works discussed there.

[66] '[T]he Principles of European Contract Law have become well-known and strangely influential in the sense that they have spurred a veritable industry of restatements'. Beale (2006) at p. 6.

At first sight the differences are vast: apart from contingencies of time and space, one can point to some striking contrasts:

- In Europe the issues relate to unification of laws of different nation states rather than within one single, albeit federal, sovereign state; but in both instances there is an issue about the extent to which the states have sovereign power over private law;
- In the United States the Restatements and Uniform Laws were felt to be needed because under the Constitution private law was largely within the jurisdiction of the several states; in the European Union there is no such restriction and there is therefore more scope for initiatives channelled through a single, if complex, centre, subject to the principle of subsidiarity;[67]
- In Europe unification involves transcending several legal traditions (civil, common law, Scandinavian, international law) and differences within those traditions; in America the problem was largely one of maintaining the unity (and dominance) of the imported English common law;
- In Europe the Member States chose to develop a multilingual community, so unification has to cope with a multiplicity of languages as opposed to American legal culture that was underpinned by one version of the English language;
- In Europe unification of laws is being attempted in a political context in which unity is strongly contested; in America after the Civil War national unity was not such an issue so far as law was concerned;
- In Europe unification is being attempted across diverse traditions, cultures, and religions at a time when 'diversity' is more openly recognised than it was in the United States in the first half of the twentieth century;
- In Europe most of the efforts at unification are directed at persuading the European Parliament and Council (usually via the Commission) to adopt measures of unification; in the United States, as we have seen, the Restatements were conceived as a means of by-passing the legislative and executive branches of the various states.

Despite these and many other differences, there are some apparent similarities that might justify treating the American and European efforts as analogous:

- The main focus of attention in both cases has been on private law, especially commercial law and contract – which are sometimes subsumed under the contested category of 'lawyers' law';[68]
- Some, but not all, of the main initiatives have come from non-governmental organisations and individuals;[69]

---

[67] However, the EU has been harmonising regulatory law for a long time, but only in respect of consumer protection has it intervened significantly in respect of private law (in the narrow sense).

[68] On the problematic concept of 'lawyers' law' see p. 270 above.

[69] A striking example is the Lando Commission, which broke away from UNIDROIT in 1980.

- Apart from the movement for a European Civil Code (or a Code of Contract), many of the projects aim at constructing forms of 'soft law' short of legislation, several taking the form of 'restatements';[70]
- Most of the end-products seek to render existing doctrine as formal statements of legal principles or rules, some supplemented by notes similar to those of the American Restatements;
- Most of the European projects are expressly directed to quite specific practical purposes rather than as academic exercises.[71]

There are thus some similarities between the American Restatements and some European projects on unification, especially in respect of juridical form, in having limited (though varied) practical objectives, in being concerned with rather cautious incremental legal development, and in being in large part the work of private sector organisations and academics. It is also tempting to suggest that the main initiators of the European projects are Euro-philes and the opponents and sceptics have been Euro-sceptics or legal nationalists, such as Pierre Legrand.[72] That may be partly true, but on its own it is too simple. So too is the argument that the outcome of such efforts will be merely surface law – obscuring local differences, misleading as descriptions, emphasising superficial similarities, and likely to be of little practical importance.

The targets of such generalised scepticism are quite varied. They include the ideas that (i) there is a common core of principles and concepts of European contract, or more generally private law; (ii) codification of European contract or private law is feasible and desirable; and (iii) a common European legal culture will develop over time.

There are strong grounds for arguing that such scepticism is over-generalised: First, as Hugh Beale has pointed out:

> In one sense we already have a European private law in the form of legislation from Brussels. Firstly, some of the articles of the Treaty, for example those dealing with competition, give direct rights of action to those who are injured by anti-competitive practices. Secondly, there are many regulations that affect

---

[70] On soft law in the EU, see Chapter 4, n. 132 above.

[71] 'Some hope that their projects will be treated as preliminaries to codification. Others, who may be opposed to large scale codification, conceive of more limited practical uses.' Beale lists the following uses for some projects: (i) concretising the *lex mercatoria*; (ii) enabling parties to a transnational contract to adopt principles expressly (subject to any mandatory applicable national laws); and (iii) providing suitable models for legislation, (sometimes by stating what is thought to be 'the best modern rule', echoing an ALI dilemma, see above); (iv) as a translation tool; (v) as guides to future sectoral harmonisation, short of codification, (as exemplified by existing EU Directives and regulations on consumer contracts). (Beale (2006)). See also Miller (2007).

[72] The debate about codification is sometimes represented as a power struggle between representatives of the common law and civil law traditions. As Legrand argues, codification or large-scale unification would probably be dominated by the civilians. (Legrand (1997) at Chapter 9). That is probably too simple, but one might interpret the use of the 'restatement idea' as a concession to common law incrementalism.

matters of private law, for example, in the field of jurisdiction. And, thirdly, there are European Directives, which Member States are obliged to implement though the precise means of implementation is left to the Member State.[73]

This legislation, especially on competition and consumer law, can hardly be dismissed as unimportant, ineffective, or a mere façade.[74]

Second, the European projects in the field are quite varied: UNIDROIT, the Trento Project, the Lando Commission, the European Commission on European Contract Law, the movement for codification of private law or contract, and the study group on Social Justice in European Law all have different agendas and methods.[75] Most have quite specific and nuanced objectives that fall short of codification. For example, the Common Frame of Reference, which is being developed for the European Commission, is likely to be used as a legislative and interpretive 'toolbox' of standard principles, concepts and terminology that will guide the revision and extension of sectoral harmonisation, but does not aim for codification. Indeed, some of those involved with this project and its predecessors are specifically opposed to codification.[76] The European Commission has backed away from ambitious legislative projects designed to replace national legislation in deference to the doctrine of subsidiarity; and some governments, including that of the United Kingdom, have opposed unifying legislation that would replace national laws – although a good deal of unifying has been done in respect of consumer protection.

Third, the processes involved and the conceptions of the enterprise are a good deal more complex and sophisticated than the original American Restatements. One major difference is that the main strategic aim is to work with the European legislative authorities rather than to by-pass them. Even if the main preparatory work is quite abstract and technocratic in tendency, political concerns (e.g. the protection of weaker parties) will have an opportunity to be weighed in an allegedly democratic legislative process.

Thus, although the current projects on unification of European private law aim at the production of code-like statements of principles and/or rules, the processes involved and the institutional context are likely to make them less vulnerable to charges of 'formalism' or the production of mere 'surface law' than the ALI Restatements.

(e) Under the radar: unnoticed, secret and invisible legal orders

In Esmeralda, city of water, a network of canals and a network of streets span and intersect each other. To go from one place to another you have always the choice

---

[73] Beale (2006). On the EU and harmonisation see also Sauter and Vos (1998).
[74] These are comparable to European legislation in other fields.
[75] These are usefully surveyed in Beale (2006). For a recent analysis, see Fazio (2007).
[76] Beale (2006).

between land and boat: and since the shortest distance between two points in Esmeralda is not a straight line, but a zigzag that ramifies in tortuous optional routes, the ways that open to each passserby are never two, but many, and they increase further for those who alternate a stretch by boat with one on dry land.

And so Esmeralda's inhabitants are spared the boredom of following the same streets every day. And that is not all: the network of routes is not arranged on one level, but follows instead an up-and-down course of steps, landings, cambered bridges, hanging streets. Combining segments of the various routes, elevated or on ground level, each inhabitant can enjoy every day the pleasure of a new itinerary to reach the same places. The most fixed and calm lives in Esmeralda are spent without any repetition.

Secret and adventurous lives, here as elsewhere, are subject to greater restrictions. Esmeralda's cats, thieves, illicit lovers move along higher, discontinuous ways, dropping from a rooftop to a balcony, following guttering with acrobats' steps. Below, the rats run in the darkness of the sewers, one behind the other's tail, along with conspirators and smugglers: they peep out of manholes and drainpipes, they slip through double bottoms and ditches, from one hiding-place to another they drag crusts of cheese, contraband goods, kegs of gunpowder, crossing the city's compactness pierced by the spokes of underground passages.

The map of Esmeralda should include, marked in different coloured inks, all these routes, solid and liquid, evident and hidden. It is more difficult to fix on the map the routes of swallows, who cut the air over the roofs, dropping long invisible parabolas with their still wings, darting to gulp a mosquito, spiraling upward, grazing a pinnacle, dominating from every point of their airy paths all the points of the city.[77]

In *Globalisation and Legal Theory* I used this quotation to illustrate the idea of a user's perspective on law and to suggest that from that kind of standpoint a legal order is in some respects analogous to a city.[78] The idea of 'surface law' suggests that beneath formal accounts of a given legal order in terms of rules or doctrine there may lurk other normative or legal orders that are arcane, ignored, or even 'invisible'. Commonly cited examples of such phenomena include Santos' account of Pasagarda law (the unofficial property regime of a Brazilian *favela*)[79] or gypsy law as described by Weyrauch and others,[80] or the Common Law Movement in the United States (the legal arm of the militias) as described by Koniak,[81] or '*angrezi shariat*' (the institutionalised and partly anglicised social practices of some Muslim communities in Britain).[82] That such normative orders exist is an established social fact. That some satisfy broad criteria of identification of non-state law, such as those suggested in Chapter 3, is

---

[77] Italo Calvino (1974) *Invisible Cities* at pp. 88–9. Calvino's notion of 'invisibility' is concerned with the elusiveness of depicting the 'reality' of a city; much of it is applicable to the difficulties of describing law, see *GLT*, pp. 168–73.

[78] *GLT*, pp. 137–8, 168–73; see *GJB*, pp. 1–2.   [79] Santos (2002), Chapter 5.

[80] Weyrauch *et al.* (1993), (2001).   [81] Koniak (1996), (1997). See also Hendges (1997).

[82] Menski and Pearl (1998) at pp. 51–61 On South Asians in Britain as 'skilled cultural navigators', see Ballard (1994), discussed in Menski (2006) at pp. 60–5; see also Bano (2007).

arguable.[83] However, Calvino's evocation of Esmeralda provides a warning against talking loosely of 'invisible' or 'arcane' or 'unnoticed' legal orders for several reasons.

First, some of the routes in Esmeralda are *part* of the 'official' structure of the city – the canals, the streets, and the bridges, for example. Similarly previous examples of what lies beneath 'the surface' discussed in this chapter are defined by their relationship to a legal system: interposed norms, enforcement or compliance practices, 'soft law' documents such as the American *Restatements*, are not independent of the legal orders to which they are attached. Rather they implement, supplement, modify, or subvert an existing regime of surface law. The idea of an independent legal order is different from this: the common law regimes of the militias are in opposition to, and aspire to replace, 'official' American municipal law.[84] Similarly, residents of Pasagarda leased, conveyed, and inherited property, although in the eyes of the 'asphalt law' (as they referred to municipal law) they were trespassers on the land in which they claimed interests according to Pasagarda law.[85]

'Independence' in this context is a relative matter. The institutionalised practices of Muslim communities typically modify some of their traditions and customs in order to conform to the 'host' legal system. For example, Muslim pre-nuptial contracts and Islamic banking practices try to accommodate both state and religious legal ideas.[86] Even in respect of matters on which they diverge from 'official' law, non-state legal orders often echo or caricature the concepts and forms of the state legal system. For example, Pasagarda residents use simplified versions of official documents.[87] Even more strikingly the discourse of the Common Law Movement draw heavily on traditional common law terms (e.g. lien, sovereignty, affidavit, equity) as well as basing their regime on the original wording of the American Constitution, the first ten Amendments, and, bizarrely, the Uniform Commercial Code.[88] Thus while it serves clarity to treat Pasagarda law, Gypsy law, and the Common Law Courts as discrete entities, they are all involved in complex interrelationships and interactions with state legal systems.[89]

Secondly, to talk of 'invisible' or 'ignored' legal orders leaves open the question 'invisible to or ignored by whom?' Most of the standard examples referred to above are not recognised as legal by the state legal system. There is an important difference between official recognition of Islamic or customary law in Tanzania

---

[83] See Chapter 4.4 above. Whether these examples are treated as 'law' is not important in the present context.

[84] Koniak (1996). This article is entitled 'When Law Risks Madness'.

[85] Santos (2002), Chapter 5.

[86] Bano 2007. On Islamic Banking see, for example, Iqbal and Llewellyn (eds.) (2002). On minority communities in Britain see Menski (2006) at pp. 60–5 and works cited there. See further Chapter 13, n. 110.

[87] Santos (2002) at 106–7, pp. 117–22.   [88] Koniak (1996) at pp. 71–3, 89–91.

[89] On interlegality see Chapter 16.2 on the web.

for certain purposes as part of the 'official' legal system (state legal pluralism) and courts taking into account non-state customs or beliefs in specific cases, for example in a plea in mitigation[90] or a 'cultural defence'.[91] Terms like 'invisible' and 'arcane' suggest something more than non-recognition. A non-state normative or legal order may not be officially recognised, but may nevertheless be in public view. For example, Islamic legal ideas are in the public domain: whether or not the customs and practices of a given community have been studied or publicly described is often a matter of happenstance. Only since the mid-1980s has 'Gypsy law' begun to receive sustained detailed attention from legal scholars; the Romani people have been quite reticent about their beliefs and practices, but they have been described in general terms in the non-legal literature for many years. Santos' description of the situation in 'Pasagarda' in the 1980s is often cited as a classic case study, but analogous practices in other Latin American *favelas* are generally undocumented.[92] In short, 'invisibility' is a contingent fact. The significant point in the present context is that surface accounts of municipal law rarely mention non-state legal orders, however important or prominent they are.[93]

It is tempting to treat 'invisible' legal systems as analogous to 'informal economies', which have a more developed literature. There are, indeed, some points of contact, even overlap. For example, 'a black economy' may have its own *lex mercatoria*. The terminology is similarly rather varied:

> The phenomenon is known, and has been discussed in literature, under many different names: informal, unofficial, regular, parallel, second underground, subterranean, hidden, invisible, unrecorded, and shadow economy or moonlighting. In several languages, the term most often used is 'black economy' ('le travail au noir' in French, 'Schwarzarbeit' in German, and 'svarta sektor' in Swedish).[94]

Most of these terms could be applied to examples of non-state legal orders. However, the main focus is on contrasting 'black economies' to recorded GNP, usually with a negative orientation, emphasising tax evasion, connections with crime, drugs, and prostitution and the relative merits of policies of deterrence.

---

[90] Since 1994 Judges in England have been issued with a *Handbook on Ethnic Minority Issues*. See www.jsboard.co.uk/publications.

[91] There is a rapidly growing literature on 'cultural defence' (e.g. Renteln (2004) and Phillips (2007)). Of course, under conflicts of law rules foreign laws and foreign judgments may be recognised in specific cases, but that is a different issue.

[92] However, there is a growing literature on urban poverty in Latin America, including the legal aspects, (e.g., Fernandes (eds.) (1995) and, more broadly, Fernandes and Varley (eds.) (1998), McAuslan (2003)).

[93] In 1990 an informal survey of literature on Brazilian Law in English found no references to Pasagarda or *favelas*. In a more detailed survey of the primary and secondary legal literature on Mauritius (1995) I found almost no mention of religious law even though nearly 70 per cent of the population are Hindu and Muslim (ethnically Indo-Pakistani) and 27 per cent are Christian (mainly Creole or African). The municipal legal system is typically described as a 'hybrid' mixture of common law and civil law. The significant point is that such literature is completely uninformative about the importance or otherwise of religious law, custom, or other forms of non-state law.

[94] Frey and Schneider (2001) at p. 7441; See also Hansen (2001), Benton (1994).

A prominent exception is Hernando de Soto, *The Other Path* (1989).[95] While some non-state legal orders are opposed to the state legal system (e.g. the Common Law Courts), there is no presumption that they are in conflict. Rather 'interlegality' encompasses a great variety of relations.[96]

Of course, some normative and legal regimes are purposely secretive. Secret regulations and tribunals are not unknown as subordinate parts of a state legal regime.[97] Official or semi-official interposed norms relating to enforcement or compliance are typically not publicised. The interposed appointments committee that Sophie found came under threat as soon as its existence became known. Resort to alternative dispute resolution, including domestic and international arbitration, is in part motivated by the fact that many such proceedings are not in public and in important respects may be protected by strict requirements of confidentiality. And, of course, Esmeralda's cats, thieves, and illicit lovers will often choose particular routes to escape observation. Understanding law in a broad sense requires knowledge of normative and non-state legal orders 'in action' and their inter-relations ('interlegality'). Even understanding a state legal system involves knowledge of its relationship to other co-existing normative orders, whether or not they are characterised as 'legal'. This inevitably involves penetrating beneath the 'surface' of formal statements of legal rules.

10.3 Meanings and referents of 'surface law'

I have so far avoided defining 'surface law'. The foregoing case studies suggest that the standard dichotomies that we have explored are regularly used (often quite loosely) in a variety of contexts, that they reflect some persistent concerns that need to be differentiated, that what is treated as being on the surface varies, and that the vocabulary has a strong emotive bias along the lines of 'we know best': deep/superficial; appearance/reality; what is meant to happen/what actually happens. It is also clear from these examples that familiar formalist/ realist differences of perspective are a recurrent theme.

Of course, what appears 'on the surface' depends on standpoint. In order to keep things simple let us postulate as a paradigm case an outside observer (student, scholar or citizen) encountering a legal order for the first time in the form of legal rules articulated in formal texts such as codes, statutes, treaties, regulations, textbook statements, restatements, and the like.[98] Let us treat as

---

[95] See Chapter 12 below.   [96] See Chapter 16.2 on the web.

[97] The story of Guantanamo Bay and 'extraordinary rendition' created a more complex 'legal Black Hole', see Steyn (2004), Gross and Ní Aolaín (2006), Lichtblau (2008).

[98] Since some of the most important contrasts have been between the surface and what lies beneath what judges say, it is sensible to include legal judgments or opinions. But, especially in the common law, these do not always embody 'rules in fixed verbal form'. An elusive category is 'official views', beloved of ironic sociologists. For example, generalised secondary accounts of the kind that McBarnet accused criminologists of relying on to make contrasts between 'appearance' and 'reality' in the 1960s. (McBarnet (1978)).

extensions other standpoints (e.g. a legal draftsman, or a 'foreign' lawyer or businessman visiting another legal system) and other legal phenomena such as ideologies, buildings, public legislative processes, trials, and so on which may be what newcomers and others first encounter 'on the surface'.

Confining ourselves to legal texts and external observers simplifies the analysis. However, in the present context it is sensible to have a reasonably broad conception of 'law' because some of the standard contrasts are made between explicit statements of legal rules and something else: 'the law in action', 'real rules', 'unofficial law', hidden normative and legal orders, interposed norms and institutions, underlying principles, ideologies and so on. In diffusion a common contrast is often made between 'official' imported law and pre-existing 'unofficial law' – typically customary or religious normative orders that exist below the surface, the interaction with which is often overlooked.[99] So without entering into debates about definitions or conceptions of 'law', I shall here treat these contrasted phenomena as falling within the ambit of the 'legal'.[100]

(a) 'Surface' as metaphor

The Oxford English Dictionary devotes nearly three pages to the usages of 'surface'. The definition that most closely matches its most common usage in the present context is figurative:

> Usually denoting that part or aspect of anything which presents itself to a slight or casual mental view, or which is perceived without examination; outward appearance often in such phrases as *on the surface* = superficially. Also, to scratch the surface....[101]

'Surface' in this context is a metaphor suggesting the exterior of a physical object or the top of a body of liquid (a lake, the sea, a cup of coffee). The liquid metaphor suggests a vertical plane, with an observer looking down on the surface.[102] There is a common, but not a necessary, suggestion that the surface

---

[99] E.g. Pistor and Wellons, (1999). Of course, the converse can be the case – that is it is state law that is the 'host' – for example, the growing interaction between Muslim law and custom and pre-existing state law in the United Kingdom (See Menski and Pearl (1998) at pp. 51–83), or the interaction between Brazilian state law (ashphalt law) and 'upstart' Pasagarda law of the *favelas* (Santos (2002), Chapter 4).

[100] For a broad conceptualisation of the 'legal ' that would fit this contrast see above Chapter 4.4. The conception of law developed there or, more succinctly, MacCormick's conception of 'institutionalised normative order' will fit my purpose here. (MacCormick (2007) Part I). The argument in this chapter would not be changed radically if a narrower conception of 'law' were insisted on – for the standard contrasts could be expressed in terms of legal/non-legal phenomena. However, some examples, such as the Cheyennes or Sophie's project might be excluded from such an analysis because they do not involve 'law' so conceived at all.

[101] *Oxford English Dictionary* (2nd edn, 1989).

[102] See my exchange with Westbrook about diffusion: Westbrook (2006) at pp. 490–1 and Twining (2006a) at p. 511. Of course, the metaphor is sometimes mixed – (e.g. veneer, façade, shell contrasted with core, heart, root).

is opaque and what lies beneath it may be different from what is observable on top. In that case it may be hidden, arcane, secret, invisible, and more or less 'deep'. The metaphor can be dangerous in several obvious respects:

First, it may suggest that the surface is opaque; but, of course, many liquids are more or less transparent.

Second, it suggests that what is below the surface is not or may not be the same. There is, of course, a whole spectrum of possibilities from the liquid having the same consistency throughout, as in a well mixed cocktail, to multiple layering (as with oil and water) or to a whole complex world of different phenomena hiding or hidden 'beneath the surface'.[103]

Third, what appears on the surface depends in part on standpoint. What is obvious or apparent to one may be hidden from another. In most of the examples used here it is reasonable to postulate an outside observer. But there are of course many other standpoints, including those in which what is first encountered is not a legal text, but for example, a fatal road accident, a policeman, a writ or summons, a standard form contract, a court building, an actual trial, or a court-room drama – in all of which, the official legal rules are 'in the background'.[104]

Fourth, quite what conception of 'law' is adopted in the circumstances and what 'law' presents itself to a particular observer may vary. So, for example, rules embodied in texts are most commonly treated as the law on the surface: the university's published rules in Sophie's project; formal human rights instruments; codes or doctrinal statements of contract rules; the texts of the American Restatements and Uniform laws; and so on. But, in his approach to comparative law, Markesenis treats judicial opinions rather than abstract rules as being on 'the surface' and contrasts the styles of common law and civil law judges in respect of openness about policy and willingness to articulate precise rules. Llewellyn when talking about 'paper rules' was similarly contrasting what judges say and what they do in the context of common law adjudication. However, McBarnet's complaint against criminologists was that they focused on 'official' legal ideology (due process, the rule of law, defendant's rights) and contrasted this with what happened in practice, while ignoring the details of the intermediate formal legal rules.[105]

10.4 Some health warnings

In pursuing her research Sophie needs to bear in mind some salutary 'health warnings' about using, or at least over-using, these contrasts. Some of the important ones could be summarised as follows:

---

[103] *Ibid.*

[104] Even in respect of legal texts there are variants from formal statements of legal rules to which other considerations might apply (e.g. the Comments of the Uniform Commercial Code, 'the small print' in a standard form contract (is this 'on the surface'?), or judicial opinions (judgments) where there is no explicit 'holding' or *ratio decidendi*).

[105] McBarnet (1978).

(a) Do not be seduced by the emotive charge in these terms. Nearly all these dichotomies involve terms that privilege one branch of a dichotomy against the other: reality, real rules, action, practice, back stage, depth all imply some kind of superiority when contrasted with appearance, aspiration, paper rules, books, theory, and superficiality. In the present context it is especially important to be wary of contrasts between superficiality and depth and not to confuse 'surface' with 'superficial.' If such contrasts are to be analytically useful, they need, so far as is feasible, to be purged of any strong emotive associations.

(b) Because of (a) there may be a temptation to focus attention on one branch of the dichotomy and to neglect the other (e.g. to claim to be only concerned with real rules or the law in action or what goes on backstage). A healthy corrective is McBarnet's criticism of socio-legal scholars and criminologists for ignoring legal rules or treating them as unimportant.[106]

(c) Obviously, more than one kind of 'gap' is suggested by these contrasts, but they are often not clearly differentiated. Gaps between appearance and reality and aspiration and reality are quite different – and 'reality' is a notoriously question-begging term. The distinction between 'paper rules' and 'real rules' was originally used to draw a distinction between empirical description and normative prescription of judicial behaviour. Karl Llewellyn was careful to emphasise that even 'pure paper rules' remain an actuality in adjudication.[107] Similarly, the contrast between law in books and law in action is often used in ways that assume that law books only contain bare statements of rules of law and nothing else. That is hardly true of most law books, let alone books about law.[108] For some of us, a persistent challenge has been to get more of the action into the books.[109]

(d) The extent of a 'gap' varies considerably. Gaps can be immense, minor, or almost non-existent as a matter of continuous variation. In empirical enquiries nothing about the extent of a gap should be taken for granted.

(e) Perhaps, most important, is the point that treating these familiar contrasts as binary and talk of 'gaps' both suggest that the two poles of each dichotomy are separate, perhaps even unrelated alternatives.[110] However, this is not the case with nearly all the alternatives considered here. When rules are flouted, not enforced, manipulated, or misinterpreted the activity tales place with reference to those rules. 'Underlying' problems, principles, policies and rationales are intimately related to 'surface' law. 'Interposed' norms and institutions are inserted between surface phenomena and actual practices. Overlooked or 'invisible' legal and normative orders may sometimes proceed independently and without reference to official or state law, but more often than not there is some interaction: the relationship can involve

---

[106] *Ibid.*   [107] See p. 300 above.   [108] Abel (1973).   [109] *LIC*, Chapter 3.
[110] I am grateful to Andrew Halpin for emphasising this point.

rules about following rules'.[114] Griffiths' research led him to accept that social behaviour is much more rule-guided than is generally recognised and that '[t]he continuities between "legal" and "non-legal" rules are thus much more manifold and more profound than one had realized.'[115] The important point in the present context is that a great part of Galligan's 'social spheres' and Griffiths' 'rules about following rules' are beneath the surface in that all of the elements cannot be divined from the text alone. They may be expressed, but not in fixed verbal form, or tacit, implicit, and, as with rules of grammar, not fully understood by those who follow them.

To sum up: (i) these recurring dichotomies are indeed significant, but they often reflect different underlying concerns; (ii) accounts of 'surface law' are often on their own inadequate, mainly because they are uninformative ('the study of rules alone is not enough'); (iii) 'surface' as a metaphor conceals a number of pitfalls, not least in the bias in terms such as superficial, deep, action, reality; (iv) not all 'surface law' is superficial, soft, or unimportant; (v) as I hope Henrik Zahle would have agreed, the idea of surface law is an important dimension of polycentricity;[116] and, finally, (vi) the various examples discussed contain some suggestive distinctions and ideas that are more nuanced than the crude standard dichotomies. They may help to inform discussions of diffusion, convergence, unification and harmonisation of laws and other topics.

---

[114] Griffiths (2003) at p. 1(abstract).

[115] *Ibid.* This chapter raises important questions for any general theory of rules – see Chapter 15.4 on the web.

[116] Petersen and Zahle (1995).

Chapter 11

Is law important? Law and the Millennium Development Goals[1]

It has required great vision, great holiness, great wisdom to keep alive and vivid the sense of unity of man. It is precisely the saints, the poets, the philosophers, and the great men of science who have borne witness to the underlying unity which daily life has denied. But now the distances are abolished. It is at least possible that our new technological resources, properly deployed, will conquer ancient shortage. Can we not at such a time realize the moral unity of our human experience and make it the basis of a patriotism for the world itself?[2] (Barbara Ward)

11.1 Introduction

The purpose of this chapter is to give an interpretation of a range of views about the importance of law in economic, social and political development in the context of changing theoretical and technical approaches to 'development' from 1945 to the Millennium and a little beyond. Is law important? If so, why and in what respects?

My standpoint is that of an English jurist who has been concerned about economic, social and political development throughout his career, mainly as a theorist, scholar and teacher of law, but also from time to time as a consultant and advisor on a range of specific issues and projects that have been 'developmentally relevant'. In this regard, I have been more of an observer than a participant.

I am conscious of significant biases in three respects. First, my main experience of, and concerns about, 'development' have been rooted in Eastern Africa. I have had some limited professional experience in other Commonwealth countries, including West Africa, Papua New Guinea, Lesotho, Hong Kong, and India, but my main geographical reference points have been Sudan, Kenya, Uganda and Tanzania and, to a lesser extent, Ethiopia and Rwanda. The largely unhappy stories of development in that region are significantly different from those relating to Latin America, South East Asia, the Middle East, and African countries that were colonised by imperial powers other than the British. One

---

[1] I am grateful to Patrick McAuslan, Brian Tamanaha, Bronwen Morgan, Clare Williams, and participants in seminars in Miami, London, and Berlin for helpful comments and suggestions.
[2] Ward (1966).

theme of this chapter is the obvious one that generalisation about problems of development beyond the local and the national are quite dangerous.

Second, I am an enthusiast for my discipline: I am a 'legal nationalist' in that I believe that law can pervade nearly all aspects of social life, that it is a marvellous subject of study, and that a legal perspective can provide important lenses on social and political events and phenomena. Law *is* important – for better or for worse. From time to time I have had to make 'the case for law' – usually in the parochial context of arguing the claims of my academic discipline for a reasonable share of funding, but also because of the elusive values embodied in ideas about human rights and the rule of law.[3]

A third bias is that I believe that it is a scandal and a tragedy that over half of humankind lives and dies in conditions of radical poverty. As a realist I am well aware of the many obstacles to achieving even the minimal standards of decency and justice that are prescribed by the Millennium Development Goals (MDGs). I am even quite pessimistic about the prospects for achieving the less than half loaf promised by the MDGs. But as an unreconstructed idealist I believe that our continuing acceptance of the present situation and the modest, often cynical, commitments of political leaders are shameful. We have the means, we have the know-how, it is in everyone's long-term self-interest, but ultimately we seem to lack the political will 'to make poverty history'.

From a global perspective 'law and development' raises important issues for general jurisprudence. The intention of this chapter is not polemical. The purpose is to make a modest contribution to the theoretical understanding of 'law and development' from a particular, quite limited, perspective. The thesis is that not much can be expected of law as an instrument for directly or indirectly controlling or guiding human behaviour, but nonetheless it is potentially important not only in obvious ways – as one precondition of security and stability – but in some less obvious ones that deserve attention.

The chapter is structured as follows: Section 11.2 sketches a broad historical context; Section 11.3 constructs five ideal types of assumptions and perceptions about the importance of law in development derived from both the contemporary literature and my own experiences in this broad and confusing field. The five categories, which overlap, are: (a) that law is only important insofar as it contributes to pre-conditions for development; beyond that, like water in marriage, its role is incidental, contingent and largely uninteresting; (b) law is important because the Rule of Law (formal legality) is important; (c) law is mainly important for providing structures and processes for ensuring the efficient operation of free markets; (d) that in addition to (a) – and possibly (b) and (c) – law is important at various levels and in necessary ways for constituting, structuring and regulating practices and procedures that enable development activities (the multifunctional view); (e) that human development

---

[3] See Chapter 11.3 (d) and (e) below.

is largely a matter of attaining human rights and that law is a critical element in rights-based approaches to development.[4] Section 11.4 considers these five perspectives in relation to the Millennium Development Goals – their underlying theory, and the main texts of the Millennium Project – with special reference to Uganda.[5] Section 11.6 considers the relevance of non-state law and other normative orders to 'development'.

One preliminary point: the concepts of 'law' and 'development' have both generated a great deal of literature and for good reason. So conceptual clarification is a necessary preliminary to addressing questions about the relationship between law and development. In this context, I propose to apply Occam's Razor to both terms. I shall adopt the concept of 'human development' pioneered by Ul Haq and given a philosophical justification by Amartya Sen and others. A useful formulation is by Sen:

> Development requires the removal of major sources of unfreedom: poverty as well as tyranny, poor economic opportunities as well as systematic social deprivation, neglect of public facilities as well as intolerance or overactivity of repressive states.[6]

This conception was constructed mainly in reaction to a tendency to confine or reduce the idea of poverty to low income in the case of individuals and low GDP in the case of countries. It is now widely, if not universally, accepted that poverty involves multiple deprivations which are interrelated – including health, food, water, sanitation, housing, and literacy. In talking of 'development' wealth is not, and cannot be, the only value.

While the Human Development Index and related indicators are recent, at no stage since World War II have most significant leaders confined the idea of 'development' to economics. The Universal Declaration of Human Rights covered civil and political and social and economic rights. War on 'poverty, ignorance, and disease' was the rallying cry of Julius Nyerere and others in the 1960s.[7] Concern with social development and welfare has been a continuous theme in the discourses of development. What is new is first, that the range of quantifiable indicators has been expanded and reformed and second, that a very broad consensus has crystallised around the Human Development Index and a broad conception of poverty.

---

[4] This range of ideal types is not comprehensive. For example, it does not include strong socialist (command economy) or anarchist views, but reference is made to the idea, not uncommon among economists, that law is mainly a brake or an obstacle to economic development.

[5] A detailed analysis of the Uganda Poverty Reduction Action Plan, 2004 is included in Appendix I on the web.

[6] Sen (1999) at p. 3. Compare the statement by Sen's close friend and colleague, Mahbub Ul Haq: 'Human development has four essential pillars: equity, sustainability, productivity and empowerment. It regards economic growth as essential but emphasizes the need to pay attention to its quality and distribution, analyses at length its link with human lives and questions its long-term sustainability'. 'The Human Development Paradigm' in Ul Haq (1995), pp. 13–23, at p. 21.

[7] E.g. Nyerere (1967), (1968).

'While it is true that, sixty years on, we may not be that much closer than the founders of the UN were to knowing how to achieve 'development' (how to overcome the global inequality that has grown over the last two centuries), we *are* closer to agreeing on what development really is.[8]

Earlier chapters have made the case for a broad conception of law when adopting a global perspective.[9] However, nearly all of the discourse and debate about law and development have made state (municipal) law the almost exclusive focus of attention. Even those who favour a limited role for the state in economic and social life have been state-centric in this respect. So the question: 'What is the role of law in development?' has almost invariably referred to municipal law. This, I think, is a mistake because it underestimates the importance of other levels of legal and normative ordering and it reinforces a tendency to assume that tradition, custom, religious law and 'unofficial law' are generally obstacles to development, which is associated with 'modernisation'. In order to engage with the literature, most of this chapter follows convention in concentrating on state law. However, Section 11.6 argues that in considering the future, much more attention needs to be paid to other levels of legal ordering and to the potential roles of non-state law in furthering, as well as impeding, the attainment of development goals. Just as in diffusion studies it is a common error to assume that legal importation and law reform generally fills a legal vacuum ('the empty vessel fallacy'),[10] so in considering law and development it is a mistake to assume that non-state law is non-existent, unimportant, or just an obstacle to be overcome.[11]

11.2 'Law and development': An historical excursus

Some standard accounts of 'development' (and of 'law and development') start the story after World War II. It is true that 'development' took on special significance after 1945 and, as one commentator put it, was used as 'shorthand for the process of socioeconomic change that has shaped contemporary societies, particularly those of Africa, Asia, and Latin America.'[12] It might seem pedantic to point out that Lord Hailey's classic African Survey was published in 1938,[13] the League of Nations Mandate for Tanganyika in 1919 explicitly refers to a duty to promote 'the social progress of it inhabitants' and the 'development of the natural resources of the territory'; that Sir Henry Maine specifically called his argument in *Ancient Law* 'a theory of legal development';[14] and that consciously induced change was central to Bentham's ideas. Related ideas of progress, evolution, and reform have long intellectual histories. What was new

---

[8] Murphy (2006) at p. 353.   [9] See Chapters 1 and 4. See further Chapter 12.

[10] Everett M. Rogers (1995), discussed at chapter 9.4(j).

[11] Jeffrey Sachs, the Director of the Millennium Project, fairly consistently treats custom and tradition as obstacles to development and, in a period of religious revival, barely considers the role of religion (Sachs (2005)). See Chapter 11.6 below.

[12] P. B Evans (2001) at p. 3557.   [13] Hailey (1938).   [14] Maine (1884) (Preface to 10th edn).

after 1945 was not the idea itself, nor governmental interest in the idea (perhaps with an enhanced priority), but rather that the processes and theories about them became a major focus of attention in the social sciences in the period. Thus histories of 'development' tend to be inward-looking and parochial accounts by academics about recent academic writings.

This is especially true of 'law and development', an American phrase that I first heard about 1964, several years after I had begun to take a jurist's interest in law in Africa.[15] There has been no detailed history of efforts to relate law to development. However, there is now a standard legend about the American Law and Development Movement from the 1960s to the 1990s. It is largely focused on the activities based in a few elite American Law Schools and funded mainly by the Ford Foundation, perhaps with tacit support from the US Government. This legend may or may not be broadly accurate about the involvement of American academic lawyers, but for present purposes it is not suitable. It is parochial, exporter-oriented, geographically selective, and the time-scale is too short.[16]

For present purposes, a much better overview, but not a comprehensive history, is in a semi-autobiographical paper by Patrick McAuslan, who began his legal career as my colleague in Dar-es-Salaam, but unlike me, continued to work in the field, building up a vast experience of problems of land tenure, land reform and urban planning in more than forty countries over nearly forty years.[17] He would be the first to admit that his account is impressionistic and has an East African bias. But it fits both my impressions and my reading of the literature and it has some clear advantages over the narrower American accounts. First, it has a longer time span – tracing law and development back to the Middle Ages and starting the modern, more detailed account in the late colonial period (the 1940s). Second, it has a broader geographical reach,

[15] In Eastern Africa, where I worked from 1958 to 1965, the phrase 'law and development' was hardly used. The discourses and controversies centred on 'colonialism', 'nation-building', 'colonial law', 'African Law', 'Law in Africa', 'customary law', 'technical co-operation' and so on. There were occasional references to 'legal development'. One interesting exception was that in the early 1960s University College Dar-es-Salaam invited Wolfgang Friedmann to advise on setting up a course on 'Law and Economic Development' (Friedmann (1964). On the history of 'African Law' as a subject see Harrington and Manji (2003).

[16] I am not here concerned to take another swipe at American parochialism. Referring to American-sponsored activities as '*The* Law and Development Movement' may have not been appreciated in SOAS, Paris, and Louvain, let alone in law faculties in former French, British, Dutch, and Portuguese colonies, but it was not unreasonable for American scholars to be concerned about the state of a fragile field in their own universities. The most-cited work is 'Scholars in Self-estrangement' by Galanter and Trubek (1974), but there are more solid studies by Merryman (2000a) (2000b), Snyder (1980) Sutton (1990), Gardner (1980), and more recently by Dezalay and Garth (2002a), (2000b). For a sharp critique of this kind of literature see Tamanaha (1995). Recent writings have taken account of some non-American scholars but they are very largely confined to the 'anglophone' world and Latin America. (e.g Trubek and Santos (eds.) (2006)). An exception is Carty (ed.) (1992).

[17] McAuslan (2004). This summary is based on an unpublished paper presented at a conference in Cornell University in 2004. A revised version is in preparation for McAuslan (forthcoming 2009).

although it focuses mainly on the former British Empire, with an emphasis on Africa. Third, and most important, unlike much of the development literature, McAuslan's account is not solely exporter-oriented or focused on foreign interventions. Most of the law-and-development literature does not treat local activities directed to legal change as 'development'. Some of these reflect local responses to foreign imports, but others are largely home grown. For example, in most African countries national Law Reform Commissions and similar bodies continued to operate in times of foreign apathy and neglect as well as in times of foreign interventions, benign or otherwise.

Finally, McAuslan emphasises the difficulties and dangers of generalisation given the enormous variations in colonial legacies, local histories, cultures, conditions, and ruling elites. There are very significant differences between and within regions. The stories of 'law and development' in East Asia, India, Latin America, the Middle East, North Africa, and Africa south of the Sahara are all different. Talk of 'law and development' is a largely conventional expatriate Anglophone discourse.[18] Accounts of law in the histories of colonies of the other major imperial powers could well be substantially different. It is even difficult to generalise about Kenya, Uganda and Tanzania despite some shared history and geography. In short, there is no substitute for local legal histories.

McAuslan nevertheless sees some patterns in the perceptions of law and development in the period 1940 to the present. In particular he contrasts the views of producers (external) and importers (local) in a table that is highly suggestive, even if it is a simplification (see Table 11.1: The Evolution of Law and Development). If one interprets this as applying mainly to common law Africa and if one accepts that there is likely to be more homogeneity in the international donor community than in local stories of legal development, then this suggests that these are intelligent hypotheses, if not evidence-based generalisations, about the intellectual history of law and development in the late twentieth century.

What this highly suggestive overview brings home is the need for more detailed histories – especially local histories – of law in less developed countries and its significance for stability and political, social and economic development. There are a few examples – Pistor and Wellons's historical account of the role of law and legal institutions in six Asian countries between 1960–1995 is one model.[19] However, we are a long way from having the basics for a well-grounded theory of the relationships of law and development in different contexts.[20]

---

[18] See n. 15 above.

[19] Pistor and Wellons (1999). Outstanding earlier examples are Palley (1966), Ghai and McAuslan (1970).

[20] See, however, the ambitious, but highly contentious macro-economic work of Rafael La Porta and associates attempting to establish correlations between legal traditions and economic development (e.g. La Porta et al. (1996)). They argue that 'common law countries generally have the best, and French civil law coutries the worst, legal protection of investors, with German and Scandinavian civil law countries located in the middle.'). See Dam (2006) and Balas et al. (2008) and references there. For criticisms see Siems (2005) and Roe (2006).

Table 11.1 The Evolution of Law and Development (McAuslan)

Perceptions – * Phases	Producers (External)	Consumers (Internal)
Empire 15 – mid 20th century	Law in the acquisition of empire. The use of force to acquire and maintain empire. State creation: law and order: acquisition of land and its productive use; development of legal systems to facilitate European commerce.	Law in the acquisition of empire. State destruction: breakdown of legal order: disruption of commerce; land seizure; unequal application of the law; colonies as 'undeveloped estates'; slavery and forced labour. The use of force to resist and overthrow empire.
The 40s and 50s	The decades of benign colonialism. Use of law at both national and international levels to provide for the orderly transfer of power to new independent states: and to create rudiments of welfare state: education: health care	The decades of 'hanging on'. Using national and international law as a tool to prolong colonialism by purporting to confer rights and responsibilities while ensuring effective power resided in the metropolises.
The 60s	The decade of optimism. Law and development as part of the process of throwing off the shackles of colonialism and building a new polity; development of legal education and research; 'modern' laws from the metropolises introduced to provide for a 'modern' society and state.	The decade of nationalism. Law was used to reassert the national identity, national concerns; repatriate national assets and a national approach to exercising political and economic power via autochthonous constitutions, home-grown political systems and parastatal authorities.
The 70s	The decade of disillusion. Law and development 'doesn't work': new democratic structures and practices do not spring up overnight; transplants don't work.	The decade of consolidation. National legal systems were developed, operated and written about by home-grown lawyers. National legal solutions to national problems were developed and brought into operation.
The 80s	The decade of neglect but transition. IFIs and donors did not see law as a particularly important tool for development. Academics had better things to do than work in a field where there was a paucity of funding. New approaches began to enter the field.	The limits of legal radicalism. Law was ignored in the increasingly lawless competition for power and access to resources or used as a weapon in the struggle. Official state law had less and less relevance to the lives of the citizen.
The 90s	The decade of (re)-discovery. Perhaps law is important as a tool for the development of markets, the key to 'real' development and as an input to good governance; re-thinking transplants – perhaps they do work if the conditions are right.	The decade of challenge. Pressures both internal and external mount to change the structure of the state, political and economic systems and rethink the role of law in these developments. Constitutional and economic reforms via law.
The 00s	The decade of (re)-colonisation. The importation of Western law as the key to economic growth and entry into the global market place. The World Bank seeks to extend its empire by appropriating holistic legal systems and 'rule of law' reform. Law used to justify colonial re-occupation, new imposed constitutions, market-led land reform. New states recognised. Elites and resources appropriated.	The decade of (re)-colonisation. The imposition of Western law as a key to re-assert political and economic control over developing countries; IFIs and donors require national legal reforms. International law used to justify colonial occupation, regime change, semi-imposed constitutions; foreign acquisition of national resources. New states *as a colonial tool? Back to the future?*

Source: McAuslan unpublished. Reproduced by permission of the author.

11.3 Contemporary perceptions of the role of law in development: five models

This section considers five models of assumptions or attitudes to the question: What is the role of law in development? In much of the development literature and discourse by non-lawyers, law is hardly explicitly mentioned at all, either because it is taken for granted or because it is considered largely irrelevant. This changed with the American Law and Development Movement in its first phase (late 1960s to late 1970s), partly because law is given more emphasis in American culture and tradition than elsewhere. From time to time, national and international development agencies have given law a modest priority and, recently, development has increasingly surfaced in human rights discourse. These different attitudes can be roughly categorised into five ideal types: (a) the social control view; (b) the Rule of Law as formal legality; (c) law as a facilitator of free markets; (d) the multifunctional ('legal nationalist') view; and (e) rights-based perspectives.

These ideal types are an attempt to represent attitudes and expectations about the roles of law (law's point), not claims about what law in fact does (its effects).[21] To some extent they reflect different ideological views of the role of the state, but for the sake of clarity, it is best to keep expectations of law and models of the role of the state conceptually separate as the relationship is not one to one. These models or ideal types are not mutually exclusive. In particular, (c) and (d) will often include (a) or (b) or both, for (a) to (d) are ranked in increasing order of expansiveness. However, rights-based approaches are part of a different story.

(a) The Law and Order model: Like water in marriage?

In the early 1960s American academic lawyers began to ask: 'What is the role of law in development?' When I first heard the question, my initial reaction was sceptical. It sounded odd to English ears, inviting a response along the following lines:

> That is rather like asking: what is the role of water in marriage? Only a plumber would ask such a question. The answer is obvious: a necessary pre-condition, but beyond that there is no general answer, for the uses of water in this context are manifold, serendipitous, and not very interesting.

This rather flippant response probably reflected the views of most English lawyers and non-lawyers interested in development at the time.[22] Social order is

---

[21] See Chapter 4.3 (d) above.

[22] An exception was the International Commission of Jurists, a non-governmental organisation set up 'to foster understanding of and respect for the Rule of Law'. A number of English lawyers, including Lord Shawcross and Norman Marsh, played a significant part in its activities that included a series of conferences, which produced a number of pronouncements, including the

a pre-condition of development, but beyond that law is no more than a technical body of rules and a flexible instrument of particular policies.

Something like this view is implicit in writings about development that hardly mention law or do not mention it at all. That includes nearly all writings about economic and social development during the twentieth century, with a few notable exceptions.[23] Law is tacitly assumed to be a taken-for-granted pre-condition for security and stability rather than a salient feature of development strategies. A commonly stated view was: generally, law and order is one thing, development quite another. For example, McAuslan reports that between the mid-1960s and the early 1990s '[t]he World Bank did not rate law as a significant development discipline ... and Law was not a discipline which found a place in Habitat'.[24]

Theoretical support for this view can be found in the writings of some sociologists of law. For example, John Griffiths in his inaugural lecture at Groningen in 1977 asked: 'Is law important?' and gave the following answer:

> Legal rules are the *form* in which the political decisions taken by a nation state generally appear. ... The question 'is law important?' must be taken to ask what legal rules *add* to the political decisions they embody: the question is about law and it would be wrong to try to answer it by observing that politics are important.[25] ... [t]he sociology of law is more than one among many subcategories of sociology: it deals, rather, with one way by which the *sine qua non* of social life – collective goods – is maintained ... Law does not stand in a relation of a *cause* to collective goods (and hence to social phenomena); it is rather an aspect, however modest, of the overall social investment in collective goods – it is one of the forms which the social control effort as a whole exhibits[26] ... yes, legal rules are 'important', in the sense that they are an aspect of the maintenance of collective goods, and hence of social life itself.[27]

In short, law is mainly important for its contributions to social control.[28] By 'collective goods' Griffiths means: 'A preferred state of affairs which has [the]

Act of Athens, the Declaration of Delhi, and the Law of Lagos. When I was in Sudan and Tanzania I used to receive free copies of both the *Journal of the International Commission of Jurists* and the socialist *Review of Contemporary Law*, produced by the International Association of Democratic Lawyers – a regular reminder of the Cold War.

[23] In the period of decolonisation, constitution-making naturally became a focus of attention, but this was seen as related to political development. Land tenure and reform became an important topic in some countries, for instance in East Africa from the 1950s. The East African Royal Commission Report of 1955 devoted a chapter to recommending the individualisation of land tenure in order to 'enable access to land for economic use' Cmnd. 9475 (London: HMSO, 1955) CH. XXX (at 428). Lord Hailey, *An African Survey* (Revised) (1957).

[24] McAuslan (2003) at pp. 110–11

[25] John Griffiths 'Is Law Important?' (Inaugural Lecture, Groningen, 1977)) published as Griffiths (1978) at p. 357.

[26] *Ibid.*, p. 368.

[27] *Ibid.*, p. 369. This argument is developed and modified in Griffiths (2003) and (2006).

[28] Griffiths uses 'social control' more broadly than I have done in Chapter 4.1(c), but it is narrower than my 'ordering of relations' in that it is confined to the basic institutions of a society. At some points Griffiths implies that law is *necessary* for social control in complex societies, a view that is challenged by Tamanaha (2001) at p. 224.

property of depending upon simultaneous sacrifice by many actors – a preferred state of affairs, which, so long as actors remain free from collective
control, will not be maintained.'[29] Collective goods include basic institutions
such as the family, contract, property, and authority. Beyond that Griffiths is
sceptical of the extent to which legal rules have direct effects on behaviour and
on the feasibility of explaining behaviour in terms of such effects. Legal rules
may have indirect effects, but it is very difficult to separate these from other
factors.[30]

Griffiths acknowledges that law could be important instrumentally, but it is
virtually impossible to prove causal relations between legal rules as independent
variables and social behaviour.

> [N]ot all legal rules are involved with the maintenance of collective goods. …The
> other sort of legal rules, those which concern goods which could be secured by
> individual action, seem much less interesting; anything which needs to be known
> about them can be investigated within the bounds of the traditional, instrumen-
> talist conception of law, but without the illusion that legal rules, as such, will be an
> important explanatory variable.[31]

In short, instrumental questions about law are uninteresting beyond its
contribution to social control, just as questions about the incidental uses of
water in marriage are uninteresting because they are contingent, serendipitous
and incidental. In most instances law/water are not independent variables, and
if they have effects on behaviour they are generally unimportant.[32]

(b) The Rule of Law as formal legality

Jeremy Bentham treated publicity as the most important 'security against
misrule'.[33] However, his sovereign was not subject to law nor limited by it. So
'securities against misrule' were a matter of politics, not law. Since Bentham's
time, the idea of the 'Rule of Law' has been at the centre of efforts to limit state
power and to make government accountable. It has been the main doctrine for

---

[29] Griffiths (1978) at p. 365 In the outline for the lecture he gives a formal definition: '*Collective
goods*: those goods which cannot be achieved by individual preference-maximizing behavior, but
which depend on mutual coercion. Example: a stable optimum population' (Groningen 1977
version at iv). Griffiths gives slavery as another example to make the point that 'goods' carries no
moral connotation. On the use of 'public goods' in the Uganda PEAP see Appendix 1 on the web.

[30] This conclusion follows from Griffiths' sharp critique of 'legal instrumentalism', discussed in
Chapter 16.4 on the web.

[31] Ibid., p. 374: 'For again, the relation between the two conceptions is not one of mutual exclusion;
it is just that the instrumental conception deals with the least interesting part of the phenomenon
of law'.

[32] On development Griffiths asserts: '[T]here is not really, so far as I know, a scrap of respectable
evidence that law is important one way or the other – either to promote development, as all the
[law-related] foreign assistance activity supposes, or to frustrate it as the more recent criticism
alleges. On the other hand there *is* some respectable ground for skepticism.' (Griffiths (1978) at
p. 350 citing Pozen (1976)).

[33] Bentham (1990) (ed. P. Schofield).

law's self-legitimation, in that the idea of governance being subjected to rules, which serve as a check on arbitrary power is considered a specifically legal value. For many people, the answer to the question: 'Why is law important?' is because the Rule of Law is a fundamental human good. This goes beyond, but typically includes, the idea that law promotes security and stability.

Because of its importance as a political concept, 'the Rule of Law' has attracted many shades of meaning. In 2002 the World Bank claimed to have supported 330 'Rule of Law' Projects in over 100 countries.[34] These included such a variety of enterprises that it is doubtful whether this label has much coherence or analytical significance. In the present context, we need a narrower interpretation.[35] Most commentators on Rule of Law theory distinguish between formal and substantive conceptions. Paul Craig put the matter as follows:

> Formal conceptions of the rule of law address the manner in which the law was promulgated (was it by a properly authorised person. ...); the clarity of the ensuing norm (was it sufficiently clear to guide an individual's conduct so as to enable a person to plan his or her life, etc.); and the temporal dimension of the norm (was it prospective ...). Formal conceptions of the rule of law do not however seek to pass judgment upon the actual content of the law itself. They are not concerned with whether the law was in that sense a good or bad law, provided that the formal precepts of the rule of law were themselves met. Those who espouse substantive conceptions of the rule of law seek to go beyond this. They accept that the rule of law has the formal attributes mentioned above, but they wish to take the doctrine further. Certain substantive rights are said to be based on, or derived from, the rule of law. The concept is used as the foundation for these rights, which are then used to distinguish between 'good' laws, which comply with these rights, and 'bad' laws, which do not.[36]

In his excellent book *On The Rule of Law* Brian Tamanaha indicates 'thicker' and 'thinner' accounts as per table 11.2, overleaf.[37]

The most important version in the present context is formal legality (2). Rule *by* or *through* law as an instrument of power (1) lacks the crucial ideas of governance under law and accountability and hardly counts as rule *of* law. Linking democracy to formal legality is a common, but not a necessary, extension.[38] Linking the Rule of Law to property rights, civil and political rights, social welfare, and justice is also common, but this has the effect of tying the concept to one or other versions of political liberalism or social

[34] Cited by Alvaro Santos in Trubek and Santos (2006) at p. 253, n.1.

[35] See the criticisms of this as incoherent at *ibid.*, pp. 298–300. The term 'Rule of Law' is sometimes used to refer to the rebuilding of judicial and legal institutions in post-conflict situations. (I am grateful to Patrick McAuslan for this point.)

[36] Craig (1997) at p. 467. Compare the analysis of the formal theory in Summers (1993).

[37] Tamanaha (2004). This gives an excellent account of the intellectual history of the concept of the Rule of Law, an insightful analysis of contemporary debates, and a strong defence of the core ideas of both formal and substantive versions. On these issues my views are close to Tamanaha's.

[38] Summers (1993) and (1999) does not accept this extension.

Table 11.2

	ALTERNATIVE RULE OF LAW FORMULATIONS		
	Thinner ------------> to -----------> Thicker		
FORMAL VERSIONS:	**1. Rule-by-Law**	**2. Formal Legality**	**3. Democracy+ Legality**
	– law as instrument of government action	– general, prospective, clear, certain	– consent determines content of law
SUBSTANTIVE VERSIONS:	**4. Individual Rights** – property, contract, privacy, autonomy	**5. Right of Dignity and /or justice**	**6. Social Welfare** – substantive equality, welfare, preservation of community

Source: Brian Tamanaha (2004), p. 91. Reproduced with permission.

democracy and so narrowing the scope and application of the concept. For many people the idea of formal legality is worth defending independently of these other values.

The basic idea, shared by all of the categories in Tamanaha's taxonomy except perhaps the first, is that law operates as a constraint on arbitrary power. In the present context, where we are concerned with different perceptions of the importance of law in development, formal legality represents the first step away from a minimalist law-and-order view. Formal legality, as conceived by its leading proponents, requires that laws should be general, prospective, public, clear, and certain, but it makes no requirement about the content of law. The basic intuition according to Raz is that 'law must be capable of guiding the behaviour of its subjects'.[39] Others place more emphasis on the idea of public accountability. Most proponents of this version consider an independent judiciary, fair and public hearings according to the principles of natural justice, and some provision of judicial oversight over the exercise of discretion by other branches of government to be necessary means to implement the idea.[40] For liberal supporters of formal legality, the rule of law is a bastion of individual liberty, enabling individuals to plan their lives and take decisions on the basis of settled expectations (i.e. a broad view of 'security').[41] But not all supporters of this version of the Rule of Law are liberals in this sense.

Formal legality is largely procedural. It does not deal with the content of law. It claims to be neutral between different substantive policies and ideologies;

---

[39] Raz derives a number of principles from this formal interpretation of the Rule of Law, while maintaining that it is separate from ideas of democracy, basic rights, equality or justice (Raz (1979) at pp. 214.–17). His list is only slightly different from Fuller's principles of the inner morality of law (Fuller (1969) Chapter 2); see also Dyzenhaus (2006).

[40] The varied history of judicial review shows the range of views about the scope of this idea.

[41] See Chapter 5.4 (b) above.

it says almost nothing about justice, rights, or social welfare.[42] Its supporters generally acknowledge that on its own this conception of the Rule of Law is quite compatible with bad or even wicked government. Formal legality can authorise slavery, and co-exist with denial of human rights, segregation, discrimination, and abject poverty.[43] The claim is that even a wicked legal system which observes formal legality is less bad than a wicked legal system that ignores it. Supporters treat this ideal as worth defending in itself, because it is a means of making power accountable and providing guidance to subjects about what they must, may, can, and may not do.

It may not be surprising to find jurists as diverse as Dicey, Hayek, Fuller, Raz, and Tamanaha defending the idea of formal legality as a fundamentally important political good. However, orthodox Marxists were shocked when the revered Marxian historian Edward Thompson concluded in *Whigs and Hunters* that the rule of law is 'a cultural achievement of universal significance'[44] and 'an unqualified human good'.[45] Previously, Marxists had considered state law as an instrument of oppression in the interests of the ruling class and claims about legality an obfuscation that needed to be demystified. Thompson, on the basis of his studies of English liberalism, concluded that the forms of law did operate to constrain the exercise of power and like other forms of hypocrisy, it was the homage paid by vice to virtue and a great deal better than nothing. The significance of Thompson's conclusion, which persuaded some but not all,[46] is that if one accepts his argument then the idea of formal legality as a political virtue is compatible with ideologies other than liberalism.

Generally, those who support the Rule of Law as formal legality also assume or explicitly claim that law is essential to social ordering. However, it is worth remembering that Brian Tamanaha criticised strong versions of the social order thesis.[47] In challenging naive assumptions about the functions of law he argued that social order can exist without law; contributing to social order is by no means the only function of law; law is not the only institution that contributes to social ordering; and that:

> The traditionally assumed relationship [between law and social order] gets things precisely upside down. It is state law that is dependent on these other sources of social order if it is to have a chance of exerting an influence.[48]

---

[42] However, the idea of justice under the law (expletive justice) is sometimes included within the formal conception of the Rule of Law.

[43] Tamanaha (2004) at pp. 95–6.   [44] Thompson (1975) at p. 265.   [45] *Ibid.* at p. 266.

[46] Some still dwell on the potential for abuse of the formal Rule of Law. Because legal formality is sometimes used as a cynical façade to mask repressive or nefarious policies, it does not follow that it is worthless. As Edward Thompson argued, such hypocrisy is often the tribute paid by vice to virtue (or is just a good habit) and, as such, has real value. It is a necessary, but not a sufficient, condition for good governance.

[47] See Chapter 4.1 at p. 97–9, 113.

[48] Tamanaha (2001) at p. 224. Tamanaha's view can find support in the Uganda Poverty Eradication Action Plan, discussed in Appendix 1 on the web. To end cattle rustling in Karamoja, the army and diplomacy must restore 'normal' order before handing back responsibility to the police.

This position is not as radical as it may sound. Tamanaha's aim was to draw a conceptual distinction between the criteria of identification of law (what law is) and the functions of law (what law does) and to argue that the extent to which law actually contributes to social order (or undermines it) is an empirical question that depends on the circumstances. Like Griffiths, Tamanaha is sceptical of general assumptions about the actual effects of law on social order. Tamanaha is also strongly committed to the ideal of the Rule of Law, both in respect of formal legality and of some versions of substantive legality. It follows from this that the law-and-order view and the formal legality view of the importance of law should be kept conceptually separate, although many people subscribe to both.

(c) Strong free market views

For a relatively short period in the late 1980s and the early 1990s the leading international financial institutions and many foreign aid agencies were driven by dogmatic and doctrinaire versions of laissez faire economics. These ideas have a long history that can be traced back through the Chicago school of economics, and F.A. Hayek, to selective interpretations (some would say perversions) of the ideas of Adam Smith. Although, no longer fashionable in their purest forms in international development circles, at least on the surface, such ideas are still influential, for instance, in business, in business schools, and in those American law schools that are still strongly influenced by 'economic analysis of law'.

There are many variants and modifications of free market ideology. By no means all adherents to this approach adopt the brutal version that I encountered at the University of Chicago in the period 1957–1963.[49] Although the approach is often associated with their names, as pragmatic politicians neither President Reagan nor Mrs Thatcher acted consistently with the more dogmatic versions. Similarly, it is wrong to assume that even during the heyday of these ideas the World Bank, IMF and other development agencies acted consistently in implementing strategies based on a pure form of these ideas.[50] Nevertheless, for a period this kind of thinking was very influential and in the eyes of many it had disastrous consequences.

---

[49] Elsewhere I have recounted the story of my clashes with Aaron Director, one of the pioneers of 'law and economics'. Twining (2007b). Director, *inter alia*, said of persons displaced by an urban slum clearance project to provide 'low cost housing' that those who could not afford the rents were 'not economically fit to survive'.

[50] An interesting example of 'the jurisprudence of the World Bank' is the writings of Ibrahim Shihata, the very influential General Counsel and Vice-President (later Senior Vice-President) of the World Bank from 1983–1999. Although in favour of free markets, his juristic ideas are quite close to the kind of social engineering espoused by Roscoe Pound (Shihata (1991)). On Shihata's defence of the World Bank's involvement with governance as 'apolitical', using a substantive version of the Rule of Law, see Alvaro Santos in Trubek and Santos (2006) at pp. 269–75. See generally, Schlemmer-Schulte and Ko-Yung Tung (eds.) (2001).

The basic ideas are familiar and need not be expounded at great length. Wealth creation is the over-riding 'value';[51] capital investment in a free market with minimum state intervention is the (only) road to wealth creation; in poorer countries, with relatively limited capital, foreign direct investment is a necessity; therefore, the conditions for attracting and retaining FDI need to be established.

The strategy of structural adjustment driven by these ideas was retroactively labelled 'the Washington Consensus' by John Williamson in 1990. The key elements were fiscal discipline; redirecting public expenditure priorities; tax reform; deregulation; promoting foreign direct investment; financial liberalisation; a single exchange rate; trade liberalisation; privatisation; security of property rights.[52]

The structural adjustment programmes of the international financial institutions have been hugely controversial. Economists still debate the exact consequences of particular programmes and whether any achieved their goals.[53] But there is widespread agreement that, even if GDP was raised, it was at a great social cost; that the main beneficiaries were often the middle class and foreign investors; and that for many the effects were disastrous, often leaving the poor worse off and even creating an enlarged underclass. For example, in 2001 one observer in Tanzania reported:

> While economists continue to praise the improvement in Tanzania's macro-economic indicators, I, as an economically illiterate visitor, see no signs of anything other than a deterioration in the standard of life of the bulk of the population. The prices of coffee, cashew nuts and cotton, three of the principal cash crops, have fallen severely. Unemployment among the young is high. Health and education facilities remain poorer than they were 15 years ago. It is true that a small proportion of the population lives very well, in good housing, with private transport, servants and household amenities, but the contrast with the lives of the many is stark. In this respect, Tanzania is similar to many countries in both the developing and developed worlds. So far, the Tanzanian people bear up under this with remarkable fortitude, cheerfulness and friendly hospitality. I confess, however, that I do not share the view, apparently widely held in the North and West of the world, that the supply of investment from outside and the globalisation of 'free' trade, is about to bring increasing prosperity to the Tanzanian population. It may well bring increasing prosperity to the investors and middle-

---

[51] See the powerful critique by Ronald Dworkin in a paper entitled 'Is Wealth a Value?' Dworkin (1980/85).

[52] Williamson (1994). Williamson allowed for some differences of opinion within this 'consensus'. A good critical discussion is Kelsey (1995). 'Structural adjustment' meant adjusting to the new structure of the global economy; from early on 'the Washington Consensus' was opposed by 'the New York dissent' which, in relation to Africa, emphasised the need to take more account of 'the human dimension' and the burden of external debt. This could be read as a predecessor of the human development approach pioneered by Ul Haq and Sen in the 1990s. (Murphy (2006) at pp. 228–9) (see below). On 'chastened neo-liberalism' see pp. 339–41 below.

[53] E.g. Easterly (2006), Stiglitz (2002) and Sachs (2005) are examples of economists who initially favoured 'the strong medicine' of structural adjustment and subsequently retreated or recanted.

ranking Tanzanian employees, but I see no signs at present of any benefit to the majority of the people who are, in my view (unsupported by any real research on my part) less well off, worse educated and less well provided with health services than in the first twenty years after independence. This may seem strange to those struck by the building of great new office blocks, smart hotels, well-stocked shops and luxurious houses in the new Dar-es-Salaam, but I suggest they talk to the ordinary people and examine a few statistics of social conditions.[54]

Economic fundamentalism in its purest form restricts the role of the state to maintaining security and holding the ring to enable the free play of market forces. From this point of view, one might expect strategies that envisaged a lesser and more limited role for law and, indeed, policies of privatisation and deregulation are directed at removing state 'interference' and 'rolling back' the influence of the state in economic life. However, in the international development context, law was given considerably increased emphasis in development strategies from about 1990. At a general level, the ideology that requires a strong state with limited functions, nevertheless emphasises protection of property rights, enforcement of contracts, and facilitation of commerce through the constitutive role of law, for example in respect of companies, banks, and other financial institutions. But in the 1990s there were also special historical reasons for emphasising law and law reform. First, the 'collapse of communism' in Eastern Europe led not only to the dismantling of the institutions and laws of command economies, but also their replacement by a modern, market-friendly regime in almost all areas of economic and financial life – not just commercial law broadly conceived (including anti-trust), but labour law, financial regulation, intellectual property, banking, insolvency and many other less obvious legal fields related to 'transitional justice'.[55] Furthermore, investor confidence was said to require an independent and upright judiciary, reliable enforcement mechanisms, an independent legal profession, local government and all the familiar paraphernalia of a modern Western liberal state, which typically is closer to welfare state and mixed economy models.[56]

---

[54] Trevor Jagger (2002). This article stimulated a lively debate at a Britain-Tanzania Society seminar, in 2002. Some of Jagger's account was questioned, but there appears to have been a consensus that in Tanzania poverty had increased, especially in the towns, at the same time as, but not necessarily because of, improved economic performance. Britain-Tanzania Society *Newsletter* Vol. 3 Issue 9 (2002). Even if the underlying theory of structural adjustment had been broadly correct, its application was often very crude: if tariff barriers are forced down in a poor country *before* corresponding protectionist measures are removed in richer countries, the result will be that the poor country may be importing subsidised foodstuffs from richer countries to the detriment of its local agriculture, let alone its exports; in Uganda over-rapid decentralisation and the ending of subsidies have been among the main objects of criticism (see Appendix 1 on the web). Muwanga (2001) provides a very interesting account of different perceptions of poverty in Uganda.

[55] Czarnota, Krygier, and Sadurski (eds.) (2005).

[56] Writing of Eastern Europe and Africa from the mid-1960s to the mid-1990s, McAuslan points out that while external pressures were directed at removing constraints on the market, including legal restraints, other pressures led to both market reform and governance reform both having a

Second, and not entirely coincidentally, the early 1990s saw a huge rise in interest and activity in respect of human rights and democracy, not only in Eastern Europe, but in many other parts of the world. Since World War II the international human rights regime has grown steadily, so that many consider 'human rights' to be the predominant moral discourse in international and transnational relations. At least as significant as the global regime, has been the development of regional regimes, of which the European Convention on Human Rights is the most developed. Equally important, especially since the Cold War, has been the rapid proliferation of domestic regimes of civil rights in post-colonial states, Eastern Europe, and longer established democracies, including the United Kingdom.[57] Not long after the emergence of the Washington Consensus, the World Bank and other major institutions qualified their prioritisation of market reform with the phrase 'human rights, good governance and democracy'. The reasons for this are too complex to pursue here, but what emerged has been aptly labelled 'chastened neoliberalism'.[58] The following is a fairly typical statement:

> The legal framework in a country is as vital for economic development as for political and social development. Creating wealth through the cumulative commitment of human, technological and capital resources depends greatly on a set of rules securing property rights, governing civil and commercial behaviour, and limiting the power of the state. The legal framework also affects the lives of the poor and, as such, has become an important dimension of strategies for poverty alleviation in the struggle against discrimination, in the protection of the socially weak and in the distribution of opportunities. In society, the law can make an important contribution to a just and equitable society and thus to prospects for social development and poverty alleviation.[59]

There is considerable doubt as to whether these ideas can be interpreted in a way that makes them coherent. The unfettered pursuit of wealth creation is difficult to reconcile with concerns about distributive justice, participatory

---

substantial legal component (including judicial, local government, and tax reform), which sometimes pointed in different directions (McAuslan (2003) at pp. 110–13).

[57] 'Over the past twenty-five years, and particularly since the end of the Cold War, a commitment to judicially enforceable bills of rights has quite quickly become part of the legal mainstream in all democracies, even in those places whose deep democratic pedigrees might have been expected to have insulated them from this new human rights wave.' (Gearty (2006), pp. 64–5).

[58] David Kennedy in Trubek and Santos (eds.) (2006) at pp. 150–58.

[59] World Bank (1994). At the 1998 memorial service for Mahbub ul Haq, the pioneer of the Human Development Index and broader conceptions of 'poverty', the President of the World Bank, James Wolfensohn, is reported to have said:

> If Mahbub is flying around up there around my head, if he is, he'll be laughing, because I have one thing to say to him, 'Mahbub – you were right!'

> Murphy (2006) at p. 246. However, many are sceptical about the extent to which the actual practices of international financial institutions reflect the public pronouncements of 'chastened neo-liberalism'.

democracy, environmental protection, poverty reduction, and social and economic rights. What is clear is that such perspectives envisage a much broader and varied role for state law than economic fundamentalism. So the simple neo-liberal model no longer fits the declared approaches of the donor community and of the MDGs.

(d) Law as multi-functional[60]

The first three ideal types of answers to the question: Why is law important? – the social control, formal legality, and free market models – are all quite narrow, although they can be and often are combined. Broader answers go beyond all of these, but not necessarily in a single direction. For example, 'substantive Rule of Law' ideas, of which there are many varieties, tend to be linked to Western ideas of liberal democracy. Similarly, chastened neo-liberalism, which sometimes marches under the banner of The Rule of Law, may be more or less chastened, and can pursue a number of quite different strategies.[61] Moreover, chastened neo-liberalism has to some extent shed its 'one size fits all' tendencies and, as is apparent in respect of the MDGs, there is now a wider acceptance that strategies for 'development' have to take account of local conditions, histories, and culture and, at least in theory, need to be arrived at by participatory processes and to be genuinely 'owned' by all the important stakeholders. So the ideas cater for diversity, but the extent to which respect is actually accorded to local knowledge and specific poverty reduction planning concerns also varies considerably.[62] So generalisation is difficult. Constructing an ideal type of broader perceptions and expectations of the role of state law is correspondingly difficult.

I acknowledged earlier[63] that I am an enthusiast for my discipline and that I have sometimes been called on to make 'the case for law' in order to try to win a bigger share of the higher education budget for legal education. Underlying this attitude is a judgement that non-lawyers, especially economists and other social scientists, regularly underestimate the social and political importance of law, especially in the context of development. As a self-interested advocate, I have probably overstated the case, but it may be helpful to look at one example of this 'legal nationalist' perspective. In 1974–1975 I was a member of an International Legal Center Committee that produced a report on *Legal Education in a*

---

[60] Because of the vagueness of 'the Rule of Law' there are grey areas between categories (c) and (d) in the text: (b) is restricted to formal legality, but (d) is much wider even than the broadest interpretations of 'the Rule of Law'.

[61] See Trubek and Santos (2006) on the variety and incoherence of World Bank 'Rule of Law' projects. On 'the Rule of Law revival' see Carothers (1999).

[62] On charges that preparation of PRSPs in Uganda and Tanzania involved too little consultation, and that in the case of Tanzania the second draft of its PRSP was done within the World Bank, see below.

[63] See p. 324 above.

Changing World. I helped to draft and signed the report which contained the following passages:

> 96. In the majority of the countries within our review, law has been chosen as an instrument of change and development. In such countries a heavy burden is laid on the legal system. It is required to discharge a variety of different tasks, to innovate and facilitate complex transactions, to define the rights of the citizens *inter se*, and between them and the institutions of government, to establish incentives for desirable activities and disincentives for undesirable ones, to provide procedures for participation in the affairs of the nation, to provide access to justice, to persuade, to cajole, to coerce. While the choice of law as an instrument of development and its specific uses are political matters, we consider that institutions of legal education and research have an important role to play in ensuring an effective use of law, once that choice has been made.
>
>   97. Important human values – of justice, fairness, and equity – should underlie the basic principles of the law, although particular laws and indeed whole legal systems have been and are unjust. In the situation in many developing countries where technocratic and growth oriented considerations tend to dominate, sometimes at the cost of a just and fair society, an emphasis on legal principles can do much to redress the balance, and help to give development a more complete orientation. It is the task of legal education to lead in this movement.[64]

This passage needs to be read in connection with an even more ebullient statement about the potential role of law schools in a national system of higher education.[65] I take full responsibility for this piece of advocacy, even though I might have cavilled at some of the wording. Today, I read it with some reservations.

First, I think that this passage, and the report as a whole is over-generalised insofar as it purported to apply to almost all developing countries. Even as an aspirational statement I now believe that legal cultures, law schools and systems of higher education are more diverse than this assumes. Second, the passage needs to be read as part of a self-interested piece of advocacy, making the case for law to have its share of resources alongside other disciplines. It was part of a bid by a group of lawyers for a share of the budget at a time when interest in law

---

[64] International Legal Center (1975), paras 96–7.

[65]   '*98. Legal Education and the Generation of Human Skills Which Contribute to Processes of Development*. People in law roles are often active participants in transactions which may be very significant to development. They may define and analyze problems; counsel and plan a course of action; negotiate and settle disputes; define and advocate a position; frame and implement rules. Good professionals exercise these skills – indeed, such skills are part of the essence of 'lawyering'; good legal education can encourage (in the view of some, it should demand) the use and development of these skills through various methods of legal education. Precisely because legal education can be developed in ways which engage students in hypothetical problem solving and other forms of simulated participation in transactions, it has much potential as a kind of education useful to development ... (*ibid*).

had diminished in development circles.[66] It was special pleading, but in a worthy cause. Third, I would now use the word 'instrument' more cautiously than we did at the time.[67]

These reservations aside, I still believe in the essentials of the message: that state law is relevant to development in various ways at a number of levels and that it is important not only because of what it contributes to order and stability.[68]

Despite the wording, this passage – and the report as a whole – can be defended against charges of crude or naïve instrumentalism. It does not claim that law contributes much directly to development; it emphasises equity, fair procedures, and by implication the Rule of Law. And it suggests that, beyond basic social order, law has important functions other than serving as simple instruments of policy or power. Unlike 'the water in marriage' view, this perspective treats law as important in a variety of ways at a number of levels, by no means all of them obvious.[69]

A more reflective and sober version of this view of the potential roles of law is made by Patrick McAuslan on the basis of his very wide practical experience of problems of land reform and urban planning in many countries. In his excellent book, *Bringing the Law Back In*,[70] he makes a passionate and informed case for law being more important than just as a pre-condition for development or holding the ring for the free market to operate. So far as land law and planning is concerned law is important in establishing structures and enabling the operation of an equitable, efficient and appropriate market in land and a democratically responsive, efficient and accountable urban government.[71] He recounts how in the past too little law has enabled the uncontrolled use of arbitrary power;[72] the wrong kind of law could be used to maintain racial and class segregation in housing;[73] or ruthlessly to destroy the fragile security of the urban poor.[74] Too much law can create a bureaucratic morass that can

---

[66] Trubeck and Galanter's famous lament 'Scholars in self-estrangement' was written about the same time and published in 1974. Our report was more optimistic and more assertive in making the case for law. See also similar arguments at later dates by Keith Patchett (1987) and Dawn Oliver (reported in Twining (1994) at pp. 60–61).

[67] On 'instrumentalism' see Chapter 16.4 on the web.

[68] I still deliver similar messages about my discipline in order to try to capture the imagination and enthusiasm of first-year law students. (See Twining (1994), p. 4–11.)

[69] Another area where law has considerable potential for furthering strategies of social justice, but which has had little sustained attention until recently is procurement (using public spending power to further anti-discrimination and like policies). See now McCrudden (2007).

[70] McAuslan (2003).   [71] *Ibid.*, p. 113.

[72] E.g. planning by bulldozer in developing Dodoma, the new capital of Tanzania (*ibid.*, p. 148).

[73] *Ibid.*, p. 140–1.

[74] McAuslan acknowledges that there can be some truth in 'an alternative development' argument that [in some contexts]: '[L]aw impedes the efforts of ordinary people to house themselves, to obtain an income, to get access to potable water, electricity and other urban services and thereby to survive and better themselves in an urban environment. Law turns homesteaders into squatters, self-build houses into "slums" and "nuisances", which must be demolished; petty traders into criminals and job seekers into vagrants.' (p. 143)

overwhelm development and land management as in Madras in the mid-1980s.[75] McAuslan gives a rich array of examples of the disastrous consequences of either too little law or a cavalier attitude to its observance on the part of officials. In the end law is important:

> A general, albeit western liberal-democratic answer is that government in accordance with the law is likely to be fairer, more respected, more effective in the long run than government in defiance or in disregard for the law.[76]

Using the Habitat Agenda and Global Strategy Plan of 1996[77] as a template and illustrating its application in the special circumstances of Tanzania in the mid-1990s, McAuslan shows how land law is not and cannot be either simply a 'neutral' technology for implementing state policy nor just a pre-condition for security and development. Rather it has multiple roles in providing an overarching framework for decision-making and management; as the institution for providing security of tenure and title; as prescribing procedures for regulating participation, market transactions, dispute resolution and remedying grievances. In short a whole range of functions, some of which involve complex technicalities.[78]

I call scholars who have made 'the case for law', such as McAuslan and myself, 'legal nationalists' because we argue that law can be important over and above both its contributions to social order and stability and the idea of the formal Rule of Law as a constraint on arbitrary power. 'Legal nationalism' in

---

[75] *Ibid.*, at pp. 149–50. Robert Chambers, an influential specialist in rural development, treated lawyers as one of the missing professions from this area, whose influence could either help or harm the rural poor: 'Law is a profession which, like management, has a strong urban, industrial, and commercial orientation. One does not find a rural Legal Department equivalent to a Department of Community Development or Agricultural Extension. Yet there are many laws in many countries which, if enforced, would help the rural poor. As it is, the laws of property, invoked by the "haves" against the "have-nots", maintain and defend gross disparities of wealth.' (Chambers (1983) at p. 183).

[76] McAuslan (2003) at p. 144. An extreme example of the price of disregard for law is the tragic history of Uganda (1970–1990) 'where a civilian government careless of legal niceties and constitutional forms was rudely replaced by a military regime careless of human rights, liberties and life, which in turn was replaced by a succession of civilian administrations utterly unable to restore law or respect for law within the country and equally unable therefore to mount any programmes of urban or rural development. A totally new beginning ultimately became necessary.' (*Ibid.*)

[77] The Habitat Agenda and the Global Plan of Action came out of the UN City Summit in Istanbul, in 1996. See *The Challenge of Sustainable Cities* (1997), which sets out principles and a framework for urban management and development in relation to market enablement, political enablement, and community enablement. It is discussed in detail in McAuslan (2003), Chapter 6.

[78] McAuslan illustrates the roles of law envisaged by the Habitat Agenda in relation to the National Land policy adopted by Parliament in Tanzania in 1995 and embodied in the Land Act 1999 and Village Land Act 1999 (p. 116). McAuslan is highly critical of 'one-size-fits-all' assumptions and emphasises the importance of concern for technical detail along with genuine local 'ownership', competence and probity among officials. See also the similar argument made about the pervasiveness of law as illustrated by legal records. Twining and Quick (eds.) (1994). McAuslan's approach to land reform in Tanzania has been controversial see Manji (2006), Chapters 3 and 4; Shivji (1998).

this sense involves no necessary commitment to naïve instrumentalism – that is views that law is an important form of social engineering.[79] Rather, at the level of detail, legal rules need to be imbricated with ideas of equity, fairness, and concern for basic rights. Of itself, law does not *cause* development to happen; and if it contributes at all to conditions that can result in lowering infant mortality or creating jobs or preventing famines or establishing universal primary education, such contributions vary according to context, and, if relevant at all, may equally well be negative as positive.

The connection between legal nationalism and 'legal liberalism' is more complex. The latter term was attributed to a 'paradigm' that was the main target of critical legal studies in the United States from the early 1970s. In a famous critique Marc Galanter and David Trubeck used it as their butt in a famous paper 'Scholars in Self-estrangement' that was part recantation, part lament for lost funding, but mainly sharp criticism of the body of assumptions that they claimed underlay almost all American 'Law and Development' activities in the prior decade, including their own.[80] It was also a lament for the absence of social theory informing most scholarly research. Above all it was a sharp political critique of 'liberal' political theory underlying American academic culture at the time – in particular the idea that law could be 'neutral' and be kept clearly separate from politics.

Trubek and Galanter characterised the 'liberal legalist paradigm' as follows:

The literature stressed the centrality of the state: the state is seen as the primary agent of social control and change, which will use law as a purposive instrument to transform society and yet will itself be constrained by law.

It focused on higher agencies of the legal system and showed little interest in nonstate forms of legal or other social ordering; indeed, one detects a subtle bias against informal legal systems and customary law.[81]

It manifested a pervasive belief in the ultimate efficacy of legal rules as instruments of social change. Paradoxically, this belief is underscored by the widespread awareness of the gap between 'law in action' and 'law in the books'. Where it becomes apparent that immediate rule change will not affect social behavior, attention shifts to the institutional changes that will be needed to guarantee that this *will* occur. ...

The literature assumed that changes in law would change behavior....

It further assumed that legal professions were, or could come to be, representative of the public interest (the interests of 'development') rather than agents of relatively narrow segments of society.

---

[79] See Chapter 16.4(a) on the web.

[80] Trubek and Galanter (1974). This paper originated as a report to the Research Advisory Committee of the International Legal Center, which was concerned with 'Law and Development' research generally, not just in the United States. The final report glossed over the sharp differences within the Committee (International Legal Center (1974)).

[81] The literature on the MDGs illustrates how most contemporary development literature is still state-centric. See below. On why and when non-state law is important, see Chapter 11.6 and Chapter 12 below.

Finally, it took for granted the existence of some natural tendency for legal systems in the Third World to evolve in the direction of the model of legal liberalism....[82]

This critique has so many targets that it is difficult to respond to it. First, a legal nationalist today would agree with some of the criticisms. They are persuasive insofar as American contributions to 'law and development' involved naive instrumentalist views of law as social engineering; or were ethnocentric in assuming the superiority and suitability for export of American ideas and institutions; or were dismissive of tradition, custom, or religious law; or were based on a rosy view of law in the United States; or were quiet adjuncts of self-interested, sometimes sinister, foreign policies. Similarly, it would have been naive to assume that a well-trained legal elite would naturally favour the interests of the poor over the rich.

It is difficult to apply this paradigm or its critique to non-American involvement in 'law and development' from 1950 to 1975, let alone before then. First, it is a recantation and critique by Americans of Americans with some peculiarly American assumptions, not least about 'liberalism' and critical legal studies.[83] It takes no account of the views of non-Americans, especially those in less developed countries.

Second, one has doubts about 'liberal legalism' as a useful paradigm even within the United States, and it is hardly a fair characterisation of some of the leading American scholars who were involved in 'law and development' in Africa in the 1960s, 1970s and beyond – for example, Jim Paul, Ann and Robert Seidman, Burnett Harvey, Cliff Thompson and Iain McNeill. Nevertheless, some of the ideas and assumptions under attack were influential, not only among Americans.

Third, in my view, the Galanter-Trubek critique was too sweeping and, if taken seriously, threw the baby out with the bathwater. Perhaps unduly influenced by one version of critical legal studies' rule-scepticism they poured scorn on ideas and institutions associated with 'the Rule of Law' at a time when many newly independent countries were struggling to establish it. As McAuslan puts it:

> [I]t is easy to forget that for many peoples all over the world, the advent of independence, a written constitution, popularly elected legislatures, independent judiciaries, the rule of law and social and economic reforms brought about through legal mechanisms were a major advance on the previous system of governance to which they were subjected.[84]

---

[82] *Ibid.*, at pp. 1078–9.

[83] In American usage 'liberalism' seems to refer to two different ideas: free market ideology and individual freedom. In England the term is also used ambiguously, typically with less emphasis on economics.

[84] McAuslan cites an eloquent passage from a paper by Telford Georges, the much admired Trinidadian Chief Justice of Tanzania in favour of a broad conception of the Rule of Law (Georges (1973) at p. 26) and treats that as close to the ideas of Julius Nyerere. See also the biography of Georges' successor, Chief Justice Nyalali (Widner (2001)). McAuslan also points out that American disillusionment with Law and Development took place at a time when American foreign policy had moved away from support for democracy and equity in the developing world.

The legal nationalist values both security and the Rule of Law, but makes an additional claim for law's importance. It is a claim that is difficult to express in general terms: that law provides structures, procedures, devices, and ways of argumentation which are necessary if the implementation and enforcement of policies are to be equitable, fair, participatory and so on. But law can also undermine such values. Law is a practical and often technical subject. The devil is in the detail. To some extent law is in part a technology, in part a vehicle for values, in part an instrument of policy.[85] To say that it is important does not mean that its influence is inherently benign. But subjecting behaviour, especially the behaviour of the powerful, to the governance of rules, is important and usually requires mastery of technical details.

(e) Rights-based approaches

We saw in Chapter 7 that a strong philosophical case can be made for a basic moral right to be free from poverty. We also saw that there is a substantial difference between asserting a basic human right as a moral right and establishing the same idea, or something very similar, as an enforceable legal right in international, regional, or municipal law.[86]

In recent years 'rights-based' approaches to development have been strongly advocated and, in some contexts, have even become fashionable:

> Rights-based approaches – increasingly popular with many development agencies – focus not so much on people's needs, but more on what they have a right to expect – both in terms of basic human rights such as the right to life, food, water, shelter, etc., and in terms of their right to have their views represented to agencies that have an impact on their lives (DFID, 2000; Crook, 2001). If governments sign up to the targets, this means in principle that the people whose interests they are meant to serve can lobby them to behave in the manner most consistent with meeting the targets. In this conception, 'beneficiaries' of aid have a right to expect that agencies will act fairly in pursuing stated objectives.[87]

---

[85] See Chapter 9.4(k) above. On the idea that different kinds of law have different functions see Tamanaha (2001), Chapter 8.

[86] This section is concerned with invoking human rights as legal or political rights to combat poverty. This is different from, though related to, the approach of Hernando de Soto and others who advocate 'another path' through strengthening and invoking individual legal rights to property under domestic law to give small businessmen and farmers greater security (de Soto (1989)).

[87] Black and White (eds.) (2004) at 14. See also 'In the parallel field of international humanitarian assistance, a rights-based approach stresses how people's rights as defined by international humanitarian law have been violated, and sees international intervention as helping people to regain those rights. This positions the beneficiaries of aid as claimants, rather than as beggars. ... Nonetheless, it should be remembered that UN conference resolutions do not have *legal* status. In this sense, for a rights-based argument to be fully convincing in terms of the international development targets, "Southern" governments need to reflect their commitment to the targets by passing relevant legislation (e.g. making school attendance compulsory).' (*Ibid.*).

The claims made in favour of such approaches have been summarised as follows:

> The case that the human rights framework can contribute significantly to efforts to promote equitable and sustainable development has been laid out extensively elsewhere. In essence the reasons include: the advantage of building upon legal obligations already voluntarily undertaken by governments that have ratified human rights treaties; the mobilizational potential of rights discourse; the added value and credibility brought to the MDGs by applying norms of non-discrimination and equality to ensure that aggregated approaches do not neglect certain groups of individuals; the specificity given to vague terms such as participation and empowerment when particular civil and political rights norms are invoked; the potential role of human rights institutions that already exist at the national level in many countries; and the potential contribution of increasingly sophisticated international accountability mechanisms in the human rights arena.[88]

There are, of course, dissenters from this view. First, there are general human rights sceptics, who believe that human rights discourse is fatally flawed. Such views have been supported by thinkers as different as Bentham, Burke, and Marx and their modern successors.[89] Second, there are supporters of thin theories of human rights, who deplore the unconstrained, sometimes anarchical, proliferation of human rights claims. Third, there are those who support civil and political rights, but who resist the idea that it is useful to talk of either moral or legal rights, where no correlative obligations and responsibilities have been allocated.[90] And, fourth there are some who, whether or not they support the existing human rights regime, argue that the discourse of rights is inappropriate in the context of strategic policy making, where the central issues involve difficult political choices about priorities.[91]

---

[88] Alston (2005) at p. 779. Advocates of 'rights-based approaches' are not always clear whether they are referring to human rights as moral rights, or as 'soft law' (e.g. directive principles of state policy), or as legally enforceable rights. It is one thing to remind governments of their public political commitments or their existing international obligations (legally binding, but typically not practically enforceable), it is quite another to suggest that policy documents such as poverty reduction/eradication structure plans should be enacted in forms that would give individual citizens extensive legally enforceable rights against government. Most of the arguments made by advocates of 'rights-based' approaches seem to rely mainly on the rhetorical power of rights discourse as a means of political pressure, as is illustrated by the quotations from Black and White and Alston. However, some stress the discourse as a first step towards the institutionalisation of machinery for making claims and their enforcement.

[89] Waldron (1987) cf. Glendon (1991), Dembour (2006) (discussed in Ch. 7); Baxi (2006).

[90] E.g. Onora O'Neill (2000a), criticised by Tasioulas (2007a). (See Chapter 7 above).

[91] A good example of this view is Lucia Zedner's critique of 'right-based' approaches to policy-making in relation to Control Orders in England and Wales: 'It remains an open question, however, whether critical analysis of Control Orders need necessarily be confined to the domain of human rights or whether it is best furthered there. It is arguable that human rights discourse is too narrowly focused on the defence of particular individual rights. In seeking only compliance it fails to question the very existence of the Control Order. It cannot challenge the presumptions upon which it is based nor the end to which it is aimed.' (Zedner (2007a) at pp. 183–4). See further Zedner (2007b)).

Especially important is the fact that, in the context of development, Governments are notoriously reluctant to turn their public 'commitments' into legally binding obligations. As we shall see, this is what has happened with the Millenium Development Goals (MDGs).

What is the relationship between the MDGs and human rights? In an important article, Philip Alston has made the case for stronger links between the supporters of the MDGs and human rights activists.[92] Whilst there is considerable overlap between the MDGs and existing human rights conventions,[93] he acknowledges that the MDGs do not at present create legal obligations and that, given the attitudes of most governments, this is not likely to change in the foreseeable future. Nevertheless, he deplores the situation in which, like 'ships passing in the night' neither community has 'embraced this linkage with enthusiasm or conviction'.[94] He puts much of the blame on the human rights community, which has been quite critical of the MDGs, and he calls on them 'to engage more effectively with the development agenda, to prioritize its concerns rather than assuming that every issue needs to be tackled simultaneously, and to avoid being over prescriptive.'[95] In short, the best that can be hoped for is a highly selective rights-based approach to the MDGs. We shall see later that the Government of Uganda has conspicuously avoided using the discourse of human rights in its Poverty Eradication Action Plan.[96] In a survey of fifty-nine national MDG reports in August 2004, Alston found only one (Bosnia and Herzegovina) that could be said to have adopted a rights-based approach.[97]

11.4 The Millennium Development Goals (MDGs)

At the Millennium Summit in September 2000 the United Nations' Millennium Declaration was adopted unanimously by 189 countries.[98] The Declaration set out eight major goals, supported by eighteen targets to be monitored against forty-eight indicators (See Table 11.3). The goals are:

---

[92] Alston (2005).

[93] Alston notes that the Human Development Report for 2003 (UNDP, 2003) maintained that: 'The Millennium Development Goals not only "mirror the fundamental motivation for human rights," but they also "reflect a human rights agenda–rights to food, education, health care and decent living standards."' The UN High Commissioner for Human Rights Mary Robinson also reported in 2002 that '[t]he strategies to reach the Millennium human rights goals and the Millennium development goals reinforce and complement each other.' In her view, 'most if not all of the strategies to achieve the [MDGs] operate within a human rights framework'. (Alston (2005) at p. 759). Mary Robinson has been a leading advocate of rights-based approaches, see Robinson (2007).

[94] Alston (2005) (abstract).   [95] Ibid.

[96] See pp. 355–7 below.   [97] Alston (2005). See n. 127 below.

[98] See United Nations Millennium Declaration, A/RES/55/2 (18 September 2000), online: www.un.org/millennium/declaration/ares552e.pdf; and United Nations Statistics Division, Millennium Development Goal Indicators Database, ST/ESA/STAT/MILLENNIUMINDICATORSDB/WWW (30 July 2005), online: http://millenniumindicators.un.org/unsd/mi/mi_goals.asp.

1. Eradicate extreme poverty and hunger.
2. Achieve universal primary education.
3. Promote gender equality and empower women.
4. Reduce child mortality.
5. Improve maternal health.
6. Combat HIV/AIDS, malaria and other diseases.
7. Ensure environmental sustainability.
8. Develop a global partnership for development.

A sceptic might ask: is this not just one more in the long line of aspirational documents that have been promulgated over the years by UN and other agencies without resulting in any discernible difference to the plight of the world's poor? Why should we take this more seriously than its predecessors? It is true that most of these ideas are to be found in earlier UN documents in the 1990s, that the history of earlier efforts to create co-ordinated strategies for development had been disappointing, that the impact of foreign technical assistance has been at best uneven, and that there are many obstacles and pitfalls between idealistic aspirational statements and even partial realisation on the ground. And there are already predictions that many of the MDGs will not be met.[99]

These are reasonable doubts. But there are several grounds for believing as well as hoping that the strategy behind the MDGs marks a watershed in the history of 'development' for the following reasons: (i) the goals are based on a coherent underlying philosophy focused on poverty reduction; (ii) the goals and targets are SMART (specific, measurable, achievable, realistic and time-bound); (iii) the strategy is operationalised at country level, allowing for sensitivity to differing histories and conditions and local 'ownership' in respect of planning and implementation; (iv) the mechanisms for monitoring and reporting outcomes and for delivering aid draw on the experience of prior successes and failures and are more technically sophisticated than all prior efforts, especially in respect of monitoring and reporting; (v) crucially, there is a very high degree of consensus among stakeholders about the goals, the strategies, and the underlying technologies; (vi) there is a global compact with incentives for both developing countries and the international community, including IFIs, NGOs, and foreign donor agencies to work together towards

---

[99] Balanced assessments about the prospects include Black and White (eds) (2004) and Cheru and Bradford (eds.) (2005). Global figures on each of the goals can be highly misleading, not least because they can conceal vast discrepancies between and within countries. At present, the most reliable projections are to be found in country-specific plans. The main *general* threat to attainment of the MDGs may be global warming: 'At first blush, it might appear that only number seven, "Ensure environmental sustainability", is linked to climate change. But, as agricultural lands shift, water availability changes, and disease vectors move, our ability to provide food, improve health, provide clean water, and sustain natural resources will be degraded. As climate changes the baseline against which we intended to measure progress on these goals shifts, and so climate change becomes absolutely central to goals one, four, five, seven and, eight. However, all the Millennium Development Goals will become difficult to achieve as the climate changes because economic, ecological, and socio-political stability are inextricably linked.' (Bierbaum (2008) at p. 33.)

Table 11.3 Millennium Development Goals: A compact among nations to end human povety

Millennium Development Goals and targets		
Goal 1: Eradicate extreme poverty and hunger	*Target 7: Have halted by 2015 and begun to reverse the spread of HIV/AIDS*	*(includes tariff- and quota-free access for exports, enhanced program of debt relief for and cancellation of official bilateral debt, and more generous official development assistance for countries committed to poverty reduction)*

Goal 1: Eradicate extreme poverty and hunger

Target 1: Halve, between 1990 and 2015, the proportion of people whose income is less than $1 a day

Target 2: Halve, between 1990 and 2015, the proportion of people who suffer from hunger

Goal 2: Achieve universal primary education

Target 3: Ensure that, by 2015, children everywhere, boys and girls alike, will be able to complete a full course of primary schooling

Goal 3: Promote gender equality and empower women

Target 4: Eliminate gender disparity in primary and secondary education, preferably by 2005 and in all levels of education no later than 2015

Goal 4: Reduce child mortality

Target 5: Reduce by two-thirds, between 1990 and 2015, the under five mortality rate

Goal 5: Improve maternal health

Target 6: Reduce by, three-quarters, between 1990 and 2015, the maternal mortality ratio

Goal 6: Combat HIV/AIDS, malaria and other diseases

Target 7: Have halted by 2015 and begun to reverse the spread of HIV/AIDS

Target 8: Have halted by 2015 and begun to reverse the incidence of malaria and other major diseases

Goal 7: Ensure environmental sustainability

Target 9: Integrate the principles of sustainable development into country policies and programmes and reverse the loss of environmental resources

Target 10: Halve by 2015 the proportion of people without sustainable access to safe drinking water

Target 11: Have achieved by 2020 a significant improvement in the lives of at least 100 million slum dwellers

Goal 8: Develop a global partnership for development

Target 12: Develop further an open, rulebased, predictable, nondiscriminatory trading and financial system (includes a commitment to good governance, development, and poverty reduction – both nationally and internationally)

Target 13: Address the special needs of the least developed countries

(includes tariff- and quota-free access for exports, enhanced program of debt relief for and cancellation of official bilateral debt, and more generous official development assistance for countries committed to poverty reduction)

Target 14: Address the special needs of landlocked countries and small island developing states (through the Program of Action for the Sustainable Development of Small Island Developing States and 22nd General Assembly provisions)

Target 15: Deal comprehensively with the debt problems of developing countries through national and international measures in order to make debt sustainable in the long term

Target 16: In cooperation with developing countries, develop and implement strategies for decent and productive work for youth

Target 17: In cooperation with pharmaceutical companies, provide access to affordable essential drugs in developing countries

Target 18: In cooperation with the private sector, make available the benefits of new technologies, especially information and communications technologies

Source: UNDP (2002)

some clear common goals. Thus, there are grounds for believing that, in the words of Jeffrey Sachs 'our generation can choose to end [radical] poverty by 2025'.[100]

The degree of consensus is truly remarkable. All of the heads of state, who attended the special meeting of the General Assembly that adopted them, signed the Millennium Declaration. By 2002 all member Governments of the UN had endorsed the MDGs. More important, by 2004 the UN Secretary-General, Kofi Annan, could report that the MDGs have 'generated unprecedented, coordinated action' by both developing countries and major international organisations, including UN agencies, the World Bank, the IMF, and major state and private donors of technical assistance.[101] For the first time in history nearly all the major donor agencies were singing to the same hymn sheet. The great campaign in 2005 to 'Make Poverty History' gave an encouraging indication of popular support, though how far that is sustainable in the longer term remains to be seen. By August 2004 many, but not all, less developed countries had produced Poverty Reduction Strategy Plans (PRSPs), which are seen as a key element in carrying the strategy forward.[102]

Specified goals and targets, a clear but flexible strategy, optimism about technical feasibility, popular support, and mechanisms for monitoring, naming and shaming are important, sometimes necessary, ingredients of a workable consensus. But in the end three further ingredients are necessary for such a consensus to be sustainable: sincere belief in the worthwhileness of the goals, genuine commitment on the part of the key actors, and perception that it is in one's self-interest to support them.

A striking point about the MDGs is that they are minimalist. 'Extreme poverty' is the target, not relative deprivation. One target for 2015 is reducing the proportion of people with incomes of under $1 a day to 50 per cent.[103] Reducing child mortality, improving maternal health, combatting HIV/AIDS, malaria and other diseases as priorities are hardly controversial. Achieving universal primary education, promoting gender equality, and empowering women may need justification in some quarters and subscription to these will not be universally sincere. But the human development conception of poverty emphasises the interdependence of all these elements and for nearly all belief systems the situation described in standard accounts of the North–South divide

---

[100] Sachs (2005) at p. 1 *et passim*.

[101] Annan (2005) ('In Larger Freedom' Report to Security Council, March 2005).

[102] Some plans are referred to as Poverty Eradication Action Plans (PEAPS). The document analysed below is Uganda's PEAP for 2004. By 2006 140 national MDG reports had been published (UNDP Country Reports 2 (2007)). For a useful analysis of some of the earlier country reports from a human rights perspective see Alston (2005a), p. 792–98. On public attitudes to foreign aid in the USA see nn. 108 and 115 below.

[103] Proportion of Population Below $1 Purchasing Power Parity (PPP) per day. Controversy has surrounded the formulation of this goal and the meaning of this figure (see e.g. Pogge (2002) at p. 254, n. 333).

is wrong. Almost all can agree that this situation is bad, unacceptable, unjust, terrible, or obscene.

Who would dissent? One can imagine some arguments: 'They are not economically fit to survive';[104] 'Charity begins at home – starving children in Africa and floods in Bangladesh are not my concern'; 'The poor will get their reward in heaven'; 'The female sex *is* inferior'; 'The poor will always be with us'; 'Foreign aid is counterproductive' and so on.[105] Some consider a global perspective on poverty too abstract.[106] Of course, there will be some dissenters (informed or uninformed) and some other mavericks – a few in public, more in private.[107] But the indications are that at global, regional, and national levels the overwhelming weight of public opinion supports the values of the MDGs,[108] but one will find resistance to some of them (e.g. gender equality) at some local levels. In the present context I do not need to accord such views any more attention.

[104] See n. 49 above.

[105] In *World Poverty and Human Rights*, Thomas Pogge devotes several pages to rejecting 'four easy reasons to ignore world poverty': preventing poverty deaths is counterproductive; a gigantic global project is not politically feasible because it would involve unacceptable sacrifices by the better off; 'throwing money at the problem is no solution'; the problem is disappearing anyway. Pogge (2002) Introduction. Other grounds for scepticism include fears that richer nations will not deliver on their promises, that local political leaders have other priorities, that the attainment of the goals will require centralised direction in respect of problems that need genuine local 'ownership', that IFIs and human rights groups were slow to take the MDGs seriously, and some powerful nations only signed up because there was no specific price tag. A great deal of UNDP's promotional efforts are directed to countering such attitudes. Most of these points are discussed in the text.

[106] David Wiggins, in discussing the indispensability of implicit particular knowledge for moral understanding, expresses guarded scepticism about the MDGs as formulated in general terms: 'Well, who can be against any of these things? The question is not of course whether one is for or against them, but the danger that such approved formulations should upstage local perceptions and interpretations of what is locally needed or intended.' (Wiggins (2006) at pp. 350–1). This is not so much a criticism of the Millennium Project, as an important part of the case for making the hub of the enterprise more local than global. That, in turn, rests on the sincerity and determination of local leaders.

[107] Perhaps the most corrosive, and not necessarily unrealistic, attitude is that radical poverty reduction is not in the interest of ruling elites in some poorer countries. For elaboration of such pessimistic views see van der Walle (2001) and Lockwood (2005). Of course, for many regimes poverty reduction has not been their highest priority.

[108] An important survey suggests that public opinion is ahead of the US Government in supporting efforts to reduce world poverty and the MDGs: 'A large majority of Americans favor the US committing to the goal of devoting seven-tenths of one-percent of GDP to reducing world poverty, provided that other developed countries do so as well. An equally large majority favors the US committing up to $50 a year per taxpaying household to meet the Millennium Development Goals by the year 2015 – once again provided that other countries do so as well.' (Program on International Policy Attitudes June 29, 2005). The same survey suggests that while a strong majority favours farm subsidies for small farmers, 70 per cent oppose giving subsidies to large farming businesses, which are estimated to receive about 80 per cent of farm subsidies. This opinion is independent of the effects of US farm subsidies on ldcs, because the connection is not well understood (*ibid*). See further n. 115 below. By 2007 five countries had already met or surpassed the 0.7 per cent target and six others (including the UK) had committed to meeting this target by 2015.

Jeremy Bentham listed four 'principles subordinate to utility': security, subsistence, abundance, and equality. He suggested that even utilitarians, who are not given to hierarchies of priorities, would give priority to basic security and subsistence over the other two. So do most other belief systems. Whether one talks in terms of 'basic needs' or 'fundamental rights' or human interests, food, water, shelter and health together with security will usually be at or near the top of the list. So do surveys of what people want. There are, of course, conceptual difficulties about security and subsistence and both are relative matters.[109] But Bentham was surely right in his perception that questions about the relative importance of abundance and equality generally arise after some minimum basic requirements of security and subsistence have been met.[110] So it is reasonable to proceed on the basis that the minima prescribed by the Millennium Goals are broadly compatible with most major contemporary belief systems.

Ecumenical arguments typically appeal to both idealism and self-interest.[111] It is clearly in the self-interest of poorer countries, and of their governments, if they are well-intentioned, for poverty to be reduced or, better still, eradicated.[112] It is in the interest of the donor community to have a coherent and credible strategy towards agreed goals, although donor rivalry will not be completely eliminated. Most important, the case needs to be made to people and governments in rich countries that contributing to the Millennium Goals is in their self-interest.

Apart from appealing to humanitarian ideals, two main arguments support this case. First, the Millennium Goals have been kept modest in respect of costs as well as targets. The issues are complex, but the main point is put by Jeffrey Sachs as follows:

> The truth is that the cost now is likely to be small compared to any relevant measure – income, taxes, the costs of further delay, and the benefits from acting. Most important, the task can be achieved within the limits that the rich world had already committed: .07 percent of gross national product of the high income world, a mere 7 cents out of every $10 in income.[113]

However, there is general agreement that to achieve the MDGs some increased expenditure will be needed in the form of targeted foreign aid and debt relief. More difficult in practice, is the point that to achieve 'fair trade' will involve some significant alteration to existing protectionist practices, especially in the European Union and North America.[114] Supporters of the MDGs cannot

---

[109] See Quinn (2008).   [110] Dinwiddy (2004), pp. 84–9.

[111] On 'ecumenical arguments' see pp. 145 and 172 above.   [112] See n. 107 above.

[113] Sachs (2005) at p. 288. The whole of Chapter 15 is entitled 'Can the Rich Afford to Help the Poor?'. Estimates of the total costs of the MDGs vary, but have converged in recent years (p. 301).

[114] On the role of the WTO see Bermann and Petros (eds.) (2007).

plausibly claim that they involve no sacrifices or concessions; their point is that these are affordable and much less than might be expected.[115]

There are several grounds of appeal to enlightened self-interest: expanded markets, increased economic stability, and reduction of war and terrorism are frequently cited. The difficulty is that these mainly affect interests in the long-term. Bentham, the arch-priest of enlightened self-interest, would have grasped the main point: when colonies are no longer profitable 'Rid yourselves of Ultramaria'.[116] Support poverty eradication as it strengthens security. Divest from colonies, invest in the MDGs!

Of course, the MDGs have been a subject of controversy. Apart from criticisms on points of detail (e.g. the costs have not been properly calculated, not all the targets are measurable, this or that should be added), the most powerful objections relate to ambition and feasibility. Thomas Pogge and others emphasise the modesty of the goals: to reduce the *proportion* of those with under *$1 a day* by *50 per cent* sets the target below subsistence level, is lower than some prior targets, and does not preclude an actual increase in numbers in countries where population is growing (mainly the poorest countries).[117] And what of the other 50 per cent, asks Upendra Baxi, are they not entitled to justice or rights?[118] The standard response to these points is that this is only a first step in a long process, twenty-five years is almost nothing in the time frame of world history, and that modesty of aim was necessary to obtain consensus. Pogge's points are part of a larger argument about the basic structure of world society being fundamentally unjust and that only a radical reform of existing institutions can achieve a truly just international order.

The converse line of criticism is that the targets are over-ambitious, will raise false expectations, and may prove to be counter-productive.[119] In short, history suggests that even these modest goals are not realistic or feasible. The most powerful line of argument supporting this view is that time-bound targets, state-centrism and uniform global strategies cannot achieve the projected goals and that it is basically contradictory to try to *plan* markets. It is beyond the scope of this chapter to consider these arguments in depth. Suffice to say here that despite some misgivings about the MDGs, I am prepared to give them strong support on the ground that

---

[115] Repeated studies have shown that US citizens tend greatly to overestimate the percentage of public expenditure devoted to foreign aid; when asked what would be reasonable, they often suggest figures that are several times greater than actual expenditure (e.g. 'we give 15%, it should be 5%', when in fact it is less than 1%). (Program on International Policy Attitudes (PIPA) 2 Feb. 2001 www.pipa.org. A *Washington Post* survey in 1995 put the figures even higher (cited by Singer (2004) at pp. 182–4).

[116] Bentham, *Colonies, Commerce and Constitutional Law: Rid Yourselves of Ultramaria and Other Writings on Spain and Spanish America* (1993) (*CW*)

[117] Pogge (2002) (2005)   [118] Baxi (2007) at p. 83.

[119] Clemens, Kenny and Moss (2004) cited by Alston; Alston (2005a) summarises the main lines of argument relating to ambition and feasibility and neglect of the human rights dimension at pp. 762–7.

they offer the best hope at hand to mitigate world poverty, even if the goals are modest and not all will be achieved.[120] A quarter loaf is better than no bread.

11.5 The Millennium Development Goals and Uganda: A case-study of Uganda's Poverty Eradication Action Plan, 2004

The purpose of this chapter is to consider different perceptions of the roles and significance of law (especially state law) in the processes of development with particular reference to the most important contemporary development effort. The MDGs, quite rightly in my view, are largely focused at national level. Indeed, to rely on global figures in this respect can be seriously misleading, especially averages and aggregates. Generalisations in this area are particularly dangerous. In January 2007 I undertook a case study of the perceptions of the role of law in one national plan, that of Uganda, one of the world's poorest countries in sub-Saharan Africa, the region about which there is currently the most pessimism about MDGs.[121] A detailed report of this study is included in the Appendix. Uganda is a party to the MDG 'global compact'.[122]

Uganda's Poverty Eradication Action Plan, 2004 (hereafter UPEAP) is the main document embodying the strategy for poverty eradication/reduction of the Government of Uganda (hereafter GOU). The GOU's highest priority is stated to be eradication of poverty, 'defined as low incomes, limited human development, and powerlessness'.[123] The aim is to transform Uganda into a middle-income country, largely by private investment in competitive enterprises with industrialisation of agriculture (especially local processing of agricultural products) being a key element. Protectionism is rejected. While emphasising private investment, competition, and income enhancement, the report is not based on an extreme version of free market ideology. 'Poverty' is not defined solely in economic terms, but by reference to the indicators in the Human Development Index. Social and human development is treated as being closely interrelated with economic development. Throughout the report great stress is placed on gender issues and concerns about increasing inequality, both for individuals and for geographical areas, especially the North. Indeed the document is quite *dirigiste*: planning and government intervention are central,

---

[120] My personal attitude to the MDGs is not really relevant to the central argument of this chapter. However, I have been asked to state a view. Very briefly, I think that (i) the MDGs are admirable so far as they go; (ii) the success of the enterprise should be judged country by country. One can be optimistic about the prospects for some countries, pessimistic about others, with the outcome very much in the balance for the rest; (iii) the biggest obstacles to attainment of the MDGs are civil strife, natural disasters, global warming, pandemics, large scale corruption, and perhaps, most important, no substantial change in the protectionist agricultural policies of Europe and North America. Numerous estimates of the progress or otherwise towards realising the MDGs at the half-way stage are to be found on the Internet.

[121] See Black and White (eds.) (2004) *passim*, especially Chapter 14 (Fairhead).

[122] See Appendix 1 available on the web.   [123] For page references see Appendix 1.

'development'.[130] For example, nearly all the literature on the MDGs is state-centric and either ignores non-state law and other normative orders altogether or accords a passing acknowledgement to 'customary law.' The Uganda PEAP hardly mentions customary law (except in relation to land) and makes one passing reference to 'customary and indigenous knowledge'.[131] Jeffrey Sachs, the Director of the Millennium Project, in his powerful book, *The End of Poverty*, does not mention customary law, or religion, but tellingly has a significant heading in the index for 'cultural barriers'.[132] This is not untypical of writing about development by economists, though there are some exceptions.

Ignoring non-state law in this context may be attributable to ignorance, state-centric perspectives, deliberate policy, indifference, or downright hostility. A fairly extreme example of hostility to customary law is a speech in 2006 by the Right Hon. Don McKinnon, the Secretary-General of the Commonwealth Secretariat:[133]

> The drawbacks of customary law are manifold. For a start, just take its perceived failure to adapt to the expectations created by modern statehood, education, new technology, and global development. It lacks a contemporary comprehensiveness. It fails to address the emerging issues and needs of children, women and the disadvantaged.[134]

After listing a series of 'deep-seated and harmful social values and practices',[135] he concluded:

> From these examples, it is clear that the greatest single damage done by the persistence of customary law is to women, children and the poor. How far this has been a bar to our achievement of the Millennium Development Goals – particularly the 2nd to achieve universal primary education; the 3rd, to promote gender equality and empower women; and the 5th, to promote maternal health – remains a matter for concern.[136]

---

[130] There are some discussions of customary international law in relation to human rights. For example, Alston argues that at least some of the MDGs reflect norms of customary international law, especially the first six goals, but this view is explicitly rejected by the United States (Alston (2005a) at pp. 774–7).

[131] *Ibid.*, at p. 178.

[132] Sachs (2005) index. The longest passage reads: 'Even when governments are trying to advance their countries, the cultural environment may be an obstacle to development. Cultural or religious norms in the society may block the role of women, for example, leaving half of the population without economic or political rights and without education, thereby undermining half of the population in its contribution to overall development. Denying women their rights and education results in cascading problems. Most important, perhaps, the demographic transition from high fertility to low fertility is delayed or blocked altogether.' (Sachs (2005a) pp. 60–1); see also pp. 36–7, 72.

[133] McKinnon (2006). The Rt Hon. Don McKinnon was addressing a legal conference on 'Courting Justice: Rule of law reform in Africa' in London in April 2006.

[134] McKinnon (2006) at p. 651.

[135] His list included female genital mutilation, enforced female servitude (*trokosi*), prolonged and cruel mourning rites for widows, unfair inheritance practices, trafficking in children for forced labour and the sex trade, accusations and practices of witchcraft (*ibid.*).

[136] McKinnon (2006) at p. 651.

Fortunately, not all discussions of customary law are so sweeping and dogmatic. There is a large and growing body of literature, much of it based on detailed empirical research, that presents a more complex and balanced view.[137] The kind of negativity illustrated by this, admittedly extreme, example tends to be based on a number of dubious assumptions: that women are always at a disadvantage under customary law; that customary law is static rather than dynamic; that it is rigid rather than flexible; that it is incompatible with sustainable development; that it is always economically inefficient; that it is not concerned to conserve resources; and that values involved in economic development strategies (including the Millennium Development Goals) are instrinsically morally superior to customary values.[138]

Because generalised hostility to customary law tends to be ignorantly ethnocentric, it does not follow that there are no problems. Of course there are. It is probably true, for example, that by and large women have historically had by far the worse deal under most religious and customary traditions. How to respond to such judgements philosophically, socially, and politically is an immensely complex task.[139] In the last fifteen years (especially since the Beijing conference of 1995) Western feminists have begun to confront contradictions and dilemmas that women in more traditional cultures have had to live through, contend with, and struggle over throughout history. Few Western feminist scholars now embrace the kind of simplicities exemplified by McKinnon's attack on customary law, but that does not mean that they are backtracking on their commitment to furthering the equality and well-being of all women. The issues are far too complex to do justice to here.[140] In the present context the important point is that custom, religion, and various forms of non-state law are directly relevant to the attainment of projects such as the Millennium Development Goals, but it is far too simple to assume that they are inherently either a barrier or a

[137] E.g. Ørebach *et al.* (2005). A central theme of this book is that: '[E]ach customary law system needs to be evaluated on its merits'. (Bosselman, at p. 441). See also Perreau-Saussine and Murphy (2007), Rajagopal (2007), pp. 276–82. A useful general bibliography on customary law in Africa is Okupa (1998). There has been a striking revival of theoretical interest in custom and customary law recently, for example Polanski (2007) (internet law), Tasioulaas (2007b) (international law), Perreau–Saussine and Murphy (2007) (general).

[138] Counter-examples to most of these over-generalisations can be found in Ørebech *et al.* (eds.) (2005). On 'chthonic law' and the environment see Glenn (2004) 72–80.

[139] One possible starting point is Martha Nussbaum's critique of secular feminism from a feminist perspective that is explicitly universalist: '[One] pragmatic error of the secular humanist is to fail to pursue alliances with feminist forces within each religious tradition. Religious traditions have indeed been powerful sources of oppression for women; but they have also been powerful sources of protection for human rights, of commitment to justice, and of energy for social change.' (Nussbaum (2000) at p. 178.) Nussbaum next identifies three doubts about secular feminism at a deeper level: *the instrinsic value of religious capabilities*; *respect for persons*, (including their beliefs); and *political liberalism* (in the Rawlsian sense of a non-comprehensive moral theory) (*ibid.*, at pp. 178–80).

[140] Bennett (1999), Nussbaum (2000), Okin (1999), Mukhopadhyay and Singh (eds.)(2007), Stewart (2009).

motor to 'development', unless perhaps that is interpreted solely in terms of national GDP.[141]

There is a sophisticated, if patchy, literature on customary law. However, a great deal of this literature, especially by lawyers, adopts the perspective of state legal pluralism and treats those aspects that are, or in the opinion of the authors should be, recognised as *part* of municipal law. My own early writings on the subject focused on the place of customary law in the national legal systems of East Africa.[142] It is hardly surprising that even those who write sympathetically about custom, tradition, and religion in the context of development, generally have a top-down, technocratic perspective concerned with how policy-makers might incorporate them and build on local 'folk wisdom' as part of strategies of state-sponsored development. These are legitimate concerns, but it is important to bear in mind that from a subaltern or user perspective[143] customary and religious norms often have much wider scope than and may be interpreted differently from those aspects that are recognised by the state as part of municipal law. Sometimes they are used as bastions of resistance against foreign incursions.[144] From almost any perspective non-state norms (whether or not they are classified as 'legal') are important just because they may be deeply rooted in people's practices and beliefs.

11.7 Conclusion

In 1969 Barbara Ward, who inspired Mahbub Ul Haq and Amartya Sen, among others, argued that we already had the technological resources to conquer world poverty and what was needed was a moral vision of humankind as a community.[145] Since then the story of 'development' has been an uneven, often unhappy one. Technology has progressed, the world has become more interdependent, the Millennium Development Goals suggest that there is a moral unity, or at least a very broad consensus, about basic needs. What is still required is sustained political will on the part of the leaders of poor countries as well as rich ones, backed by public opinion. Jeremy Bentham believed that the interests of the rulers, however they are chosen, are in all respects potentially opposed to the interests of the governed.[146] For this reason, he became a reluctant convert to democracy and emphasised transparency, freedom of speech, and other forms of publicity as securities against misrule.[147] In recent years Amartya Sen has reached similar conclusions by a different route, linking democracy and

---

[141] See generally de Soto (1989), (2000).   [142] Twining (1963).

[143] On user perspectives see Nader (1984): MacCormick (2007) Chapter 1, *passim*; GLT, pp. 125–6.

[144] The post-colonial literature on 'resistance' is now well-developed, see especially Chanock (1985), Benton (2002), Rajagopal (2003).

[145] Ward (1966) cited at the start of this chapter.

[146] This was a constant theme of his later political writings. See, e.g. 'Constitutional Code Rationale' in Bentham (1989) at pp. 232–7. See generally, Rosen (1983), Schofield (2006).

[147] On Bentham's conversion to democracy, see Dinwiddy (2004), Chapter 2.

sustainable development under the mantra 'Development as Freedom'.[148] Despite the 'challenges' of natural disasters, civil wars, epidemics, corruption and other obstacles to development, the Millennium Development Goals offer the best hope yet of combining technological know how, with moral vision and political will to greatly reduce, if not totally eradicate, extreme poverty. In this cause law has a largely unobtrusive, but significant, role to play.

[148] Sen (1999).

Chapter 12

The significance of non-state law[*]

12.1 Taking non-state law seriously

The great bulk of mainstream Western legal theory and legal scholarship in the twentieth century focused on the domestic law of municipal legal systems, sometimes extending to public international law in the narrow sense of law governing relations between states ('The Westphalian Duo'). Hart, Rawls, Dworkin, Kelsen, and Raz are examples of this perspective. The main exceptions have been legal anthropologists and other scholars who have emphasised the importance of legal pluralism. Recently some jurists interested in the implications of 'globalisation' – including Glenn, Santos, Tamanaha, and Twining – have advanced arguments in favour of broader conceptions of law that include at least some examples of 'non-state law'. This, not surprisingly, has met with some resistance.

In the immediate context, viewing our discipline and its subject matters from a global perspective, both geographically and historically, my argument for a broad conception of law is that focusing solely on the municipal law of nation states (or the Westphalian Duo) leaves out too much that should be the proper concern of legal scholarship. A reasonably inclusive cosmopolitan discipline of law needs to encompass all levels of relations and of ordering, relations between these levels, and all important forms of law including supra-state (e.g. international, regional) and non-state law (e.g. religious law, transnational law, chthonic law i.e. tradition/custom) and various forms of 'soft law'. A picture of law in the world that focuses only on the municipal law of nation states and public international law would for many purposes be much too narrow.[1] For example, it is difficult to justify omitting Islamic law or other major traditions of religious law from such a picture. Yet, to include only those examples of religious law or custom officially recognised by sovereign states (state legal pluralism) would be seriously misleading.[2] To try to subsume European Union

---

[*] This is a revised version of section IId of Twining (2005) and is reproduced here by permission.
[1] On legal and normative orders that are invisible or pass unnoticed see Chapter 10.2(c) above. On the tendency in development circles either to ignore custom or treat it as an obstacle to progress see Chapter 11.6 above.
[2] It is hardly controversial to say that to recognise Islamic or other religious law only insofar as it is recognised by sovereign states involves crude distortion. It would be odd to accept the idea of a

Law or *lex mercatoria* or international commercial arbitration or all examples of 'human rights law' under public international law similarly stretches that concept to breaking point, without any corresponding gains.[3]

A move to extend the conception of law to encompass the main phenomena that are appropriately treated as subject matters of our discipline[4] undoubtedly raises a number of conceptual difficulties, but that is not a good reason for retreating back to the familiar orbit of a state law plus a few 'law-like' analogies. In the present context, the key step is to cease to treat modern municipal law as a paradigm case by reference to which one can decide on the closeness of the analogy of other candidates for inclusion. Glenn, Tamanaha, and Griffiths, for example, in different ways de-centre the state from their pictures of law in the world without denying that it is for most purposes the most powerful, complex, and sophisticated form of law around.[5]

In the present context the issue is not mainly a semantic one nor a matter of status – a plea that specialists in religious legal traditions or African law or Romani law should be recognised as jurists and legal scholars. It concerns the health of our discipline and especially our collective ignorance and marginalisation of the ideas, norms, institutions and practices of non-Western legal traditions. My thesis in this context is that we can no longer afford to maintain such a narrow focus, that this involves significant redeployment of attention and resources, and that this re-orientation of our discipline raises fundamental

---

Jewish, Islamic or Romani legal tradition, but to refuse to talk about Jewish and Islamic or Romani law – that is a corollary of thinking in terms of law as a system of rules. Huxley (2002). On the differences between looking at Jewish legal tradition from the perspective of a theologian and a jurist see Bernard Jackson (2005).

[3] A theory of state law such as Hart's provides an inadequate theoretical framework for grounding our discipline as it becomes more cosmopolitan and more concerned with multiple levels of legal relations and legal ordering. Hart's conception of law cannot easily fit European Union Law, contemporary Public International Law, religious law, canon law, medieval and modern *lex mercatoria*, let alone other forms of traditional and customary law that are candidates for our attention as legal scholars and jurists. In short, none of our stock of theories of municipal law can provide an adequate theoretical basis or organising concept for a cosmopolitan and reasonably inclusive discipline of law.

[4] Of course 'understanding law' involves understanding much else besides. Studying law in context does not involve defining law as context. Our concern here is with what constitute legal phenomena as the main subject matters of our discipline. That implies some means of differentiating between legal and other phenomena, between legal and 'non-legal' rules, institutions, practices, and processes. Scepticism about a general definition of law does not involve denial of the need to be able to make appropriate differentiations and clarifications in given contexts.

[5] Glenn (2004), Tamanaha (2001), Griffiths (1986) (2003). MacCormick (2007) concentrates on state law but emphasises: 'One point which has been repeated throughout this book is that law as institutional normative order can be found in many contexts other than that of each single state. That is so, both because of the way international and transnational organizations have developed beyond state boundaries, and because many of the organizations active in civil society have their own internal institutional ordering. States may indeed claim primacy over such organizations (e.g., churches, international sporting associations), but the organizations need not in turn, and some do not, acknowledge that primacy in the form in which it is asserted by one or another state.' (MacCormick (2007) at p. 288 (discussed Twining (2009)).

problems of comparison and generalisation across legal traditions, cultures and other boundaries[6] that we may not yet be well equipped to tackle.

Some colleagues may readily concede that more attention needs to be paid to other legal traditions and cultures and that this has implications for legal theory. They may also concede that if one adopts a global perspective at the start of the twenty-first century there are good reasons for arguing that an *exclusive* focus on municipal law is too narrow for many practical and theoretical purposes and for a balanced view of the subject matters of a genuinely cosmopolitan discipline of law. But they may still be concerned about a sharp break with state-centred conceptions of law, or what Simon Roberts has called 'attempts to loosen the conceptual bonds between law and government'.[7] These concerns need to be addressed not only in relation to my specific argument, but also to broader claims about the importance of non-state law in a variety of other contexts.

The literature on globalisation is replete with talk of the decline of sovereignty, the changing significance of national boundaries, religious revivals, the increase in migration and displacement, the extension of multi-culturalism, the decline of private international law and the rise of private transnational justice, the importance of informal horizontal transnational networks of officials and judges, the increasing roles of non-state actors, and so on. The more ebullient forms of 'g-talk' contain such catch-phrases as 'the end of sovereignty', 'the decline of the nation state', 'global governance', 'a borderless world'. Clearly these developments deserve the attention of jurists, but their significance is contested and difficult to interpret. However, to argue that non-state law deserves more attention from legal scholars and jurists involves no specific commitment to a firm position on any of these developments. Whether the nation state is in fact declining in relative importance is an extremely complex and elusive question, which is usually best tackled at lower levels of generality. For present purposes it is sufficient to restate briefly why non-state law needs our attention.

Patrick Glenn, among others, has made the general case at some length for taking non-state law seriously.[8] His argument provides a useful starting point for this chapter. The nation state as the primary form of governance emerged slowly in Europe, roughly between the thirteenth and sixteenth centuries. The modern conception of a sovereign nation state with a monopoly of legitimate authority over defined territory has been the predominant form in the West for barely two centuries. Even during that period that predominance has not been universal:

> There has been considerable correspondence between statist legal theory and actual legal practice in Europe and the United States, but elsewhere it has been

---

[6] On the analytic value of the concepts of culture, tradition, civilisation, and religion see Chapter 3.4(b) above and Foster (ed.) (2006) *passim*.

[7] Roberts (2005) (abstract).   [8] Glenn (2003a) (2003b).

taken *cum grano salis*. States in the colonized world (the rest of the world) lived through the eighteenth, nineteenth, and twentieth centuries in a delicate equilibrium between local law (in non-state form) and the metropolitan law of the colonial power. Identities here were complex and shared, law was conceived in a pluralistic manner, state law was necessarily limited, and conquered peoples played an active role in the law applicable to them. ... Law here has been conceived for centuries in a transnational manner.[9]

Apart from variations in the power and reach of state law, Glenn emphasises the variety of forms in which states exist and the lack of analytical purchase of the concept of a national legal system. There may be nearly 200 members of the United Nations, but these include failed states, small states,[10] fragmented states, states caught up in lengthy civil wars, and states with corrupt, despotic, or anarchic regimes. In most parts of the world the modern form of the state, with its great variety and fluidity, is a quite recent phenomenon with shallow roots. Often the result of colonialism and imperialism, in the post-colonial period its stability and hegemony have often been challenged (e.g. through boundary disputes, civil wars, revolution, and conquest).

The conception of a nation state (which is the basis for membership of the United Nations), is essentially formal, obscuring both the diversity of kinds of states, the variation in the extent of each state's actual effective control over its territory, and the fragility and susceptibility to change of this political form.[11]

Glenn treats nation-state law as one tradition among many. In addition to various forms of non-state law at sub-national levels, he examines the contributions of the *ius commune*, the *lex mercatoria*, natural law, personal laws, 'binding' custom, self-regulation, and best practices to the development of transnational law. He links this to his general thesis about tradition and persuasive authority:

Ancient justifications for law beyond the state are once again of relevance since transnational law is not (generally) considered to be binding law [subject to exceptions] ... . Pre-state and post-state law, however, share the general characteristic of being suppletive law, law which is at the disposition of the parties as

---

[9] Glenn (2003a) at p. 842, see also Glenn (1987).

[10] Braithwaite and Drahos (2000) at p. 492 report that in the 1990s more than 50 per cent of the largest economies in the world were corporations rather than states, cited by Glenn (2003a) at p. 846.

[11] 'The definition of a state suggests uniformity, since all states are composed of uniform elements – a government and a defined territory. International law supports this impression of uniformity, since all states are treated as equal, at least in principle. Yet, national legal traditions crystallize in many different forms, some close to the European model, or models, others far removed from them. Diversity emerges in the choice which the members of each state make as to its constituent elements. The tradition of a national legal system creates no obstacle to this, since systems are defined only in terms of ensembles with interacting elements. That is why the notion of state is not *féconde;* it is a formal descriptor and almost anything can be conceived of in terms of system. Hence the ubiquity of the expression "legal system" in describing wildly disparate legal phenomena in the world.' (Glenn (2003b) at pp. 90–1.) See *GLT*, pp. 178–84. Glenn's emphasis on the diversity of states and the formal nature of the category contrasts sharply with Simon Roberts' emphasis on the distinctiveness of state law as a form of ordering, discussed below. On the concept of system see Chapter 15.4 on the web.

opposed to binding them. The notion of binding people together was necessary for the purposes of construction of collective identities, as in the case of organized religion and the state.[12]

12.2 Four concerns

Patrick Glenn's account of legal traditions of the world may be controversial,[13] but this is the most comprehensive and persuasive general argument for taking non-state law seriously if one adopts a global perspective. Given that this appears to involve quite a radical break from the dominant Western traditions of academic law, it is hardly surprising if it gives rise to some anxieties among scholars and jurists. Such concerns also deserve attention. I shall argue that while a global perspective opens up some exciting possibilities for our discipline, the break with tradition need not be quite as sharp as might at first sight appear. I shall consider these concerns under a four heads:

(a) A threat to liberal democracy?
(b) Diluting the discipline of law?
(c) Conceptual difficulties I: the problem of the definitional stop.
(d) Conceptual difficulties II: the distinctiveness of state law.

(a) A threat to liberal democracy?

In recent years, a great deal of modern Anglo-American jurisprudence has been focused on the development of liberal democratic theory, as exemplified by the work of Rawls, Dworkin, Raz, and MacCormick. This kind of political philosophy has been almost as state-centric as legal theory.[14] For much of the twentieth century it has been concerned with a tug of war between the minimalist/reactive state, the welfare state, and the administrative state.

Some political scientists have noted a strong change of mood. There was a period in which the state was looked on with suspicion by the libertarian Right, but was considered by the Left to provide the best hope for popular sovereignty, social justice and the rights of the citizen. But in recent years the predominant mood has changed to one of suspicion of both the state and of nationalism.[15]

---

[12] Glenn (2003a) at p. 849.   [13] See Foster (ed.) (2006).

[14] However, for some social scientists the concept of governance extends beyond the state to include, for example, economy, family, and community. Two recent books (Galligan (2007) and MacCormick (2007)) acknowledge the significance of 'non-state' law, but explicitly focus on state law as being sufficiently distinctive and important to warrant special attention. This is, of course, not inconsistent with the argument of this chapter, except perhaps they may underestimate the practical importance of non-state law in some parts of the world.

[15] 'Associated, above all, with the impact of Foucault and his brethren, the new prevailing sentiment on the left is anti-state, libertarian, fearful of authoritarianism, and suspicious of collectivism. … Here I shall argue that only a strong polity can hold out the prospect of democratic self-governance with individual liberty and social justice; only a strong state can protect against the disintegrative forces of global capitalism and the divisive forces of particularism and identity.' (Abraham (2007) at p. 210.)

These tendencies have in turn bred a fear that the decline of the state will lead to anarchy, repression and injustice. Surely, it can be argued, political ideals such as democracy, the Rule of Law, citizenship, human rights, due process, social welfare, and social justice depend for their realisation on relatively strong and stable forms of centralised governance?

Such concerns may be well-founded. Within jurisprudence, they may not be good grounds for refusing to acknowledge the importance of the phenomena that a broad conception of law would subsume under 'non-state law', but they provide an important warning: legal scholars should no more romanticise non-state law than they should view state law through rose-tinted spectacles.

It is worth noting that several of those arguing for a broad conception of law, have given a similar warning: for example, Santos explicitly argues that 'there is nothing inherently good, progressive, or emancipatory about legal pluralism'.[16] Teubner criticises the vagueness and confusion of post-modern treatments of legal pluralism.[17] Interestingly, Brian Tamanaha, having devoted a whole book to arguing strenuously for a broad conception of law, focused almost exclusively on state law in writing about the Rule of Law as an ideal.[18] The lesson is clear: a positivist conception of law that includes examples of non-state law does not involve a commitment to the approval of non-state law in general, or specific examples thereof. Nor does it imply that the nation-state and democratic government are in terminal decline.

(b) Diluting the discipline of law?

A major concern of some legal scholars and educators is that an enthusiastic response to 'globalisation' will result in the discipline of law becoming detached from its roots in a particular legal tradition and local legal practice. This concern might be expressed as follows: Our tradition of academic law has been state-centred and rightly so for three main reasons. First, municipal state law is by far the most important form of normative ordering (or of law in a broad sense). Second, I myself have argued that law is a participant-oriented discipline closely connected in fact with legal practice in a broad sense.[19] Professional lawyers – judges, government lawyers, private practitioners, and even law-makers – deal almost entirely with state law, mainly local municipal law. They do not practice non-state law. Third, academic law is intimately linked with preparation for legal practice. To a large extent legal scholarship services legal education and training. Basic competence involves the mastery of practical details and socialisation into the local legal culture, especially the intellectual skills and 'mentality' of lawyers practising within a particular system or tradition. Even when legal education is presented as a good vehicle for a general liberal education, the core of the discipline is concerned

---

[16] Santos (1995) at pp. 114–15; see Santos (2002) at pp. 90–2.   [17] Teubner (1992) at pp. 1443–5.
[18] Tamanaha (2004) at pp. 26–35.   [19] E.g. LIC, pp. 126–8, *GJB*, pp. 31–3.

with intellectual skills that involve analysis, interpretation, application, and argumentation about detailed particulars. Study of other traditions in perspectives courses may have value as a secondary activity, but it usually involves study *about* generalities rather than studying *how* to participate in a particular legal system.[20] Experience has shown that the sources of non-state law, even when they are available, are often less suitable as vehicles for developing intellectual and practical skills than codes, statutes, cases and other traditional materials of the study of law.[21] Heightened awareness of other legal traditions may be admirable, but it is no substitute for the disciplined study of local particulars. For the discipline of law to be internally coherent and manageable it must continue to focus on domestic state law.

This is not the place to dwell on the implications of globalisation for legal education, vocational training, and legal practice. In this context, the best I can do is confess and avoid. I have argued elsewhere that different considerations arise in relation to legal scholarship and legal education, for much the same reasons that are stated in the objection.[22]

However, the case for maintaining the traditional focus can easily be overstated. Non-state law is more directly relevant to many kinds of legal practice than is generally acknowledged. Legal practice in a multi-cultural society should to some extent be multi-cultural: to insist on a unitary legal culture can be viewed as a conservative ploy or as a delusion.[23] Our discipline has never been entirely local and it is becoming more cosmopolitan. Legal scholarship and legal

---

[20] On the distinction between studying about and studying how, see *LIC*, pp. 181–3. Part of Ronald Dworkin's appeal is that his theory focuses on detailed argumentation about specific issues (especially in hard cases) within a given system, whereas descriptive theories such as those of Hart and Tamanaha operate at a more abstract level largely from external points of view. A Hartian description of the form and structure of a state legal system is likely to be rather thin and provides little or no guidance to judges and other participants. On Dworkin's limited conception of legal practice see pp. 28–9 above. On difficulties surrounding the external/internal distinction see *GJB*, pp. 30–2, 181 and *LIC*, pp. 217–21.

[21] This is confirmed by my experience of trying to teach 'customary law' in the Sudan and East Africa. See *LIC*, Chapter 2.

[22] Twining (2001) This book is concerned in first instance with legal scholarship and legal theory – with what is involved in advancing understanding of law from a global or transnational perspective and only indirectly with the implications of this for the teaching of law. I am personally somewhat sceptical about the rapid development of global or radically transnational legal education, at least at first degree level. (See Preface, n. 8 above.) A cosmopolitan discipline does not mandate neglect of local knowledge. For the time being the rule of thumb should be 'think global, focus local'. It might be argued that one of the implications of adopting a broad conception of law is that the concept of 'legal education' is correspondingly broadened. As, Lawrence Friedman has said, 'Life in America, and the West in general, is a vast, diffuse school of Law.' (Friedman (1989) at p. 1598). Socio-legal studies of legal awareness and knowledge and opinion about law could usefully be extended to cover how ordinary people learn about non-state law. However, in writing about legal education I have usually followed convention in focusing on law schools and professional training programmes, which are mainly concerned with state law. (See, however, *LIC*, Chapter 15.)

[23] The case for viewing domestic law as inescapably pluralistic in Western countries that have significant ethnic minorities is made convincingly by Menski (Chapter 1) and Ballard (Chapter 2) in Shah and Menski (2006). See also Bano (2007). It is to be hoped that those law

education have in fact been quite responsive to changes associated with 'global-isation'. For example, in the United Kingdom every law student is exposed to European Community Law and, at least via the Human Rights Act, 1998, to the European Convention on Human Rights. More and more options are offered with an explicitly transnational focus (e.g. international trade, human rights, immigration law, Internet Law). As important, perhaps, is the fact that many subjects are recognised as having important transnational dimensions (e.g. regulation, commercial law, environmental law, intellectual property, and labour law). Family law and feminist legal theory are becoming more sensitive to multi-culturalism; challenges to rigid views of sovereignty are explored in constitutional law as well as international law and jurisprudence; more attention is being paid to Muslim law, not only in separate courses as a form of 'foreign law', but also in courses on domestic law, such as family law, finance, and criminal law as it affects minority communities;[24] a leading textbook on the English legal system gives a prominent place to 'alternative dispute resolution'[25] and courses of that name are placing an increasing emphasis on cross-cultural and transnational negotiation, mediation, and arbitration. In 1994, it was estimated that over two-thirds of the courses in the London Intercollegiate LLM dealt mainly with international, transnational, foreign, or comparative subjects.[26]

To sum up: concern that our discipline should not lose touch with the local and the particular and with professional legal practice is well founded and nothing in this chapter is intended to suggest otherwise.

(C) Conceptual difficulties I: The problem of the definitional stop

A more traditional concern has been with a version of 'the floodgates argu-ment'. If one opens the door to some examples of non-state law, then we are left with no clear basis for differentiating legal norms from other social norms, legal institutions and practices from other social institutions and practices, legal traditions from religious or other general intellectual traditions and so on. Let us call this the problem of the definitional stop. Within the literature of legal pluralism there have been three main reactions to this problem.

First, some have tried to produce a general definition that differentiates the legal from the non-legal. For example, in the first edition of *Toward a New*

---

schools that reassert that their main concern is still the detailed study of local domestic law include under that rubric minority religious and customary practices that have a significant bearing on such matters as family, finance, crime, and community-based tribunals. The Judicial Studies Board in England and Wales publishes an *Equal Treatment Bench Handbook* (2007) that addresses issues of diversity and sensitivity to the customs and beliefs of ethnic minorities.

[24] See Pearl and Menski (1998).   [25] Bradney and Cownie (2000).

[26] GLT, pp. 55–6. Law schools in the United States have been somewhat less responsive to 'globalisation', in part because of the influence of bar examinations on the curriculum and students' choice of options. But there has been an expansion of interest in foreign and com-parative law, Islamic law etc. See, for example, recent issues of the *Journal of Legal Education*. In Miami I teach a course on 'Globalisation and Law', which attracts a modest number of students.

Common Sense, Santos produced a general definition of law that was very close to that of the anthropologist E. Adamson Hoebel.[27] Teubner also feels the need to do this.[28] This is one of Tamanaha's central concerns in his *General Jurisprudence of Law and Society*. He explicitly seeks to establish criteria of identification that differentiate legal institutions from institutions such as hospitals, schools, and sports leagues. This concern leads him to set up his 'labelling test', which several critics, including myself, have rejected on the grounds that it conflates analytic and folk concepts and that it is unworkable.[29] This deserves to be seen as a valiant failure.

Second, there are those who take the position that the search for a general definition of 'law' is a futile pursuit. Many writers just beg the question. '"*It just doesn't matter*"' writes Glenn, 'whether or not "Cthonic law" is classified as law'.[30] In some contexts, whether a particular set of phenomena is classified as legal or not may be insignificant. Very little turns on whether the phenomena under consideration are designated as 'law' or not in Weyrauch's accounts of Romani ('Gypsy') law, or Bradney and Cownie on 'Quaker law', or Santos' account of 'Pasagarda law' or many of the classic studies of dispute processes in pre-literate societies, such as those of Gulliver on the Arusha.[31] Similarly Pistor and Wellons, in their excellent study of law and economic development in Asia, conclude that nearly all receptions of state law involve complex interactions between imported official law and local 'unofficial law'.[32] It would not make much difference to their study if they had not used the term 'law' in relation to local normative orders. Conversely, in contexts where the focus is exclusively on state law, there would be little change of substance if a convention developed of referring to 'state law' or 'municipal law' in such contexts. If Hart's classic work were re-named *The/A Concept of State Law*, very little of the text would need to be changed.[33]

---

[27] Santos (1995) at p. 112. 'A social norm is legal if its neglect or infraction is regularly met, in threat or in fact, by the application of physical force by an individual or group possessing the socially recognized privilege of so acting' (Hoebel (1954) at p. 28). This was the general definition that Llewellyn refused to include in *The Cheyenne Way*. (See *KLRM*, pp. 177–9.)

[28] Teubner (1992).   [29] Twining (2003); Himma (2004), Roberts (2005) at pp. 20–2.

[30] Glenn (2004) at p. 69. See the criticisms of Glenn's failure to distinguish clearly between legal and religious aspects of a tradition in the context of his general theory of legal traditions in Foster (ed.) (2006). However, Glenn may be defended on the ground that he is comparing phenomena which are *conventionally* viewed as major legal traditions by outside observers, but each conceptualises religion and law and their relations differently.

[31] Weyrauch and Bell (1993), Weyrauch (ed.) (1997); Bradney and Cownie (2000); Gulliver (1963).

[32] Pistor and Wellons (1999); Berkowitz, Pistor and Richard (2003) at pp. 163–201.

[33] Galligan, whose main concern is modern legal systems/societies, nevertheless opens the door to the idea of non-state law: ' … [T]he persistent intuition of legal pluralists that there is something potentially legal about some social spheres is well-founded. Once law is located prior to rules as the expression of social relations, it becomes clear that informal spheres may express important social relations, and in that sense are potentially legal. However, in modern societies, their potential is smothered by the claims of state law'. (Galligan (2007) at p. 191.) This is a grudging recognition of 'informal law', but the emphasis on potentiality links it too closely to Hart's idea of the pre-legal. Galligan's book is about law in *modern* society and does not address all societies. Nevertheless, his last sentence is probably an overstatement.

However, sometimes the categorisation may have some significance. For example, it could be argued that Glenn needs a distinction in the context of his argument, for he treats legal traditions as the main unit of comparison, without clearly distinguishing between law and religion in respect of several intellectual traditions.[34]

Third, there are some, like Marc Galanter, who see the indicia of 'the legal' as a complex mix of attributes along one or more continua so that it is artificial and misleading to prescribe precise general boundaries – at least outside a particular context.[35] In practice, Galanter ends up with a conception of 'the legal' which is broader and vaguer than Tamanaha's. Karl Llewellyn refused to include a general definition of law in the *Cheyenne Way* for similar reasons,[36] but as I argued above one can construct some general indicia for differentiating legal from non-legal phenomena from his law-jobs theory on the basis of a kind of 'thin functionalism' while leaving borderline cases to be settled in a specific context.[37] In the context of mapping law from a global perspective, I have been willing to indicate some broad criteria of identification not very different from Llewellyn's, but subject to three caveats: first, that this is intended for no more than clarification in a quite specific context; second, that it is not intended that this characterisation should bear much theoretical weight; and, third, that this conception represents only one way among several for categorising the phenomena for this particular purpose.[38]

If one is interested in the relations between municipal law and other normative orders there are conceptual problems however one defines or conceptualises law. The definitional stop is only one of several problems in this area, most of which are unlikely to be resolved by conceptual analysis or formal definitions alone.

(d) Conceptual difficulties II: The distinctiveness of centralised governance

A somewhat different concern has recently been expressed by Simon Roberts. In his elegant Chorley Lecture for 2004, Simon Roberts criticised attempts 'to loosen the conceptual bonds between law and government' and to broaden representations of law to include negotiated orders, which have distinct rationalities and values.[39] Roberts is a distinguished legal anthropologist who can hardly be accused of being narrowly focused or indifferent to social context. Indeed, his main concern seems to be that broadening our conceptions of law may de-stabilise 'the comparative project', obscure the differences between state law and other forms of normative orders, and in the process weaken our capacity to grasp the nature of negotiated orders.

Roberts' lecture is an extension of an argument that he made in his paper 'Against Legal Pluralism' in which he suggested 'that it is inevitably problematic to attempt to fix a conception of law going beyond the robust self-definitions of

[34] Foster (ed.) (2006), Glenn (2007).   [35] Galanter (1981).   [36] KLRM, pp. 177–9 (1973).
[37] See Chapter 4.3(d) above.   [38] See p. 117 above.   [39] Roberts (2005).

state law'.[40] In both papers Roberts is concerned that when enthusiastic jurists turn their attention to non-state normative orders they are likely to try to interpret other cultures through what are essentially lawyers' 'folk concepts' or else to indulge in an undisciplined and 'eclectic resort to the theoretical resources of the social sciences.'[41] While acknowledging that a sharp distinction between folk and analytic concepts can be problematic, Roberts insists that only by working with this distinction and looking for meaning at an analytic level can 'the comparative project' hope to achieve any stability.[42]

I find Roberts' argument puzzling because I agree with nearly all of his main points, but I do not share his fears about the consequences of adopting a broad conception of law for some purposes. Like him, I think that one of the main challenges to comparative law and legal anthropology is the development of usable analytic concepts.[43] For example, in the present context, I have no reason to dissent from the following propositions:

(a) That there are aspects of the form and structure of state law that are clearly linked to centralisation, leadership, and governance. In some respects, state law represents a distinctive social form worthy of conceptualisation in a rigorous and precise fashion.[44]

(b) That state/municipal law has been and is likely to continue to be the main focus of attention of legal scholars and legal practitioners and is likely to be of great political and economic significance for the foreseeable future.

(c) That broadening the concept of law to include some non-state normative orders poses a number of conceptual difficulties, including problems of differentiating legal from 'non-legal' phenomena in different contexts and individuating orders, systems, and semi-autonomous social fields.[45]

(d) That confining one's conception of law to state law does not involve a commitment to the idea that other forms of normative ordering are unimportant or unworthy of the attention of legal scholars.[46]

---

[40] Roberts (1998) at p. 105. Roberts is justified in warning of the dangers of juricentrism. Lawyers may tend to view the world through juricentric lenses, much as human beings tend to view the world through ethnocentric lenses. This is the message of auotopoiesis. However, not all jurists are confined by narrow legalistic perspectives and it is one of the aims of a humanistic jurisprudence to counter such tendencies, not least by acknowledging the continuities between legal and other social phenomena.

[41] See Roberts at p. 95. On 'folk' concepts see Chapter 2, n. 63 above.

[42] Roberts (1998) at pp. 102–5; see also Roberts (2005) at pp. 23–4.

[43] See Chapter 2 above. Here Patrick Glenn, writing about traditions, appears to diverge, arguing against looking for a *tertium comparationis* in comparing traditions. Glenn (2004) at pp. 46–7.

[44] Joseph Raz justifies confining his concept of law to municipal legal systems because they are sufficiently important and sufficiently different from most other normative systems to be made the object of a separate study. Raz (1979) at p. 105. But Roberts makes further claims. See also Galligan (2007) at Chapter 1.

[45] See Chapter 4 above and Chapter 15.4 on the web.

[46] However, one implication of Roberts' argument appears to be that our colleagues in the Law Department of the School of Oriental and African Studies who specialise in Islamic law, Buddhist law, Hindu law etc, are only studying law insofar as the phenomena they study are closely

I also agree with some of Roberts' criticisms of Pospisil, Sacco, Teubner, and Geertz[47] and with many, but not all, of his other specific points. So I am left puzzled as to what we might be disagreeing about. Surely it cannot be just another return to obsession with 'the definition of law'? Maybe there is more to it than that. Let me suggest two reasons.

First, Roberts' central concern is that '[a]s radically different modes of ordering and decision are represented together as "legal", law loses analytic purchase'.[48] Here it is useful to distinguish between law as an analytic concept, law as an organising concept, and law as a rough way of designating a scholarly field or focus of attention. Many of us feel that the concept of law has so many varied associations that it is unwise to expect it to have much analytic purchase: it is too abstract, too ambiguous, with too many contested associations to perform that function, unless a particular conception is specified with precision in a particular context. On the other hand, the concept of state or municipal law as one form of law (e.g. as elucidated by Hart) can perform that function. It is difficult to see why substituting the term 'state law' or 'municipal law' or something similar for 'law' will not satisfy Roberts' concern.[49] Furthermore, the history of jurisprudence and comparative law suggests that law is itself unlikely to be satisfactory as a generic concept, with species and sub-species that can be elucidated by reference to clear differentiae and criteria of identification. Failed typologies of 'legal families' illustrate that rather clearly – the families were not species of a single genus.[50] The familiar complexities surrounding the conceptualisation of law are also not simply resolved by resort to Wittgenstein's method of family resemblances, although that can be of some assistance.[51]

In Chapter 4 we considered Brian Tamanaha's attempt to construct a core conception of law that would serve as 'an organising concept', (i.e. as the basis for a theoretical framework within which a wide range of different forms of law can be accommodated and compared). Here, Tamanaha seems to have expected his umbrella concept to have to do less work than Roberts' analytic concepts – Tamanaha makes it clear that most analysis, comparison and explanation has to take place at lower levels of abstraction.

connected with centralised governance. My objection to this is not primarily to do with semantics or status; rather it is that it reinforces their marginalisation within our discipline and does not really allow for the possibility of scholars studying religious law from a juristic, as opposed to theological or historical or social scientific, perspective.

[47] I have made a similar critique of Tamanaha's labelling test for law, but I sense that Roberts has unfairly characterised Tamanaha's project.

[48] Roberts (2005) at p. 23.

[49] Hart's own method helps to explain why he thought law, apart from its various meanings in ordinary usage, is not readily susceptible to definition *per genus et differentiam*. (Hart 1953). It is too abstract to be satisfactorily elucidated as a species of some even more abstract genus. However, see my formulation which treats law as a species of the genus social practice, differentiated by its primary orientation (see Chapter 4.4 above) and MacCormick on 'explanatory definition' (MacCormick (2007) at pp. 281–9.

[50] Most commonly comparatists have referred to families of legal systems, but have used 'legal system' ambiguously. (See Chapter 3.4 above.)

[51] See p. 102 above.

A third use of an abstract conception of law is to do no more than roughly indicate a broad area of study. As we have seen terms like legal theory, legal philosophy, and jurisprudence tend to be used rather loosely. For special reasons, I have felt it important to stipulate a rough working distinction between legal theory and legal philosophy as its most abstract part.[52] The terms are nevertheless vague and rightly so. Few think it worthwhile to make them more precise; indeed, false precision would be a fault. As we saw, Herbert Hart said of legal philosophy that it has no very clear boundaries. This is generally accepted. For the purpose of my specific thesis about the focus of the discipline of law I have argued for a broadened view of the discipline and a correspondingly inclusive conception of law for this purpose. But what are or should be the subject matters of particular fields of study is historically contingent. In some contexts adopting a broad conception of a field rather than a narrow one can have important intellectual consequences, but in this context the consequences need not be nearly so dire as Roberts suggests.[53]

A second point about Roberts' concern is that by subsuming centralised systems of governance and negotiated orders under the same conceptual roof, the distinctive nature of the latter will be lost sight of. Echoing the classic distinction between chiefly and acephalous societies, he is keen to emphasise the differences between the two categories. Roberts has done important work on 'alternative dispute resolution'[54] and he has interesting things to say about the appropriateness of trying to design institutions of third-party adjudication (such as international criminal tribunals) in the absence of a strong centralised order.[55] But he seems to postulate centralised governance and negotiated orders as antiphonal ideal types in some kind of binary opposition rather than providing for other variations along a complex range of overlapping continua or some other more complex picture. So what Roberts presents is a narrow conception of law and a typology of two main types of normative order along a continuum of centralisation/decentralisation. This is unnecessarily

---

[52] See pp. 21–25 above.

[53] Roberts alleges that I have left myself 'free to hold forth about whatever aspect of the social world interests him from within the secure stockade of jurisprudence.' Roberts (2005) at p. 22. 'Beyond its normative character, "law" seems to have no specificity whatever.' *Ibid.* This is unfair in several respects. First, he quotes a passage in a paper on diffusion (Twining (2005) in which I say that I will not repeat what I have said about the conceptual issues elsewhere, but he does not give the cross-reference, which to some extent meets his point. (Twining 2003a.) Second, it is not the case that I am prepared to include 'any old normative order' in my conception(s) of law in that specific context (or some others). For example, I have made it clear that I do not usually include the rules of ping pong, spelling, grammar, or many social conventions in my conception(s) of legal rules. Nor do I treat social institutions such as hospitals, schools or businesses as specifically legal institutions. However, unlike Tamanaha, I believe that the internal governance of some such institutions can be usefully viewed as a form of legal order in some contexts. Often, in writing about legal education, I have in the past proceeded on the assumption that we are mainly concerned with domestic municipal law in that context (see, however, *LIC*, Chapter 15, especially pp. 298–301).

[54] Roberts (1979), Roberts and Palmer (2005).   [55] Roberts (2005) at p. 23.

reductionist. For example, some of the standard candidates for inclusion under a broad conception of non-state law do not fit easily into this binary divide: Pasagarda Law as described by Santos, the Common Law Movement in the United States as described by Koniak, Quaker law as described by Bradney and Cownie, Romani ('Gypsy') law as described by Weyrauch, and Hindu law as described by Menski are examples that just do not fit either ideal type at all comfortably.[56] Similarly, in setting up his ideal type of centralised authority, Roberts lumps together weak states, fragmented states, failed states, tyrannies, states bedevilled by civil war, and so on.[57] We need a much more complex framework of explication.

To sum up: Some of the concerns behind resistance to the idea of non-state law deserve to be taken seriously. What is at stake is not mainly to do with definitions or labelling or semantics. The central point is that relations between municipal law and other forms of normative ordering (however they are labelled) and other interactions (interlegality) deserve the sustained attention of jurists because they are a crucial part of understanding legal phenomena.

---

[56] Santos (2002), Koniak (1996), Bradney and Cownie (2000), Menski (2006) at Chapter 4. Some of these examples are discussed at Chapter 3, nn. 27–30

[57] See Glenn's comments above. Galligan comments: 'While [Roberts'] analysis deflates some of the more fanciful claims of legal pluralism, his tying of law to the state, a position that would have the concurrence of Hume, Bentham, and Hart, is insupportable. It rests on the notion that (a) law is tied to governing and (b) that governing is exclusively a state activity'. Galligan (2007) at p. 192.

Chapter 13

Human rights: Southern voices

Francis Deng, Abdullahi An-Na'im, Yash Ghai and Upendra Baxi*

13.1 Introduction

In Ahdaf Soueif's novel, *The Map of Love*, an Egyptian woman, Amal, is expecting an American visitor: 'Wary and weary in advance: an American woman – a journalist, she had said on the phone. But she said Amal's brother had told her to call and so Amal agreed to see her. And braced herself: the fundamentalists, the veil, the cold peace, polygamy, women's status in Islam, female genital mutilation – which would it be?'[1]

Amal is a cosmopolitan scholar, who moves easily between the worlds of Cairo, New York, and Europe. She is weary of the simplistic repetitious stereo-typing of Egypt, Arab culture, and Islam by Westerners. Western normative jurisprudence faces similar charges of a repetitious parochialism about its agenda and about the bearing of other traditions on normative questions.

Western juripudence has a long tradition of universalism in ethics. Natural law, classical utilitarianism, Kantianism, and modern theories of human rights have all been universalist in tendency. But nearly all such theories have been developed and debated with at most only tangential reference to, and in almost complete ignorance of, the religious and moral beliefs and traditions of the rest of humankind. When differing cultural values are discussed, even the agenda of issues has a stereotypically Western bias. How can one seriously claim to be a universalist if one is ethnocentrically unaware of the ideas and values of other belief systems and traditions?

As the discipline of law becomes more cosmopolitan, it needs to be backed by a truly cosmopolitan general jurisprudence.[2] My objective here is to make a

---

* This is an extended version of the 17th Annual McDonald Lecture, delivered at the Centre for Constitutional Studies, University of Alberta, 31 March 2005. It was first published in 11 *Review of Constitutional Studies* 203–79 (2006) and is reprinted here with minor revisions by kind permission of the journal. (See also www2.warwick ac.uk/fac/soc.law/elj/lgd/2007.) A reader, containing selected works by the four jurists and updated, is planned for 2009. I am grateful to Terry Anderson, Bill Conklin, Marie Dembour, Andrew Halpin, Janna Promislow, Carl Wellman, and participants in seminars at the University of Miami, the University of Sussex and the University of Ulster for helpful comments and suggestions. I also wish to thank the four subjects of this article for answering questions, and pointing out errors and omissions, while leaving me space to make my own interpretations, for which I am solely responsible.

[1] Soueif (1999) at p. 6.   [2] Above Chapter 1.

small contribution to this cause by exploring the work of four non-Western jurists who are from 'the South' and who have made substantial contributions to the theory and practice of human rights: Francis Deng (Sudan), Abdullahi An-Na'im (Sudan), Yash Ghai (Kenya), and Upendra Baxi (India). I shall finish with some remarks on why I have selected these four individuals, who else might have been included, the similarities and contrasts in their perspectives, in what sense they can be claimed to be 'voices' from or of the South, and their relationship to some familiar strands in Western liberal democratic theory.

Since my immediate objective is to make the views of these four jurists better known, I shall try to provide a clear and fair exposition of their ideas about human rights, based on a finite number of accessible texts. This is part of the larger enterprise of de-parochialising our own traditions of jurisprudence at a time when we need to take seriously the implications of the complex processes of globalisation for our understanding of law.

Let me begin with a brief overview of the four individuals, each of whom emphasises seemingly different aspects of 'voice'. Francis Deng, justifiably, claims to speak for the traditions and culture of his own people, the Ngok Dinka of Kordofan in the Sudan. He argues that traditional Dinka values are basically compatible, in most respects, with the values underlying the Universal Declaration of Human Rights[3] and related international conventions and declarations. Abdullahi An-Na'im argues that a 'modernist' interpretation of Islam involves ideas that are, for the most part, similarly reconcilable with international human rights ideas, but that acceptance of such ideas (their internalisation within Islamic belief systems) depends far more on conversations and debates *within* Islam than on cross-cultural dialogue, let alone external attempts at persuasion or imposition. Yash Ghai is sceptical of most claims to universality that are made for human rights; however, adopting a pragmatic materialist stance, he reports that he has found through practical experience of postcolonial constitution making that human rights discourse provides a workable framework for negotiating political and constitutional settlements among politicians and leaders claiming to represent different majority, minority, and ethnic interests in multi-ethnic societies. Such discourse also facilitates popular participation in constitutive processes. Upendra Baxi argues that as human rights discourse becomes commodified, professionalised by technocrats, and sometimes hijacked by powerful groups, it is in grave danger of losing touch with the experience of suffering and the needs of those who should be the main beneficiaries – the poor and the oppressed. They are the main authors of human rights. To take human rights seriously is to take suffering seriously.

All four have been activists as well as theorists, but in different ways. Francis Deng has had a very distinguished career in international diplomacy. Abdullahi

---

[3] GA Res. 217(III), UN GAOR, 3d Sess., Supp. No. 13, UN Doc. A/810 (1948) [Universal Declaration].

An-Na'im has been a human rights activist within the Sudan and several other countries, and a publicist for human rights internationally. Yash Ghai has played a major role in post-independence constitution making and reform, especially in the South Pacific and Kenya. Upendra Baxi has been an influential publicist and campaigner in India and on the international stage, as well as serving as vice-chancellor of two Indian universities. For the last twenty years, he has campaigned and litigated on behalf of the victims of the Bhopal disaster.

13.2 Francis Mading Deng[4]

(a) Introduction

God asked man, 'Which one shall I give you, black man; there is the cow and the thing called "What", which of the two would you like?'

The man said, 'I do not want "What."'

God said: 'But "What" is better than the cow!'

God said, 'If you like the cow, you had better taste its milk before you choose it finally.'

The man squeezed some milk into his hand, tasted it, and said, 'Let us have the milk and never see "What."'[5]

What you have said, you Mading, we are very pleased. Things we have told you, you will give them a purpose; you will write them down and that is a big thing. ...

If this machine of yours writes and records what a man really says, and really records well, then if what we have said is bad, it will search for our necks; if it is good, then we will say these words have saved our country. Now we have trusted you ... we trust in you fully. Whatever you think we have missed, whatever you think we should have said that we missed, let it be said that we are the people who said it.[6]

---

[4] A note on sources: Francis Deng is a prolific writer who has dealt with many topics. The main sources for this section are: (i) Francis M. Deng, *Tradition and Modernization: A Challenge for Law Among the Dinka of the Sudan*, 2nd edn. (1971) [*Tradition and Modernization*]; *The Dinka of the Sudan: Case Studies in Cultural Anthropology* (1972) [*The Dinka of the Sudan*]; *The Dinka and Their Songs* (1973); [*Songs*]; *Africans of Two Worlds: The Dinka in Afro-Arab Sudan* (1978) [*Africans of Two Worlds*]; *The Man Called Deng Majok: A Biography of Power, Polygyny and Change* (1986) [*Deng Majok*]; 'The Cow and the Thing Called "What": Dinka Cultural Perspectives on Wealth and Poverty' (1998) ['Cow'], which condenses a series of articles in the *Sudan Democratic Gazette* in 1998 [referred to by date, e.g. *SDG* 9/98]; 'The Cause of Justice Behind Civil Wars' in Ifi Amadiume and Abdullahi An-Na'im (eds.) *The Politics of Memory* (2000) c. 11 [*Politics of Memory*]; Abdullahi An-Na'im and Deng (eds.) *Human Rights in Africa: Cross-Cultural Perspectives* (1990) [An-Na'im and Deng, *Human Rights in Africa*]; Francis M. Deng, *Talking it Out: Stories in Negotiating Human Relations* (2006) and (ii) interviews, conversations, and correspondence with myself conducted over the years. A selection of other works by Deng, not specifically cited here, are listed in the Bibliography. On the Dinka, see also, Lienhardt (1958), (1961), and (1982); and Ryle *et al.* (1982).

[5] Dinka folk tale related to Deng by Loth Adija, quoted in *Africans of Two Worlds* at p. 71. See also 'Cow,' at p. 101. Francis Deng interprets 'What' in this creation myth to refer to curiosity and the search for scientific knowledge, and hence the tale becomes a rationalisation of Dinka conservatism and backwardness in relation to modern science and technology. *Africans of Two Worlds* at p. 71, n. 7.

[6] Chief Ayeny Aleu, interview with Francis Deng, reported in *Africans of Two Worlds* at pp. 34–5.

Francis Mading Deng was born in 1938 near Abyei in Kordofan in the west of the Sudan. His father, Deng Majok, was paramount chief of the Ngok Dinka, the only Nilotic inhabitants in the Northern Sudan. It is commonly said that 'Abyei is to the Sudan as the Sudan is to Africa,' a bridge between the African and Arab worlds. Deng Majok was an outstanding tribal leader, a national figure, especially prominent for his bridging role between the Arab north and the Nilotic south. He was also known as the creator of a huge family through marrying more wives than any other man in Dinka history. Francis, one of his senior sons, became both the leading interpreter of Dinka tradition and a committed proponent of human rights, maintaining that they are basically compatible. How could this be?

Francis was the eldest son of Deng Majok's fourth wife. Although he did not groom any of his sons to succeed him, Deng Majok believed in education. The education of Francis Deng is a story of a remarkable journey through different cultures. It began in Deng Majok's compound in Abyei and continued in a boarding school for sons of chiefs run on similar lines to a British preparatory school. Francis Deng then proceeded to Khor Taaqqat, a secondary boarding school in the North, where the great majority of the boys were Muslims. He read law at the University of Khartoum, where he was taught in English mainly by expatriate teachers, including myself. The course was largely based on English law, but included an introduction to Shari'a law. Some attempt was made to discuss the role of customary law in the national legal system of the Sudan, but there was not sufficient literature to carry this very far. With encouragement, Deng spent some of his vacations studying customary law by sitting in his father's court, reading the court records, interviewing chiefs and elders, and starting a collection of recordings of several hundred Dinka songs.[7] This was the start of his very extensive explorations of Dinka traditions, culture, and law over many years.

Francis Deng graduated with a good LLB in 1962 and obtained a scholarship to pursue postgraduate studies in London, where he stayed for a year, before proceeding to Yale Law School, from which he obtained a doctorate in 1967. Before the age of thirty, he had been exposed to Dinka, Christian, British colonial, Northern Sudanese, Muslim, and both English and American common law ideas. So it is hardly surprising that one of the central concerns of all his writing has been the problem of identity.

On leaving Yale, Francis Deng worked as an officer in the Human Rights Division of the United Nations Secretariat in New York from 1967 to 1972. During this period he met and married Dorothy Ludwig and became part of an American family. They have four sons, who have grown up mainly in Washington, DC, but who have kept in touch with their Dinka heritage.

In 1972 Deng joined the Sudanese diplomatic service. He served as Ambassador to the United States and Scandinavia, becoming Minister of

---

[7] *The Dinka of the Sudan* at p. 8.

State for Foreign Affairs between 1976 and 1980. From 1980 to 1983, he was Sudan's ambassador to Canada. Subsequently he has held a number of academic positions, mainly in the United States. He has continued to be involved in public affairs, most notably in efforts to end the civil war in the Sudan and, from 1992 to 2004 as Representative of the Secretary-General of the United Nations on Internally Displaced Persons, rising to the status of Undersecretary-General. In this capacity he has had enormous influence in bringing the plight of 25 million people in forty countries to public attention, and in persuading governments that this neglected problem is a matter both of sovereign responsibility and legitimate international humanitarian concern.[8] In 2007 he was appointed Special Adviser to the UN Secretary-General for Prevention of Genocide and Mass Atrocities.

Even when holding responsible full-time public positions, Francis Deng has been a prolific writer. His first book, *Tradition and Modernization:A Challenge for Law Among the Dinka of the Sudan*,[9] was based on his doctoral thesis at Yale. Of it, Harold Lasswell, his main supervisor, wrote: 'Dr Deng has brought to the task of examining his own culture an impressive objectivity of outlook that testifies to his success in acquiring the essential characteristic of a scientific frame of reference.'[10] This frame of reference, based on Lasswell and McDougal's 'law, science, and policy' approach, represented a significant departure for Deng:

> There was a time when I would have been reticent to speak of values because my earlier legal training made me suspicious of such terms as falling within the realm of metaphysics and therefore irrelevant to hard legal analysis. But then I was fortunate, I would say, to go to Yale Law School, where Myres McDougal and Harold Lasswell attached considerable importance to values. In their jurisprudence of law, science and policy, values were defined in concrete terms, embracing deference values such as power, rectitude, affection and respect, and welfare values like wealth, well-being, skills and enlightenment. Another major principle introduced by the Yale School of Jurisprudence was the concept of human dignity as an overriding goal of community and social processes. Again, human dignity was one of those concepts that I had been conditioned by my earlier legal training to dismiss as metaphysical. The Yale school gave it an empirical meaning by defining it in terms of the broadest shaping and sharing of values.[11]

For Francis Deng, these concepts resonated with Dinka values as he perceived them and at the same time provided a direct link with universal principles applicable to all societies.

---

[8] Roberta Cohen and Francis Deng, *Masses in Flight: The Global Crisis of Internal Displacement* (1998). Further examples of his work as an intellectual leader in international relations include Reinicke and Deng (2000); and Deng and Minear (eds.) (1992).

[9] *Tradition and Modernization*.

[10] Harold Lasswell, Foreword to *Tradition and Modernization* at p. xi.

[11] *Politics of Memory* at pp. 186–7.

Tradition and Modernization is unusual in another respect. It is one of the few books about law ever to be based quite substantially on songs. Rarer still, the author was qualified by birth to be a poet. This extraordinary feat arose out of necessity: because of the security situation, Deng was unable to return home to do more fieldwork, so he partly made up for this gap in his data by making an extensive collection of songs from fellow Dinkas in the United States and from his earlier recordings and his memory. In time he produced two volumes of translations of Dinka songs and folk tales. His early writings bring out the special role played by song in Dinka social relations in relation to courtship, bridewealth, cattle, disputes, war, religious ceremonies, and celebrations:[12]

> Among the Dinka, songs and dance have a functional role in everyday life. They do not deal with constructed situations; they concern known facts, known people, and defined objectives. But, above all they are skills of splendor in which a Dinka finds total gratification and elevation. The vigor and rhythm with which they stamp the ground, the grace with which they run in war ballets, the height to which they jump, the manner of pride and self-approval with which they bear themselves, and the way in which the high-pitched solo receives the loud unified response of the chorus combine to give the Dinka a euphoria that is hard to describe. As the singing stops, the drums beat even louder, the dance reaches its climax, and every individual, gorged with a feeling of self-fulfillment, begins to chant words of self-exaltation.

> > I am a gentleman adorned with beads
> > I dance to the drums and level my feet
> > The girls of the tribe gather before me
> > The wealth of the tribe comes to me.[13]

Francis Deng has produced over twenty books, including two novels. Many of them concern the Dinka or the problems of North–South conflict in the Sudan. Even when writing about broader issues such as human rights, displaced persons, and dispute resolution, he regularly draws on Dinka examples and reaffirms that at the core of his multi-layered identity remains a commitment to

---

[12] Deng writes:

> 'To give some examples of the general significance of songs, the social structure, particularly territorial grouping, is reinforced by age-set group-spirit dramatized in initiation, warfare, and other age-set activities, which without songs would be barren. The concept of immortality through posterity receives a great deal of its support and implementation through songs. Singers not only give genealogical accounts of their families, but also stress and dramatize those aspects which express their relevance to contemporary society. Young members of competitive families have been known to compose songs or have songs composed for them in reply to each other's allegations about incidents affecting the relative position of their families. In this process a young man may do a special investigation into the history of his family and of the tribe, to find additional evidence to sing about and bolster his family'.

Songs at 78. In this book Deng anthologises ox songs, cathartic songs, initiation songs, age-set insult songs, war songs, women's songs, hymns, fairy tale songs, children's game songs, and school songs.

[13] *The Dinka of the Sudan*, see n. 4 at p. 17.

central Dinka values. A central concern of his work is to reconcile tensions between tradition and modernity, between Dinka culture and universal standards, and between national unity and diversity in a conflicted Sudan.

(b) The historical context

Francis Deng's writings need to be viewed in the context of the history of the Sudan. At Independence in 1956, the Dinka were one of the largest peoples in Africa. In the 1956 census they were estimated to number nearly 2 million, divided into twenty-five independent groups living a semi-nomadic, semi-pastoral life in settlements dispersed over nearly a million square miles within the Sudan. During the Condominium period they were perceived by outsiders to be strongly religious, immensely proud, exclusive, and resistant to change.[14] For many years they fiercely resisted foreign rule, but under the British they also found that the policy of indirect rule was a convenient way of maintaining their heritage and distinct identity. Whether the motives of the British in maintaining the isolation of the Southern Sudan are attributed to a respect for Nilotic culture amounting almost to romance, or to a policy of divide and rule, or to a mixture of both, until Independence the Dinka enjoyed the security and exclusiveness resulting from the policy, while resenting being ruled by outsiders, whether British or Northerners.

The Sudan became independent in 1956. During the past half-century, except for a ten-year break, the Dinka have suffered terribly, experiencing repression, massacres, starvation (sometimes deliberately induced), decimation, enslavement, and displacement. The civil war in the Sudan began in 1955. From 1972 to 1983, there was a break following the Addis Ababa Agreement, which gave the Southern Sudan regional autonomy.[15] War resumed in 1983 after the military regime of Gafaar Nimeiry instituted a strategy of Islamisation. The latest peace agreement, in 2005, still holds precariously at the time of writing.[16] Over the years, Francis Deng has been involved in attempts to broker a peace as a statesman and diplomat, but above all as a writer.

Here I shall concentrate on Deng's treatment of universalism and relativism with respect to human rights by focusing on a few of his very extensive writings, especially his biography of his father, the volume *Human Rights in Africa*, edited jointly with Abdullahi An-Na'im,[17] and a series of articles published in

---

[14] Between 1898 and 1956, Sudan was in theory jointly governed by the United Kingdom and Egypt, but in fact, the British were the sole rulers. The human side of the story is recounted in Collins and Deng (eds.) (1984).

[15] On the background of the Addis Ababa Agreement on the Problem of the Southern Sudan, 1972, see Woodward (1990).

[16] A Peace Accord was signed in Nairobi on 9 January 2005. For details, see Sudan Peace Agreements, online: United States Institute of Peace: www.usip.org/library/pa/_sudan.html. Last visited – July 2007.

[17] *Supra* n. 4.

The Sudan Democratic Gazette[18] and the *Journal of International Affairs*[19] that set out his general position in summary form.

Despite this terrible history of death, suffering, and displacement, Francis Deng emphasises the resilience and vitality of Dinka culture which has formed the basis of their identity. He has documented this culture in rich detail through interviews, folk tales, legends, biographies, cases, and historic events. In his early work he had to rely quite heavily on his own experience, a sparse but generally excellent scholarly literature,[20] and his own recordings of Dinka songs. After he returned to the Sudan, he was able to update his knowledge and supplement these sources with extensive recordings of interviews with Dinka chiefs and other informants.

In his scholarly writings about the Dinka, Deng adopted an approach that now might be considered unfashionable in its use of 'the ethnographic present' and the rather rigid framework of analysis of Lasswell and McDougal.[21] However, Dinka history and culture are also powerfully evoked through Dinka folk tales, songs, oral history, and novels. He identifies the unity of Dinka culture in a changing and tragic situation through a few core concepts and values that form a distinctive Dinka identity.[22] His interpretation is in a sense 'idealised' in that he focuses on core values of a tradition that were never fully lived up to and, as he makes very clear, have been threatened not only by modernity but by nearly half a century of suffering.[23] What follows is a brief outline of his interpretation of these ideas and how they relate to international norms of human rights, democracy, and good governance.

---

[18] *SDG* (1998 and 1999).   [19] 'Cow,' n. 4 above.

[20] Several works on the ethnography of the Dinka and neighbouring Nilotic peoples became anthropological classics: E.E. Evans-Pritchard, *Witchcraft, Oracles and Magic Among the Azande* (1937); *The Nuer* (1940); and *Nuer Religion* (1956); P.P. Howell (1954); and Lienhardt (1961). See *Tradition and Modernization*, see n. 4 at p. xlii–iii.

[21] Deng drew heavily on Harold D. Lasswell and Myres S. McDougal, *Law, Science and Policy* (mimeographed materials, 1964), which in due course developed into Lasswell and McDougal (1992). Deng also cites a number of articles, the best known of which is Harold D. Lasswell and Myres S. McDougal, 'Legal Education and Public Policy' (1943). See further *Tradition and Modernization, ibid.* at p. xxviii n. 12.

[22] Godfrey Lienhardt emphasises the point that: 'cultural homogeneity is by no means accompanied by political unity. The million or so Dinka of the Southern Sudan and their neighbours the Nuer, are culturally very similar indeed; but politically they are divided into many mutually exclusive and often hostile tribes.' Lienhardt (1964) at p. 155.

[23] It is important to emphasise that most of Deng's research and writing on the Dinka took place in the 1970s, before some of the worst traumas in Dinka history and before academic anthropology took a self-critical, and sometimes post-modern, turn. In the present context, the significance of Deng's work in that period is that it provides a rich and detailed reconstruction and interpretation of Dinka culture as an 'ideal type,' which emphasises its distinctive aspects, is quite frank, and is not uncritical. It has the strengths and limitations of 'insider research'. See, for example, Adler and Adler (1987). The debate over Deng Majok's marriages (discussed below) illustrates, in extreme form, the divide between Dinka values and international human rights norms that Francis Deng has sought to transcend. His account is remarkably detached and open, yet he manages to maintain the posture of a loyal and respectful son.

(c) Dinka culture

The Dinka were said to be among the most religious of African peoples. They believe in a single God who has similar characteristics to the God of other monotheistic religions, including Christianity and Islam, but they have no concept of heaven or hell. 'The overriding goal of Dinka society is *koc e nohm*, a concept of procreational immortality which aims at perpetuating the identity of every individual male. Respect for the dignity of any person is central to this principle.'[24]

Both men and women are immortalised by procreation. It determines their social status, wealth, and place in history. Immortality maintains the identity of the dead and enables them to continue to participate in social processes in this world and to influence them.[25]

Two central concepts are *cieng* and *dheng* (or *dheeng*). The concept of *cieng* sets the standard of good social relations. It has no counterpart in English. As a verb it can mean to treat a person well, to live in harmony, to be generous, hospitable, and kind. A person's character or behaviour can be evaluated in terms of having good or bad *cieng*: 'Cieng places emphasis on such human values as dignity, integrity, honor, and respect for self and others, loyalty and piety, compassion and generosity, and unity and harmony. … Good *cieng* is opposed to coercion and violence, for solidarity, harmony, and mutual coop-eration are more fittingly achieved voluntarily and by persuasion.'[26]

Cieng sums up central values of human relations. Dinka society provides various avenues for developing individual and collective pride through attain-ing values that demand respect. A person attains the status of *dheng* by his or her conduct: 'Among the many positive meanings of *dheng* are nobility, beauty, handsomeness, elegance, charm, grace, gentleness, hospitality, generosity, good manners, discretion, and kindness.'[27] As with virtue, there are many paths to *dheng* – through ancestry, cattle, sexual prowess, graciousness, generosity, bravery, or wealth in the form of cattle.[28]

Dinka values are believed to be sanctioned by God and the ancestors. Harold Lasswell commented on the powerful processes of early socialisation that created an 'inner policeman' which can continue to operate after an individual has moved from his original setting and come into contact with other norms,

---

[24] *SDG* 9/98. See also 'Cow'.

[25] *Human Rights in Africa* at p. 264. For example: 'When a man dies before marrying, even as an infant, he leaves his kinsmen with a religious obligation to marry on his behalf and beget children to his name.' *Human Rights in Africa* at p. 265. On levirate, see *Tradition and Modernization* at pp. 137–9.

[26] *Human Rights in Africa* at p. 266.   [27] *Ibid.* at p. 267.

[28] *Ibid.* Deng illuminatingly explores the complexities and nuances of the concepts of *cieng* and *dheng* in their social context in *Tradition and Modernization* at pp. 24–30 and *The Dinka of the Sudan* at pp. 9–24. *Cieng* sets social standards for ideal human relations that promote harmony and unity; *dheng* categorises individuals according to how they have earned respect through their conduct. It is easy to see why Francis Deng finds that these concepts resonate with more abstract (and usually vaguer) Western concepts such as dignity and respect for persons.

values, and temptations.[29] In traditional society, living up to these values was largely left to individual conscience, social approval and disapproval, and persuasion rather than force. Dinka tradition makes no sharp distinction between law, custom, and morals. All are backed by religious and social pressures and especially by individual conscience:

> These moral and spiritual principles are also applied to guide and control the exercise of political and legal authority. Dinka law is not the dictate of the ruler with coercive sanctions. Rather it was an expression of the collective will of the community, inherited from the ancestors, generally respected and observed, sanctioned largely through persuasion, or if need be, spiritual sanctions.[30]
>
> Despite the martial culture of the Dinka as herders and warriors, killing, even in a fair fight, is believed to be spiritually contaminating and dangerous according to ritual practices. Killing by stealth or ambush is considered particularly depraved and requires even more elaborate procedures of redress and rites of atonement. Theft was hardly heard of in traditional society and, when it occurred, was met with degrading sanctions that were severely damaging to one's social standing. Virtually every wrong threatens the wrongdoer with misfortune and death.[31]

Dinka norms on killing, marriage, the family, harms, insult, and defamation (including defamation of the dead), social hierarchy, and economic relations are all directly related to the overriding importance of immortality through procreation and the values embodied in the concepts of *cieng* and *dheng*. These values integrate the individual and the community. They are illustrated in concrete form by the role of cattle in Dinka society. 'It is for cattle that we are liked, we the Dinka. The government likes us because we keep cattle. All over the world people look to us because of cattle. And when they say "Sudan," it is not just because of our color, it is also because of our wealth; and our wealth is cattle.'[32]

Cattle are wealth, but they signify much more than that. Cattle constitute bridewealth that ensures continuity through procreation; cattle are prepared for special sacrifices to God, the spirits, and ancestors. A great many songs are about oxen or the need for oxen – for marriage, for sacrifice, or just for *dheng*. Young men exalt themselves and their lineage through identification with their personality ox, a castrated bull of little practical value:

> When I rise I sing over my ox,
> gossipers disperse
> I am like my forefathers
> I rise to be seen by my ancient fathers

[29] Lasswell said that 'the basic norms of society are rather fully incorporated into the emerging personality system at an early age. ... The inner policeman continues to operate after the individual has moved from his original social setting and is exposed to novel norms and sanctions'. Foreword to *Tradition and Modernization* at xi.

[30] *SDG* 9/98.   [31] *Ibid.* at p. 10.

[32] Chief Ayeny Aleu, quoted in *Africans of Two Worlds*, at p. 71.

I rise to be seen walking with pride
As it was in the distant past
When our clan was born.[33]

(d) Leadership

The Dinka lacked any centralised institutions for making or enforcing law, and some anthropologists have maintained that they were an example of an 'acephalous' or chiefless society and that 'chiefs' were a colonial creation. However, this is misleading. The Dinka did have leaders whom anthropologists have variously referred to as 'master of the fishing spear' (Lienhardt) or 'The Leopard Skin Chief' (Evans-Pritchard and Paul Howell).[34] These titles emphasise the religious nature of traditional leadership which contrasted with British secular conceptions of the role of chiefs. According to Deng, the traditional leader was the embodiment of Dinka values, mediating between God, the ancestors, and the living: 'Viewed in local terms, these qualities are often associated with "the tongue" and "the belly." By the tongue is meant the ability to speak soothing and conciliatory words that bring harmony and mutual co-operation to human relations. The belly connotes showing hospitality to visitors, but also generosity to the needy.'[35]

During the condominium period, chieftainship among the Dinka became more secular and political. Persuasion remained a prime requirement of leadership, but over time authority came to rely more on secular punishments than on religious sanctions. Such punishments as prison and flogging offended Dinka conceptions of dignity and were resented, although over time they came to be accepted to some extent.[36] Pressures on traditional chiefs to meet their material obligations sometimes led to accusations of corruption or abuse.[37] The move from religious to secular leadership opened the way to criticism of chiefs and even to political opposition.

Francis Deng's father, Deng Majok, lived through all of these strains between tradition and modernity and was regarded by many as the embodiment of a great Dinka leader. He was widely admired for many qualities, including wisdom, generosity, strong leadership, and progressiveness, and for building good relations with neighbouring Arabs while safeguarding the security and independence of his own people.[38] However, he was often criticised for 'excessive marriage'. At first sight this provides a rather striking example of a conflict

---

[33] *SDG* 6/99. See also the Cow creation myth, n. 5 above.
[34] *Africans of Two Worlds* at p. 118.   [35] *Deng Majok* at p. 278.
[36] 'The alienation of the people from modern-day secular authority may be illustrated by the fact that the Dinka refer to the government, even that represented by the Chief, as '*ju*' [foreigner].' *Africans of Two Worlds* at p. 142.
[37] *Deng Majok* at p. 278, suggesting this is a cause of corruption in Africa generally.
[38] *Ibid.* at pp. 273–4. See also Deng, *Seed of Redemption* (1986) (novel) at pp. 165–6.

between Dinka tradition and modern 'universal' values. But the story is more complex than that.

In his biography of his father, Francis Deng deals frankly and in detail with Deng Majok's prodigious uxoriousness. Chapter Twelve is significantly entitled 'The Economics of Polygyny'.[39] By Dinka tradition there is no limit to the number of wives that a man can marry provided that he can afford them. In Deng Majok's case, estimates of the total number of wives he acquired during his life vary between 200 and 400. This appears to have been a record in Dinka history and it occasioned continuing controversy. On the one hand, he was clearly fulfilling the imperatives of procreation and immortality. According to his son, he generally treated his wives and offspring generously and fairly, but he maintained control and surface order within the family through the strict discipline of an authoritarian patriarch. He 'granted equal opportunities for procreation,'[40] but there was often 'turmoil beneath the calm'.[41] Within Ngok Dinka society the situation was problematic.

The size of his family was a matter of prestige rather than shame. But marriage was costly and the family was worried about the draining of their wealth; others hinted at corruption, though no formal accusations were ever made. Deng Majok's defenders maintained that he always acted in accordance with Dinka mores, if not European ones. Nearly all the arguments seem to have centred on issues of power, wealth, and procreation, rather than on sexual morality. His son reports:

> In defending his marriages, Deng Majok gave different reasons to different people. To some, especially his family, he might talk of marriage as an investment and a source of economic and social security. To others he might mention the need to broaden the circle of relatives and the relationships by affinity as a strategy of extending political influence. But the reason he stressed most often and which cut across all others was procreation. And, in a curious way, all those who discussed the matter with him now report his arguments with considerable sympathy and nearly always end up agreeing with his point of view, if only in retrospect.
>
> 'When his marriages began to be excessive', said Nyanbol Amor [his second wife], we went and said to him: 'Deng, what is this? Cattle should be allowed to remain for some time to increase in number. You now seize a cow a woman uses for making butter and you send it off to marriage; why is that? Aren't we enough? We do not want you to continue with your marriages!'
>
> He replied: 'Are you people fools? Have you no sense of judgment? I am marrying these wives for your own good. These women will have children. And it is these children who will remain with you.'[42]

It was not only his wives who tried to dissuade him. Sons, elders, fellow chiefs, and ordinary people raised the issue with him. The discussions appear to have been quite frank and open, but Deng Majok never relented. In respect of marriage, Deng Majok was treated as a spendthrift investor in wives, but in

---

[39] *Deng Majok* at pp. 190–209.   [40] *Ibid.* at p. 174.   [41] *Ibid.*   [42] *Ibid.* at p. 203.

other respects he was considered to be a great moderniser. He invested in the education of his sons, but was more reluctant to educate his daughters. He built good relations with his Arab neighbours, he emphasised ideas of due process, and he resorted to modern medicine. During the period of the Condominium, Deng Majok also exactly fitted the British policy of indirect rule:

> Deng Majok's leadership represented a peak in the evolution of tribal authority from the role of spiritual and moral functionary to an autocratic government institution backed by the coercive power of the state. The erosion of the egalitarianism and democracy of traditional society has been counterbalanced by the effectiveness of the new institutions in establishing and consolidating broad-based adherence to the rule of law in the broader framework of the nation-state. Deng Majok and other tribal chiefs in both the North and the South were indispensable in the maintaining of order and security among the masses of the rural population and in the context in which the central government machinery was otherwise remote and costly.[43]

When Deng writes about reconciling Dinka values with 'modernity',[44] he is concerned more with the relationship to human rights norms than to values of the colonial (or Condominium) state.

(e) Universal values

In his early writings Francis Deng did not make much reference to human rights, but he has always emphasised human dignity as a basic value. After completing his doctorate at Yale, he worked for five years as a human rights officer in the UN Secretariat and acquired considerable professional expertise in the area, especially in relation to women's rights. Since then he has been a firm, quite orthodox, upholder of the international human rights regime and of basic principles of democracy, both of which he considers to be universal. On human rights he emphasises the *United Nations Charter*[45] and the *Universal Declaration of Human Rights*,[46] especially such general phrases as 'the recognition of the inherent dignity and of the equal and inalienable rights of all members of the human family.'[47] On democracy he states:

> Among the principles of democracy that have gained universal validity are that governments rule in accordance with the will of the people and adhere to the rule of law, separation of powers, and independence of the judiciary, and respect for fundamental rights and civil liberties. These principles should be safeguarded by transparency, freedom of expression (and of the press), access to information and accountability to the public. Given the tendency of Africans to vote according to their ethnic or tribal identities, democracy will have to mean more than electoral votes. In the context of ethnic diversity, devolution of power through

---

[43] *Ibid.* at p. 140.   [44] *Tradition and Modernization* at pp. xxv–xlii.
[45] *Charter of the United Nations*, adopted 26 June 1945, entered into force 24 October 1945.
[46] See n. 3.   [47] *SDG* 6/98 at p. 9, citing the *Universal Declaration*, Preamble.

decentralisation down to the local level, combined with some methods of ensuring the representation of those who would otherwise be excluded by the weight of electoral votes, would be necessary. In any case, democracy, however defined or practiced, implies accommodation of differences and a special responsibility for the protection of minorities.[48]

At first sight, these familiar ideas of modern liberal democracy seem a long way from Dinka tradition with its emphasis on immortality – especially through the male line – polygyny, a non-monetary economy, divine chieftainship, and cattle. Nor does this fit with his father's autocratic style. How could a UN human rights officer working on international women's rights continue to respect and honour his father, a patriarch who had over 200 wives? Are Dinka concepts of *cieng* and *dheng* quite the same as the meaning of 'dignity' in the *UN Declaration on Human Rights*? How can one reconcile the immortality of ancestors with so earthbound and secular an ideology as modern human rights? Is Dinka tradition really democratic?

Francis Deng adopts an elaborate strategy to confront these issues. The following is just a brief summary.

First, Deng is not a cultural relativist.[49] Following Abdullahi An-Na'im, he emphasises that for institutions and particular norms to be accepted as legitimate and to be effective they must be debated, interpreted, and applied within the concepts and internal logic of local cultures. However, this does not preclude using universal standards as a basis for judging particular features of a culture or tradition. Relativism that rejects all external standards is unacceptable, but relativism in the sense of taking very seriously the beliefs and values of a given culture complements universalism. In respect of the details of institutional design and specific prescriptions, culture is an essential part of legitimating any social change.[50] In short, a cultural approach to human rights and democracy involves seeing tradition as supplementing abstract values and principles. *Cieng* and *dheng* are conceptions that concretise, localise, and enrich abstract notions of human dignity.

Second, human rights and the principles of democracy are universal, but only at a very abstract level. At that level, Dinka ideals that emphasise respect for persons, dignity, and harmony are fundamentally compatible; indeed, Deng goes so far as to say that the Dinka 'clearly had notions of human rights that formed an integral part of their value system'.[51] Furthermore, although the principles of democracy are universal, 'democracy should be home grown to be sustainable'.[52] Independence constitutions in Africa tended to fail, not because of their ideals, but because they were essentially imposed from above and in a form that was not the result of a genuine local constitutive process. The ideals,

---

[48] *SDG* 5/98 at p. 11.   [49] See especially *Human Rights in Africa*; *SDG* 8/9 at p. 4.
[50] Contrast with Ghai, who plays down the importance of 'culture' as compared with material interests.
[51] *SDG* 8/98 at p. 9.   [52] *SDG* 5/98 at p. 12.

he claims, were already part of African tradition: 'In traditional Africa, rulers governed with the consent of the people who participated broadly in their own self-administration; were free to express their will; and held their leaders to high standards of transparency and accountability. In that sense, indigenous societies were more democratic than most modern states in Africa.'[53]

Third, the Dinka are changing. They have become more open to learning from the outside world and some are less confident about the superiority of their own culture. There is even talk of giving up the Cow for the pursuit of 'What'. After over forty years of conflict and suffering they yearn for peace. How far these terrible years and the dislocation of so many have weakened the grip of Dinka culture and its 'internal policeman' is uncertain. But for many the core values embodied in *cieng* and *dheng* have sustained their identity. After conducting a series of interviews with chiefs and elders in 1999, Francis Deng concluded that the civil war had been both a destabilising and a radicalising factor, ironically increasing motivation for development, but in ways that are compatible with basic elements of their cultural integrity.[54] For example, in an integrated rural development project, the Dinka strongly resisted any suggestion that cattle could be used as draft animals, but they were prepared to sell them for cash, or use them in ways 'that are compatible with the dignity of the animals as they see it'.[55]

Fourth, Deng acknowledges that, judged by the standards of human rights norms, some aspects of Dinka culture are open to criticism. In 1990 he summarised the main points as follows:

> There are, however, severe constraints on the Dinka cultural system of values in terms of objective universal human rights standards. One set of negative effects derives from the inequities inherent in the logic of the lineage system and its stratification on the basis of descent, age, and sex. Another set of negative characteristics lies in the conservative nature of the system and its resistance to change or cross-cultural assimilation. And yet another shortcoming of the system lies in the fact that its human rights values weaken as one goes away from the structural center of Dinka community.[56]

---

[53] *Ibid.* Not everyone will agree with this generalised account of African political traditions, but there is a recognisable affinity with Deng's accounts of Dinka political tradition. His argument is that the institutions and processes might be different, but the values are closely compatible.

[54] 'Whether it is a manifestation of characteristics hitherto hidden by their isolationism, the result of the impact of the civil war, or simply adaptability to their present circumstances, the Dinka are demonstrating a degree of commitment to development that would surprise the observers of the 1950s.' *SDG* 10/98 at p. 13.

[55] *Ibid.* at p. 11.

[56] *Human Rights in Africa* at p. 273. See also the following summary: 'Although Dinka cultural values, in particular the emphasis on procreational continuity, idealised human relations, and the dignity of the individual in the communal context, engendered [sic] the elements of human rights principles, the system had built-in shortcomings, embodied in structural inequities, resistance to change, and a condescending view of the outside world.' *SDG* 9/98 at 11. See also *ibid.* at p. 9, explicitly linking Dinka values to human rights, but with similar reservations.

(f) Women in Dinka society

Perhaps the biggest test of Deng's argument about the compatibility of Dinka tradition with human rights is the subject of the status and treatment of women, as it is for many of the world's cultures, traditions, and religions. Deng's own accounts of Dinka cosmology and of his father's uxoriousness, although clearly an extreme case, suggest a large gulf between central aspects of Dinka tradition and the norms and standards embodied in such instruments as the Convention on the Elimination of All Forms of Discrimination Against Women (*CEDAW*).[57] Deng acknowledges this. He accepts that polygamy is inconsistent with equal respect and that Dinka women have a subordinate role in Dinka cosmology and tradition. He himself is committed to UN values on the status of women. He is monogamous, and the Dinka heroes in his two novels are monogamous – indeed, one resists pressure to take additional wives.[58] He can point out, in mitigation, that the central concept of *thek* applies to women, as well as to men and clan divinities. *Thek* includes, but is broader than, the English concepts of respect and deference. As Lienhardt points out: '*Thek* ... is a compound of behaviour which shows unagressiveness and deference to its object, and of behaviour which shows esteem for it.'[59]

Francis Deng is quite explicit about the position of women. After acknowledging the inequities of the social structure in the passage quoted above, he continues:

> The problem lies not only in the injustices of the system but also in the fact that those who are less favoured by it tend to react to the inequities, thereby creating paradoxes in the social system. For instance, although women are the least favored by the ancestral values, society depends on them not only as sources of income through the custom of marriage with cattle wealth but also as mothers who perform the educational role of inculcating ancestral values in their children at an early age. Yet women have no legitimate voice in the open channels of decisionmaking and can participate only through indirect influence on their sons and husbands. But because of the close association between mothers and children and the considerable influence wives have over their husbands, women are regarded as most influential in the affairs of men. Nevertheless, because of the inequities of polygyny, women are known for jealousies, divisiveness, and even disloyalty to clan ideals. Their influence, especially on the children, must therefore be curtailed.
>
> The Dinka reconcile these conflicting realities by recognizing the love and affection for the mother as functions of the heart, while those feelings for the father are functions of the mind. ...
>
> As a result of these contradictions, the position of women among the Dinka is a complex one in which deprivations and inequities are compensated by devices that ensure a degree of conformity and stability, despite ambivalences.[60]

[57] Adopted December 1979, entered into force September 1981, UN Doc. A/34/46, at 193 (1979)
[58] *Seed of Redemption*, see n. 38.   [59] Lienhardt (1961) at p. 126.
[60] *Human Rights in Africa* at pp. 273–4.

This is to state a problem rather than to resolve it. The status and treatment of women in Dinka tradition are closely bound up with Dinka cosmology, with its emphasis on procreation and veneration of male ancestors, a pastoral economy, its practices and attitudes to cattle, and many other matters. This raises a host of complex questions about how far Dinkas living in rural communities could retain their strong sense of cultural identity over time if they were to adjust to the standards of the outside world in respect of monogamy, the education of women, participation in decision making, non-discrimination, and other requirements of even minimalist versions of feminism. How far can the specifics of traditional Dinka values and beliefs justify a margin of appreciation that modifies abstract principles of women's equality? And what of the situation of Dinka women who live outside traditional society? Francis Deng does not attempt to address these issues in a sustained way. In the light of the tragic history of the Dinka over the last thirty years, they may not even be the most pressing questions.

(g) Conclusion

Francis Deng has been a prolific writer on a wide range of topics, and he has addressed a variety of audiences. For present purposes, his most relevant writings can be treated as falling into three groups: First, there is an extensive collection of books and essays that describe, evoke, and explain Dinka culture, with tradition and modernisation as a central theme. Most of these writings are scholarly works addressed to mainly Western audiences and published in the 1970s. A second, more varied, group deals with political and social relations between the North and South Sudan. In some instances, the explicit aim is to encourage a more sympathetic understanding of Southern culture and aspirations by Northern Muslims. In these, identity is a central theme. For over thirty years, Deng has supported a unified, but pluralistic Sudan in which a strong national identity is forged through an open recognition of cultural diversity.[61] Third, since about 1990 and partly influenced by Abdullahi An-Na'im, he has addressed issues concerning the compatibility of human rights with African traditions. In this context he has adopted an explicitly cross-cultural perspective. These writings are less extensive than the other groups and are addressed to rather varied audiences.[62]

---

[61] Francis Deng has sometimes been accused of being too conciliatory and too optimistic. He reports how at a dinner party Nelson Mandela was criticised for being too indulgent, but Francis defended him, arguing that everyone has a good side and a bad side, and in relations with others one should build on their good side. He is well known for the diplomatic way in which he has dealt with heads of government and other political leaders when confronting them about their responsibilities for displaced persons. And he has over the years sought rapprochement with the Northern Sudanese leaders. He claims that this represents the Dinka way. *Politics of Memory* at pp. 185–86.

[62] The main ones are *Human Rights in Africa* (academic, mainly addressed to the human rights community in the United States), 'Cow,' and *SDG* (articles addressed to fellow Southerners).

In the present context, the first group of writings is probably the most significant. Francis Deng's account of Dinka traditions may now seem somewhat idealised, even outdated, but he has provided a rich body of authentic material that is open to interpretation from other perspectives. Above all, he has given Dinka tradition and values a voice in the outside world. He has also illustrated in a vivid and specific way the more general theme of the complex relationship between long-established traditional values and modern conceptions of human rights.

13.3 Abdullahi Ahmed An-Na'im[63]

I am arguing for secularism, pluralism, constitutionalism and human rights from an Islamic perspective because I believe this approach to these principles and institutions is indispensable for protecting the freedom for each and every person to affirm, challenge or transform his or her cultural or religious identity.[64]

To seek secular answers is simply to abandon the field to fundamentalists, who will succeed in carrying the vast majority of the population with them by citing religious authority for their policies and theories. Intelligent and enlightened Muslims are therefore best advised to remain within the religious framework and endeavour to achieve the reforms that would make Islam a viable modern ideology.[65]

On 18 January 1985, Mahmoud Mohamed Taha was publicly executed in Khartoum on the grounds that he was an apostate and a heretic. Taha was the leader of a small radical modernising movement in the Sudan, known as

---

[63] This section is based mainly on the following works by Abdullahi Ahmed An-Na'im: *Toward an Islamic Reformation: Civil Liberties, Human Rights, and International Law* (1990) [*Islamic Reformation*]; *Human Rights in Cross-Cultural Perspectives: A Quest for Consensus* (1992) [*Quest for Consensus*]; 'Human Rights in the Arab World: A Regional Perspective' (2001) 23:3 *Human Rights Quarterly* 701; *Islamic Family Law in a Changing World: A Global Resource Book* (2002) [*Islamic Family Law*]; 'Promises We Should All Keep in Common Cause' in Susan Moller Okin *et al., Is Multiculturalism Bad for Women?* (1999) 59 ['Promises']; 'The Future of Shari'a Project' [unpublished manuscript, 2004a]; *The Future of Shari'a* (2005) at c. 1. [unpublished manuscript, cited with permission of the author] [*Future of Shari'a*] now completed as *Islam and the Secular State* (2008) [*Secular State*] Abdullahi Ahmed An-Na'im, ed., *Human Rights Under African Constitutions: Realizing the Promise for Ourselves* (2003); and An-Na'im and Deng, *Human Rights in Africa* (1990). See also: Tori Lindholm and Kari Vogt (eds.) *Islamic Law Reform and Human Rights: Challenges and Rejoinders* (1993) (Proceedings of a symposium held in Oslo 14–15 Feb. 1992, which focused on An-Na'im) (Lindholm and Vogt (1993)); Ann Elizabeth Mayer, 'Universal Versus Islamic Human Rights: A Clash of Cultures or a Clash with a Construct?' (1994) 15: 2 *Michigan J. of International Law* 307 [Mayer, 'Universal Versus Islamic Human Rights']; Ann Elizabeth Mayer, *Islam and Human Rights: Tradition and Politics* (3rd edn) (1990) [Mayer, *Islam and Human Rights*]; and Mahmoud Mohamed Taha, *The Second Message of Islam*, trans and intro by Abdullahi Ahmed An-Na'im (1987) [Taha]. Mashood A. Baderin, *International Human Rights and Islamic Law* (2003) contains a mildly critical account of An-Na'im's treatment of international law.

[64] An-Na'im, *Future of Shari'a* at c. 1, para. 15.

[65] An-Na'im, cited by John O. Voll, 'Foreword' to An-Na'im, *Islamic Reformation*.

the Republican Brothers (or Republicans), founded in the late 1940s during the struggle for independence. For the previous two years the Republicans had been peacefully protesting against human rights violations that resulted from President Ja'far Nimeiry's programme of Islamicisation that had begun in 1983. Their protest had included bringing several unsuccessful suits in the courts alleging that the introduction of a traditionalist version of Islamic law (Shari'a) was unconstitutional because it involved discrimination against women and non-Muslims.[66] Taha and some of his followers had been interned in 1983. They were released about eighteen months later, but Taha and some others were re-arrested in January 1985.

Apostasy was not then an offence under Sudanese law. Taha was originally charged and tried for offences under the Penal Code and the State Security Act. However, the appellate court, without any serious trial of the issue, or even a pretence of due process, convicted Taha of heresy and apostasy and sentenced him to death. The President swiftly confirmed the sentence, which was immediately carried out. This blatantly political and unlawful killing shocked many ordinary Sudanese, Northerners as well as Southerners, who were opposed to Islamisation. It was without precedent and quite contrary to Sudanese ways of handling political disagreements. Instead of representing a great victory for Islam, as Nimeiry proclaimed, Taha's execution strengthened the opposition to his regime, which was overthrown in a peaceful revolution in April 1985, only three months after Taha's death. Human rights activists proclaimed Taha to be a martyr and established Arab Human Rights Day to commemorate the anniversary of his death.[67]

Among Taha's followers was Dr Abdullahi An-Na'im, who at the time was an associate professor of law at the University of Khartoum. An-Na'im had joined the Republicans in the late 1960s when he was still a law student. After graduating from Khartoum in 1970, he went to Britain for postgraduate work, first in Cambridge and then in Edinburgh, where he obtained a doctorate in criminology in 1976. He returned to Sudan to teach and practice law and to resume his association with the Republicans. Mahmud Mohamed Taha had been banned from public activity since the early 1970s.[68] An-Na'im was one of his most loyal followers and soon became a leading spokesman for his ideas. In 1983, with Taha and others, he was interned without charge for about eighteen months. They were released in late 1984, but then Taha was arrested again, tried, and executed. Having unsuccessfully campaigned for Taha's reprieve. An-Na'im left the Sudan in 1985, resolved to promote and develop the ideas of his master. He has remained in exile ever since (except recently for occasional visits), first holding some short-term appointments, including as executive director of Africa Watch from 1993 to 1995. Since 1995, he has been a professor of law at Emory University in Atlanta. An-Na'im is now well known, not only as Taha's most prominent follower, but also as a prominent Islamic jurist in his own right.

---

[66] Mayer (1994) at p. 361.   [67] *Ibid.* at p. 387.   [68] Voll (1990) at p. 65.

By 2005, An-Na'im had published several books and nearly fifty articles. He has written about public law, family law, international law, and many other particular topics. Here I shall concentrate on his writings about human rights in relation to Islamic law. In order to understand these, it is first necessary to outline Taha's main ideas, as expounded in his most important book, which was first published in Arabic in 1967 and was translated into English in 1987 by An-Na'im as *The Second Message of Islam*.[69]

Mahmud Mohamed Taha was considered a revolutionary in many quarters of the Islamic world. He had been declared an apostate by Al-Azhar as early as 1973, and he was regularly attacked by Muslim Brothers and other 'fundamentalists'. His main concern was to adapt Islamic law to modern conditions and to interpret it in a way that would be compatible with human rights as expressed in basic international documents, such as the *Universal Declaration of Human Rights*. Taha's key idea was methodological – what he called 'the evolution of Islamic legislation'.[70] He advanced a method of interpretation that would allow the abrogation of some texts of both the *Qu'ran* and the *Traditions of the Prophet* (the Sunna) in favour of other texts in the same sources. The texts should be read in their historical context in order to distinguish between fundamental principles and transitional provisions, which were relative to time and place, and which were never meant to be binding for all time. This method opens the door to the idea of continuous reform of the Shari'a to suit changing conditions, even in respect of doctrines based directly on the holy *Qu'ran*, which many Muslims consider to be immutable.

The historical argument pointed out that Islamic law was only systematised during the periods of the Medina and Ummayed states some 150–250 years after the death of the Prophet (in the seventh century).[71] In this view, the early generations of Muslims, who are considered to have been among the most holy, were not the subject of the Shari'a in the form that it came to be accepted by most subsequent believers. Moreover, much of the early medieval Shari'a itself was legislation responsive to its immediate social, economic, and political context and could now be discarded as out-dated. Thus Taha (and his followers) treat Shari'a as a medieval construct and advance an Islamic alternative to Shari'a. Only by using this radical method of interpretation would it be possible to bring Islamic law into line with modern needs, conditions, and standards. Furthermore, significant aspects of the received Shari'a could be shown to be incompatible both with human rights and relevant passages in the *Qu'ran*. By far the most important clashes concern the Shari'a's differential treatment of 'the other' – slaves, women, and non-Muslims. Taha argued for a strong egalitarian principle of equal treatment of all human beings irrespective of race, gender, nationality, or status.[72]

---

[69] Taha (1987).   [70] *Islamic Reformation* at pp. 34–5.   [71] Ibid. at pp. 14–19.

[72] An-Na'im, *Islamic Reformation* Chapter 7, entitled 'Shari'a and Basic Human Rights', is an excellent statement of a general position that is fleshed out in more detail in many subsequent writings.

An-Na'im's intellectual development is marked by several stages, but he has remained faithful to the basic methodology and conclusions of his teacher. He first promulgated Taha's own ideas in both Arabic and English. His first major book, *Toward an Islamic Reformation* (1990), built explicitly on Taha's ideas, but developed them in more detail in respect of political structure, criminal justice, civil liberties, human rights, and international law. Written in a clear and concise style, it provides 'the intellectual foundations for a total reinter-pretation of the nature and meaning of Islamic public law'.[73] His method is to contrast the Medina version of the Shari'a with international human rights standards and a liberal human rights philosophy.

An-Na'im is a strong supporter of the international regime of human rights. His approach 'is based on the belief that, despite, their apparent peculiarities and diversity, human beings and societies share certain fundamental interests, concerns, qualities, traits and values that can be identified and articulated as the framework for a common 'culture' of universal human rights'.[74] Human rights are not universal merely because they are posited in international law. 'Rather, the rights are recognized by the documents because they *are* universal human rights'.[75] He sums up his basic theory as follows:

> The criteria I would adopt for identifying universal human rights is that they are rights to which human beings are entitled by virtue of being human. In other words, universal standards of human rights are, by definition, appreciated by a wide variety of cultural traditions because they pertain to the inherent dignity and well-being of every human being, regardless of race, gender, language, or religion. It follows that the practical test by which these rights should be identified is whether the right in question is claimed by the particular cultural tradition for its own members. Applying the principle of reciprocity among all human beings rather than just among the members of a particular group, I would argue that universal human rights are those which a cultural tradition would claim for its own members and must therefore concede to members of other traditions if it is to expect reciprocal treatment from those others.
>
> In content and substance, I submit that universal human rights are based on two primary forces that motivate all human behavior, the will to live and the will to be free.[76] Through the will to live, human beings have always striven to secure their food, shelter, health, and all other means for the preservation of life. … At one level, the will to be free overlaps with the will to live, in that it is the will to be free from physical constraints and to be secure in food, shelter, health, and other necessities of a good life. At another level, the will to be free exceeds the will to live

---

[73] Voll (1990) at p. ix.   [74] *Human Rights in Africa* at p. 21.

[75] An-Na'im, *Islamic Reformation* at pp. 165–6 (emphasis in original).

[76] A footnote at this point reads: 'Here I am adopting the analysis of *Ustadh* Mahmoud Mohamed Taha, *Second Message of Islam* … ' *Ibid*. It is significant that until recently, An-Na'im made hardly any reference to Western political theorists. See however, n. 77 below.

in that it is the driving force behind the pursuit of spiritual, moral, and artistic well-being and excellence.[77]

An-Na'im's method is to contrast the Medina version of the Shari'a (and the Mecca texts that were intended to be universal) with 'enlightened' international standards and his liberal theory of human rights. He is critical of the tendency for some to play down or be evasive about conflicts between the historical Shari'a and international human rights norms. For example, some governments in Muslim countries sign up to international human rights conventions, but do not abide by them; others enter vague reservations. Islamic declarations of human rights are silent on key issues relating to the position of women and non-Muslims, and religious freedom.[78] An-Na'im criticises the selective nature of many reforms of family law in Muslim countries.[79] He also criticises Dr Hassan el Turabi, the leader of the Islamic National Front in Sudan, in that he was vague and evasive on the status and role of women though claiming that Islam treats all believers equally.[80] Only a few Muslim commentators on human rights are more candid. For example, Sultanhussein Tabandeh indicates clear inconsistencies between the Shari'a and the Universal Declaration of Human Rights in arguing that Muslims are not bound by the latter.[81] Conversely, An-Na'im argues that Shari'a needs to be radically reformed because it is

---

[77] *Ibid.* at p. 164 (footnote omitted). An-Na'im's interpretation of human rights is recognisable as being within the mainstream of democratic or humanistic liberalism. He appeals to the principle of reciprocity (Kant's Golden Rule), he emphasises dignity and well-being as values (an echo of Lasswell via Francis Deng?), and he talks of achieving an 'overlapping consensus' (Rawls' term) between cultures. He is aware of affinities with Kant, Rawls, and Habermas, but claims that he reached his conclusions by a different route or at least that he was not consciously influenced by them. (Interview with author 16 August 2003). Rawls, in a solitary discussion of An-Na'im in a footnote, says of his discussion of constitutionalism, 'This is a perfect example of overlapping consensus'. Rawls (1999b) at pp. 590–1. As discussed below, An-Na'im has recently emphasised the role of the idea of 'ciric reason' in Islamic debates about public policy and reform.

[78] For forceful critiques of some Islamic declarations, see Mayer (1999); see also Bassam Tibi (1993) at pp. 80–9. Referring to a series of declarations of the late 1980s and early 1990s (by Al-Azhar, the London-based Islamic Council, and others), and mentioning specifically the treatment of women and religious minorities, Tibi states: 'The Islamization programs supported by these self-professed and alleged exponents of specifically Islamic human rights schemes repudiate rather than embrace the standards of international human rights law' (at pp. 87–8). For a detailed analysis of the 1990 *Cairo Declaration on Human Rights*, see Mayer (1994) at pp. 327–35.

[79] See especially *Islamic Family Law*.

[80] *Islamic Reformation* at pp. 39–41. In 2006 Hassan Al-Turabi issued a surprisingly liberal *fatwa*, arguing that beliefs that are 'merely cultural' should be purged, including prohibitions on women becoming imams, strict interpretations of the *hijab*, and requirements that non-Muslim spouses convert to Islam (Al-Turabi (2006) discussed in Jenkins (2007b), pp. 203–4). Whether this is a sign of some convergence among Muslim intellectuals is a matter of contention.

[81] Sultanhussein Tabandeh, *A Muslim Commentary on the Universal Declaration of Human Rights*, trans. by Charles Goulding (1970) at pp. 171–2. See also Mayer 'A Critique of An-Na'im's Assessment of Islamic Criminal Justice' in Lindholm and Vogt Chapter 3. 'An-Na'im is committed to the proposition that public law in Muslim countries should be based on Islam – unlike many other Muslims who believe that Islamic law should be relegated to the sphere of personal status and private law matters such as contracts, a belief that has dictated the role Islamic law has played in most actual legal systems in the twentieth century.' (Ibid., 36–7).

inconsistent with human rights standards, especially in respect of discrimination against women and non-Muslims,[82] freedom of religion, and slavery.[83]

His general conclusion is summarised as follows:

> Unless the basis of modern Islamic law is shifted away from those texts of the Qur'an and Sunna of the Medina stage, which constituted the foundation of the construction of Shari'a, there is no way of avoiding drastic and serious violation of universal standards of human rights. There is no way to abolish slavery as a legal institution and no way to eliminate all forms and shades of discrimination against women and non-Muslims as long as we remain bound by the framework of Shari'a. ... The traditional techniques of reform within the framework of Shari'a are inadequate for achieving the *necessary* degree of reform. To achieve that degree of reform, we must be able to set aside clear and definite texts of the Qur'an and Sunna of the Medina stage as having served their transitional purpose and implement those texts of the Meccan stage which were previously inappropriate for practical application but are now the only way to proceed. ... In view of the vital need for peaceful co-existence in today's global human society, Muslims should emphasize the eternal message of universal solidarity of the Qur'an and of the Mecca period rather than the exclusive Muslim solidarity of the transitional Medina message.[84]

For much of the twentieth century, debates and struggles about interpretation of Islamic theology and jurisprudence have tended to be framed either as debates between schools or as disagreements between fundamentalists and secularists. An-Na'im's aim is to establish an Islamic foundation for 'the

---

[82] An-Na'im is unequivocal about his own position on the treatment of women and non-Muslims. In a response to Susan Okin, he stated:

> I am not suggesting, of course, that either minority or majority should be allowed to practice gender discrimination, or violate some other human right, because they believe their culture mandates it. In particular, I emphasize that all women's rights advocates must continue to scrutinize and criticize gender discrimination anywhere in the world, and not only in Western societies. But this objective must be pursued in ways that foster the protection of all human rights, and with sensitivity and respect for the identity and dignity of all human beings everywhere.

'Promises,' at p. 61. On religious toleration, see *Islamic Reformation*, at pp. 175–7.

[83] An-Na'im's treatment of slavery is a good example of his approach. During the formative stages of Shari'a, a person's status was normally determined by their religion. At that time women were not regarded as full persons, and slavery was an established institution in many places. The medieval Shari'a reflected these practices: 'The most that Shari'a could do, and did in fact do, in that historical context was to modify and lighten the harsh consequences of slavery and discrimination on grounds of religion or gender. ... Shari'a as a practical legal system could not have disregarded the conception of human rights prevailing at the time it purported to apply in the seventh century, modern Islamic law cannot disregard the present conception of human rights if it is to be applied today.' *Islamic Reformation* at p. 170. Recently, An-Na'im has emphasised a continuing role for a re-interpreted Shari'a: 'Thus Shari'a does indeed have a most important future in Islamic societies and communities for its foundational role in the socialization of children, sanctification of social institutions and relationships, and the shaping and development of those fundamental values that can be translated into general legislation and public policy through democratic political process. But it does not have a future as a normative system to be enacted and enforced as such as public law and public policy.' *Future of Shari'a* at c. 1.

[84] An-Na'im, *Islamic Reformation* at pp. 179–80 (emphasis in original).

benefits of secularism', among which he includes religious toleration, equality between Muslims and non-Muslims and men and women, constitutional democracy, and equal status for Muslim and non-Muslim states.[85] Some Islamic reformers believe that such 'benefits' can only be achieved through a secular democratic system, which takes priority over religious doctrine.[86] An-Na'im, on the contrary, believes that liberal democratic ideas will never be accepted by Muslims unless they are persuaded that they are backed by Islamic premises. He therefore sets out to show that Islam, as interpreted by Mohamed Taha, does support the same values.[87]

For An-Na'im, the different schools of Islam are themselves a product of the Middle Ages (although they are probably here to stay) and few devout Muslims will be persuaded by secular arguments. He writes: 'To seek secular answers is simply to abandon the field to the fundamentalists, who will succeed in carrying the vast majority of the population with them by citing religious authority for their policies and theories. Intelligent and enlightened Muslims are therefore best advised to remain within the religious framework and endeavour to achieve the reforms that would make Islam a viable modern ideology.'[88]

This passage provides a link to the next stage of An-Na'im's intellectual development. In considering the debate about universalism and cultural relativism in respect of human rights, he began to focus on the problems of persuasion and effectiveness in the context of cultural diversity and pluralism of beliefs. While maintaining a universalist stance in respect of basic values, he concluded that cultural legitimacy of human rights ideals could only be achieved by internal dialogue within a culture rather than by external pressure. Dialogue between cultures is also important in order to achieve an overlapping consensus on human rights and the necessary conditions for peaceful co-existence, but acceptance of the legitimacy of human rights standards requires internal cultural support.

In the next stage of his work, An-Na'im placed more emphasis on what he called 'cultural legitimization'.[89] He argues that the legitimacy of human rights standards will only be plausible to a given constituency if members believe that they are sanctioned by their own cultural traditions. Since people understand things through their own cultural lenses, such legitimacy can mainly be attained by dialogue and struggle *internal* to that culture. As he put it recently:

> While this approach raises the possibility of local culture being invoked as the basis for violating or rejecting the existence of a human right, I am unable to see an alterative to a basic methodology of cultural legitimacy which can be

---

[85] *Ibid.* at p. 8; *cf.* 'Promises' at p. 107: 'I am proposing an understanding of Islam which will achieve the benefits of secularism with an Islamic rationale.'

[86] For example, 'Promises' at p. 73.

[87] 'Taha's methodology, however, would not abolish *hudud* as a matter of Islamic law.' *Ibid.* at p. 108.

[88] An-Na'im, quoted by Voll (1990) at p. xii.

[89] See especially An-Na'im & Deng, *Human Rights in Africa*; An-Na'im, 'Promises'.

constantly improved through practice and over time. For example, culture may be used to justify discrimination against women or the use of corporal punishment against children as being in their own 'best interest'. Rejecting the cultural argument presented in support of such views is unlikely to work in practice. Indeed, women themselves are likely to support their own repression if they believe it to be 'the will of God' or the immutable tradition of their communities. In contrast, an approach that acknowledges the underlying value of respecting the will of God or local tradition, and then continues to question what that means under present circumstances is more likely to be persuasive.[90]

Outsiders purporting to advance an interpretation of a culture (as happened in the Salman Rushdie affair) will nearly always be viewed with suspicion.[91] An-Na'im is critical both of universalist positions based solely on Western or liberal perspectives and of militant cultural relativist positions. He himself explicitly defends a weak form of cultural relativism partly for tactical reasons, but also because belief in human rights can only be internalised when reconciled with other aspects of one's system of beliefs.[92] Cross-cultural dialogue has a role not only in identifying shared values but also in a building a richer new consensus, provided that the dialogue is genuinely reciprocal.[93] Both internal and external dialogue can be constructive and dynamic; they do not merely identify existing similarities and differences, but they can also generate new ideas and enriched understandings:

> This bonding through similarities does not mean, in my view, that international peace and cooperation are not possible without total cultural unity. It does mean that they are more easily achieved if there is a certain minimum cultural consensus on goals and methods. As applied to cooperation in the protection and promotion of human rights, this view means that developing cross-cultural consensus in support of treaties and compacts is desirable. Cultural diversity,

---

[90] *Future of Shari'a* at p. 18. The passage continues:

> 'As a Muslim, if I am presented with a choice between Islam and human rights, I will always choose Islam. But if presented with an argument that there is in fact consistency between my religious beliefs and human rights, I will gladly accept human rights as an expression of religious values and not as an alternative to them. As a Muslim advocate of human rights, I must therefore continue to seek ways of explaining and supporting the claim that these rights are consistent with Islam, indeed desirable from an Islamic perspective, though they may be inconsistent with certain human interpretations of Shari'a'.

Ibid. at p. 18.

[91] Nearly all Western discussions ignored scholarly *internal* Islamic debate on the Rushdie affair. See, e.g. M.M. Ahsan and A.R. Kidwai (eds.) (1993).

[92] Discussing a comment by Mohammed Arkoun, 'The Concept of Islamic Reformation' in Lindholm and Vogt (1993), An-Na'im replies: '[T]here is an important tactical difference between our approaches. Whereas Arkoun wishes to problematize the text of the Qu'ran itself immediately, I seek to explore the possibilities of transforming the understanding of that text.' His constant theme is the practicalities of achieving consensus.' (An-Na-im in Lindholm and Vogt at p. 98).

[93] An-Na'im's conception of reciprocal dialogue seems quite analogous to Habermas' 'ideal speech situation', but he disclaimed first-hand knowledge of Habermas's work at the time he developed these ideas (interview 16 August 2003). However, in *Islam and the Secular State* he briefly discusses the relationship of his ideas to those of Rawls and Habermas at pp. 97–101.

however, is unavoidable as the product of significant past and present economic, social and environmental differences. It is also desirable as the expression of the right to self-determination and as the manifestation of distinctive self-identity.[94]

An-Na'im recognises that 'culture' is neither monolithic nor static and typically provides space for internal dialogue, as is well illustrated by the rich tradition of debate within Islamic jurisprudence. He recognises that the possibilities of genuine dialogue can be curtailed or suppressed if a powerful group claims to have a monopoly of authoritative or correct interpretation.[95] An-Na'im illustrates his conception of internal dialogue by reference to the controversial topic of Islamic punishments.[96] Many Islamic countries, including Saudi Arabia and Iran, are signatories to the International Covenant on Civil and Political Rights (ICCPR).[97] Article 7 of the ICCPR prohibits 'torture or cruel, inhuman, or degrading treatment or punishment'. Under Islamic law, serious criminal offences are classified as *hudud* and carry with them mandatory punishments that include amputation of the right hand for theft and whipping, stoning to death, and exact retribution (eye for an eye) for specific offences. These offences are defined and punished by the express terms of the *Qu'ran* and/or Sunna. Taking the example of theft, the question arises: can amputation of the right hand be treated as cruel, inhuman, or degrading *as a matter of Islamic law*?

An-Na'im gives a qualified answer to this question. First, he distinguishes sharply between the actual practices of particular regimes and the theoretical, or theological, interpretation of the principles governing punishment. Thus he argues that enforcement of *hudud* in Saudi Arabia, Sudan, by the Taliban in Afghanistan, or recently in Northern Nigeria is illegitimate from an Islamic point of view.[98] Second, he points to some of the interpretive resources available to a sincere liberal Muslim who privately is repelled or uneasy about these provisions: 'Islamic law requires the state to fulfil its obligation to secure social and economic justice to ensure decent standards of living for all its citizens *before* it can enforce these punishments. The law also provides for very narrow definitions of these

---

[94] *Human Rights* at p. 27. The passage continues: 'Nevertheless, I believe that a sufficient degree of cultural consensus regarding the goals and methods of cooperation in the protection and promotion of human rights can be achieved through internal cultural discourse and cross-cultural dialogue. Internal discourse relates to the struggle to establish enlightened perceptions and interpretations of cultural values and norms. Cross-cultural dialogue should be aimed at broadening and deepening international (or rather intercultural) consensus.'

[95] 'The claim may of course be made that a certain policy or law is Shari'a, but that is always false because it is nothing more than an attempt to invoke the sanctity of Islam for the political will of the ruling elite.' *Future of Shari'a*.

[96] See especially *Islamic Reformation* at pp. 111–15, 123–4; *Quest for Consensus* at pp. 32–7; and 'Promises' at pp. 108–13. See also Baderin (2003) at pp. 78–85.

[97] *International Covenant on Civil and Political Rights*, 19 December 1966, 999 UNTS 171 arts. 9–14 (entered into force 23 March 1976).

[98] Personal communication to the author, 24 August 2005. In his view, *hudud* should not be enforced by the state at all, unless it were adopted as part of the criminal code through the political process, without reference to religious beliefs and subject to constitutional safeguards. Even then An-Na'im would take a very narrow view of its applicability. *Future of Shari'a* at c. 1.

offenses, makes an extensive range of defences against the charge available to the accused person, and requires strict standards of proof. Moreover, Islamic law demands total fairness and equality in law enforcement.'[99]

An-Na'im personally believes that these prerequisites are extremely difficult to satisfy in practice 'and are certainly unlikely to materialise in any Muslim country in the foreseeable future'.[100] Nevertheless, he concludes, '[n]either internal Islamic reinterpretation nor cross-cultural dialogue is likely to lead to the total abolition of this punishment as a matter of Islamic law'.[101] Given the political will, much can be done to restrict the scope of *hudud* and its implementation. A strong case can be made for not applying religious sanctions to non-Muslims, and in some predominantly Muslim countries Shari'a has been displaced by secular law. But outright abolition of *hudud* punishments is not likely. The basic idea is embodied in texts that express the will of God, backed by internally coherent theological rationales.[102] In this kind of case, 'the internal struggle cannot and should not be settled by outsiders';[103] what counts as cruel, inhuman, or degrading in a given society must be settled by the standards of that society.

In the process, as in his treatment of *hudud*, An-Na'im appears to concede that there are points at which human rights and Islamic principles may conflict and that here Islamic principle 'trumps' secular values. However, he emphasises that the range and extent of application would be severely constricted. Again, his concern seems to be the practicability of reaching consensus through persuasion: 'I agree with Ann Mayer that many Muslims today would probably prefer to continue within the Western-style criminal justice systems introduced in these countries during the colonial period. However, as increasingly stronger Islamist movements are demanding the enforcement of *hudud*, Muslims in general may find it difficult to maintain the status quo without appearing to be anti-Islamic. In this light, I believe that there is a growing need for thinking about Islamic criminal justice.'[104]

This is the considered view of a thoughtful scholar who is regarded as an extreme liberal by many Muslims.[105] It sets out with discomforting clarity his view of the possibilities and limitations of building a worldwide consensus by

---

[99] *Human Rights* at p. 34.   [100] *Ibid.*   [101] *Ibid.* at p. 36.

[102] For example, a *hudud* punishment may be considered lenient because it is not carried over to the next life. *Ibid.* at p. 35.

[103] *Ibid.*

[104] 'Promises' at p. 109. An-Na'im distinguishes (*ibid.* at p. 107) between his own personal beliefs and arguments that are likely to persuade fellow Muslims: 'If the reform of Islamic law suggested in [*Islamic Reformation*] is not achieved through one methodology or another, then my personal choice as a Muslim would be to live in a secular state rather than one ruled in accordance with Shari'a. But I seriously doubt if this would be the choice of the majority of Muslims today.' For a reflective and generally sympathetic critique of An-Na'im's approach to criminal justice, see Mayer (1993).

[105] Despite his vulnerability to marginalisation or dismissal as the follower of a heretic, An-Na'im seems to attract large audiences and his writings have been widely circulated in (parts of) the Middle East. He is, of course, not alone as a liberal reformer, but he is unusual, first as a jurist writing in English and, second, as a reformer who insists on basing his arguments on Islamic ideas.

dialogue. An-Na'im is not a strong cultural relativist. He believes that most of the values embodied in the current human rights regime can be reconciled with interpretations of Islam that would be widely, if not universally acceptable; too much attention, in his view, is paid to headline-grabbing examples (e.g female circumcision) many of which are contested within Islam.

(a) A third stage[106]

An-Na'im has always been an activist as well as a scholar. He was involved in Taha's Islamic Reform Movement from the late 1960s and, a quarter-century later, became executive director of Human Rights Watch (Africa) in Washington, DC. He has always stressed the importance of implementation and enforcement of human rights. He has been active in many committees and non-governmental organisations (NGOs) concerned with human rights in Africa and the Middle East. He has been involved in projects to promote human rights values at grass roots level through linking to specific local concerns and promoting cross-cultural dialogue about relevant issues such as problems of women's access to land or reform of family law. He has been especially interested in ways of lessening 'human rights dependency', professionalising local non-governmental organisations, and encouraging their withdrawal from dependence on foreign funding and dissociation from being perceived as agents of some 'Western agenda'. All of such 'advocacy for social change' is based on his two central ideas: a liberal modernist interpretation of Islam, and the need to strengthen the cultural legitimacy and effectiveness of international human rights standards.

An-Na'im's latest project on 'The Future of Shari'a' has resulted in a book entitled *Islam and the Secular State: Negotiating the Future of Shari'a* (2008).[107] The objective 'is to ensure the institutional separation of Islam and the state, despite the organic and unavoidable connection between Islam and politics'. It

---

[106] During the 1990s, An-Na'im developed his cross-cultural approach to legitimation of human rights (partly in association with Francis Deng). Subsequently, his main activities have been concerned with detailed, often practical applications of his general approach, especially modernisation of Shari'a. He is especially concerned with human rights advocacy. He sees the relationship between state and religion as a crucial issue. At the time of writing his latest initiative is 'The Future of Shari'a Project', which is 'particularly concerned with the constitutional and legal dimensions of the post-colonial experiences of Islamic societies, especially issues of the relationship among Islam, State and Society. ... The fundamental concern of this project is how to *ensure the institutional separation of Shari'a and the state, despite the organic and unavoidable connection between Islam and politics.*' 'The Future of Shari'a Project', (emphasis in the original). See now An-Na'im (2008) discussed below.

[107] *Islam and the Secular State* was published while the present work was in the press. The Preface begins: 'This book is the culmination of my life's work, the final statement I wish to make on issues I have been struggling with since I was a student at the University of Khartoum, Sudan, in the late 1960s. I speak as a Muslim in this book because I am accountable for these ideas as part of my own religion and not simply as a hypothetical academic argument. But the focus of my proposal is the public role of Shari'a, not matters of religious doctrine and ritual practice in the private, personal domain' (Preface at p. vii).

challenges 'the dangerous illusion of an Islamic state that can enforce Shari'a principles through the coercive power of the state':

> The central argument of the book is that 'coercive enactment' of Shari'a by the state betrays the Qur'an's insistence on voluntary acceptance of Islam. Just as the state should be secure from the misuse of religious authority, Shari'a should be freed from the control of the state. State policies or legislation must be based on civic reasons accessible to citizens of all religions.
>
> Showing that throughout the history of Islam, Islam and the state have normally been separate, An-Na'im maintains that ideas of human rights and citizenship are more consistent with Islamic principles than with claims of a supposedly Islamic state to enforce Shari'a. In fact, he suggests, the very idea of an 'Islamic state' is based on European ideas of state and law, and not on the Shari'a or Islamic tradition.[108]

It is not possible to do justice here to this rich and powerful work, which develops a number of themes: that human agency has been central to the development of Shari'a and is necessary for its continuing interpretation and for motivation for social and cultural change; that whatever the state or other authority tries to enforce in the name of Shari'a is necessarily secular; and that the separation of Islam and the state does not involve the relegation of Islam to the private domain – it still has a role in the formation of public policy and legislation, but this role needs to be performed through civic reason rather than coercion.[109] Chapter 3 contains a succinct restatement of his views on constitutionalism, human rights, and citizenship.[110]

A significant development in An-Na'im's thinking concerns secularism. If, as is widely assumed, 'secularism' implies hostility to religion or its decline or exclusion of all considerations drawn from belief in God, this is naturally opposed to an Islamic point of view. But, more narrowly interpreted as a principle for mediating between different religious beliefs through separation of religion and state, it is necessary for ensuring a stable basis for co-existence and co-operation in conditions of pluralism of beliefs (now almost universal) and for facilitating the unity of diverse communities in one political

---

[108] An-Na'im (2008) cover abstract.

[109] 'By civic reason, I mean that the rationale and the purpose of public policy or legislation must be based on the sort of reasoning that most citizens can accept or reject. Citizens must be able to make counterproposals through public debate without being open to charges about their religious piety. Civic reason and reasoning, and not personal beliefs and motivations, are necessary whether Muslims constitute the majority or the minority of the population of the state.' (2008 at pp. 7–8.) An-Na'im substitutes 'civic reason' for 'public reason' in order to differentiate the idea from the meanings given to it by Rawls and Habermas.

[110] The main, but not exclusive, focus of An-Na'im (2008) is on societies in which Muslims are a majority and the role of the state is in issue. There is now an extensive literature on the interaction between state law and the laws and customs of religious minorities in Europe, e.g. Aluffi *et al.* (2004), Goody (2004), Ramadan (2004), Pearl and Menski (1998), Shah and Menski (eds.) (2006). There is also a growing number of empirical studies on how ethnic minorities in Europe adjust to and navigate situations of pluralism, e.g. Ballard (1994), Bano (2007), Yilmaz (2005).

community. In this narrow sense 'secularism' is an important part of
An-Na'im's political theory:

> The conception of the secular state I am proposing offers an alternative vision to
> perceptions of secularism and the secular state that many Muslims find objec-
> tionable. Instead of sharp dichotomies between religion and secularism that
> relegate Islam to the purely personal and private domain, I call for balancing
> the two by separating Islam from the state and regulating the role of religion in
> politics. This view combines continuity of histories of the secular realm in Islamic
> societies with reform and adaptation of these traditions to offer future possibil-
> ities for these societies. In particular I argue that there is nothing 'un-Islamic'
> about the concept of a secular state as negotiating the organic and legitimate role
> of Islam in public life. The Qu'ran addresses Muslims as individuals and com-
> munity, without even mentioning the idea of a state, let alone prescribing a
> particular form for it. It is also clear that the Qu'ran does not prescribe a
> particular form of government.[111]

(b) Conclusion

An Na'im's views are, not surprisingly, controversial in the Muslim world. In
internal debates within Islam he is in danger of being dismissed as an
extremist – as the disciple of Taha who was condemned as an apostate, and
as an open subscriber to 'Western values'. Clearly his overt challenges to a
number of cherished beliefs may be felt to be shocking. However, his views are
not quite as extreme as may appear at first sight. His account of history is close
to that of many respected scholars.[112] All Muslim countries have accepted the
form of the nation state, most with 'modern' constitutions. Most of these states
are signatories to the bulk of human rights conventions, with surprisingly few
reservations. Many of the reforms that An-Na'im advocates have been adopted
in several, sometimes most, Muslim countries, but in a more piecemeal fashion
than he suggests. His main contribution is to provide a coherent religious
justification for reforms that have been, or might be, made in the name of
'modernisation' or 'secularisation'.

An-Na'im is controversial, but there is a danger that he should be perceived
as the darling of Western liberals, a liberal Muslim who is importing 'enlightened' ideas into Islam. But his message to non-Muslims is not so comfortable.
First, participants in a debate need to be prepared to learn as well as to teach.
There is much in the Islamic tradition from which Westerners can learn – for
instance in relation to commercial morality.[113] Secondly, there is the problem
of ignorance. Before rushing to judgement, non-Muslims need to try to understand the internal logic of views that may seem strange or abhorrent to them;

---

[111] An-Na'im (2008) at p. 267.
[112] See, for example, Kamrava (2006), Ramadan (2004), and the apparent softening of his
position by Hassan al Turabi above n. 80.
[113] E.g. Khurshid Ahmed (2003).

they need to be aware of the ways in which such views are contested and debated within the culture of Islam; they should not exaggerate the gap between Islamic beliefs and the values embodied in international human rights norms at this stage in their history; and, above all, before labelling some practices as 'barbaric', they need to consider how some of their own practices appear to members of other cultures. They also need to be aware of the extent of the leeway for interpretation within traditions such as Islam, as is vividly illustrated by recent scholarship on law reform in Malaysia and other predominantly Muslim countries.[114]

13.4 A realist and materialist interpretation: Yash Ghai[115]

Yash Pal Ghai was born in Kenya in 1938. He is still a Kenyan citizen. He went to school in Nairobi and then studied law at Oxford and Harvard and was called to the English Bar. He started teaching law as a lecturer in Dar-es-Salaam in 1963, eventually becoming professor and dean, before leaving in 1971. Since then he has held academic posts at Yale, Warwick, and Hong Kong. In addition to numerous visiting appointments, he was research director of the International Legal Center in New York in 1972–1973 and a research fellow at Uppsala University from 1973 to 1978. He has written or edited nearly twenty books, mainly about public law and constitutionalism in Commonwealth countries.

---

[114] For example, Donald L. Horowitz (1994). See also Norman Anderson's earlier classic work, *Law Reform in the Muslim World* (1976). On Islamic banking, see Siddiqi, 11 (1997); Edge (ed.) (1996); El-Gamal (2006) and, since 1991, the journal *Review of Islamic Economics*.

[115] Yash Ghai's recent writings on human rights are only one part of his very extensive list of publications. (i) The biographical section draws on publicly available sources, personal knowledge, and Ghai's 'Legal Radicalism, Professionalism and Social Action: Reflections on Teaching Law in Dar-es-Salaam' ['Legal Radicalism'] in Issa G. Shivji (ed.) (1986) 26 [Shivji, *Limits of Legal Radicalism*]. (ii) The section on negotiating claims in multi-ethnic societies draws heavily on two of his publications: 'Universalism and Relativism: Human Rights as a Framework for Negotiating Interethnic Claims' (2000b) ['Universalism']; and Yash Ghai (ed.) *Autonomy and Ethnicity: Negotiating Competing Claims in Multi-Ethnic States* (2000a). (iii) The section on the Asian Values debate is based mainly on 'Human Rights and Asian Values' (1998a) ['Human Rights']; 'The Politics of Human Rights in Asia' in Wilson (ed.) (1995) at p. 203 ['Politics of Human Rights']; 'Asian Perspectives on Human Rights' (1993) ['Asian Perspectives']; 'Rights, Duties and Responsibilities' in J. Caughelin, P. Lim and B. Mayer-Konig (eds.) *Asian Values: Encounter with Diversity* (1998b) at p. 20 ['Rights, Duties']; *Asian Human Rights Charter: A People's Charter* (1998c); 'Rights, Social Justice and Globalization in East Asia' ['Social Justice'] in Joanne R. Bauer and Daniel A. Bell (eds.) (1999) at p. 241 (Bauer & Bell). (iv) The section on the role of judges in implementing rights is mainly based on Yash Ghai and Jill Cottrell (eds.) (2004) (Ghai & Cottrell). (v) Other writings are cited as they are mentioned. Ghai's views are further developed in two important recent papers: 'Redesigning the State for Right Development' (forthcoming) (arguing that the UN Declaration on the Right to Development provides a coherent structure for constitution-making and the design of institutions at a national level); and 'A Journey Around Constitutions' (2005) (Beinart Lecture, University of Cape Town, 2002) ['Journey'] reflecting on his experiences as a constitutional scholar and adviser.

Ghai is highly respected as a scholar, but he is even better known as a legal adviser to governments and agencies, especially in the South Pacific and East Africa. He has been highly influential on post-independence constitutional development in the South Pacific, serving as constitutional adviser in Papua New Guinea, Vanuatu, Fiji, Western Samoa, and the Solomon Islands, among others. He has also been involved in a variety of peacekeeping and trouble-shooting activities in Bougainville, Sri Lanka, Afghanistan, East Timor, and Nepal. He has been prominent in debates about public law in Hong Kong and has recently served as a constitutional adviser in Iraq and Nepal. Since 2005 he has been Special Adviser to the UN Secretary–General on human rights in Cambodia. Over the years he has received numerous honours, including election as a corresponding fellow of the British Academy in 2005.

From November 2000 to July 2004 he was full-time chair of the Constitution of Kenya Review Commission, on leave from Hong Kong. Despite enormous difficulties, the commission produced a draft constitution in December 2002, almost simultaneously with the ouster of President Moi and the ruling party, KANU (Kenya African National Union), in an election that was accepted by foreign observers as being generally 'free and fair.' Unfortunately, once in power the new leaders were less keen on reform than they had been when in opposition. At the time of writing no new constitution has been enacted.[116]

Ghai has unrivalled experience of constitution making in post-colonial states. Besides his unquestioned academic and practical expertise, he has succeeded in winning the trust of many rival political leaders of different persuasions, often in tense situations, not least because of the obvious sincerity of his commitment to opposing all forms of colonialism and racism. He has shown great courage in standing up to domineering heads of government, such as President Moi. His courage and negotiating skills are legendary.

Almost all of the constitutions that Yash Ghai has helped to design and introduce have included a bill of rights.[117] They have generally fitted broadly liberal ideals of parliamentary democracy, judicial independence, and the rule of law. He has been an outspoken critic of governmental repression, especially detention without trial and torture, but there is a discernible ambivalence in his attitude to human rights. For example, he was editor and principal draftsman of an important report by the Commonwealth Human Rights Initiative, entitled *Put Our World to Rights: Towards a Commonwealth Human Rights Policy*, published in 1991.[118] Yet in 1987 he was co-editor (with Robin Luckham and

---

[116] Ghai comments on the constitutive process in Kenya in two recent papers cited above.

[117] The most influential model has been the Nigerian Bill of Rights (1959/1960), which in turn was heavily influenced by the European Convention on Human Rights. The 1960 Independence Constitution of Nigeria represented a change of attitude by the colonial office in London, which until then had been lukewarm about bills of rights. Thereafter, the Nigerian bill of rights became a model for many Commonwealth countries in the period of decolonisation. The story is told in Simpson (2001) at pp. 862–73.

[118] London: Commonwealth Human Rights Initiative.

Francis Snyder) of *The Political Economy of Law: A Third World Reader*, which presented a distinctly Marxian perspective and which contains no mention in the index of rights, human rights, or constitutional rights, except a few references to *habeas corpus*.[119]

After the 'collapse of communism', symbolised by the fall of the Berlin Wall, some former Marxist intellectuals adopted the discourse of human rights.[120] However, Ghai's ambivalence has deeper roots. Perhaps the key is to be found in his own account of his intellectual development.[121] In a refreshingly frank memoir, he tells how he moved from orthodox legal positivism (Oxford and the English Bar), through a phase of liberal reformism (Harvard and the early years in Dar-es-Salaam) to accepting the basics of Marxist critiques of neo-colonialism and of Julius Nyerere's African Socialism from about 1967. He acknowledges that his acceptance of Marxism was not wholehearted. He recognised the value of Marxian structural analysis of political economy, but this was tempered by three concerns: First, as an East African Asian he was especially sensitive to racist attitudes that he discerned among locals as well as expatriates: 'What passed in general for radicalism in those days included a large amount of racism and xenophobia.'[122] Second, he had a 'predilection for free debate,'[123] which was beginning to be stifled by a local form of political correctness. And third, while his university colleagues were academically stimulating, most lacked any sense of the importance of legal technicality and practical sense. They taught their students to despise the law, but not how to use it:

> My experience seemed to point to the problems when fidelity to the law weakens – the arrogance of power, the corruption of public life, the insecurity of the disadvantaged. I was not unaware, of course, of other purposes of the law which served the interests of the rich and the powerful. But the fact was that it did increasingly less and less so; a whole body of statutory law since TANU [the ruling party] came to power had begun to tip the scales the other way. I retained my ambivalence about the legal system, and was not attracted to the attitudes of many private practitioners I met (or the interests they served). At the same time I knew the evasion of the law or the dilution of its safeguards harmed many of the people the radical lawyers were championing.[124]

Ghai's experiences in Dar-es-Salaam were formative in important respects. In nearly all of his work since then, three tensions are apparent: a strong commitment to certain basic values, tempered by a pragmatic willingness to settle for what is politically feasible in the circumstances; a genuine interest in theory, especially political economy, and a determination to be effective in the role of a good hard-nosed practical lawyer;[125] and a materialist, Marxian

---

[119] Ghai, Luckham and Snyder (1987).   [120] For example, Shivji (1989).

[121] This essay, revealingly entitled 'Legal Radicalism, Professionalism and Social Action,' appears in a volume (Shivji, *Limits of Legal Radicalism* (1986)) commemorating the twenty-fifth anniversary of the Faculty of Law, University of Dar-es-Salaam.

[122] Ghai 'Legal Radicalism,' at pp. 29–30.   [123] *Ibid.*   [124] *Ibid.* at p. 27.   [125] *Ibid.* at p. 31.

perspective on political economy sometimes in tension with a sincere belief in liberal values embodied in the rule of law, an independent judiciary, and human rights. For the last thirty years he has also had to balance the demands of teaching, research, and writing with practical involvement in high-level decision making in a continually expanding range of countries. As a consultant he has also had to reconcile his belief in the importance of local context – historical, political, and economic – with a general approach to constitutionalism and constitution making. He is a rare example of a foreign consultant who genuinely rejects the idea that 'one size fits all'.

In the early years of his career, Ghai wrote about many topics mainly from a public law perspective. He joined in East African debates about the arguments for and against bills of rights[126] and he addressed particular topics, such as *habeas corpus*, racial discrimination, and the position of ethnic minorities.[127] However, it was not until about 1990 that he focused his attention regularly on human rights as such. This is perhaps due to 'the increased salience' that human rights discourse achieved during this period.[128] Even then, he has consistently viewed bills of rights and the international human rights regime as one means among many that may serve to protect the interests of the poor and the vulnerable as well as satisfy majority and minority interests.[129] As we shall see, his approach has generally been more pragmatic than idealistic and it is only quite recently that he has devoted much space to writing about human rights theory. Rather than try to attempt to trace his intellectual development or summarise his general constitutional theory, I shall here focus on three recent papers that illustrate more general aspects of his approach to human rights: the role of human rights discourse in reaching constitutional settlements in multi-ethnic societies, his critique of the 'Asian values' debate of the early 1990s, and his exchange with Abdullahi An-Na'im about the justiciability of economic and social rights. In considering these particular pieces, it is important to bear in mind that Yash Ghai is primarily a public lawyer for whom bills of rights are

---

[126] Ghai and McAuslan, (1970) at c. XI, XIII. At Independence, Kenya opted for a weak bill of rights, while Tanganyika (later Tanzania) decided against one at that stage of development and nation building. See Nyerere (1966) *passim*, esp. c. 62. Ghai and McAuslan argued that even a limited bill of rights is one way of making a government publicly accountable, but after the disillusioning experience of the Kenya Bill of Rights in the immediate post-Independence period, they reluctantly concluded that 'an ineffective Bill is worse than no Bill at all, as it raises false hopes. ... The total effect of the Bill of Rights in practice is occasionally to require Government to do indirectly what it cannot do directly – a strange mutation of its normal role.' Ghai & McAuslan at pp. 455–6. This theme is echoed in Ghai's more recent writings: e.g. 'Sentinels of Liberty or Sheep in Wolf's Clothing? Judicial Politics and the Hong Kong Bill of Rights' (1997a). On the post-Independence history of human rights in Tanzania, see Widner (2001).

[127] See especially Ghai (1967); D.P. Ghai and Y.P. Ghai (eds.) (1971); and Ghai and McAuslan (1970).

[128] 'Universalism'.

[129] For example, in discussing issues and prospects for constitution making in post-war Iraq, 'full respect for the principles of universal human rights' is only one of nine principles to be accommodated in a settlement likely to be acceptable to the Shia and other groups. Ghai, 'Constitution-Making in a New Iraq' in Ghai, (2003b) at p. 34, online: www.minorityrights.org/admin/download/Pdf/IraqReport.pdf.

only one aspect of constitutionalism and human rights discourse is but one aspect of constitutional and political theory.

(a) Negotiating competing claims in multi-ethnic societies[130]

Yash Ghai, as a Kenyan Asian, comes from an embattled minority. One of his first monographs, written with his brother, D.P. Ghai, a distinguished economist, was entitled 'Asians in East and Central Africa'.[131] In nearly all of the countries where he has served as a constitutional adviser, protecting the interests of significant ethnic or religious minorities has presented a major problem. And, of course, multiculturalism is a pervasive phenomenon in most societies today. So it is hardly surprising that this theme has been in the foreground of his more general writings on human rights.

In a symposium published in the *Cardozo Law Review* (February 2000),[132] Ghai drew on his experiences of constitution-making to make what is perhaps his fullest statement of a general position on human rights. His central thesis is that both of these debates often obscure the political realities and the potential practical uses of human rights discourse as a flexible framework for negotiating acceptable compromises between conflicting interests and groups.

Ghai warns against interpreting human rights discourse too literally or solely in ideological terms. Rather, he adopts 'a more pragmatic and historical, and less ideological, approach'.[133] In his experience, concerns about 'culture' have in practice been less important than the balance of power and competition for resources. Human rights rhetoric may be used – sometimes cynically manipulated – to further particular interests or, as in the Asian values debate, to give legitimacy to repressive regimes by emphasising the right to self-determination of sovereign states (but not necessarily of peoples or minorities within those states).

Nevertheless, in his view, human rights discourse has provided a useful framework for mediating between competing ethnic and cultural claims, and in combating repressive regimes, just because it is flexible and vague and not rigidly monolithic.[134] In domestic constitutive processes and constitutional law,

---

[130] For the main sources of this section, see *supra* n. 115.
[131] Ghai and Ghai (1971), reprinted in Whitaker (ed.) (1973).
[132] 'Universalism'.   [133] *Ibid.* at p. 1099.
[134] He proceeds to clarify:

'By the "framework of rights" I mean the standards and norms of human rights reflected in international instruments and the institutions for the interpretation and enforcement of rights. This means that no permissible policies are arbitrary. Instead, they must be justified by reference to a recognized right, the qualifications that may be lawfully imposed on the right, or a balance between rights. The procedures and guidelines for the balance and tradeoffs must be included within the regime of rights. The notion of framework also refers to the process of negotiations or adjudication which must be conducted fairly within certain core values of rights. There must also be the acceptance of the ultimate authority of the judiciary to settle competing claims by reference to human rights norms'.

'Universalism' at pp. 1103–4.

the international human rights regime has provided a crucial reference point for local debates. In a study of constitution making in four quite different countries – India, Fiji, Canada, and South Africa – he found that the relevance of rights was widely acknowledged, much of the content and orientation of competing viewpoints was drawn from foreign precedents and international discourse, and groups presented their claims in terms of different paradigms of rights, drawn largely from transnational sources. In short, international norms and debates were used as resources for local arguments and negotiations in the process of achieving a constitutional settlement:

> For multicultural states, human rights as a negotiated understanding of the accept-able framework for coexistence and the respect for each culture are more important than for monocultural or mono-ethnic societies, where other forms of solidarity and identity can be invoked to minimize or cope with conflicts. In other words, it is precisely where the concept or conceptions of rights are most difficult that they are most needed. The task is difficult, but possible, even if it may not always be completely successful. And most states today in fact are multicultural, whether as a result of immigration or because their peoples are finding new identities.[135]

Ghai uses his four case studies to explode a number of myths: First, he challenges the assumption that culture is the salient element in determining attitudes to rights, a matter of significance when 'cultural relativism' is invoked to undermine the case for human rights.[136] 'Culture' is not irrelevant, but it operates in complex ways. Culture is not monolithic, but protean; no community has a static culture;[137] cultures change and intermix; homogeneity of culture within a nation state is nowadays exceptional, and indeed much state effort is devoted to artificially creating a common culture as a prop for national unity. Questions of the relation of rights to culture arise *within* communities, as when women or minorities have invoked rights to challenge or interrogate 'tradition'. As Santos and others have suggested, cross-cultural discourse can generate new forms and enrich the culture of rights.[138] Perhaps, most important, Ghai

---

[135] *Ibid.* at p. 1102.

[136] In respect of the four case studies he concluded:

> 'Culture' has nowhere been a salient element determining attitudes to rights. It has been important in Fiji, Canada, and South Africa, but it has been important in different ways. ... With the exception of the Canadian first nations ['the Aborigines'], the proponents of the cultural approach to rights were not necessarily concerned about the general welfare of their community's cultural traditions. They were more concerned with the power they obtain from espousing those traditions. ... The manipulation of 'tradition' by Inkatha is well documented. Fijian military personnel and politicians who justified the coup were accused of similar manipulation by a variety of respectable commentators.

> *Ibid.* at pp. 1135–6.

[137] See Lisa Fishbayn's insightful paper on judicial interpretations of 'culture' in family cases in South Africa, Fishbayn (1999).

[138] 'Universalism' at p. 1098, citing Santos (1995) See Jeremy Webber's thesis that Aboriginal rights in Canada are best understood to be the product of cross-cultural interaction rather than as the result of some antecedent body of law (Webber (1995)).

emphasises that 'the material bases of "rights" are stronger than cultural bases'.[139]

Second, Ghai attacks as a myth the idea that the origins and current support for universal rights are solely Western. Historically, the sources of the international regime are quite diverse, with different 'generations' having different supporters.[140] During the colonial period, for example, the British were among the strongest opponents of rights talk, especially in relation to self-determination or local bills of rights. At that time, nationalist leaders were strong supporters of human rights, especially the right to self-determination, but that enthusiasm did not always survive beyond Independence. Bentham, Burke, and Marx were among the critics of rights within the Western tradition. During the Cold War, the Eastern bloc generally championed social and economic rights, the Western powers individual civil and political rights. In South Africa it was the whites who historically opposed universal human rights, and, after the end of apartheid, it was the black majority who were the most committed to them.[141] In modern times, political leaders have invoked 'the right to self-determination' as a defence against external criticism of internally repressive regimes and at the same time dismiss 'rights discourse' as a form of Western neo-colonialism – as in the Asian values debate.

It is no doubt true that the current international regime of rights derives largely from Western intellectual traditions, but Ghai points out that today 'there is very considerable support for rights in Asia, among parliamentarians, judges, academics, trade unionists, women's groups, and other non-governmental organizations'.[142] When Western-dominated organisations, such as the World Bank, the International Monetary Fund, and state foreign aid agencies promote 'human rights and good governance and democracy', they tend to emphasise a narrow band of individual and property rights rather than the whole spectrum that were included in the original Universal Declaration of Human Rights.[143] Such selectivity illustrates the flexibility, and possibly the incoherence, of the general framework of rights discourse. Whatever the origin, the general framework and current support are not specifically Northern or Western.

Third, Ghai strongly challenges the use of sharp dichotomies in this context. For example, he identifies at least five types of relativist positions that need to be distinguished:[144] (i) strong cultural relativism (i.e. that rights depend upon

---

[139] 'Universalism,' at pp. 1100, 1136–7.

[140] Compare Upendra Baxi's account of alternative human rights histories, *infra* at pp. 432–7.

[141] 'Universalism' at pp. 1137–8.   [142] 'Human Rights' at p. 169.

[143] The Universal Declaration of Human Rights included social, economic and cultural rights as well as civil and political rights, and recognised the importance of duties. See 'Human Rights' at p. 170.

[144] 'Universalism' at pp. 1095–9. The formulation in the text is mine. Ghai's categories are recognisable, but some writers distinguish between many more positions. On the ambiguities of 'relativism', see Haack (1998) at p. 149.

culture rather than upon universal norms); (ii) that cultural differences do indeed exist, but only the Western concept of human rights is acceptable as a basis for universal norms (conversely, some Asian politicians argue that their societies are superior to the West because their cultures emphasise duty and harmony rather than individual rights and conflict); (iii) moderate cultural relativism (i.e. that a common core of human rights can be extracted from overlapping values of different cultures);[145] (iv) that cultural pluralism can be harmonised with international standards by largely internal re-interpretation of cultural tradition – the basic approach of Abdullahi An-Na'im; and (v) that an enriched version of rights can be developed by intercultural discourse, which can lead towards a new form of universalism. Ghai concludes:

> On the more general question of universalism and relativism, it is not easy to generalize. It cannot be said that bills of rights have a universalizing or homogenizing tendency, because by recognizing languages and religions, and by affirmative policies a bill of rights may in fact solidify separate identities. Nevertheless, a measure of universalism of rights may be necessary to transcend sectional claims for national cohesion. Simple polarities, universalism/particularism, secular/religious, tradition/modernity do not explain the complexity; a large measure of flexibility is necessary to accommodate competing interests. Consequently most bills of rights are Janus-faced (looking towards both liberalism and collective identities). What is involved in these arrangements is not an outright rejection of either universalism or relativism; but rather an acknowledgement of the importance of each, and a search for a suitable balance, by employing, for the most part, the language and parameters of rights.[146]

On the basis of these four case studies, backed by his wide practical experience, Ghai suggests some further general conclusions: First, rights provide a framework not only for cross-cultural discourse and negotiation, but also 'to interrogate culture' within a given community, as when women have used them to challenge traditionalists in Canada, India, and South Africa.[147] Second, 'in no case are rights seen merely as protections against the state.

---

[145] A prominent modern example is Renteln (1988), (1990). This continues a tradition that can be traced back to the search for cultural universals by George P. Murdock and the attempts by Father Thomas Davitt, SJ to find an empirical support for natural law in universal values and norms in preliterate societies, e.g. Thomas Davitt, SJ, 'Basic Value Judgments in Preliterate Custom and Law' (Paper presented to the Council for the Study of Mankind, Conference on Law and the Idea of Mankind, Chicago, 1963/4) (unpublished). Apart from problems of the 'naturalistic fallacy' (deriving 'ought' propositions from 'is' premises), such efforts tend to encounter two main lines of objection: (i) General prescriptions of the kind 'killing is condemned in all known societies' are so hedged with exceptions and qualifications as to have virtually no content. (ii) Such accounts tend to play down or pass over in silence unattractive near-universals such as aggression and the subordination of women. In 'Universalism' at p. 1098, Ghai cites Charles Taylor's argument that although human nature is socially constructed, there is often sufficient overlap to ground a workable common core of human rights. See Charles Taylor, 'Conditions of an Unenforced Consensus on Human Rights' (Taylor (1999)).

[146] 'Universalism' at pp. 1139–40.   [147] *Ibid.* at p. 1137.

They are instruments for the distribution of resources, a basis for identity, and a tool of hegemony, and they offer a social vision of society. Rights are not necessarily deeply held values, but rather a mode of discourse for advancing and justifying claims.'[148] Third, in multi-cultural societies, balancing of interests requires recognition of collective as well as individual rights, including rights connected with being a member of a group, as with affirmative action in India.[149] Fourth, where rights are used for balancing interests, there is no room for absolutism of rights. They have to be qualified, balanced against each other, or reconceptualised.[150] Fifth, a stable settlement in a multi-ethnic society often involves recognition and appropriate formulation of social, economic, and cultural rights. This in turn requires an activist state.[151] Sixth, 'since interethnic relations are so crucial to an enduring settlement, and past history may have been marked by discrimination or exploitation, a substantial part of the regime of rights has to be made binding on private parties.'[152] Finally, the requirements of balancing conflicting interests within a framework of rights give a major role to the judiciary in interpreting, applying, and reinterpreting the constitutional settlement in a reasoned and principled way.[153]

Ghai's approach is illustrated by his treatment of the so-called 'Asian values' debate. This is widely perceived as a concerted attack on human rights by spokesmen for what is wrongly regarded as representing some kind of Asian consensus. Ghai argues that the debate has obscured both the complexity and the richness of debates about rights within Asia.

(b) The 'Asian values' debate[154]

> The authoritarian readings of Asian values that are increasingly championed in some quarters do not survive scrutiny. And the grand dichotomy between Asian values and European values adds little to our understanding, and much to the confounding of the normative basis of freedom and democracy (Amartya Sen).[155]

'The Asian values debate' refers to a controversy that flared up in the run-up to the Vienna World Conference on Human Rights in 1993. After the collapse of communism, increased attention to human rights issues had led to growing criticism of human rights violations in China and also in countries that had been allies in the Cold War. This was also the period of increased conditionalities being imposed by international financial institutions and Western aid agencies in the name of 'human rights, good governance and democracy'. In a regional meeting preparatory to the Vienna Conference, many Asian

---

[148] *Ibid.*   [149] *Ibid.* at p. 1138.   [150] *Ibid.*   [151] *Ibid.*   [152] *Ibid.*
[153] *Ibid.* at pp. 1138–9. See also, however, his caveats about the role of the judiciary in relation to economic and social rights, discussed below.
[154] For sources of this section, see n. 115 above.
[155] Amartya Sen, 'Human Rights and Asian Values: What Lee Kuan Yew and I Peng Don't Understand about Asia' (1997) at p. 40.

governments signed *The Bangkok Declaration*,[156] which was widely interpreted as an attempt to present a united front against growing Western hegemony. Lee Kuan Yew (and the Government of Singapore) and Muhathir Mohamed (and the Government of Malaysia), who could hardly be considered representative of the whole of Asia, framed this North–South confrontation in terms of a fundamental conflict between 'human rights and Asian values'.

The Asian values debate has rumbled on for over a decade and has surfaced in a number of different contexts, of which one of the most interesting and important is the positions taken by China both internally and externally in response to Western criticism.[157] Yash Ghai was one of a number of 'Southern' intellectuals who jumped to the defence of ideas about human rights and democracy as not being peculiarly Western. In a series of papers published between 1993 and 1999, he sharply criticised the arguments and positions adopted by the leaders of Singapore and Malaysia and in the process developed his own general position on human rights.[158]

We need not enter into the details of Ghai's criticisms of the Singapore and Malaysian versions of the Asian values position, which he treats as both insincere and confused.[159] He suggests that the true motive for their campaign was to justify authoritarian regimes at a time when they were being subjected to criticism both internally and internationally for repression of dissent and civil liberties. However, participating in the debate sharpened Ghai's focus on the connections between culture, the market, and human rights. Here it is sufficient to quote his own summary of his treatment of one phase of the debate as it

---

[156] Final Declaration of the Regional Meeting for Asia of the World Conference on Human Rights, A/CONF.157/ASRM/8, A/CONF.157/PC/59 (7 April 1993), online: www.unhchr.ch/html/menu5/wcbangk.htm. Other accessible documents include Government of Singapore, *Shared Values* (Singapore: Government of Singapore Printers, 1991); and a useful symposium in 1994 in *Foreign Affairs*, including Fareed Zakaria, 'A Conversation with Lee Kuan Yew' (1994) and the response by Kim Dae Jung (1994). See also Ghai 'Social Justice'.

[157] See Kent (1999); and Foot (2000).

[158] In the version of 'the Asian values position' advanced by Lee Kuan Yew and the Government of Singapore, Ghai summarises the core of the argument as follows: (i) The West is decadent – lawless, amoral, and in economic decline. This decadence is due to its emphasis on democracy and human rights based on extreme individualism. 'Rights consciousness has made people selfish and irresponsible and promoted confrontation and litigiousness.' (ii) Asian societies have maintained social stability, economic progress, and a sense of moral purpose on the basis of a culture and ethos that emphasises duties and subordinates individual interests to the welfare of the community. (iii) There is a Western conspiracy to subvert Asian political independence and economic success by imposing decadent alien values on Asian culture. Ghai challenges all of these positions in 'Human Rights' (1998) at pp. 176–7; see also the more detailed critique in 'Politics of Human Rights' (1995).

[159] Ghai tended to dismiss the Bangkok Declaration as an incoherent and self-contradictory document, a political compromise that was hardly worth deconstruction (e.g. 'Politics of Rights' at p. 209; 'Human Rights' at p. 174) and to concentrate on the arguments of Lee and Muhathir, about whom he was equally scathing ('Human Rights,' *ibid*): 'To draw from their pretentious and mostly inconsistent statements a general philosophy of Asian values is like trying to understand Western philosophy of rights and justice from statements of Reagan and Thatcher.'

surfaced before and during the Bangkok meeting in March and April 1993, preceding the Vienna World Conference on Human Rights:

> Asian perceptions of human rights have been much discussed, particularly outside Asia, stimulated by the challenge to the international regime of rights by a few Asian governments in the name of Asian values. Placing the debate in the context of international developments since the Universal Declaration of Human Rights 50 years ago, [the author] argues that international discussions on human rights in Asia are sterile and misleading, obsessed as they are with Asian values. On the other hand, the debate within Asia is much richer, reflecting a variety of views, depending to a significant extent on the class, economic or political location of the proponents. Most governments have a statist view of rights, concerned to prevent the use of rights discourse to mobilize disadvantaged or marginal groups, such as workers, peasants, or ethnic groups, or stifle criticisms and interventions from the international community.[160] However, few of them [i.e. governments] subscribe to the crude versions of Asian values, which are often taken abroad as representing some kind of Asian consensus. [The author] contrasts the views of governments with those of the non-governmental organizations (NGOs) who have provided a more coherent framework for the analysis of rights in the Asian context. They see rights as promoting international solidarity rather than divisions. Domestically, they see rights as means of empowerment and central to the establishment of fair and just political, economic and social orders.[161]

To start with, Ghai was quite dismissive of arguments that human rights represent a form of cultural imperialism – the imposition of values that are atomistic, confrontational, and self-seeking on a culture that stresses harmony, consensus, hard work, and solidarity. This argument, in his view, exaggerated the homogeneity of 'Asian' cultures, distorted the nature of human rights, and overemphasised the place of culture in economic success. However, in a later paper on 'Rights, Duties and Responsibilities' he decided to take more seriously the argument that some Asian traditions, notably Hinduism and Confucianism, emphasise duties rather than rights, and that this is a superior way to organise society.[162] 'Duty' in this context is more abstract than the Hohfeldian idea of duty: it refers to obligations or responsibilities attached to office or status or class, rather than merely being the correlative of claim rights. Such responsibilities prescribe right and proper conduct in respect of a given role or relationship, like father–son, husband–wife, friend–friend, and, most important, ruler-subjects. In one interpretation of Confucianism, such duties could be said to be less self-regarding than rights, more communitarian, oriented to harmony rather than conflict, and more informal, emphasising honour, peace,

---

[160] Ghai points to the highly selective presentation of Asian values by some protagonists, glossing over the hierarchical structures of relationships, subordination of women, the exploitation of children and workers, nepotism and corruption based on family ties, and the oppression of minorities. *Ibid.* at p. 177.

[161] This is based on the Abstract to 'Human Rights'.   [162] 'Rights, Duties'.

and stability. 'The key duties are loyalty, obedience, filial piety, respect, and protection'.[163] Ghai acknowledges that in some societies this version of Confucianism can be attractive:

> I do not wish to oppose a broader notion of duty in the sense of responsibilities or civic virtue. There is clearly much that is attractive in persons who are mindful of the concerns of others, who wish to contribute to the welfare of the community, who place society above their own personal interests. No civilized society is possible without such persons. There is also much that is attractive in societies that seek a balance between rights and responsibilities and emphasize harmony. Nor do I wish to underestimate the potential of duty as a safeguard against abuse of power and office. I am much attracted to the notion of the withdrawal of the Mandate of Heaven from rulers who transgress upon duties of rulers (although I am aware that this was largely impotent as a device of responsiveness or account-ability or discipline of rulers).[164]

However, these virtues mainly concern social relations of human beings within civil society rather than relations between citizens and the state, which is the primary sphere of human rights. Moreover, as modern Confucian scholarship suggests, there is a downside to such a philosophy:[165] a duty-based society tends to be status oriented and hierarchical, and in some societies, Confucian duties rarely extended beyond family and clan, promoting corruption rather than a genuine civic sense. Confucius himself emphasised the moral responsibilities of the ruler, was contemptuous of merchants and profits, and was against strong laws and tough punishments – for authoritarian, market-oriented, and often corrupt governments to invoke Confucius is hypocritical. By conflating the ideas of state and community, the official protagonists of Asian values obscure the role of the regime of rights to mediate between state and community: 'That the contemporary celebration of duty has little to do with culture and much to do with politics is evident from the various contra-dictions of policies and practices of governments heavily engaged in its exhortation.'[166]

In the present context, perhaps the important point is a warning against taking any debates and discourse about human rights too literally. The context is typically political, and the same discourse can be used or abused for a wide range of different political ends. Above all, such discourse is historically contingent:

> I believe that rights are historically determined and are generally the result of social struggles. They are significantly influenced by material and economic conditions of human existence. It is for that reason unjustified to talk of uniform

---

[163] *Ibid.* at p. 29.   [164] *Ibid.* at pp. 37–8.

[165] *Ibid.* at p. 38, citing de Barry (1991). He also points out (*ibid.*) that traditional Confucianism placed more emphasis on the individual than has generally been recognised, citing Yu-Wei Hsieh (1967); and Tu Wei-Ming, (1985).

[166] 'Rights, Duties' at p. 34.

attitudes and practices in such a diverse region as Asia. Rights become important, both as political principles and instruments, with the emergence of capitalist markets and the strong states associated with the development of national markets. Markets and states subordinated communities and families under which duties and responsibilities were deemed more important than entitlements. Rights regulate the relationship of individuals and corporations to the state. Despite the lip service paid to the community and the family by certain Asian governments, the reality is that the State has effectively displaced the community, and increasingly the family, as the framework within which an individual or group's life chances and expectations are decided. The survival of community itself now depends on rights of association and assembly.[167]

(c) The role of judges in implementing economic, social, and cultural rights

The UN Declaration covered both civil and political rights (CPR) and economic, social, and cultural rights (ESCR). It made no formal distinction between the two classes. However, during the Cold War, the distinction became significant and was sharpened in the ideological battles between the Western powers and the Eastern bloc, the former prioritising CPR, the latter ESCR. This distinction became further entrenched both in international covenants and through the influence of the colonial powers and the Soviet Union on subordinated countries. Thus the European Convention on Human Rights[168] is restricted to civil and political rights, and this limitation has spread to many Commonwealth countries. The distinction still lives on (e.g. in the domestic and foreign policies of the United States and of the People's Republic of China). However, the constitutions of India (1949) and South Africa (1994) are significant exceptions to this privileging of one set of rights to the exclusion of the other.

The validity of the distinction has long been a matter of contention, and the claim that 'human rights are interdependent and indivisible'[169] is widely supported by the human rights community. At the start of the Millennium the debate became sharply focused within Interights, an influential London-based NGO, by the responses to a memorandum prepared by Yash Ghai that was intended to focus the program of Interights on ESCR:

> It was not my intention to expound a theory of ESCR, but to suggest a focus for work. I acknowledged the importance of ESCR as rights, but cautioned against an over-concentration on litigation strategies and pointed to limitations of the judicial process in view of the nature of ESCR. The memo implied the need to

---

[167] 'Human Rights' at p. 169. Pressure of space precludes my doing justice to Ghai's analysis of the complex relationship between economic globalisation and human rights in Asia, on which see 'Social Justice'.

[168] Convention for the Protection of Human Rights and Fundamental Freedoms (4 November 1950), CETS No. 005, online: Council of Europe www.conventions.coe.int/Treaty/en/Summaries/Html/005.htm.

[169] On Baxi's criticism of this and other 'mantras,' see Baxi (2006a) Chapter 1.

avoid polarities or dichotomies (such as justiciability and nonjusticiability and civil and political/economic and social rights). In this as other instances of enforcement of the law, there was a division of labour between court-oriented strategies and other modes of enforcement. It was important, in discussions of the enforceability of ESCR, to pay attention to the relationship between judicial enforcement and the supporting framework that other institutions could provide, as well as to the effects of litigation on wider participation in the movements, and lobbying, for human rights.[170]

The memorandum provoked mixed reactions. The ensuing debate culminated in a valuable collection of essays edited by Yash Ghai and Jill Cottrell.[171] This volume throws light not only on issues such as justiciability, but also on the specific nature of ESCR, different methods of implementation, and the experience of the courts in several countries in dealing with them. The final chapter by the editors represents a significant development of Ghai's views.[172]

In this volume, the debate was initially framed by contrasting positions asserted by Abdullahi An-Na'im and Lord (Anthony) Lester.[173] An-Na'im objected in principle to the classification of human rights into two broad classes. He argued that this distinction leads to the perception that ESCR are inferior,[174] it denies the claim that human rights are indivisible and interdependent,[175] it is not based on any consistent or coherent criteria of classification, and it undermines 'the universality and practical implementation *of all human rights*'.[176] In particular, An-Na'im attacked the idea that no ESCR should be enforced by the judiciary. All human rights need to be supported by a variety of mechanisms, and the role of each mechanism should be assessed and developed in relation to each right. But it is not appropriate to leave promotion and enforcement to national governments, for the fundamental aim of protecting human rights 'is to *safeguard them from the contingencies of the national political and administrative processes*'.[177] The judiciary has a vital role to play in this. An-Na'im placed great emphasis on the importance of human rights as universal standards incorporated in the international regime and backed by international co-operation in their implementation. The framework of international standards is crucial for the recognition of ESCR as *human rights*.

Lord Lester and Colm O'Cinneide developed a familiar response: while acknowledging that ESCR are indeed human rights and the poor and the vulnerable need protection from violations of both classes of rights, they argued

---

[170] Ghai & Cottrell, *supra* n. 115 at p. vi.   [171] *Ibid.*   [172] Ghai and Cottrell at p. 58

[173] Abdullahi An-Na'im, (2004b) in Ghai and Cottrell (2004b) at p. 7 Lester and O'Cinneide, 'The Effective Protection of Socio-Economic Right' in Ghai and Cottrell, *ibid.*, at p. 16.

[174] For example, '[W]ithin the European system, ESCR has been relegated to non-binding charters and optional protocols.' An-Nai'im, *ibid.* at p. 11.

[175] For example, a right to freedom of expression is not much use to the vulnerable without a right to education; conversely, implementation of a right to education is dependent on freedom to research and communicate freely. *Ibid.*

[176] An-Na'im, *ibid.* emphasis added.   [177] *Ibid.* at p. 8.

that ESCR are best protected by non-judicial mechanisms. For reasons of democratic legitimacy and practical expertise, the judiciary should have a very limited role in those aspects of governance that involve allocation of resources, setting priorities, and developing policies.[178]

In the ensuing debate it became clear that the range of disagreement was quite narrow. This is hardly surprising within a group of human rights experts (mainly lawyers) arguing in the context of an NGO that is committed to promoting ESCR. There appears to have been a consensus on a number of points: that ESCR should be treated as *rights*, that their effective enforcement and development was a matter of concern, that this requires a variety of mechanisms, that the idea of the interdependence of rights is of genuine practical importance, and that the concept of 'justiciability' is too abstract and too fluid to provide much help in delineating an appropriate role for the judiciary in respect of ESCR.

Ghai took issue with An-Na'im on two main grounds: An-Na'im placed too much emphasis on the international regime as the foundation for national policies on rights,[179] and he was wrong in suggesting that those who want a restricted role for the judiciary are necessarily opposed to ESCR as rights. Nevertheless, Ghai suggested that the differences between An-Na'im and the proponents of judicial restraint can easily be exaggerated – they are mainly differences of emphasis about a role that is contingent on local historical and material conditions. Several of the commentators made the point that courts have taken ESCR into account when interpreting CPR provisions.

One senses that Ghai may have been somewhat impatient with a debate which seems to have been based largely on mutual misunderstandings of seemingly conflicting viewpoints. No one denied that courts had some role to play in this area, while An-Na'im was not asking that they should be seen as the only relevant mechanism. However, the debate stimulated Ghai to develop his own ideas about the nature of ESCR and the role of human rights discourse in framing state policies. Without claiming to do justice to a rich and detailed analysis, one can perhaps pinpoint three key ideas underlying his position:

First, he was stimulated to articulate his view of the role of courts in relation to EHCR. This should not be static, but generally speaking should be less prominent than their role in relation to CPR. After a survey of the case law developed so far, especially in India and South Africa, including cases in which courts had been felt by critics to have become too involved, Ghai and Cottrell concluded:

---

[178] Lester and O'Cinneide (2004).

[179] 'Reliance on international norms brings in all of the difficulties of hegemony and alleged imposition; and it ignores the national character of the constitution as a charter of the people themselves to bind their rulers … and it ignores the critical importance of local action, democracy etc.' Ghai and Cottrell (2004) at p. 2. Interestingly, as discussed below, Baxi makes a similar criticism of Ghai in a different context.

Courts can play an important role in 'mainstreaming' ESCR by (a) elaborating the contents of rights; (b) indicating the responsibilities of the state; (c) identifying ways in which the rights have been violated by the state; (d) suggesting the frameworks within which policy has to be made, highlighting the priority of human rights (to some extent the South African courts have done this, by pointing to the need to make policies about the enforcement of rights, and Indian courts by highlighting the failure of government to fulfil [Directive Principles of State Policy] so many years after independence). There is a fine balance here, for there is always a risk that courts may cross the line between indicating failures of policy and priorities and indicating so clearly what these priorities ought to be that they are actually making policy.[180]

The primary decision-making framework must be the political process.[181]

The main contribution of courts in Ghai's view should be 'in developing core or minimum entitlements'.[182] However, once policies have been formulated by government or other agencies, backed by standards and benchmarks, courts may also have a role in implementing such standards.

Second, Ghai and Cottrell point out that issues about justiciability cannot turn on the difference between CPR and ESCR, or on some untenable distinction between negative and positive rights.[183] They distinguish between two aspects of justiciability that are often confused:[184] (i) *explicit non-justiciability*, when a constitution or law explicitly excludes the jurisdiction of the courts, for example the Directive Principles of State Policy in the Indian Constitution; and (ii) *non-justiciability as a matter of appropriateness*, a more delicate and complex matter. This may be based on arguments about separation of powers, or legitimacy, or the competence of courts, or some concept of what is a 'political' question or a combination of these. These are contested matters in which no clear consensus has emerged in the case law, except a tendency to reject sharp distinctions.[185]

---

[180] Ghai and Cottrell (2004) at p. 86. They cite with approval (at pp. 86–7) dicta in the South African case of *Government of the Republic of South Africa & Ors v Grootboom & Ors* [2000] ICHRL 72 (4 October 2000), 2000 (11) BCLR 1169 (CCSA) (QL), and of Madam Justice Louise Arbour (as she then was) dissenting in *Gosselin v Québec (Attorney General)* [2002] 4 SCR 429 (QL), 2002 SCC 84, where she draws a distinction between recognition of the kinds of claims individuals may assert against the state and questions of how much the state should spend and in what manner: 'One can in principle answer the question whether a Charter right exists – in this case, to a level of welfare sufficient to meet one's basic needs – without addressing how much expenditure by the state is necessary in order to secure that right. It is only the latter question that is, properly speaking, non-justiciable' (at para. 332).

[181] *Ibid.* at p. 89.   [182] *Ibid.* at p. 87.   [183] *Ibid.* at pp. 70–1.   [184] *Ibid.* at pp. 66–70.

[185] 'Courts are considered an unsuitable forum where there may be no clear standards or rules by which to resolve a dispute or where the court may not be able to supervise the enforcement of its decision or the highly technical nature of the questions, or the large questions of policy involved may be thought to present insuperable obstacles to the useful involvement of courts.' *Ibid.* at p. 69. The Supreme Court of India case of *Upendra Baxi v State of Uttar Pradesh & Ors* (1986) 4 SCC 106 is cited as an example of the courts getting involved in an unsuitable activity. (Here the court supervised a home for women for five years.)

Third, the discussion of the role of the courts throws light on the nature of ESCR. Ghai rejects any sharp distinction between ESCR and CPR, but nevertheless argues that there are certain tendencies that characterise ESCR and suggest a more limited role for the courts in relation to many, but not all of them.[186] For example, in many domestic and international instruments, there is a tendency for ESCR provisions to be drafted in terms that allow considerable discretion in respect of standards, timing, and methods of enforcement.[187] Such notions as 'progressive realisation', 'margin of appreciation', and 'to the extent of its available resources' further limit the role of courts. No human rights are costless, but all implementation of all human rights depends on 'a complex interaction of policies in numerous sectors, institutions, and entitlements.'[188] However, as the Indian and South African cases have shown, there is scope for courts to define what is the minimum core of any given right (a notoriously difficult and contentious matter), to sanction state violation of established rights, and to point out that 'progressive realisation' implies that the state has a constitutional duty to start implementation and a further duty to ensure that there is no deterioration of standards. Ghai's essentially evolutionary and pragmatic argument is consistent with An-Na'im's insistence that what are appropriate mechanisms of implementation should be decided on the merits in respect of each right in particular contexts rather than by reference to abstract categories. But in light of the experience of the case law, there may be a considerably more significant role for courts in the long run than An-Na'im suggests.

Fourth, and more important, Ghai's main concern was to focus attention on other means of implementing and developing ESCR and to make a general case for the idea that human rights discourse can provide a broad overarching framework for constructing state policies and priorities.[189] One trouble with the debates about 'justiciability' has been that 'human rights' has tended to be treated as doctrine (often legal doctrine) rather than as discourse and that it focuses attention on litigation (usually a last resort) and away from the range of other possible mechanisms and resources that need to be employed in the realisation of all human rights, including ESCR.

(d) Conclusion

One senses that Ghai is sometimes impatient with theoretical debates about rights and prefers to work at less general levels. Like many others, he rejects strong versions of both universalism and relativism; he criticises a tendency to over-emphasise 'culture' rather than material interests; he argues that the

---

[186] See the excellent discussion by Ghai and Cottrell (2004) at pp. 76–82, of the way these considerations affect rights to education, medical treatment, housing, environment, and social security.

[187] But there are exceptions (e.g. the right to free and compulsory primary education). *Ibid.* at p. 61.

[188] *Ibid.* at p. 62.   [189] *Ibid.* at p. 61.

debate on Asian values greatly exaggerated the uniformities of 'East Asian culture' and was used to divert attention away from the failings of repressive regimes and human rights violations – the result being to obfuscate genuine issues about human rights in different contexts in East Asia. Similarly, the debate about the justiciability of ESCR amounted to little more than differences of emphasis among lawyers about the proper role of courts – a role that should depend on timing and context in any given country. Most of the protagonists have been lawyers who have tended to argue on the basis of human rights as legal doctrine rather as a discourse that provides a workable framework for mediating conflicting interests and providing a basis for settlements that are accepted by local people as legitimate.

Many of these themes are illustrated in specific ways in Ghai's recent writings about Hong Kong, in which the same dichotomies between theory and practice, socialism and liberalism, and idealism and pragmatism are discernible in creative tension. After a generally pessimistic diagnosis of the situation, he ends on a pragmatic note of hope about the future by appealing to enlightened self-interest:

> It is easy for the Central Authorities, if they were so minded, to bypass or undermine the Basic Law, and they would presumably always find people who are willing to collaborate with them in this enterprise. However, China stands to gain more from a faithful adherence to the Basic Law, to keep promises of autonomy, to permit people of all persuasions to participate in public affairs, to respect rights and freedoms, and to let an independent judiciary enforce the Basic Laws and other laws. This is a more effective way to win the loyalty of Hong Kong people. An adherence to legal norms and consultative and democratic procedures would ultimately benefit the Central Authorities as they grapple with the difficult task of managing affairs on the mainland as economic reforms and the movement for democracy generate new tensions.[190]

Yash Ghai advances a pragmatic materialist interpretation that is broadly supportive of the current international human rights regime. He stresses the uses and limitations of bills of rights as devices for limiting governmental power and increasing accountability. He focuses on the use and abuse of human rights discourse in real-life political contexts, especially by governments that invoke the right to self-determination against external critics of their treatment of their own citizens. His views are not surprisingly controversial.[191] But he provides a uniquely realistic perspective on the practical operation of human rights discourse, especially in the context of constitutional negotiation and settlement.

---

[190] Ghai, (1999a) at p. 500.

[191] For example, 'naturalists' believe that human rights embody universal values. Cultural relativists might argue that he is too dismissive of the core of truth in the idea that there are strong communitarian traditions in Asia that are far less individualistic than Western ideologies of individual rights; and his views are likely to be anathema to free-market 'liberals'. He has also been attacked from the left by Upendra Baxi for too readily taking the international regime of human rights as the starting-point for constitutionalism and for failing to emphasise how human rights discourse can obfuscate 'the real historical struggles' of 'subaltern' peoples, as discussed further below.

13.5 Upendra Baxi[192]

For hundreds of millions of 'the wretched of the earth,' human rights enunciations matter, if at all, only if they provide shields against torture and tyranny, deprivation and destitution, pauperization and powerlessness, desexualization and degradation.[193]

[T]he task of human rights, in terms of making the state ethical, governance just, and power accountable, are tasks that ought to continue to define the agendum of activism.[194]

Human rights languages are perhaps all we have to interrogate the barbarism of power, even when these remain inadequate to humanize fully the barbaric practices of politics.[195]

(a) Introduction[196]

Upendra Baxi was born in Rajkot, Gujerat in 1938. His father, Vishnuprasad Baxi, was a senior civil servant and a noted scholar of Sanskrit. Upendra was brought up in a large household, which sometimes numbered as many as seventy people under one roof, excluding servants. He remembers his childhood environment as a mix of perpetual pregnancies, relentless micro-politics, and a complete lack of privacy. His view of the extended communal family has remained decidedly unromantic. In his words, he reacted against this aspect of Hindu culture, and 'I declared UDI [Unilateral Declaration of Independence] at the first opportunity'. He went to university, did well, and soon embarked on a career as an academic, public intellectual, and legal activist.

After graduating in law from the University of Bombay (LLM, 1963), he taught at the University of Sydney (1968–1973). There he worked closely with

---

[192] This section is based mainly on Upendra Baxi: (i) *The Future of Human Rights* (Delhi: Oxford University Press, 2002a) (*Future of Human Rights*) a second edition was pubished in 2006, but as the first edition is more readily available references to it have been retained, except where there is a significant change; (ii) 'Voices of Suffering, Fragmented Universality, and the Future of Human Rights' ('Voices of Suffering, 1998') (1998) 8: 2 *Transnational Law & Contemporary Problems* 125; (iii) 'Voices of Suffering, Fragmented Universality, and the Future of Human Rights' in Burns H. Weston and Stephen P. Marks (eds.) *The Future of International Human Rights* (1999) 101 ('Voices of Suffering, 1999') (This 1999 piece contains a succinct restatement of Baxi's basic ideas. For many it is probably the best place to start, even though there are many more recent writings); and (iv) a draft introduction to Upendra Baxi & Shulamith Koenig, *The People's Report on Human Rights Education* (2002) (Baxi & Koenig, *Human Rights Education*). (A revised version was published in 2006 as *The Human Right to Human Rights Education? Some Critical Perspectives* (Baxi (2006b)); (v) *Human Rights in a Posthuman World: Critical Essays* (2007a) (*Posthuman World*). Reference will also be made to a number of articles and to three books published in 1994: *Inhuman Wrongs and Human Rights: Some Unconventional Essays* (1994a); *Mambrino's Helmet: Human Rights for a Changing World* (1994b); and Uprendra Baxi and O. Mendelsohn (eds.) *The Rights of Subordinated Peoples* (1994).

[193] 'Voices of Suffering', at p. 103.   [194] *Future of Human Rights* at p. xii.

[195] 'Voices of Suffering' at p. 102.

[196] The biographical information is based in part on conversations and correspondence with Professor Baxi over a number of years, especially 27 August 2005, 12 December 2005 and 9 December 2005.

Julius Stone, the well-known legal theorist and public international lawyer. During this period he spent two years at Berkeley, where he obtained the degrees of LLM (1966) and JSD (1972), having written a thesis on private international law under the supervision of Professor Albert Ehrenzweig. On his return to India he held the post of professor of law at the University of Delhi from 1973 to 1996. During this period he also served as vice-chancellor of South Gujerat (1982–1985), director of research at the Indian Law Institute (1985–1988), and vice-chancellor of the University of Delhi (1990–1994). Since 1996, he has been professor of law and development at the University of Warwick. He has also held visiting appointments at several American law schools.

Baxi has been a prolific writer. In addition to producing over twenty books and many scholarly articles, he has been a frequent broadcaster and contributor to the Indian press. His early work was largely concerned with public law and law and society in India, and he consciously addressed mainly Indian audiences. As an activist he has been very influential both in India and South Asia. He contributed much to legal education. He was a leading commentator and critic of the Indian Supreme Court and a pioneer in the development of social action litigation and 'the epistolary jurisdiction' that gave disadvantaged people direct access to appellate courts. He was also extensively involved in legal action and law reform concerning violence against women and was opposed to major dam projects. He has also been very actively involved in the aftermath of the Bhopal catastrophe.[197] Over time, Baxi's interests and audiences expanded geographically, but he has maintained his concern and involvement with Indian affairs. His more recent interests have included comparative constitutional law, the legal implications of science and technology, law and development, responses to terrorism, and above all the strategic uses of law for ameliorating the situation of the worst off.[198]

Baxi describes his perspective on human rights as that of a comparative sociologist of law. Julius Stone, his main academic mentor, was a student of the sociological jurist, Roscoe Pound. Baxi embraced the sociological perspective, but as a follower of Gandhi and Marx (later Gramsci), and an active participant in protests at Berkeley from 1964 to 1967,[199] he gave the ideas of Pound and

---

[197] Upendra Baxi, *Mass Torts, Multinational Enterprise Liability and Private International Law* (2000b) (*Mass Torts*).

[198] Baxi has written a great deal about the uses and limitations of law in furthering the interests of the worst off, but his views on human rights extend beyond law to include ideas, discourse, and praxis.

[199] In one communication Baxi wrote to this author:

It was 'heaven to be alive' those days! To go to the Greek Amphitheater adjoining the International Student House and to hear Joan Baez singing protest melodies. To read the classic text *Soul on Ice*, the first to utter the now heavily jargonised phrase: 'When confronted with a logical impossibility, you have the choice to be part of the problem or part of the solution.' Before Berkeley, I never marched with the processions carrying placards.

'Radicalization' occurred on a wholly different learning curve as well as when I attended … Professor David Daube's seminars on the notion of impossibility in Roman and Greek law! Professor Daube's charismatic problematic of course was the situation when a horse was sworn in as a Roman Senator! … David taught me memorably – long before the Derridean/ postmodernist vogue – the ways in which the law makes the impossible possible.

Stone a distinctly radical twist. Stone called him a 'Marxist natural lawyer';[200] others have pointed to his lengthy engagement with postmodernism. But such labels do not fit him. Marxism proved too rigid and doctrinaire,[201] and post-modernism is too irresponsible to be of much use to a practical political agenda.[202] Neither quite fits his not uncritical sympathy for the ideas of Amartya Sen and Martha Nussbaum.[203] Above all, Baxi's concern has been for those whom, following Gramsci, he calls 'subaltern peoples'. Perhaps more than any other scholarly writer on human rights he consistently adopts the point of view of the poor and the oppressed.

Since the early 1990s most of Baxi's work has concerned human rights. Much of what he writes is critical of discourses of human rights, the complexities and compromises involved, and the misuses to which the discourses have been put. The tone is passionate, polemical, and radical, but the style is learned, allusive, and quite abstract.[204] Some of the distinctions that he emphasises have occasioned puzzlement: for example, the distinction between the politics *of* human rights and politics *for* human rights,[205] between human rights movements, human rights markets, and market-friendly human rights,[206] between justified and unjustifiable human suffering,[207] and between 'modern' and 'contemporary' human rights[208] – all of which will need explication. While much of his argument is complex, dialectical, and often ironic, one clear message rings out: taking human rights seriously must involve taking human suffering seriously.

At first sight, Baxi seems deeply ambivalent about rights: he is a fervent supporter of universal human rights, yet he is sharply critical of much of the talk and practice associated with it, and he emphasises many of the obstacles and threats to the realisation of their potential. Much of his account relates 'to the narratives of unrealised and even unattainable human rights'.[209] Rather than

---

[200] Upendra Baxi, 'From Human Rights to Human Flourishing: Julius Stone, Amartya Sen, and Beyond?' (Julius Stone Lecture, University of Sydney, 2001) (Baxi 2007c) (Stone Lecture), parts of which are included in revised form as chapter 2 of *Posthuman* (2007a) with the title 'Amartya Sen and Human Rights'.

[201] While there is a distinct Marxian strain in Baxi's thought, especially through Gramsci, he has been as critical of Soviet ideology and praxis as of free market capitalism: 'Both the triumphal eras of bourgeois human rights formations and of revolutionary socialism of Marxian imagination marshalled this narrative hegemony for remarkably sustained practices of the politics of cruelty.' *Future of Human Rights* at pp. xiv, 35, 137–8. Anyway, Baxi is far too eclectic intellectually to be categorised as a Marxist.

[202] *Ibid.* at pp. 78–80, 97–100.   [203] Baxi (2007c); also Baxi and Koenig, (2006) at p. 50.

[204] He moves smoothly from his Indian intellectual heritage (Gandhi, Ambedkar, the Supreme Court of India) to Western (especially Anglo-American) jurisprudence (he has written about Bentham, Kelsen, Rawls, Dworkin, and Stone), through Marxian theory (Marx, Gramsci, Benjamin) and Natural Law (Aquinas, Gewirth), drawing on contemporary sociology (e.g. Beck, Bourdieu, and Castells) and Continental European philosophy (Foucault, Derrida, Laclau, Levinas), engaging with but distancing himself from post-modernism (especially Rorty) and critical legal studies, and dealing more sympathetically with Nussbaum and Sen.

[205] E.g., *Future of Human Rights* at pp. x–xi, 13–14, 42–4 *et passim*.

[206] E.g. *ibid.* at pp. vi, 121–31.   [207] *Ibid.* at pp. 27–8.   [208] *Ibid.* at pp. 17–18.

[209] *Ibid.* at p. xii.

accept this as ambivalence, he recalls Gramsci's distinction between pessimism of the intellect and optimism of the will.[210] Although he writes about human rights futures, Baxi is more concerned with struggle than with prediction.

In the writings that we have already considered, Francis Deng, Abdullahi An-Na'im, and Yash Ghai use the international human rights regime as their starting point. As lawyers, they are aware that this regime is changing, dynamic, complex, and open to competing interpretations. However, they treat it and especially the Universal Declaration of Human Rights as being sufficiently stable and clear to provide standards for appraising and giving direction to other normative orders.[211] Like them, Upendra Baxi opposes all forms of imperialism, colonialism, racism, and patriarchy. He steers a subtle path between universalism and relativism.[212] He agrees that humankind as a whole should be the subject of our moral concern. He treats the Universal Declaration as one high point of the development of the current human rights regime, but he sees that regime as being inherently fragile and problematic. And his general tone and positions are more radical than the other three.

Like Ghai, Baxi's initial attitude to human rights is pragmatic: we need to work within human rights discourse not because it clearly embodies universal moral principles,[213] but because in the second half of the twentieth century it became the dominant mode of moral discourse in international relations, edging out other moral tropes such as distributive justice or 'solidarity'.[214] Just because they have become so dominant, the discourses of human rights have been used to support a wide variety of often incompatible interests, and this in turn has led to complexity, compromise, contradiction, and obfuscation

[210] In writing about attempts to develop 'enlightened' policies for the construction of major dams, rather than ceasing their construction as inevitably involving major human rights violations, Baxi comments: 'Human rights violations urge us to, however, profess pessimism of will and the optimism of intellect. We need to hunt and haunt all erudite discourses that seek to over-rationalize development. We need to defend and protect people suffering everywhere who refuse to accept that the power of a few should become the destiny of millions.' Upendra Baxi, 'What Happens Next Is Up to You: Human Rights at Risk in Dams and Development' (2001b) at p. 1529.

[211] For Baxi's criticisms of Ghai in the 2000 *Cardozo Law Review* symposium on the theme of 'Universal Rights and Cultural Pluralism' see n. 215 below.

[212] Chapter 6 of *Future of Human Right*s is entitled 'What is Living and Dead in Relativism?'

[213] Baxi makes interesting points that I cannot pursue here about the intellectual history of who counts as 'human' (*Future of Human Rights, ibid.* at pp. 28–9), the Hegelian idea of concrete universality – what it is to be fully human (*ibid.* at pp. 92–7), and the implications of biotechnology for ideas of 'human dignity' (*ibid.* at pp. 161–3). Baxi distances himself from strong relativist positions, while acknowledging that post-modernists and anti-foundationalists have usefully problematised ideas of universality (e.g. *ibid.* at pp. 97–118). (Compare Ghai at p. 413 above and accompanying text.) Baxi concludes: 'The universality of human rights symbolizes *the universality of the collective human aspiration to make power increasingly accountable, governance progressively just, and the state incrementally more ethical.' Ibid.* at p. 105 (emphasis in original).

[214] Like me, Baxi does not think that human rights discourse can adequately capture the concerns of distributive justice; unlike me he is surprisingly kind to John Rawls' much-criticised *The Law of Peoples* (1999). See GLT, pp. 69–75 and Chapter 5.5 above.

in both the discourse and the practices of human rights. More than Ghai, Baxi consistently adopts the standpoint of the worst off.[215]

Baxi presents the international human rights scene as fragile, contradictory, and riddled with myths, false histories, and ambiguities. It is marked by frenetic activity, explosive articulation of human rights standards and norms, and varied critiques and scepticisms about this dominant discourse. Global capitalism, new technologies, and both global terrorism and post-9/11 responses to 'terrorism' ('terrorism wars')[216] further threaten the fragile, contingent advances made by human rights movements. Small wonder then that there is a crisis of confidence even among the most committed and 'progressive' activists and NGOs:

> The astonishing quantity of human rights production generates various experiences of scepticism and faith. Some complain of exhaustion (what I call 'rights-weariness'). Some suspect sinister imperialism in diplomatic maneuvers animating each and every human rights enunciation (what I call 'rights-wariness'). Some celebrate human rights as a new global civic religion which, given a community of faith, will address and solve all major human problems (what I call 'human rights evangelism'). Their fervor is often matched by those NGOs that tirelessly pursue the removal of brackets in pre-final diplomatic negotiating texts of various United Nations' summits as triumphs in human solidarity (what I call 'human rights romanticism'). Some other activists believe that viable human rights standards can best be produced by exploiting contingencies of international diplomacy (what I call 'bureaucratization of human rights'). And still others (like me) insist that the real birthplaces of human rights are far removed from the ornate rooms of diplomatic conferences and are found, rather, in the actual sites (acts and feats) of resistance and struggle (what I call 'critical human rights realism').[217]

---

[215] In a comment on Ghai's 'Universalism', Baxi criticises Ghai from a 'subaltern perspective on constitutionalism', for too readily treating international standards as the starting-points for modern constitutionalism ('Constitutionalism' at pp. 1190–1), for masking the suffering involved in human rights struggles, for 'a wholly utilitarian construction of rights,' (*ibid.* at p. 1191) and for accepting too readily the views of political elites at the expense of ordinary people (*ibid.* at pp. 1208–10). Some of this criticism is, in my view, unduly harsh. The sharp tone may have spilled over from his criticism, in the same symposium, of Kenneth Karst (2000) for painting an idealised picture of American constitutional history without mentioning slavery.

[216] This theme is developed at length in Baxi, and the (2005) ('Two 'Wars''). See also 'Human Rights in Times of Terror' Posthuman (2007) Chapter 5.

[217] 'Voices of Suffering' at p. 116 (footnotes omitted). A longer version adds: 'Some activists celebrate virtues of dialogue among the communities of perpetrators and those violated (what I term human rights *dialogism*).' *Future of Human Rights* at p. 51. Baxi is sympathetic to 'moderate forms of dialogism' (*ibid.* at pp. 58–9), exemplified by truth and reconciliation commissions and the writings of Abdullahi An-Na'im, but warns that dialogue with the worst kinds of perpetrators of violations may delegitimate the idea of human rights in the eyes of the violated (*ibid.* at p. 60). For example, 'The idea that a handful of NGOs can dialogue with a handful of CEOs of multinationals to produce implementation of human rights is simply Quixotic.' *Ibid.* at p. 58. See also Baxi's more pragmatic approach to the UN's proposed Norms on Human Rights Responsibilities of Transnationals and Other Business Corporations in 'Market Fundamentalisms: Business Ethics at the Altar of Human Rights' (2005a) ('Market Fundamentalisms') (arguing for a pragmatic negotiated compromise between the competing ideologies of business and international regulation).

(b) The future(s) of human rights

The Future of Human Rights contains the most comprehensive statement of Baxi's views on human rights.[218] Since 1990, Baxi has published at least four books and many articles on the subject. More are in the pipeline. Nevertheless, the core of his thinking is quite stable. Perhaps it can be rendered in four parts: first, the starting point is a concern for and a quite complex idea of human suffering as it is actually experienced anywhere, but especially in the South; second, a comprehensive assessment, often sharply critical, of the past history and current state of human rights discourse, theory, and praxis; third, an aspirational vision of a just world in which all human beings know and genuinely own human rights as resources that can empower vulnerable communities and individuals to interpret their own situations, to resist human rights violations, and to participate in genuine dialogues about alternate and competing visions for a better future in a world that will continue to be pluralistic, ever changing, and possessed of finite resources to meet infinite human wants;[219] and, finally, pragmatic suggestions about possible strategies and tactics in the perpetual struggle to move realistically towards realising this vision (the politics *for* human rights).

Baxi's aim in *The Future of Human Rights* is 'to decipher the future of protean forms of social action assembled by convention, under a portal named "human rights". It problematises the very notion of "human rights", the standard narratives of their origins, the ensemble of ideologies animating their modes of production, and the wayward circumstances of their enunciation.'[220]

In short, his objective is to mount a sustained and complex critique of much of the discourse and many of the practices that surround human rights at the start of the twenty-first century and to present a vision, rooted in experiences of suffering, that can serve as a secular equivalent of liberation theology.[221] For Baxi, such a vision – 'critical human rights realism' – should become part of the symbolic capital of the poor and the dispossessed to be used as a resource in their struggles for a decent life.

---

[218] This account is based on the first edition of *Future of Human Rights* (2002). In the new edition, Baxi develops these ideas at greater length, and often more concretely in lectures, speeches, articles, and pamphlets scattered around websites, learned journals, and activist magazines that are spread widely both geographically and intellectually. Some take the form of detailed commentaries on particular reports or draft texts. Among the most substantial of these are ' "A Work in Progress?": The United States Report to the United Nations Human Rights Committee' (1996a) at p. 34; ' "Global Neighbourhood" and the "Universal Otherhood": Notes on the Report of the Commission on Global Governance' (1996b) (review essay on the *Brandt Report* (1995)); comment on the UN Draft Code of Conduct of Transnational Corporations and Businesses (2003a) ('Market Fundamentalisms,' *ibid.*). *Posthuman* (2007), as the title implies, explores the implications of technology, including biotechnotology, digitalisation, neurobiology, robotics, and nanotechnology for theorising about human rights.

[219] This formulation is constructed from several passages in Baxi (2006b) and Baxi and Koenig (2006).

[220] *Future of Human Rights* at p. v.   [221] Baxi & Koenig, *Human Rights Education*.

Baxi claims that *The Future of Human Rights* advances a distinctive 'subaltern' activist perspective on human rights futures.[222] His central theme is that human rights discourse only has value if it fulfils the axiom 'that the historic mission of contemporary human rights is to give voice to human suffering, to make it visible and to ameliorate it'.

Baxi considers this task to be formidable. The second half of the twentieth century has been called 'the Age of Rights',[223] and discourses of human rights have been said to be 'the common language of humanity',[224] yet what difference in fact have human rights made to human suffering?[225] 'The number of rightless people grow even as human rights norms and standards proliferate'.[226]

The Future of Human Rights is diffuse, polemical, and difficult to summarise. Perhaps the main themes can be succinctly stated largely in Baxi's own words as follows:[227]

- Human rights discourse is fraught with haunting ambiguities, complexity, and contradiction.[228] It is intensely partisan and cannot be reduced to a single coherent set of ideas. A crucial distinction is between the statist discourses of the powerful and educated (*illustrado*) and the subversive discourses of the violated (indigenous/*indio*).[229]
- Taking rights seriously must involve *taking human suffering seriously*.
- *Suffering is ubiquitous*; it can be both creative and destructive of human potential. It is not confined to poor or undemocratic countries.
- *How suffering is justified* must be a central concern of human rights discourse. Historically, human rights discourse has been used to legitimate state power, colonialism, imperialism, and patriarchy in various forms, and to exclude large sectors of humanity from moral concern.[230] Conversely, successful human rights movements create new forms of justifiable suffering.[231]
- *The true authors of rights* are communities in struggle, not Western thinkers or modern states.[232] Linking human rights to experienced human suffering is

---

[222] *Future of Human Rights* at p. xiii.   [223] *Ibid.* at c. 1.

[224] Boutros Boutros Ghali, 'Human Rights. The Common Language of Humanity' in UN World Conference on Human Rights, the Vienna Declaration and the Programme for Action (1993), cited in 'Voices of Suffering' at p. 101.

[225] See also 'Voices of Suffering' at p. 102: 'But politics of cruelty continue even as sonorous declarations of human rights proliferate.'

[226] *Future of Human Rights supra* at p. viii.

[227] This outline is based on *Future of Human Rights*, 'Voices of Suffering', and a talk given by Baxi at the University of Essex in May 2003.

[228] In *Future of Human Rights* at p. 14, Baxi focuses mainly on human rights discourses, but he insists that '[t]he non-discursive order of reality, the materiality of human violation, is just as important, if not more so, from the standpoint of the violated.'

[229] *Ibid.*   [230] See text at nn. 257–60 below.

[231] 'Gender equality makes patriarchs suffer. The overthrow of apartheid in the United States made many a white supremacist suffer. ... People in high places suffer when movements against corruption gain a modicum of success.' *Future of Human Rights* at p. 17.

[232] A vivid example of this thesis is Linebaugh and Rediker, (2000), which argues that freed slaves were among the main originators of Western human rights ideas.

the best hope of ensuring that human rights discourse: (i) is not hijacked by a trade-related, market-friendly paradigm of human rights,[233] (ii) is not obfuscated by the politics *of* human rights (e.g. competition between NGOs) rather than political struggles *for* human rights,[234] and (iii) is not dominated by the complacent discourse of the powerful.[235]

- Modern human rights discourse is secular. It has severed the connection between human rights discourses and religious cosmologies.[236] This involves a radical acceptance of human finitude (no life after life/death); justifications are only of this world; it problematises custom and tradition; and creates a secular civic religion, a community of faith.[237]
- The contemporary production of human rights is exuberant (even 'carnivalistic'), producing a riot of perceptions. Clearly there are too many 'soft' human rights enunciations, but very few 'hard' enforceable rights.[238] To some, human rights inflation is a threat; others point to the glacial progress made in the direction of 'hard', enforceable human rights norms; yet others read the uncontrolled production of human rights as, perhaps, the best hope for a participative creation of human futures; attempts by the UN or other agencies to control the rate of production are likely to favour the rights of global capital.
- Increasingly, human rights movements and NGOs 'organize themselves in the image of markets',[239] competing with each other (in fundraising, advertising, building capital) like entrepreneurs in a spirit of nervous 'investor rationality'[240] and being forced into the trap of commodifying human rights.[241]
- Economic 'globalisation' threatens to supplant the ideals of the Universal Declaration of Human Rights with a trade-related, market-friendly paradigm, which emphasises the right to property, the rights of investors, and even the rights of corporations (sidelining the poor to feed off the drips from the alleged trickle-down effects of capitalist prosperity).[242]

---

[233] *Future of Human Rights* at p. 8; see also Baxi's satirical Draft Charter of the Human Rights of Global Capital. *Ibid.* at pp. 149–51. Compare the more pragmatic tone of 'Two Wars'.

[234] The former serves the ends of *Realpolitik*, with 'the latter seeking to combat modes of governance (national, regional, or global) that command the power to cause unjustifiable human suffering and impose orders of radical evil.' *Future of Human Rights* at pp. ix, 40–1.

[235] To the powerful, the World Food Summit goal of halving the number of starving people by 2015 appears ambitious, even unrealistic; to the poor it appears remote and 'rather callous'. *Ibid.* at p. vii. Baxi regularly contrasts the glacial pace of response to the *misfortune* of poverty and hunger with the urgency for pursuing the war on terrorism after the *injustice* of 9/11.

[236] '[H]uman rights education symbolizes a secular, or multi-religious equivalent of "liberation theology"'. *Human Rights Education* at p. 18.

[237] *Future of Human Rights* at p. 14.   [238] *Ibid.* at p. 71.

[239] 'Voices of Suffering' at p. 144; *Future of Human Rights* at p. 121.

[240] 'Voices of Suffering' at p. 145.   [241] *Future of Human Rights* at p. 8.

[242] *Ibid.* at pp. 125–9. Committed supporters of human rights have objected to this economic analogy. Baxi concedes (*ibid.* at p. 121) that non-governmental human rights praxis can be interpreted analytically in terms of both social movements and 'quasi markets', but he maintains that the comfortable language of 'networks' and 'associational governance' glosses over the contradictions and complexity of human rights movements.

- Postmodernism, ethical and cultural relativism, and sceptical critiques of rights discourse draw attention to some genuine difficulties, but they fail to provide constructive strategies for action to alleviate suffering and, however well-intentioned, they make possible toleration of vast stretches of human suffering.[243]
- The politics of difference and identity views human rights as having not just an emancipative potential but also a repressive one.[244]
- Globalisation and the development of techno-scientific modes of production threaten to make contemporary human rights discourse obsolescent.[245]
- Rights have several different uses as symbolic resources in politics *for* human rights: (i) as markers of policies – testing whether policy enunciations recognise, respect, or affirm human rights; (ii) as constraints on policy implementation (self-conscious restraint and positive disincentives); (iii) as resources for policy – processes and structures of policy implementation legitimated by reference to specific human rights regimes; (iv) as providing access to effective legal redress; and (v) as resources for collective action (e.g. to mobilise discontent with policy or its implementation).[246]

Each of these themes is developed in *The Future of Human Rights*, some of them at greater length and more concretely in other works. Rather than attempt a comprehensive exposition, I shall focus on a topic that is pivotal in Baxi's argument and among his more original contributions: different conceptions of the history of human rights.

(c) Two paradigms of human rights in history: 'the modern' and 'the contemporary'

A standard account of the history of human rights is presented in terms of 'generations':[247] The first phase in response to the Holocaust and the horrors of

---

[243] See n. 204 above.

[244] 'Voices of Suffering' at p. 103. This is the converse of Santos's argument that, even though law is often repressive, it has the potential to be emancipatory. (Santos (1995) Chapter 9, (2005) Chapter 9.) The difference is mainly one of emphasis.

[245] *Future of Human Rights* at p. 156. This means that the increasing dominance of science and technology, as a mode of production and as an ideology that presents itself as progressive, 'threatens us all with the prospect of rendering human rights language *obsolescent*' (e.g. in civilian use of nuclear energy, expanding information technology, and development of new biotechnologies). *Ibid.* (emphasis in original). See now *Posthuman* (2007).

[246] This formulation is a paraphrase of a passage on 'the place of rights' in policy making and implementation. Although written specifically in the context of a discussion of population policies in India, it has a broader significance. Upendra Baxi, 'Sense and Sensibility' (2002) at p. 511 *Seminar*, online: www.india-seminar.com/semframe.htm ('Sense and Sensibility'). In respect of international law, Baxi emphasises that the strategic aims should include enforcing positive law, expanding the range and refining the content of *ius cogens*, and moving beyond positive law to address the processes of norm formulation and using the discourse of rights to 'write against the law' ('that is [using] subversive forms of story telling against totalizing narratives of human rights') Baxi & Koenig, *Human Rights Education* (2006) at pp. 15–18.

[247] E.g., *Put Our World to Rights* at pp. 34–5. Ghai would clearly agree that it is a simplification.

World War II was marked by a preoccupation with civil and political rights. The second generation was represented by the International Covenant on Economic, Social and Cultural Rights (ICESCR).[248] The third phase marked a move from emphasis on individual rights to recognition of collective rights, including concern for the environment ('green rights') in tension with 'the right to development'. A fourth phase involved a progressive recognition of the rights of peoples. While talk of 'generations' of international human rights has sometimes been a convenient simplifying device, most commentators distance themselves from this taxonomy. At best it can describe one phase of international law. It is generally accepted that such 'history' is too crude. For example, the Universal Declaration of Human Rights, which is the starting point of modern development, covered economic and social rights as well as civil and political – but these became split in the period of the Cold War. Today, most orthodox commentators at least pay lip service to the claim that human rights are universal, interdependent, and indivisible.[249]

Upendra Baxi advances a more fundamental critique of such 'history'. In his view, it represents a complacent, patronising, Euro-centric or rather 'Northern-centric', top-down view of the sources of human rights, suggesting that rights are 'the gifts of the West to the Rest'.[250] It entirely overlooks the contribution of struggles by the poor and the oppressed to the slow recognition of human rights as universal.[251]

To make sense of human rights, Baxi argues, one must see the basic ideas not as emanating from Christian natural law or the liberal Enlightenment or the reactions of Western governments to the horrors of World War II. The main context of the production of human rights has been local communities in struggle against the diverse sources of suffering; the main impetus has been direct experience of suffering; the main authors have been those involved in grass-roots struggles[252] – some having become well-known, while the great majority have been unsung:

---

[248] G.A. res. 2200A (XXI), 21 U.N.GAOR Supp. (No. 16) at 49, UNDocA/6316 (1966), 993 UNTS3, *entered into force* Jan. 3, 1976, online: Office of the United Nations High Commission for Human Rights www.ohchr.org/english/law/cescr.htm.

[249] See, for example, the skilful way in which H. Steiner and P. Alston, in *International Human Rights in Context: Law, Politics, Morals* (Oxford: Clarendon Press, 1996) – the leading student course book on international human rights – bring out the complexity of the story, first by acknowledging that most development of human rights issues has been local (at pp. 24–5), and second by identifying the different sources out of which the current international regime developed: 'It would be possible to study human rights issues not at the international level but in the detailed contexts of different states' histories, socio-economic and political structures, legal systems, cultures, religions and so on' (*ibid.* at p. 24). See now Steiner and Alston (2008) Chapter 2. Baxi might criticise this as too top-down or state-centric, underplaying the significance of social movements, but he would no doubt concede that the state would still be a major player in any history written from below.

[250] *Future of Human Rights* at p. vi.   [251] See Linebaugh and Rediker (2000).

[252] 'Almost every global institutionalisation of human rights has been preceded by grassroots activism.' 'Voices of Suffering' at p. 124.

After all it was a man called Lokmanya Tilak who in the second decade of this century gave a call to India: *swaraj (independence) is my birthright and I shall have it,* long before international human rights proclaimed a right to self-determination. It was a man called Gandhi who challenged early this century racial discrimination in South Africa, which laid several decades later the foundation for international treaties and declarations on the elimination of all forms of racial discrimination and apartheid. Compared to these male figures, generations of legendary women martyred themselves in prolonged struggles against patriarchy and gender inequality. The current campaign based on the motto 'Women's Rights *Are* Human Rights' is inspired by a massive history of local struggles all around.[253]

Even within the Eurocentric perspective, narratives articulated in terms of 'generations' of rights radically foreshorten history in ways that hide the fragmented ideas that preceded the *Universal Declaration*. For example, human rights doctrine *preceded* abolition and often condoned slavery. The right to property and the right to govern were used to justify various forms of colonialism and imperialism. Only very recently in the long history of rights talk has there been reason to celebrate the maxim that 'Women's Rights are Human Rights', but this does not mark the beginning or the end of women's struggle for equality.[254]

Instead of a linear history, Baxi substitutes two contrasting 'paradigms' (or ideal types) of conceptions of human rights, both of which mask the continuities in the historiography of these two forms: the modern (or modernist) paradigm[255] and the 'contemporary' paradigm:

> The distinction between 'modern' and 'contemporary' forms of human rights is focused on *taking suffering seriously.* In the 'modern' human rights paradigm it was thought possible to take human rights seriously without taking human suffering seriously. Outside the domain of the laws of war among and between 'civilized' nations, 'modern' human rights regarded large-scale imposition of human suffering as *just* and *right* in pursuit of a Eurocentric notion of *human 'progress'.* That discourse silenced human suffering. In contrast, the 'contemporary' human rights

---

[253] Uprendra Baxi, 'The Reason of Human Rights and the Unreason of Globalization' (A.R. Desai Memorial Lecture, Bombay, 1996), cited in *ibid.* at pp. 124–5.; see also *Posthuman* (2007) pp. 97–103.

[254] Like Deng, An-Na'im, and Ghai, Baxi is unequivocal in his assertions that women's rights are human rights. He sees the phrase 'the rights of man' as an example of the logic of exclusion in human rights discourse; and he is cautious of the rhetoric of some claims about progress (e.g. 'The near-universality of ratification of the CEDAW, for example, betokens no human liberation of women; it only endows the state with the power to tell more Nietzschean lies.' *Future of Human Rights* at p. 87). He is a friendly critic of the feminist movement in India: *Memory and Rightlessness* (15th J.P. Naik Memorial Lecture, New Delhi: Centre for Women's Development Studies, 2003); see also, 'Gender and Reproductive Rights in India: Problems and Prospects for the New Millennium' (Lecture delivered for the UN Population Fund, New Delhi, 2000).

[255] *Future of Human Rights* at pp. 27–8. Baxi's labels can be confusing. 'Modern' here refers to modernity with its associations with the Enlightenment, liberalism, and rationality; 'contemporary' is associated with, but deliberately distanced from, post-modernism. This distinction seems to me to be quite close to Santos's contrast between 'regulatory' (modern) and 'emancipatory' forms of law (Santos (1995) Chapter 9 (2002) Chapters 1, 2, and 9.

paradigm is animated by a politics of activist desire to render problematic the very *notion of politics of cruelty.*[256]

This passage needs some unpacking. Baxi presents the two paradigms in terms of four main contrasts:

Modern	Contemporary
1. Logics of exclusion	1. Inclusiveness
2. Right to govern	2. Radical self-determination
3. Ascetic (a thin conception of rights)	3. Exuberant (proliferation of rights)
4. Rhetoric of ' progress'	4. Voices of suffering

First, while the 'contemporary' paradigm is inclusive, the 'modern' paradigm for most of its history interpreted 'human' to exclude all those who were not to be regarded as human by virtue of having the capacity to reason and an autonomous moral will: 'In its major phases of development, "slaves", "heathens", "barbarians", colonised peoples, indigenous populations, women, children, the impoverished, and the "insane" have been, at various times and in various ways, thought unworthy of being bearers of human rights... These discursive devices of Enlightenment rationality were devices of *exclusion*. The "Rights of Man" were human rights of all men capable of autonomous reason and will.'[257]

Baxi is cautious about universalism in relation to claims that there are moral principles that are valid for all times and all places, but he emphasises the enormous normative significance of the inclusive claim that human rights apply to all human beings by virtue of their humanity.[258]

Second, the logic of exclusion led to the justification of colonialism. The language of 'modern' human rights was often used to justify colonialism, imperialism, and patriarchy through the right of property (especially occupation of 'terra nullius' – ignoring the presence of indigenous people) and 'a natural collective human right of the superior races to rule the inferior ones'.[259] In contrast, the contemporary human rights paradigm is based on the premise of radical self-determination, insisting that every human person 'has a right to a voice, a right to bear witness to violation, a right to immunity from disarticulation by concentrations of economic, social, and political formations. Rights

---

[256] *Future of Human Rights, ibid.* at pp. 34–5; 'Voices of Suffering' at p. 114.

[257] 'Voices of Suffering' at pp. 109–10; *Future of Human Rights* at p. 29.

[258] All human beings are included, but it is 'an anthropomorphic illusion that the range of human rights is limited to human beings; the new rights to a clean and healthy environment ... take us far beyond such a narrow notion.' 'Voices of Suffering' at pp. 104–105.

[259] *Ibid.* at p. 110. See also *Future of Human Rights* at pp. 29–30. 'The construction of a collective right to colonial/imperial governance is made sensible by the co-optation of languages of human rights into those of *racist* governance abroad and *class* and *patriarchal* domination at home.' *Ibid.* at p. 31.

languages, no longer so exclusively at the service of the ends of governance, open up sites of resistance'.[260]

Third, 'modern' human rights are state-centric and ascetic, treating the state as the only legitimate source of rights and limiting their scope.[261] The sources of 'contemporary' human rights are ebullient, leading to 'a carnival of production', though this in turn creates problems. They extend not only to discrete minorities but also to 'wholly new, hitherto unthought of, justice constituencies':[262] 'Contemporary enunciations thus embrace, to mention very different orders of example, the rights of the girl child, migrant labour, indigenous peoples, gays and lesbians (the emerging human right to sexual orientation), prisoners and those in custodial institutional regimes, refugees and asylum seekers, and children'.[263]

Fourth, the 'modern' human rights cultures traced their pedigree to ideas of progress, social Darwinism, racism, and patriarchy. They used these ideas to justify 'global imposition of cruelty as "natural", "ethical", and "just"'.[264] Because of the exclusionary logic, the suffering of large numbers of 'sub-human' peoples were rendered invisible. By contrast, especially in the wake of the revulsion occasioned by the Holocaust and Hiroshima/Nagasaki, '"contemporary" human rights discursivity is rooted in the illegitimacy of all forms of politics of cruelty'.[265] The ensuing regime of international human rights and humanitarian law outlawed some barbaric practices of state power and 'this was no small gain' from the standpoint of those violated.[266]

Baxi presents the 'modern' as state-centric, top-down, technocratic, exclusionary, lean and mean, and used by those in power to legitimate their position and their actions; he presents the 'contemporary' as bottom-up, rooted in experience of suffering, ebullient, and involving radical self-determination, with human rights serving as a weapon of protest and empowerment of the dispossessed. These two paradigms are not meant to represent successive stages in history; rather they are two ideal types of conceptions of human rights that have been used discursively, sometimes concurrently and sometimes sequentially, mainly in connection with state-oriented Western discourses.

---

[260] *Ibid.*

[261] For instance, in the conventional discourse, torture, cruel, inhuman, and degrading treatment are classified as violations of human rights, but starvation and domestic violence are not. *Ibid.* at p. 13, n. 21.

[262] *Ibid.* at p. 32.   [263] *Ibid.*; 'Voices of Suffering' at p. 112.

[264] *Future of Human Rights* at p. 32. Baxi also uses this idea to attack technocratic justifications of dams and population control in the name of 'progress'. For example: 'Policy-makers as well as human science specialists are not persuaded, on available evidence, by the rights approach. The reasons for this "benign neglect" of rights vary. Malthusians and neo-Malthusians are wary of a rights approach, in general, because they perceive "over-population" as a social scandal and menace; the hard core among them are not perturbed by excesses in "family planning" programmes and measures implementing these. In their view, "man"-made policy disasters are as welcome as "natural" disasters that in net effect reduce population levels.' Some argue that reduction in population levels may serve better futures for human rights. 'Sense and Sensibility'.

[265] *Future of Human Rights* at p. 33.   [266] *Ibid.* at p. 34.

Baxi suggests that an adequate account of the future(s) of human rights requires a developed social theory of human rights, as well as a re-imagined history. At present we lack both. Baxi has been a leading pioneer of socio-legal studies in India, although it is fair to say that he has no more than hinted at what such a social theory might be like.[267] But he has sketched a general approach to the kind of history needed to underpin his vision of a healthy future for human rights. Clearly such history would need to be based on the kind of detailed 'history from below' exemplified by Edward Thompson, Peter Linebaugh, or George Rudé,[268] as well as the kind of sardonic work on official archives of a Brian Simpson.[269] But it would also need the grand sweep of world history that one associates with Eric Hobsbawm, Immanuel Wallerstein, or Patrick Glenn.[270] Baxi does not claim to have written a history of human rights, but he has made a devastating critique of the predominant mode of complacent, self-congratulatory narratives that dominate much human rights literature.

(d) Conclusion

Baxi characterises human rights discourse as ebullient, even carnivalistic. These adjectives might be applied to his own writings on human rights. The bibliography illustrates his energy and passion as well as the breadth of his interests. Recently he has written extensively on the subject. He has produced a substantially revised edition of *The Future of Human Rights* and no doubt more lectures, speeches, and articles. He has written specifically on population control, bio-technology, international business ethics, environmental issues, globalisation, terrorism and responses to terrorism, and good governance – all in relation to human rights. There are recent essays on the right to food and the right to development. In short, he is a prolific writer who presents a continuously moving target. Some of his most colourful passages are found in quite particular studies. Nevertheless, they are given coherence by a single theme:

---

[267] 'By a social theory of human rights I wish to designate bodies of knowledge that address (a) genealogies of human rights in "pre-modern", "modern" and "contemporary" human rights discursive formations; (b) contemporary dominant and subaltern images of human rights; (c) tasks confronting projects of engendering human rights; (d) exploration of human rights movements as social movements; (e) impact of science and high-tech. on the theory and practice of human rights; (f) the problematic of the marketization of human rights; (g) the economics of human rights.' (*Future of Human Rights* at p. 32, n. 18). The whole of this book could be said to be a contribution to such a social theory in that it comments briefly on most aspects of this agenda, but mainly in a preliminary and very general way, with very little empirical basis or relationship to mainstream social theory. Baxi cites a number of general books by Santos, Unger, Shivji, and others that mark the 'beginnings' of such an enterprise, but he acknowledges that we are a long way from achieving the kind of 'grand theory' that he thinks is needed. *Ibid.*

[268] E.P. Thompson (1977) and (1963); Linebaugh and Rediker (2000); and Rudé (1959). See also Balakrishnan Rajagopal (2003) at pp. 1–2. Like Baxi, Rajagopal locates much of the history of human rights in resistance to colonialism.

[269] Simpson (2001).

[270] E.g., Eric Hobsbawm (1995) (3 vols.); Wallerstein (1979); and Glenn (2004). See also Benton (2002).

Human rights futures, dependent as they are upon imparting an authentic voice to human suffering, must engage in a discourse of suffering that moves the world.[271]

13.6 Four Southern voices

A just international order and a healthy cosmopolitan discipline of law need to include perspectives that take account of the standpoints, interests, concerns, and beliefs of non-Western people and traditions. The dominant scholarly and activist discourses about human rights have developed largely without reference to these other perspectives. Claims about universality sit uneasily with ignorance of other traditions and parochial or ethnocentric tendencies.

Writings about human rights from non-Western perspectives need to be better known in the West. The four individuals whose more general ideas on human rights are summarised here cannot be considered to be a representative sample of 'Southern' viewpoints on human rights; nor can they claim to be spokespersons for any group or people any more than can other public intellectuals. There are many other individuals and groups who deserve such attention. For instance, two Nobel Prize winners, Shirin Ebadi and Aung San Suu Kyi, might help to right the gender balance. There are other contemporary scholars from outside Europe who have written about human rights. Some, like Amartya Sen, Nelson Mandela, and Mr Justice Christie Weeramantry, are world famous. Others, such as Issa Shivji of Tanzania, several Latin America jurists, or the late Neelan Tiruchelvan of Sri Lanka, are well known in their own regions and in specialist circles. A later generation of scholars are also coming into prominence.[272] And there is an extensive literature on Islam, human rights, and law reform. But for my own ignorance and linguistic deprivation, these and many others could be added – especially if one goes back in time, to include for instance Mahatma Ghandi or B.R. Ambedkar.

I have selected these four mainly because I believe that their ideas deserve to be better known, many of their writings are accessible, and I am familiar with their work and know them personally. Each has made a distinctive contribution to both the theory and praxis of human rights. The works we have considered are accessible just because most of them are written in English by Western-trained scholars and are addressed mainly to Western academics and human rights activists. This makes these writings just one potential route to a broader perspective on human rights discourse and action.[273]

---

[271] 'Voices of Suffering' at p. 156.

[272] For example, Tariq Ramadan, Makau Mutua, Mahmood Mamdani, and Balakrishnan Rajagopal.

[273] There are, of course, anthologies and commentaries on the ideas of contemporary non-Western thinkers who are not jurists, (e.g. Cooper, Nestler and Mahmoud (eds.) (2000), Esposito and Voll (eds.) (2001), Kamrava (ed.) (2006). See also the writings of Tariq Ramadan, especially Ramadan (2004). For an interesting commentary on Muslim intellectuals in Europe, see Jenkins (2007) esp. Chapter 6.

These four thinkers are both significantly similar and strikingly different – in short, they are suitable objects for comparison. They belong to a single post-colonial generation (three were born, coincidentally, in 1938; An-Na'im is a decade younger, but started early).[274] All four have been concerned with the problems of racism, colonialism, post-Independence politics, weak and corrupt regimes, poverty, and injustice in the South. They have given expression to ideas that are rooted in these concerns without claiming to represent any particular constituency. All four were trained in the common law, have spent substantial periods in the United States and the United Kingdom, and write in English. They have been all been activists as well as scholars, but in quite varied ways. Each has a distinctive voice and says different things. They make a fascinating study in contrasts. But, although they differ, they do not disagree on most fundamentals; rather they complement each other.

In recent years their ideas seem to have converged in some significant ways. Two aspects of this deserve emphasis. First, all four are acutely aware that we live in a world characterised by a diversity of beliefs, both within and across national boundaries, and that this creates profound problems of co-existence and co-operation. None sees much prospect of papering over such differences. Francis Deng's writings evoke a cosmology and way of life that is beyond the experience and imagination of most of us. Much of Ghai's practice has been concerned with reaching constitutional settlements and handling conflicts in multi-ethnic societies in which civil strife and protection of minorities are acute problems. So far as I can tell, each of them would opt for what Patrick Glenn calls 'sustainable diversity'[275] rather than some bland homogenisation in which one size is made to fit all. All emphasise the significance of local particularities.

Secondly, the fact of pluralism (of beliefs, cultures, traditions) raises issues that are fashionably discussed in terms of universalism versus cultural relativism. My sense is that all four are impatient about such debates. Each steers a path between strong versions of universalism and particularism. In interpreting them, it is important to distinguish between four different meanings of universalism: (i) *formal universalisability*, as embodied in Kant's categorical imperative or the Golden Rule; (ii) *empirical universalism*, the position that human nature and systems of belief grounded in this nature are in their essentials universal or near-universal and that this can form the basis for an over-arching metaphysics of humanism (a view that has gone out of fashion in anthropology and most social sciences, which tend to emphasise the diversity, plasticity, and contingency of social cultures and belief systems, but that still finds some

---

[274] All four belong to the post-Independence generation of public intellectuals in their own country or region. India became independent in 1946, in Baxi's eighth year; the Sudan in 1956, when Deng and An-Na'im were still at school; Kenya became independent in 1963, the year that Ghai took up his first teaching post at Dar-es-Salaam, where Tanzania had attained Independence two years earlier. For each of them, local, regional, and international post-Independence politics formed a crucial part of the context of their intellectual development.

[275] Glenn (2004) at p. 10.

support in genetics, socio-biology, and more 'hard-wired' perspectives on the human psyche); (iii) *ethical universalism*, the position that there are universal moral principles, including principles underpinning human rights, that apply to all persons at all times and in all places; and (iv) *procedural universalism*, the hope that despite diversity of beliefs and conflicting interests, humankind can through reasonable dialogue and negotiation construct sufficient consensus to ground stable institutions and practices to sustain co-existence and co-operation.

On my interpretation, all four are very close to each other on these points. All appear to accept formal universalism and to reject strong empirical claims to universality of cultures and beliefs; in other words, they accept diversity of beliefs as a psychological and social fact. On ethical universalism, their positions are somewhat different: all four are politically committed to fighting for the basic values embodied in the Universal Declaration of Human Rights.[276] An-Na'im comes close to espousing a religion-based form of ethical universalism; Deng in all of his writings emphasises human dignity as a basic value, but seems to use international human rights documents as a consensual working premise rather than as embodying a single set of universal moral precepts; Ghai and Baxi pragmatically plugged into human rights discourse quite late in their careers, because it was so dominant in the spheres in which they operated. Ghai sees it as a historically contingent workable framework for negotiating constitutional and political settlements and developing constitutions through genuinely democratic constitutive processes, but he stresseses material interests rather than cultural differences as the main recurrent basis of conflict. Baxi also treats human rights as a form of discourse and underlines its potential for abuse and obfuscation, passionately arguing for it to be allowed to be the medium for expressing 'voices of suffering', especially in the half of the world that is deprived of food, water, health, education, and other necessities for a life worth living.[277]

All four reject strong cultural relativism. They respect cultural diversity and value tolerance, but this involves no commitment to 'tolerating the intolerable'. Each believes in the value of dialogue, but with different emphases: Deng, the diplomat, has always relied on persuasion and mediation; An-Na'im stresses the importance of internal dialogue; Ghai points to the value of human rights discourse as a framework for political negotiation and compromise between people with different interests, concerns, and ethnicities; Baxi, more pugnacious, sees dialogic human rights as the gentler part of struggle.

---

[276] None of them treats the fact of pluralism of beliefs as a ground for abdicating moral commitments or refusing to criticise particular cultural practices.

[277] One encouraging sign is that the United Nations Development Program (UNDP)'s social indicators embodied in the Millennium Goals appear to be a basis for a genuinely broad consensus about basic needs, if not about priorities or strategies for achieving them. See Chapter 11.4 above.

See United Nations Millennium Declaration, A/RES/55/2 (18 September 2000), online: www.un.org/millennium/declaration/ares552e.pdf; and United Nations Statistics Division, Millennium Development Goal Indicators Database, ST/ESA/STAT/MILLENNIUMINDICATORSDB/WWW (30 July 2005), online: www.millenniumindicators.un.org/unsd/mi/mi_goals.asp.

What of differences? One can point to differences in ethnicity,[278] mother tongue (English was for each of them a second or third language), attitudes to religion,[279] professional fields of specialisation,[280] the arenas in which they have been activists, and the historical events they have witnessed. By and large they have read different things.[281] In the present context, perhaps the main differences in their treatment of human rights are differences of concerns, emphasis, and style rather than any profound disagreements.[282]

It would be tempting to end by trying to compare and contrast these quite different perspectives on human rights with some familiar strands in Western liberal democratic theory.[283] There are indeed some interesting issues that could be pursued. But in the present context this would undermine my purpose, which is to point to one possible route out of the intellectual isolationism and parochialism of Western legal theory.

To sum up:

- For a case study of the relationship between an exotic traditional nomadic culture and the international human rights regime, read Francis Deng.
- If you wish to learn how a devout Muslim scholar has developed a strategy for reconciling Islamic beliefs with Western liberal democratic ideals, read Abdullahi An-Na'im.

---

[278] Ethnically Deng is Nilotic, An-Na'im is Northern Sudanese (Arab), Ghai is Kenyan Asian (Hindu), Baxi is Indian (also Hindu background).

[279] Each has somewhat different specialisms: Deng in ethnography, international relations, and diplomacy; An-Na'im in Islamic theology and public international law; Ghai in public law and constitutionalism (and to a lesser extent public international law); Baxi in Indian law, especially public law, and recently environmental protection and responses to terrorism. All converge under the umbrella of 'law and development'.

[280] An-Na'im is a committed Muslim. The others are generally secular and agnostic or even atheist.

[281] Ghai and Baxi are well read in both Marxist theory and Anglo-American jurisprudence; Deng and An-Na'im less so. Although some of An-Na'im's ideas seem to echo liberal thinkers such as Rawls (overlapping consensus, public reason), or Habermas (deliberative democracy, ideal speech situation), he denied having read them before he developed his own ideas (interview with author, see nn. 77 and 109 above.). None is an out-and-out postmodernist, but Baxi has flirted with postmodernism and is more familiar with modern Continental European ideas.

[282] Baxi's criticism of Ghai, and Ghai's exchange with An-Na'im about the role of judiciaries in protecting economic, social, and cultural rights, seem to me to involve relatively minor differences. Dembour (2006) puts forward a general taxonomy of schools of thought about human rights: the Natural School, the Deliberative School, the Protest School, and the Construction School (typified or inspired by Kant, Habermas, Levinas, and Derrida, respectively). It is fairly obvious that Baxi belongs to the Protest School, but how the others might fit this classification is open to debate (Dembour communication to the author, 29 March 2005).

[283] See, e.g. Rawls on 'overlapping consensus' and 'public reason'; Habermas's 'ideal speech situation' and 'the principle of universalization"; Lasswell, among others, 'values' and 'dignity', see n. 21 and Dworkin's ideas of 'equal concern and respect' for persons and 'rights as trumps' in *Taking Rights Seriously* (1977). An-Na'im (2008) at pp. 97–101 includes a section discussing Rawls and Habermas in relation to 'civic reason', 'public reason' and 'overlapping consensus'. He expresses reservations about applying concepts derived from Western experience directly to Islamic societies (see n. 109 above).

- If you are interested in a pragmatic, materialist argument about the practical value of using human rights discourse to reach political settlements and compromises in multi-ethnic or other conflicted societies, read Yash Ghai.
- And, if you are interested in an impassioned plea that human rights discourse should first and foremost be interpreted and used to further the interests of the worst off, read Upendra Baxi.

Chapter 14

Conclusion

At the risk of some repetition, this chapter draws together the main threads of the argument so far. The later chapters (published at www.) further concretise the general thesis. The purpose of this book is to explore the implications of globalisation for the discipline of law and for jurisprudence as its theoretical, or more abstract, part. The primary objective of the institutionalised discipline of law is understanding law (i.e. the main subject matters of the discipline). The scope and nature of these subject matters has long been contested with differing views falling into two internally varied camps: a narrow view that treats law as doctrine – rules, principles, concepts, and rule systems – and a more expansive view, which extends beyond doctrine to include social practices, institutions, processes, and personnel, as well as rules. This book adopts an expansive conception of our discipline and uses a broad conception of law as a form of institutionalised social practice as its organising concept. However, this in no way suggests that doctrine, concepts, and rules are unimportant. It recognises that law as ideas, which have not necessarily been institutionalised as social practices, is a central aspect of the concept of a legal tradition; that the precept 'for purposes of understanding law, the study of rules alone is not enough' applies as much to studies focused on doctrine (one version of 'law in context') as to broader studies that extend to actual practices and institutions.

Adopting an extensive conception of the subject matters of law as a discipline is not derived from nor dependent on a particular conception of law. But there is a connection. I have adopted a broad conception of law in this context because from a global perspective conceptions of law confined to state law leave out too many forms of normative ordering that require the attention of a reasonably inclusive cosmopolitan discipline – especially religious law, some forms of custom, important examples of institutionalised self-regulation, and various forms of 'soft law', such as *lex mercatoria* or non-binding declarations of rights. These forms of law may not have been salient in the domestic law of modern industrialised states, at least until recently, but they are important in more traditional societies, in the global South, and at the various levels of supranational and transnational ordering that are of increasing significance. Concepts such as 'non-state law', 'soft law', and 'religious law' are problematic and their elucidation is one of the many tasks for the analytical part of general jurisprudence.[1]

Jurisprudence, viewed as the theoretical or more abstract, part of law as a discipline has a number of tasks to perform to assist in the enterprise of advancing knowledge and understanding of law. These tasks include: construction and elucidation of concepts; synthesis; addressing fundamental philosophical issues ('high theory'); middle order theorising (conceptual, normative, empirical); constructing working theories; exploring connections with neighbouring disciplines; intellectual history; and critical examination of assumptions and presuppositions of particular sub-disciplines or specialisms (e.g. comparative law, human rights, diffusion) and of legal discourse generally. In the present context, the primary role of jurisprudence is to perform these tasks in assisting academic law and academic lawyers to adjust to the implications and demands of globalisation.

In this view, the relationship between theory and specialised scholarship is reflexive. One of the strengths of law as an institutionalised discipline is that it is continuously stimulated by, and has to be responsive to, events, problems, examples, and ideas from outside itself – from other disciplines and 'the real world'. For the most part, it does not create its own agenda or feed off its own questions and examples. It is to be expected that practice and specialised scholarship will often be in advance of theory, as is illustrated by recent trends and developments in many specialised fields of law in response to globalisation. Thus an important, perhaps the main, role of legal theorising is to respond to and reflect on trends in specialist areas that are developing anyway. The role of the theorist is not merely or mainly to construct grand overarching or synthesising theories (although these have their uses), but also to interpret, make sense of, provide tools for, and to critically assess such developments.

This book is rooted in Western traditions of academic law, especially the Anglo-American tradition. It is addressed primarily to jurists, scholars, and students within these traditions. It is not an attempt to launch a brand new Global Jurisprudence divorced from these historical roots. If this were desirable, it would be premature, for we are not yet well-equipped to generalise about legal phenomena from a global perspective. When I talk of 'our' discipline I speak mainly as a common law trained jurist, based in the United Kingdom and the United States and with links to Europe and the post-colonial Commonwealth. The central argument is that our discipline in this quite local sense needs to become more genuinely cosmopolitan and to broaden its perspectives both geographically and intellectually. From a global perspective our predominant traditions of academic law have focused mainly on the domestic municipal law of modern nation states, have assumed that doctrine is the core of the subject matters of the discipline, and have tended towards universalism and secularism in respect of values despite the phenomena of belief pluralism and religious

---

[1] On non-state law see Chapter 12 above; on 'soft low' see Chapter 4, n. 132.

revival. Collectively we have generally been ignorant of other legal traditions and belief systems and generally indifferent to legal phenomena and problems in other parts of the world. My argument is not that our discipline should abandon its local roots and its concern with immediate detailed practical problems, but rather that building on the strengths of our heritage it should broaden its vision to include other levels of ordering, other forms of law, understandings of other legal traditions and belief systems, and to engage more with pressing global and transnational issues. Insofar as our discipline has already been responsive to such challenges, the role of general jurisprudence is to take stock of these responses and make sense of them, as well as to guide, suggest, stimulate, and criticise.

Most of the processes of 'globalisation' take place at sub-global levels. Interdependence is a relative matter. A global perspective is useful in setting a context and constructing overviews, but increasing interdependence generally operates more locally through regions, diasporas, alliances, networks, and former empires. A great deal of diffused 'modern' law is quite urban, with limited reach into rural areas or urban or peri-urban ghettoes.[2] General jurisprudence should be as concerned with sub-global phenomena and issues, rural as well as urban, not just with those that are genuinely global.

In approaching the task of broadening our vision, I have adopted a strategy of starting with quite abstract themes and illustrating them selectively in order to concretise the argument. Chapters 2 to 8 discussed general jurisprudence in terms of three broad, but inter-related areas, but with particular reference to individual thinkers, mainly in the Anglo-American tradition. This has served to introduce some of the leading contemporary theorists of globalisation and law – Glenn, Santos, Tamanaha, Pogge, Singer, and Sen – while relating them directly to classic predecessors in that tradition.

In respect of analytical jurisprudence, my central thesis is that there is more than ever a central role for conceptual analysis, but the agenda needs to be broadened to include analytical concepts that can be used across legal traditions, and basic concepts of empirical legal studies, as well as the relatively narrow range of concepts studied by analytical jurists working with one or other narrow doctrinal conceptions of law. The 'naturalist turn' in philosophy can be interpreted as fortifying the idea of continuities between analytical and empirical legal studies, provided that it is not interpreted as making conceptual analysis redundant.

Globalisation also has implications for normative jurisprudence. It has stimulated a revival of concern about universalism and relativism in ethics, it has provoked the 'Asian values' debates, and it has contributed to a new wave of rethinkings of the scope and justifications of human rights as moral, political, and legal rights. Singer's development of Benthamite utililitarianism and

---

[2] On the neglect of law in rural development circles, see Robert Chambers (1983), cited in Chapter 11, n. 75 above.

Pogge's critical extension of Rawls illustrate how classic Western theories can be adapted and applied at transnational levels. The work of Pogge, Griffin, Tasioulas, Ul Haq, and Sen shows how perennial issues of moral philosophy can be approached from a genuinely global perspective.

In some places, empirical legal studies have made significant headway in recent years and broader contextual and realist approaches to the study of law have become part of the mainstream. But empirical legal work at supra-state, trans-state, and sub-state levels is relatively underdeveloped. Genuinely 'scientific' empirical studies maintain a precarious foothold. Empirical approaches to comparative law, human rights, and international law are still in their infancy. Symptomatic of this backwardness is the almost complete lack of reliable global statistics about legal phenomena compared to neighbouring fields such as health, education, transport, welfare, let alone economics. Recently data banks and even league tables have started to develop, largely outside academic law. They deserve constructive critical attention. Both macro- and micro-theoretical approaches have responded unevenly to globalisation. Social theory is responding at a number of levels, but a healthy cosmopolitan discipline of law needs to be thoroughly contextualised and empirically informed in respect of all mainstream subjects rather than having empirical legal studies regarded as an optional, often marginal, supplement or add-on.

With or without major contributions from theory globalisation is already having, and will continue to have, a major impact on the landscape of specialised legal fields. Some clear trends are already apparent. First, greater emphasis is being placed on established transnational fields, such as public international law, regional law, international trade and finance (including Islamic banking and finance).[3] New transnational fields are emerging, such as Internet law,[4] procurement,[5] and transitional justice.[6] From a global perspective the North–South divide is of crucial importance, and this makes issues of 'law and development' (however characterised) much more central for the discipline of law and for legal theory than they have been in the past. For example, such ideas as 'a right to freedom from poverty' and 'the right to development', as well as moral issues surrounding humanitarian intervention, should be seen to be as much a concern of normative jurisprudence as they are of political and moral theory. These are points at which boundaries between disciplines dissolve.

Second, there will be greater emphasis on the legal dimensions of issues and phenomena that are genuinely global, such as climate change and other

---

[3] The future of private international law is less assured.

[4] E.g Mifsud Bonnici (2007), Reed (2004), Polanski (2007), and the writings of Michael Froomkin, e.g. Froomkin (2002), (2003), Froomkin et al. (2007).

[5] McCrudden (2007).

[6] E.g. Teitel (2000); Symposium (2007). See the webpage of the Transitional Justice Institute (University of Ulster) www//transitional justice.Ulster.ac.uk.

environmental issues, radical poverty, regional integration, the common heritage of mankind, migration, war, terrorism, pandemics, and the media.

Third, there is likely to be a greater emphasis on the transnational dimensions of subjects previously perceived as domestic, such as contract, criminal law, family law, intellectual property, and labour law.[7] For example, in family law, issues relating to the interests and rights of children in respect of labour, custody, adoption, and abduction across national borders, and the sex trade.[8]

Fourth, there should be a greater awareness of the significance of religious movements and diasporas. For example, increasing attention is being paid to the religious and customary practices of ethnic minorities (both immigrant and indigenous) and their interface with municipal state law in Northern countries (e.g. how Muslim minority communities in the West finance their property and business transactions).[9]

Fifth, empirically informed comparative law will be crucial for the development of our capacity to make well-grounded generalisations about legal phenomena across legal traditions and cultures. Like it or not, we are all comparatists now, but very few are socio-legal comparatists.[10]

Sixth, there are perspectives, of which feminism, human rights, critical theory, and post-modernism are currently the most salient, that cut across conventional classifications of specialist fields and lead to fundamental, sometimes radical, rethinking of received ideas.

It is contrary to the spirit of this book to set forth a comprehensive agenda for general jurisprudence. But this account of general trends can be usefully concretised by looking at one such attempt. In 1995 Boaventura de Sousa Santos conducted a magisterial survey of areas that are central to rethinking law from a global perspective and constructed an agenda for research.[11] His framework was a set of assumptions about the struggle between the 'hegemonic forces' of global capitalism and the rather more fragmented forces of 'cosmopolitan anti-hegemonic and utopian legalities'. The three forces of transnationalisation of law in the service of global capital were: (a) the transnationalisation of nation state law through harmonisation, structural adjustment, and other forms of diffusion; (b) the development of legal regimes of regional integration; (c) transnational commercial regulation through non-state law, including

---

[7] *The Global Issues Series* (edited by Franklin A. Gevurtz and published by West) provides supplementary texts for use in American courses on domestic law. This is an encouraging development.

[8] E.g Estin and Stark (2007).

[9] E.g Pearl and Menski (1998) Chapter 3, Ballard (ed.) (1994). On religious minorities in Europe see Chapter 13, nn. 110–112 above.

[10] On the centrality of comparative legal studies to developing a genuinely cosmopolitan discipline, see GLT, Chapter 7 and Nelken and Örücü (2007) *passim*.

[11] Santos (1995) Chapter 4 (modified in Santos (2002) Chapter 5). For a longer discussion of the earlier chapter, see GLT, 239–42. The later version adds 'global reform of courts' (including the exportation of 'Rule of Law' and ideas of representative democracy and judicialisation of politics). On other agendas, see Falk (1998), (2002), Santos and Rodriguez-Garavilo (2005).

lex mercatoria, international commercial arbitration, the World Trade Organization, and self-regulation. In opposition to these, he set (d) The law of people on the move (i.e. the rights of migrants, refugees and internally displaced persons), and the 'deterritorialisation of citizenship'; (e) the law of indigenous peoples (e.g. Maoris, aborigines, and native North Americans); (e) the protection and development of human rights; and (f) an extended conception of the common heritage of mankind (*ius humanitatis*).[12]

Even within Santos' ideological framework, this list is not comprehensive: he might have added control of the media, the arms trade, nuclear proliferation, the transnationalisation of legal practice, and labour law. Santos' provocative survey is especially interesting for three reasons: first, despite envisaging globalisation as mainly economic (or at least politico-economic), he sets out an agenda for research that covers vast areas of law which he considers need to be reconceived and researched in the context of globalisation. Second, his framework is avowedly that of the sociology of law, an interesting attempt at fusion of neo-Marxist and post-modern ideas that involve a blending of normative, conceptual, and empirical perspectives. Third, with the partial exception of human rights, almost all of these lines of enquiry have not received much attention from mainstream Western legal theory. Santos' vision of a cosmopolitan discipline of law seems to be radically different from, and more adventurous than, the kinds of thinking that has gone on to date in respect of 'internationalising' the curriculum in law schools in the United Kingdom and the United States.

If one adopts a wider and less ideological conception of 'globalisation', as I have done in this book, one could add an almost endless number of topics not on Santos' agenda (e.g. climate change, the internet, diffusion of technological and biological developments, international crime, the drug trade, transnational epidemics). But the agendas of our discipline and of general jurisprudence are too open-ended for it to be sensible to try to be comprehensive.

One of the most important tasks of theorising is the articulation and critical appraisal of the presuppositions and working concepts of legal discourse generally and of more specialised areas. As the processes of globalisation impact on and give greater prominence to transnational fields such as comparative law, public international law, human rights law, international economic and financial law, regional regimes and so on, there is a corresponding need to subject their assumptions and discourses to critical scrutiny. Such 'rethinkings' have already begun to a significant extent in some areas. For example, in the late 1980s anthropologists, including legal anthropologists, recognised that they had often erred in treating small-scale societies as timeless, self-contained units and since then have been more sensitive to the broader contexts of history and geography.[13] The writings of Philip Allott, Richard Falk, Fernando Téson,

---

[12] On *ius humanitatis*, see Chapter 5, n. 238 above.

[13] Collier and Starr (1989) marks the change of perspective in legal anthropology. See also Moore (ed.) (2005).

Martti Koskenniemi and critical theorists of international law are clearly contributions to general jurisprudence.[14] Similarly, in recent years mainstream
comparative law has been the subject of sustained critique from a number of
directions.[15] Chapter 9, on diffusion, is included here as an example of this kind
of critical jurisprudence. Perhaps some of the most important developments are
taking place in relation to empirical legal studies, usually at the level of middle
order theory. For example, some of the best theoretical work in recent years has
been done in relation to transnational aspects of regulation, regional governance, and environmental protection.[16]

Three particular tasks for jurisprudence as an activity have been recurrent
themes in this book: conserving and mining the heritage of juristic texts; critical
assessment of the underlying assumptions of significant specialist fields of
scholarship and practice; and helping to keep our discipline in touch with
developments in other disciplines and important issues of the age. A critical
approach in an era of rapid change suggests the need for quite radical changes.
But a conception of jurisprudence as heritage emphasises tradition and continuity. Accordingly, it may be appropriate to end by revisiting the idea of
mining our rich heritage of texts and ideas and theories. In connection with this,
I suggest three tasks:

(a) *Extending the canon and reducing our ignorance of other traditions.*
    Western jurists need to become better acquainted with the leading thinkers
    and salient ideas and controversies in other legal traditions. Some of the
    literature of non-Western legal traditions that have until now been con-
    sidered the province of specialists need to be assimilated into the main-
    stream. That is a pre-condition for genuine cross-cultural dialogue and
    for serious aspirations to universalism. The task is daunting not least
    because of problems of selection, accessibility, translation, interpretation,
    and depth – to say nothing of the manageability of such a vast heritage.
    Fortunately, that heritage includes much excellent writing by Western
    scholars (notwithstanding criticisms of 'orientalism')[17] and, to a lesser
    extent, accessible writings by contemporary 'Southern' jurists. The task is
    huge, but it will continue to be an essential part of developing a genuinely
    cosmopolitan jurisprudence.

(b) *Reviewing the canon.* It is worth asking to what extent are there relevant
    texts in our own tradition that have been marginalised or forgotten and that

---

[14] See Chapter 1, n. 38.   [15] See Chapter 1, n. 38.

[16] E.g. on EC law and constitutionalism see e.g. Weiler (1999), Walker (2003), (2005), Tsagourias
(2007); On regulation see, e.g. Parker, Scott and Lacey (eds.) (2004), Chayes and Chayes (1995),
Morgan and Yeung (2007); On environment, see Ebbeson and Okowa (eds.) (2008).

[17] Edward Said's *Orientalism* (1978) alerted us to the subtle dangers of racism, stereotyping, and
ideological biases in Western writings about the Arab world and, more generally, 'the Orient'.
However, it was unfair in its sweeping denigration of the small band of genuine scholars who, in
respect of law, include Joseph Schacht, Anthony Allott, Duncan Derrett, and Marc Galanter. For
a forceful critique of Said, see Irwin (2006).

deserve to be reinstated as being of particular relevance to a more cosmopolitan legal theory. To some extent that is happening already, as is illustrated by the attention being paid to Kant's 'To Perpetual Peace'.[18] Thinkers such as Grotius, Leibniz, and Vico may also warrant renewed attention. So may some of the classics of world history and comparative history.[19] And, of course, we need to be better acquainted with the classics of other legal traditions.

Of Anglo-American texts that deserve to be resurrected, I would include some of the works of Sir Henry Maine, Jeremy Bentham's writings on colonialism, international law and his (to me disappointing) essay on 'Matters of Place and Time in Legislation',[20] and a refinement and development of Karl Llewellyn's 'law-jobs' theory[21] – but that is just a list of personal preferences.

(c) *Reinterpreting the mainstream.* Third, it is worth taking a critical look at ideas of our own current canonical jurists from a global perspective. As we have seen in Chapter 5, one example is Thomas Pogge's transfer of Rawls' theory of justice to the world stage, exploring much more convincingly than *The Law of Peoples* the application of Rawls' principles of justice to the design and operation of transnational and international institutions and practices. The result is to transform a fairly comfortable theory of domestic justice into one that provides a potentially radical critique of existing institutional arrangements in the world as a whole. Tamanaha's interpretation of Hart is another example.[22] Some of Peter Singer's writings can be read as the modern application of Benthamite utilitarianism to global and transnational issues.[23] Interesting questions arise about the applicability of Dworkin's Hercules to reasoning and interpretation in other juristic traditions.[24] And one notes that there have been significant shifts in feminist theory as its geographical horizons have broadened.[25] The reinterpretation of familiar texts from a global perspective is well under way.

Finally, there is the question of 'relevance'. We have seen that there is a quite widespread feeling that some recent legal philosophising has lost touch with mainstream legal scholarship and legal practice. By contrast, legal scholars have been quite responsive to the stimuli of 'globalisation', perhaps to the extent that others may feel that some transnational fields have become too fashionable. Legal theory can develop on the back of specialised areas of legal scholarship; of course, it can also respond directly to what are perceived to be major global issues, such as war and peace, poverty, economic and social development,

---

[18] Kant (1795). Recent commentaries include Kleingeld (ed.) (2006) and Senghaas (2007).

[19] Interestingly, David Goldman (2007) has found inspiration in the work of Eugen Rosenstock-Huessy (1938).

[20] See Chapter 5.4(d) above.   [21] See Chapter 4.2 above.   [22] See Chapter 4.1 above.

[23] See Chapter 5.5 above.   [24] *GLT*, 40–7.

[25] See Okin (1999), Nussbaum (2000), Riles (2002), Stewart (2009) See further Chapter 6, n. 100 above.

environment, pandemics, genocide, terrorism and so on.[26] Again there are many lists and agendas, representing different standpoints, ideologies, and interests. One should not expect a consensus. But adopting a global perspective and asking what the implications of 'globalisation' are for jurisprudence and the discipline of law can at least stimulate thought and debate about potential new lines of enquiry and the directions in which we, as jurists and scholars, should be heading.

[26] Nearly forty years ago Julius Stone wrote a paper on 'Trends in Jurisprudence in the Second Half Century' (1967) printed in Hathaway (1980). This can make for quite depressing reading in that the agenda of issues still looks quite contemporary, some debates that he treated as overworked are still alive, and some of the issues in his programme have not yet been implemented, including the better integration of analytical and socio-legal approaches.

Bibliography

Abel, Richard (1973a) 'A Comparative Theory of Dispute Institutions in Society' 8 *Law and Society Rev.* 212.

(1973b) 'Law Books and Books about Law', 26 *Stanford L. Rev.* 175.

(1988) *The Legal Profession in England and Wales* Oxford: Blackwell.

(1989) *American Lawyers* Oxford: Oxford University Press.

(2001) 'Lawyers' 12 *IESBS* 3358.

and Philip Lewis (eds.) (1988–9) *Lawyers in Society. Vol 1. The Common Law World; Vol 2 The Civil Law World; Vol 3 Comparative Theories* Berkeley, CA: University of California Press.

Abel-Smith, Brian & Robert Stevens (1967) *Lawyers and the Courts: A Sociological Study of the English Legal System 1750–1965* Cambridge, MA: Harvard University Press.

Abimbola, Wande and Kola Abimbola (2007) *Orisa: Yoruba Religion and Culture in Africa and the Diaspora* Birmingham: Iroko Academic Publishers.

Abraham, David (2007) 'The Boundaries and Bonds of Citizenship: Recognition and Redistribution in the United States, Germany and Israel' 7 *Migration in History* 210.

Adler, Matthew D. and Eric A. Posner (eds.) (2001) *Cost–Benefit Analysis: Legal, Economic and Philosophical Perspectives* Chicago: University of Chicago Press.

Adler, P.A. and P. Adler, (1987) *Membership Roles in Field Research* London: Sage.

Ahmed, Khurshid (2003) '*The Challenge of Global Capitalism: An Islamic Perspective*' in Dunning (ed.) Chapter 8.

Ahsan, M.M., and A.R. Kidwai (eds.) (1993) *Sacrilege versus Civility: Muslim Perspectives on The Satanic Verses Affair* rev. edn. Leicester: The Islamic Foundation.

Alfieri, Anthony (1993) 'Impoverished Practices: Critical Theories and Legal Ethics' 81 *Georgetown L. Jo.* 2567.

Allen, Layman E. and Hans Baade (eds) (1963) *Jurimetrics* New York: Basic Books.

Allison, John W.F. (1996) *A Continental Distinction in the Common Law* Oxford: Oxford University Press.

Allott, Anthony N. (1970) *New Essays in African Law* London: Butterworth.

(1980) *The Limits of Law* London: Butterworth.

(2000) 'The Hunting of the Snark or the Quest for the Holy Grail: The Search for Customary Law' in Ian Edge (ed.) Chapter 3.

Allott, Philip (1990) *Eunomia: New Order for the World* Oxford: Oxford University Press.

(2002) *The Health of Nations: Society and Law beyond the State* Cambridge: Cambridge University Press.

Alston, P. (2005a) 'Ships Passing in the Night: The Current State of the Human Rights and Development Debate Seen Through the Lens of the Millennium Development Goals', 27 *Human Rights Qrtly* 755.

(ed.) (1999) *The EU and Human Rights* Oxford: Oxford University Press.

(ed.) (2005b) *Labour Rights as Human Rights* Oxford: Oxford University Press.

Alter, N. (2001) 'Diffusion, Sociology of', 6 *IESBS* 3681.

Al-Turabi, Hassan (2006) 'Sudanese Scholar Hassan Al-Turabi Elaborates on his Revolutionary *Fatwa*' www.memritv.org/Transcript.asp?P1=1112.

Aluffi, Roberta B.-P. and Giovanna Zincone (eds.) (2004) *The Legal Treatment of Islamic Minorities in Europe* Leuven: Peeters.

Amadiume, Ifi and Abdullahi An-Na'im (eds.) (2000) *The Politics of Memory* London: Zed Books.

American Bar Association (1992) *Legal Education and Professional Development* (The MacCrate Report) Chicago: American Bar Association.

American Law Institute, 75th Anniversary 1923–98 (1998) Philadelphia: ALI.

Andersen, Camilla Basch (2006) 'Scandinavian Law in Legal Traditions of the World' 1 *Jo. Comparative Law* 142.

Anderson, Norman (1976) *Law Reform in the Muslim World* London: Athlone.

An Na'im, Abdullahi (1990) *Toward an Islamic Reformation: Civil Liberties, Human Rights and International Law* Syracuse, NY: Syracuse University Press, Preface by John Voll.

(1993) 'Toward an Islamic Reformation; Responses and Reflections' in Lindholm and Vogt (eds.) Chapter 6.

(1999) 'Promises We Should All Keep in Common Cause' in Okin *et al.*

(2001) 'Human Rights in the Arab World: A Regional Perspective' 23 *Human Rights Qtrly* 701.

(2002) *Islamic Family Law in a Changing World: A Global Resource Book* London: Zed Books.

(2004a) 'The Future of Shari'ah Project' (Memo.)

(2004b) 'To Affirm the Full Human Rights Standing of Economic, Social and Cultural Rights' in Ghai and Cottrell (eds.).

(2005) *The Future of Shari'a* (Unpublished manuscript).

(2006) *African Constitutionalism and the Role of Islam* Philadelphia: University of Pennsylvania Press.

(2008) *Islam and the Secular State: negotiating the future of Shari'a* Cambridge, MA: Harvard University Press.

(ed.) (1992) *Human Rights in Cross-Cultural Perspectives: A Quest for Consensus.* Philadelphia: University of Pennsylvania Press.

(ed.) (2003) *Human Rights Under African Constitutions: Realizing the Promise for Ourselves* Philadelphia: University of Pennsylvania Press.

and Francis Deng (eds.) (1990) *Human Rights in Africa: Cross-Cultural Perspectives* Washington, DC: Brookings Institution.

Jerald Gort, Henry Jansen, and Hendrik M. Vroom (eds.) (1995) *Human Rights and Religious Values* Amsterdam: Eerdmans.

Annan, Kofi (2005) 'In Larger Freedom' Report to Security Council, March 2005.

Antokolskaia, Masha (2007) 'Comparative Family Law: Moving with the Times?' in Őrűcű and Nelken (eds.).

Arkoun, Mohd. (1993) 'The Concept of "Islamic Reformation"' in Lindholm and Vogt (eds.).

Arminjon, Pierre, Baron Boris Nolde and Martin Wolff (1950–51) *Traité de Droit Comparé* Paris: Librarie Generale de droit et de jurisprudence (3 vols).

Association of Democratic Lawyers (1958–81) *Review of Contemporary Law* Brussels.

Atiyah, Patrick (1970/2006) *Accidents, Compensation and the Law London*: Weidenfeld and Nicolson; (7th edn., (ed.) P. Cane) Cambridge: Cambridge University Press.

and Robert Summers (1987) *Form and Substance in American Law* Oxford: Oxford University Press.

Atkinson, Max and Paul Drew (1979) *Order in Court: The Organization of Verbal Interaction in Judicial Settings* London: Macmillan.

Atria, Fernando (2002) *On Law and Legal Reasoning.* Oxford: Hart

Attfield, Robin and Barry Wilkins (eds.) (1992) *International Justice and the Third World* London: Routledge.

Austin, John (1832/1863/1954) *The Province of Jurisprudence Determined and The Uses of the Study of Jursprudence* (ed. H.L.A. Hart). London: Weidenfeld and Nicolson.

Ayer, Alfred J. (1948) 'The Principle of Utility' in G. W. Keeton and G. Schwarzenberger (eds.).

(ed) (1956) *The Revolution in Philosophy* London: Macmillan.

Ayres, Ian and John Braithwaite (1992) *Responsive Regulation: Transcending the Deregulation Debate* New York: Oxford University Press.

Baderin, Mashood A. (2003) *International Human Rights and Islamic Law* Oxford: Oxford University Press.

Baghramian, M. (2001) 'Relativism: Philosophical Aspects' 19 *IESBS* 13012.

Bainbridge, John (1972) *Study and Teaching of Law in Africa* South Hackensack: Rothman.

Bainham, Andrew (ed.) (1994) *The International Survey of Family Law* Netherlands: International Society of Family Law.

Baker, John H. (1977) 'University College and Legal Education, 1826–1976' 1 *Current Legal Problems* 13.

Balas, Aron, Rafael La Porta, Florencio Lopez-de-Silanes, and Andrei Schleifer (2008) *The Divergence of Legal Procedures* (NBER Working Paper 13809) Cambridge, MA: National Bureau of Economic Research.

Baldwin, John and Gwynn Davis (2003) 'Empirical Research in Law' in Cane and Tushnet (eds.) Chapter 39.

and Keith A. Bottomley, (1978) *Criminal Justice: Selected Readings* London: Martin Robertson.

Balkin, John (1987) 'Deconstructive Practice and Legal Theory', 96 *Yale Law Jo.* 743.

Ballard, Roger (2006) 'Ethnic Diversity and the Delivery of Justice: The Challenge of Plurality' in Shah and Menski (eds.) Chapter 2.

(ed.) (1994) *Desh Pardesh: The South Asian Presence in Britain* London: Hurst.

Banakar, Reza (2002) 'Sociological Jurisprudence' in Banakar and Travers Chapter 2.

and Max Travers (eds.) (2002) *A Introduction to Law and Social Theory* Oxford: Hart.

(eds.) (2005) *Theory and Method in Socio-legal Research* Oxford: Hart.

Bangkok Governmental Declaration (1993).

Bano, Samia (2007a) 'Islamic family Arbitration, Justice and Human Rights in Britain' 2007(1) Law, Social Justice and Global Development Jo. www2.warwick.ac.uk/fac/soc/law/elj/lgd/2007_1/bano

(2007b) 'Muslim Family Justice and Human Rights: The Experience of British Muslim Women' 1 *Jo. Comparative Law* 38.

Barcello, John J. III and Roger C. Cramton (eds.) (1999) *Lawyers' Practice and Ideals: A Comparative View*. The Hague and London: Kluwer Law International.

Barfield, Thomas (ed.) (1997) *The Dictionary of Anthropology* Oxford: Blackwell.

Barnett, Hilaire (1995) 'The Province of Jurisprudence Determined – Again!' 15 *Legal Studies* 88.

and Diana Yach (1985) 'The Province of Jurisprudence Determined' 5 *Legal Studies* 151.

Barrett, David, George T. Kurian and Todd M. Johnson (eds.) (2001) *World Christian Encyclopedia: A Comparative Study of Churches and Religions in the Modern World* Oxford: Oxford University Press.

Barry, Brian (1972) *The Liberal Theory of Justice* Oxford: Clarendon Press.

Barry, Christian and Thomas Pogge (eds.) (2005) *Global Institutions and Responsibilities: Achieving Global Justice* Oxford: Blackwell.

Barton, John, Jack P. L. Gibbs, and John H. Merryman (1983) *Law in Radically Different Cultures*. St. Paul, Minn.: West.

Baslar, Kemal (1998) *The Concept of the Common Heritage of Mankind in International Law* The Hague: Marinus Nijhoff.

Bauer, Joanne R. and Daniel A. Bell (eds.) (1999) *The East Asian Challenge to Human Rights* Cambridge: Cambridge University Press.

Bauman, Jon R. (1999) *Pioneering a Global Vision: The Story of Baker and McKenzie* Chicago: Harcourt Professional Education Group.

Bavinck, Maarten and Gordon Woodman (forthcoming 2009) 'Can There be Maps of Law?' in Franz von Benda-Beckmann, Keebet von Benda-Beckmann and Anne Griffiths, *Spatialising Law: An Anthropological Geography of Law in Society* Aldershot: Ashgate Publishing.

Bavink, Maarten (2003) 'How to Start Mapping Law: A Rejoinder to Woodman'. Paper delivered at xiv International Congress of the Commission on Folk Law and Legal Pluralism, August 26–29, 2004, University of New Brunswick, Fredericton, Canada, Law, Plural Society and Social Cohesion in the 21st Century.

Baxi, Upendra (1985) *Courage, Craft and Contention: The Indian Supreme Court in the Eighties* Bombay: Tripathi.

(1986a) Introduction to *Bentham's Theory of Legislation* (revised reprint) Bombay: Tripathi.

(1991a) 'Conflicting conceptions of legal cultures and conflict of legal cultures' 33 *Jo. of the Indian Law Institute* 173.

(1991b) 'Decay and Destruction Today: Social Reality and Social Theory' (Presidential Address: Indian Academy of Social Sciences) Delhi: University of Delhi.

(1994a) *Inhuman Wrongs and Human Rights: Some Unconventional Essays* New Delhi: Har Anand.

(1994b) *Mambrino's Helmet?: Human Rights for a Changing World* Delhi: Har Anand.

(1995a) '"Summit of Hope" in the Depths of Despair? Social Development as a Realization of Human Rights' xxiii 21 *Mainstream* 19.

(1995b) 'The Myth and Reality of the Indian Adminstrative Law' An Introduction to I. P. Massey, Lucknow: Eastern Book Company.

(1996a) 'A Work in Progress?': The United Nations Report to the United Nations Human Rights Committee' 38 *Indian Jo. International Law* 34.

(1996b) "'Global Neighbourhood' and the 'Universal Otherhood': Notes on the Report of the Commission on Global Governance" 22 *Alternatives* 525.

(1996c) 'The Unreason of Globalization and the Reason of Human Rights' A.K. Desai Memorial Lecture Bombay: Mumbai: University of Mumbai.

(1996d) 'Human Rights Education: A Promise for the Third Millennium?' 8th Zakir Hussain Memorial Lecture, Delhi.

(1997) 'Judicial Activism: Usurpation or Re-democratization?' 47 *Social Action* 342.

(1998) 'Voices of Suffering: Fragmented Universality, and the Future of Human Rights' 8 Transnational Law and Contemporary Problems 125 and in Weston and Marks (eds.) (1999).

(2000a) 'Gender and Reproductive Rights in India: Problems and Prospects for the New Millennium' Lecture delivered for the UN Population Fund, New Delhi.

(2000b) *Mass Torts, Multinational Enterprise Liability and Private International Law* The Hague: Martinus Nijhoff, reprinted from vol. 276 *Recueil des Cours*, Hague Academy of International Law.

(2000c) 'Constitutionalism as a Site of State Formative Practices' 21 *Cardozo L. Rev.* 1183.

(2001a) 'Failed decolonization and the future of social rights: some preliminary reflections' Tel Aviv: Minerva Centre of Human Rights.

(2001b) 'What Happens Next is Up to You: Human Rights at Risk in Dams and Development', 16 *American U. International Law Rev.* 1507.

(2001c) 'Operation 'Enduring Freedom': Towards a New International Order' 1.

(2001d) 'Too many, or too few, human rights?' 1 *Human Rights Law Rev.* 1.

(2002a) *The Future of Human Rights* Delhi: Oxford University Press.

(2002b) 'Memory and Rightlessness' Fifteenth J.P. Naik Lecture Delhi: Centre for Women's Development Studies.

(2002c) 'Sense and Sensibility' Online *Seminar* www.india-seminar.com/semframe.htm

(2002d) 'Rule of Law in India: Theory and Practice' HKU seminar (revised 2003).

(2003a) Comment on the UN Draft Code of Conduct of Transnational Corporations and Businesses.

(2003b) 'The Colonialist Heritage' in Legrand and Munday (eds.) Chapter 3.

(2003c) 'A Known but an Indifferent Judge': Situating Ronald Dworkin in Contemporary Indian Jurisprudence' 1. *I.CON* 557.

(2005a) 'Market Fundamentalisms: Business Ethics at the Altar of Rights' 59 *Human Rights L. Rev.* 3.

(2005b) 'The War *ON* Terror and the War *OF* Terror: Nomadic Multititudes, Aggressive Incumbents, and the "New" International Law: Prefatory Remarks on Two "Wars".' 43 *Osgoode Hall L. Jo.* 7.

(2006a) *The Future of Human Rights* (2nd edn) New Delhi: Oxford University Press.

(2006b) *The Human Right to Human Rights Education? Some Critical Perspectives* New Delhi: Universal Law Book Co.

(2006c) 'Development as a Human Right or as Political Largesse? Does it make any Difference?' (Founder' Day Lecture) Madras: Madras Institute of Development Studies.

(2007a) *Human Rights in a Posthuman World* New Delhi: Oxford: University Press.

(2007b) 'Amartya Sen and Human Rights' in Baxi (2007a) Chapter 2.

(2007c) 'From Human Rights to Human Flourishing: Julius Stone, Amartya Sen, and Beyond?' Julius Stone Lecture, University of Sydney.

Baxi, Upendra (ed.) (1986b) *Inconvenient Forum and Convenient Catastrophy: The Bhopal Case* Bombay: Tripathi.

(1989) *Law and Poverty* Bombay: N.M. Tripathi.

and A. Dhandha (eds.) (1990) *Valiant Victims and Lethal Litigation: The Bhopal Case* Bombay: Tripathy.

and Shulamith Koenig (2006) *The People's Report on Human Rights Education.*

Beale, Hugh (2006) 'The European Civil Code movement and the European Union's Common Frame of Reference', 6 *Legal Information Management* 4

Becher, Tony (1989) *Academic Tribes and Territories* Milton Keynes: Open University Press.

Beck, Ulrich (1992) *The Risk Society* London: Sage.

Bedau, Hans (2000) 'Anarchical Fallacies: Bentham's Attack on Human Rights' 22 *Human Rights Quarterly* 261.

Beecher-Monas, Erica (2007) *Evaluating Scientific Evidence* New York: Cambridge University Press.

Beer, Lawrence W. and Hiroshi Itoh (1996) *The Constitutional Case Law of Japan, 1970 through 1990* Seattle: University of Washington Press.

Beetham, David (1993) *Auditing Democracy in Britain* University of Essex: Democratic Audit Paper No. 1.

Beitz, Charles (1979) *Political Theory and International Relations* Princeton: Princeton University Press.

Beitz, Charles *et al.* (eds) (1985) *International Ethics: A Philosophy and Public Affairs Reader* Princeton: Princeton University Press.

Bell, Christine (2006) 'Peace Agreements: Their Nature and Status' 100 *Am. Jo. International Law* 373.

Bell, Christine, Colm Campbell, and Fionnuala Ní Aolaín (2004) 'Justice Discourses in Transition' 13 *Social and Legal Studies* 325.

(2005/6) 'The Paradox of Transition in Conflict Democracies' 27 *Human Rights Qrtrly* 172.

Bell, Christine *et al.* (eds.) (2007) Special Issue: 'Transitional Justice' 3 *International Jo. of Law in Context* No.2.

Bell, John (2001) *French Legal Cultures* London: Butterworth.

(2006) 'Chapter Five: Civil Law Tradition' (Review of Glenn) (2004) in Foster (ed.) p. 130.

Belvedere, Andrea (1997) 'Some Observations on the Language of the Italian Civil Code' in Pintore and Jori (eds.) p. 339.

Bennett, T.W (1999) *Human Rights and Customary Law Under the South African Constitution* Cape Town: Juta.

Bentham, Jeremy (1777–79) 'Of Torture' (ed. P.E and W.L. Twining (1973) in M. James (ed.)).

(1780) *Place and Time* (manuscript ed. P. Schofield (2007), (partly published in *1 Works* 168–94).

(1786–9) *Principles of International Law* 2 *Works* 561.

(1795) *Supply Without Burden or Escheat vice Taxation* 2 *Works* 585–98.

(1802) Traité de législation civile et pénale (ed. E. Dumont) Paris: Bentham, Jeremy.

(1989) 'Constitutional Code Rationale' in *First Principles Preparatory to Constitutional Code* (ed. P. Schofield.) Oxford: Oxford University Press.

(1825) *A Treatise on Judicial Evidence* (ed. Dumont, anon trs.) London: J. W Paget.

(1827) *Rationale of Judicial Evidence* (ed. J.S Mill, 5 vols.) London: Hunt and Clarke.

(1831) *Parliamentary Candidate's Proposed Declaration of Principles* (reprint from *Constitutional Code* Ch. VII).

(1838–43) *Principles of the Civil Code 1 Works* 297–364.

(1970) *Introduction to the Principles of Morals and Legislation* (ed. J.H. Burns and H.L.A Hart, *CW*) London: Athlone Press; (2nd edn. (1996) Oxford: Clarendon Press).

(1977) *Comment on the Commentaries and A Fragment on Government* (ed. J.H. Burns and H.L.A Hart *CW*) London: Athlone Press.

(1983a) *Constitutional Code* I (ed. F. Rosen and J.H. Burns, (*CW*)) Oxford: Oxford University Press.

(1983b) *Deontology* (ed. Amnon Goldworth *CW*) Oxford: Oxford University Press.

(1990) *Securities Against Misrule and Other Constitutional Writings for Tripoli and Greece* (ed. Philip Schofield, *CW*) Oxford: Oxford University Press.

(1995) *Colonies, Commerce and Constitutional Law: Rid Yourselves of Ultramaria and other Writings on Spain and Spanish America* (ed. Philip Schofield *CW*) Oxford: Oxford University Press.

(1998a) *'Legislator of the World': Writings on Codification, Law and Education* Philip Schofield and Jonathan Harris (eds.) (*CW*) Oxford: Oxford University Press.

(1998b) *Codification Proposal* in *'Legislator of the World'* (1998a).

(2001) *Writings on the Poor Laws* (Michael Quinn (ed.) *CW*) Oxford: Oxford University Press.

(2002) *Nonsense Upon Stilts* in *Rights, Representation and Reform: Nonsense Upon Stilts and Other Writings on the French Revolution* (Philip Schofield, Catherine Pease-Watkin, and Cyprian Blamires (eds.) *CW*) Oxford: Clarendon Press. (Also known as *Anarchical Fallacies*.)

Benton, Lauren (1994) 'Beyond Legal Pluralism: Towards a New Approach to the Informal Sector' 3 *Social and Legal Studies* 223.

(2002) *Law and Colonial Cultures: Legal Regimes in World History 1400–1900* Cambridge: Cambridge University Press.

Berelson, Bernard and Gary A. Steiner (1964) *Human Behavior: An Inventory of Scientific Findings* New York: Harcourt Brace.

Bergin, Thomas (1968) 'The Law Teacher: A Man Divided against Himself' 54 *Virginia L.Rev* 637.

Berg-Schlosser, D (2001) 'Comparative Studies: Method and Design' 4 *IESBS* 2427.

Berkowitz, Daniel, Katharina Pistor and Jean-Francois Richard, (2003) 'The Transplant Effect', 51 *American Jo. Comparative Law* 163.

Berman, Harold J. (1950) (2nd edn 1963) *Justice in Russia: An Interpretation of Soviet Law* Cambridge, MA.: Harvard University Press.

(1983) *Law and Revolution: The Formation of the Western Tradition* Cambridge, MA.: Harvard University Press.

(1995) 'World law' 18 *Fordham International Law Jo.* 1617.

(2003) *Law and Revolution II: The Impact of the Protestant Reformations on the Western Legal Tradition* Cambridge, MA: Harvard University Press.

Bermann, George A. and Petros C. Mavroidis (2007) *WTO Law and Developing Countries* New York: Cambridge University Press.

Besson, Samantha and John Tasioulas (eds.) (2008) *Philosophy of International Law* Oxford: Oxford University Press.

Beveridge, Fiona and Sue Nott (1998) 'A Hard Look at Soft Law' in Craig and Harlow (eds.) Chapter 14.

Bierbaum, Rosina M. (2008) 'Energy and Climate Change' 61 *Bulletin of the American Academy of Arts and Sciences* 32.

Binder, Gyorah and Robert Weisberg (2000) *Literary Criticisms of Law*. Princeton, NJ: Princeton University Press.

Bix, Brian (1995) 'Conceptual Questions and Jurisprudence' 1 *Legal Theory* 465.

 (2000) 'Conceptual Jurisprudence and Socio-Legal Studies'. 32 *Rutgers Law Jo.* 227.

Black, Donald (1976) *The Behavior of Law* London: Academic Press.

 (1989) *Sociological Justice*. New York: Oxford University Press.

 (1993) *The Social Structure of Right and Wrong* San Diego: Academic Press.

 (1995) 'The Epistemology of Pure Sociology' 20 *Law and Social Inquiry* 829.

 (2007) 'Relativity, Legal' in David S. Clark (ed.) Vol. 3, 1292.

Black, Max (1952) *Critical Thinking* (2nd edn) Englewood Cliffs, NJ: Prentice-Hall.

 (1962) *Models and Metaphors*. Ithaca: Cornell University Press.

Black, Richard and Howard White (eds.) (2004) *Targeting Development: Critical Perspectives on the Millennium Development Goals* London: Routledge.

Blankenburg, Erhard and Freek Bruinsma, (1994) *Dutch Legal Culture* (2nd edn) Deventer: Kluwer.

Blaustein, Albert P. and Charles O. Porter (1954) *The American Lawyer* Chicago: University of Chicago Press.

Blomley, Nicolas (1994) *Law, Space and the Geographies of Power* New York: Guilford Press.

Bodenheimer, Edgar (1955–56) 'Modern Analytical Jurisprudence and the Limits of its Usefulness' 104 *U. Pennsylvania. Law Rev.* 1680.

Bohannan, Paul (1957) *Justice and Judgement Among the Tiv of Nigeria* Oxford: Oxford University Press.

Bosselman, Fred (2005) 'Adaptive resource management through customary law' in Ørebach *et al.* Chapter 6.

Bottomley, Anne (1997) 'Lessons from the Classroom: Some aspects of the 'Socio' in 'Legal' Education' in Thomas (ed.) Chapter 8.

Bowring, John (ed.) (1838–43) *The Works of Jeremy Bentham* Edinburgh: W. Tait.

Boyle, Kevin (ed.) (2007) see Mary Robinson (2007).

Bradney, Anthony and Fiona Cownie (2000) *Living Without Law: An Ethnography of Quaker Decision-making, Dispute Avoidance and Dispute Resolution*. Aldershot: Ashgate.

Bradney, Tony (1998) 'Law as a Parasitic Discipline' 25 *Jo. Law and Society* 71.

Braithwaite, John and Peter Drahos (2000) *Global Business Regulation* Cambridge: Cambridge University Press.

Brandt, Richard (1967) 'Ethical Relativism' in *Encyclopedia of Philosophy* P. Edwards (ed).

Braudel, Fernand (1993) *A History of Civilizations* (trs. Richard Mayne) Viking Press, New York; (1st edn) *Grammaire de Civilizations* Paris: Les Editions Arthaud, 1987.

Brewer, Neil and Kipling D. Williams (2005) *Psychology and Law: An Empirical Perspective* New York: Guilford Press.

Brierley, James L (1963) *The Law of Nations: An Introduction to the Law of Peace* Oxford: Oxford University Press, (6th edn by Sir H. Waldock) (1st edn 1928).

British Academy (2004) *That Full Complement of Riches, The Contributions of the Arts, Humanities and Social Sciences to the Nation's Wealth* London: The British Academy (The Langford Report).

Brooks-Gordon, Belinda and Michael Freeman (eds.) (2006) *Law and Psychology* Oxford: Oxford University Press.

Brown, L. A. (2001 'Diffusion: Geographical Aspects' 6 *IESBS* 3676.

Brown, Peter and Henry Shue (eds.) (1977) *Food Policy* New York: Free Press.

Buchanan, Allen (2000) 'Rawls's Law of Peoples: Rules for a Vanished Westphalian World' 110 *Ethics* 697.

Buckland, William W. (1890) 'Difficulties of Abstract Jurisprudence' 24 *LQR* 436.
    (1945) *Some Reflections on Jurisprudence* Cambridge: Cambridge University Press.

Bullard, Robert D. (ed.) (2005) *The Quest for Environmental Justice* San Fransisco: University of California Press.

Bunn, Isabella (2006) *The Right to Development and International Economic Law: Legal and Moral Dimensions* Oxford: Hart.

Burman, Sandra and Barbara Harrell-Bond (eds.) (1979) *The Imposition of Law* New York: Academic Press.

Burns, James (1966) 'Bentham and the French Revolution' Transactions of the Royal Historical Society, 5th series, Vol. 16, p. 95.
    (1973) 'Bentham on Sovereignty: An Exploration' in M. James (ed.) 133.

Busumtwi-Sam, James (2002) 'Development and Human Security: Whose Security, and Security from What?' 57 *International Journal* 253.

Butler, William E (2006) 'Russia, *Legal Traditions of the World*, and Legal Change' 1 *Jo Comparative Law* 142.

Cairo Declaration on Human Rights (1990).

Cain, Maureen and Alan Hunt (eds.) (1979) *Marx and Engels on Law* London: Academic Press.

Calvino, Italo (1974) *Invisible Cities*. (trs. William Weaver) San Diego: Harcourt Brace.
    (1986) *Mr. Palomar* (trs. William Weaver) San Diego: Harcourt Brace.

Campbell, Tom (2007) 'Poverty as a Violation of Human Rights: Inhumanity or Injustice?' in Pogge (ed.) (2007b) Chapter 2.

Campbell, Tom, Jeffrey Goldsworthy, and Adrienne Stone (eds.) (2003) *Protecting Human Rights: Instruments and Institutions* Oxford: Oxford University Press.

Campbell, Tom, Keith Ewing and Adam Tomkins (eds.) (2001) *Sceptical Essays on Human Rights* Oxford: Oxford University Press.

Cane, Peter and Mark Tushnet (eds.) (2003) *The Oxford Handbook of Legal Studies* Oxford: Oxford University Press.

Carlin, Jerome (1962) *Lawyers on their Own* New Brunswick: Rutgers University Press.
    (1966) *Lawyers' Ethics* New York: Russell Sage Foundation.

Carothers, Thomas (1999) *Aiding Democracy Abroad: The Learning Curve* Washington, DC: The Carnegie Endowment for International Peace.

Carson, David and Ray Bull (eds.) (2003) *Handbook of Psychology in Legal Contexts* Chichester: John Wiley.

Carson, David, Becky Milne, Francis Pakes, Karen Shalev, and Andrea Shawyer (eds.) (2007) *Applying Psychology to Criminal Justice* Chichester: John Wylie.

Carty, Tony (ed.) (1992) *Law and Development* New York: New York University Press.

Cassese, Antonio (2003) (2nd edn) *International Criminal Law* Oxford: Oxford University Press.

Castellino, Joshua and Elvira Dominguez Redondo (2006) *Minority Rights in Asia: A Comparative Legal Analysis* Oxford: Oxford University Press.

Castells, Manuel (2000) *End of Millennium* Oxford: Blackwell.

Cauquelin, Josiane, Paul Lim and Birgit Mayer-Konig (eds.) (1998) *Asian Values: An Encounter with Diversity* Richmond: Curzon Press.

Chaliand, Gérard and Jean-Pierre Rageau, (1995) *The Penguin Atlas of Diasporas* New York: Viking.

Chambers, Robert (1983) *Rural Development* London: Longman Scientific and Technical.

Chang, Ruth (ed.) (1997) *Incommensurability, Incomparability and Practical Reason* Cambridge, MA: Harvard University Press.

Chanock, Martin (1985) *Law, Custom, and Social Order: The Colonial Experience in Malawi and Zambia* Cambridge: Cambridge University Press.

Charlesworth, Hilary, Christine Chinkin and Shelley Wright (1991) 'Feminist Approaches to International Law' 85 *American Jo. International Law* 613.

Chayes, Abraham and Antonia Chayes (1995) *The New Sovereignty: Compliance with International Regulatory Agreements*. Cambridge, MA.: Harvard University Press.

Cheru, Fantu and Colin Bradford (eds.) (2005) *The Millennium Development Goals: Raising the Resources to Tackle World Poverty* London: Zed Books.

Chiba, Masaji (1989) *Legal Pluralism: Towards a General Theory through Japanese Legal Culture* Tokyo: Tokai University Press.

   (1993) *Sociology of Law in Non-Western Countries* Onati: Onati Institute for the Sociology of Law.

   (1998) 'Other Phases of Legal Pluralism in the Contemporary World' 11 *Ratio Juris* 228.

   (ed.) (1986) *Asian Indigenous Law: In Interaction with Received Law* London: Kegan Paul International.

Chinkin, Christine (1989) 'The Challenge of Soft Law: Development and Change in International Law' 38 *International and Comparative Law Quarterly* 850.

Chua, Amy (1998) 'Markets, Democracy, and Ethnicity: Toward a New Paradigm for Law and Development', 108 *Yale L. Jo.* 1.

   (2003) *World on Fire* New York: Doubleday.

Cingranelli, David (1988) *Human Rights: Theory and Measurement* New York: St Martin's Press.

Clark, David S. (ed.) (2007) *Encyclopedia of Law and Society: American and Global Perspectives* Thousand Oaks, CA: Sage.

Clark, Philip (2006) 'The Rules (and Politics) of Engagement: Aiming at Truth, Justice, Healing and Reconciliation through Gacaga', in Clark and Kaufman (eds.).

   and Zackery Kaufman (eds.) (2009) *Rebuilding after Genocide: Transitional Justice, Post-Conflict Resolution and Reconciliation in Rwanda* New York: Columbia University Press.

Clarke, Alison and Paul Kohler (2005) *Property Law: Commentary and Materials* Cambridge: Cambridge University Press.

Clemens, Michael A., Charles J. Kenny and Todd J. Moss (2004) 'The Trouble with the MDGs: Confronting Expectations of Aid and Development Success' Washington, DC: Centre for Global Development Working Paper 40.

Cohen, David and E.S. Atieno (1992) *Burying S. M.: The Politics of Knowledge and the Sociology of Power in Africa* London: James Currey.

Cohen, L. Jonathan (1954) *The Principles of World Citizenship* Oxford: Blackwell.

(1992) *An Essay on Belief and Acceptance* Oxford: Clarendon Press.

Cohen, Roberta and Francis Deng, (1998) *Masses in Flight: The Global Crisis of Internal Displacement* Washington, DC: The Brookings Institution.

Coleman, Jules (ed.) (2001) *The Practice of Principle*. Oxford: Oxford University Press.

Collier, Jane and June Starr (eds.) (1989) *History and Power in the Study of Law*. Ithaca, NY: Cornell University Press.

Collins, Hugh (1982) *Marxism and Law* Oxford: Oxford University Press.

Collins, Robert O. and Francis Deng (eds.) (1984) *The British in the Sudan, 1898–1956* Stanford: Hoover Institute.

Comair-Obeid, Nayla (1996) *The Law of Business Contracts in the Middle East* London: Kluwer International.

Conaghan, Joanne, Richard M. Fischl and Karl Klare (eds) (2002) *Labour Law in an Era of Globalization* Oxford: Oxford University Press.

Conklin, William E. (2008) *Hegel's Laws: The Legitimacy of a Modern Legal Order* Stanford: Stanford University Press.

Cook, Rebecca (ed.) (1994) *Human Rights of Women: National and International Perspectives* Philadelphia: University of Pennsylvania Press.

Cooper, John, Ronald Nettler and Mohamed Mahmoud (eds.) (2000) *Islam and Modernity: Muslim Intellectuals Respond* London: Tauris.

Cooper, Robert L. (ed.) (1982) *Language Spread: Studies in Diffusion and Social Change* Bloomington, Ind.: University of Indiana Press.

Coser, Lewis, A. (1956) *The Functions of Social Conflict* London: Routledge and Kegan Paul.

Cotran, Eugene (1966) 'The Place and Future of Customary Law in East Africa' in *East African Law Today*.

Cotterrell, Roger (1992) *The Politics of Jurisprudence: A Critical Introduction to Legal Philosophy* Philadelphia: University of Pennsylvania Press.

(1995) *Law's Community* Oxford: Oxford University Press.

(1997) 'The Concept of Legal Culture' in David Nelken (ed.) Chapter 1.

(1998) 'Why Must Legal Ideas be Interpreted Sociologically?' 25 *Jo. Law and Society* 171.

(1999) *Emile Durkheim: Law in a Moral Domain* Edinburgh: Edinburgh University Press.

(2006) *Law, Culture and Society: Legal Ideas in the Mirror of Social Theory* Aldershot: Ashgate.

and J.C. Woodliffe (1974) 'The Teaching of Jurisprudence in British Universities' *JSPTL* (NS) 89.

Cownie, Fiona (2004) *Legal Academics: Culture and Identities* Oxford: Hart.

Anthony Bradney, and Mandy Burton (2003) *English Legal System in Context* (3rd edn) London: LexisNexis (4th edn 2007).

Craig, Paul (1997) 'Formal and Substantive Conceptions of the Rule of Law' *Public Law* 467.

and Carol Harlow (eds.) (1998) *Lawmaking in the European Union* London: Kluwer Law International.

Cranston, Maurice (1973) *What are Human Rights?* (2nd edn) London: Bodley Head.

Crisp, Roger and Brad Hooker (eds.) (2000) *Well-Being and Morality: Essays in Honour of James Griffin* Oxford: Clarendon Press.

Cusson, M. (2001) 'Social Control' 4 *IESBS* 2730.

Czarnota, Adam, Martin Krygier, and Wojciech Sadurski (eds.) (2005) *Rethinking the Rule of Law under Communism* Budapest: Central University Press.

D'Agostino, Fred (2003) *Incommensurability and Commensuration: The Common Denominator* Aldershot: Ashgate.

Dalgano, Melvin (1975) 'The Contemporary Significance of Bentham's Anarchical Fallacies: A Reply to William Twining' 61 *Archiv fur Rechts–und Sozialphilosophie* 357.

Dam, Kenneth (2006a) 'Institutions, History and Economic Development' (Olin Law and Economics Working Paper No. 271) Chicago: University of Chicago Law School.

(2006b) 'The Law-Growth Nexus: The Rule of Law and Economic Development' Washington DC: Brookings Institution Press.

Damaska, Mirjan (1986) *The Faces of Justice and State Authority: A Comparative Approach to the Legal Process* New Haven: Yale University Press.

Daniels, Norman (ed.) (1975) *Reading Rawls: Critical Studies of A Theory Of Justice* Oxford: Blackwell.

Darwin, Charles (1859) *On the Origin of the Species* Facsim. 1st edn, Cambridge, MA: Harvard University Press. (1st edn) London: John Murray.

Daube, David (1956) *Forms of Roman Legislation* Oxford: Clarendon Press.

Dauvergne, Catherine (ed.) (2003) *Jurisprudence for an Interconnected Globe* Aldershot: Ashgate.

David, René (1964) (1st edn) *Les grandes systèmes du droit contemporain* Paris: Dalloz.

Davis, J. (ed.) (1982) *Religious Organization and Religious Experience* London and New York: Academic Press.

Davitt S.J. Father Thomas (1963/4) 'Basic Value Judgments in Preliterate Custom and Law', Council for the Study of Mankind, Conference on Law and the Idea of Mankind (Chicago) (unpublished paper).

de Barry, W.T. (1991) *The Trouble with Confucianism* Cambridge, MA: Harvard University Press.

De Burca, Grainne and Joanne Scott (eds.) (2006) *Law and New Governance in the EU and the US* Oxford: Hart.

Del Mar, Maksymilian (forthcoming 2009) *Law as Institutional Normative Order: Essays in Honour of Sir Neil MacCormick* Aldershot: Ashgate

De Mulder, Richard (2004) 'Jurimetrics – New Impulses' Berkeley: Gruter Institute www.gruter.org.

De Soto, Hernando (1989) *The Other Path* London: I. B. Tauris.

(2000) *The Mystery of Capital: Why Capitalism Triumphs in the West and Fails Everywhere Else* New York: Basic Books.

Deakin, Simon (2005) 'Social Rights in a Globalized Economy' in Alston (ed.) Chapter 2.

Dembour, Marie-Bénédicte (2006) *Who Believes in Human Rights? Reflections on the European Convention* Cambridge: Cambridge University Press.

Deng, Francis M. (1971) *Tradition and Modernization: A Challenge for Law among the Dinka of the Sudan* (2nd edn) New Haven: Yale University Press.

(1972) *The Dinka of the Sudan* New York: Holt, Reinhart and Winston Prospect Heights, IL.: Waveland Press.

(1973) *The Dinka and their Songs* Oxford: Clarendon Press.

(1974) *Dinka Folktales* New York: African Publishing Co.

(1978) *Africans of Two Worlds* New Haven: Yale University Press.

(1980) *Dinka Cosmology* London: Ithaca Press.

(1982) *The Recollections of Babo Nimir* London: Ithaca Press.

(1986a) *Seed of Redemption: A Political Novel* New York: Lilian Barber Press.

(1986b) *The Man Called Deng Majok: A Biography of Power, Polygyny and Change* New Haven: Yale University Press.

(1989) *Cry of the Owl* New York: Lilian Barber Press.

(1993) *Protecting the Dispossessed: A Challenge to the International Community* Washington DC: Brookings Institution.

(1995) *War of Visions: Conflict of Identities in the Sudan* Washington DC: Brookings Institution.

(1998) 'The Cow and the Thing Called "What": Dinka Cultural Perspectives on Wealth and Poverty', 52 *Jo. of International Affairs* 101.

(1998) *Sudan Democratic Gazette* 5/98.

(1998) *Sudan Democratic Gazette* 8/98.

(1998) *Sudan Democratic Gazette* 9/98.

(1999) *Sudan Democratic Gazette* 3/99.

(1999) *Sudan Democratic Gazette* 6/99.

(1999) *Sudan Democratic Gazette* 10/99.

(2000) 'The Cause of Justice Behind Civil Wars' in Amadiume and Abdullahi An-Na'im (eds.) Chapter 11.

(2006) *Talking It Out: Stories in Negotiating Human Relations* London: Kegan Paul.

and Adbdullahi An Na'im (eds.) (1990) *Human Rights in Africa: Cross-Cultural Perspectives* Washington DC: Brookings Institution.

and Abdullahi An Na'im (1997) *Their Brothers' Keepers: Regional Initiative for Peace in the Sudan* Addis Ababa: Inter-Africa group.

and Gifford Prosser (1987) *The Search for Peace and Unity in the Sudan* Washington, DC: The Woodrow Wilson Press.

and F.M. Daly (1989) *Bonds of Silk: The Human Factor in the British Administration of the Sudan* East Lansing, MI: Michigan State University.

and William Zartman (eds.) (1991) *Conflict Resolution in Africa* Washington DC: Brookings Institution.

and Larry Minear (eds.) (1992) *The Challenges of Famine Relief: Emergency Operations in the Sudan* Washington, DC: The Brookings Institution.

and Terrence Lyons (1998) *African Reckoning* Washington DC: The Brookings Institution.

Denman, Thomas (1824) Review of Dumont's *Traité des Preuves Judiciaires* 40 Edinburgh Review 169.

Derrett, J. Duncan M. (1961–62) 'The Ministration of Hindu Law by the British', 4 *Comparative Studies in Society and History* 10.

(1968) *An Introduction to Legal Systems* London: Sweet and Maxwell.

(1999) 'An Indian Metaphor in St. John's Gospel', 9 *Jo. Royal Asiatic Society* 271.

Devlin, Patrick (1965) *The Enforcement of Morals* (Maccabaean Lecture in Jurisprudence (1959)) Oxford: Oxford University Press.

Dews, Peter (ed.) (1999) *Habermas: A Critical Reader* Oxford: Blackwell.

Dezalay, Yves & David Sugarman (eds.) (1995) *Professional Competition and Professional Power: Lawyers, Accountants and the Social Construction of Markets* London: Routledge.

and Bryant G. Garth (1996) *Dealing in Virtue: International Commercial Arbitration and the Construction of a Transnational Legal Order.* Foreword by Pierre Bourdieu. Chicago, IL: University of Chicago Press.

(2002a) *Global Prescriptions: The Production, Exportation and Importation of a New Legal Orthodoxy* Ann Arbor: University of Michigan Press.

(2002b) *The Internationalization of Palace Wars: Lawyers, Economists, and the Contest to Transform Latin American States* Chicago, IL: University of Chicago Press.

DFID (Department for International Development (UK)(2002) Draft Evaluation Guidelines www.eldis.org./static/DOC 13188.

Dhavan, Rajeev, Neil Kibble and William Twining (eds.) (1989) *Access to Legal Education and the Legal Profession* London: Butterworth.

Diamond, Jared (2005) *Collapse: How Societies Choose to Fail or Succeed* New York: Vintage Penguin.

Dias, Clarence J., Robin Luckham, Dennis O. Lynch, James C.N. Paul (eds.) (1981) *Lawyers in the Third World: Comparative and Developmental Perspectives* Uppsala: Institute for African Studies and New York: International Legal Center.

Dias, R.W.M. (1964, 1st edn)(1976, 4th edn)(1985, 5th edn) *Jurisprudence* London: Butterworth.

(1979, 3rd edn) *Bibliography of Jurisprudence* London: Butterworth.

and Graham J.B. Hughes (1957) *Jurisprudence* London: Butterworth.

Dickinson, Laura (ed.) (2007) *International Law and Society: Empirical Approaches to Human Rights* Aldershot: Ashgate.

Dine, Janet (2005a) 'Researching globalisation' 61 *Amicus Curiae* 7.

(2005b) *Companies, International Trade and Human Rights* New York: Cambridge University Press.

Dinwiddy, John (2004) *Bentham: Selected Essays of John Dinwiddy* William Twining (ed.) Stanford: Stanford University Press.

Dixon, Julie (2001) *Evaluation and Legal Theory*. Oxford: Hart.

Drobnig, Ulrich and Manfred Rehbinder (eds.) (1994) *Rechtrealismus, multikulturelle Gesellschaft und Handelsrecht: Karl N. Llewellyn unde seine Bedeutung heute.* Berlin: Duncker & Humblot.

Duff, R. Anthony (ed.) (1998) *Philosophy and the Criminal Law* Cambridge: Cambridge University Press.

Dumont, Étienne (1802) *see* Bentham, Jeremy (1802).

Dunning, John H. (ed.) (2003) *Making Globalization Good* Oxford: Oxford University Press.

Duxbury, Neil (1995) *Patterns of American Jurisprudence* Oxford: Oxford University Press.

(2003) 'A Century of Legal Studies' in Cane and Tushnet (eds.) Chapter 42.

Dworkin, Ronald (1977) *Taking Rights Seriously* London: Duckworth.

(1980/1985) 'Is Wealth a Value?' 9 *Jo. Legal Studies* 191 reprinted in *A Matter of Principle* (1985) Chapter 12.

(1985) *A Matter of Principle*. Cambridge, MA: Harvard University Press.

(1986) *Law's Empire*. London: Fontana.

(2002) 'Thirty Years On', 115 *Harvard Law Rev.* 1655.

(2006a) 'Hart and the Concepts of Law' 119 *Harvard Law Review Forum* 95.

(2006b) *Justice in Robes* Cambridge, MA: Harvard Belknap Press.

Dyzenhaus, David (2006) *The Constitution of Law: Legality in a Time of Emergency* Cambridge: Cambridge University Press.

East African Law Today (1966) London: BIICL.

East African Royal Commission (1955) *Report Cmnd.* 9475 London: HMSO.

Easterley, William (2006) *The White Man's Burden* Oxford: Oxford University Press.

Ebbesson, Jonas and Phoebe Okowa (eds.) (2008) *Environmental Justice in Context* Cambridge: Cambridge University Press.

Economides, Kim (1996) 'Law and Geography: New Frontiers' in Philip Thomas (ed.).

Edge, Ian (ed.) (1996) *Islamic Law and Legal Theory* New York: New York University Press.

(ed.) (2000) *Comparative Law in Global Perspective* Ardley, NY: Transnational Publishers.

Edwards, Paul (ed.) (1967) *Encyclopedia of Philosophy*. New York: MacMillan and Free Press.

Eekelaar, John (1978/1984) *Family Law and Social Policy* London: Weidenfeld & Nicolson.

El-Gamal, Mahmoud A. (2006) *Islamic Finance: Law, Economics and Practice* New York: Cambridge University Press.

Ellickson, Robert (1991) *Order Without Law: How Neighbors Settle Disputes* Cambridge, MA: Harvard University Press.

(1998) 'Law and Economics Discovers Social Norms' 27 *Journal of Legal Studies* 537.

Ellis, Anthony (ed.) (1985) *Ethics and International Relations* Manchester: Manchester University Press.

Empson, William (1947) *Seven Types of Ambiguity* (2nd edn) London: Chatto and Windus.

Endicott, Timothy (2000) *Vagueness in Law* Oxford: Oxford University Press.

Epstein A.L. (ed.) (1967) *The Craft of Social Anthropology* London: Tavistock.

Escamilla, M. and M. Saavedra (eds.) (2005) *Law and Justice in Global Society* Granada: University of Granada. (World Congress of Philosophy of Law and Social Philosophy).

Espeland, Wendy and Michael Sauder (2007) 'Rankings and Reactivity: How Public Measures Create Social Worlds' 113 *Am. Jo. Sociology* 1.

and Mitchell L. Stevens (1998) 'Commensuration as a Social Process', 24 *Annual Review of Sociology* 313.

Esposito, John L (ed.) (1999) *The Oxford History of Islam* New York: Oxford University Press.

and John H. Voll (eds.) (2001) *Makers of Contemporary Islam* New York: Oxford University Press.

Estin, Ann L and Barbara Stark (2007) *Global Issues in Family Law* St Paul, MN: West.

Evans, Malcolm D. (ed.)(2006) (2nd edn) *International Law* Oxford: Oxford University Press.

Evans, P.B. (2001) 'Development and the State' 6 *IESBS* 3557.

Evans-Pritchard, E.E. (1937) *Witchcraft, Oracles and Magic Among the Azande* Oxford: Oxford University Press.

(1940); *The Nuer* Oxford: Oxford University Press.

(1956) *Nuer Religion* Oxford: Oxford University Press.

Ewald, William (1995a) 'Comparative Jurisprudence I: What was it like to try a rat?' 143 *U. Pennsylvania L. Rev.* 1889.

(1995b) 'Comparative Jurisprudence II: The Logic of Legal Transplants' 43 *American. Jo. Comparative Law* 489.

Ewing, Alfred C. (1929) *The Morality of Punishment* London: K. Paul, Trench, Trubner.

Ewing, Keith (1994) 'The Bill of Rights Debate: Democracy or Juristocracy in Britain' in Ewing, Gearty, and Hepple (eds.).

and Conor Gearty (1990) *Freedom under Thatcher: Civil Liberties in Modern Britain* Oxford: Oxford University Press.

Conor Gearty, and Bob Hepple (eds.) (1994) *Human Rights and Labour Law* London: Mansell.

Falk, Richard (1998) *Law in an Emerging Global Village.* Ardsley, NY: Transnational Publishers.

(2002) 'Reframing the Legal Agenda of World Order in the Course of a Turbulent Century' in Likosky (ed.) Chapter 17.

Fallers, Lloyd (1969) *Law Without Precedent* Chicago: University of Chicago Press.

Faundéz, Julio, Mary Footer, and Joseph Norton (eds.) (2000) *Governance, Development and Globalization* London: Blackstone.

Fazio, Sylvia (2007) *The Harmonization of International Commercial Law* Alphen, Ned.: Kluwer International.

Feeley, Malcolm (1976) 'The Concept of Laws in Social Science: A Critique and Notes on an Expanded View' 10 *Law and Society Rev.* 497.

Fernandes, Edesio (ed.) (1995) *Law and Urban Change in Brazil* Aldershot: Avebury.

and Ann Varley (eds.) (1998) *Illegal Cities: Law and Urban Change in Developing Countries* London: Zed Books.

Feteris, Eveline T. (1999) *Fundamentals of Legal Argumentation* Dordrecht: Kluwer Academic.

Finnis, John (1972) 'Some Professorial Fallacies About Rights', 4 *Adelaide L. Rev.* 377.

(1980) *Natural Law and Natural Rights* Oxford: Clarendon Press.

(1983) *Fundamentals of Ethics* Oxford: Oxford University Press.

Fishbayn Lisa (1999) 'Litigating the Right to Culture: Family Law in the New South Africa', 13 *Int. Jo. of Law, Policy, and the Family* 147.

Fisher, Roger, William Ury, with Bruce Patten (ed.) (1991) *Getting To Yes* (2nd edn) New York: Penguin.

Fishkin, James (1985) 'Theories of Justice and International Relations: The Limits of Liberal Theory' in Beitz *et al.* (ed.).

Fitzpatrick, Peter (1992) *The Mythology of Modern Law* London: Routledge.

Fletcher, George (1993) *Loyalty: An Essay on the Morality of Relationships* New York: Oxford University Press.

(1996) *Basic Concepts of Legal Thought*. Oxford: Oxford University Press.

Flood, John (1983) *Barristers' Clerks* Manchester: Manchester University Press.

(1996) 'Megalwayering in the Global Order: The Cultural, Social and Economic Transformation of Global Legal Practice' 3 *Int. Jo Legal Profession* 169.

(2002) 'Globalisation and Global Elites: Transnational Legal Processes, Globalisation and Power Disparities' in Likosky (ed.) p. 114.

(2007) 'Lawyers as Sanctifiers: The Role of Elite Law Firms in International Business Transactions' 14 *Indiana Journal of Global Legal Studies* 35.

and Fabian Sosa (2008) 'Lawyers, Law Firms and the Stabilization of Transnational Business' *Northwestern Jo. of International Law and Business*.

Fontana, David (2001) 'Refined Comparativism in Constitutional Law' 49 *U.C.L.A. L. Rev.* 539.

Food and Agriculture Organization (FAO) (2005) *Food Insecurity in the World* Rome: FAO.

Foot, Rosemary (2000) *Rights Beyond Borders: The Global Community and the Struggle over Human Rights in China* Oxford: Oxford University Press.

Foster, Nick (ed.) (2006) Symposium on Glenn's *Legal Traditions of the World*, (2nd edn) 1 *Jo. Comparative Law* 100.

Franck, Thomas M. (1972) 'The New Development: Can American Law and Legal Institutions Help Developing Countries?' 12 *Wisconsin L. Rev.* 767.

(1995) *Fairness in International Law and Institutions* Oxford: Oxford University Press.

Frandberg, Ake and Mark Van Hoecke (eds.) (1998), *The Structure of Law*. Uppsala: Iustus Forlag.

Freedom House (2005) *Freedom of the Press: A Global Survey of Media Independence* New York: Freedom House.

Freeman, Michael (ed.) (2006) *Law and Sociology* 8 *Current Legal Issues* 49 and Oxford: Oxford University Press.

Freeman, Michael D.A. (2001) *Lloyd's Introduction to Jurisprudence* (7th edn) London: Sweet and Maxwell.

Frey, B.S. and F. Schneider (2001) 'Informal and Underground Economics' 11 *IESBS* 7441.

Friedman, Lawrence (1985) *A History of American Law* (2nd edn) New York: Simon and Schuster.

(1989) 'Law Lawyers and Popular Culture' 98 *Yale Law Jo.* 1579.

(1994) 'The Law and Society Movement' 38 *Stanford L. Rev.* 763.

(1996) 'Borders: On the Emerging Sociology of Transnational Law' 32 *Stanford Jo. Int. Law* 65.

(1997) 'The Concept of Legal Culture: A Reply' in David Nelken (ed.) Chapter 2.

(2002) *American Law in the Twentieth Century* New Haven: Yale University Press.

(2005) 'Law and Society Comes of Age' 1 *Annual Review of Law and Social Science* 1.

and Rogelio Pérez-Perdomo (eds.) (2003) *Legal Culture in the Age of Globalization: Latin America and Latin Europe* Stanford, CA: Stanford University Press.

Friedmann, Wolfgang (1960) *Legal Theory* (4th edn) London: Stevens.

(1964) 'The Role of Law and the Functions of Lawyers in Developing Countries' 17 *Vanderbilt L. Rev.* 181.

Friedrich, Carl (1972) *Tradition and Authority* London: Macmillan.

Froomkin, A. Michael (2002) 'ICANN's UDRP: Its Causes and (Partial) Cures' 67 *Brooklyn L. Rev.* 605.

(2003) 'Habermas@discourse.net: Toward a Critical Theory of Cyberspace' 116 *Harvard L Rev.* 749.

Froomkin, Michael, Tim Wu, Esther Dyson, and David Gross (2007) 'On the Future of Internet Governance' 101 *Proceedings of American Society of International Law.*

Fuchs, Alan (1992) 'Review of T. Pogge *Realizing Rawls*' 10 *Ethics* 395.

Fuller, Lon (1949) 'The Case of the Speluncean Explorers' 62 *Harvard L. Rev.* 616.

(1957–8) 'Positivism and Fidelity to Law – A Reply to Professor Hart', 71 *Harvard Law Review* 630.

(1969) *The Morality of Law* (2nd edn) New Haven: Yale University Press.

Galanter, Marc (1974) 'Why the 'Haves' Come Out Ahead: Speculation on the Limits of Legal Change' 9 *Law and Society Rev.* 95.

(1981) 'Justice in Many Rooms: Private Ordering and Indigenous Law' 19 *Journal of Legal Pluralism and Unofficial Law* 1.

(1991) *Competing Equalities: Law and the Backward Classes in India* (rev. edn.) Delhi: Oxford University Press.

(1992) *The Debased Debate on Civil Justice.* University of Wisconsin Dispute Processing Research Papers, No. 10.

(1998) 'Oil Strike in Hell: Contemporary Legends about the Civil Justice System', 40 *Arizona L. Rev.* 717.

(2005) *Lowering the Bar: Lawyer Jokes and Legal Culture* Madison, WI: University of Wisconsin Press.

and David Trubek (1974) 'Scholars in Self-estrangement: Some Reflections on the Crisis of Law and Development Studies in the United States' 14 *Wisconsin L. Rev.* 1062.

and Thomas Palay (1991) *Tournament of Lawyers: The Transformation of the Big Law Firm* Chicago: University of Chicago Press.

Galison, Peter (1997) *Image and Logic: A Material Culture of Microphysics*, Chicago: University of Chicago Press.

Gallie, W.B. (1956) 'Essentially Contested Concepts' *Proceedings of the Aristotelian Society* 167.

Galligan, Denis (2007) *Law in Modern Society* Oxford: Oxford University Press.

(ed.) (1995) *Socio-Legal Studies in Context: The Oxford Centre, Past and Future* Oxford: Blackwell.

Gardner, James A. (1980) *Legal imperialism: American Lawyers and Foreign Aid in Latin America* Madison, WI: University of Wisconsin Press.

Gardner, John P. (ed.) (1990) *United Kingdom law in the 1990s: Comparative and Common Law Studies for the XIIIth International Congress of Comparative Law* London: United Kingdom National Committee of Comparative Law.

(ed.) (1997) *Human Rights as General Norms and a State's Right to Opt Out: Reservations and Objections to Human Rights Conventions* London: BIICL.

Garth, Bryant (2001) 'Law and Society: Socio-legal Studies' 12 *IESBS* 8484.

and Joyce Sterling (1998) 'From Legal Realism to Law and Society: Reshaping the Last Stages of the Social Activist State' 32 *Law and Society Rev.* 409.

Gavison, Ruth (ed.) (1987) *Issues in Contemporary Legal Philosophy: The Influence of HLA Hart* Oxford: Oxford University Press.

Gearty, Conor (2004) *Principles of Human Rights Adjudication* Oxford: Oxford University Press.

(2005) 'Human Rights in an Age of Counter-Terrorism: Injurious, Irrelevant or Indispensable?' 58 *Current Legal Problems* 25.

(2006) *Can Human Rights Survive?* (Hamlyn Lectures) Cambridge: Cambridge University Press.

(2007) 'Reply' *Symposium Public Law* 227.

Geertz, Clifford (1983) *Local Knowledge: Further Essays in Interpretative Anthropology*, New York: Basic Books.

Gellner, Ernest (1959/1978) *Words and Things*. London: Routledge.

Genn, Hazel, Martin Partington, and Sally Wheeler (2006a) *Law in the Real World: Improving Our Understanding of How Law Works* London: Nuffield Foundation (The Genn Report).

(2006b) *Law in the Real World: Improving Our Understanding of How Law Works* (Report summary) London: Nuffield Foundation.

Georges, Telford (1973) 'The Rule of Law In Tanzania' in James and Kassam (eds.)

Gerber, David J. (2004) 'The Common Core of European Private Law: The Project and Its Books' 52 *American Jo. Of Comparative Law* 995.

Gessner, Volkmar and David Nelken (eds.) (2007) *European Ways of Law: Towards a European Sociology of Law* Oxford: Hart.

Geuss, Raymond (2001) *History and Illusion in Politics*. Cambridge: Cambridge University Press.

Gevurtz, Franklin A. (ed.) (2006–) *Global Issues Series* St Paul, MN: West.

Gewirth, Alan (1988) 'Ethical Universalism and Particularism', LXXXV *The Journal of Philosophy* 288.

Ghai, Dharam and Yash Ghai (1971) *Asians in East and Central Africa* London: Minority Rights Group, (reprinted in Whitaker (ed.), (1974)).

Ghai, Yash (1967) 'Independence and Safeguards in Kenya' 3 *East African Law Jo.* 177.

(1974) 'The Asian Minorities of East and Central Africa' in Whitaker (ed.).

(1986) 'Legal Radicalism, Professionalism and Social Action: Reflections on Teaching Law in Dar-es-Salaam' in Shivji (ed.), Chapter 3.

(1987) 'Law, Development and African Scholarship' 50 *M. L. R* 750.

(1993) 'Asian Perspectives on Human Rights' 23 *Hong Kong L.Jo.* 342.

(1995) 'The Politics of Rights in Asia' in G.P. Wilson (ed.) p. 203.

(1997a) 'Sentinels of Liberty or Sheep in Woolf's Clothing? Judicial Politics and the Hong Kong Bill of Rights' 60 *Modern Law Rev.* 459.

(1997b) 'The Rule of Law and Capitalism: Reflections on the Basic Law' in Wacks (ed.) Chapter 12.

(1998a) 'Human Rights and Asian Values' 9 *Public Law Review* 168.

(1998b) 'Rights, Duties and Responsibilities' in Cauquelin, Lim and Mayer-Konig (eds) Chapter 2.

(1998c) *Asian Human Rights Charter: A People's Charter* Hong Kong: Asian Human Rights Commission.

(1999a) *Hong Kong's New Constitutional Order* (2nd edn) Hong Kong: Hong Kong University Press.

(1999b) 'Rights, Social Justice and Globalization in East Asia' in Bauer and Bell (eds.) Chapter 10.

(2000a) *Autonomy and Ethnicity: Negotiating Competing Claims in Multi-ethnic States* Cambridge: Cambridge University Press.

(2000b) 'Universalism and Relativism: Human Rights as a Framework for Negotiating Interethnic Claims' 21 *Cardozo L Rev.* 1095.

(2003a) *Public Participation and Minorities* (Report) London: Minority Rights Group International.

(2003b) 'Constitution-making in a new Iraq' in Ghai, Lattimer and Said 27.

(2005) 'A Journey Around Constitutions' (Beinart Lecture, University of Capetown, 2002) 122 *S.African L. Jo.* 804.

(forthcoming) 'Redesigning the State for Right Development'.

and Patrick McAuslan (1970) *Public Law and Political Change in Kenya: A Study of the Legal Framework of Government from Colonial Times to the Present* Nairobi: Oxford University Press.

Mark Lattimer and Yahia Said (2003) *Building Democracy in Iraq* (Report) London: Minority Rights Group International.

(ed.) (1991) *Put Our World to Rights* London: Commonwealth Human Rights Initiative.

and Jill Cottrell (eds.) (2004) *Economic, Social and Cultural Rights in Practice: The Role of Judges in Implementing Economic, Social and Cultural Rights* London: Interights.

Ghali, Boutros Boutros (1993) 'Human Rights. The Common Language of Humanity' in UN World Conference on Human Rights, the Vienna Declaration and the Programme for Action.

Ghosh, Amitav (2005) *The Hungry Tide* London: Harper Collins.

Gibbs, James P. (1989) *Control: Sociology's Central Notion* Urbana: University of Illinois Press.

Giddens, Anthony (1990) *The Consequences of Modernity* Stanford: Stanford University Press.

Glendon, Mary Ann (1991) *Rights Talk: The Impoverishment of Political Discourse* New York: The Free Press.

(2001) *A World Made New: Eleanor Roosevelt and the Universal Declaration of Human Rights* New York: Random House.

Glenn, H. Patrick (1987) 'Persuasive Authority' 32 *McGill L. Jo.* 261.

(2001) 'Are Legal Traditions Incommensurable?' 49 *Am. Jo. Comp. Law* 133.

(2003a) 'A Transnational Concept of Law' in Cane and Tushnet (eds.), p. 839.

(2003b) 'The Nationalist Heritage' in Legrand and Munday (eds.) Chapter 4.

(2004) *Legal Traditions of the World: Sustainable Diversity in Law* (2nd edn.) (1st edn, 2000) Oxford: Oxford University Press.

(2007a) 'Legal Traditions and *Legal Traditions*' 2 *Jo. Comparative Law* 69.

(2007b) *Legal Traditions of the World: Sustainable Diversity in Law* (3rd edn) Oxford: Oxford University Press.

Goffman, Erving (1959) *The Presentation of Self in Everyday Life* New York: Anchor.

Goldman, Alvin (1986) *Epistemology and Cognition* Cambridge MA: Harvard University Press.

Goldman, David B. (2007) *Globalisation and the Western Legal Tradition: Recurring Patterns of Law and Authority* Cambridge: Cambridge University Press.

Goodale, Mark and Sally Merry (2007) *The Practice of Human Rights: Tracking Law Between the Global and the Local* New York: Cambridge University Press.

Goode, Roy (1998) *Commercial Law in the Next Millennium* Hamlyn Lectures. London: Sweet and Maxwell.

Goodman, Nelson (1955) *Fact, Fiction and Forecast* Cambridge, MA: Harvard University Press.

Goodrich, Peter and David G. Carlson (eds.) (1998) *Law and the Postmodern Mind: Psychoanalysis and Jurisprudence* Ann Arbor: Michigan University Press.

Goody, Jack (2004) *Islam in Europe* Cambridge: Polity Press.

Goold Benjamin J. and Liora Lazarus (eds.) (2007) *Security and Human Rights* Oxford: Hart.

Gordley, James (1991) *The Philosophical Foundations of Modern Contract Doctrine.* Oxford: Oxford University Press.

Government of Singapore, (1991) *Shared Values* Cm 1 of 1991, Singapore: Government Printers.

Gray, Christopher B. (ed.) (1999) *The Philosophy of Law: An Encyclopedia* New York: Garland.

Gray, John C. (1909) *The Nature and Sources of Law* New York: Columbia University Press.

Graziadei, Michele (2003) 'The functionalist heritage' in Legrand and Munday (eds.), p. 100

Green, Leslie (2005) 'General Jurisprudence: A 25th Anniversary Essay' 25 *Oxford Jo. Legal Studies* 565.

Green, Maria (2001) 'What We Talk About When We Talk About Indicators: Current Approaches to Human Rights Measurement' 23 *Human Rights Qtrly* 1062.

Greenberg, Karen J. (ed.) (2006) *The Torture Debate in America* New York: Cambridge University Press.

Greenhalgh, Trisha (2004) 'Meta-narrative Mapping: A New Approach to the Synthesis of Complex Evidence' in Hurwitz, Greenhalgh, Skultans (eds.).

Glenn Robert, Fraser Macfarlane, Paul Bate and Olympia Kyriakidou (2004) 'Diffusion of Innovations in Health Service Organizations: Systematic Literature Review and Recommendations' 82 *Millbank Quarterly* 581.

Glenn Robert, Paul Bate, Olympia Kyriakidou, Fraser Macfarlane and Richard Peacock (2005) *Diffusion of Innovations in Health Service Organisations: A Systematic Literature Review* Oxford: Blackwell.

Griffin, James (1986) *Well-Being: Its Meaning, Measurement, and Moral Importance* Oxford: Clarendon Press.

(1996) *Value Judgement: Improving our Ethical Beliefs* Oxford: Oxford University Press.

(2000) 'Replies' in Crisp and Hooker (eds.).

(2001a) 'Discrepancies Between the Best Philosophical Account of Human Rights and the International Law of Human Rights' CI Proceedings of the Aristotelian Society (Presidential Address) 1.

(2001b) 'First Steps in an Account of Human Rights' 9 *European Jo. of Philosophy* 306.

(2003a) 'A Short Intellectual Biography' 10 *Telos* 157.

(2003b) 'Group Rights' in Meyer, Paulson, and Pogge (eds.) Chapter 10.

(2008) *On Human Rights* Oxford: Oxford University Press.

Griffiths, Anne M. (1997) *In the Shadow of Marriage: Gender and Justice in an African Community* Chicago: University of Chicago Press.

Griffiths, John (1978) 'Is Law Important?' 54 *N.Y.U. L.Rev.* 339.

(1983) 'The General Theory of Litigation – A First Step' 5(2) *Zeitschrift fur Rechtssoziologie* 145.

(1986) 'What is Legal Pluralism?' 24 *Jo. Legal Pluralism* 1.

(2003) 'The Social Working of Legal Rules' 48 *Jo. Legal Pluralism and Unofficial Law* 1.

(2006) 'The Idea of Sociology of Law and its Relation to Law and to Sociology' in Michael Freeman (ed.) Chapter 4.

Heleen Weyers, and Maurice Adams (2008) *Euthanasia and Law in Europe* Oxford: Hart.

Gross, Oren and Fionnuala Ní Aoláin (2006) *Law in Times of Crisis: Emergency Powers in Theory and Practice* New York: Cambridge University Press.

Guardiola-Rivera, Oscar (2003) 'The Question Concerning Law' 66 *Modern Law Review* 792.

Guest, Stephen (1997) *Ronald Dworkin* (2nd edn) Edinburgh: Edinburgh University Press.

Gulliver, Philip (1963) *Social Control in an African Society* London: Routledge.

Haack, Susan (1993) *Evidence and Inquiry: Towards Reconstruction of Epistemology* Oxford: Blackwell.

(1998) *Manifesto of a Passionate Moderate* Chicago: University of Chicago Press.

(2003) *Defending Science Within Reason: Between Scientism and Cynicism* Amherst, NY: Prometheus Books.

(2005) 'On Legal Pragmatism: Where Does 'The Path of the Law' Lead Us?' 50 *American Jo. of Jurisprudence* 71.

Habermas, Jurgen (1995) 'Reconciliation Through the Use of Public Reason: Remarks on John Rawls' Political Liberalism', 92 *Jo. of Philosophy* 109.

(1996) *Between Facts and Norms: Contributions to a Discourse Theory of Law and Democracy* (trs. W. Rehg) Oxford: Polity Press.

Hailey, Lord (1938) *An African Survey* RIIA: Oxford: Oxford University Press.

(1957) *An African Survey: A Study of Problems arising in Africa South of the Sahara* London: Oxford University Press.

Hale, Brenda, David Pearl, and Elizabth Cooke (2002) (5th edn) *The Family, Law and Society* London: Butterworth.

Hall, Kermit *et al.* (eds.) (2002) *The Oxford Companion to American Law* New York: Oxford University Press.

Halliday, Simon and Patrick Schmidt (eds.) (2004) *Human Rights Brought Home: Socio-legal Perspectives on Human Rights in the National Context* Oxford: Hart.

Halliday, Terence (1987) *Beyond Monopoly*. Chicago: University of Chicago Press.

and C. Lucien Karpik (1997) *Lawyers and the Rise of Western Political Liberalism* Oxford: Oxford University Press.

Hallis, Frederick (1930) *Corporate Personality* Oxford: Oxford University Press.

Halme, Miia (2007) *Human Rights in Action* PhD thesis, University of Helsinki.

(2008) *Human Rights in Action* Helsinki: University of Helsinki Press.

(ed.) (2004) 'Symposium on Law and Anthropology – An Interrelationship of Fantasies and Utopias' 15 *Finnish Yearbook of International Law* 3.

Halpin, Andrew (1997) *Rights and Law: Analysis and Theory* Oxford: Hart.

(2003) 'Fundamental Legal Conceptions Reconsidered', 16 *Canadian Jo. Law and Jurisprudence* 41.

(2004) *Definition in Criminal Law* Oxford: Hart.

(2006a) 'Glenn's *Legal Traditions of the World*: Some Broader Philosophical Issues' in Foster (ed.), p. 116.

(2006b) 'Ideology and Law' 11 *Jo. Political Ideologies* 153.

(2006c) 'The Methodology of Jurisprudence: Thirty Years off the Point' 19 *Canadian Jo. Law and Jurisprudence* 67.

(2007) 'A Rejoinder to Glenn' 2 *Jo. Comparative Law* 88.

Hamilton, Walton (1932) 'Institution' 8 *Enc. Soc. Sci.* 84.

Hampshire, Stuart (1983) *Morality and Conflict* Oxford: Blackwell.

(1989) *Innocence and Experience* London: Allen Lane.

Hansen, K.T. (2001) 'Informal Sector' 11 *IESBS* 7450.

Harding, Christopher and Chin L. Lim (eds.) (1999) *Renegotiating Westphalia: Essays and Commentary on the European and Conceptual Foundations of Modern International Law* The Hague: Martinus Nijhoff.

Hare, R.M. (1981) *Moral Thinking* Oxford: Oxford University Press.

Harrington, John and Abreema Manji (2003) 'The Emergence of African Law as an Academic Discipline' 102 *African Affairs*, 109–34.

Harrison, Ross (1983) *Bentham* London: Routledge and Kegan Paul.

Hart H.L.A. (1953) *Definition and Theory in Jurisprudence* (Inaugural Lecture) Oxford: Oxford University Press (reprinted in Hart (1983) and elsewhere).

(1954) 'Definition and Theory in Jurisprudence' 70 *LQR* 57.

(1957) 'Analytic Jurisprudence in Mid-Twentieth Century: A Reply to Professor Bodenheimer.' 105 *U. Pennsylvania L. Rev.* 953.

(1958) 'Dias and Hughes on Jurisprudence' [1958] *Jo. Society of Public Teachers of Law (N.S.)* 143.

(1961/1994) *The Concept of Law* (2nd edn including Postscript) Oxford: Oxford University Press.

(1963) *Law, Liberty, and Morality*. London: Oxford University Press.

(1967) 'Problems of Philosophy of Law' in P. Edwards (ed.) Vol.6, p. 264 (reprinted in Hart (1983). Chapter 3).

(1968) *Punishment and Responsibility* Oxford: Oxford University Press.

(1973a) 'Between Utility and Rights' reprinted in Hart (1983).

(1973b) 'The Demystification of the Law' reprinted in Hart (1982).

(1982) *Essays on Bentham*. Oxford: Oxford University Press.

(1983) *Essays in Jurisprudence and Philosophy* Oxford: Oxford University Press.

(1987) Comment on Ronald Dworkin, 'Legal Theory and the Problem of Sense' in Gavison (ed.), p. 35.

and Tony Honoré (1985) *Causation and the Law* (2nd edn) Oxford: Oxford University Press.

Hathaway, Barbara Drexler (1980) *Julius Stone: A Bio-Biography* Austin: University of Texas Press.

Hathaway, Oona A. (2002) 'Do Human Rights Treaties Make a Difference?' 111 *Yale L. Jo* 1935.

and Harold H. Koh (eds.) (2005) *Foundations of International Law and Politics*. New York: Foundation Press.

Haupt, H-G (2001) *'Comparative History'* 4 *IESBS* 2397.

Hayek, Friedrich (1944) *The Road to Serfdom* Chicago: University of Chicago Press.
    (1979) *Law, Legislation and Liberty* Chicago: University of Chicago Press.

Hazard, John N. and Wenceslas J. Wagner (1974) *Law in the United States in Social and Technical Revolution* Brussels: Establissements Emile Bruylant.

Headland, Thomas, Kenneth Pike, and Marvin Harris (eds) (1990) *Emics and Etics: The Insider/Outsider Debate.* London: Sage.

Heinz, John P., and Edward O. Laumann (1982) *Chicago Lawyers: The Social Structure of the Bar* New York: Russell Sage; Foundation.

Held, David (1995) *Democracy and the Global Order: From the Modern State to Cosmopolitan Governance* Stanford: Stanford University Press.
    (2006) *Models of Democracy* (3rd edn) Stanford: Stanford University Press.

Heller, Thomas C. (2003) 'An Immodest Postscript' in Jensen and Heller.

Hendges, Phillip A. (1997) 'An Analysis of People, For Michigan Republic, Ex Rel v. State of Michigan' 30 *John Marshall L. Rev.* 937.

Hendly, Kathryn (2001) 'Demand for Law in Russia – A Mixed Picture' 10 *East European Constitutional Review* 72.

Herrestad, Henning (1996) *Formal Theories of Rights.* Oslo: Juristforbundets Forlag AS.

Hilson, Chris and Tony Downes (1999) 'Making Sense of Rights in Community Law' 24 *European L. Rev.* 121.

Himma, Kenneth Einar (2004) 'Do Philosophy and Sociology Mix? A Non-essentialist Socio-legal Positivist Analysis of the Concept of Law' 24 *Oxford Jo. Legal Studies* 717 (Review of Tamanaha 2001).

Hirst, Paul Q. and Grahame Thompson (1999) *Globalization in Question* Cambridge: Polity Press.

Hobsbawm, Eric (1995) *The Age of Capital 1848–1875, The Age of Empire 1875–1914, The Age of Extremes 1914–1991* NY: Abacus.
    and Terence Ranger (eds.) (1983) *The Invention of Tradition* Cambridge: Cambridge University Press.

Hodgkin, Thomas (1956) *Nationalism in Colonial Africa* London: Muller.

Hoebel, E. Adamson (1954) *The Law of Primitive Man* Cambridge, MA: Harvard University Press.
    (1964) 'Karl Llewellyn: Anthropological Jurisprude' 18 *Rutgers L. Rev.* 735.

Hoffman, Donald (1995) *Understanding Frank Lloyd Wright's Architecture* New York: Dover.

Hoffman, Roald (1995) *The Same and not the Same* New York: Columbia University Press.

Hohfeld, Wesley N. (1913/1919/1964) *Fundamental Legal Conceptions as Applied in Judicial Reasoning* (re-issued W.W. Cook (ed.) 1919, 1964) New Haven, CT: Yale University Press.
    (1914) 'A Vital School of Jurisprudence and Law' *Proceedings of the 14th Annual Meeting of AALS* 76.

Holder, Jane and Carolyn Harrison (eds.) (2003) *Law and Geography* Oxford: Oxford University Press.

Holder, Jane (2004) *Environmental Assessment: The Regulation of Decision-making* Oxford: Oxford University Press.

Holmes, Oliver Wendell Jr. (1897) 'The Path of the Law' 10 *Harvard L. Rev.* 457.

Horowitz, Donald L. (1994) 'The Qu'ran and the Common Law: Islamic Law Reform and the Theory of Legal Change' 42 *Am Jo. Comp. L.* 233 and 543.

Horwitz, Morton (1997) 'Why is Anglo-American Jurisprudence Unhistorical?' 17 *Oxford Jo. Legal Studies* 551.

Howell, Paul (1954) *A Manual of Nuer Law* London: Oxford University Press for the International African Institute.

Howells, Geraint (1998) ' "Soft Law" in EC Consumer Law' in Craig and Harlow (eds.) Chapter 15.

Howse, Robert (ed.) (2007) *The WTO System: Law, Politics and Legitimacy* London: Cameron May.

Hseih, Yu-Wei (1967) 'The Status of the Individual in Chinese Ethics' in Moore (ed.).

Hsu, C. Stephen (ed.) *Understanding China's Legal System* New York: New York University Press.

Hull, Natalie (1997) *Roscoe Pound and Karl Llewellyn: Searching for an American Jurisprudence* Chicago: University of Chicago Press.

Human Rights Watch (1993) *Global Report on Prisons* New York: Human Rights Watch.

Hume, David (1839) *A Treatise of Human Nature* London: John Norton (reprinted (1955) L.A. Selby-Bigge (ed.) Oxford: Oxford University Press.

Hunt, Alan (1978) *The Sociological Movement in Law* London: MacMillan.

Huntington, Samuel (1968) *Political Order in Changing Societies*. New Haven, Conn: Yale University Press.

   (1997) *The Clash of Civilizations and the Remaking of World Order* New York: Simon and Schuster.

Hurwitz, Brian, Trisha Greenhalgh, and Vieda Skultans (eds.) (2004) *Narrative Research in Health and Illness* London: BMJ Publications.

Hutton, Will and Anthony Giddens (2000) *On the Edge: Living with Global Capitalism* London: Cape.

Huxley, Andrew (ed.) (2002) *Religion, Law and Tradition* London: Routledge Curzon.

Hyland, Richard (1996) 'Comparative Law' in Patterson (ed.).

Ignatieff, Michael (ed.) (2005) *American Exceptionalism and Human Rights* Princeton: Princeton University Press.

Inoue, Kyoko (1991) *MacArthur's Japanese Constitution* Chicago: University of Chicago Press.

International Association of Democratic Lawyers (1958–81) *Review of Contemporary Law* Brussels.

International Commission of Jurists (1957–68) *Journal of the International Commission of Jurists* The Hague.

   (1961) *African Conference on the Rule of Law* Geneva: ICJ

   (1976) *Human Rights in a One Party State* Geneva: ICJ.

International Legal Center (1974) *Law and Development: The Future of Law and Development Research* Uppsala: Scandinavian Institute of African Studies and New York: ILC.

   (1975) *Legal Education in a Changing World* New York and Uppsala: ILC.

Iqbal, Munawar and David Llewellyn (eds.) (2002) *Islamic Banking and Finance* Cheltenham: Edward Elgar.

Irwin, Robert (2006) *For Lust of Knowing: The Orientalists and their Enemies* London: Allen Lane.

Ishay, Micheline (2004) *The History of Human Rights: From Ancient Times to the Globalization Era* Berkeley: University of California Press.

Jabine, Thomas P. and Richard Claude (1992) *Human Rights and Statistics: Getting the Record Straight* Philadelphia: University of Pennsylvania Press.

Jackson, Bernard (2006) 'Internal and External Comparisons of Jewish Law' 1 *Jo. Comparative Law* 177.

Jackson, Frank (1998) *From Metaphysics to Ethics: In Defence of Conceptual Analysis* Oxford: Oxford University Press.

Jagger, Trevor (2002) Britain-Tanzania Society Newsletter, Vol. 3 Issue 9.

Jagtenberg, R., E. Örücü and A.J. De Roo (1995) *Transfrontier Mobility of Law* The Hague: Kluwer Law International.

James, Michael (ed.) (1974) *Bentham and Legal Theory* (reprinted from 24 *Northern Ireland Legal Quarterly* (1973)) Belfast: NILQ.

James, Rudi W and Firoz M Kassam (eds.) (1973) *Law and its Administration in a One Party State: Selected Speeches of Telford Georges* Nairobi: East Africa Literature Bureau.

Jamieson, Dale (ed.) (1999) *Singer and his Critics*. Oxford: Blackwell.

Jasso, Guillermina and Berndt Wegener (1997) 'Methods for Empirical Justice Analysis: Part I Framework, Models and Quantitities' 10 *Social Justice Research* 393.

(1998) 'Exploring the Justice of Punishments: Framing, Expressiveness, and the Just Prison Sentence' 11 *Social Justice Research* 397.

Jenkins, Philip (2007a) *The Next Christendom: The Coming of Global Christianity* (Revised edn.) Oxford: Oxford University Press.

(2007b) *God's Continent: Christianity, Islam and Europe's Religious Crisis* Oxford: Oxford University Press.

Jenks, C. Wilfrid (1958) *The Common Law of Mankind* London: Stevens.

Jensen, Eric and Thomas C. Heller (2003) *Beyond Common Knowledge: Empirical Approaches to the Rule of Law* Stanford: Stanford University Press.

Jenson, Jane and Boventura de Sousa Santos (eds.) (2000) *Globalizing Institutions: Case Studies in Regulation and Innovation* Aldershot: Ashgate.

Jessup, Philip (1956) *Transnational Law* New Haven: Yale University Press.

Joerges, Christian and Ernst-Ulrich Petersmann (eds.) (2006) *Constitutionalism, Multilevel Trade Governance and Social Regulation* Oxford: Hart.

Johnson, Terence (1972) *Professions and Power* London: MacMillan.

Johnstone, Quentin and Dan Hopson Jr. (1967) *Lawyers and Their Work: An Analysis of the Legal Profession in the United States and England* Indianapolis: Bobbs-Merrill.

Jolowicz, J. Anthony (ed.) (1970) *The Division and Classification of the Law* London: Sweet and Maxwell.

Jones, William C. (2003) 'Trying to Understand the Current Chinese Legal System' in C. Stephen Hsu (ed.).

Jordana, Jacint and David Levi-Faur (eds.) (2004) *The Politics of Regulation* Cheltenham: Edward Edgar.

Judicial Studies Board (1999–) *Handbook on Ethnic Minority Issues* www.jsboard.co.uk.

Judicial Studies Board (2007) *Equal Treatment Bench Handbook* London: Judicial Studies Board.

Jung, Kim Dae (1994) 'Is Culture Destiny?' 73 *Foreign Affairs* 189.

Kadish, Mortimer R. and Sanford H. Kadish (1973) *Discretion to Disobey: A study of Lawful Departure from Legal Rules* Stanford: Stanford University Press.

Kagan, Robert A., Martin Krygier and Kenneth Winston (eds.) (2002) *Legality and Community: On the Intellectual Legacy of Philip Selznick* Lanham, MD: Rowman and Littlefield.

Kahn-Freund, Otto (1974/1978) 'On Uses and Misuses of Comparative Law' (1978) in *Selected Writings* 294 (originally published in (1974) 37 *Modern Law Rev.* 1).

(1978) *Selected Writings* London: Stevens.

Kalman, Laura (1986) *Legal Realism at Yale 1927–1960* Chapel Hill: University of North Carolina Press.

Kamp, Allen R (1995) 'Between the Wars Social Thought: Karl Llewellyn's Legal Realism, and the Uniform Commercial Code in Context' 59 *Albany L. Rev.* 325.

Kamrava, Mehran (2006) *The New Voices of Islam: Reforming Politics and Modernity* London: Tauris.

Kant, Immanuel (1795/2003) *To Perpetual Peace: A Philosophical Sketch* (trs. and ed. Ted Humphrey) Indianapolis: Hackett.

(1970) *Political Writings* (ed. H. Reiss) Cambridge: Cambridge University Press.

Karst, Kenneth (2000) 'The Bonds of American Nationhood' 21 *Cardozo Law Rev.* 1095

Kaufmann, Donald, Aart Kray, and Massimo Mastruzzi (July 2007) NBER Paper No. 4280.

Kay, Sean (2006) *Global Security in the Twenty-first Century: The Quest for Power and the Search for Peace* Lanham, Md.: Rowman and Littlefield.

Keeton, George W. (1949) *The Elementary Principles of Jurisprudence* (2nd edn.) London: Pitman.

and George Schwarzenberger (eds.) (1948) *Jeremy Bentham and the Law* London: Stevens.

Kelly, John M. (1992) *A Short History of Western Legal Theory* Oxford: Oxford University Press.

Kelly, Paul (1990) *Utilitarianism and Distributive Justice: Jeremy Bentham and the Civil Law* Oxford: Oxford University Press.

Kelsen, Hans (1945) *General Theory of Law and State* (trs. Anders Wedberg) Cambridge MA: Harvard University Press.

Kelsey, Jane (1995) *Economic Fundamentalism* London: Pluto Press.

Kennedy, David (2003) 'The Methods and the Politics' in Legrand and Munday (eds.) Chapter 11.

(2004) *The Dark Sides of Virtue: Reassessing International Humanitarianism* Princeton: Princeton University Press.

(2006) 'The 'Rule of Law' in Development Assistance: Past, Present, and Future' in Trubek and Santos (eds.).

Kennedy, Duncan (1997) *A Critique of Adjudication* Cambridge, MA: Harvard University Press.

(2006) 'Three Globalizations of Law and Legal Thought: 1850–2000' in Trubek and Santos.

Kent, Ann (1999) *China, the United Nations, and Human Rights: The Limits of Compliance* Philadelphia: University of Pennsylvania Press.

Khorshid, Aly (2004) *Islamic Insurance: A Modern Approach to Islamic Banking* London: Routledge Cavendish.

Kim Dae Jung (1994) 'Is Culture Destiny? The Myth of Asian Anti-democratic Values' 73 *Foreign Affairs* 89.

King, B.E. (1963) 'The Basic Concept of Professor Hart's Jurisprudence: the Norm out of the Bottle' (1963) *Cambridge Law Jo.* 270.

Kleingeld, Pauline (ed.) (2006) *Immanuel Kant: Toward Perpetual Peace and other Writings on Politics, Peace, and History* New Haven: Yale University Press.

Klug, Franseca, Keith Starmer, and Stuart Weir (1996) *The Three Pillars of Liberty: Political Rights and Freedoms in the United Kingdom* London: Routledge.

Klug, Heinz (2000) *Constituting Democracy: Law, Globalism, and South Africa's Political Reconstruction* Cambridge: Cambridge University Press.

Kocourek, Albert (1936) 'Factors in the Reception of Law' 10 *Tulane Law Rev.* 209.

    (ed.) (1941) *My Philosophy of Law: Credos of Sixteen American Scholars* Boston: Law Book Co.

Koh, Harold (2003) 'American Exceptionalism' 55 *Stanford L.Rev.* 1479.

Koniak, Susan (1996) 'When Law Risks Madness' 8 *Cardozo Studies in Law and Literature* 65.

    (1997) 'The Chosen People in our Wilderness' 95 *Michigan Law Review* 1761.

Kontos, Alkis (ed.) (1979) *Powers, Possession and Freedom: Essays in Honor of C.B. MacPherson* Toronto: University of Toronto Press.

Kornhauser, Lewis A. (2004) 'Governance Structures, Legal Systems and the Concept of Law' 70 *Chicago-Kent L. Rev.* 355.

Koschaker, Paul (1953) *Europa und das römische Recht* Munich: Biederstein (2nd edn 1953).

Koskenniemi, Martti (1999) 'The Effects of Rights on Political Culture' in Philip Alston (ed.).

    (2001) *The Gentle Civilizer of Nations: The Rise and Fall of Modern International Law, 1870–1960* New York: Cambridge University Press.

    (2005) *From Apology to Utopia: The Structure of International Legal Argument* Cambridge: Cambridge University Press.

Kroeber, Adolph E. and Clyde Kluckhohn (1952) *Culture: A Critical Review of Concepts and Definitions* Chicago: Papers of the Peabody Museum.

Kronman, Anthony (1983) *Max Weber* Stanford: Stanford University Press.

Krygier, Martin (1986) 'Law as Tradition' 5 *Law and Philosophy* 237.

    (1988) 'The Traditionality of Statutes', 1 *Ratio Juris* 20.

Kung, Hans (2007) *Islam: Past, Present and Future* Oxford: Oneworld (trs. John Bowden).

Kuol, Monyluak Alor (1997) *Administration of Justice in the (SPLA/M) Liberated Areas: Court Cases in War-Torn Southern Sudan* Oxford: Refugee Studies Programme.

Kuper, Andrew (2000) 'Rawlsian Global Justice', 28 *Political Theory* 640.

Kuran, Timur (2003) 'The Islamic Commercial Crisis: Institutional Roots of Economic Underdevelopment in the Middle East' 63 *Jo. Economic History* 414.

Lando, Ole and Hugh Beale (eds.) (2000–2003) *Principles of European Contract Law* The Hague: Kluwer Law International.

La Porta, Rafael, Florencio Lopez-de-Silanes, Andrei Schleifer, and Robert W. Vishny (1996) *Law and Finance* (NBER Working Paper 5661) Cambridge, MA.: National Bureau of Economic Research.

(1998) 'Law and Finance' 106 *Jo. Political Economy*, 1113.

(1999) 'The quality of government' 15 *Jo. Law, Economics and Organization* 222.

Lacey, Nicola (1998a) *Unspeakable Subjects: Feminist Essays in Legal and Social Theory* Oxford: Hart.

(1998b) 'Contingency, Coherence, and Conceptualism' in Duff (ed).

(2004) *A Life of H.L.A. Hart: The Nightmare and the Noble Dream* Oxford: Oxford University Press.

(2006) 'Analytical Jurisprudence versus Descriptive Sociology Revisited' 88 *Texas L. Rev.* 945.

Lambsdorff, Johann G. (2007) 'Corruption Perceptions Index 2006' in Transparency International, *Global Corruption Report*.

Larson, Magali (1977) *The Rise of Professionalism: A Sociological Analysis* Berkeley CA: University of California Press.

Lasswell, Harold D. (1971) *Preface* to Deng, *Tradition and Modernization*.

and Myres S. McDougal (1943) 'Legal Education and Public Policy' 52 *Yale Law J.* 203.

and Myres S. McDougal (1964) *Law, Science and Policy* mimeographed materials, New Haven.

and Myres S. McDougal (1992) *Jurisprudence for a Free Society: Studies in Law, Science and Policy* Dordrecht: Kluwer.

Latour, Bruno (1996) *Aramis or the Love of Technology* (trs. Catherine Porter) Cambridge MA: Harvard University Press.

Layard, Richard (2005a) *Happiness: Readings from a New Science* London: Allen Lane.

(2005b) 'Happiness is Back' *Prospect, Issue* 108, March 2005, p. 22.

Lazega, Emmanuel (2001) *The Collegial Phenomenon: The Social Mechanism of Cooperation among Peers in Corporate Law Partnership* New York: Oxford University Press.

Leach, Barton (1938) 'The Restatements as they were in the Beginning, are Now and Perhaps Thenceforth Shall Be' 23 *ABAJ* 517.

Legrand, Pierre (1996) 'European Legal Systems are not Converging', 45 *Int. and Comp. Law Qrtly.* 52.

(1997a) 'Acts of Repression' reprinted in Legrand (1999b) Chapter 9.

(1997b) 'Against a European Civil Code' 60 *MLR* 44.

(1997c) 'The Impossibility of Legal Transplants', 4 *Maastricht Jo. Of European and Comparative Law* 111.

(1999a) 'John Henry Merryman and Comparative Legal Studies: A Dialogue' 47 *American Jo. Comparative Law* 3.

(1999b) *Fragments on Law-as-Culture* Deventer: Tjeenk Willink.

(2003a) 'The Same and the Different' in Legrand and Munday (eds.) at p. 240.

and Roderick Munday (eds.) (2003b) *Comparative Legal Studies: Traditions and Transitions* Cambridge: Cambridge University Press.

Leiter, Brian (1997) 'Is there an "American" Jurisprudence?' (Review of Neil Duxbury's *Patterns of American Jurisprudence*) 17 *OJLS* 367.

(2004a) 'Naturalism in Legal Philosophy' in *Stanford Encyclopedia of Philosophy*. Stanford: Stanford University Press.

(2004b) 'The End of Empire: Dworkin and Jurisprudence in the 21st Century', 36 *Rutgers Law Jo.* 165.

Leiter, Brian (2007) *Naturalising Jurisprudence: Essays on American Legal Realism and Naturalism in Legal Philosophy* Oxford: Oxford University Press.

Lester, Lord of Herne Hill and Colm O'Cinneide, (2004) 'The Effective Protection of Socio-economic Rights' in Ghai and Cottrell (eds.).

Lett, James (1990) *'Emics and Etics: Notes on the Epistemology of Anthropology'* in Headland, Pike, and Harris (eds.) Ch. 9.1.

Levine, R.A. (2001) 'Ethnocentrism' 7 *IESBS* 4852.

Levinson, Sanford (ed.) (2004) *Torture: A Collection* New York: Oxford University Press.

Lewis, William Draper (1937) Introduction to *Restatement of Restitution* Philadelphia American Law Institute.

Leys, Colin (1965) 'What is the Problem of Corruption?' 3 *J. Modern African Studies* 215.
    (1996) *The Rise and Fall of Development Theory* London: Currey.

Lichtblau, Eric (2008) *Bush's Law: The Remaking of American Justice* New York: Pantheon.

Lienhardt, Godfrey (1958) 'Western Dinka' in Middleton and Tait (eds.).
    (1961) *Divinity and Experience: The Religion of the Dinka* Oxford: Clarendon Press.
    (1964) *Social Anthropology* Oxford: Oxford University Press.
    (1982) *'The Dinka and Catholicism'* in Davis (ed.).

Lijnzaad, Liesbeth (1995) *Reservations to UN- Human Rights Treaties: Ratify and Ruin?* Dordrecht, Boston: M.Nijhoff.

Likosky, Michael (ed.) (2002) *Transnational Legal Processes* London: Butterworth.

Lindholm, Tori and Kari Vogt (eds.) (1993) *Islamic Law Reform and Human Rights; Challenges and Rejoinders* Copenhagen: Nordic Human Rights Publications, Oslo.

Lindsey, Timothy (ed.) (2007) *Law Reform in Developing and Transitional Societies* Abingdon: Routledge.

Linebaugh, Peter and Marcus Rediker, (2000) *The Many-headed Hydra: Sailors, Slaves, Commoners and the Hidden History of the Revolutionary Atlantic* London: Verso.

Lipton, Peter (2001) 'Empiricism, History of' 7 *IESBS* 44815.

Liu, Sida (2006) 'Client Influence and the Contingency of Professionalism: The Work of Elite Corporate Lawyers in China' 40 *Law and Society Rev.* 751.

Llewellyn, Karl N. (1930a) *The Bramble Bush* (1960 reprint), NY: Oceana.
    (1930b) 'A Realistic Jurisprudence – The Next Step' reprinted in Llewellyn, (1962) at p. 23.
    (1931) 'Some Realism about Realism' reprinted in Llewellyn, (1962), at p. 42.
    (1934) 'The Constitution as an Institution' 34 *Columbia L. Rev* 1 (extract reprinted in Llewellyn (1962) Chapter 10).
    (1940) 'The Normative, the Legal, and the Law-Jobs: The Problem of Juristic Method' 49 *Yale L. J.* 1355 (NLLJ).
    (1949) 'Law and the Social Sciences – Especially Sociology' 62 *Harv. L. Rev.* 1286 (reprinted in Llewellyn (1962) as Chapter 15).
    (1950) *Law in our Society: A Horse-sense Theory of the Institution of Law* Unpublished materials, University of Chicago Law School, parts updated 1950–58. (LIS).
    (1960) *The Common Law Tradition: Deciding Appeals* Boston: Little Brown.
    (1962), *Jurisprudence: Realism in Theory and Practice.* Chicago: University of Chicago Press (JRTP).
    and E. Adamson Hoebel (1941) *The Cheyenne Way.* Norman: University of Oklahoma Press (CW).

Lloyd, Dennis (1959) *Introduction to Jurisprudence* (1st edn) London: Stevens.

(ed.) (1981) *Psychology in Legal Contexts: Applications and Limitations* London: MacMillan.

Lloyd-Bostock, Sally (1988) *Law in Practice: Applications of Psychology to Legal Decision-making and Legal Skills* London: Routledge.

(ed.) (1981) *Psychology in Legal Contexts* London: Macmillan.

Lockwood, Matthew (2005) *The State They're In: An Agenda for International Action on Poverty in Africa* London: IDTG Publishing.

Lombay, Julian (1998) 'Free Movement of Persons, Recognition of Qualifications, and Working Conditions' 47 *International & Comparative Law Quarterly* 224.

(2001) 'Lawyer Ethics in the Twenty-first Century: The Global Practice Reconciling Regulatory and Deontological Differences – The European Experience' 34 *Vanderbilt Jo. of Transnational Law* 907.

(2004) 'The Free Movement of Persons' 53 *International & Comparative Law Quarterly* 479.

Lord, Christopher (2004) *A Democratic Audit of the European Union* Basingstoke: Palgrave Macmillan.

Loughlin, Martin and Neil Walker (eds.) (2007) *The Paradox of Constitutionalism: Constituent Power and Constitutional Form* Oxford: Oxford University Press.

Lustgarten, Lawrence (2006) 'Human Rights: Where Do we Go from Here?' 69 *MLR* 843.

Lyons, David (1973/1991) *In the Interest of the Governed* Oxford: Oxford University Press.

Macauley, Stuart (1963) 'Non-Contractual Relations in Business: A Preliminary Study' 28 *American Sociological Rev.* 28.

(1979) Review of Merryman, Clark and Friedman in 29 *Am. Jo. Comp.L* 542.

MacCormack, Geoffrey (1985) 'Historical Jurisprudence' 5 *Legal Studies* 251.

MacCormick, Neil (1981a) *H.L.A. Hart* London: Edward Arnold.

(1981b).'Law, Morality and Positivism' 1 *Legal Studies* 131.

(1999) *Questioning Sovereignty: Law, State, and Nation in the European Commonwealth* Oxford: Oxford University Press.

(2007) *Institutions of Law: An Essay in Legal Theory* Oxford: Oxford University Press.

(2008) *H.L.A. Hart* (2nd edn) Stanford: Stanford University Press.

and Zenon Bankowski (eds.) (1989) *Enlightenment, Rights and Revolution* Aberdeen: Abderdeen University Press.

(ed.) (1997) *Constructing Legal Systems: 'European Union' in Legal Theory*. Dordrecht: Kluwer Academic.

and Robert Summers (eds) (1991) *Interpreting Statutes: A Comparative Study*. Aldershot: Dartmouth.

and Robert Summers (eds.) (1997) *Interpreting Precedents: A Comparative Study*. Aldershot: Dartmouth.

and William Twining (1986), 'Theory in the Law Curriculum' LTCL Chapter 13 reprinted in *LIC* (1997), Chapter 7.

Machura, Stefan (2001) 'German Sociology of Law' 32 *The American Sociologist* 41.

Mack, Mary (1962) *Jeremy Bentham: An Odyssey of Ideas 1748–1792* London: Heinemann.

Maine, Sir Henry Sumner (1861) *Ancient Law: Its Connection with the Early History of Society and its Relation to Modern Ideas* (10th edn 1884) London: J. Murray.

Mair, Lucy (1962) *Primitive Government* Harmondsworth: Penguin.

Maitland, Frederick W. (1936) *Selected Essays* (eds. H.D. Hazeltine, G. Lapslely and P.H. Winfield) Cambridge: Cambridge University Press.

Maliyamkono, T.L. and M.S.D. Bagachwa (1990) *The Second Economy in Tanzania* London: J. Currey.

Mallat, Chibli (1993) *The Renewal of Islamic Law* Cambridge: Cambridge University Press.

(2000) 'Commercial Law in the Middle East: Between Old Transactions and Modern Business' 48 *American Jo. Comparative Law* 81.

Manji, Abreema (2002) 'Of the Laws of Kenya and Burials and All That' 14 *Law and Literature* 463.

(2006) *The Politics of Land Reform in Africa: From Communal Tenure to Free Markets* London: Zed Books.

Maritain, Jacques (1951) *Man and the State* Chicago: University of Chicago Press.

(1954) *The Rights of Man and Natural Law* London: Bles.

Markesenis, Basil (1997) *Foreign Law and Comparative Methodology*. Hart: Oxford.

(2001) 'Unity or Division: The Search for Similarities' 54 *Current Legal Problems* 591.

Markovits, Inga (1989) 'Playing the Opposites Game: On Mirjan Damaska's *The Faces of Justice and State Authority*' 41 *Stanford L. Rev.* 1313.

Marmor, Andrei (1998) 'Legal Conventionalism' 4 *Legal Theory* 509.

Martin, Rex (1993) *A System of Rights*. Oxford: Oxford University Press.

and David A. Reidy (eds.) (2006) *Rawls's Law of Peoples: A Realistic Utopia?* Oxford: Blackwell.

Marx, Karl (1844) 'On the Jewish Question' reprinted in Waldron (1987).

Massey, I.P. (1995) *Administrative Law* Lucknow: Eastern Book Company.

Mattei, Ugo (1994) 'Efficiency in Legal Transplants: An Essay in Comparative Law and Economics' 14 *Int. Rev. of Law and Economics* 3.

(1997a) 'Three Patterns of Law: Taxonomy and Change in the World's Legal Systems' 45 *Am. Jo. Comp. Law* 5.

(1997b) *Comparative Law and Economics* Michigan: University of Michigan Press.

Mayer, Ann Elizabeth (1993) 'A Critique of An-Na'im's Assessment of Islamic Criminal Justice' in Lindholm and Vogt Chapter 3.

(1994) 'Universal Versus Islamic Human Rights: A Clash of Cultures or a Clash with a Construct?' 15 *Michigan Jo. Int. Law* 307.

(1999) (3rd edn) *Islam and Human Rights: Tradition and Politics* Boulder: Westview Press.

McAuslan, Patrick (1975) *Land, Law and Planning: Cases, Materials and Text* London: Weidenfeld and Nicolson.

(1998) 'Urbanization, Law and Development: A Record of Research' in Fernandes and Varley Chapter 2.

(2003) *Bringing the Law Back In: Essays in Land, Law and Development* Aldershot: Ashgate.

(2004/08) 'In the Beginning was the Law – An Intellectual Odyssey' Unpublished paper.

(2007) 'Law and the Poor: The Case of Dar-es-Salaam' in Philippopoulos-Mihalopoulos (ed.) Chapter 9.

(2009 forthcoming) *Property and Empire* London: Routledge Cavendish.

McBarnet, Doreen (1978) 'False Dichotomies in Criminal Justice Research' in Baldwin
and Bottomley (eds.)
(2004a) 'Looking for Loopholes: From Enforcement to Enforceability: Creative
Accounting and the Cross-eyed Javelin Thrower' in McBarnet (2004) at p. 231.
(2004b) *Crime, Compliance and Control* Aldershot: Ashgate.
McCrudden, Christopher (2006) 'Legal Research and the Social Sciences' 122 *LQR* 632.
(2007a) 'Judicial Comparativism and Human Rights' in Örücü and Nelken
Chapter 15.
(2007b) *Buying Social Justice: Equality, Government Procurement and Legal Change*
Oxford: Oxford University Press.
(2007b) 'Equality Legislation and Reflexive Regulation: a Response to the
Discrimination Law Review's Consultative Paper' 36 *Industrial Law Journal* 255.
(2008) 'Human Dignity and the Judicial Interpretation of Human Rights' 20 *European
Journal of International Law 1.*
and Gerald Chambers (eds.) (1995) *Individual Rights and the Law in Britain* Oxford:
Clarendon Press.
McDougal, Myres and David Haber (1948) *Property, Wealth, Land: Allocation, Planning
and Development; Selected Cases and Other Materials on the Law of Real Property,
and Introduction* Charlottesville, VA: Michie Casebook Corp.
McKinnon, Don (2006) 'The Rule of Law in Today's Africa' 32 *Commonwealth Law
Bulletin* 649.
McLellan, David (1972) *Karl Marx: Early Texts* Oxford: Blackwell.
Memon, Amina, Aldert Vrij, and Ray Bull (eds.) (2003) *Psychology and Law:
Truthfulness, Accuracy, and Credibility* (2nd edn) Chichester: Wylie.
Mendes, E.P. (1996) *Asian Values and Human Rights: Letting the Tigers Free* Ottawa:
Human Research and Education Center.
Mendelsohn, Oliver and Upendra Baxi (eds.) (1994) *The Rights of Subordinated Peoples*
Delhi: Oxford University Press.
Menski, Werner (2006a) *Comparative Law in a Global Context: The Legal Systems of
Asia and Africa* London: Platinum. (2nd edn) Cambridge: Cambridge University
Press.
(2006b) '*Rethinking legal theory in the light of South–North migration*' in Shah and
Menski (eds.) Chapter 1.
Mercuro, Nicholas and Steven G. Medema (eds.) (2006) *Economics and the Law:
From Posner to Postmodernism and Beyond* Princeton, NJ: Princeton University Press.
Merry, Sally (1988) 'Legal Pluralism', 22 *Law and Society Rev.* 869.
(2001) 'Law: Anthropological Aspects' 12 *IESBS* 8489.
Merryman, John (1954) 'The Authority of Authority' 6 *Stanford L. Rev.* 613.
(1974) '*Comparative Law and Scientific Explanation*' in Hazard and Wagner (eds.).
(1999) *The Loneliness of the Comparative Lawyer and other essays in foreign and
comparative law* The Hague: Kluwer Law International.
(2000a) 'Law and Development Memoirs I: The Chile Law Program' 48 *American
Journal of Comparative Law* 481.
(2000b) 'Law and Development Memoirs II: SLADE' 48 *Am. Jo Comp. L.* 713.
(2003) 'SLADE: A Memoir' in Friedman and Pérez-Perdomo Chapter 14.
David Clarke and Lawrence Friedman (eds.) (1979) *Law and Social Change in
Mediterranean Europe and Latin America: A Handbook of Legal and Social*

Indicators for Comparative Study Stanford: Stanford Law School; Dobbs Ferry, NY: distributed by Oceana Publications.

Merton, Robert K. (1949/1967) *On Theoretical Sociology* New York: Free Press.

Mertus, Julie (1999) 'Mapping Civil Society Transplants: A Preliminary Comparison of Eastern Europe and Latin America' 53 *U. Miami Law Rev.* 921.

Meyer, Lukas, Stanley Paulson, and Thomas Pogge (eds.) (2003) *Rights, Culture, and the Law* Oxford: Oxford University Press.

Middleton, John and David Tait (eds.) (1958) *Tribes without Rulers* London: Routledge and Kegan Paul.

Mifsud Bonnici, Jeanne (2007) *Self-Regulation in Cyberspace* Malta: (Doctoral dissertation).

Mill, John Stuart (1973) *A System of Logic, Ratiocinative and Inductive* (*Collected Works*, Vols 7–8, (ed.) J.M. Robson *et al.* Toronto: 1st edn, London 1843).

Miller, Daniel and Don Slater (2000) *The Internet: An Ethnographic Approach* Oxford: Berg.

Miller, Jonathan (2003) 'A Typology of Legal Transplants' 51 *Am. Jo. Comparative Law* 839.

Miller, Lucinda (2007) 'The Common Frame of Reference and the Feasibility of Common Contract Law in Europe' *Journal of Business Law* 378.

Milne, Alan (1974) 'Bentham's Principle of Utility and Legal Philosophy' in M. James (ed).

Mistelis, L. (2000) 'Regulatory Aspects: Globalization, Harmonization, Legal Transplants, and Law Reform – Some Fundamental Observations' 34 *The International Lawyer* 1055.

Misztal, Bronislaw and Anson Shupe (eds.) (1992) *Religion and Politics in Comparative Perspective: Revival of Religious Fundamentalism in East and West* Westport, CT: Praeger.

Molotch, Harvey (2003), *Where Stuff Comes From* New York: Routledge.

Mommsen, Wolfgang and Ann de Moor (eds.) (1992) *European Expansion and Law: The Encounter of European and Indigenous Law in 19th and 20th Century Africa and Asia* Oxford: Berg.

Moore, Charles (ed.) (1967) *The Chinese Mind: Essentials of Chinese Philosophy and Culture* Honolulu: University of Hawaii Press.

Moore, George Edward (1903) *Principia Ethica* Cambridge: Cambridge University Press.

Moore, Ray. A. and Donald L. Robinson (2004) *Partners for Democracy: Crafting the Japanese State after MacArthur* Oxford: Oxford University Press.

Moore, Sally Falk (1978) *Law as Process* Boston: Routledge and Kegan Paul.
  (ed.) (2005) *Law and Anthropology: A Reader* Malden, MA: Blackwell.

Moorehead, Richard, Avrom Sherr, and Alan Paterson (2003) 'What Clients Know: Client Perspectives on Legal Competence' 10 *Int. Jo. of the Legal Profession* 5.

Moosa, Ebrahim (ed.) (2000) *Revival and Reform in Islam* Boston, MA: One World.

Morgan, Bronwen (2007) 'The Berlin Mega-meeting: Counter-trend to the Nuffield Inquiry Findings?' 53 *Socio-legal Newsletter* 3.
  and Karen Yeung (2007) *An Introduction to Law and Regulation* Cambridge: Cambridge University Press.

Morrison, Wayne (1997) *Jurisprudence: From the Greeks to Post-Modernism* London: Cavendish Publishing.

Mukhopadhyay, Maitrayee and Navsharan Singh (eds.) (2007) *Gender Justice, Citizenship and Development* New Delhi: Zubaan.

Mulgan, Geoff (1991) *Communication and Control: Networks and the New Economics of Communication* New York: Guildford Press.

Munger, Frank (1995/6) 'Crossing Boundaries: Traditions and Transformations in Law and Society Research' Paper prepared for Law and Society Summer Institute, Niagara Ontario.

   (2001) 'Inquiry and Activism in Law and Society' 35 *Law and Society Rev.* 1 (Presidential address).

   and Caroll Seron (1984) 'Critical Legal Studies versus Critical Legal Theory: A Comment on Method' 6 *Law and Policy* 257.

Murphy, Craig N. (2006) *The United Nations Development Programme: A Better Way?* Cambridge: Cambridge University Press.

Myrdal, Gunnar (1944) *An Asian Drama: An Inquiry Into The Poverty of Nations* New York: Pantheon.

Nader, Laura (1984) 'A User Theory of Law' 38 *Southwestern Law Jo.* 951.

   (2002) *The Life of the Law: Anthropological Projects* Berkeley: University of California Press.

   (ed.) (1969) *Law in Culture and Society*. Chicago: Aldine.

Naffine, Ngaire (1990) *Law and the Sexes* London: Allen and Unwin.

Nagel, Thomas (2005), 'The Central Questions' *London Review of Books*, 27, 3 Feb. 2005 (review of Lacey 2004).

Nair, M.M. (1986) *A Handbook of Jurisprudence and Legal Theory* Kerala: Travancore Law House.

Nardin, Terry (1983) *Law, Morality, and the Relations of States* Princeton: Princeton University Press.

   and Melissa Williams (eds.) (2006) *Humanitarian Intervention* (Nomos XLVII) New York: New York University Press.

Nash, Christopher (ed.) (1986) *Narrative and Culture* London: Routledge.

Nelken, David (1981) 'The "Gap Problem" in the Sociology of Law: A Theoretical Overview', 1 *Windsor Yearbook of Access to Justice* 35.

   (2003) 'Comparatists and Transferability' in Legrand and Munday (eds.)

   (2007) 'Defining and Using the Concept of Legal Culture' in Örücü and Nelken (eds.) Chapter 5.

   (ed.) (1997) *Comparing Legal Cultures* Aldershot: Dartmouth.

   and Johannes Feest (eds.) (2001) *Adapting Legal Cultures* Oxford: Hart.

Nelson, John H., Allan Megill, and Donald M. McCloskey (eds.) (1987) *The Rhetoric of the Human Sciences* Madison: University of Wisconsin Press.

Newton, Scott (2007) 'Law and Power in Rwanda in the Shadow of Genocide' 2 *Jo Comparative Law* 151.

Nkrumah, Kwame (1961) *I Speak of Freedom: A Statement of African Ideology* New York: Praeger.

Noonan, John T. (1984) *Bribes* New York: Macmillan.

Norman, T.J. (1990) Review of Pogge *Realizing Rawls*.

North, Douglass C. (1990) *Institutions, Institutional Change and Economic Performance* Cambridge: Cambridge University Press.

Northrop, Filmer (1960) *The Meeting of East and West* New York: MacMillan.

Nussbaum, Martha (1999) *Sex and Social Justice* Oxford: Oxford University Press.

  (2000) *Women and Human Development: The Capabilities Approach* Cambridge: Cambridge University Press.

  (2001) '*The Costs of Tragedy: Some Moral Limits of Cost-benefit Analysis*' in Adler and Posner (eds.) at p. 169.

  and Jonathan Glover (eds.) (1995) *Women, Culture and Development: A Study of Human Capabilities* Oxford: Oxford University Press.

Nyerere, Julius (1966) *Freedom and Unity* Dar-es-Salaam: Oxford University Press.

  (1968) *Ujamaa: Essays on Socialism* Dar-es-Salaam: Oxford University Press.

O'Donnell, Guillermo, Jorge Vargas Cullell and Osvaldo M. Iazzetta (eds.) (2004) *The Quality of Democracy: Theory and Applications* Notre Dame, Ind: University of Notre Dame Press.

O'Neill, Nick, Simon Rice and Roger Douglas (2004) *Retreat from Injustice: Human Rights Law in Australia* Leichhart, NSW: Federation Press.

O'Neill, Onora (1974) 'Lifeboat Earth' 4 *Philosophy and Public Affairs* 273 reprinted in Beitz *et al.* (1985) at p. 262.

  (1986) *Faces of Hunger* London: Allen and Unwin.

  (2000) *Bounds of Justice* Cambridge: Cambridge University Press.

  (2002) *A Question of Trust* BBC Reith Lectures, Cambridge: Cambridge University Press.

Ogus, Anthony (2006) *Costs and Cautionary Tales: Economic Insights for the Law* Oxford: Hart Publishing.

Ojwang, J. Beckton and J. Kanyua Mugambi (eds.) (1989) *The S. M. Otieno Case* Nairobi: Nairobi University Press.

Okin, Susan Moller with respondents (1999) *Is Multiculturalism Bad for Women?* Joshua Cohen, Matthew Howard and Martha C. Nussbaum (eds.) Princeton, N.J: Princeton University Press.

Okupa, Effa (1998) *International Bibliography of African Customary Law: ius non scriptum* Hamburg: LIT verlag.

Ørebech, Peter, Fred Bosselman, Jes Bjarup, David Callies, Martin Chanock, and Hanne Peterson (2005) *The Role of Customary Law in Sustainable Development* Cambridge: Cambridge University Press.

Örücü, Esin (1987) 'An Exercise on the Internal Logic of Legal Systems', 7 *Legal Studies* 310.

  (1992) 'The Impact of European Law on the Ottoman Empire and Turkey'. in Mommsen and De Moor (eds.) at p. 39.

  (1994) 'Diverse Issues, Continuing Debates' in Andrew Bainham (ed.) at p. 449.

  (1995) 'A Theoretical Framework for Transfrontier Mobility of Law' in Jagtenberg, R., E. Örücü and A.J. de Roo (eds.) at p. 5.

  (1996a) 'Turkey: Change Under Pressure' in Örücü, Attwool, and Coyle (eds.) at p. 89.

  (1996b) 'Mixed and Mixing Systems: A Conceptual Search' in Örücü, Attwooll, and Coyle (eds.) at p. 335.

  (1999) *Critical Comparative Law: Considering Paradoxes for Legal Systems in Transition* Nederlandse Verenigning Voor Rechtsvergelijking No. 59 Deventer: Kluwer.

  (2000) 'Turkey Facing the European Union – Old and New Harmonies' 25 *European Law Rev.* 57.

  (2002) 'Law as Transposition' 51 *International and Comparative Law Quarterly* 205.

(2003) 'Comparatists in extraordinary places' in Legrand and Munday (eds.) Chapter 13.

(2004) *The Enigma of Comparative Law: Variations on a Theme for the 21st Century* Leiden: Martinus Nijhoff.

and David Nelken (eds.) (2007) *Comparative Law: A Handbook* Oxford: Hart.

E. Attwooll and S. Coyle (eds.) (1996) *Studies in Legal Systems: Mixed and Mixing* London: Kluwer Law International.

The Oxford Atlas of the World (1994) Oxford: Oxford University Press.

Oxford English Dictionary (2nd edn 1989).

Palley, Claire (1966) *The Constitutional History and Law of Southern Rhodesia, 1888–1965; With Special Reference to Imperial Control* Oxford: Clarendon Press.

Palmeter, David (ed.) (2003) *The WTO as a Legal System: Essays on International Trade Law and Policy* London: Cameron May.

Parekh, Bhiku (ed.) (1993) *Jeremy Bentham: Critical Assessments* London: Routledge. 4 vols.

Parker, Christine, Colin Scott, Nicola Lacey, and John Braithwaite (eds.) (2004) *Regulating Law* Oxford: Oxford University Press.

Passmore, John (1970) *The Perfectibility of Man* London: Duckworth.

Patchett, Keith (1987) 'The Role of Law in the Development Process' 48 *Commonwealth Legal Education Association Newsletter* 33.

Paton, George W. (1951, 2nd edn)(1972, 4th edn. with David Derham) *A Textbook of Jurisprudence* Oxford: Oxford University Press.

Patterson, Dennis (ed.) (1996) *A Companion to Philosophy of Law and Legal Theory* Oxford: Blackwell.

Peacock, J. (2001) 'Values, Anthropology of' 24 *IESBS* 16145.

Pearl, David and Werner Menski, (1998) *Muslim Family Law* (3rd edn) London: Sweet & Maxwell.

Peerenboom, Randall P., Carole J. Petersen and Albert H.Y. Chen (eds.) (2006) *Human Rights in Asia: A Comparative Study of Twelve Asian Jurisdictions, France and the USA* London: New York: Routledge.

Penner, James, David Schiff, and Richard Nobles (eds.) (2002) *Jurisprudence and Legal Theory* London: Lexis Nexis.

Pérez Perdomo, Rogelio (ed.) (1993) *Sociology of Law in Non-Western Countries* Onati: Onati Institute for the Sociology of Law.

Perreau-Saussine, Amanda and James Murphy (eds.) (2007) *The Nature of Customary Law: Legal, Historical and Philosophical Perspectives* Cambridge: Cambridge University Press.

Perry-Kessaris, Amanda (2003) 'Finding and Facing Facts about Legal Systems and Foreign Direct Investment in South Asia' 23 *Legal Studies* 649.

Petersen, Hanne and Henrik Zahle (eds.) (1995) *Legal Polycentricity: Consequences of Pluralism in Law*. Aldershot; Brookfield, VT: Dartmouth Pub. Co.

Petersen, Hanne, Anne Lise Kjaer, and Mikael Madsen (eds.) (2008) *Paradoxes of European Integration* Aldershot: Ashgate.

Petersmann, Ernst-Ulrich and James Harrison (2005) *Reforming the World Trading System: Legitimacy, Efficiency and Democratic Governance* Oxford: Oxford University Press.

Philippopoulos-Mihalopoulos, Andreas (ed.) (2007) *Law and the City* London: Routledge Cavendish.

Phillips, Anne (2003) 'When Culture Means Gender' 66 *MLR* 510.

(2007) *Multiculturalism without Culture* Princeton: Princeton University Press.

Pintore, Anna and Mario Jori, (eds.) (1997) *Law and Language: The Italian Analytical School*. Liverpool: Deborah Charles.

Pistor, Katarina and Philip A. Wellons (1999) *The Role of Law and Legal Institutions in Asian Economic Development 1960–1995* Oxford: Oxford University Press.

Pocock, John G.A. (1968) *Time, Institutions and Action: An Essay on Traditions and their Understanding* London: Methuen.

(1971) *Politics, Language, and Time: Essays on Political Thought and History* London: Methuen.

Podgorecki, Adam *et al.* (1973) *Knowledge and Opinion About Law* London: Martin Robertson.

Pogge, Thomas and Christian Barry (eds.) (2005) *Global Institutions and Responsibilities: Achieving Global Justice* Malden, MA: Oxford: Blackwell.

Pogge, Thomas (1989) *Realizing Rawls* Ithaca: Cornell University Press.

(2001b) 'Rawls and International Justice' 51 *Philosophical Qrtrly* 251.

(2002) *World Poverty and Human Rights* (2nd edn 2008) Cambridge: Polity Press.

(2005) 'Real World Justice' 9 *Jo. of Ethics* 29.

(2007a) *John Rawls: His Life and Theory of Justice*, translated by Michelle Kosch, Oxford: Oxford University Press.

(ed.) (2001a) *Global Justice* Oxford: Blackwell.

(ed.) (2007b) *Freedom from Poverty as a Human Right: Who Owes What to the Very Poor?* Paris: United Nations Educational, Scientific and Cultural Organization; Oxford: Oxford University Press.

Polanski, Przemyslaw P. (2007) *Customary Law of the Internet* The Hague: T.M.C. Asser Press.

Pollock, Sir Frederick (1882) *Essays in Jurisprudence and Ethics*, London: Macmillan.

Posner, Richard (1996) *Law and Legal Theory in England and America*. Oxford: Oxford University Press.

(2007) *Economic Analysis of Law* (7th edn) Austin, Texas: Wolters Kluwer for Aspen Publishers.

Postema, Gerald (1986) *Bentham and the Common Law Tradition* Oxford: Clarendon Press.

(1989) 'In Defence of 'French Nonsense': Fundamental Rights in Constitutional Jurisprudence' in MacCormick and Bankowski (eds.).

(ed.) (2002) *Bentham: Moral, Political and Legal Philosophy* Aldershot: Ashgate.

Pound, Roscoe (1910) 'Law in Books and Law in Action' 44 *American Law Review* 12.

(1917) 'The Limits of Effective Legal Action' 3 *American Bar Association Journal* 56.

(1959) *Jurisprudence* (5 vols.) St Paul, MN: West.

Powell, Walter W. and Paul J. DiMaggio (eds.) (1991) *The New Institutionalism in Organisational Analysis* Chicago: University of Chicago Press.

Power, Michael (1997) *The Audit Society: Rituals of Verification* Oxford: Clarendon Press.

Pozen, Robert (1976) *Legal Choices for State Enterprises in the Third World* New York: New York University Press.

Pradhan, R. (ed.) (2003) *Legal Pluralism and Unofficial Law in Social, Economic, and Political Development* Kathmandu: Commission on Folk Law and Legal Pluralism Press.

Program on International Policy Attitudes (PIPA) (2001) *Americans on Foreign Aid and World Hunger: A Survey of US Public Attitudes* Baltimore: University of Maryland Press.

Quayle, Dan (1991) Speech to the American Bar Association, reported in the *New York Times*, 14 August.

Quine, William van Orme (1951) 'Two Dogmas of Empiricism' 60 *Philosophical Review* 20.

  (1953) *From a Logical Point of View* Cambridge, MA: Harvard University Press.

  (1969) *Ontological Relativity and Other Essays* New York: Columbia University Press.

Quinn, Michael (2008) 'A Failure to Reconcile the Irreconcilable? Security, Subsistence and Equality in Bentham's Writings on the Civil Code and on the Poor Laws' 29 *History of Political Thought* 320.

Radinowicz, Leon (1957) *Sir James Fitzjames Stephen* London: Selden Society Lecture.

Rahman, Fazlur (2000) *Revival and Reform in Islam: A Study of Islamic Fundamentalism* (Ebrahim Moosa (ed.)) Boston, MA: One World.

Rajagopal, Balakrishnan (2003) *International Law from Below: Developing Social Movements and Third World Resistance* Cambridge: Cambridge University Press.

  (2007) 'Introduction: Encountering Ambivalence' in Goodale and Merry (eds.).

Ramadan, Tariq (2004) *Western Muslims and the Future of Islam* Oxford: Oxford University Press.

Ramasatry, Anita (2002) 'What Local Lawyers Think: A Retrospective on the EBRD's Legal Indicator Surveys' in 1 *Law in Transition: Ten Years of Legal Transition*. Autumn London, European Bank for Reconstruction and Development.

Ranney, Austin (1996) *Courts and the Political Process*. Berkeley, CA: Institute of Government Studies.

Rawls, John (1955) 'Two Concepts of Rules', 64 *Philosophical Review* 72.

  (1971) *A Theory of Justice* Cambridge, MA: Harvard University Press; Oxford: Oxford University Press.

  (1980) 'Kantian Constructivism in Moral Theory' (reprinted in *Collected Papers* Chapter 16).

  (1985) 'Justice as Fairness: Political, not Metaphysical' (reprinted in *Collected Papers*, Chapter 18).

  (1987) 'The Idea of an Overlapping Consensus' (reprinted in *Collected Papers*, Chapter 20).

  (1993) *Political Liberalism* New York: Columbia University Press.

  (1995) 'Political Liberalism: Reply to Habermas', 92 *Jo of Philosophy* 132.

  (1999a) 'The Idea of Public Reason Revisited' (1997) in *Collected Papers* Chapter 26.

  (1999b) *Collected Papers* (ed.) S. Freeman, Cambridge, MA: Harvard University Press.

  (1999c) *The Law of Peoples* Cambridge, MA: Harvard University Press.

Raz, Joseph (1970) *The Concept of a Legal System* Oxford: Clarendon Press.

  (1979a) 'The Rule of Law and its Virtue' in Raz (1979b).

  (1979b) *The Authority of Law: Essays on Law and Morality* Oxford: Clarendon Press.

  (1984) 'On the Nature of Rights' 93 *Mind* 194.

  (1994a) 'Facing Diversity: The Case of Epistemic Abstinence' in Raz (1994b) Chapter 4.

  (1994b) *Ethics in the Public Domain* Oxford: Oxford University Press.

  (1998) 'Multiculturalism' 11 *Ratio Juris* 193.

  (1999) *Engaging Reason*. Oxford: Oxford University Press.

(2001) *Value, Respect, and Attachment* Cambridge: Cambridge University Press.

(2003) 'Comments and Responses' in Meyer *et al.* p. 253.

Reed, Chris (2004) *Internet Law: Text and Materials* (2nd edn) Cambridge: Cambridge University Press.

Reimann, Mathias (1996) 'The End of Comparative Law as an Autonomous Discipline', 11 *Tulane Civil and European Law Forum* 49.

(2002) 'The Progress and Failure of Comparative Law' 50 *Am. Jo. Comparative Law* 671.

(ed.) (1993) *The Reception of Continental Ideas in the Common Law World* Berlin: Duncker and Humblot.

and Reinhard Zimmerman (eds.) (2006) *The Oxford Handbook of Comparative Law* Oxford: Oxford University Press.

Reinicke, Wolfgang H., and Francis Deng, (2000) *Critical Choices: The United Nations, Networks, and the Future of Global Governance* Global Public Policy Project, Ottawa: International Development Research Center.

Renteln, Alison Dundas (1990) *Relativism and the Search for Human Rights* London: Sage. (See also 90 *American Anthropologist* 64 (1988).)

(2004) *The Cultural Defense* New York: Oxford University Press.

Resnick, Judith (2001) 'Procedure: Legal Aspects' 18 *IESBS* 12140.

Rezsohazy, R. (2001) 'Values, Sociology of' 24 *IESBS* 116153.

Richards, Ivor A. (1943/67) *How To Read a Page* London: Routledge and Kegan Paul.

Riles, Annelise (2000) *The Network Inside Out* Ann Arbor: University of Michigan Press.

(2002) 'The Virtual Sociality of Rights: The Case of Women's Rights are Human Rights' in Likosky (ed.).

(2004) 'Anthropology, Human Rights and Legal Knowledge: Culture in the Iron Cage' 15 *Finnish Yearbook of International Law* 9.

(2006) *Documents: Artifacts of Modern Knowledge* Ann Arbor: University of Michigan Press.

(ed.) (2001) *Rethinking the Masters of Comparative Law* Oxford: Hart.

Risse, Mathias (2005) 'How Does the Global Order Harm the Poor?' 33 *Philosophy and Public Affairs* 349.

Roberts, Simon (1979) *Order and Dispute: An Introduction to Legal Anthropology* Harmondsworth: Penguin.

(1998) 'Against Legal Pluralism: Some Reflections on the Contemporary Enlargement of the Legal Domain' 42 *Jo. Legal Pluralism* 95.

(2005) 'After Government? On Representing Law Without the State' 68 *MLR* 1.

and Michael Palmer (2005) *Dispute Processes: ADR and the Primary Forms of Decision-Making* (2nd edn) Cambridge: Cambridge University Press.

Robinson, Mary (2007) *A Voice for Human Rights* (Kevin Boyle (ed.)) Philadelphia: University of Pennsylvania Press.

Robinson, Richard (1950) *Definition* Oxford: Oxford University Press.

Rodley, Nigel (1999) *The Treatment of Prisoners Under International Law* (2nd edn) Oxford University Press.

Roe, Mark J. (2006) 'Legal Origins, Politics, and Modern Stock Markets' 120 *Harvard L. Rev.* 460.

Rogers, Ben (1999) 'John Rawls' *Prospect*, June.

Rogers, Everett M. (1995) *Diffusion of Innovations* (4th edn) (1st edn 1962) New York: The Free Press.

Rorty, Richard (1987) 'Science as Solidarity' in Nelson, Megill, and McCloskey (eds.).

(1989) *Contingency, Irony, and Solidarity* Cambridge: Cambridge University Press.

(1991) *Objectivity, Relativism and Truth* Cambridge: Cambridge University Press.

(1993) 'Human Rights, Rationality and Sentimentality' in Shute and Hurley (eds.) at p. 111.

Rosen, Frederick (1983) *Jeremy Bentham and Representative Democracy* Oxford: Oxford University Press.

(1996) Introduction to Bentham *Introduction to the Principles of Morals and Legislation* Oxford: Oxford University Press.

(1997) 'Utilitarianism and the Punishment of the Innocent: The Origins of a False Doctrine' 9 *Utilitas* 23.

Rosen, Lawrence (1989) *The Anthropology of Justice: Law as Culture in Islamic Society* Cambridge: Cambridge University Press.

(2000) *The Justice of Islam* Oxford: Oxford University Press.

Rosenstock-Huessy, Eugen (1938) *Out of Revolution: Autobiography of Western Man* New York: Morrow.

Roshier, Bob and Harvey Teff (1980) *Law and Society in England* London: Tavistock Publications.

Ross, Hamish (2001) *Law as a Social Institution* Oxford: Hart.

Rossi, Peter H. and Stephen Nock (1982) *Measuring Social Judgments: The Factorial Survey Approach* Beverly Hills, CA: Sage.

and Richard A Berk (1997) *Just Punishments: Federal Guidelines and Public Views Compared* New York: Aldine De Gruyter.

Rothman, David (1971) *The Discovery of the Asylum* Boston: Little, Brown.

Rowland, Stephen (2006) *The Enquiring University* Maidenhead: Open University Press.

Royal Anthropological Institute (1950) *Notes and Queries in Anthropology* (6th edn.), London.

Rubin, Paul H. (1994) 'Growing a Legal System in the Post-Communist Economies' 27 *Cornell Int. L. J.* 1.

Rudé, G. (1959) *The Crowd in the French Revolution* Oxford: Clarendon Press.

Ryle, John *et al.*, (1982) *Warriors of the White Nile: The Dinka* Amsterdam: Time-Life Books.

Sacco, Rudolfo (1991) 'Legal Formants: A Dynamic Approach to Comparative Law II', 39 *Am. Jo. Comparative Law* 343.

Sachleben, Mark (2006) *Human Rights Treaties: Considering Patterns of Participation 1948–2000* New York: Routledge.

Sachs, Jeffrey (2005) *The End of Poverty: How We Can Make It Happen In Our Lifetime* London: Penguin.

Said, Edward (1994) *Orientalism* (1st edn, 1978) New York: Vintage Books.

Salamon, Lester M. (ed.) (2002) *The Tools of Government* Oxford: Oxford University Press.

Salmond, John William, Sir (1947) *Jurisprudence* (1996 12th edn) London: Sweet and Maxwell.

Sandel, Michael (1982) *Liberalism and the Limits of Justice* Cambridge: Cambridge University Press.

(ed.) (1984) *Liberalism and its Critics* Oxford: Blackwell.

Sands, Philippe (2005) *Lawless World: America and the Making and Breaking of Global Rules* London: Allen Lane; Penguin.

Santos, Alvaro (2006) 'The World Bank's Uses of "The Rule of Law" Promise in Economic Development' in Trubek and Santos (2006) at p. 253.

Santos, Boaventura and Cesar Rodriguez-Garavito (2005) *Law and Globalization from Below: Towards a Cosmopolitan Legality* Cambridge: Cambridge University Press.

Santos, Boaventura de Sousa (1995) *Toward a New Common Sense* London: Routledge.

(2002) *Toward a New Legal Common Sense: Law, Globalisation and Emancipation* (2nd edn) London: Butterworth.

Sarat, Austin and William Felstiner (1995) *Divorce Lawyers and Their Clients* New York: Oxford University Press.

Sarat, Austin and Susan Silbey (1988) 'The Pull of the Policy Audience' 10 *Law and Policy* 97.

Sarkar A.K. (1973) (ed.) *Summary of Salmond's Jurisprudence* (3rd edn 1981) Bombay: Tripathi.

Sarkar, Subodh C. (1913, 1971) *Sarkar on Evidence* (1st edn 1913; 12th edn 1971 (eds.) P.C. and S. Sarkar) Calcutta: Sarkar and Sons.

Sartorius, Rolf (1969) 'Utilitarianism and Obligation' 66 *Jo. Philosophy* 67.

Sauter, Wolf and Ellen Vos (1998) 'Harmonisation under Community Law: The Comitology Issue' in Craig and Harlow (eds.) Chapter 8.

Scanlon, Thomas M. (1998) *What We Owe Each Other* Cambridge MA: Belknap Press of Harvard University.

Schacht, Joseph (1964) *Introduction to Islamic Law* Oxford: Oxford University Press.

Schama, Simon (2005) *Rough Crossings* London: BBC Books.

Schauer, Frederick (1991) *Playing by the Rules*. Oxford: Oxford University Press.

(2006) '(Re)Taking Hart' 119 *Harvard L. Rev.* 852 (Review of Lacey (2004)).

Schlegel, John Henry (1995) *American Legal Realism and Empirical Social Science* Chapel Hill: University of North Carolina Press.

Schlemmer-Schulte, Sabine and Ko-Yung Tung (2001) *Liber amicorum Ibrahim F.I. Shihata: International Finance and Development Law* The Hague: Kluwer Law International.

Schlesinger, Rudolph B. (ed.) (1968) *Formation of Contracts – A Study of the Common Core of Legal Systems*. 2 vols. Dobbs Ferry, New York: Oceana.

et al. (1998) *Comparative Law: Cases, Text, Materials* (6th edn) New York: Foundation Press.

Schofield, Philip (2006) *Utility and Democracy: The Political Thought of Jeremy Bentham* Oxford: Oxford University Press.

Schum, David (1994/2001) *Evidential Foundations of Probabilistic Reasoning* New York: Wylie; reprinted (2001) Evanston: Northwestern University Press.

Scott, Colin (2004) 'Regulation in the Age of Governance: The Rise of the Post-regulatory State' in Jordana and Levi-Faur (eds.).

Scott, W. Richard (1995) *Institutions and Organizations* Thousand Oaks, CA.: Sage.

(2001) 'Organization: Overview' 16 *IESBS* 10910.

(1998) (4th edn) *Organizations: Rational, Natural, and Open Systems* Upper Saddle River, NJ: Prentice Hall.

Sedley, Sir Stephen (2005) 'Are Human Rights Universal and Does it Matter?' Holdsworth Lecture, University of Birmingham.

Seidman, Robert (1965) 'The Inarticulate Premiss' 3 *Jo. Modern African Studies* 567.

(1978) *The State, Law and Development* London: Croom Helm.

Seidman, Ann and Robert Seidman (1994) *State and Law in the Development Process* New York: St Martin's Press.

Selznick, Philip (1949) *TVA and the Grass Roots: A Study in the Sociology of Formal Organizations* Berkeley, CA: University of California Press.

Sen, Amartya and Jean Drèze (1999) *The Amartya Sen and Jean Drèze Omnibus* New Delhi: Oxford University Press.

Sen, Amartya (1981) *Poverty and Famines: An Essay on Entitlement and Deprivation* Oxford: Clarendon Press.

(1997) 'Human Rights and Asian Values: What Lee Kuan Yew and Li Peng Don't Understand about Asia' July 14 & 21 *The New Republic*, 33.

(1999) *Development as Freedom* Oxford: Oxford University Press.

(2004), 'Elements of a Theory of Human Rights' 32 *Philosophy and Public Affairs* 315.

Senghaas, Dieter (2007) *On Perpetual Peace: A Timely Assessment* New York: Berghan Books.

Shah, Prakash and Werner Menski (eds.) (2006) *Migration, Diasporas and Legal Systems in Europe* London: Routledge Cavendish.

Shapiro, Martin (1981) *Courts: A Comparative and Political Analysis* Chicago: University of Chicago Press.

Sherr, Avrom, Alan Paterson and Richard Moorehead (1994) *The Quality Agenda Volume One: Assessing and Developing Competence and Quality in Legal Aid – The Report of the Birmingham Franchising Pilot* London: HMSO.

Sherr, Avrom, Lisa Webley, S. Rogers, Alan Paterson and Simon Domberger (2000) *Quality and Cost: Final Report on the Contracting of Civil, Non-Family Advice and Assistance* Pilot Norwich: Stationery Office.

Shihata, Ibrahim F. (1991) *The World Bank in a Changing World* Dordrecht: Nijhoff.

Shils, Edward (1981) *Tradition* Chicago: University of Chicago Press.

Shivji, Issa (1989) *The Concept of Human Rights in Africa* London: Codesria.

(1998) *Not Yet Democracy: Reforming Land Tenure in Tanzania* London: International Institute for Environment and Development.

(ed.) (1986) *The Limits of Legal Radicalism* Dar-es-Salaam: Faculty of Law.

Short J.F. Jr. (2001) 'Crime: Sociological Aspects' 5 *IESBS* 2934.

Shue, Henry (1980) *Basic Rights* Princeton: Princeton University Press.

Shute, Stephen and Susan Hurley (eds.) (1993) *On Human Rights* (The Oxford Amnesty Lectures) New York: Basic Books.

Siddiqi, Muhammad Nejatullah (1997) *Banking Without Interest* Leicester: The Islamic Foundation.

Sidgwick, Henry (1907) *The Methods of Ethics* London: MacMillan.

Siedentop, Larry (2000) *Democracy in Europe* London: Penguin.

Siems, M.M. (2005) 'What Does Not Work in Comparing Securities Laws: A Critique of La Porta *et al.*'s Methodology' 16 *International Company and Commercial Law Rev.* 300.

Silbey, Susan and Austin Sarat (1987) 'Critical Traditions in Law and Society Research'
    21 *Law and Society Rev.* 165.

Simmonds, Nigel (1986, 1st edn) *Central Issues in Law and Jurisprudence: Justice, Law
    and Rights* London: Sweet & Maxwell.

Simmons, Paul A. (1992) 'Government by Unaccountable Private Non-Profit
    Corporation' 10 *Jo. of Human Rights* 67.

Simpson, A.W. Brian (2001) *Human Rights and the End of Empire: Britain and the
    Genesis of the European Convention* Oxford: Oxford University Press.

  (ed.) (1984) *Biographical Dictionary of the Common Law* London: Butterworth.

Singer, Peter (1972) 'Famine, Affluence and Morality' in 1 *Philosophy and Public Affairs*
    229. Reprinted in Beitz *et al.* (eds.) (1985) at p. 247.

  (1975/1990/1) *Animal Liberation* New York: Random House.

  (1977) '*Reconsidering the Famine Relief Argument*' in Brown and Shue (eds.)

  (1979/1993) *Practical Ethics* Cambridge: Cambridge University Press.

  (1980) *Marx* Oxford: Oxford University Press.

  (1983) *The Expanding Circle: Ethics and Sociobiology* Oxford: Oxford University Press.

  (2002/2004) *One World: The Ethics of Globalization* (2nd edn), New Haven: Yale
    University Press.

  (ed.) (1991) *A Companion to Ethics* Oxford: Blackwell.

Slaughter, Anne-Marie (1994) 'A Typology of Transjudicial Communication' 29
    U. Richmond Law Rev. 99.

  (2004) *A New World Order* Princeton: Princeton University Press.

Smart, J.J.C. (1967) 'Utilitarianism' 7 *Encyclopedia of Philosophy* P. Edwards (ed.).

Smelser, Neil and Paul Baltes (eds.) (2001) *International Encyclopedia of the Social and
    Behavioral Sciences* New York: Elsevier (*IESBS*).

Smigel, Erwin O. (1964) *The Wall Street Lawyer, Professional Organization Man?* New
    York: Free Press.

Smith, Adam (1776) *An Inquiry into the Nature and Causes of the Wealth of Nations*
    Dublin: Whitestone.

Smits, Jan M. (2007) 'Convergence of Private law in Europe: Towards a new *ius
    commune*?' In Őrűcű and Nelken (eds.) Chapter 10.

Snyder, Francis G. (1980) 'Law and Development in the Light of Dependency Theory' 14
    Law and Society Rev. 723.

  (1993) 'The Effectiveness of European Community Law: Institutions, Processes, Tools
    and Techniques' 56 *MLR* 19.

Soros, George (2002) *George Soros on Globalization* New York: Public Affairs.

Soueif, Ahdaf (1999) *The Map of Love* London: Bloomsbury.

Stade, R. (2001) 'Diffusion: Anthropological Aspects' 6 *IESBS* 3673.

Starr, June and Jane Collier (1989) *History and Power in the Study of Law: New
    Directions in Legal Anthropology* Ithaca: Cornell University Press.

Stein, Peter (1980) *Legal Evolution: The Story of an Idea* Cambridge: Cambridge
    University Press.

  (1984) 'Maine, Sir Henry James Sumner' in Simpson (ed.) at p. 341.

  (1988) *The Character and Influence of the Roman Civil Law: Historical Essays* London:
    Hambledon Press.

Steiner, Henry and Philip Alston (eds.) (1996) *International Human Rights in Context: Law,
    Politics, Morals* (3rd edn 2008 with Ryan Goodman) Oxford: Oxford University Press.

Stephen, J. Fitzjames (1883) *A Digest of the Law of Evidence* (12th edn 1948) London: Macmillan.

Stern, Vivien (1998) *A Sin Against the Future: Imprisonment in the World* Harmondsworth: Penguin.

Stevens, Robert B (1983) *Law School: Legal Education in America from the 1850s to the 1980s* Chapel Hill: University of North Carolina Press.

Stewart, Ann (2007) 'Who Do We Care About? Reflections on Gender Justice in the Global Market' 58 *Northern Ireland Legal Quarterly* 359.

    (forthcoming 2009) *Gender, Law and Justice in a Global Market* Cambridge: Cambridge University Press.

Steyn, Johan (2004) 'Guantanamo Bay: The Legal Black Hole' 53 *Int. and Comp. L. Qtrly* 1.

Stiglitz, Joseph (2002) *Globalisation and its Discontents* New York: W.W. Norton: London: Allen Lane.

Stone, Christopher (1996) *Should Trees have Standing?: And Other Essays on Law, Morals and the Environment* Dobbs Ferry, NY: Oceana.

Stone, Julius (1950) *The Province and Function of Law*. Cambridge, MA: Harvard University Press.

    (1959) 'The Ratio of the Ratio Decidendi' 22 *MLR* 597.

    (1966) *Law and the Social Sciences in the Second Half Century* Minneapolis: U. Minnesota Press.

    (1966) *Social Dimensions of Law and Justice* London: Stevens.

    (1967) 'Trends in Jurisprudence in the Second Half Century' printed in Hathaway (1980).

Stotzky, Irwin P. (1993) *Transition to Democracy in Latin America: The Role of the Judiciary* Boulder: Westview Press.

Strang, David and Sarah A. Soule (1998) 'Diffusion in Organizations and Social Movements: From Hybrid Corns to Poison Pills', 24 *Annual Review of Sociology* 265.

Suchman, M.C. (2001) 'Organizations and the Law' 16 *IESBS* 10948.

Sugarman, David (2005) 'Hart Interviewed: H.L.A. Hart in Conversation with David Sugarman' 32 *Jo. of Law and Society* 267.

Summers, Robert S. (1971) 'The Technique Element in Law' 59 *California L. Rev.* 733.

    (1993) 'A Formal Theory of the Rule of Law' 6 *Ratio Juris* 127.

    (1999) 'Propter Honoris Respectum: The Principles of the Rule of Law' 74 *Notre Dame L. Rev.* 1691.

Sumner, William Graham (1906) *Folkways* New York: Ginn.

Supiot, Alain (ed.) (2001) *Beyond Employment: Changes in Work and the Future of Labour Law in Europe* (The Supiot Report) Oxford: Oxford University Press.

Sutton, Francis X (ed.) (1990) *A World to Make: Development in Perspective* New Brunswick, NJ: Transaction Publishers.

Symposium (1956) on The Reception of Foreign Law in Turkey, Annales de la Faculté de Droit d'Istanbul No.6; Symposium in 9 *Int. Social Science Bulletin*.

    (1992) 'Do Lawyers Impair Economic Growth?' 17 *Law and Social Inquiry* No.4 (contributions by Epp, Magee, Gilson, Kefer, Cross and Sander).

    (1995) 'Donald Black and the Sociology of Law' 20 *Law and Social Inquiry* 777–870.

    (2000) John Rawls's *Law of Peoples* in 110 *Ethics* 669.

(2006) 'Empirical Studies of the Legal Profession: What Do We Know about Lawyers' Lives?' 84 *N. Carolina L. Rev* No. 5 1415.

(2007) 'Globalization of the Legal Profession' 14 *Indiana Jo. Global Legal Studies* 1.

Szabo, D. (2001) 'Criminal Justice, Sociology of' 5 *IESBS* 2954.

Tabandeh, Sultanhussein (1970) *A Muslim Commentary on the Universal Declaration of Human Rights* London: Goulding.

Taha, Mahmoud Mohamed (1987) *The Second Message of Islam* (trs. and ed. Abdullahi An Na'im). Syracuse: Syracuse University Press.

Tamanaha, Brian (1993) *Understanding Law in Micronesia: An Interpretive Approach to Transplanted Law* Oxford: Oxford University Press.

(1995) 'The Lessons of Law-and-Development Studies', 89 *Am. Jo. Int. L.* 470. (Review Article).

(1997) *Realistic Socio-Legal Theory: Pragmatism and a Social Theory of Law* Oxford: Oxford University Press.

(2001) *A General Jurisprudence of Law and Society* Oxford: Oxford University Press.

(2004) *On the Rule of Law: History, Politics, Theory* New York: Cambridge University Press.

(2006) *Law as a Means to an End: Threat to the Rule of Law* New York: Cambridge University Press.

(2007) 'Enhancing Prospects for General Jurisprudence' 15 *University of Miami International and Comparative Law Rev* 69.

Tanenbaum, Sandra J. (2006) 'Evidence by Any Other Name: Commentary on Tonnelli (2006)' 12 *Jo. Of Evaluation of Clinical Practice* 273.

Tarde, Gabriel (1979) *Les lois de l'imitation* (lst edn 1890) Paris: Slatkine Reprints.

Tasioulas, John (2002a) 'Human Rights, Universality and the Values of Personhood: Retracing Griffin's Steps' 10 *European Jo. of Philosophy* 79.

(2002b) 'From Utopia to Kazanistan: John Rawls and the Law of Peoples' 22 *Oxford Jo. Legal Studies* 367.

(2002c) 'International Law and the Limits of Fairness' 13 *European Jo. of International Law* 993.

(2005) 'Global Justice without End' 36 *Metaphilosophy* 3.

(2006) 'Punishment and Repentance' 81 *Philosophy* 279.

(2007a) 'The Moral Reality of Human Rights' in Pogge (ed.) at p. 75.

(2007b) 'Customary International Law and the Quest for Justice' in Perreau-Saussine and Murphy (eds.) at p. 307.

(2008) 'The Legitimacy of International Law' in Besson and Tasioulas (eds.) Chapter 3.

Taylor, Charles (1979) 'Atomism' in Kontos (ed.).

(1995) *Philosophical Arguments* Cambridge, MA: Harvard University Press.

(1999) 'Conditions of an Unenforced Consensus on Human Rights' in Bauer and Bell (eds.).

(2007) *A Secular Age* Cambridge, MA: Harvard University Press.

Taylor, Veronica (2007) 'Law Reform Olympics: Measuring the Effects of Law Reform in Transitional Economies' in Lindsey (ed.) Chapter 4.

Teitel, Ruti (2000) *Transitional Justice* Oxford: Oxford University Press.

Terry, Laurel S. (2007) 'The Bologna Process and its Implications for U.S. Legal Education' 57 *Jo. Legal Education* 237.

Téson, Fernando R. (1998) *A Philosophy of International Law* Boulder: Westview Press.

Téson, Fernando (1999) 'The Rawlsian Theory of International Law' 9 *Ethics and International Affairs* 79.

Teubner, Gunther (1992) 'The Two Faces of Janus: Rethinking Legal Pluralism' 13 *Cardozo Law Rev.* 1443.

(ed.) (1997a) 'Global Bukowina': Legal Pluralism in World Society' in Teubner (1997b).

(ed.) (1997b) *Global Law Without a State* Aldershot: Dartmouth.

Thatcher, Margaret (1993) *The Downing Street Years* London: HarperCollins.

Thomas, Philip (ed.) (1996) *Legal Frontiers* Aldershot, Hants; Brookfield, VT: Dartmouth.

(ed.) (1997) *Socio-Legal Studies* Aldershot: Dartmouth.

Thompson, Edward P. (1963) *The Making of the English Working Class* London: Victor Gollancz.

(1975) *Whigs and Hunters: The Origin of the Black Act* London: Allen Lane.

Tibi, Bassam (1993) 'Islamic Law/Shar'ia and Human Rights: International Law and Relations' in Lindholm and Vogt (eds.) Chapter 5.

Tonelli, Mark R. (2006) 'Integrating Evidence into Clinical Practice: An Alternative to Evidence-based Approaches' 12 *Jo. of Evaluation of Clinical Practice* 248.

Toynbee, Arnold Joseph (1947) *The Study of History* Oxford: Oxford University Press.

Transparency International (2007) *Global Corruption Report: Corruption in Judicial Systems* Cambridge: Cambridge University Press.

Trubek, David and Marc Galanter (1974) 'Scholars in Self-Estrangement: Reflections on the Crisis of Law and Development Studies in the United States' 1974 *Wisconsin L. Rev.* 1062.

Alvaro Santos (eds.) (2006) *The New Law and Economic Development* New York: Cambridge University Press.

Tsagourias, Nicholas (ed.) (2007) *Transnational Constitutionalism: International and European Models* Cambridge: Cambridge University Press.

Tufte, Edward R (1983) *The Visual Display of Quantititative Information* Cheshire Conn.: The Graphics Press.

(1990) *Envisioning Information* Cheshire, Conn: The Graphics Press.

(1997) *Visual Explanations* Cheshire, Conn: The Graphics Press.

Tur, Richard and William Twining (eds.) (1986) *Essays on Kelsen* Oxford: Oxford University Press.

Twining, William (1957) 'Some Aspects of Reception', *Sudan Law Jo. and Reports* 229.

(1963) 'The Restatement of African Customary Law: A Comment' 1 *Jo. Modern African Studies* 221.

(1964) *The Place of Customary Law in the National Legal Systems of East Africa* Chicago: University of Chicago Law School.

(1968) *The Karl Llewellyn Papers* Chicago: University of Chicago Law School.

(1973) *Karl Llewellyn and the Realist Movement.* London: Weidenfeld and Nicolson; Norman: University of Oklahoma Press (1985) (KLRM).

(1974a) 'Law and Social Science: The Method of Detail', *New Society*, 27 June.

(1974b) 'Some Jobs for Jurisprudence' 1 *British Jo. Of Law and Society* 149.

(1975) 'The Contemporary Significance of Bentham's Anarchical Fallacies' 61 *Archiv fur Rechts – und Sozialphilosophie* 325.

(1976) *Academic Law and Legal Development* Lagos: Faculty of Law, University of Lagos (Taylor Lectures, 1975).

(1979), 'Academic Law and Legal Philosophy: The Significance of Herbert Hart' 95 *Law Quarterly Rev.* 557 (reprinted in *GJB* Chapter 4).

(1983) 'Alternative to What?' 56 *MLR* 380.

(ed.) (1986) *Legal Theory and Common Law* Oxford: Blackwell (*LTCL*).

(1993a) 'Karl Llewellyn's Unfinished Agenda: Law and Society and the Job of Juristic Method.' *Chicago Papers in Legal History* Chicago: University of Chicago Law School (reprinted in *GJB*, Chapter 6) (*JJM*).

(1993b) 'Constitutions, Constitutionalism and Constitution-making' in Stotzky (ed.) Chapter 25.

(1994) *Blackstone's Tower: The English Law School* London: Sweet and Maxwell (Hamlyn Lectures) (*BT*).

(1996), 'Rethinking Law Schools', 21 *Law and Social Inquiry* 1007.

(1997a) 'Other People's Power: The Bad Man and English Positivism 1897–1997' 63 *Brooklyn L. Rev.* 189. (reprinted in *GLT*, Chapter 5).

(1997b) *Law in Context: Enlarging a Discipline*. Oxford: Oxford University Press (*LIC*).

(1998) 'Thinking about Law Schools: Rutland Reviewed' 25 *Jo. Law and Society* 1.

(2000a) 'Comparative Law and Legal Theory: The Country and Western Tradition' in Edge, Ian (ed.) at p. 21.

(2000b) *Globalisation and Legal Theory* London: Butterworth and Evanston: Northwestern University Press (*GLT*).

(2001) 'A Cosmopolitan Discipline? Some Implications of "Globalisation" for Legal Education', 8 *Int. Jo. Legal Profession* 23, also in *1 Jo. of Commonwealth Law and Legal Education* 13.

(2002a) 'Cosmopolitan Legal Studies', 9 *Int. Jo. Legal Profession* 1.

(2002b) 'Reviving General Jurisprudence'. in M. Likosky (ed.) Ch. 3 (reprinted in *GJB*, Chapter 10).

(2002c) *The Great Juristic Bazaar: Jurists' Texts and Lawyers' Stories* Aldershot: Ashgate. (*GJB*).

(2002d) 'Talk About Realism' in *The Great Juristic Bazaar* Chapter 5.

(2003a) 'A Post-Westphalian Conception of Law' 37 *Law and Society Review* 199.

(2003b) 'The Province of Jurisprudence Re-examined' (Julius Stone Lecture) in Dauvergne (ed.) Chapter 2.

(2003c) '*The Role of Academics in the Legal System*' in Cane and Tushnet (eds.) 920.

(2005a) 'Diffusion of Law: A Global Perspective' 49 *Jo. Legal Pluralism* 1.

(2005b) 'Have Concepts, Will Travel' 1 *Int. Jo. Law in Context* 5.

(2005c) 'Human Rights: Southern Voices' 11 *Review of Constitutional Studies* 203.

(2005d) 'Social Science and Diffusion of Law' 32 *Jo. Law and Society*, 203.

(2005e) 'General Jurisprudence' Proceedings of World Congress of Philosophy of Law and Social Philosophy, Granada in Escamilla and Saavedra (eds.).

(2006a) 'Diffusion and Globalization Discourse' 47 *Harvard International Law Jo.* 507.

(2006b) 'Glenn on Tradition. An Overview' 1 *Jo. Comparative Law* 107.

(2006c) *Rethinking Evidence: Exploratory Essays* (2nd edn) (1st edn 1990) Cambridge: Cambridge University Press (*RE*).

(2006d) 'Schauer on Hart' 119 *Harvard L Rev Forum* 122.

(2007a) 'Globalisation and Comparative Law' in Örücü and Nelken (eds.) Chapter 3.

(2007b) 'Law and Development: Sketches for a Memoir' (unpublished).

(2007c) 'The Challenge of Authority – a Post-Modern Foundationalist?' *Public Law* 210. (Comment on Gearty (2006)).

(2007d) 'General Jurisprudence' 15 *University of Miami International and Comparative Law Rev.* 1.

(2008a) 'The Law in Context Movement' in Cane and Conaghan (eds.).

(2008c) 'Law, Justice and Rights: Some Implications of a Global Perspective' in Ebbeson and Okowa (eds.).

(2009) '*Institutions of Law*: Globalization, non-state law and legal pluralism' in Macksymillian Del Mar (ed.).

and David Miers (1999) *How to Do Things With Rules* London: Butterworth, (4th edn) (*HTDTWR*).

and Emma V, Quick (eds.) (1994) *Legal Records in the Commonwealth* Aldershot: Ashgate.

and Iain Hampsher-Monk (eds.) (2003) *Evidence and Inference in History and Law: Interdisciplinary Dialogues* Evanston: Northwestern University Press.

and Penelope Twining (1973) '*Bentham on Torture*' in James (ed.).

UK Department for International Development (DFID) (2000) *Justice and Poverty Reduction* London.

Ul Haq, Mahbub (1995) *Reflections on Human Development* New York: Oxford University Press.

Ullmann-Margalit, Edna (1977) *The Emergence of Norms* Oxford: Oxford University Press.

UNCS (Habitat) (1997a) *The Istanbul Declaration and the Habitat Agenda* New York: Habitat.

(1997b) *The Challenge of Sustainable Cities* New York: Habitat.

Unger, Roberto M. (1996) *What Should Legal Analysis Become?* New York: Verso.

United Nations Development Programme (2003a) *Human Development Report 2003: Millennium Development Goals: A Compact Among Nations to End Poverty* New York and Oxford: Oxford University Press.

(2003b) *Indicators for Monitoring the Millennium Development Goals* New York: United Nations.

(2004) *2015: Mobilizing Global Partnerships* (UNDP Annual report).

(2005) *A Time for Bold Ambition: Together We Can Cut Poverty in Half* (Annual Report).

(2007) Country reports www.undp.org/mdg/countryreports2.shtml

United Nations (2000) Millennium Declaration http://un.org/millennium/declaration/ares552e.pdf.

United Nations Statistics Division (2005) Millennium Development Goal Indicators Database http://millenniumindicators.un.org/unsd/mi/mi_goals.asp.

United States Institute of Peace (2005) *Sudan Peace Agreements* www.usip.org/library/pa/-sudan.html/.

Upham, Frank (1987) *Law and Social Change in Postwar Japan* Cambridge, MA: Harvard University Press.

Van de Ven, A.H. (1986) 'Central problems in the management of innovation' 32 *Management Science* 590.

Van der Walle, Nicholas (2001) *African Economies and the Politics of Permanent Crisis 1979–99* Cambridge: Cambridge University Press.

Van Doren, John (1988) 'Death African Style: The Case of S.M. Otieno' 36 *American Jo. Comparative Law* 329.

Van Hoecke, Mark (1986) *What is Legal Theory?* Leuven: Acco.

   (2002) *Law as Communication* Oxford: Hart.

Vico, Giambattista (1744/2002) *The First New Science* (ed. and trs. Leon Pompa) New York: Cambridge University Press.

Vinogradoff, Sir Paul (1920–22), *Outlines of Historical Jurisprudence* 2 vols London: Oxford University Press.

Vizard, Polly (2006) *Poverty and Human Rights: Sen's 'Capability Perspective' Explored* Oxford: Oxford University Press.

Voll, John (1990) Preface to An Na'im *Toward an Islamic Reformation: Civil Liberties, Human Rights and International Law* Syracuse, NY: Syracuse University Press.

Wacks, Raymond (ed.) (1993) *Hong Kong and China 1997* Hong Kong: Hong Kong University Press.

Waldron, Jeremy (1987) *Nonsense Upon Stilts: Bentham, Burke, and Marx on the Rights of Man* London: Methuen.

   (1994) 'Vagueness in Law and Language: Some Philosophical Issues' 82 *California L. Rev.* 509.

   (1999) *The Dignity of Legislation* Cambridge: Cambridge University Press.

   (2001) *Law and Disagreement* Oxford: Oxford University Press.

Walker, Clive (2002) *Blackstone's Guide to the Anti-terrorism Legislation.* Oxford: Oxford University Press.

Walker, Neil (2005) 'Legal Theory and the European Union: A 25th Anniversary Essay' 25 *Oxford Jo. Legal Studies* 581.

   (ed.) (2003) *Sovereignty in Transition* Oxford: Hart.

Wallerstein, Immanuel (1979) *The Capitalist World Economy* New York: Cambridge University Press.

   (1980) 'The Withering Away of States' 8 *International Journal of Sociology of Law* 369.

   (1984) *The Politics of the World-Economy: The States, Movements, and Civilizations.* Cambridge: Cambridge University Press.

   (1991) *Unthinking Social Science* Cambridge: Polity Press.

   (2002) 'Legal Restraints in the Capitalist Economy' in Likosky (ed.).

Walton, Douglas (1989) *Informal Logic.* Cambridge: Cambridge University Press.

Walzer, Michael (1983) *Spheres of Justice* New York: Basic Books.

   (1985) 'The Moral Standing of States: A Response to Four Critics' in Beitz *et al.* (1985) 217.

Ward, Barbara (1966) *Spaceship Earth* New York: Columbia University Press.

Ward, Ian (2003a) *Justice, Humanity, and the New World Order* Aldershot: Ashgate.

   (2003b) *A Critical Introduction to European Law* (2nd edn) London: Butterworth.

Watson, Alan (1974) *Legal Transplants* (revised edn. 1993) Edinburgh: Scottish Academic Press.

(1976) 'Legal Transplants and Law Reform' 92 *Law Qtrly Rev.* 79.

(2000a) *Legal Transplants and European Private Law* Ius Commune Lecture, Maastricht.

(2000b) *Law Out of Context* Athens: U. Georgia Press.

(2007) *Comparative Law: Law, Reality and Society* Lake Mary, FL: Vandeplas Publications.

Wattles, Jeffrey (1996) *The Golden Rule* New York: Oxford University Press.

Webber, Jeremy (1995) 'Relations of Force and Relations of Justice: The Emergence of Normative Community Between Colonists and Aboriginal Peoples', 33 *Osgoode Hall L. Jo.* 624.

Weiler, Joseph H.H. (1999) *The Constitution of Europe*. Cambridge: Cambridge University Press.

Wei-Ming, Tu (1985) *Confucian Thought: Self-hood as Creative Transformation* Albany: State University of New York Press.

Weldon, T.D. (1953) *The Vocabulary of Politics*. Harmonsworth: Penguin.

Westbrook, David A. (2006) 'Theorizing the Diffusion of Law: Conceptual Difficulties' 47 *Harv. International Law Jo.* 489.

Westbrook, J.L. (1999) 'The Globalisation of Currency Reform', *New Zealand Law Review* 401.

Weston, Burns and Stephen P. Marks (eds.) (1999) *The Future of International Human Rights* Ardsley, NY: Transnational.

Weyrauch, Walter (1964) *The Personality of Lawyers* New Haven: Yale University Press.

and Maureen A. Bell (1993) 'Autonomous Lawmaking: The Case of the Gypsies' 103 *Yale Law Jo.* 323.

Weyrauch, Walter *et al.* (ed.) (1997) Symposium on Gypsy Law (Romaniya) 45 *American Jo Comparative Law* 2.

Whitaker, Ben (ed.) (1973) *The Fourth World: Victims of Group Oppression* New York: Schocken Books.

Whitman, James Q. (1999) Review of Wieacker (1995) 17 *Law and History Review* 400.

(2003) 'The Neo-Romantic Turn' in Legrand and Munday (eds.) at p. 312.

(2005) 'The Comparative Study of Criminal Punishment' 1 *Annual Review of Law and Social Science* 17.

Widner, Jennifer A. (2001) *Building the Rule of Law: Francis Nyalali and the Road to Judicial Independence in Africa* New York: Norton.

Wieacker, Franz (1952) *Privatrechtsgeschicte der Neuzeit* (revised 1967) (translated by Tony Weir as *A History of Private Law in Europe, with particular reference to Germany* Oxford: Oxford University Press 1995).

(1981) 'The Importance of Roman Law for Modern Western Civilization and Western Legal Thought', IV *Boston College International and Comparative Law Review* 257.

(1990) 'Foundations of European Legal Culture' 38 *American. Jo. Comparative Law* 1.

Wiggins, David (2006) *Ethics: Twelve Lectures on the Philosophy of Morality* Cambridge, MA: Cambridge University Press.

Wigmore, J.H. (1928) *A Panorama of the World's Legal Systems* (3 vols.) St. Paul, MN: West.

Williamson, John (1994a) *The Political Economy of Policy Reform* Washington DC: Institute for International Economics.

(1994b) 'In Search of a Manual for Technopols' in J. Williamson (ed.) Chapter 2.

Wilson, Geoffrey (ed.) (1995) *Frontiers of Legal Research* Chichester: Chancery Lane Publishing.

Wilson, Richard (ed.) (1997) *Human Rights, Culture and Context* London: Pluto Press.

Wing, Adrien K. (ed.) (2000) *Global Critical Race Feminism: An International Reader* New York: New York University Press.

Wise, Edward M. (1990) 'The Transplant of Legal Patterns', 38 *Am. Jo. Comp.* L.1.

Wittgenstein, Ludwig (1922) *Tractatus Logico-Philosophicus* (C.K. Ogden, trs.1990) London: Routledge.

(1953) *Philosophical Investigations* (G.E.M. Anscombe trs.) Oxford: Basil Blackwell.

(1969) (2nd edn) Preliminary studies for the 'Philosophical Investigations' generally known as *The Blue and Brown Books* Oxford: Blackwell.

Wolfe, Tom (1988) *The Bonfire of the Vanities* New York: Bantam Books.

Wollheim, Richard (1954) 'The Nature of Law' 2 *Political Studies* 128.

Wood, Philip (2005) *Maps of World Financial Law* (5th edn) London: Allen and Overy.

Woodman, Gordon (2003) 'Why There Can be No Map of Law' in Pradhan (ed.).

(2006) 'The Cthonic Legal Tradition – on Glenn's *Legal Traditions of the World*' 1 *Jo. Comparative Law* 123.

Woodman, Gordon R, Ulrike Wanitzek, Harald Sippel (eds.) (2004) *Local Land Law and Globalization: A Comparative Study of Peri-urban Areas in Benin, Ghana, and Tanzania* Munster: Lit Verlag.

Woodruffe, John G. and Ameer Ali (1979–81) *The Law of Evidence* (14th edn.) Allahabad: Law Book Co.

Woodward, Peter (1990) *Sudan 1898–1989: The Unstable State* Boulder: Lynne Rienner.

World Bank (2007) *Governance Matters VI: Governance Indicators for 1996–2006* New York.

World Conference on Human Rights (1993) *Final Declaration of the Regional Meeting for Asia* A/CONF/157/ASRM/8, A/CONF.157/PC/59.

Wrase, Michael (2006) 'Rechtssoziologie und Law and Society – die deutsche Rechtssoziologie zweschen Krise und Neuaufbruch' 27 *Zetschrift fur Rechtssoziologie* 289.

Wrong, Dennis H. (1994) *The Problem of Order: What Unites and Divides Society* New York: The Free Press.

Yilmaz, Ihsan (2005) *Muslim Laws, Politics and Society in Modern Nation States* Aldershot: Ashgate.

Zakaria, Fareed (1994) 'Culture is Destiny: A Conversation with Lee Kuan Yew' 73 *Foreign Affairs* 2.

Zander, Michael (1973) *Cases and Materials on the English Legal System* London: Weidenfeld & Nicolson; (10th edn 2007 Cambridge University Press).

Zedner, Lucy (2003) 'The Concept of Security: An Agenda for Comparative Analysis' 23 *Legal Studies* 153.

Zedner, Lucia (2007a) 'Preventive Justice or Pre-Punishment? The case of Control Orders' 60 *Current Legal Problems* 174.

(2007b) 'Seeking Security in Eroding Rights: The Side-Stepping of Due Process' in Goold and Lazarus (eds.).

Zeigert, Klaus A. (2002) 'The Thick Description of Law' in Banakar and Travers (eds.).

Ziemele, Ineta (ed.) (2004) *Reservations to Human Rights Treaties and the Vienna Convention Regime: Conflict, Harmony or Reconciliation* Leiden: Boston: M. Nijhoff.

Zweigert, Konrad and Hein Kötz (1971) *An Introduction to Comparative Law* (First edition in German, Vol. I, 2nd edn 1987, 3rd edn. trans. Tony Weir 1998) Oxford: Oxford University Press.

(1998) (3rd edn) *An Introduction to Comparative Law* trans. Tony Weir, Oxford: OUP.

Index